The New Media Edition...
with memorable content, engaging full-color art and photographs, and fascinating examples.

Visual excitement that makes anthropology come to life!

Now with a text-specific action-packed Web site that works hand-in-hand with the book!

*I*t's all here in *Humanity: Introduction to Cultural Anthropology, Fifth Edition*, and more! Thoroughly revised and entirely current, the Fifth Edition of this respected text remains research-based while it emphasizes the cultural diversity of humanity. Peoples and Bailey succeed like no other author team in revealing the excitement the field holds, and they go a step further: they show why an appreciation for and tolerance of cultural difference is critical in today's modern world.

The text contains a rich selection of ethnographic examples, vivid photographs, exciting art, and timely research references—all of which work seamlessly together to present the concepts and content of humanity to introductory students in a clear, coherent way. Cultural differences and similarities are examined throughout the book, and the authors suggest anthropological explanations whenever appropriate.

Over the next few pages, you'll see what is new and exciting about the Fifth Edition, and you'll be introduced to the technologically advanced and comprehensive array of resources that accompany the text. You haven't seen technological support like this before!

In this thorough revision, you'll find:

NEW! The *Media Edition* works hand-in-hand with an incomparable Web site. No other text makes the discovery of anthropology as real and exciting! (see pages 2-3 for details.)

NEW! *Internet Exercises* at the end of every chapter show students some of the material available via the World Wide Web and encourage its use in study and research.

NEW! The already compelling information on race, language, and ethnicity has now been expanded throughout the text.

NEW! A chapter that focuses on the arts— including the visual and performance arts—from an anthropological viewpoint (Chapter 14.)

NEW! *Other Voices* boxes that present the perspectives of non-Western anthropologists, as well as Native Americans, women, and people of color.

NEW! *A Closer Look* boxes that discuss additional relevant topics and provide interesting examples that make concepts real to students.

Preview

The exciting new Media Edition

of *Humanity: An Introduction to Cultural Anthropology, Fifth Edition*

. . . anthropology that jumps out and pulls the stude

Now your students can see anthropology come to life!

The new Media Edition of *Humanity: An Introduction to Cultural Anthropology, Fifth Edition* features an interactive and vivid Web site that works hand-in-hand with the new edition and combines high-level interactivity with video, sound, and graphics to get your students involved in the excitement of anthropology in ways never before possible! For every chapter of the book, the Web site includes:

- Discussion questions
- Internet exercises
- Access to InfoTrac® College Edition
- Text resources, including quizzes and essays

And that's just the beginning!

The *Media Edition* expands the content of *Humanity* in exciting ways. The chapter-opening photos of selected chapters (for example, Chapter 5's *Margaret Mead in New Guinea, 1964*) refer students to the Web for an exciting multimedia experience. When they click the Margaret Mead photo on the Web, students are instantly transported to the world of field anthropology through streaming audio and video. The Web video clips are drawn from full-length films from Document Education Resources and are available to qualified adopters to complete the students' learning experience.

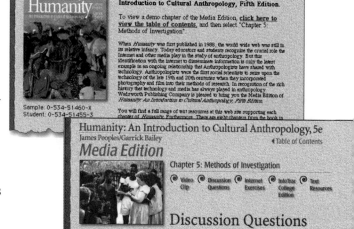

Humanity: An Introduction to Cultural Anthropology, 5e
James Peoples/Garrick Bailey
Media Edition

Welcome to the Media Edition of Humanity: An Introduction to Cultural Anthropology, Fifth Edition.

To view a demo chapter of the Media Edition, **click here to view the table of contents**, and then select "Chapter 5: Methods of Investigation".

When *Humanity* was first published in 1988, the world wide web was still in its relative infancy. Today educators and students recognize the crucial role the Internet and other media play in the study of anthropology. But this identification with the internet to disseminate information is only the latest example in an ongoing relationship that Anthropologists have shared with technology. Anthropologists were the first social scientists to seize upon the technology of the late 19th and 20th centuries when they incorporated photography and film into their methods of research. In recognition of the rich history that technology and media has always played in anthropology, Wadsworth Publishing Company is pleased to bring you the Media Edition of *Humanity: An Introduction to Cultural Anthropology, Fifth Edition*.

Sample: 0-534-51460-X
Student: 0-534-51455-3

Humanity: An Introduction to Cultural Anthropology, 5e
James Peoples/Garrick Bailey
Media Edition   ◄ Table of Contents

Chapter 5: Methods of Investigation

● Video Clip   ● Discussion Questions   ● Internet Exercises   ● InfoTrac College Edition   ● Text Resources

Discussion Questions

Take a Book Tour
What's New with 5th Edition

1. Early in the history of anthropology photography joined the traditional tools of pencil and note pads as ethnographic field tools. When motion picture film, audio recording and video became available some anthropologists, like Margaret Mead embraced the new technologies

o an exciting journey of discovery!

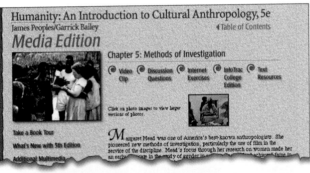

Preview this powerful site for yourself!

Visit **http://www.wadsworth.com/humanity/**
today to see all it has to offer—including
video clips, exercises, and more!

Anthropology is about discovery. . .

The Media Edition helps
students discover new
ways to study and new
ways to experience the
fascinating cultural
variability of the world's
diverse peoples.

There are two excellent comprehensive readers covering
the history of anthropological theory. Both include introductions by the editors as well as key original works by
important anthropologists:

Bohannan, Paul, and Mark Glazer, eds. *High Points in
Anthropology*, 2nd ed. New York: Knopf, 1988.
McGee, R. Jon, and Richard L. Warms, eds. *Anthropological
Theory: An Introductory History*. Mountain View, Calif.:
Mayfield, 1996.

**To understand the contemporary divisions between materi-
alists and idealists, consult some of the following works:**

Geertz, Clifford, *The Interpretation of Cultures*. New York:
Basic Books, 1973.
 • *Assorted works by an idealist and interpretivist. Good
place to start to understand this approach.*

Johnson, Allen W., and Timothy Earle. *The Evolution of Human
Societies*. Stanford: Stanford University Press, 1987.
 • *Outstanding and up-to-date theoretical and factual
treatment of cultural evolution. Conceptualizes increasing
complexity as shifting from family level through local level
to regional level, with examples illustrating the cultures of
each level.*
Marcus, George E., and Michael M. J. Fischer. *Anthropology
as Cultural Critique*. Chicago and London: University of
Chicago Press, 1986.
 • *An influential book written from the idealist perspective.
Discusses changes in anthropology and ethnography since
the 1970s. Argues that the time is right for anthropologists
to take on the task of critiquing their own culture.*

Internet Exercises

A good place to begin inquiring into anthropological theory is a website created for anthropology students. There are several websites that focus on theory. One is "Anthropological Theories: A Guide by
Students for Students" from the Department of Anthropology at The University of Alabama
(http://www.as.ua.edu/ant/murphy/anthros.htm). The discussion of the theories in this site were
developed by graduate students under the direction of Dr. Michael Murphy. Another website is "Theory in Anthropology" from Indiana University at (http:www//indiana.edu/~wanthro/theory.htm).
    To find out more about the major theorists in anthropology go to the "Anthropological Biogra-
phies" website at (http://kroeber.anthro.mankato.msus.edu/bio/index.htm). The biographies are part
of Minnesota State University at Mankato's E-Museum at (http:kroeber.anthro.mankato.msus.edu/).

Internet Exercises at the end of
every chapter in the book show
students some of the material
available via the World Wide Web
and encourage its use in study
and research.

Preview

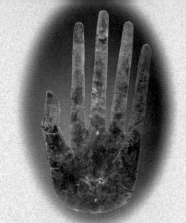

Compelling prose...
Vivid art...
Photographs that jump from the printed page...

The Fifth Edition makes an impact, any way you look at it!

Preview

This innovative new edition is authoritative, rich, and compelling on every single page! Key ideas and concepts are presented clearly and succinctly, and interesting ethnographic examples interspersed throughout the book make it easy for students to gain a true understanding of diverse people and cultures. And, once students gain an understanding of cultural anthropology, they are more aware of how their own lives are affected by it and may be empowered to make a difference in helping to solve the problems of our world.

The Fifth Edition now includes more information on *race, language,* and *ethnicity* while it emphasizes an applied approach to anthropology throughout, addressing such topics as world hunger and population growth.

actions, the objective being the maintenance of harmony and cooperation. The most serious deviations from acceptable behavior, which threaten the cohesiveness of the group, fall under that aspect of social control known as law, also discussed in this chapter. In the least organized societies, law and political organization exist independently of each other. As political organization becomes increasingly formalized and structured, governmental institutions take over legal institutions, until legal institutions become part of the formal political structure.

Forms of Political Organization

When we speak of the political organization of a particular cultural system, we frequently are left with the impression that political boundaries and cultural boundaries are the same. But the boundaries of a *polity*, or politically organized unit, may or may not correspond with the boundaries of a particular way of life. For example, the Comanche of the Great Plains shared a common

societies were unable to compete for resources. Thus, bands survived until the modern period only in regions of the world with limited natural resources. Most known band-level societies were found in the deserts and grasslands of Australia, Africa, and the Americas. A few others lived in the tropical forests of Africa, Asia, and South America and in the boreal forest and tundra regions of North America and Asia.

Bands consist of a number of families living together and cooperating in economic activities throughout the year. Band-level organization most frequently was found among peoples with foraging economies, which usually dictated low population densities and high seasonal mobility. As a result, only a relatively small number of people could stay together throughout the year. Bands ranged in size from only a dozen to several hundred individuals. The adaptive significance of the band's size and

This photo of a Northwest Coast house and family crest ("totem") pole was taken in the late nineteenth century. The painting on the house is identified as a bear by the prominent teeth, large central nostrils, paws, and ears protruding from the house top. Notice how the bear's image is split down the middle making a symmetrical image. Both halves of the image still contain the essential design attributes of the bear.

of the participants. The shared experience of singing in unison may help draw the congregation together, enhancing what many Christian denominations call their fellowship. In these and other ways, music is important in making the congregation receptive to the messages delivered by the sermon and prayers.

Music and other forms of performance arts are essential to the religious experience for diverse peoples from all parts of the world. The voudon ("voodoo") religion of the Caribbean heavily incorporates performance arts into religious ceremonies. Followers of voudon consider themselves to be people who "serve the spirits" (*loa*). Many *loa* originated and now live in West Africa, from where the ancestors of modern Afro-Caribbean peoples were enslaved during the era of slave trade begin-

ning about 1500. Voudon temples are elaborately decorated with sacred objects, paintings, and symbolic representations of various *loa*, which show the devotion of the worshippers and make the temple attractive to the spirits. Through drumming, music, and energetic dancing, voodoo worshippers induce the *loa* to leave their spiritual homes and take over the bodies of those who worship them. When the *loa* possess their human servants, the latter speak with the voices of the *loa*, wear the *loa*'s favorite clothing, eat their foods, drink their beverages, and generally assume their identity. Visiting petitioners with problems can ask questions of the worshipper/*loa*, who may answer with directions about what course of action to take. Voudon drumming, music, and dancing are so totally integrated into temple rituals that the religion is unimaginable without it.

Among many peoples, music, dance, and other forms of performance arts are essential elements of curing ceremonies. !Kung shamans (see Chapters 6 and 13) use percussion, song, and dance to induce the trance state they believe is necessary for curing sick people. The power to heal, !Kung believe, comes from a substance called n!um, which when heated up by dancing and

A new chapter that focuses on the arts is now a part of the Fifth Edition. In this chapter, Peoples and Bailey cover a broad range of topics—including visual and performance arts, body expression, music, and dance—from an anthropological viewpoint (Chapter 14).

Innovative, useful, in-text tools

Other Voices is an exciting new element designed to help broaden various topics. *Other Voices* presents the perspectives of non-Western anthropologists, as well as Native Americans, women, and people of color. Some of the topics examined in this feature are: *Conflicting anthropological interpretations of Native Hawaiians' response to Captain Cook; The Concept of the Sacred among Native Americans*; and *Orientalism and the Western View of the Arab/Islamic World.*

A Closer Look boxes highlight and provide additional information on topics such as peasant culture, ethnic conflicts, youth culture and the media, and the survival of indigenous cultures. These examples add interest and help make concepts real to students.

P r e v i e w

Chapter openers, detailed summaries, and other pedagogy help students grasp and retain important material

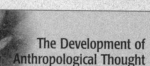

Preview

The Development of Anthropological Thought

Nineteenth-Century Origins

Early Twentieth-Century Contributions

American Historical Particularism (ca. 1900–1940)

British Functionalism (ca. 1920–1950)

Mid-Century Evolutionary Approaches (ca. 1940–1970)

Anthropological Thought Today

Materialism

Idealism

Interpretive Anthropology

Either/Or?

Why Can't All Those Anthropologists Agree?

Anthropology arose out of the encounter of Westerners with people of other continents, such as these inhabitants of the South American Andes.
Visit http://www.wadsworth.com/humanity to learn more about the material covered in this chapter and to access activities, exercises, and tutorial quizzes.

Anthropology began as a result of the encounter between Western Europeans and peoples of other lands—the Americas, Africa, the Middle East, Asia, and the Pacific Ocean. As Western intellectuals after about 1500 struggled to understand people who felt, thought, and acted differently from

...na. They address different questions and ...hypotheses. They are complementary, not ...methodologies.

...nthropologists (especially idealists—see Chap-... that both kinds of comparative studies dis-...ural system in the sample so much that the ...d is invalid. They think that ripping each ele-...he particular context in which it is embedded ...significance because each element acquires its ...y in its local historical and cultural context. ...these and other problems, comparative meth-...only practical means available for determining whether a hypothesis is valid among human cultural systems. Those who use these methods are aware of the difficulties, yet they believe that the advantage of being able to process information on large numbers of societies outweighs the problems.

...matrilineal societies are, under certain conditions, more adaptive than patrilineal societies, we still cannot directly say why.

Cross-cultural comparisons and controlled historical comparisons give us distinctly different measures of cul-

Summary

Anthropological methods fall into two overall categories. Ethnographic methods involve the collection of information on a specific cultural system, whereas comparative methods are used to test hypotheses or to investigate theoretical ideas by comparing information on numerous cultural systems. The basic aims of ethnographic methods are descriptive, whereas comparative investigations aim to determine whether some hypothesis or theoretical idea is supported by the accumulated data on human cultures.

The kinds of methods used by anthropologists depend on whether they are investigating a contemporary or a past way of life. Research into the past usually involves ethnohistory (perusal of written documents). This method requires considerable interpretation by the researcher. Sometimes those who wrote the documents used in ethnohistoric reconstructions misinterpreted events because of their cultural backgrounds and ethnocentrism. The contents of documents often are affected by the private interests of their authors.

Fieldwork is the primary method of acquiring data about living people. Fieldworkers usually live among those they study for at least a year, conducting formal interviews and surveys and engaging in participant observation. Although the difficulties of conducting fieldwork vary with the personality and gender of the field-worker

and with the people and specific topic being studied, three problems are common. Fieldworkers must not only fight against their own ethnocentrism and tendencies to stereotype those they study, but they must also overcome the stereotypes local people have developed about foreigners. It often is difficult to establish a rapport with local people because they may have had no previous experience with the kinds of questions field-workers ask. Identifying reliable informants and finding people willing to participate in intensive surveys may pose a serious problem. Sometimes people deliberately deceive the anthropologist, because they mistrust his or her motives, do not want certain facts to become public, or are culturally forbidden to give away secrets of their religion. Today, fieldwork is viewed as an essential part of the graduate education of anthropologists, and almost a prerequisite for professionalism. It is, in some respects, a rite of passage.

Comparative methods involve ways of systematically and reliably comparing massive amounts of information collected by previous ethnographers. The use of comparative methods presents many difficulties, including stating the research hypothesis in such a way that it is testable, reliably defining and measuring the variables of interest for many societies, deciding whether similar cultural elements from two or more societies are the "same" or "different," and contending with unintentional researcher bias. The results of comparative studies can be difficult to interpret. Correlation often is confused with causation.

A descriptive and detailed *Summary* at the end of each chapter condenses and reinforces key areas of discussion, giving students an excellent review and overview of the chapter.

A truly unparalleled teaching and learning package that includes Internet and technological tools like never before...

Internet Resources

The Media Edition
More than a Web site—it's an interactive extension of the text! No other text offers this unique advantage. See pages 2–3 of this preview for a complete description.

Anthropology Online: The Wadsworth Anthropology Resource Center

http://anthropology.wadsworth.com
Specially designed for you and your students, this full-service resource center offers hyperlinks to important sites in both the cultural and physical anthropology fields. There are also newsgroups, a career center, listings of other Wadsworth titles, and many other selections that expand your students' reach beyond the classroom to anthropological research on a worldwide scale.

InfoTrac® College Edition
InfoTrac College Edition gives students access to full-length articles from hundreds of scholarly and popular periodicals, updated daily and dating back as much as four years. Students will even be able to print complete articles right from *InfoTrac College Edition*, whenever it's convenient for them! These articles are available to both instructor and student through this exclusive offer. To give your students four months FREE access to this online university library, order the text packaged with *InfoTrac College Edition* (ISBN: 0-534-74738-0).

Anthropology: Exploring the Internet
0-534-56652-9
Anthropology: Exploring the Internet is a full-color brochure that lists 75 URLs, which address all aspects of anthropology. You can offer this helpful guide to your students at no charge when you order it bundled with the text! (ISBN: 0-534-74352-8)

Let's Go Anthropology
0-534-53113-X
by Joan Ferrante and Angela Vaughn
This book directs readers to some of the most anthropologically useful information posted on the Internet. It is a resource guide and an Internet yellow pages, with URLs that enable students to do the background research necessary to complete assignments and/or find interesting and useful anthropological information.

Video Resources

Visual Anthropology Video
0-534-56651-0
From Documentary Educational Resources and Wadsworth, this 60-minute video features clips from over 30 new and classic anthropological films. To accompany this valuable resource, Wadsworth also offers you *A Visual Guide to Anthropology* (0-534-53932-7) a valuable tool that provides a complete listing of more than 50 videos, with full descriptions, discussion questions, and annotations on how to use each video effectively in teaching cultural anthropology.

CNN Today Video: Cultural Anthropology, Volumes I and II
Volume I: 0-534-56650-2
Volume II: 0-534-56653-7
CNN videos, a Wadsworth exclusive, allow you to integrate the newsgathering and programming power of CNN into the classroom to show students the relevance of anthropology to their everyday lives. Organized by course topics, these compelling clips are ideal for launching lectures and sparking discussion. Qualifying adopting instructors receive a new CNN video each year for the life of the edition. Volume II is coming soon!

Resources

Wadsworth Anthropology Video Library Series

Completely updated! Qualified instructors can select from over 20 cultural and physical anthropology videos made available from such great series as NOVA, Films for the Humanities and Sciences, The Disappearing World, Document Education Resources, and In Search of Human Origins.

NEW! AnthroLink CD-ROM

0-534-55668-X

With this presentation tool, instructors can easily assemble art and database files with lecture notes to create fluid lectures that may help stimulate even the least interested students. It includes all illustrations in the book, animations and films from the student CD, and art from other Wadsworth textbooks. *AnthroLink* also has a Kudo Image Browser with an easy drag-and-drop feature that allows file export into presentation tools such as PowerPoint. Upon its creation, a file or lecture with *AnthroLink* can be posted to the Web where students can access it for study needs. Free to adopters.

Instruction and testing resources

Instructor's Manual

0-534-51456-1

The *Instructor's Manual* offers 40-70 test items per chapter, in addition to suggested supplementary lectures, discussion questions and classroom activities, Internet resources and activity suggestions, and a Film/Video resource guide.

Transparency Acetates for *Humanity: An Introduction to Cultural Anthropology, Fifth Edition*

0-534-51457-X

This selection of quality acetates for cultural anthropology is free to qualified adopters.

Thomson Learning Testing Tools

Windows/Macintosh (0-534-51458-8)

This fully integrated suite of test creation, delivery, and classroom management tools includes Thomson Learning Test, Test Online, and Management software. *Thomson Learning Testing Tools* allows professors to deliver tests via print, floppy, hard drive or LAN. With these tools, professors can create cross-platform exam files from publisher files or existing WESTest 3.2 test banks, edit questions, create questions, and provide their own feedback to objective test questions—enabling the system to work as a tutorial or an examination. Call-in testing is also available. Visit www.itped.com for more information.

Offer your students a money-saving SmartPak!

Applying Cultural Anthropology: Readings

0-534-53324-8

This reader offers a selection of 39 articles written in the words of those cultural anthropologists who are making their discipline useful. The readings are organized into five major sections reflecting those areas that are benefiting from the practice and application of cultural anthropology. The book provides anthropology students with a wide range of examples that show how the discipline is making meaningful contributions to the mitigation of human problems. Students will enjoy reading firsthand—from the experiences of practicing anthropologists—about the challenges and rewards that are experienced when working to make cultural anthropology useful. Ask about bundling options—your Wadsworth/Thompson Learning sales representative can give you more details.

Humanity

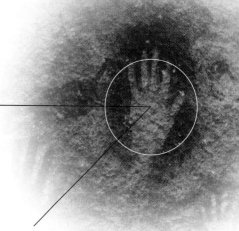

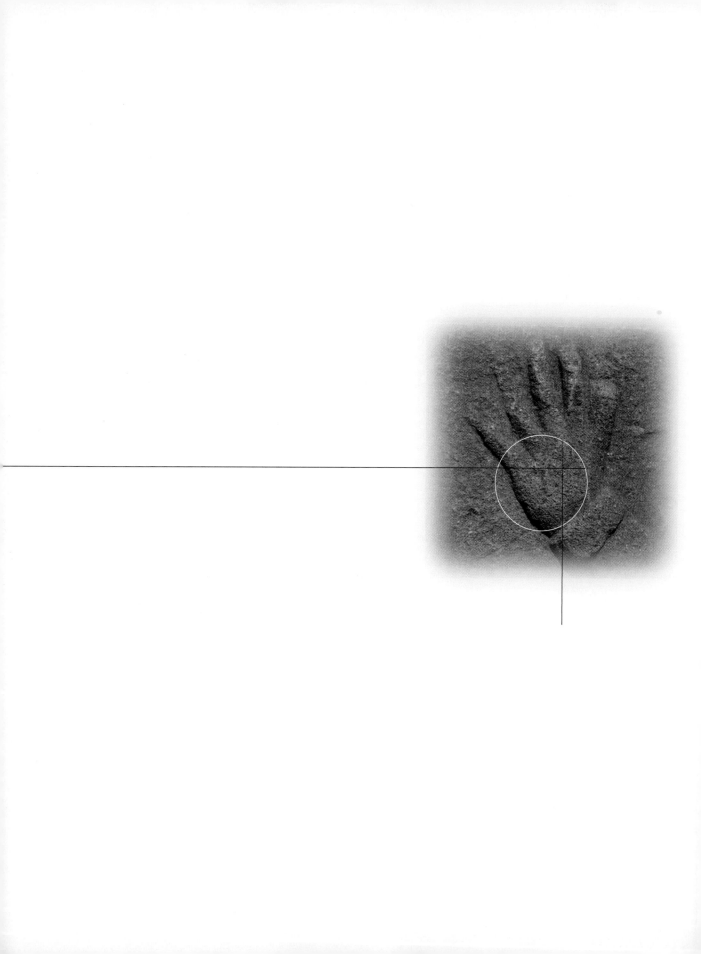

Humanity

An Introduction
to Cultural Anthropology

FIFTH EDITION

James Peoples
OHIO WESLEYAN UNIVERSITY

Garrick Bailey
UNIVERSITY OF TULSA

Wadsworth
Thomson Learning

Australia • Canada • Denmark • Japan • Mexico • New Zealand • Philippines •
• Puerto Rico • Singapore • South Africa • Spain • United Kingdom • United States

Anthropology Editor:
Eve Howard

Development Editor:
Robert Jucha

Assistant Editor:
Ari Levenfeld

Editorial Assistant:
Jennifer Jones

Marketing Manager:
Christine Henry

Print Buyer:
Karen Hunt

Permissions Editor:
Robert Kauser

Production and Composition:
Electronic Publishing Services Inc., NYC

Text and Cover Design:
Baugher Design

Cover Image:
Corbis/Brian Bikander

Copy Editor:
Electronic Publishing Services Inc., NYC

Photo Research:
Electronic Publishing Services Inc., NYC

Illustrations:
Electronic Publishing Services Inc., NYC

Index:
Electronic Publishing Services Inc., NYC

Cover Printer:
Phoenix Color

Printer/Binder:
World Color/Taunton

Printed in the United States of America
1 2 3 4 5 6 03 02 01 00 99

Library of Congress Cataloging-in-Publication Data

Peoples, James G.
   Humanity: an introduction to cultural anthropology /
James Peoples, Garrick Bailey. —5th ed.
       p.   cm.
   Includes bibliographical references and index.
   ISBN 0-534-51455-3   (pbk.)
   1. Ethnology.   I. Bailey, Garrick Alan.   II. Title.
GN316.B35   1999
306—dc21   99-20288

Instructor's Edition ISBN 0-534-51460-X

Wadsworth/Thomson Learning
10 Davis Drive
Belmont, CA 94002-3098
USA
www.wadsworth.com

International Headquarters
Thomson Learning
290 Harbor Drive, 2nd Floor
Stamford, CT 06902-7477

UK/Europe/Middle East
Thomson Learning
Berkshire House
168-173 High Holborn
London WC1V 7AA
United Kingdom

Asia
Thomson Learning
60 Albert Street #15-01
Albert Complex
Singapore189969

Canada
Nelson/Thomson Learning
1120 Birchmount Road
Scarborough, Ontario M1K 5G4
Canada

Contents in Brief

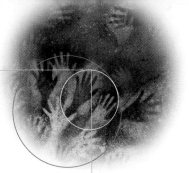

Preface   XI

CHAPTER 1
The Study of Humanity   1

P A R T   I
Humanity, Culture, and Language

CHAPTER 2
Culture   15

CHAPTER 3
Culture and Language   33

P A R T   I I
Theories and Methods
of Cultural Anthropology

CHAPTER 4
The Development of Anthropological Thought   51

CHAPTER 5
Methods of Investigation   69

P A R T   I I I
Diversity

CHAPTER 6
Adaptation: Environment and Cultures   84

CHAPTER 7
Exchange in Economic Systems   107

CHAPTER 8
Marriage, Family, and Residence   120

CHAPTER 9
Kinship   137

CHAPTER 10
Gender in Comparative Perspective   159

CHAPTER 11
The Organization of Political Life   184

CHAPTER 12
Social Inequality and Stratification   202

CHAPTER 13
Relations with the Supernatural   218

CHAPTER 14
Art and the Aesthetic   243

CHAPTER 15
Personality, Culture, and the Life Cycle   262

P A R T   I V
Anthropology in the Modern World

CHAPTER 16
The Changing Human World   279

CHAPTER 17
Ethnicity in the Modern World   306

CHAPTER 18
Applied Anthropology and World Problems   331

CHAPTER 19
The Survival of Indigenous Peoples   351

Glossary   365

Notes   370

Bibliography   374

Peoples and Cultures Index   384

Name Index   387

Subject Index   388

Contents

Preface xi

CHAPTER 1
The Study of Humanity   1
Subfields of Anthropology   2
  Physical/Biological Anthropology   2
  Archaeology   3
  Cultural Anthropology   4
  Anthropological Linguistics   5
  Applied Anthropology   5
Cultural Anthropology Today   6
Anthropological Approaches   8
  Holistic Perspective   8
  Comparative Perspective   8
  Relativistic Perspective   9
The Value of Anthropology   9
Summary   11
Key Terms   12
Suggested Readings   12
Internet Exercises   13

P A R T   I
Humanity, Culture, and Language

CHAPTER 2
Culture   15
Defining Culture   17
  Shared ...   17
  ... Socially Learned   17
  ... Knowledge   18
  ... and Patterns of Behavior.   18
Cultural Knowledge   20
  Norms   20
  Values   20
  Symbols   21
  Classifications of Reality   22
  World Views   23
Culture and Human Life   24
Cultural Knowledge and Individual Behavior   25

Biology and Cultural Differences   27
Summary   31
Key Terms   32
Suggested Readings   32
Internet Exercises   32

CHAPTER 3
Culture and Language   33
Humanity and Language   34
Some Properties of Language   34
  Multimedia Potential   35
  Discreteness   35
  Arbitrariness   35
  Productivity   36
  Displacement   36
How Language Works   36
  Sound Systems   37
  Variations in Sound Systems   38
  Words and Meanings   40
Language and Culture   41
  Language and Cultural Classifications
    of Reality   41
  Language As a Reflection of Culture   43
Language and World Views   45
Social Uses of Speech   46
Summary   49
Key Terms   50
Suggested Readings   50
Internet Exercises   50

P A R T   I I
**Theories and Methods
of Cultural Anthropology**

CHAPTER 4
The Development of Anthropological Thought   51
Nineteenth-Century Origins   52
Early Twentieth-Century Contributions   55
  American Historical Particularism   55
  British Functionalism (Ca. 1920–1950)   56

Mid-Century Evolutionary Approaches
  (Ca. 1940–1970)   58
Anthropological Thought Today   59
  Materialism   59
  Idealism   61
  Interpretive Anthropology   63
  Either/Or?   63
  Why Can't All Those Anthropologists Agree?   64
Summary   66
Key Terms   67
Suggested Readings   67
Internet Exercises   67

CHAPTER 5
Methods of Investigation   69
Ethnographic Methods   69
  Ethnographic Fieldwork   69
  Problems in Field Research   71
  Fieldwork As a Rite of Passage   73
  Ethnohistory   73
Comparative Methods   77
  Cross-Cultural Comparisons   78
  Controlled Historical Comparisons   79
Summary   81
Key Terms   82
Suggested Readings   82
Internet Exercises   83

P A R T   I I I
Diversity

CHAPTER 6
Adaptation: Environment and Cultures   84
Understanding Human Adaptation   85
Hunting and Gathering   87
  Foraging and Culture   88
Domestication   91
Agriculture   92
  Horticulture   94
  Cultural Consequences of Horticulture   95
  Intensive Agriculture   96
  Cultural Consequences of Intensive Agriculture   97
Pastoralism   100
  The Karimojong: An Example from
    East Africa   102

Adaptation and Culture   103
Summary   103
Key Terms   104
Suggested Readings   105
Internet Exercises   106

CHAPTER 7
Exchange in Economic Systems   107
Reciprocity   108
  Generalized Reciprocity   108
  Balanced Reciprocity   109
  Negative Reciprocity   111
  Reciprocity and Social Distance   112
Redistribution   113
Market Exchange   114
  Money   114
  Peasant Marketplaces   116
Summary   117
Key Terms   118
Suggested Readings   118
Internet Exercises   119

CHAPTER 8
Marriage, Family, and Residence   120
Some Definitions   121
Marriage   121
  Functions of Marriage   123
  Nayar "Marriage"   123
Marriage in Comparative Perspective   124
  Marriage Rules   124
  How Many Spouses?   125
  Marriage Alliances   129
  Marital Exchanges   130
Kinship Diagrams   131
Postmarital Residence Patterns   132
Family and Household Forms   133
Summary   135
Key Terms   135
Suggested Readings   136
Internet Exercises   136

CHAPTER 9
Kinship   137
Kinship   138
  Cultural Variations in Kinship   138

Unilineal Descent   139
  Unilineal Descent Groups   142
  Descent Groups in Action   143
  Avunculocality Revisited   146
Cognatic Descent   147
  Cognatic Descent in Polynesia   147
Bilateral Kinship   149
Influences on Kinship Systems   149
Classifying Relatives: Kinship Terminologies   151
  Varieties of Kinship Terminology   152
  Determinants of Kinship Terminology   154
Summary   157
Key Terms   157
Suggested Readings   158
Internet Exercises   158

CHAPTER 10
Gender in Comparative Perspective   159
Cultural Construction of Gender   160
The Sexual Division of Labor   163
  Patterns and Influences   165
  Intensive Agriculture and Women's Labor   169
The Status of Women   172
  Universal Subordination?   174
  Influences on Women's Status   175
  Women's Status in Industrial Societies   180
Summary   181
Key Terms   182
Suggested Readings   182
Internet Exercises   183

CHAPTER 11
The Organization of Political Life   184
Forms of Political Organization   185
  Bands   185
  Tribes   187
  Chiefdoms   188
  States   189
Social Control and Law   191
  Social Control   191
  Law   191
Legal Systems   192
  Self-Help Systems   192
  Court Systems   196
Summary   199
Key Terms   200

Suggested Readings   200
Internet Exercises   201

CHAPTER 12
Social Inequality and Stratification   202
Systems of Equality and Inequality   203
  Egalitarian Societies   203
  Ranked Societies   204
  Stratified Societies   204
Castes in Traditional India   205
Classes in Industrial Societies: The United States   207
Maintaining Inequality   210
  Ideologies   211
  American Secular Ideologies   211
Theories of Inequality   212
  Functionalist Theory   212
  Conflict Theory   214
  Who Benefits?   214
Summary   216
Key Terms   217
Suggested Readings   217
Internet Exercises   217

CHAPTER 13
Relations with the Supernatural   218
Defining Religion   219
  Supernatural Powers: Beings and Forces   219
  Myths   219
  Rituals   220
Theories of Religion   222
  Intellectual/Cognitive Functions   223
  Psychological Functions   224
  Social Functions   225
Sphere of Supernatural Intervention   226
Supernatural Explanations of Misfortune   226
  Sorcery   227
  Witchcraft   228
  Interpretations of Sorcery and Witchcraft   228
Varieties of Religious Organization   230
  Individualistic Cults   231
  Shamanism   231
  Communal Cults   233
  Ecclesiastical Cults   234
Revitalization Movements   235
  Prophets and Revelations   235
  Melanesian Cargo Cults   235
  Native American Movements   236

Summary   238
Key Terms   238
Suggested Readings   239
Internet Exercises   240

CHAPTER 14
Art and the Aesthetic   241
The Pervasiveness of Art   243
Forms of Artistic Expression   244
   Body Arts   244
   Visual Arts   248
   Performance Arts   251
Art and Culture   254
   Secular and Religious Art   254
   Art and Gender   256
   Social Functions of Art   256
Summary   260
Key Terms   260
Suggested Readings   260
Internet Exercises   261

CHAPTER 15
Personality, Culture, and the Life Cycle   262
Personality and Culture   263
   Child-Rearing Practices and the Formation
     of Personality   263
   Cultural Consequences of Modal Personality   266
Age Categories and Age Sets   268
Life Cycle   269
   Childhood   269
   Becoming an Adult   270
   Initiation Rites   271
   Adulthood   274
   Old Age   275
Summary   276
Key Terms   277
Suggested Readings   277
Internet Exercises   278

P A R T   I V
Anthropology in the Modern World

CHAPTER 16
The Changing Human World   279
Culture Change   280
History and Anthropology   280
The World in 1500   281

The World Since 1500   281
   Initial Expansion of Europe   281
   The World and the Industrial Revolution   288
   European Impact on World Cultural Systems   292
The World Since 1945   293
   The Global Economy   293
   Demographic Changes   297
   Political Fragmentation   300
Consequences of an Interdependent World   300
Summary   303
Key Terms   303
Suggested Readings   304
Internet Exercises   305

CHAPTER 17
Ethnicity in the Modern World   306
Ethnic Groups   307
   Situational Nature of Ethnic Identity   307
   Attributes of Ethnic Groups   307
   Fluidity of Ethnic Groups   310
   Types of Ethnic Groups   310
The Problem of Stateless Nationalities   311
Resolving Ethnic Conflict   322
   Homogenization   322
   Accommodation   325
   Resolution   325
Summary   329
Key Terms   329
Suggested Readings   330
Internet Exercises   330

CHAPTER 18
Applied Anthropology and World Problems   331
Applied Anthropology   332
Population Growth   333
Anthropological Perspectives on Population Growth   334
   Consequences of Population Growth   334
   Costs and Benefits of Children
     in North America   335
   Costs and Benefits of Children in the LDCs   336
World Hunger   338
   Scarcity or Inequality?   339
   Is Technology Transfer the Answer?   341
   Agricultural Alternatives   344
The Uses of Fieldwork: Two Studies   345
   Planting Trees in Haiti   345
   Delivering Health Care Services in Swaziland   347

Summary   348
Key Terms   349
Suggested Readings   349
Internet Exercises   350

CHAPTER 19
The Survival of Indigenous Peoples   351
Indigenous Peoples Today   352
Vanishing Knowledge   355
   Medicines We Have Learned   357
   Adaptive Wisdom   358
   Cultural Alternatives   362
Summary   363
Key Term   363
Suggested Readings   364
Internet Exercises   364

Glossary   365
Notes   370
Bibliography   374
Peoples and Cultures Index   384
Name Index   387
Subject Index   388

A Closer Look

Into the Wild Unknown of Workplace Culture   7
The Cultural Construction of Race   28
Indian Givers   41
Things or Texts?   60
Marshall Sahlins, Gananath Obeyesekere,
   and Captain James Cook   76
Domesticates in the Old and New Worlds   92
"Insulting the Meat" among the !Kung   110
Group Marriage in the United States   127
Backbone of the Nation?   148
Alternative Sex Roles among the Plains Indians   164
Murder among the Cheyenne   197
Occupational Prestige in the United States   208
The Ethnic Art Market   258
Liminality and Becoming a Soldier   274
Importance of the Horse to Plains Indians   284
The Bankers and the Sheiks   296
Acadians and Cajuns   312
Collapse of the Soviet Union   320
Reclaiming the Past   356
Amish Communities in North America   360

Other Voices

Alice Fletcher and Francis La Flesche   74
Understanding the Sacred   221
A Native View of Maori Art   247
Orientalism and the Western View of the
   Arab/Islamic World   300
What Is Development?   342

Preface

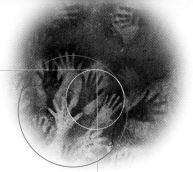

Humanity is intended as a textbook to be used in introductory college and university courses in cultural anthropology. Anthropology studies and tries to explain or interpret the fascinating cultural variability of the world's diverse peoples. In *Humanity,* we try to convey to students the educational value of discovering and understanding this variability. In the process of discovery, we hope all our readers will experience a change in their attitudes about other cultures. Equally important, anthropology should lead people to reconsider their own identities as individuals and as members of a culture with its own distinctive beliefs and behaviors. We also hope our readers will come away with a new way of looking at some of the problems that afflict the world in the year 2000, particularly those involving so-called ethnic conflicts, population growth, global hunger, and the survival of indigenous cultures. Finally, we want students to grasp the significance of some of the changes that have affected them in the twentieth century and that will so profoundly affect their lives in the third millennium.

The diverse peoples of the world now interact more intensively and affect one another more profoundly than ever before. The main reasons for this increasing interdependence of peoples and nations are well-known from the popular media: increasing integration of the global economy, growing international migration, cultural exchanges, the worldwide spread of the consumer culture, and new political conflicts and cooperations related to the breakup of the Soviet Union and its allies. Multiculturalism and multinationalism have become everyday words in just a couple of decades. Anthropology has much to say about these specific changes, but just as importantly anthropology—at least, anthropology taken seriously—makes those who study it aware of how their own lives are affected by such changes.

Changes in the Fifth Edition

Many of the substantial revisions in the previous (fourth, 1997) edition of *Humanity* reflected an increased emphasis on the practical applications of anthropological approaches, methods, ideas, and empirical studies. In this edition, we have retained virtually all of these changes and added several others. Most notably, we have added a completely new chapter—Chapter 14, "Art and the Aesthetic." This chapter focuses on the expressive dimension of human existence. To make room for this new material without lengthening the text, we have deleted an entire chapter (Chapter 6 in the fourth edition, titled "The Peoples of the World"), and integrated material from two previous chapters into a single chapter (Chapter 6 in the new edition, titled "Adaptation: Environment and Cultures").

The fifth edition includes three completely new special features.

- The material discussed in what we called "Boxes" in previous editions is replaced by inserts now called "A Closer Look." Mainly, the material is intended to discuss additional relevant topics that cannot be readily integrated into the body of the main discussion. In some cases, the material is the same as in the former boxes, but new discussions appear in A Closer Look in Chapters 1, 2, 4, 14, and 18.
- A new kind of insert, called "Other Voices," appears in several chapters of this edition (Chapters 5, 13, 14, 16, and 18). In most cases, the material discussed under Other Voices presents the insights and opinions of non-Western scholars on particular topics.
- "Internet Exercises" are provided at the end of every chapter to show interested students some of the material that can be acquired on the World Wide Web. These exercises were written by Michael Murphy of Ohio State University, whose assistance is greatly appreciated by the authors and editors.

As in previous editions, we have revised all chapters to streamline selected discussions, update the factual material, reflect recent changes in the field's emphasis, and delete any remaining redundancies. Many of the most substantial revisions directly reflect the insightful comments of reviewers of the fourth edition. Throughout, numerical data have been updated with the most recently available statistics. Most chapters contain new introductions to make the chapter material more engaging.

For instructors who have used previous editions of *Humanity,* the following chapter-by-chapter overview of the primary revisions in this fifth edition will be helpful:

Chapter 1 again introduces the entire discipline of anthropology and its five subfields. There are minor reorganizations and condensations, but the major change is in the addition of A Closer Look, which focuses on anthropologists studying the modern workplace.

Chapter 2 (culture) retains its basic orientation. We removed the box on the relationship between "race" and sports performance. Instead, a new discussion describes why so many anthropologists claim that "race" is a culturally constructed concept rather than a biologically given classification of people. Some of the material in this chapter has been reorganized and the formal definition of culture is slightly altered.

Chapter 3 (language) begins with a new section describing some of the reasons why language is such a remarkable capacity of humankind. In the interest of space and readability, we no longer cover syntax at all. The section on universal grammar also is deleted.

Chapter 4 (theory) is reduced in length by condensing material on unilineal evolutionism, British functionalism, and mid-century evolutionary approaches (White and Steward). However, the discussion of contemporary theoretical orientations is somewhat more detailed in its treatment of the scientific and humanistic approaches. An entirely new concluding section discusses reasons why ethnologists disagree so much on theoretical matters.

Chapter 5 (methods) contains A Closer Look describing the debate between Sahlins and Obeyesekere regarding the interpretation of historical events.

Chapter 6 (adaptation) now combines the information on hunting and gathering and domestication (cultivation and pastoralism) into a single chapter. Necessarily, this resulted in condensing some information, especially ethnographic cases. We were still able, though, to both cover the major adaptations themselves and discuss their main effects on cultural systems in aspects such as relative sedentism, group size, resource control, exchange, and leadership patterns. This chapter continues to provide the material framework to which many other institutions (family and descent form, gender, political organization, and so forth) are related.

Chapter 7 contains many changes in terminology (e.g., "goods" are now "products") and the example of Haitian marketplace *pratik* relationships is deleted.

Chapter 8 (marriage and family forms) features a streamlined discussion of the functions of family groupings and the forms of marriage.

Chapter 9 (kinship, descent, and terminology) is reduced in length and complexity by eliminating coverage of phratries and moieties, reducing the subsection on cognatic descent, and reducing as far as practical the description of kin terminological systems.

Chapter 10 (gender) continues to focus around the cultural construction of gender, the sexual division of labor, and "the" status of women in diverse societies. The

subsection on intensive agriculture and women's labor is simplified by eliminating some peripheral points, and the subsection on overall societal complexity and women's status is now more focused. The box on how the roles of American women have been affected by increasing female employment is eliminated, but its main points are incorporated into the main discussion.

In Chapter 11 (politics and law), the section titled "Attributes of Law" is deleted and some passages are reworded.

Chapter 12 (inequality and stratification) is updated statistically and, in some places, reworded. The example of Indian *jajmani* is deleted.

In Chapter 13 (religion), we removed the tabular comparison showing the relation between social classes and the belief in supernatural retribution. We also clarify the distinction between *cult* and *religion,* in the context of comparing forms of religious organization.

Chapter 14 (art) is a totally new chapter. After defining art broadly, we cover body arts, visual arts, and performance arts. Each subsection is enriched with ethnographic examples focusing on the place of artistic objects, designs, movements, and music in the cultural context that gives them their local meanings. The concluding section explicitly addresses the place of art in cultural and social existence, covering specific topics like its social functions and its use as symbols of identity.

Chapter 15 (personality and life cycle) continues to emphasize the complexity of the relationship between personality and culture. The concept of *modal personality* is clarified (we hope!). We condensed parts of the discussion of life-cycle changes, but retained the discussion of age sets in this chapter (over the objections of some reviewers, who felt age sets best fit into Chapter 9).

In Chapter 16 (changing human world), the box on the clash of civilizations is replaced by an Other Voices insert on Edward Said's views on Western misinterpretations of the Islamic world. Statistical data also are updated.

Chapter 17 (ethnicity) has new material on the conflict in Kosovo, the rise of the Hindu nationalist party in India, and recent nuclear testing by Pakistan and India.

In Chapter 18 (applied anthropology and world problems), the section on population growth is reduced and statistical data are updated. The specific contributions anthropologists have made to the understanding of childbearing decisions are stated more clearly and forcefully. In the section on world hunger, we condensed the example of El Salvador, which clarifies its relevance to the scarcity/inequality issue. The box on the energy requirements of different agricultural methods is deleted, but its main point is integrated into the main text.

Chapter 19 (cultural survival) includes some rewrites and new examples, but is otherwise retained as the most appropriate conclusion to the text.

Of course, the glossary, notes, and bibliography have been revised to reflect the preceding changes in the content of the chapters. Despite the addition of a few new key terms for Chapter 14, the glossary actually contains fewer entries than earlier editions, as we believe a minimalist approach to key terms is appropriate. As in previous editions, we assemble notes and works consulted for each chapter at the end of the book to keep readers' attention focused on the content. Wherever possible, we nonetheless attempt to give full credit to the scholars whose theoretical ideas or ethnographic information we use by integrating their names into the discussion.

Pedagogical Features

The fifth edition continues to include the following aids to learning:

Engaging previews that open each chapter
Summaries that close each chapter
Boldfaced Key Terms at first mention or definition
Listings of Key Terms at the end of each chapter
Suggested Readings—selected to be suitable for introductory students—on each chapter's content
An alphabetized Glossary at the end of the book that defines every Key Term as concisely as possible
Three Indexes: one by subject, one by people or nation mentioned or discussed, and one by name of scholar mentioned or cited

Like other textbook authors, we had to make hard choices about many of the preceding features: How detailed should the summaries be? What should and should not be listed as Key Terms? On such issues, we have tried to strike a balance between breadth and depth, recognizing that not everyone will agree with our choices.

Media Edition

When *Humanity* was first published in 1988, the World Wide Web was still in its relative infancy. Today educators and students recognize the crucial role the Internet and other media play in the study of anthropology. But this use of the Internet to disseminate information is only the latest example of an ongoing relationship that anthropologists have shared with technology. Anthropologists were the first social scientists to seize upon the technology of the late nineteenth and twentieth centuries when they incorporated photography and film into their methods of research. In recognition of the rich history that

technology and media have always played in anthropology, Wadsworth is pleased to bring you the Media Edition of *Humanity: An Introduction to Cultural Anthropology,* Fifth Edition.

You will find a full range of text resources at this website supporting each chapter of *Humanity.* At the beginning of each chapter you will locate the website for the text. Log on at http://www.wadsworth.com/ humanity. Furthermore, there are eight chapters from the book for which additional enrichment material is provided on the website. A banner at one corner of the chapter-opening photograph identifies these chapters. The photographs were selected in conjunction with Documentary Educational Resources, the leader in anthropology film and video. Click on the small camera or audio icons appearing alongside these chapters to view the multimedia resources available. You will be taken to an essay about the photograph where more images have been provided on this subject and have the option to view a short video clip from which the image was taken. The enriched site also provides hot links to valuable discussion questions online and exercises students may conduct using the Internet.

Student Supplements

The Wadsworth Anthropology Resource Center   The website for this text, The Wadsworth Anthropology Resource Center (http://anthropology.wadsworth.com) contains numerous useful study aids for students. This site includes hyperlinks to some of the most useful anthropology and other Internet sites, a career center, a discussion forum, and other resources. You will find a text-specific page for *Humanity.* Also, you will have access to text-specific quizzes, flash cards, Internet projects, hypercontents, and much more.

InfoTrac® College Edition   Your instructor may have requested the addition of InfoTrac College Edition in adopting *Humanity* for your course. If this is the case you will have received a special pass code shrink-wrapped with the text. The pass code will allow access to InfoTrac College Edition for three months during the times you are enrolled in your anthropology course. InfoTrac College Edition is an online source of both scholarly and popular articles from hundreds of periodicals. This is a fantastic resource for conducting research, writing papers, or stimulating discussions in the classroom.

Let's Go Anthropology, by Joan Ferrante   This URL directory was specifically designed for anthropology and contains detailed descriptions of each website listed. This handy guide can be used as a resource for additional classroom assignments and exercises, and can be packaged with your text at a discount price.

Anthropology: Exploring the Internet   *Anthropology: Exploring the Internet* is a full-color, trifold brochure containing 75 URLs covering all aspects of anthropology. This item can be shrink-wrapped free with the textbook.

Supplements for the Instructor

The Instructor's Manual with Test Bank, prepared by Bruce Wheatley of the University of Alabama at Birmingham, has been extensively revised for the Fifth Edition. The Instructor's Manual contains suggested supplementary lectures, suggested uses for each chapter of videos available from the publisher, extensive classroom discussion questions, and a new section on Internet and InfoTrac College Edition exercises. The Test Bank has also been extensively revised and consists of multiple-choice, true/false, and essay questions. Full-color Transparency Acetates of the figures and tables from the text are available to instructors.

Media Supplements

AnthroLink   With this tool, you can create multimedia lectures easily. Just make your selection from the searchable database of hundreds of pieces of art and media, import information from your own lecture notes if you wish, and present in class or post your presentations on the Web.

CNN Cultural Anthropology Today Video: Volumes I and II   Available exclusively from Wadsworth, these exciting videos feature riveting clips from CNN, the world's leading 24-hour global news network. Organized by topics covered in a typical cultural anthropology course, the 60-minute videos are divided into clips ranging from 2 to 7 minutes long. Clips are followed by questions designed to spark class discussion.

A Guide to Visual Anthropology   This valuable teaching tool helps instructors select outstanding videos and use them in the classroom. It contains a listing of over 50 top-quality videos and includes the following information for each: a complete description, discussion questions, and annotations on using the video effectively in teaching cultural anthropology. *The Visual Anthropology Video* (see below) is also available for use with this guide. 0-534-53932-7

The Visual Anthropology Video   Produced exclusively for Wadsworth by Documentary Educational Resources, a leading producer of anthropological films, this 60-minute video contains clips on approximately 20 different films with discussion questions for each clip. These excellent, carefully chosen clips covering a variety of topics in anthropology are engaging and effective lecture launchers. The video is even more effective when used in conjunction with *The Guide to Visual Anthropology.*

The Wadsworth Anthropology Video Library   Choose from a collection of videos selected for their timeliness and relevance. Contact your Wadsworth/Thomson Learning representative for a complete list of videos and policy by adoption size.

Acknowledgments

Since 1988, when the first edition of *Humanity* was published, the book has benefited enormously from the comments of dozens of reviewers. For this edition, we thank the following scholars for their suggestions and criticisms of the fourth edition:

Howard Campbell
University of Texas at El Paso

William L. Coleman
North Carolina, Greensboro

Richard T. Curley
University of California, Davis

Lucy Laufe
Montgomery College

William M. Leons
University of Toledo

David Paul Lumsden
York University

Frank C. Miller
University of Minnesota

Brian L. Molyneaux
University of South Dakota

Martin Ottenheimer
Kansas State University

Carter Pate
University of Tennessee at Chattanooga

Frances M. Slaney
University of Regina

Mark Tromans
Broward Community College

Paul Wohlt
Ball State University

We have not always agreed with the scholars' recommendations, of course; in some cases, their suggestions proved to be beyond our competence. However, in a great many cases, their specific comments are incorporated.

Our personal friends and colleagues not only lent moral support, but also their expertise in particular topics. Jim thanks his Ohio Wesleyan colleagues Ted Cohen, John Durst, Dick Fusch, Mary Howard, Akbar Mahdi, and Jan Smith. Janice Schroeder's cheerfulness and diligence continues to be helpful. Timothy Roden's help with the section on music was valuable. Tom Love of Linfield College corrected some specific errors. Over the years, the kind words of Tom McKenna and Doug Raybeck about the book have meant a lot. I thank Dick Curley, Bill Davis, and Henry Rutz for training me broadly enough in graduate school to contribute to an introductory level text.

The staff at Wadsworth was always helpful and tolerant of our occasional tardiness. In particular, thanks to Halee Dinsey, Robert Jucha, Jennifer Jones, production editor Lake Lloyd, copy editor Cheryl Robbins, and photo researcher Francis Hogan. Bruce Wheatley contributed an Instructor's Manual and Test Items, for which we are extremely grateful. Michael Murphy did a fine job on the new Internet Exercises that appear at the end of each chapter. Finally, we thank our spouses for their tolerance of our workloads.

James Peoples
Garrick Bailey

CHAPTER 1

The Study of Humanity

C
O
N
T
E
N
T
S

Subfields of Anthropology

Physical/Biological Anthropology

Archaeology

Cultural Anthropology

Anthropological Linguistics

Applied Anthropology

Cultural Anthropology Today

Anthropological Approaches

Holistic Perspective

Comparative Perspective

Relativistic Perspective

The Value of Anthropology

Video · Audio · Photos
Hotlinks · Essay
http://www.wadsworth.com/humanity

Cultural anthropology studies how and why the world's diverse peoples differ so much in their customs and beliefs. The people shown here are the Ju/'hoansi, a people of southern Africa who formerly lived by means of hunting and gathering.
Visit http://www.wadsworth.com/humanity to learn more about the material covered in this chapter and to access activities, exercises, and tutorial quizzes.

W*HAT PHYSICAL and mental characteristics make humans different from other animals? Is there such a thing as "human nature" and, if so, what is it like? In what ways are all people alike? How and why do human groups differ, both biologically and culturally? In what ways have human cultures changed in the last 10,000 years? How are people who live in modernized, industrialized, urbanized nations different from people living a more "traditional," "indigenous" lifestyle? These are some of the questions investigated by anthropology, the field that studies all humanity.*

A*LMOST EVERYTHING about people interests anthropologists. We want to know when, where, and how the human species originated and why we evolved into what we are today. Anthropologists try to explain the many differences between the world's cultures, such as why some cultures believe people get sick because the souls of witches devour their livers, whereas others hold that tarantulas fling tiny magical darts into their victims' bodies. We want to know why so many Canadians like beef, which devout Hindus will not touch. We are interested in why some New Guineans often engorge themselves* *with the meat of pigs, which is the same animal flesh that some Middle Eastern religions believe to be unclean. In short, anthropologists of one kind or another are liable to investigate almost everything about we human beings: our evolution, our genes, our emotions, our intellects, our behaviors, our languages, and our religions.*

IF YOU HAVE the impression that anthropologists have quite diverse interests, you are correct. In fact, it is commonly said that the distinguishing characteristic of anthropology—the thing that makes it different from the many other fields that also include people as their subject matter—is its broad scope. A good way to emphasize this broad scope is to say that anthropologists are interested in all human beings—whether living or dead, Asian or African or European—and that they are interested in many different aspects of humans, including their skin color, family lives, political systems, tools, religions, and languages. No place or time is too remote to escape the anthropologist's notice. No dimension of humankind, from genes to art styles, is outside the anthropologist's attention.

Subfields of Anthropology

Anthropology, then, is a diverse field—so diverse that no anthropologist can master the whole range of subjects encompassed by the discipline. Almost all modern anthropologists specialize in one of five principal subfields. Physical (or biological) anthropology is concerned mainly with the evolutionary origins and physical diversity of the human species. Archaeology focuses on the technological and cultural development of human societies over long time periods. The subdiscipline known as cultural anthropology describes and analyzes contemporary and historically recent societies, trying to understand how and why the world's cultures are so diverse. Anthropological linguistics deals with human languages and their relation to cultures. The fifth subfield, applied anthropology, uses anthropological concepts, methods, and theories to try to solve contemporary human problems. Anthropology is even more complicated than this fivefold division implies because each of these subfields is in turn divided into several specializations. Although cultural anthropology is the primary subject of this book, a brief look at the other subfields is essential to understand the whole discipline.

Physical/Biological Anthropology

Physical (also called **biological**) **anthropology** is concerned with the biological evolution of the human species, the anatomy and behavior of monkeys and apes, and the physical variations between different human populations. As these subjects indicate, physical anthropology is closely related to the biological and zoological sciences in its goals and methods.

An important goal of physical anthropology is to understand how and why the human species evolved from prehuman, ape-like ancestors. The specialization that investigates human biological evolution is known as **paleoanthropology**. Over decades of searching for fossils and carrying out meticulous laboratory studies, paleoanthropologists have reconstructed the history of how humans evolved anatomically. The outlines of human evolution are becoming clear. Most scholars agree that the evolutionary line leading to modern humans split from those leading to modern African apes (chimpanzees and gorillas) around five million years ago. It also appears that fully modern humans, *Homo sapiens*, evolved surprisingly recently, probably less than 150,000 years ago. Of course, the fossil record is incomplete and can be interpreted in various ways, so new discoveries may alter our current understanding.

Another subfield of biological anthropology is **primatology**. Primatologists specialize in the evolution, anatomy, social behavior, and adaptation of primates, the taxonomic order to which humans belong. By conducting field studies of how living primates forage, mate, move around in their environment, and interact socially, primatologists hope to shed light on the forces that affected early human populations.

Primatological research on the behavior of group-living monkeys and apes has added significantly to the scientific understanding of many aspects of human behavior, including sexuality, parenting, cooperation, tool use, and intergroup conflict and aggression. Field studies of African chimpanzees and gorillas, the two apes genetically most similar to the human species, have been especially fruitful sources of hypotheses and information.

Yet another type of biological anthropologist is interested in how and why human populations vary physically. All humans are members of a single species, and one of the basic tenets of anthropology is that the physical similarities among the world's peoples far outweigh the differences. Nonetheless, peoples whose homelands are in Africa, Asia, Europe, Australia, the Pacific islands, and the Americas were once more isolated from one another than they are today. During this separation they evolved differences in overall body and facial form, height, skin color, blood chemistry, and other genetically determined features. Anthropologists who study **human variation** seek to measure and explain the differences and similarities among the world's peoples in these and other physical characteristics.

The field of primatology is concerned with the evolution and behavior of primates, humanity's closest biological relatives. Jane Goodall, here interacting with a chimpanzee, is famous for her pioneering field studies in east Africa.

Most physical anthropologists work in universities or museums, as teachers, researchers, writers, and curators. But many people trained in biological anthropology also work in "practical jobs", applying their knowledge of human anatomy to find answers to problems. For instance, specialists in **forensic anthropology** work for or consult with law enforcement and other agencies, where they analyze and help identify human skeletal remains. Among their contributions are determining the age, sex, height, and other physical characteristics of crime or accident victims. Forensic anthropologists gather evidence from bones about old injuries or diseases, which then are compared with medical histories to identify victims. For example, forensic anthropologist Clyde Snow has disinterred the bones of some of the northern Iraqi Kurds killed by Saddam Hussein's government in the late 1980s. In 1993, he located a mass grave in eastern Croatia, where Serb forces had gunned down 200 Croatian patients and staff from a medical center. In the 1990s, teams of forensic anthropologists have exhumed remains from graves in Bolivia, Guatemala, El Salvador, and Haiti in efforts to identify victims of political assassination and determine the exact causes of their deaths.

Archaeology

Archaeology is the investigation of the human past by excavating and analyzing material remains. Because it investigates the many ways in which human life has changed over the centuries and millennia, archaeology has much in common with history. It differs, however, in its methods and, to some extent, its goals. Modern archaeology usually is divided into two major kinds of studies: prehistoric and historic.

Prehistoric archaeology is the study of ancient cultures—those that never kept written records of their activities, customs, and beliefs. Although prehistoric peoples lacked writing, some information about their way of life can be reconstructed from the tools, pottery, ornaments, bones, plant pollen, charcoal, and other materials they left behind, in or on the ground. Through excavation and laboratory analysis of these material remains, prehistoric archaeologists reconstruct the way people lived in ancient times and trace how human cultures have changed over the centuries. In fact, research conducted by prehistoric archaeologists provides our only source of information about how people lived before the development of writing.

To learn about the more recent past, historians use written materials such as diaries, letters, land records, newspapers, and tax collection documents. Written records provide useful data, but they typically are fragmentary and provide information only on specific subjects and subgroups within a society. The growing field of **historic archaeology** supplements written materials by excavations of houses, stores, plantations, factories, and other historic structures. Historic archaeologists often uncover hard data on living conditions and other topics lacking in written accounts.

Many archaeologists today are employed not in universities, but in museums, public agencies, and for-profit corporations. Museums offer jobs as curators of artifacts and as researchers. State highway departments employ archaeologists to conduct surveys of proposed new routes in order to locate and excavate archaeological sites that will be destroyed. The U.S. Forest Service and National Park Service hire archaeologists to find sites on public lands so that decisions about the preservation of cultural materials can be made. Those who work in the growing field of **cultural resource management** locate sites of prehistoric and historic significance, evaluate their importance, and make recommendations about total or partial preservation. Since the passage of the National Historic Preservation Act in 1966, private corporations and government bodies who wish to construct factories, buildings, parking lots, shopping malls, and other structures must file a report on how the construction will affect historical remains and on the steps taken to preserve them. Because of this law, the business of **contract archaeology** has boomed in the United States. Firms engaged in contract archaeology bid competitively for the privilege of locating, excavating, and reporting on sites affected or destroyed by construction. Hundreds of (mostly small) contract archaeology companies exist.

Cultural Anthropology

Cultural anthropology (also called **ethnology**) is the study of contemporary and historically recent human societies and cultures. As its name suggests, the main focus of this subfield is culture—the customs and beliefs of some human group (the concept of culture is discussed at length in Chapter 2).

Cultural anthropologists study an enormous number of specific subjects, far too many to even be listed here. But some of their main overall objectives are:

- studying firsthand and reporting about the ways of living of particular human groups;
- comparing diverse cultures to one another to determine if there are any principles that operate universally in human culture;
- trying to understand how various dimensions of human life—economics, family life, religion, art, communication, and so forth—relate to one another in particular cultures and in cultures generally;
- understanding the causes and consequences of cultural change; and
- making the public at large aware and tolerant of the cultural differences that exist in the human species.

This last objective is especially important in the contemporary world, in which individuals with diverse cultural backgrounds increasingly come into contact with one another.

Prehistoric archaeologists investigate the remote past by the careful excavation of material remains.

To some people, ethnological studies seem a bit eso-teric—"interesting," some say, "but of little practical value." Most anthropologists disagree. We think that what we learn by our descriptions, comparison, and analyses of cultures helps to improve the human condition. We believe that our studies of other cultures will help us to understand our own way of life. And, as we shall see later in this book, specific studies carried out by cultural anthropologists have helped solve practical problems in real human communities.

To do their research and collect their information, ethnologists conduct **fieldwork**. Fieldworkers ordinarily move into the community under study, communicate in the local language, and live in close contact with the people. Daily interaction with the members of a community provides ethnologists with firsthand experiences that yield insights that could not be gained in any other way. Fieldworkers usually report the findings of their research in books or scholarly journals, where they are available to the general public. A written account of how a single human population lives is called an **ethnography** (which means "writing about a people"). We have more to say about fieldwork in Chapter 5.

Anthropological Linguistics

Defined as the study of human language, linguistics is a field all its own, existing as a separate discipline from anthropology. Linguists describe and analyze the sound patterns and combinations, words, meanings, and sentence structures of human languages. As discussed in Chapter 3, language has some amazing properties, and the fact that humans are able to learn and use language at all is truly remarkable.

Language interests anthropologists for several reasons. For one thing, the ability to communicate complex messages with great efficiency may be the most important capability of humans that makes us different from primates and other animals; certainly our ability to speak is a key factor in our evolutionary success. Cultural anthropologists, especially, are interested in language because of how the language and culture of a people affect each other. The subfield of **anthropological linguistics** is concerned with the complex relations between language and other aspects of human behavior and thought. For example, anthropological linguists are interested in how language is used in various social contexts: What style of speech must one use with people of high status? What does the way people attach labels to their natural environment tell us about the way they perceive that environment? We return to these and other topics in anthropological linguistics in Chapter 3.

Applied Anthropology

In the past, almost all professional anthropologists spent their careers in some form of educational institution, either in colleges and universities or in museums. Today, hundreds of anthropologists hold full-time positions that allow them to apply their expertise in governmental agencies, nonprofit groups, private corporations, and international bodies. Hundreds of others make their living as consultants to such organizations and institutions. These institutions and organizations employ anthropologists because they believe that people trained in the discipline will help them in problem solving. In recognition of the growth of noneducational employment opportunities, the American Anthropological Association (the professional organization of anthropologists) officially recognizes **applied anthropology** as a separate subfield. In the 1990s, about half of those with new anthropology Ph.D.s acquire jobs in some federal, state, or local governmental agency or in the private sector.

We discuss some of the ways applied anthropologists have contributed to the alleviation of human problems in later chapters. For now, a few examples will illustrate some of the work they do.

Medical anthropology is one of the fastest growing specializations. Medical anthropologists investigate the complex interactions between human health, nutrition, social environment, and cultural beliefs and practices. Because the transmission of viruses and bacteria are greatly affected by people's diets, sanitation, sexual habits, and other behaviors, one role of medical anthropologists is to work with epidemiologists to identify cultural practices that affect the spread of disease. Different cultures have different ideas about the causes and symptoms of disease, how best to treat illnesses, the abilities of traditional healers and doctors, and the importance of community involvement in the healing process. By studying how a human community perceives such things, medical anthropologists can provide information to hospitals and agencies that help them deliver health care services more effectively.

Development anthropology is another area in which cultural anthropologists apply their expertise to the solution of practical human problems, usually in the Third World. Working both as full-time employees and as consultants, development anthropologists provide information on communities that help agencies adapt projects to local conditions and needs. Examples of agencies and institutions that employ development anthropologists include the U.S. Agency for International Development, the Rockefeller and Ford Foundations, the World Bank, and the United Nations Development Program. Perhaps the most important role of the anthropologist in such institutions is to provide policymakers with knowledge of local-level ecological and cultural conditions, so that projects will avoid unanticipated problems and minimize negative impacts.

Educational anthropology offers jobs in public agencies and private institutions. Some roles of educational anthropologists include advising in bilingual education, conducting detailed observations of classroom interactions, training personnel in multicultural issues, and adapting teaching styles to local customs and needs. An increasingly important role for North American educational anthropologists is to help teachers understand the learning styles and behavior of children from various ethnic and national backgrounds.

Increasingly, corporations employ cultural anthropologists. Especially since the 1980s, the growth of overseas business opportunities led North American companies to need professionals who can advise executives and sales staff on what to expect and how to speak and act when they conduct business in other countries. Because of their training as acute observers and listeners, anthropologists are employed in the private sector in many other capacities as well. The article reprinted in "A Closer Look" illustrates some of the ways the contemporary business world is finding the training and talents of anthropologists useful.

As these examples show, anthropologists apply their knowledge and skills to the solution of practical human problems in many ways. Speaking broadly, cultural anthropologists are valuable to agencies, companies, and other organizations because they are trained to do two things very well: first, to observe, record, and analyze human behavior; and, second, to look for and understand the cultural assumptions, values, and beliefs that underlie that behavior.

Cultural anthropology is the largest subfield. Of the doctoral degrees awarded in the United States in 1996-7, 53% were in cultural anthropology, 26% in archaeology, 12% in physical/biological anthropology, 1% in linguistics, and 7% in applied anthropology. However, these figures are misleading in one respect. New Ph.D.s in other specializations—especially in cultural anthropology—often acquire jobs that use their research and analytical skills in solving institutional problems and providing human services; such people may also consider themselves applied anthropologists.

Cultural Anthropology Today

As the foregoing overview of the five subdisciplines confirms, anthropology is indeed a broad field. Even by itself, cultural anthropology—the main subject of this text—is enormously broad, for modern ethnological fieldworkers live among and study human communities from all parts of the world, from the mountains of Tibet to the deserts of the American Southwest, from the streets of Calcutta to the plains of East Africa.

In the popular imagination, cultural anthropological fieldworkers go to far-off places and study exotic peoples, or "natives." Except for the stereotypes about the "natives," this image was reasonably accurate until the 1970s. Until then, ethnology differed from sociology and other disciplines that studied living peoples and cultures mainly by the kinds of cultures studied. Cultural anthropologists mainly focused on small-scale, non-Western, preindustrial, subsistence-oriented cultures, whereas sociologists mainly dealt with large Euro-American, industrial, money-and-market countries. Cultural anthropologists themselves often sought out pristine, untouched tribal cultures to study because living among the "primitives" brought prestige and enhanced one's reputation in the discipline.

Since the 1970s, all this has changed. You are about as likely to find a contemporary anthropological fieldworker studying a Canadian medical clinic as a New Guinea village. A few subjects of recent studies done in modern settings include: American bodybuilders, the cultural significance of Elvis, British witches' covens, Appalachian towns, New Jersey fraternities, courts of law, the decline of the middle class, and family life in the Silicon Valley. As these examples indicate, more and more cultural anthropologists are working "here at home" rather than "far away." One reason for this trend is the realization that anthropological concepts and fieldwork methods can yield insights about modern societies that other disciplines overlook. Another is that increasing numbers of ethnologists are using their knowledge and training to solve real-world problems.

The boundaries between cultural anthropology and other disciplines (especially sociology) are much less firm than they were even a few decades ago. Most ethnological fieldwork, however, still occurs in relatively small communities (on the order of a few hundred to a few thousand) where the researcher can participate firsthand in the lives of the people. More than any other single factor, the fieldwork experience distinguishes cultural anthropology from other disciplines concerned with humankind. Also, cultural anthropology remains far more comparative and global in its scope and interests than the other social sciences and humanities. Ethnologists are far more likely to conduct research in a country other than their own than are sociologists or psychologists, for example.

In many ways, modern cultural anthropology overlaps with numerous other disciplines that study people. For example, a fieldworker may be especially interested in the agriculture, leadership patterns, legal system, or art of a culture or region. He or she will, therefore,

A CLOSER LOOK

Into the wild unknown of workplace culture

Anthropologists revitalize their discipline

by Brendan I. Koerner

When anthropologists get together, they like to swap stories about the joys of their profession: trekking among the Masai in Northern Tanzania, combating queasy stomachs in Chiapas.

But cultures like these that once seemed exotic are no longer isolated; if pioneering anthropologist Margaret Mead returned to Samoa today, she wouldn't have to miss her favorite MTV shows. Anthropology has had trouble keeping pace with these changes, to the point that some of its biggest names say it risks being absorbed by sociology and other disciplines. But the science is not dead yet: Researchers increasingly are plying their trade in Xerox rooms and union halls, where they are as exotic as Mead was on the island of Ta'u.

Many of the 1,500 researchers at last week's International Congress of Anthropological and Ethnological Sciences, in Williamsburg, Va., blamed anthropology's funk on a "post-modernism" fad. Since the late 1970s, many anthropologists have abandoned traditional field-work for academic critique. "They retreated to discussing issues at a level so jargon filled and academic—and I am using that word in a bad sense—that they became totally irrelevant," says E. Liza Cerroni-Long, an Eastern Michigan University anthropologist. She says that post-modernism took hold partly in response to anthropology's "guilty past," buttressing the superiority of European colonialists. Post-modern anthropology is still very much alive—papers presented last week included "Liminality as a Temporal Construct" and "The Unbearable Whiteness of Barbie: Ethnography and Feminist Theory Confront the Ethnically Correct Doll."

Fortunately, such insular discourse is on the wane, and a growing legion of anthropologists is battling to prove their relevance to contemporary society. Indeed, of the 2,000-plus anthropologists in the United States practicing outside academia, more than 40 percent work as consultants to the business world. They are hired to record the "folk knowledge" of workers, such as the way experienced refrigeration technicians can test a unit's performance with a mere wave of a hand above the fan. Others are enlisted to gauge workers' needs; an anthropologist helped officials at a Chicago union learn that their rank and file was upset that shop stewards spent more time recruiting new members than responding to grievances. Corporate giants such as Motorola and Nestlé also have seen fit to enlist the aid of anthropologists in the workplace.

Mexican Poker

Last week, Ken Erickson of the University of Missouri-Kansas City spoke of his work in a Garden City, Kan., slaughterhouse, investigating the relationship between immigrant meatpackers and their supervisors after a wildcat strike. Management had thought the walkout was due to language barriers. By spending months on the shop floor slicing loins and playing Mexican poker after hours, Erickson learned that the workers understood their supervisors but resented being treated as unskilled labor, compelled to wear bulky armor as if they were too incompetent to avoid injuring themselves. Erickson discovered that the employees possessed valuable skills not taught in training: the trick to boning an unusual cut of meat, or tips for keeping one's leg from being nicked. The strike was prompted not by language problems, Erickson concluded, but because management didn't respect the value of workers' knowledge. As a result, the plant incorporated that knowledge into training programs.

As industrial anthropologists have found new cultures to explore, physical anthropologists also are revitalizing the science by applying new technology to the study of human remains. Already famed for excavating mass graves in Bosnia or dredging up clues about mysterious murders, physical anthropologists now are helping skeletons speak with unprecedented eloquence. Their most exciting new tool is the analysis of mitochondrial DNA, the genetic material in a cell's engine. Mitochondrial DNA is passed intact from mother to daughter and can trace ancestry back through many centuries. This method is being used to establish genetic links between ancient Mayan civilization and modern ethnic groups in Central America. Different Mayan populations sometimes clashed violently, and skeletons of decapitated prisoners of war litter sites such as Guatemala's Iximche. Stephen Whittington of the University of Maine believes that mitochondrial DNA testing of those victims may reveal that modern ethnic conflicts in places such as Guatemala have centuries-old roots. "You could say it's a politically loaded type of question," he says. "When you're looking at ethnic relations, when you're looking at who is a traditional enemy of whom, you can't just come out and say this is all academic." Straying from the purely academic, of course, is exactly what's needed to get anthropology to stop treading water.

become acquainted with the work of economists, agronomists, political scientists, and artists or art historians—disciplines that have made some particular dimensions of human life their specialization. Likewise, an ethnologist who specializes in some geographical region (such as West Africa, China, or Brazil) will read the works of historians, sociologists, novelists, and political scientists who also have written about the region. Cultural

In the past, most fieldworkers travelled to distant places to study non-Western peoples and cultures, like this French fieldworker in the Moluccas, Indonesia. Although this is less true today, anthropological fieldwork still focuses largely on small communities, allowing researchers to interact closely with local people.

anthropologists regularly study subjects that are the specializations of other disciplines, as is nicely illustrated by anthropological specializations in such areas as ethnomusicology, ethnopoetics, ethnobotany, and ethnolinguistics. (Here's an at least half-true general principle: Any subject can be made into a subject for ethnological research by prefixing it with "ethno.") Cultural anthropology thus cuts across many disciplines, encompassing many of the subjects that other scholars consider their special province—law, religion, literature, music, and so on.

Anthropological Approaches

Because cultural anthropologists study many of the same kinds of things studied by other scholars, obviously it is not *what* they study that makes the field distinct. Most ethnologists believe that the main difference between their discipline and other social sciences and humanities lies not so much in the *kinds* of subjects they investigate as in the *approach* they take to studying humankind. We believe it is important that cultures and communities be studied holistically, comparatively, and relativistically. Because it is these perspectives as much as anything else that make cultural anthropology distinctive, they need to be introduced.

Holistic Perspective

To study a subject holistically is to attempt to understand all the factors that influence it and to interpret it in the context of all those factors. The **holistic perspective** means that no single aspect of a human culture can be understood unless its relations to other aspects of the culture are explored. Holism requires, for example, that a fieldworker studying the rituals of a people must investigate how those rituals are influenced by the people's family life, economic forces, political leadership, relationships between the sexes, and a host of other factors. The attempt to understand a community's customs, beliefs, values, and so forth holistically is one reason why ethnographic fieldwork takes so much time and involves close contact with people.

Taken literally, a holistic understanding of a people's customs and beliefs is probably not possible because of the complexity of human societies. But cultural anthropologists have learned that ignoring the interrelations between language, religion, art, economy, family, and other dimensions of life results in distortions and misunderstandings. The essence of the holistic perspective may be stated fairly simply: *Look for connections and interrelations between things, and try to understand parts in the context of the whole.*

Comparative Perspective

As we have already seen, in the early decades of its existence ethnological research focused mainly on non-Western peoples, many of whom thought and acted quite differently from the citizens of the anthropologist's own (usually European or North American) nation. Anthropologists soon learned that the ideas and concepts that applied to their own societies often did not apply to those of other peoples, whose cultural traditions were vastly different. They learned, for example, to mistrust the claims put forth by French scholars about human nature when the only humans these scholars had ever encountered lived in Western Europe!

More than most people, anthropologists are aware of the enormous diversity of the world's cultures. This diversity means that any general theories or ideas scholars might have about humans—about human nature, sexuality, warfare, family relationships, and so on—must take into account information from a wide range of societies. In other words, general theoretical ideas about humans or human societies or cultures must be tested from a **comparative perspective**.

The main reason why anthropologists insist on comparison is simple: Unless we compare and contrast cultures to one another, we have no way of discovering whether some custom or behavior is unique to one culture (e.g., your own), or found among only certain cultures, or universal among all cultures. And unless we know whether a custom or behavior is found in one, in some, or in all cultures, we cannot investigate why it exists. The main danger here is that many people think that the customs and behavior that are familiar to them are characteristic of people everywhere—but this is usually not the case. Anthropologists know that the cultural ideas and practices of people living in different times and places are far too diverse for any general theory to be accepted until it has been tested in a wide range of human groups. The comparative perspective that anthropologists use to investigate their ideas may be stated as: *Generalizations about humans are likely to be mistaken unless they take the full range of cultural diversity into account.*

Relativistic Perspective

Fundamentally, **cultural relativism** means that no culture is inherently superior or inferior to any other. The reason anthropologists adopt this perspective is that concepts such as "superiority" require judgments about the relative worthiness of behaviors, beliefs, and other characteristics of a culture. But such judgments are usually rooted in one's values, and one's values, by and large, depend on the culture in which one was raised. (You may think, incidentally, that surely there are universally valid standards for judging and evaluating cultures. Perhaps you are right; the trouble is, people don't agree on what they are!)

To see why approaching the study of cultures relativistically is important, we may contrast cultural relativism with **ethnocentrism**. Ethnocentrism is the belief that the moral standards, manners, attitudes, and so forth of one's own culture are superior to those of other cultures. Most people are ethnocentric, and a *certain degree* of ethnocentrism probably is essential if people are to be content with their lives and if their culture is to persist. Mild ethnocentrism—meaning that people hold certain values dear but don't insist that everyone else hold and live by those values—is unobjectionable to ethnologists. But extreme ethnocentrism—meaning that people believe that their values are the only correct ones and that all people everywhere should be judged by how closely they live up to those values—breeds attitudes and behaviors of intolerance that are anathema to cultural anthropology.

Ethnocentric attitudes are detrimental to the objectivity of ethnographic fieldworkers. However difficult in practice, anthropologists should try to avoid evaluating the behavior of the people being studied according to the standards of the fieldworker's own culture. Like the holistic and comparative perspectives, the essential point of cultural relativism may be stated simply: *In studying another culture, do not evaluate the behavior of its members by the standards and values of your own culture.*

Anthropologists know that generalizations about humans must take the full range of cultural diversity into account. These women are of the Kaimanga people of Papua New Guinea.

The Value of Anthropology

What insights does anthropology offer about humanity? What is the value of the information anthropologists have gathered about the past and present of humankind? We have already seen that applied anthropologists help in planning and implementing programs, and in future chapters we look further at how anthropological research contributes to the solution of human problems. For now, we note some of the general insights of the field.

First, because of its broad scope, anthropology helps to understand the biological, technological, and cultural development of humanity over long time spans. Most of the reliable data now available about human biological evolution, prehistoric cultures, and non-Western peoples were collected by anthropologists. Much of this knowledge has become part of our cultural heritage. Because it is recorded in textbooks and taught in schools, we too easily forget that someone had to discover these facts and interpret their significance. For example, only in the late nineteenth century did most scientists accept that people are related to apes, and only in the late twentieth century did the closeness of this relation become apparent.

But anthropology has contributed more than just "facts." Concepts first developed or popularized by anthropologists have been incorporated into the thinking of millions of people. To illustrate, in this chapter we have used the term *culture*—a concept that we assume our readers are aware of and a word that commonly is used in everyday life. You may not know that the scientific meaning of this word, as used in the phrase "Japanese culture," is not very old. Well into the nineteenth century, people did not fully understand the importance of the distinction between a people's culture (the *learned* beliefs and habits that made them distinctive) and their biological makeup (their *inherited* physical characteristics). Patterns of acting,

thinking, and feeling often were thought to be rooted in a group's genetic makeup. For example, because there often are obvious differences in the physical appearances of various peoples, it was thought that these physical differences accounted for differences in beliefs and habits as well. In other words, differences that we now know are caused largely or entirely by learning and cultural upbringing were confused with differences caused by biological inheritance. Early twentieth-century anthropologists such as Franz Boas, Alfred Kroeber, and Ruth Benedict marshaled empirical evidence showing that race and culture are independent of each other. As this example shows, anthropologists have in fact contributed much to our understanding of the human condition, although most people are not aware of these contributions.

Another value of anthropology (ethnology, especially) is that it teaches us the importance of understanding and appreciating cultural diversity. Anthropology urges us not to be ethnocentric in our attitudes toward other peoples. The orientation known as cultural relativism is not only important to the objectivity of ethnologists but also one of the main lessons anthropology offers to the general public. Mutual toleration and understanding among the world's peoples is increasingly important in this era of world travel, international migration, global business, and ethnic conflicts. The world's problems will not be solved simply by eliminating ethnocentrism. But a relativistic outlook on cultural differences might help to alleviate some of the prejudices, misunderstandings, interethnic

One message anthropologists teach their students is understanding and appreciating the diversity of the world's many cultures. As interaction between peoples increases, the lesson of cross-cultural understanding becomes ever more important.

conflicts, and outright racism that continues to victimize so many people in all continents.

A related point is that anthropology helps people to avoid some of the miscommunication and misunderstandings that commonly arise when people from different parts of the world interact with one another. As we shall see in future chapters, our upbringing in a particular culture influences us in subtle ways. For instance, Canadians know how to interpret one another's actions on the basis of speech styles or body language, but these cues do not necessarily mean the same thing to people from different cultures. A Canadian salesperson selling products in Turkey may wonder why her host will not cut the chitchat and get down to business, whereas the Turk can't figure out why the visitor thinks they can do business before they have become better acquainted. An Anglo-American trying to appear self-confident in his dealings with a Latin American may instead come across as arrogant or egotistical. Anthropology teaches people to be aware of and sensitive to cultural differences—people's actions may not mean what we take them to mean, and much misunderstanding can be avoided by taking cultural differences into account in our dealings with other people.

Because of its insistence on studying humanity from a comparative perspective, anthropology helps us to understand our own individual lives. By encouraging you to compare and contrast yourself and your ways of thinking, feeling, and acting with those of people living in other times and places, anthropology helps you see new things about yourself. How does your life compare to the lives of other people around the world? What assumptions do you unconsciously make about the world and other people? Do people in other cultures share the same kinds of problems, hopes, motivations, and feelings as you do? Or are individuals raised in other societies completely different? How does the overall quality of your existence—your sense of well-being and happiness, your self-image, your emotional life, your feeling that life is meaningful—compare with people who live elsewhere? Anthropology offers the chance to compare yourself to other peoples who live in different circumstances. By studying others, we gain insight into ourselves.

Finally, anthropology gives new insights about modern society. Many citizens of the wealthy nations of North America, Europe, and East Asia are dissatisfied with their lives in spite of the fact that, compared to most humans living today, they are highly privileged. In North America, widespread unhappiness and dissatisfaction seem common. In the United States, affluent New Agers move to Sedona, Arizona, or to Santa Fe, New Mexico, in search of enhanced self-awareness, harmonic convergences, shamanic knowledge, Hindu philosophy, and other alternative "lifestyles" they hope will lend meaning to their lives. Baby boomers who have made it into the middle class enter middle age in fear of losing their middle management jobs, all the while doubting that Social Security will be there for them. Members of Generation X worry that they will never get a chance to live the American Dream no matter how many goods and how much education their frazzled parents buy for them. Are people of the late twentieth century in fact more stressed out than people were in previous centuries? Have people always lived in fear and uncertainty? No one truly knows the answers to such questions, but anthropologists do have contributions to make, some of which are discussed in future chapters of this book.

Summary

Defined as the study of humanity, anthropology differs from other disciplines in the social sciences and humanities primarily because of its broad scope. The field as a whole is concerned with all human beings of the past and present, living at all levels of technological development. Anthropology is also interested in all aspects of humanity: biology, language, technology, art, politics, religion, and all other dimensions of human life.

Individual anthropologists of today usually specialize in one of five subdisciplines. Physical anthropology studies the biological dimensions of human beings, including our biological evolution, the physical variations between contemporary populations, and the biology and behavior of nonhuman primates. Archaeology uses the material remains of prehistoric and historic cultures to investigate the past, focusing on the long-term technological and social changes that occurred in particular regions of the world. Cultural anthropology, or ethnology, is concerned with the social and cultural life of contemporary and historically recent human societies. By conducting fieldwork in various human communities and describing their findings in ethnographies, cultural anthropologists contribute to the scientific understanding of cultural diversity and to making the general public more aware and tolerant of cultural differences. Anthropological linguistics studies language, concentrating on nonwritten languages and investigating the interrelations between language and other elements of a people's way of life. Finally, applied anthropology uses the concepts, methods, and theories of the discipline of anthropology to solve real-world problems in such areas as health, development, and education.

Until around 1970 cultural anthropology (the main subject of this text) concentrated on human cultures that are popularly known as "tribal," "premodern," or "preindustrial." This is not as true today, when anthropologists often do their research in the complex urbanized and industrialized nations of the developed world. It is increasingly difficult to distinguish ethnology from the kindred discipline of sociology. However, firsthand, extended fieldwork in villages or relatively small towns or neighborhoods continues to be a hallmark of cultural anthropology. Also, ethnologists are far more comparative in their interests and research than other social sciences.

Cultural anthropologists also differ from other scholars who study living people by their approach. There are three main characteristics of this approach. Holism is the attempt to discern and investigate the interrelations between the customs and beliefs of a particular society. The comparative perspective means that any attempt to understand humanity or explain cultures or behaviors must include information from a wide range of human ways of life, for anthropologists have learned that most customs and beliefs are products of cultural tradition and social environment, rather than of a universal human nature. The perspective known as cultural relativism refers to fieldworkers' efforts to understand people's behaviors on their own terms, not those of the anthropologist's own culture. This requires that anthropologists avoid being ethnocentric in their research, for each people have their own history and values.

Anthropology has practical value in the modern world, and it is not as esoteric as many people think. Only anthropology allows us to see the development of human biology and culture over long time spans. Most of the knowledge we have about human evolution, prehistoric populations, and modern tribal societies was discovered by anthropologists. Early anthropologists were instrumental in popularizing the concept of culture and in showing that cultural differences are not caused by racial differences. The value of inculcating understanding and tolerance among citizens of different nations is another practical lesson of anthropology, one that is increasingly important as the economics of the world become more interdependent and as the development of weaponry makes the consequences of international misunderstanding more serious. The information that ethnographers have collected about alternative ways of being human allows us to become more self-aware. The comparative perspective of anthropology also gives us insights into our own society.

Key Terms

physical/biological anthropology
paleoanthropology
primatology
human variation
forensic anthropology
archaeology

prehistoric archaeology
historic archaeology
cultural resource management
contract archaeology
cultural anthropology (ethnology)
fieldwork
ethnography
anthropological linguistics
applied anthropology

medical anthropology
development anthropology
educational anthropology
holistic perspective
comparative perspective
cultural relativism
ethnocentrism

Suggested Readings

The following four books are among the best introductions to some of the subdisciplines of anthropology:

Fagan, Brian. *People of the Earth: An Introduction to World Prehistory*. 9th ed. New York: Addison-Wesley, 1997.
 • *Comprehensive textbook, written for undergraduates, covering the prehistory of all continents.*
Fromkin, Victoria, and Robert Rodman. *An Introduction to Language*. 5th ed. San Diego: Harcourt Brace Jovanovich, 1992.
 • *A thorough and witty introduction to linguistics.*

Jurmain, Robert, Harry Nelson, Lynn Kilgore, and Wendy Trevathan. *Essentials of Physical Anthropology*. 3rd ed. Belmont, Calif.: Wadsworth, 1998.
 • *A relatively brief introduction to primatology, human evolution, and genetic and physical variation among human populations.*
Renfrew, Colin, and Paul Bahn. *Archaeology: Theories, Methods, and Practice*. 2nd ed. London: Thames and Hudson, 1996.
 • *Comprehensive yet user-friendly textbook focusing on the methods archaeologists use to investigate the past.*

The following ethnographies are excellent for introducing the ways of life of various people around the world. All are highly readable.

Chagnon, Napoleon A. *Yanomamö: The Last Days of Eden.* San Diego: Harcourt Brace Jovanovich, 1992.
  • *A readable ethnography of an Amazonian people who are threatened by the incursions of missionaries, miners, tourists, and other outsiders.*

Farrer, Claire R. *Thunder Rides a Black Horse: Mescalero Apaches and the Mythic Present.* 2nd ed. Prospect Heights, Ill.: Waveland, 1996.
  • *Concise account of ethnographer's experience with the modern Apache. Focuses on girl's puberty ceremonies, interweaving Apache culture into the account.*

Fernea, Elizabeth. *Guests of the Sheik.* Garden City, N.Y.: Anchor, 1969.
  • *A writer, journalist, and academician's account of her experiences in an Iraqi village with her anthropologist husband.*

Kraybill, Donald B. *The Puzzles of Amish Life.* Intercourse, Penn.: Good Books, 1990.
  • *Focuses on how the Amish of Lancaster County, Pennsylvania, have maintained intact communities and their values by selectively using modern technologies.*

Shostak, Marjorie. *Nisa: The Life and Words of a !Kung Woman.* New York: Vintage, 1983.
  • *An outstanding biographical account of a San woman.*

Thomas, Elizabeth Marshall. *The Harmless People.* 2nd ed. New York: Vintage, 1989.
  • *A wonderfully written account of the customs and beliefs of the San (formerly called "Bushmen") of southern Africa.*

Turnbull, Colin. *The Forest People.* New York: Simon & Schuster, 1962.
  • *A readable and sympathetic ethnography about the traditional culture of the BaMbuti pygmies of the African rain forest.*

Ward, Martha C. *Nest in the Wind.* Prospect Heights, Ill.: Waveland, 1989.
  • *A delightful account of a fieldworker's experiences and difficulties on a tropical Pacific island.*

Internet Exercises

Introduction to the Internet

The Internet is a growing resource of information that is becoming more widely used by anthropologists. Internet exercises follow each chapter in this book. These exercises will point out material available via the Internet that relate to the content of each chapter. The exercises are also designed to give the student experience using the Internet as a research tool. Considering the growing amount of information that can be accessed through the Internet, it is important to learn the search skills necessary to find the best and most relevant information on specific topics.

Those of you who are not yet familiar with using the Internet should not be intimidated. Ask a friend or a site assistant at a public computing site to help you with getting started. Once you learn how to log on and find out how to get around on the "Information Superhighway" you will realize that it is not very complicated. A good starting point, even for those who have some experience on the Internet, is a tour of the World Wide Web designed by Hugh Jarvis, a professor of archaeology at the State University of New York at Buffalo (http://wings.buffalo.edu/go?tour). Other sites which discuss the Internet and its implications for anthropology are Brian Schwimmer's "Anthropology on the Internet: A Review and Evaluation of Networked Resources" (http://www.artsci.wustl.edu/~anthro/ca/papers/schwimmer/intro.html). Both of these sites explain what the Internet is and how it works.

There are many anthropology resources available on the Internet; there are websites, discussion groups, and newsgroups. Wadsworth Publishing Company maintains a website with useful information, many links to other anthropology resources, and the homepage for this textbook at (http://anthropology.wadsworth.com).

Another web-based Internet feature unique to this textbook is Infotrac College Edition. Infotrac College Edition is an online university library with access to over 600 periodicals. To get started you can link to Infotrac College Edition from this text's homepage at (http://anthropology.wadsworth.com) or by pointing your web browser to (http://infotrac-college.com/wadsworth). Click on Enter Infotrac

College-Wadsworth Edition. Next you will be asked for a password provided with your textbook. After typing in the password click on Log in. To see a list of the journal titles available click on Power Trac. Then select "Journal Name List" under Choose Search Index and click on submit search. Besides having a number of anthropology journals such as: *The Australian Journal of Anthropology, The Canadian Review of Sociology and Anthropology,* and *Journal of the Royal Anthropological Institute,* you will also find there are many other social science journals that are related to anthropological interests.

The American Anthropological Association, the world's largest organization of anthropologists, also has a list of links to anthropology resources on the Internet (http://ameranthassn.org/). Other sites that provide a wide variety of links are *Nicole's AnthroPage,* a website created by Nicole Noonan (http://wsu.edu:8000/~i9248809/anthrop.html) and *Anthropology Resources on the Internet,* compiled by Allen H. Lutkins (http://www.nitehawk.com/alleycat/anth-faq.html).

Please note that the websites listed in this text were all current at the time of publication, but Internet addresses often change. Usually the authors of the website will provide a link to the new site (if there is one), but not always. Sites are pointed out in this book because of their pertinence to the material covered in the chapter and the overall quality of the site. This is far from an exhaustive list however. The number of Internet resources relating to anthropology is growing at an ever-increasing rate. Treat the sites mentioned in the text as starting points for your own web surfing. If you find something new, report it to a site that maintains lists of links. Some sites, such as *Nicole's AnthroPage* (http://wsu.edu:8000/~i9248809/anthrop.html), have a place on their pages where you can add a link; most others have a place to contact the webmaster of the site.

CHAPTER 2

Culture

Defining Culture

Shared . . .

. . . Socially Learned . . .

. . . Knowledge . . .

. . . and Patterns of Behavior.

Cultural Knowledge

Norms

Values

Symbols

Classifications of Reality

World Views

Culture and Human Life

Cultural Knowledge and Individual Behavior

Biology and Cultural Differences

The culture of a particular human group largely determines how its members think, act, and feel.

Visit http://www.wadsworth.com/humanity to learn more about the material covered in this chapter and to access activities, exercises, and tutorial quizzes.

*C*ULTURE IS A WORD *many people use practically every day. For example, you may think that you increase your "appreciation of culture" by going to the symphony or art gallery. Or you may have heard someone in the "cultural elite" complain about the "popular culture" of TV sitcoms, movies, computer games, nose rings, afternoon soap operas, and rap music. Perhaps you even use peoples' speech style or personal tastes to conclude that some individuals are more "cultured" than others because of their education, social class, or upbringing.*

TAKEN IN CONTEXT, these ways of using the word culture are fine. But anthropologists define and use the term in quite a different way, for we want people to appreciate the full significance of culture for our understanding of humanity. In the anthropological conception, the distinction between "high culture" and "low culture" is largely meaningless, and it is impossible for one group of people to be more "cultured"—to "have more culture"—than others.

IN THIS CHAPTER, *we discuss the anthropological conception of culture. After giving the word a fairly precise definition, we cover some of its main elements, introducing some terms along the way. We then discuss why culture is so important to the human species. Finally, we explain the modern anthropological view of how cultural differences and physical/biological differences between human populations are related.*

One of the first explicit definitions of culture was given over a century ago by E.B. Tylor, one of the founders of anthropology. In 1871, Tylor defined culture as "that complex whole which includes knowledge, belief, art, morals, law, customs, and any other capabilities and habits acquired by man as a member of society." Notice that this definition is very broad, including almost everything about a people's overall way of life, from their "knowledge" to their "habits." Notice also that culture is something individuals acquire as "a member of society," meaning that people obtain their culture from growing up with and living among a particular group.

Since Tylor's day, anthropologists have defined *culture* in hundreds of ways, although the main elements of Tylor's original conception of culture are still valid. (In fact, many modern ethnologists have their own favorite definitions!) Practically all modern definitions share certain key features. Anthropologists say that culture

- is learned from others in the process of growing up in a particular human society or group;
- is widely shared by the members of that society or group;
- is responsible for most of the differences in ways of thinking and behaving that exist between human societies or groups; and
- is so essential in completing the psychological and social development of individuals that a "culture-less" individual would not be considered normal by other people.

Culture, then, is learned, shared, largely responsible for group-level differences, and necessary to make individuals into complete persons.

Cultural anthropologists often use the term *culture* when they want to emphasize the unique or most distinctive aspects of a group of peoples' customs and beliefs. When we speak of Japanese culture, for example, we usually mean whatever beliefs and customs the Japanese people share that make them different from other people. How the Japanese think and act differs in some ways from how the North Americans, Iranians, Chinese, and Indians think and act, and the phrase *Japanese*

culture concisely emphasizes these differences. So to speak of the culture of a people is to call attention to all the things that make that people distinctive from others and, hence, that make that people unique in some respects.

Notice that there are some things that anthropologists do *not* mean when we use the word culture. We do not mean that Japanese culture is better or worse than, say, French or Indian culture. We mean only that the three differ in certain identifiable ways. Anthropologists also do not mean that Japanese, French, or Indian culture is unchanging. We mean only that they remain in some ways distinct despite the changes that have occurred in them over the years. Above all, anthropologists do not mean that Japanese, French, or Indian cultures are different because of the physical (biological) differences between the three peoples. We mean only that Japanese, French, and Indian children are exposed to different ways of thinking and acting as they grow up, so that they *become* Japanese, French, or Indian because of their upbringing in different social environments.

In what kinds of ways do cultures differ? How do cultures vary? As a first look, we can say that cultures vary in their ways of thinking and ways of behaving. *Ways of thinking* means what goes on inside people's heads: how they perceive the world around them, how they feel, what they desire, what they fear, and so forth. *Ways of behaving* refers to how people commonly act: how they conduct themselves around parents and spouses, how they carry out ceremonies, what they do when they are angry or sad, and so forth. Obviously, thought and behavior are connected. How we act depends, in part, on how and what we think. In turn, the ways we think depend, in part, on how people around us behave.

Although ways of thinking and behaving are interdependent, it is important to distinguish between them. To do so, many anthropologists say that culture consists of *mental* and *behavioral* components.

Culture's mental components include all the knowledge and information about the world and society that children learn while growing up. These include attitudes about family, friends, enemies, and other people; notions of right and wrong (morality); conceptions about the proper roles of males and females; ideas about appropriate dress, hygiene, and personal ornamentation (etiquette); beliefs about the supernatural; rules about sexual activity; notions about the best or proper way to live (values); and perceptions of the world. The list could, of course, be greatly expanded to include all other knowledge that the members of a society or other group have learned from previous generations. All these kinds of knowledge largely determine how members of a culture think.

In this book, we shall use the phrase **cultural knowledge** to refer to the information, attitudes, ideas, beliefs, conceptions, rules, values, perceptions, and other mental phenomena that affect people's ways of thinking. To avoid repetition, we shall use the terms *beliefs* and *ideas* as synonyms for *knowledge.*

For now, there are two key points about cultural knowledge. First, ideas and beliefs are learned as a consequence of being born into and growing up among a particular group. This means that any information or knowledge that people genetically inherit (for example, "instincts") is not—by definition—part of culture. Second, cultural knowledge exists in people's heads. Members of any given generation are carriers of cultural ideas, which they have learned from previous generations and will pass along, perhaps with some modifications, to future generations.

The behavioral components of culture include all the things people regularly do, or how they habitually act. As the terms *regularly* and *habitually* imply, members of the same culture generally adopt similar behaviors in similar situations (e.g., in church, on the job, at a wedding or funeral, visiting a friend). Anthropologists tend to be more interested in these regularities and habits—in what most people do most of the time when they are in similar situations—than in the behavior of individuals per se. We are most concerned with **patterns of behavior**. To avoid repetition, we use the terms *behavior(s)* and *action(s)* as synonyms for the patterns that make up a culture's ways of behaving.

Although we distinguish between the mental and the behavioral components of culture, the two are closely related and profoundly affect each other. To emphasize these interconnections, we speak of **cultural integration**, meaning that the various elements of culture fit together in a more or less coherent way. Stated differently, cultural integration means that the parts of culture are mutually interdependent. We use the phrase *cultural system* when we wish to emphasize the integration of culture.

Defining Culture

The concept of culture is so important to cultural anthropologists that it is useful to have a formal definition of the term:

> The **culture** of a group consists of shared, socially learned knowledge and patterns of behavior.

For convenience, we discuss each major component of this definition separately.

Shared . . .

By definition, culture is *collective*—it is shared by some group of people. "Shared by some group of people" is deliberately vague, because the "group" that "shares" culture depends on our interests. The people who share a common cultural tradition may be quite numerous and

geographically dispersed, as illustrated by the phrases "Western culture" and "African culture." Although we use such phrases whenever we want to emphasize differences between Africans and Westerners, the peoples to whom they refer are so diverse that the term "group" has little meaning. At the other extreme, the group that shares a common culture may be small. Some Pacific islands or Amazonian tribes, for instance, have only a few hundred members, yet the people speak a unique language and have distinct customs and beliefs.

Despite these and other complexities, when we say people *share culture* we usually mean at least one of two things. First, the people are capable of communicating and interacting with one another without serious misunderstanding and without needing to explain what their behavior means. Second, people share a common **cultural identity:** they recognize themselves and their culture's traditions as distinct from other people and other traditions. Thus, Africans (or Westerners, or Native Americans) do not share culture by the first criterion, although they do by the second.

People who share a common culture often live in the same **society**, or a territorially defined population most of whose members speak the same language and share a sense of common identity relative to other societies. The identification of a cultural tradition with a single society is sometimes convenient because it allows us to use phrases like "American culture" and "Indian culture." Societies and cultures, however, do not always share the same physical territory. For example, we usually think of a modern nation as a single society, yet many cultural groupings, identities, and traditions coexist within the boundaries of most modern nations.

. . . Socially Learned . . .

To say that culture is *socially learned* is to say that individuals acquire it from others in the process of growing up in a society or some other kind of group. The process by which infants and children socially learn the culture of those around them is called **enculturation**. The learning of one's culture, of course, happens as a normal part of peoples' childhood.

To say that culture is *learned* is to deny that culture is transmitted to new generations *genetically*, by biological reproduction. Culture is not part of a particular human group's biological makeup, but is something the people born into that group acquire while growing up among other members. Biological/genetic differences (including "racial" differences) between human populations do not explain the differences in thinking, feeling, and acting between human populations. Africans, East Asians, Europeans, and Native Americans do not differ in their cultures because they differ in their gene frequencies—they

Children acquire culture from social learning, not biological heredity. As they grow up in a community, they learn appropriate ways of feeling, thinking, and acting, a process known as enculturation.

can adopt the diet of other members of my family and culture, thus avoiding the costs (and possible danger and pain!) of learning on my own, by trial and error.

Think about the enormous advantages of humans' reliance on social learning rather than trial and error learning. First, anything that one individual learns can be communicated to others in a group, who can take advantage of someone else's experience. Second, the culture that any generation has acquired is passed down to the next generation, which transmits it to the third generation, and so on. Thus, the knowledge and behavior acquired by one generation is potentially available to future generations (some of it is lost or replaced each generation, of course). By this process of social learning, over many generations knowledge can accumulate. Because of this accumulation, people alive today live largely off the knowledge acquired and transmitted by previous generations. Members of new generations socially learn such knowledge through enculturation and, in modern societies, through formal education in schools and colleges.

. . . Knowledge . . .

When anthropologists use the phrase *cultural knowledge*, we do not mean that a people's beliefs, perceptions, rules, standards, and so forth are true, in an objective or absolute sense. In our professional role, anthropologists do not judge the accuracy or worthiness of a group's knowledge. Indeed, we recognize that the knowledge of any cultural group differs to a greater or lesser degree from the knowledge of any other group; in fact, such differences are one of the major things we attempt to describe and understand. What is most important about cultural knowledge is not its Truth Value, but that:

- the members of a culture share enough knowledge to be capable of behaving in ways that are meaningful and acceptable to others, so that they do not constantly misunderstand one another or have to explain what they are doing; and that
- the knowledge leads people to behave in ways that work at least well enough to allow them to survive and reproduce themselves and transmit their culture.

In a few words, cultural knowledge must lead to behavior that is meaningful to others and adaptive to the natural and social environment. We consider some of this knowledge in the next section.

. . . and Patterns of Behavior.

"Human behavior varies from culture to culture," as you may have heard. But even individuals who are brought

do not differ *culturally* because they differ *biologically*. Any human infant is perfectly capable of learning the culture of any human group or biological population, just as any child can learn the language of whatever group she or he happens to be born into. To state the main point in a few words: *cultural differences and biological differences are largely independent of one another.*

To say that culture is *socially learned* is to say that people do not learn culture primarily by *trial and error learning*. The main way children learn culture is by observation, imitation, communication, and inference, and not by trial and error. One important way in which humans differ in degree, though not in kind, from other primates is the ability to learn by imitating and communicating with other humans. I do not have to learn what is good to eat by trying out a variety of foods, then rejecting those that taste bad or make me sick, and retaining in my diet only those that are tasty, satisfying, and nourishing. Rather, I

up in the same culture differ in their behaviors. The behavior of individuals varies for several reasons. First, individuals have different *social identities*: males and females, old and young, rich and poor, parents and children, and so forth. Behavior appropriate for people with one identity may not be appropriate for others. Second, individual behavior varies with *context and situation*: A woman acts differently depending on whether she is interacting with her husband, child, priest, or employee. Third, each human individual is in some ways a unique human individual: We all differ in our emotional responses, interpretations of events, reactions to stimuli, and so forth. Finally, cultural standards for and expectations of behavior are not always clear, a point covered in more detail later in this chapter. For these and other reasons, it is a mistake to think of behavior as uniform within the same culture.

Despite such complexities, within a single cultural grouping there are behavioral regularities or patterns. For instance, if you were to visit an Amazonian rain forest people known as the Yąnomamö, you might be shocked by some of their behaviors. By most cultures' standards, the Yąnomamö are unusually demanding and aggressive. Slight insults often meet with violent responses. Quarreling men may duel one another in a chest-pounding contest, during which they take turns beating one another on the chest, alternating one blow at a time. More serious quarrels sometimes call for clubs, with which men bash one another on the head. A man may shave the top of his head to display proudly the scars he has received from his many club fights. Fathers sometimes encourage their sons to strike them (and anyone else) by teasing and goading, all the while praising the child for his fierceness.

If, on the other hand, you were to visit the Semai, a people of Malaysia, you might be surprised at how seldom they express anger and hostility. Indeed, you might find them *too* docile. One adult should never strike another—"Suppose he hit you back?" they ask. With this attitude toward violence, murder is nonexistent or extremely rare—so rare, in fact, that there are no penalties for it. The Semai seldom hit their children—"How would you feel if he or she died?" they ask. When children misbehave the worst physical punishment they receive is a pinch on the cheek or a pat on the hand. Ethnographer Robert Dentan suggests one reason for the nonviolence of the Semai: Children are so seldom exposed to physical punishment that when they grow up they have an exaggerated impression of the effects of violence.

A Yąnomamö and a Semai react to similar situations in different ways, with different behaviors. If one Yąnomamö demands something of another—as they often do—and the demand is refused, the asker is likely to fly into a rage and make threats, and may resort to violence.

The behavioral patterns of different human groups are quite variable. The Yąnomamö, for instance, are more prone to violence than most other peoples.

If a Semai fails to grant the request of another, the person who is refused may experience a psychological state Semai call *punan*. Punan might be translated as "accident proneness" because the Semai think that to make someone unhappy by frustrating their desires increases that person's chances of having an accident. So (and this is perfectly logical, given their beliefs) if you ask me for something and I refuse your request, I have committed an offense against you that could result in your becoming accidentally injured. You, being the victim of the punan caused by my affront, have the right to demand compensation from me.

The contrasting behavioral responses of Yąnomamö and Semai people to requests made by others illustrate an important characteristic of most human behavior: its social nature. Humans are supremely social animals. We seldom do anything alone, and even when we are alone we rely unconsciously on our cultural upbringing to provide us with the knowledge of what to do and how to act. Relationships between people are therefore enormously important in all cultures. Anthropologists pay special heed to the regularities and patterning of these social relationships, including such things as how family members interact, how females and males relate to one another, how political leaders deal with subordinates, and so forth.

The concept of **role** is useful to describe and analyze interactions and relationships in the context of a group. Individuals are often said to "have a role" in some group.

Roles usually carry names or labels. Examples are "mother" in a family, "student" in a classroom, "accountant" in a company, and "headman" of a Yąnomamö village. Attached to roles are the group's *expectations* about what people who hold the role should do. Learning to be a member of a group includes learning its expectations. Expectations include rights and duties. The *rights* (or privileges) I have as someone with a role include the benefits I and other group members agree I should receive as a member. My *duties* (or obligations) as the holder of a role include what I am expected to do for other members or for the group as a whole.

Rights and duties are usually *reciprocal*: my right over you is your duty to me, and vice versa. My duties to the group as a whole are the group's rights over me, and vice versa. If I adequately perform my duties to the group, other members reward me, just as I reward them for their own role performance. By occupying and performing a role in a group, I get some of my own wants and needs fulfilled, and I do so by behaving in ways that others find valuable and satisfying. Conversely, failure to live up to the group's expectations of role performance is likely to bring some sort of informal or formal punishment. Among Yąnomamö, young men who refuse to stand up for themselves by fighting are ridiculed and may never amount to anything.

During enculturation into a particular culture, children learn the kinds of roles that exist and the expectations people have about the rights and duties of those roles. The shared knowledge of roles and expectations is partly responsible for patterns of behavior.

Cultural Knowledge

As we have seen, cultural knowledge includes a people's beliefs, attitudes, rules, assumptions about the world, and other mental phenomena. In this section we discuss five elements of cultural knowledge: norms, values, symbols, classifications of reality, and world views. These five elements are not necessarily more important than other kinds of cultural knowledge, but they do require some discussion because they are not entirely commonsensical.

Norms

Norms are shared ideals (or rules) about how people ought to act in certain situations, or about how particular people should act toward particular other people. The emphasis here is on the words *ideal, rule, ought*, and *should*. To say that norms exist does not mean everyone follows them all the time; indeed, some norms are violated with great regularity. *Norm* implies, rather, that (1)

there is widespread agreement that people ought to adhere to certain standards of behavior, (2) other people judge the behavior of a person according to how closely it adheres to those standards, and (3) people who repeatedly fail to follow the standards face some kind of negative reaction from other members of the group. We are able to make collective judgments about someone's personal morality or character because we share common norms. Shared expectations about how roles should be performed are one kind of norm.

Sometimes people feel that norms are irrational rules that stifle their creativity or keep them from doing what they want for no good reason. People may believe that some norms about proper conduct are confining, such as norms about how to dress correctly for special occasions, or about when and to whom we must give gifts, or about fulfilling familial obligations, or about when to have sex. But in fact, norms are quite useful to us as individuals. It is mainly because we agree on norms that we know how to behave toward others and that we have expectations about how others should act toward us. For example, when you enter a roomful of strangers at a party, you are somewhat uncertain about how to act. But everyone knows how to go about getting acquainted in your cultural tradition, so you soon are introducing yourself, shaking hands, and asking the other guests what they do, what they are studying, and so forth. Here, and in many other cases in everyday life, norms are not experienced as oppressive. They serve as useful instructions on how to do something in such a way that others know what you are doing and accept your actions as—what else?—"normal."

Values

Values consist of a people's beliefs about the goals or way of life that is desirable for themselves and their society. Values have profound, although partly unconscious, effects on people's behavior. The aims we pursue, as well as our more general ideas about "the good life," are influenced by the values of the culture into which we happen to have been born or raised. Values affect our motivations—why we do what we do. Values also are critical to the maintenance of culture as a whole because they represent the qualities that people believe are essential to continuing their way of life. It is useful to think of values as providing the ultimate standards that people believe must be upheld under practically all circumstances.

An excellent example of how values provide ultimate standards is the American emphasis on certain rights of individuals, as embodied in the Bill of Rights to the Constitution. No matter how much some Americans hate what the press prints, what the right or left wing says, or the pro-life or pro-choice movements, few believe that unpopular organizations or speech should be suppressed, so long as they do not engage in or advocate violence. Freedom of the press, of speech, and of religion are ultimate standards that take precedence over the opinions and interests of the moment. People may be deeply attached to some of their values and, under certain circumstances, be prepared to sacrifice their lives for them.

Symbols

A **symbol** is an object or behavior that stands for, represents, or calls to mind something else. Just as we learn norms and values during enculturation, so do we learn the meanings that people in our group attach to symbols. And just as norms and values affect the patterns of behavior found in a culture, so do the understandings people share of the meanings of symbols. In fact, unless individuals agree that certain kinds of behavior communicate certain meanings, social interaction would be far more difficult than it usually is. Our common understandings of the meanings of behaviors allow us to interact with one another without the need to explain our intentions, or to state explicitly what we are doing and why.

For the most part, the understandings that the members of a culture share about the meanings of behaviors and objects are unconscious. We can speak to inquiring strangers about our values and explain to them why we believe they are important. But it is nearly impossible to tell someone why a wink, a tone of voice, a way of wearing jewelry, a particular gesture, a way of walking, a style of dress, or a particular facial expression carries the meaning it does, rather than some other meaning. We "just know" as "everyone knows," for such things are "common knowledge."

Two important properties of symbols are that their meanings are usually arbitrary and conventional. *Arbitrary* in this context means that there are no inherent qualities in the symbol that leads a human group to attribute one meaning to it rather than some other meaning. Thus, the wink of an eye that often means "just kidding" in some cultures is—literally—meaningless in other cultures. *Conventional* refers to the fact that the meanings exist only because people implicitly agree they exist. Thus, at an intersection, a red light means "stop," but only because all drivers agree (hopefully!) that it does.

Words provide a familiar example of the arbitrary and conventional nature of symbols. In English the word for a certain kind of large animal is *horse,* but in Spanish the same animal is called *caballo*, in German *pferd*, in Arabic *hisanun*, in French *cheval*, and so on for other languages. There is nothing about the animal itself that makes one of these words better than the others. The meaning "horse" is conveyed equally well by any of the

People often are deeply attached emotionally to the values of their culture, as this outpouring of grief in Britain at the funeral of Princess Diana illustrates.

words, which is another way of saying that the meaning is arbitrary and conventional.

The shared understandings that allow people to correctly interpret the meanings of behaviors is an enormously important part of cultural knowledge. Because you assume that the people you interact with share your understandings, in most situations you know how to act so as not to be misunderstood.

To most North Americans, for example, actions such as nodding the head to show agreement or affirmation, walking hand in hand in public, and embracing a friend or relative seem commonsensical and perhaps "natural." Yet these and other social behaviors do not mean the same thing in all cultures. An important part of enculturation consists of leaning how to interpret the behavior of other people and how to adjust our own behavior in accord with their expectations. Culture, in other words, provides us with the common understanding of how to interact with one another appropriately (that is, according to shared expectations) and meaningfully (that is, in such a way that other people usually are able to interpret our intentions).

Nonverbal communication provides a fine example of these understandings. When you interact with someone face to face, you are engaged in a continual giving and receiving of messages, communicated both by speech and behavior. Spoken messages are intentionally (consciously) sent and received. Other messages—including body language, facial expressions, hand gestures, touching, and the use of physical space—are communicated by nonverbal behavior, much of which is unconscious. Nonverbal messages emphasize, supplement, or complement spoken messages. We are not always conscious of what we are communicating nonverbally, and sometimes our body language even contradicts what we are saying. (Is this how your mother often could tell when you were lying?)

The general point is that cultural knowledge conditions social behavior in ways people do not always recognize consciously—at least until someone's behavior violates collective understandings. Furthermore, gestures and other body movements with well-known meanings in one culture have no meaning, or different meanings, in another. On a Micronesian island studied by one of the authors, people may answer "yes" or show agreement by a sharp intake of breath (a "gasp") or by simply raising the eyebrows. One may also answer "yes" by the grunting sound that carries exactly the opposite meaning to North Americans. Pointing is done with the nose, not the finger. You would signal "I don't know" or "I'm not sure" by wrinkling your nose, rather than shrugging your shoulders. "Come here" or "come closer" is indicated by moving the arm in the direction of the person you are communicating with; this motion is exactly the same one used by North Americans to mean "move further away." For two people of the opposite sex, even spouses or engaged couples, to hold hands in public is offensive and bad manners; however, it is perfectly acceptable for two same-sex friends to walk hand in hand. One should never touch the head of someone else, especially if the person is of similar or higher status. It is rude to walk between two people engaged in conversation; if possible, one walks around them; if not, one says the equivalent of "please excuse me," waits for permission, and then crouches down while passing between them.

Aside from showing the necessity of shared understandings of symbolic behavior, these examples of personal space and gestures show one way misunderstandings occur when individuals with different cultural upbringings interact. Raised in different cultures where spacing and gestures carry different meanings, each individual (mis)interprets the behavior of the other based on their own culture's understandings, often seeing the other as rude, unfriendly, insensitive, overly familiar, and so forth. Arabs and Iranians often stand "too close" for the Canadian and American comfort zone. Japanese are less likely than North Americans to express definite opinions or preferences, which often comes across as uncertainty or tentativeness. The common American tendency to be informal and friendly is viewed as inappropriate in Japan and many other cultural settings, where feelings of warmth and closeness are confined to narrow circles, or where outward manifestations of emotions are held in check.

Classifications of Reality

The members of a cultural tradition share ideas of what kinds of things and people exist. They have similar **classifications of reality**, meaning that the human and natural environments are divided up according to shared criteria.

For example, people everywhere recognize a category of people who are related to them biologically or through adoption—their relatives, we call them. But the principles by which certain kinds of relatives are placed into cultural categories vary between kinship systems. Thus, English speakers think of the sisters of both our mother and our father as a single kind of relative, and we call them by the same kinship term, *aunt*. But there are some cultural traditions in which the sister of one's mother is considered one kind of relative and the sister of one's father a different kind, and each is called by a separate kinship term. As we shall see in Chapter 9, these various ways of classifying kin are connected to other characteristics of a people's kinship system. The general point for now is that people of different cultural traditions have different ideas about social life, and vary in the way they conceive of their societies as divided up into kinds of people.

The same applies to the way people classify their natural environment. Cultural knowledge not only provides the categories by which we classify kinds of people, but also categories by which plants, animals, phases of the moon, seasonal changes, and other natural phenomena are classified into kinds. The way people classify the things in their natural environment both affects and is affected by how they relate to that environment.

For example, on the island of Mindoro in the Philippines lives a people known as the Hanunóo, who grow most of their food by a method called *shifting cultivation*. This method involves farming a plot for one or two years, abandoning it for a number of years until it has recovered its potential to yield a crop, and then replanting it. The Hanunóo judge whether a plot they abandoned some years previously has recovered enough for replanting by the quantity and kind of natural vegetation that has recolonized the plot. The need to assess the degree of readiness of a plot for recultivation has led the Hanunóo to develop an extremely complex classification of the plants found in their habitat. They are able to identify more than 1,600 "kinds" of plants, which exceeds by more than 400 the number of species that a botanist would distinguish.

Which classification is right, that of the Hanunóo or that of the botanist? Both. The point is not that the Hanunóo are right and the botanist wrong, or vice versa. Rather, the botanist uses one set of criteria to decide whether two individual plants belong to the same kind, and these criteria have been adopted because they have proved useful to science. The Hanunóo use a different set of criteria that, over the course of many generations, they have developed for their specific needs. The criteria by which various realms of nature are carved up and assigned to categories are important components of cultural knowledge because they influence the way a people perceive the natural world.

They also influence how people use the resources in their environments. Plants and animals are classified not just into various kinds but also into various categories of usefulness. Members of different cultural traditions perceive nature in different ways, and what one people consider a resource is not necessarily defined as a resource for another people. For example, Muslims and Orthodox Jews consider pork unclean. Traditional Hindus refuse to consume the flesh of cattle, their sacred animal. The fact that a given animal or plant is edible does not mean that people *consider* it edible (or else more North Americans would eat dogs, as do many east and southeast Asians, and horses, as do many French).

Taking this one step further, people of different cultures differ in their beliefs about the kinds of things that do and do not exist. For instance, some people believe that some individuals (called witches) use malevolent supernatural powers to harm their enemies. Traditional Navajo believe that witches can change themselves into wolves, bears, and other animals. The Tukano people of the Bolivian rain forest think that a spirit of the forest controls the game animals they depend on for meat. So a Tukano group's shaman periodically makes a supernatural visit to the abode of the forest spirit. He promises to magically kill a certain number of humans and to send their souls to the forest spirit in return for the spirit's releasing the animals so the hunters can find game. In sum, not only do different cultures classify objective reality in different ways, but they differ on what reality *is*; one culture's definition of reality may not be the same as that of another culture.

World Views

The **world view** of a people is the way they interpret reality and events, including their images of themselves and how they relate to the world around them. World views are affected by how people classify the social and natural world, which we have just discussed. But world views include more than just the way society and nature are carved up by a culture. People have opinions about the nature of the cosmos and how they fit into it. All cultures distinguish physical bodies from spiritual souls and have beliefs about what happens to the latter after the former dies. People have ideas about the meaning of human existence: how we were put on earth, who or what put us here, and why. They have notions of what evil is, where it comes from, why it sometimes happens to good people, and how it can be combated. They have beliefs about what supernatural powers or beings are like, what they

can do for (or to!) people, and how people can worship or control them. Everywhere we find myths and legends about the origins of living things, objects, and customs.

These examples of various aspects of world view all come from religion. But it is important not to confuse world view and religion, and especially not to think that religion and world view are synonymous. Although religious beliefs do influence the world view of a people, cultural traditions vary in aspects of world view that we do not ordinarily think of as religious.

For instance, the way people view their place in nature is part of their world view: Do they see themselves as the masters and conquerors of nature, or as living in harmony with natural forces? The way people view themselves and other people is part of their world view. Do they see themselves, as many human groups do, as the only true human beings, and all others as essentially animals? Or do they see their way of life as one among many equally human but different ways of life? Most modern scientists share a similar world view: They believe that all things and events in the universe have natural causes that we can discover through certain formal procedures of observation and experimentation and systematic logic.

A people's conception of time and space is also part of their world view. Westerners are so used to thinking of time in arbitrary units—for our seconds, minutes, and hours are not natural segments of time—that we forget that other people do not always share our ideas of how important these units are. Many North Americans frown on "wasting time" and on not "using time productively." This view of time as a resource that, like money, can be spent wisely or foolishly is not present in the world view of many other cultures. Similar considerations apply to physical space. In a North American house, unused space—areas in which little activity occurs or that are not used to display or store possessions—is often considered "wasted space."

To a large extent, such views of time and space are understandable, given other dimensions of the North American way of life. They are connected to values, such as progress and the work ethic. They also are connected to certain economic conditions not found in many other places in the world. We must pay dearly for the space of earth and air enclosed by the walls of our dwellings; in general, the larger the space, the more we pay; so unused space is viewed as wasted space because we have paid for something we are not using. If, on the other hand, spaces of earth are freely available to all who want to use them, the notion that space is a resource that can be wasted is less likely to be strong. The same applies to time. We can waste it because it is possible for us to use every bit of it in some way. Time not spent sleeping, eating, and maintaining our bodies can be spent earning money or enjoying the things that money allows us to possess or participating in social activities that we "barely can find the time for." If, on the other hand, we were to stop working whenever we satisfy our bodily needs, as was once common among humanity, we would find ourselves with "time on our hands," and the view of time as a resource that can be used wisely or foolishly would be less developed.

Culture and Human Life

Anthropologists believe that culture is absolutely essential to humans and to human life as it is usually lived—in association with other people, or in social groups.

Living in social groups certainly does not require culture. Many species of termites, bees, ants, and other social insects live in quite complex groups, yet they have no culture, as we are using the term. Gorillas, chimpanzees, baboons, macaques, and most other primates also live in groups. Research done by primatologists shows that chimpanzees learn to use and make simple tools, share food, communicate well, have intergroup conflicts in which animals are killed, and form relationships in which two individuals who are physically weaker cooperate to overpower a stronger animal. Yet few anthropologists would claim that chimpanzee groups have culture in the same sense as all human groups do. (Some use the term *protoculture* to emphasize that such animal behaviors are learned rather than instinctive.) If other group-living social animals cooperate, communicate, and survive without culture, why do people need culture at all?

The main reason boils down to the following: the culture of the society into which people are born or raised provides the information ("knowledge," we have called it) they need to survive in their natural environments and to participate in the life of groups. This knowledge, which infants begin to learn soon after birth, is necessary because humans do not come into the world equipped with a *detailed set of behavioral instructions inherited genetically from their parents.* Rather, people are born with a *propensity to learn the knowledge and behaviors of the group they were born into from observation, interaction, and communication with members of that group.* More than any other animal, humans are, as two biologists have put it, "programmed to learn."

An analogy with language will bring this point home. Humans are exposed to the language of their community almost from the moment of birth. Babies do not inherit genetically a knowledge of the sounds, words, and grammar spoken by their parents. But humans are born with a propensity to learn the language of their group, which they do quickly, automatically, and nearly perfectly (see Chapter 3).

A similar process applies to culture. As we have seen, culture is transmitted socially, not genetically, meaning that it is passed on to new generations by enculturation, not by biological reproduction. Just as the mastery of language provides people with the information they need to communicate thoughts and complex ideas to one another, so does the mastery of culture provide the knowledge and behaviors that make it possible for them to survive in their environments and live together in groups. Culture is, therefore, necessary for human existence in at least three specific ways:

1. Culture provides the skills needed to adapt to our surroundings. It gives people the knowledge they need to produce the tools, shelter, clothing, and other objects they use to survive in their natural environments. Parents and other adults teach children the techniques they need to acquire food and other essential resources and to protect themselves from nature's elements. As they grow up, children learn the behaviors useful for tracking game, gathering wild plants, making gardens, herding livestock, or finding a job, depending on how people make their living in a particular society. Since most human populations have lived in the same environment for many generations, if not centuries, the current generation is usually wise to take advantage of the adaptive wisdom learned and passed down by their cultural ancestors.

2. Culture is the basis for human social life. It provides ready-made norms, values, expectations, attitudes, symbols, and other knowledge that allow individuals to communicate, cooperate with one another, live in families and other kinds of groups, relate to members of their own and the opposite sex, and establish political and legal systems. As they grow up, people learn what is and is not acceptable behavior, how to win friends, who relatives are, how and whom to court and marry, whether to show glee or sadness, and so forth.

3. Culture affects our views of reality. It provides the categories and beliefs through which people perceive, interpret, analyze, and explain events in the world around them. The culture we acquire while growing up in a given group provides a filter or screen that affects how we perceive the world through our senses. Some objects "out there" in the world are sensed, others are not. Some events are important, others can be ignored. During enculturation, people socially learn the categories and beliefs that filter their per-

ceptions of reality and give meaning to things and events. Growing up in a given culture thus leads people to develop shared understandings of the world (keep in mind that "shared understandings" do not imply Truth).

In sum, culture is essential to human life as we know it because it provides us with the means to adapt to our surroundings, form relationships in organized groups, and interpret reality. Adaptation, organization, interpretation—these are three of the main reasons culture is essential to a normal human existence. In Part 3 of this book, we look at some of the diverse ways in which various cultures have equipped their members to adapt to their environment, organize their groups, and understand their world.

Cultural Knowledge and Individual Behavior

We have seen that anthropologists distinguish between the mental and behavioral components of culture. Having discussed cultural knowledge, we can now look at how ideas and beliefs are related to behavior.

A simplistic view sees cultural knowledge as providing rules or instructions that tell people how to behave in specific situations, how to perform their roles acceptably, and so forth. For example, there are cultural rules for how to have weddings, how to settle quarrels, and how to act toward one's mother-in-law. There are always a few individuals who do not follow the rules of their culture, but such "deviants" usually are either brought back into conformity, ostracized, or eliminated. This way of looking at how knowledge and behavior are related emphasizes the norms of culture: norms tell us how to do things; usually we do them in these ways; when we don't we are punished.

Although the preceding view applies to some behaviors, cultural knowledge consists of far more than just rules or instructions. It consists of values that provide only rough and sometimes conflicting guidelines for behavior. It includes shared classifications of reality and world views, which certainly influence behavior but only indirectly (by affecting how we perceive and interpret the world) rather than directly (as instructions). Finally, cultural knowledge includes attitudes, understandings of symbols, and other kinds of ideas and beliefs that affect how people act, but not in the same way as rules do. The effects on behavior of these and other mental components of culture are too subtle and complex to think of as rules or instructions.

At any rate, even when a culture's rules provide highly detailed behavioral instructions—and sometimes they do—the actions of individuals are not preprogrammed. People usually have some leeway to choose between alternative courses of action. In their everyday lives most people do not blindly follow their culture's "dictates." They plan, calculate, weigh alternatives, and make decisions. They think ahead (sometimes, at least!) and consider the possible benefits and consequences of alternative actions before they act. In deciding how best to approach the relation between knowledge and behavior, we must take into account people's ability to think ahead, plan, and choose.

One way to do this is to realize that formulating plans and making choices are mental processes, and therefore, they rely on and work within the existing framework of cultural knowledge. Deciding how to behave involves at least the following procedures: deciding on one's goals (or ends); determining the resources (or means) available to acquire these goals; considering which specific actions are likely to be most effective; calculating the relative costs (in resources) and benefits (rewards) of these alternative actions; and, finally, choosing between these alternative behaviors.

Cultural knowledge affects every step of this choice-making process. Norms force individuals to take into account how others are likely to react to their behavior. Values affect the goals that people have and help prevent them from acting in ways that infringe on the rights of others. Choices are affected by the existing cultural categories of people and things, world views, and the chooser's anticipation of how others will interpret the meaning of his or her actions. We can see how important cultural knowledge is when people choose between alternative behaviors: It affects goals, perceptions of resources, availability of means, relative weighting of costs and benefits, and so on. So important is the effect of cultural knowledge on individual decisions that one influential anthropologist long ago defined culture itself as "standards for deciding what is, . . . what can be, . . . how one feels about it, . . . what to do about it, . . . and how to go about doing it" (Goodenough 1961, 552).

Following this line of reasoning we can say that the main way in which cultural knowledge affects behavior is by its profound influences on choices about what to do in various situations. Another way of stating the same thing is to say that cultural knowledge supplies "boundaries" for behavior. Speaking metaphorically, culture draws the lines that behavior usually does not cross, meaning that it determines which behaviors are likely to be proper or acceptable or understandable to others. Within these boundaries, people are free to choose between alternative actions. Most people do not violate the boundaries of their culture because they believe in the moral rightness of norms, because they fear negative reactions from others, or because doing so would involve actions that others might misinterpret.

Once explicitly stated, the aforementioned might seem obvious. After all, many people in the modern world believe in what they call "individual freedom." But if our culture truly dictates our behavior then our freedom is an illusion, as is our exercise of free will. We only *think* we are free to choose. Culture in fact is pulling our strings. Many anthropologists of the past (and a few in the present) believed that culture is, in effect, all powerful in the lives of individual human beings. They viewed culture as existing independently of individuals, who were treated merely as culture's "carriers" and "transmitters." Culture became, as some anthropologists said, a *superorganism*.

Yet, most people do not experience their culture as all powerful. Although it *could* be true that your mind is mainly a vessel of your culture, you probably think there is a lot more to you than that. Indeed, although most of us recognize that our culture imposes boundaries and constraints on our behavior, we nonetheless think that we exercise our free will. But the problem is that, although many people recognize that *they themselves* exercise free will, they think that *members of other cultures* are "prisoners" of their cultures: "the Yąnomamö are so aggressive because their culture makes them act this way."

This is one reason why the distinction between knowledge and behavior is so important. Shared cultural knowledge profoundly affects the behavior of individuals in the ways we have discussed, but it does not determine behavior in detail. This applies to members of other cultures as well as members of your own culture. In fact, shared ideas and beliefs sometimes do not predict behavior very well. We cannot always say what someone will do in a given situation, even though we know what other people want and expect the person to do and even though cultural expectations are fairly clear. There are several major reasons why the behavior of individuals varies, and often departs from expectations.

The most obvious reason is that no two individuals have exactly the same life experiences, even though they are raised and enculturated in the same cultural settings. A related reason is that no two individuals (except identical twins) have the same genetic makeup, and our genes affect how we react to our life experiences. Different life experiences and biological uniqueness make individuals different (to greater or lesser degrees of course) in their behaviors.

Other reasons are more subtle. Norms and values are not always consistent and do not always provide unambiguous guidelines for behavior. Generally, you should not lie, but quite often a small lie is necessary to preserve a personal relationship or to avoid hurting someone's feelings. Here small lies are told to avoid greater harms. Often, too, small lies are so useful to achieve our personal goals that our private interests take precedence.

In many situations, pursuing one worthwhile goal or upholding one value conflicts with pursuing another goal or upholding another value, so that people must choose between them. Most North Americans believe in the work ethic, value success and getting ahead on the job, and want to be good mothers and fathers. They hold these beliefs, values, and goals simultaneously. But jobs and career advancement too often detract from the time we devote to the pursuit of "family values," so we must decide how to allocate our time and energy between activities that are all culturally defined as worthwhile.

People often find ways to justify (both to themselves and others) violations of norms and accepted standards when such norms and standards conflict with their interests. You can rationalize stealing from your employer if you think you are underpaid. Your employer can rationalize working you overtime for not much extra pay because the company must operate in a "highly competitive environment." Your classmates can rationalize cheating on a test because the instructor is boring, the textbook wordy and unclear, and the information is all B.S. anyway.

Finally, the messages people receive about proper, right, or acceptable behavior are contradictory. Sometimes the models for behavior that most people accept are contradicted by the messages and models people receive from the actions of their parents, relatives, friends, political leaders, and the media. We generally agree that adultery and violence are wrong, but we gain the impression from many sources that they are common and almost to be expected.

The plight in 1998 and 1999 of American President Bill Clinton illustrates many of these conflicts and contradictions. He admitted to an adulterous affair—morally wrong behavior, most agree, but not in itself serious enough to remove him from office, because there is a distinction between a president's private life and his public duty. He deceived The American People by denying he had sex with "that woman," but in the process he defined "sex" in such narrow, technical language that his intent to deceive was transparent. But all politicians speak double-talk: When Senate Judiciary Committee Chairman Henry Hyde's extramarital affair became public, Hyde dismissed it as a "youthful indiscretion"—he was in his forties at the time, and the affair lasted five years. President Clinton lied to a grand jury about his affair—a felony crime, clearly, but many citizens reason that the lie was not really an important one, and could have been meant to avoid personal embarrassment, public humiliation, and hurt to his family. Other values are more important than an understandable lie—how many of us would lie under the same circumstances? Clinton perhaps obstructed justice by encouraging people to withhold evidence. But evidence of what? A sexual relationship that—however loathsome in its salacious details—had little to do with his job performance.

We chose the preceding examples because they are familiar to most readers. But the main point of the examples is this: All cultures have abstract public values and publicly acknowledged norms that distinguish right from wrong, appropriate from inappropriate, and so forth. But all real people recognize that real-world situations are complicated; that real-life individuals have personal goals to pursue and sometimes yield to temptation; that in reality people have to choose between values and norms that at least in some times and circumstances are in conflict; and that—realistically—many members of their group will not behave as they "should." All human groups periodically must deal with the complicated conflicts between private interests and public duties. The behavior of individuals often is an uneasy compromise between the two. Human behavior is indeed embedded in a context of cultural knowledge, but its relation to this context is complex and variable.

Biology and Cultural Differences

In many ways, humans are like other mammals: We must regulate our body temperatures, balance our energy intakes and expenditures, and so forth. But, as you know by now, anthropologists say that humans are special mammals because we rely so heavily on culture for our survival and sense of well-being. How, then, are biology and culture related?

Although we cannot discuss this issue in depth, it is necessary to address one important dimension of this relationship: that between biological differences and cultural differences. Do biological/genetic/physical differences between groups of people have anything to do with the cultural differences between them? To rephrase the question so that its full implications are apparent: Is there any correlation between cultures and human physical forms, or *races*, as they are usually called? ("A Closer Look" shows why most anthropologists think that "race" is a cultural construct, rather than a strictly biological classification of types of people.)

Members of any race can learn any culture, which is part of the evidence that racial and biological differences between populations are not important causes of cultural differences.

Before the twentieth century it was widely thought that the physical differences between populations explained differences in how groups thought, felt, and behaved. That is, many people believed that "racial" differences partly accounted for differences in culture. According to this notion, now called **biological determinism**, cultural differences have a biological basis, meaning that groups of people differ in how they think, feel, and act because they differ in their innate biological makeup.

Biological determinism can be a convenient "theory" of what makes groups of people culturally different from one another, especially if it is combined with ethnocentric attitudes about the superiority of one's own culture. If French or English culture is superior to African or Native American culture, then it must be because the French or English are innately superior biologically to Africans or Native Americans (it is obvious how so-called inherited differences in intelligence would be brought into such opinions). Colonial rule, the expropriation of land and other resources, slavery, forced labor, mass killing, and other practices could be and were justified by the idea that groups of people differed in their customs and beliefs because of their physical differences.

Almost all modern ethnologists reject biological determinism. We believe that the physical differences between human populations do not cause differences in cultural knowledge and behavior. The diverse cultures of Africa did not and do not differ from the cultures of Europe, Asia, or the Americas because Africans, Europeans, Asians, and Native Americans differ biologically.

A CLOSER LOOK

The cultural construction of race

Race is certainly one of the most explosive topics of our time. Liberal Americans think that affirmative action policies based in part on race are necessary to redress over two centuries of discrimination against "racial minorities." Conservatives argue that "race-based" hiring and admissions practices deny equal opportunity to qualified white people, many of whom come from socioeconomic backgrounds that are just as deprived as many minorities. Citizens are asked to check off their "racial/ethnic identity" on official census forms. Pollsters often emphasize the "racial divide" that distinguishes "blacks" from "whites" on various social issues.

Most people who debate these and other such public issues assume that race is an objective, natural category into which particular individuals with their visible physical characteristics can be placed. If you don't know what race you are, it is probably because you are "mixed race." Races appear to be real. We can actually witness the physical differences between humans by visiting almost any large city in North America, where members of different races mingle. Racial differences are obvious.

Most anthropologists disagree, as do many scholars in other disciplines. They argue that race is not, in fact, an objective and natural category, but a classification of people based on perceptions and distinctions that come far more from culture than from nature. Race, they believe, is a *cultural construct* rather than a *biological reality*. What does this mean, and why do most anthropologists believe it? There are several main reasons.

First, genetic studies show that the genetic variation within a given race far exceeds the variation between races. Two randomly chosen individuals within the same racial category are about as likely to be as different from one another in their total genetic makeup as are two individuals of different races. So, genetically, races are not discrete populations. This is because fully modern humans—*Homo sapiens sapiens*—evolved only within the last 150,000 or so years, so that significant genetic divergences have not had very long to occur.

Second, most of the differences between individuals that we attribute to their race are only skin deep. We focus on certain readily visible physical traits when we place individuals into racial categories: skin color, shapes of facial features, hair characteristics, and so forth. Were we to look beyond traits that are observable, we would find that if other ("invisible") traits were used, different racial categories would often result. For example, a racial classification of the world's people based on blood groups (ABO, rH, and other factors) would yield a different classification than one based on skin color. The same applies to a racial classification based on the shape of teeth or jaws, or on the ability to digest lactose (a milk enzyme). In short, the traits we use to define "races" lead to one kind of racial classification, but a different classification would be made were we to use other traits.

Third, just how many races are there? Most people raised in North America answer "three," which used to be called "Mongoloid," "Negroid," and "Caucasoid." This threefold classification of humanity is based on the history of contacts between Europeans and certain peoples of Africa and Asia. But why only three? The so-called "pygmies" of central Africa are quite different physically from their Bantu neighbors, as are the once-widespread Khoisan peoples of southern Africa. The indigenous peoples of New Guinea, Australia, and surrounding islands are quite different not only from many of their neighbors, but from some of the Africans whom they outwardly resemble in their skin coloration. Many people of south Asia have skin as dark as some Africans, although in some other physical characteristics they resemble Europeans. Shall we also call these groups separate races?

Along the same lines, different cultures sometimes develop different racial classifications of people. In the nation of Brazil, several hundred terms refer to people of different physical types. Based on his fieldwork, Conrad Kottak reported that in a single village in northeastern Brazil, forty different terms were used in a racial classification! To non-Japanese, Japan appears to be a "racially homogeneous" country. Yet many Japanese recognize and emphasize the differences between native Japanese and descendants of immigrants from Korea. Many Japanese also discriminate against the *Burakumin*, the modern descendants of groups once engaged in low-level occupations. Yet *Burakumin* are so indistinguishable physically that some Japanese still investigate the past of potential spouses to be sure they are "pure" Japanese.

Racial classifications change over time even within the same cultural tradition. In the Americas, people who are today considered to be indistinguishable racially once were widely viewed as members of different races. When large numbers of Irish immigrated to the Americas after the potato blight struck Ireland in the late nineteenth century, they were considered a "race" by many white Americans whose ancestors had lived here somewhat longer. Jews also were seen by many as a distinct racial group. Yet such distinctions sound silly today—to most North Americans, at any rate! So the dif-

Nor do the cultures of different ethnic groups within a modern nation differ because these ethnic groups differ physically: African-Americans, Euro-Americans, and Asian-Americans do not differ in their beliefs and behaviors because of their different genetic makeup.

To claim that physical differences do not account for cultural differences might seem like a sweeping overgeneralization. Certainly, the claim that "racial," or other physical differences have little or nothing to do with explaining cultural differences is difficult to prove. But this claim is

ficulty of determining how many races there are, together with the facts that different cultures disagree on the number and definition of races, should make us suspicious that races are objectively definable biological groupings.

Does all this mean that some anthropologists deny that there are important physical differences between populations whose ancestors originated in different continents? No. What they deny is that these differences cluster in such a way that they produce discrete biological categories of people, i.e., "races." Individual human beings differ from one another physically in a multitude of visible and invisible ways. If races—as North Americans typically define them—are real biological entities, then Africans and people of African ancestry would share a wide variety of traits and Europeans and people of European ancestry would share a wide variety of different traits. But once we add traits that are less visible than skin coloration, hair texture, and the like, we find that the people we identify as "the same race" are less and less like one another and more and more like people we identify as "different races." Add to this point the fact that the physical features used to identify a person as a representative of some race (e.g., skin coloration) is continuously variable, so that one cannot say where "brown skin" becomes "white skin." We can see that although physical differences *are* real, our use of physical differences to classify people into races is a *cultural construction*.

For these and other reasons, most anthropologists agree that race is more of a cultural construction than a biological reality. So what? What does it matter? So long as people can—if not today, then someday—avoid viewing some "races" as inferior to others, why is it so important that we recognize that races are culturally constructed?

It might matter a great deal, given the past and current realities of racial divisions. Racial terms (e.g., "black,"

"white") have connotations, making it very difficult for most people to use such terms in a neutral manner. It is hard to use a racial category in a neutral manner, for stereotypes about various races are deeply embedded in our cultural knowledge. (You don't believe it? What does the term "welfare queen" call to mind?)

Further, once we have classified people into kinds or types, it is very difficult to avoid ranking the types according to some measure of quality, goodness, or talent. Familiar qualities include intelligence, work ethic, athletic ability, and musical talent. Some people believe that "Asians" are smart and work hard, whereas African-Americans are better natural athletes and more musically talented. From such seemingly innocent stereotypes, we too easily conclude that it is natural talent that puts many Asians near the top of their class, and many African-Americans near the bottom academically. Recent books such as one called *The Bell Curve*, published in 1994, argue that genetically based intellectual abilities explain much of the differential success of different "races" in America today. Such arguments are moot if race is indeed a cultural construction.

There is another reason to view race as culturally constructed: doing so helps to avoid confusing "race" with other kinds of differences that have nothing to do with physical differences. Most North Americans are unable to distinguish—or at least do not consistently distinguish—differences due to race with differences due to language, national origin, or cultural background. The latter differences, of course, are based on culture, not biology, yet the two are not distinguished by a great many people. "Race" is confused with "ethnicity." For example, "Native American" and "Hispanic" are often viewed as the same kind of identity as is race—even, apparently, on census forms! But "Hispanics" may be black or white, and many people who identify themselves as "Native American" based on

their origins and culture are indistinguishable physically from Americans with European ancestry or African ancestry.

Finally, race is currently a part of the way people identify themselves to one another; it is an important part of an individual's social identity. Such an identity often carries with it a great degree of "racial pride." Racial pride is often a positive force in the lives of people who have suffered the effects of prejudice and discrimination, as older African-Americans who were part of the 1960s Black Power movement will appreciate. Yet "racial pride" cuts both ways, as people who are familiar with the beliefs and activities of the Aryan Nation and other such groups dedicated to maintaining "racial purity" know. Although "race" may be a source of "pride," it also is a major—and perhaps *the* major—source of division in many of the world's nations. Depending on your own "racial" identity and values, it may be either comforting or disconcerting to realize that race is a division of our own making.

Some readers may draw a political conclusion from the previous argument: If it is true that There Ain't No Such Thing as Race, then there shouldn't be any such thing as preferences in hiring, admissions, promotion, and so forth based on race. But past and present discrimination was and is rooted not on the biological reality of race, but on the cultural construction of race. That is, because certain groups defined as "racial" groups historically were victims of discrimination, the legacy of discrimination is still with us. If discriminatory practices of the past and present disadvantaged certain people, then it makes no difference whether the disadvantaged persons belong(ed) to an objective biological category or to a culturally constructed category. They still may be disadvantaged, and a social policy based on notions of social justice may be used to remedy the effects of past and present prejudice and discrimination.

based on good evidence, some of which is familiar to most people. Consider the following three facts.

- Individuals of any physical type are equally capable of learning any culture. For instance, the North

American continent now contains people whose biological ancestors came from all parts of the world. Yet modern-day African-, Chinese-, Indian-, Irish-, Hispanic-, and Italian-Americans have far more in common in their thoughts and actions than any of them have in common with the peoples of their ancestral homelands. Indeed, many members of these groups have been assimilated and are culturally indistinguishable from other American citizens.

- An enormous range of cultural diversity was and is found on all continents and regions of the world. Despite the physical similarities between them, native Americans were enormously diverse culturally when the people of Europe learned of their existence after 1492. Most West Africans are biologically similar, yet they are divided into dozens of different cultural groupings. The same disjunction between physical characteristics and cultural diversity applies to people of East Asia, South Asia, Europe, and other regions. Far too much diversity occurs within populations who appear to be biologically similar for biological differences to be a significant cause of cultural variation.
- Hugely different cultural systems succeed one another in time within the same biological population and

Buddhist monks in Nepal play horns during a ritual. Religion and music are two of many cultural universals.

indeed within the same society. Cultures can and regularly do undergo vast changes within a single human generation; these changes cannot be due to genetic changes in the population, which usually take many generations to be noticeable.

Because of these and other kinds of evidence, most cultural anthropologists feel justified in reaching the following conclusion: Physical (including "racial") differences between human populations are largely irrelevant in explaining the cultural differences between them. This means that if we want to explain the differences between the Kikuyu culture of East Africa and the Chinese culture of East Asia, we should largely ignore the physical and genetic differences between the Kikuyu and the Chinese. We might argue that differences in the Kikuyu and Chinese natural environment, technology, and history make their cultures different. But for the most part we ignore the physical differences between them.

As one can infer from the preceding discussion, cultural anthropologists strongly oppose biological determinist notions. In fact, in the early decades of the twentieth century some anthropologists, such as Franz Boas, fought such ideas by marshaling evidence that—to state the point simply—culture is not determined by "race."

This does not mean that biological factors are irrelevant for culture. Human beings have physiological needs and biological imperatives just like other animals. Food, water, shelter, and the like are necessary to sustain life. Sexual activity is pleasurable for its own sake as well as necessary for reproduction. People become sick and may die from disease, so coping with the effects of viruses, bacteria, and other microorganisms is a biological necessity. Finally, no human society will survive unless its members effectively nurture and enculturate their children. To persist over many generations, all groups must develop behavioral means of meeting these biological needs and coping with these environmental problems; those that have failed to do so are no longer around.

Therefore, much behavior in all cultures is oriented around the satisfaction of biological needs for food, shelter, reproduction, disease avoidance, and so forth. Such imperatives must be dealt with in all societies. It is partly because of these universal problems that anthropologists have discovered **cultural universals**, or elements that exist in all known human societies. Some cultural universals are obvious because they are requirements for long-term survival in a species that relies on material technology and lives in highly organized social groups. Such universals include tools, shelter, methods of communication, patterns of cooperation used in acquiring food and other essential resources, ways of teaching children, and so forth. There is no great mystery about why all human groups have such things.

Other cultural universals are not so obvious. They do not seem necessary for the survival of individuals or groups, but they are nonetheless present everywhere. Among these are ways of assigning tasks and roles according to age, gender, and skill; prohibitions on sexual relationships (incest taboos) between certain kinds of relatives; organized ways of sharing and exchanging goods; games, sports, or other kinds of recreational activities; beliefs about supernatural powers, and rituals that are used to communicate with and influence them; decorative arts; ways of classifying various kinds of relatives into social categories; customary ways of handling the dead and expressing grief; myths; and rites of passage that ceremonially recognize the movement of people through certain stages of life.

More elements found in all cultures could be listed, but our point is made: All human cultures share certain characteristics whose universal existence cannot be explained simply by the fact that they are necessary for short- or long-term survival. The very existence of such cultural universals suggests that the human genetic endowment limits the forms that culture can take. It may be impossible for a human culture to exist that has no rules about sexual intercourse with relatives, no religion of any kind, no play or recreation or decorative art, no recognition of kinship ties beyond the immediate family, and no sharing or exchanging of goods.

There may be an inborn genetic or biological basis for sexual rules, religion, play, kinship, and other cultural universals precisely because they *are* universal. Yet the precise forms that these and other universal elements take vary from culture to culture. For instance, al human societies have beliefs about the supernatural (religion), but the nature of these beliefs varies enormously among cultures, as seen in Chapter 13. Likewise, people in all societies keep track of their family and kinship relationships, but they do so in a wide variety of ways, as documented in Chapters 9 and 10. Part 3 describes and analyzes the diverse ways in which cultures meet their material needs, organize their exchanges, trace their relatives, and believe in the supernatural.

Summary

Culture is the key concept of the field of ethnology. The term has been defined in hundreds of ways but usually refers to the whole way of life of some society or group. To describe and analyze culture it is useful to distinguish between its mental and behavioral components, or between cultural knowledge and patterns of behavior. Culture is defined in this book as the shared, socially learned knowledge and behavioral patterns characteristic of some group of people. The term "group" may refer to an entire society, an ethnic group, or a subculture, depending on the context of the discussion.

Culture is socially learned, meaning that it can be transmitted from one group or individual to another. Enculturation is the transmission of culture to new generations. Cultural knowledge is not true in any objective sense, but it must at least allow a society to persist in its environment and must enable people to interact appropriately and meaningfully.

Cultural knowledge has many components, some of which are norms, values, common understandings of the meanings of symbols, classifications of reality, and world views. Because these and other components of cultural knowledge are products of social learning—not inborn—we must learn them during enculturation, although they may seem natural or commonsensical.

A simplistic view would hold that cultural knowledge determines the behavior of the individuals who share that knowledge. But cultural ideas and beliefs serve as more than just rules or instructions for behavior. A more useful and realistic view sees cultural knowledge as affecting the choices people make about how to act in particular situations. Cultural knowledge limits and influences behavior but does not determine it in great details for peoples' behavior is not simply programmed by their culture.

Biological determinism is the notion that the culture of a human population derives in part from biological or "racial" factors, so that biological differences help to explain cultural differences between human groups. This idea is rejected by nearly all modern ethnologists, who consider the biological differences between groups largely irrelevant in explaining cultural differences between them. The shared biological endowment of the human species, however, certainly does affect culture, since how people meet their biologically given needs is reflected in their culture. The existence of cultural universals also suggests that the shared genetic heritage of all humanity strongly affects the kinds of cultures that are possible in the human species.

Key Terms

cultural knowledge
patterns of behavior
cultural integration

culture
cultural identity
society
enculturation
roles
norms

values
symbols
classifications of reality
world view
biological determinism
cultural universals

Suggested Readings

Barclay, Harold B. *Culture: The Human Way.* Calgary: Western Publishers, 1986.
- *A brief book about culture, its characteristics, its components, and the forces that change it.*

Barrett, Richard A. *Culture and Conduct.* Belmont, Calif.: Wadsworth, 1984.
- *In addition to serving as a short text, this book summarizes many issues in contemporary anthropology.*

Boyd, Robert, and Peter J. Richerson. *Culture and the Evolutionary Process.* Chicago and London: University of Chicago Press, 1985.
- *Viewing culture as a system of inheritance of socially learned traits, the authors use models derived from biological (genetic) evolutionary theory to enlighten cultural evolution. Theoretical and often mathematical, this book is unsurpassed in its creativity and insight on culture.*

Brown, Donald E. *Human Universals.* New York: McGraw-Hill, 1991.
- *An up-to-date description and analysis of cultural universals.*

Durham, William H. *Coevolution: Genes, Culture, and Human Diversity.* Stanford, Calif.: Stanford University Press, 1991.
- Coevolution *means that genes and learning interact to produce cultural diversity, each responding to the other. This sophisticated and detailed book explains several cultural patterns in various parts of the world as the outcome of coevolution.*

Geertz, Clifford. *The Interpretation of Cultures.* New York: Basic, 1973.
- *Collected articles by a leading American anthropologist. Two articles are especially well known: "Thick Description: Towards an Interpretive Theory of Culture" and "The Impact of the Concept of Culture on the Concept of Man."*

Internet Exercises

Log on to InfoTrac College Edition and try entering the word culture for a search. Click on <u>view</u> to look at the encyclopedia excerpt for the term culture. How is this definition the same as that given in this chapter? Are there any differences? Go back to the results of the search for the word culture. Notice that there are 110 periodical references, 32 subdivisions, and 25 related subjects. Looking through some of these will give you an idea of how many different things enter into the concept of culture and also of its importance.

The concept of culture is not easy to define, but cultural anthropologists have given us a formal definition that delimits the fundamental aspects of culture. Washington State has a website *What is Culture* (http://www.wsu.edu:8001/vcwsu/commons/topics/culture/culture-index.html). This site examines different definitions of culture and has galleries devoted to the various aspects of culture. Look at the definition of culture given by Clifford Geertz. In Chapter 4 you will be introduced to the materialist and idealist perspectives in anthropology. For now, can you guess which perspective this definition most likely belongs to?

CHAPTER 3

Culture and Language

Humanity and Language

Some Properties of Language

Multimedia Potential

Discreteness

Arbitrariness

Productivity

Displacement

How Language Works

Sound Systems

Variations in Sound Systems

Words and Meanings

Language and Culture

Language and Cultural Classifications
of Reality

Language as a Reflection
of Culture

Language and World Views

Social Uses of Speech

*Communication by means of symbolic language is one of the main abilities
that makes humans distinct from other animals.*
Visit http://www.wadsworth.com/humanity to learn more about the material covered
in this chapter and to access activities, exercises, and tutorial quizzes.

*L ANGUAGE is the shared knowledge of sounds, words, meanings,
and grammatical rules that people use to send and receive messages. Along with our extreme reliance on the social leaning of
culture, the ability to communicate complex, precise information is the main mental capability that makes humanity distinct from
other animals.*

*WE BEGIN this chapter by discussing briefly a few of the reasons why lan-
guage is so remarkable and so important. Then we describe some of the
features of language that differentiate it from the communication systems
of other animals. We show how people communicate by following unconscious rules for combining sounds and words in ways that other people
who know the language recognize as meaningful. Finally, we discuss how
language is related to certain aspects of culture and how speaking is itself
a culturally conditioned behavior.*

Humanity and Language

Although we talk to one another every day, we seldom consider how remarkable it is that we can do so. Yet the ability to speak and comprehend the spoken messages of language requires knowledge of an enormous number of linguistic elements and rules. Language and culture together are critical to the development of human individuals—unless we learn them, our psychological and social development is incomplete. In all probability, without them we would be unable to think, as the word "think" is generally understood, because language and culture provide our minds with the concepts and terms for thought itself. The importance of language for human life is revealed by mentioning several points.

First, *Homo sapiens* is the only animal capable of speech. Other animals—including honeybees, some whales and dolphins, and chimpanzees—are capable of impressive feats of communication, but only humans have and use language. By intense human effort, chimpanzees (our closest primate relatives) can learn to use sign language or to manipulate symbols standing for words and concepts into sentences. Yet no chimpanzee can respond to this simple request: "Tell me what you plan to do tomorrow."

In fact, language is so critical to humanity that it helped to shape our biological evolution. This includes, of course, our brains, but it also includes our vocal tracts. The human *vocal tract*—the parts of our respiratory tract that allow us to form distinct sounds—consists of the lungs, trachea, mouth, and nasal passages. The human vocal tract is biologically evolved for speech, for it is a remarkable resonating chamber. Distinctive vowel sounds are made by raising and lowering the tongue, or parts of the tongue, to produce sounds of different wavelengths, which our ears recognize as different sounds (compare where your tongue is for the vowels in *sit* and *set,* and in *teeth* and *tooth*). Most consonants are produced by interrupting the flow of air through our mouths. The initial sound of *tap* is formed by bringing the tongue into contact with the alveolar ridge just behind the teeth, then releasing the contact suddenly. You change *tap* to *sap* by blowing air through your mouth while almost, but not quite, touching the tip of your tongue to your alveolar ridge, thus making the initial sound into a brief hissing noise. You do all this unconsciously and with astounding speed and precision. The other vowels and consonants of English and other languages are made by articulating various parts of the vocal tract in different ways. Each sound is possible because the chamber formed by the mouth, throat, and nasal passages, and the muscles of the tongue and lips, are biologically evolved to allow us to produce them.

There is a good reason why chimpanzees cannot speak human words: Their vocal tracts are not evolved to do so. Yet, with training, any human can make the sounds found in any other human language.

Second, language makes it possible for people to communicate and think about abstract concepts, as well as about concrete persons, places, things, actions, and events. Among these abstractions are *truth, evil, god, masculinity, wealth, values, humanity, infinity, law, democracy, universal, space,* and *hatred.* Humans all understand abstractions such as these and they greatly affect our everyday behavior.

Third, the social learning by which children acquire culture would be impossible without language. Language makes it possible for the knowledge in one person's mind to be transmitted into the mind of another person. Experience is stored and transmitted to others by means of language. During enculturation, we learn not just "facts" and "lessons" about the world. We hear (or read) stories and myths, whose "lessons" are only implicit. The world view of a culture is communicated (and perhaps even shaped) by language. And, as we discuss later in this chapter, the ways in which a society or other group classify reality is encoded in their language.

Finally, language allows humans to reap the benefits of the most complete and precise form of communication in any animal. Because of language, we can communicate incredibly detailed information about past, present, and future events. Indeed, we can talk about events that might not even have occurred, events that are barely possible, events that certainly never did happen, and events that might happen tomorrow but probably won't. We can tell lies to one another about an event, a third party, or ourselves. We can discuss plans, contingencies, and possible courses of action, based on our expectations about what might happen in the future. These are things we all do so routinely that it is hard to imagine not being able to do them!

In brief, language is powerful. It makes abstract thought possible. It allows the relatively quick and easy transmission of information from one individual (and generation) to another. It allows the communication of amazingly complex and precise messages.

Some Properties of Language

We can best understand the power of language by describing some of the properties that distinguish it from the communication abilities of other animals. Nearly forty years ago, linguist Charles Hockett identified thirteen features shared by all human languages. Only five of the thirteen are important for our purposes.

Multimedia Potential

Any message uses some medium for its transmission from sender to recipient. For example, writing is the medium in which the messages of this book are transmitted. When you speak, the medium for your message is speech, transmitted by sound waves. Gestures and bodily movements are communications media, which are received by the sense of sight rather than hearing. Messages can also be transmitted through other media (including even chemicals, whose odors carry meaning to animals such as ants and dogs).

Unlike most other ways of communicating, language has *multimedia potential,* meaning that linguistic messages can be transmitted through a variety of media. The original medium for language, of course, was speech, but language's multimedia potential allowed people to take advantage of other media, such as writing and Morse codes. American sign language is a medium for the hearing impaired. Even touching and the resulting nerve signals can be a communication medium for language. Helen Keller, both blind and deaf, communicated and received linguistic messages by touch. Writing, signing, and the Internet all are possible because of language's multimedia potential.

Discreteness

We communicate linguistic messages by combining discrete units according to certain shared and conventional rules. Knowing how to speak a language means knowing the units and the rules for combining them. Thus, words are composed of discrete units of sound (e.g., j, u, m, p) that are combined to communicate a meaning (e.g., jump). Sentences are composed of discrete units of meanings (words) that are combined according to rules to communicate a message.

Alphabets are possible because of the property called *discreteness.* In alphabetic writing, people string together the letters of their alphabet to form words. The letters of the English alphabet symbolize discrete sounds, and originally each sound was pronounced in a similar way in all the words in which it appeared. For example the letter *t* appears in *student, textbook, eat,* and *today,* and so does the sound we symbolize as *t* in the English alphabet. The same applies to all other letters in an alphabet.

In the English alphabet, most letters no longer represent a single sound. The letter *a*, for example, is pronounced differently in the words *act, father, warden, assume,* and *nature.* The same is true for other letters that represent English vowels. Some single sounds in English are rendered in spelling as two letters, such as *th, ou,* and the *gh* in *rough.* Why does the spelling English now uses for certain words not reflect the way these words are pronounced? Basically, because changes in spelling have lagged behind changes in pronunciation since the invention of the printing press.

By themselves, most sounds carry no meaning: The three English sounds in the word *cat,* for example, are meaningless when pronounced by themselves. But by combining this limited number of sounds in different ways, words are formed, and words do communicate meanings. Thus, the three sounds in *cat* can be put together in different sequences to form the words *act* and *tack.* Words, then, are composed of sound combinations that have recognized, conventional meanings in a speech community. And all languages use a small number of sounds to make a large number of words.

Sounds are not the only units of language that people recombine when speaking with one another. Words are combined according to the grammatical rules of the language to convey the complex messages carried by sentences. By mastering their language's words and their meanings, and the rules for combining words into sentences, speakers and listeners can send and receive messages of great complexity with amazing precision (e.g., "In the basket of apples on you left, hand me the reddest one on the bottom.")

Discrete sounds are sometimes said to be the building blocks of language. By recombining them in different sequences and numbers, an infinite number of words can be pronounced (although most languages have only thousands of words).

Arbitrariness

The relationship between the strings of sounds that makes up words and the meanings these words communicate is *arbitrary,* which means that words are symbols (see Chapter 2). When children learn to speak and understand verbal messages, they learn the combinations of sounds that are permissible according to the rules of their language. For instance, in English, *mp, nt,* and *ld* are all possible combinations, but *pm, tn,* and *dl* are not (although these combinations are used by other languages). Children also learn to match up certain sound combinations (words) with their meanings. By the age of one, most children have learned the meanings of dozens of words. They have mastered many words that refer to objects (*ball*), animals (*doggie*), people (*mama*), sensory experiences (*hot*), qualities (*blue, hard*), actions (*eat, run*), commands (*no, come here*), emotions (*love*), and so forth. The child learns to associate meanings with words, even though the specific sound combinations that convey these various meanings have no inherent relation to the things themselves. Thus, the feelings aroused by "I love you" in English are also

Language gives humans the ability to speak and understand incredibly complex messages. Because we talk to one another almost every day, most of us are unaware of the power of language.

aroused by "Te amo" in Spanish, although the sounds of the message are different. Because the relation between meanings and words or sentences is arbitrary, our ability to communicate linguistic messages is based entirely on conventions shared by the sender and receiver of a message. When we learn a language, we master these conventions about meanings, just as we strive to master pronunciations and other things.

Productivity

Productivity refers to a speaker's ability to create totally novel sentences (and to a listener's ability to comprehend them). Productivity means that a language's finite number of words can be combined into an infinite number of meaningful sentences. The sentences are meaningful because the speaker and listener know what each word means individually and the rules by which they may be meaningfully combined. The amazing thing is that individuals are not consciously aware of their knowledge of these rules, although they routinely apply them each time they speak and hear.

Displacement

Displacement refers to our ability to talk about objects, people, things, and events that are remote in time and

space. Language has this property because of the symbolic nature of words and sentences, which means that things do not have to be immediately visible to communicate about them. We can discuss someone who is out of sight because the symbols of language (in this case, a name) call that person to mind, allowing us to think about him or her. We can speculate about the future because although its events may never happen, our language has symbols that stand for future time, and more symbols that allow us to form a mental image of possible events. We can learn about events (such as worldwide depression and civil wars) that happened long ago. Displacement makes it possible for us to talk about things that may not even exist, such as goblins, ghosts, and ghouls; indeed, we can give these imaginary things detailed characteristics in our mind's eye, although our real eyes have never seen them. Because of displacement, we can tell one another stories about things that never happened, and thus create myths, folklore, and literature. People can learn of events remote from them in space, such as Bill Clinton's troubles, the trials of O.J., and the global financial crisis. Much of culture depends on this important property of language.

Together, multimedia potential, discreteness, arbitrariness, productivity, and displacement make language the most precise and complete system of communication known among living things. Because of them, I can write the following simple (but false) sentence, which you understand perfectly although you've never read or heard it before: "Last Tuesday at 7:02 P.M., Denzel Washington chased my neighbor's dog around the yard and bit her ear." (If you find your ability to decode this sentence unremarkable, it's only because you are human!)

How Language Works

As children learn the language of their community, they master an enormous amount of information about individual sounds, sound combinations, meanings, and rules. Linguistic units (sounds, words) and the rules for combining them make up the total system of linguistic knowledge called a **grammar**. *Grammar* refers to all the knowledge shared by those who are able to speak and understand a given language: what sounds occur, rules for combining them into sequences, the meanings that are conveyed by these sequences, and how sentences are constructed by stringing words together according to precise rules.

Grammatical knowledge is *unconscious,* meaning that those who share a language cannot verbalize the nature of the knowledge that allows them to speak and comprehend one another. It also is *intuitive,* meaning that speaking and understanding are second nature—we ordinarily do not need to think long and hard about how to transform the message we want to communicate into a sentence, or how to decode a sentence we hear into a message.

This scientific use of *grammar* differs from the everyday use of the term. In everyday speech we judge people partly on the basis of whether we consider their grammar proper. In the United States there are several dialects, or regional variants, of English. One, called *Standard American English* (SAE)—the dialect we usually hear in the national news media—is culturally accepted as most correct. Other dialects, especially those spoken by many African-Americans and by southern or Appalachian whites, are looked down on by many of those whose dialect is SAE.

But there is no such thing as superior and inferior dialects (or languages) *in the linguistic sense*. That is, each language, and each dialect, is equally capable of serving as a vehicle for communicating the messages its speakers need to send and receive. So long as a person successfully communicates, there is no such thing as "bad grammar," or people who "don't know proper grammar." The exchange of messages

> *Merle*: I ain't got no shoes.
> *Pearl*: I ain't got none either.

is perfectly good English—to members of certain subcultures who speak one English dialect. So long as speakers communicate their intended meaning to listeners, then the words they use or the ways they construct their sentences are as valid linguistically as any other. The evaluations we make of someone else's grammar or overall style of speech, then, are cultural evaluations. Culturally, people define some dialects as more correct than others. But if the history of the United States had been different, some other dialect of American English might have become standard, and the sentences

> *Jennifer*: I have no shoes.
> *Christopher*: Nor do I.

might have become a cultural marker by which one segment of the population judges another as unsophisticated.

This point is so important that it is worth saying another way. Many languages are not uniform but have variations based on region, class, ethnicity, or some other difference between people. These variations in the grammar of a single language are called **dialects**. The speakers of a language or dialect share a complete knowledge of its grammar. When linguists try to discover this grammar, they call what they are investigating a *descriptive* grammar: They are trying to describe completely and objectively the elements and rules that underlie communication in some particular language or dialect. The descriptive grammar a linguist would write of Black English would differ slightly from that of SAE. But a linguist would never describe the differences between the two dialects in terms of relative superiority, since each dialect is capable of conveying the same messages.

In contrast, when some speakers of SAE label African-American or southern dialects as substandard English, they are basing their judgments on their cultural assumptions about the relative correctness of dialects. But this judgment is entirely *cultural. Linguistically,* all languages and all dialects work as well as others, meaning that all languages and all dialects have equal ability to communicate the messages their speakers need to send and receive.

With this point about the relativity of languages and dialects in mind, here we discuss two aspects of grammar: (1) sounds and their patterning, and (2) sound combinations and their meanings. (A third field studies the rules for combining words into sentences, but this complicated subject is outside the scope of this book.)

Sound Systems

When we speak, our vocal tract emits a string of sounds. Linguists are trained to describe and analyze the nature and patterning of these sounds. The sounds of a language, together with the way these sounds occur in regular and consistent patterns, make up the *phonological system* of the language. The study of this sound system is called **phonology**.

For example, when you hear the word *debt,* you hear a sequence of sounds that you associate with a certain meaning. You do not consciously think, and may even be unable to recognize, that *debt* consists of three distinguishable sounds, / d /, / ɛ /, and / t /. (The slash marks / / denote sounds recognized as distinctive in a single language.) In fact, if someone asked you, "How many sounds are there in 'debt'?" you might say "Four" because you would confuse the sounds in *debt* with its number of letters in English spelling.

But you do know what the three sounds in *debt* are, although you might not know that you know. You know because you recognize that the word *pet* is a different word that *debt,* although only its initial sound, / p /, is different. You know because you recognize *debt* and *date* as different words, although they differ only in their second sound. And you know because you recognize the profound contrast in meaning between *debt* and *dead,* although this difference is caused by a single sound at the end of the two words. If English speakers did not know, at an unconscious level, that *debt* must be pronounced / dɛt /, rather than / pɛt /, / dayt /, or / dɛd /, they would mispronounce it, and their listeners would be unable to distinguish *debt* from these other words. Conversely, if a listener did not know that / dɛt / is different from / pɛt /, she or he might expect to receive a cat or dog when the speaker said, "I'm paying my debt to you."

The particular sounds that the speakers of a language recognize as distinct from other sounds are called the **phonemes** of the language. Phonemes are the individual sounds that make a difference in the meanings of its words. For example, we can break up the word *brought* into four phonemes: / b /, / r /, / ɔ /, and / t /. The substitution of any other phoneme for any of the phonemes in the word *brought* would either change the word into another word (e.g., *bright,* in which a different vowel sound, / ay /, is substituted for / ɔ /) or make it unintelligible (e.g., *blought* or *broughk*).

Languages have different phonemes, and various languages' phonological systems are patterned differently. This means that languages recognize and distinguish between sounds based on different sound qualities, and that each language has its own logic and consistency in making these distinctions.

As an example of the patterning of the phonological system of one language, compare two phonemes of English: / b / and / p /. The phoneme / b / appears in *boy, able, probation,* and *flab.* It is made by putting the lips together and then releasing them while making a slight vibration with the vocal cords. The phoneme / p / appears *in pat, approach, mop,* and *example.* We make the / p / sound the same way as / b /, except that we do not vibrate our vocal cords.

You can hear the vibration of your vocal cords in / b / by placing your hands over your ears while saying the word *bat* slowly and listening for a slight buzz during the pronunciation of / b /. This buzz is the sound your vocal cords make when your lungs force air through them while they are constricted, or tightened, until they are nearly in contact with one another. All sounds in which the vocal cords vibrate are called *voiced.* Examples of other voiced consonants in English are / d /, / z /, / g /, and / ǰ / (/ ǰ / is the first and last sound in *judge*). All vowel sounds are voiced in English.

Now place your hands over your ears while saying the word *pat.* You will not hear a buzz during the pronunciation of / p /. This is because your vocal cords are completely open, so the flow of air from your lungs is unimpeded and no buzzy sound is created. All sounds in which the vocal cords are open, so that their vibration does not contribute to the sound, are called *voiceless.* Other voiceless phonemes in English are / t /, / s /, / k /, and / č / (/ č / is the first and last sound in *church*).

The only difference between *bat* and *pat* is this first sound, and the significant difference between the sounds / b / and / p / is that the vocal cords vibrate during / b / but are open during / p /. Stated technically, the only difference between the two phonemes is that / b / is voiced, whereas / p / is voiceless.

We discussed these two English phonemes in some detail to make a general point: Our understanding of words is based on our shared ability to hear *distinctions* between their constituent sounds and to recognize these distinctions as *significant.* People who speak English have no difficulty hearing the distinctions between the first sounds of *bill* and *pill,* although they do not consciously know what qualities make these sounds different. We also recognize the distinctions between the two sounds as significant—that is, as making a difference in the meanings of the words in which they appear. If the difference between / b / and / p / was not significant, we would not recognize any difference between words that differ only in these sounds—*pill* and *bill* would have the same meaning and therefore would be the same word!

Variations in Sound Systems

We have just put into words what every speaker of English unconsciously and intuitively knows: that we detect the difference between sounds such as / t / and / d /, and / f / and / v /, and that we recognize this difference as significant. Can't everyone in the world hear this difference, and doesn't everyone recognize this difference as significant?

No, they can't and don't. There are a great many languages in which sounds that differ only in whether they are voiced or voiceless are not recognized as different sounds. In fact, speakers may not be able to hear the difference between such sounds. For instance, in Kosraen, a Micronesian language, the distinctions between the sounds / t / and / d /, / p / and / b /, and / k / and / g / make no difference in meaning. So the two alternative pronunciations of the following words make no difference in meaning to Kosraens:

> *ki̇p* and *gi̇p* mean "satiated," "full from eating"
> *tʌn* and *dʌn* mean "color"
> *pʌk* and *bʌk* mean "sand"

It is as if English-speaking people made no distinction between *cot* and *got,* between *tan* and *dan,* and between

One of many differences between languages is the discrete sounds that their speakers recognize as distinctive. Distinctions between some sounds that are clearly heard by English speakers are not made by the Micronesian language these women speak.

pig and *big*. This does not mean that Kosraen ears are not as sensitive as Canadian, Australian, or English ears. It means only that the Kosraen and English languages do not recognize the same distinctions in similar sounds as making a difference in the meanings of words. In English, / k / and / g / are different phonemes; in Kosraen, they are alternative ways of pronouncing the same phoneme.

So differences between sounds that are meaningful in one language's phonological system do not always make a difference in meaning in another's. Conversely, one language may recognize distinctions between similar sounds that the speakers of another language do not detect. For example, we have referred to the English phoneme / p / as if it is always pronounced the same way. In fact, we use two pronunciations for / p /, depending on the sounds around it. Consider the words *pit* and *spit*. You might think that the only difference between the two is the sound / s /. If so, you are wrong. The / p / in *pit* is followed by a short puff of air (called *aspiration*) between it and the vowel; the / p / in *pit* is said to be aspirated. The / p / in *spit* is not followed by such a puff; it is unaspirated. (You cannot hear this difference, but you may be able to feel it: Put your hand immediately in front of your mouth while saying the two words, and you may feel the aspiration after the / p / in *pit*, but not after the / p / in *spit*.)

Surely such a slight difference cannot matter, but in many languages it does. In Thai, for example, / p / and / pʰ / (the ʰ stands for aspiration) are separate phonemes, which means that those who speak Thai detect the difference between many aspirated and unaspirated sounds

and recognize it as changing the meaning of many words. This is seen in the following Thai words:

paa "forest"	*pʰaa* "to split"
tam "to pound"	*tʰam* "to do"
kat "to bite"	*kʰat* "to interrupt"

Note that a difference in sound that is nearly inaudible to a speaker of English changes the meanings of the paired Thai words just listed. Hindi, the language spoken by many Asian Indians, also recognizes the differences between aspirated and unaspirated sounds.

One of the most interesting ways in which languages differ in their phonological systems is the way the pitch of the voice is used to convey meaning. (The pitch of a voice depends on how fast the vocal cords vibrate: The higher the frequency of vibration, the higher the pitch of the voice.) English speakers use pitch to convey different meanings, as you can see by contrasting the following sentences:

She went to class.
She went to class?

The first statement is turned into a question by altering the pitch of the voice. In the question, the pitch rises with the word *class*.

Speakers of English use the changing pitch of their voices over the whole sentence to communicate a message; that is, the voice pitch falls or rises mainly from word to word, rather than within a word. There are many other languages in which a high, medium, or low pitch used within an individual word, or even in a syllable, changes the fundamental meaning of the word.

Languages in which the pitch (or tone) with which a word is said (or changes in the voice pitch during its pronunciation) affects the meaning of a word are known as **tone languages**. Tone languages occur in Africa and in southeastern and eastern Asia. Chinese, Thai, Burmese,

In the process of interacting with parents and other adults, children learn the rules for forming morphemes out of sounds and the meanings people in their community attach to these morphemes.

and Vietnamese are all tone languages, which is why they have a musical quality to ears accustomed to English. As an example of how pitch can affect meaning, consider these words from Nupe, an African tone language:

bā (high tone) means "to be sour"
bā (mid tone) means "to cut"
bā (low tone) means "to count"

Here, whether the two phonemes in *ba* are pronounced with a high, mid, or low tone changes their meaning. The same principle can apply to syllables within a word—how the pitch of the voice changes between the syllables alters the meaning. This is exemplified by the following Thai words:

nâa (tone of voice falls on second vowel) means "face"
năa (tone of voice rises on second vowel) means "thick"

Because the tone with which a word is pronounced, or changes in tone between the syllables of the word, can change its meaning, the pitch of the voice is a kind of phoneme in tone languages. It has the same effect as adding / s / in front of the English word *pot*, which totally alters its meaning to *spot*.

Words and Meanings

Words are combinations of sounds (phonemes) to which people attach standardized meanings. Any language contains a finite number of words, each matched to one or more meanings. The total inventory of words in a language is called its *lexicon*. **Morphology** is the study of meaningful sound sequences and the rules by which they are formed.

Of all linguistic elements, words are the most easily transmissible across different languages. When groups who speak different languages come into contact, one or both groups often incorporates some of the "foreign" words into its lexicon. Incorporation is especially likely to happen if one language's words have no counterparts in the lexicon of the other, as is commonly the case for many nouns. Because of the way the world trading and political system has developed in the last five centuries (see Chapter 17), English words have spread widely into other languages. The Japanese language has incorporated hundreds of English words, and in France the use of English words became such a hot political issue that the government recently outlawed the "importation" of further English words. Lest English speakers become too chauvinistic about their language, it should be noted that English (a Germanic language) itself has, over the centuries, adopted words from the Romance languages (which originated from Latin), as anyone who has taken French, Spanish, Portuguese, Italian, or other Romance languages knows. Less well known is the fact that the early English colonists who settled in the Americas adopted lots of words from the Indians—words that are now incorporated into the English lexicon (see "A Closer Look").

In studying the meanings of language, morphologists need a more precise concept than *word*. To see why, ask yourself if you know the meaning of the following sound sequences, none of which qualifies as a word:

un	ed
pre	s
non	ing
anti	ist

You do, of course, recognize these sound sequences. Those in the first column are prefixes, which change the meaning of certain words when placed before them. Those in the second column are suffixes, which alter a word's meaning when they follow the word.

A CLOSER LOOK

Indian givers

The earliest European settlers of eastern North America came from the British Isles. With the exception of French-speaking Quebec, most citizens of Canada and the United States speak English as their "native language." Few of us know about the influence of the original native languages of North America—those spoken by American Indians—on the English vocabulary. As Jack Weatherford explains in his book *Native Roots*, many familiar English words, phrases, and place names are derived from one or another Native American language.

The earliest Spanish and Portuguese explorers were surprised at how many of the plants and animals in the "New World" (North and South America and the Caribbean) were unknown to them. A few animals, such as deer and wolves, were enough like familiar European fauna that European words were applied to them. Others, however, had no European counterparts. Terms taken from North American Indian languages were adopted for many of these, including cougar, caribou, moose, raccoon, chipmunk, opossum, skunk, and chigger. Other "English" terms for animals are taken from the languages of South American peoples: condor, piranha, tapir, toucan, jaguar, alpaca, vicuña, and llama. Plants, too, were unfamiliar, and Native American words were adopted for saguaro, yucca, mesquite, persimmon, hickory, and pecan, to name only some of the most common derivatives.

As we shall see in Chapter 6, Indians of the Americas were the first to domesticate numerous food plants that now have worldwide importance. All the following crops have names with Native American origins: squash, maize, hominy, avocado, tapioca (also called manioc and cassava, both also taken from native languages), pawpaw, succotash, tomato, and potato.

Indian words for natural features other than plants and animals also were adopted by European immigrants: bayou, muskeg, savanna, pampas, hurricane, chinook. Terms in various Native American languages for clothing, housing, and other material objects have made it into English: igloo, teepee, wigwam, moccasin, parka, poncho, toboggan, husky, canoe, kayak, and tomahawk. Caucus and powwow, for meetings, are two other English words with native origins.

People everywhere find it useful to name geographical locations to make it easy to discuss people, things, and events. The earliest European settlers often named American places to honor important people in their home countries—for example, Charleston, Albuquerque, Columbus, Carolina, and Virginia (the latter named after the supposed condition of England's Queen Elizabeth I). Other American place names are derived from European geography— Nova Scotia (new Scotland), New Hampshire, Maine (a province in France), and, of course, New England.

Native American peoples had their own names for places and landscape features, and often these manes were the ones that endured and appear on modern maps. River names with Indian origins include Mississippi, Ohio, Yukon, Missouri, Arkansas, Wabash, Potomac, Klamath, Minnesota, and Mohawk, to mention just a few of the most familiar. The lakes called Huron, Ontario, Michigan, Oneida, Tahoe, and Slave have Indian names, as do hundreds of other bodies of water in Canada and the United States. Whole states are named after Indian peoples such as the Illini, Massachuset, Ute, Kansa, and Dakota, while names of other states and provinces are derived from native words, such as Manitoba, Ontario, Saskatchewan, Texas, Oklahoma, Ohio, Minnesota, Iowa, and Nebraska. Miami, Chicago, Saskatoon, Ottawa, and Omaha are just a few large cities with names derived from Indian languages. Seattle was named after a particular Indian leader, Seal'th, of the West Coast. Finally, the names of two countries on the North American continent have Indian roots: *kanata* (Canada) is an Iroquoian word meaning village (although it now is applied to a much larger community), while the area formerly known as New Spain took a name meaning "the place of the Mexica" (another name for the Aztecs) after winning its independence in 1823.

Aside from the inherent interest in the historical fact that many words in the English vocabulary have Indian origins, the adoption of words is a reminder of another, wider point: The culture of those of us who live in the modern world is the product of interaction among disparate peoples. In the past five centuries, increasing contact among the major regions of the planet has led to the spread of cultural beliefs and ideas. Like our languages, our cultural traditions have multiple origins. We shall discuss some of these connections and their impacts in later chapters.

Source: Weatherford (1991); we thank Thomas Love for correcting errors in the previous edition.

Sound sequences such as these are "detachable" from particular words. Take the words *art* and *novel,* for example. By adding the suffix *-ist* to these words, we make new words meaning "a person who creates art" or "one who writes novels." That *-ist* has a similar meaning whenever it is attached to other words is shown by the made-up word *crim*; you don't know what this word means, but by adding *-ist* to it, you instantly know that a *crimist* is "a person who crims." We need a concept that will include prefixes and suffixes such as *uni-, -ing, -ly,* and so forth to analyze such compound words and their meanings.

Any sequence of phonemes that carries meaning is known as a **morpheme**. There are two kinds of morphemes in all languages. **Free morphemes** are any morphemes that can stand alone as words, for example, *type, walk, woman, establish*. **Bound morphemes** are attached to free morphemes to modify their meanings in predictable ways, for example, *dis-, bi-, -er, -ly.* Thus, by adding suffixes to the example free morphemes, we get:

typist	typed	typing
walked	walking	walks
womanly	womanhood	womanish
established	establishment	establishes

Both prefixes and suffixes—which in English are the two kinds of bound morphemes—can be attached to a free morpheme to change its meaning, as shown in the following examples:

desire	desirable	undesirable
excuse	excusable	inexcusably
possible	impossible	impossibility
health	healthy	unhealthful
complete	completely	incompletely

Note that both free and bound morphemes carry meaning (although the meaning depends on the context in which they are used), unlike most phonemes such as/ l /, / g /, / n /, and so on. Just as phonemes are a language's minimal units of sound, morphemes are the minimal units of meaning. Thus, we cannot break down the free morphemes *friend, possible, man,* or *run* into any smaller unit that carries meaning. Nor can we break down the bound morphemes *non-, -ish, -able,* or *tri-* into any smaller units and still have them mean anything in English.

There is no doubt that the speakers of a language learn its rules for forming compound words by combining free and bound morphemes. That is, people learn how to make new compound words by applying a rule of compound-word formation, not be learning each compound word separately.

For instance, take the English rule for forming a plural noun from a singular noun. It can be done by adding the bound morpheme / z /, as in: *beads, apples, colors, eggs.* (Incidentally, / z / represents one of only a few cases in English in which a phoneme is also a morpheme. When used as a bound morpheme at the end of a noun, / z / usually carries the meaning "more than one.") Children learn the morphological rule for plural formation at an early age, but it takes them a while longer to learn the many exceptions to the rule. They apply the rule consistently to all words, saying "childs," "mans," "foots," "mouses," and so on.

The same is true for the English rule for forming the past tense of a verb. Generally, the bound morpheme / d / is added as a suffix to the verb, as in *formed, bored, loaded,* and *included.* Again, children learn this rule for past-tense formation early, and they apply it consistently. We hear children say "goed," "runned," "bringed," and "doed."

Thus, one of the many things people unconsciously know when they know a language is its rules for changing the meanings of free morphemes by the addition of bound morphemes. We do not have to learn *tree* and *trees* as separate words. We need only apply a general morphological rule (i.e., add / z / as a suffix to make a noun plural) to *tree,* or to many other nouns.

Language and Culture

The major interest of anthropological linguists (see Chapter 1) is how the culture a group of people share is related to the language they speak. This topic is obviously complex and potentially very technical, so here we focus on only three areas in which language and culture might be most closely tied together. First, as we know from Chapter 2, the members of a single culture share (to a large degree) the same classification of reality. This classification is closely related to the contrasts in meaning between the words of the language. Second, many parts of language reflect the social relationships between individuals and the cultural importance people attach to different things or categories. Third, some scholars have suggested that language powerfully shapes a peoples' perception of reality and even their entire world view. These possible interconnections are discussed in the remainder of this section.

Language and Cultural Classifications of Reality

Cultures differ in how they break up the natural and social world into categories (see Chapter 2). In the 1960s, a specialization within cultural anthropology developed that is usually called *cognitive anthropology* or *ethnoscience.* Cognitive anthropologists often study how cultures construct their classifications of reality by perceiving and labeling the world according to different criteria. One conclusion of such research is that classifications are organized in consistent patterns, much like the patterns of sound systems in language.

To see how this organization works, return for a moment to phonology. As we have seen, English recognizes as significant the difference between voiced and voiceless consonants. On the other hand, many other languages do not recognize this distinction between sounds, for the meaning of a word in these languages is not affected by whether certain of its consonants are voiced or voiceless. The distinctions between the same sounds are objectively present in all languages, but they are not necessarily perceived and made significant.

Now recall that one difference between cultures is how they classify reality into categories of objects, people, other life forms, and events. This is done by perceiving or not perceiving different features of things, and by recognizing or not recognizing these differences as important (just as the speakers of a language do or do not perceive or recognize differences between sounds). On the basis of these perceptions and recognitions of contrasts and similarities between things, humans define categories of reality. We classify specific objects, people, natural phenomena, and so forth into one or another category, depending on which of their many features we notice and view as significant. Members of different cultural traditions do not necessarily base their categories on the same contrasts and similarities (just as speakers of different languages do not distinguish phonemes based on the same contrasts and similarities; recall, for example, that aspiration is not a difference that matters in English phonology, although it is the only difference between some phonemes in Hindi and Thai).

An example sheds light on how the "cognitive categories" of a people can be built up in much the same way as elements of language. Take three kinds of livestock: cattle, horses, and swine. How do North American livestock farmers categorize and classify these animals? Consider the following list:

Cattle	Horses	Swine
cow	mare	sow
bull	stallion	boar
steer	gelding	barrow
calf	foal	piglet
heifer calf	filly	gilt
bull calf	colt	shoat

(Unless you have a rural background, you may not recognize some of these terms. Farmers need to discuss cattle, horses, and swine more than do suburban or city folk, so they use a rich lexicon to talk about livestock.) Note that the same features are used to contrast the different categories of cattle, horses, and swine. *Cow* and *bull* contrast in the same way as *mare-stallion* and *sow-boar*: The first is female; the second, male. There is a special term for each kind of mature male animal that has been neutered: *steer, gelding,* and *barrow.* There are specific terms for newborn animals, regardless of their sex: *calf, foal,* and *piglet.* And there are separate terms for female and male immature animals: *heifer calf* and *bull calf, filly* and *colt, gilt* and *shoat.* Each kind of livestock is then divided into categories based on sex (female, male, neutered male) and age (adult, immature, newborn). Each category can be described by the features that distinguish it in the farmers' classification of livestock: a *filly* is an "immature female horse," a *barrow* is a "mature castrated male swine," and so on.

These are the features of animals that farmers find important enough to make the basis of their classification of livestock. Notice that this classification rests on contrasts and similarities between *selected* characteristics of the animals—just as the speakers of a language recognize only *some* features of sounds as significant. Notice also that the classification is patterned: The same contrasts and similarities (sex, age) are used to distinguish kinds of cattle, horses, and swine. Similarly, the phonological rules of a language are patterned: If a feature (e.g., voicing) of one class of sound (e.g., stop) is recognized as significant for one member of the class, it tends to be recognized as significant for other members of the class as well.

Like the sound systems of languages, the way people classify things is constructed out of selected features of those things, and these same features are the basis for distinguishing other, similar things. Thus, the part of cultural knowledge called *classifications of reality* is organized much like the sound system of language: We perceive only certain differences and similarities as significant, and build up our conception of reality from these differences and similarities. Since we generally assign labels (morphemes) to the resulting categories (and subcategories), language is closely related to a culture's classifications of reality.

Language as a Reflection of Culture

Anthropological fieldworkers try to learn the language of the community they work with, partly because it facilitates interaction, but also because knowing how to speak the language helps fieldworkers understand the local culture. In fact, many aspects of the language a people speak reflect their culture.

For example, a complex lexicon tends to develop around things that are especially important to a community, as we just illustrated with the farmer's classification of livestock. People will assign names or labels to those objects, qualities, and actions that they see as most important, which makes it easier for them to communicate complex information about these subjects.

Examples of how vocabulary reflects a people's need to communicate about certain subjects are found among individuals of different subcultural and occupational categories in North American society. Take automobile tools, for example. A professional mechanic can identify hundreds of kinds of tools; the Saturday-afternoon home mechanic can identify perhaps several dozen; and the rest of us don't know a compression tester from a feeler gauge. Numerous other examples could be cited to show that a language's lexicon responds to the needs of people to discuss certain topics easily. There are no surprises here.

But not all specialized vocabularies are developed entirely to meet the need of the members of some group to converse easily or precisely among themselves. Specialized vocabularies also serve as *status markers* for professions and other groups. Lawyers speak "legalese" only partly because they need to make fine distinctions between points of law that are obscure to the rest of us. Legalese is a secret—as well as a specialized—vocabulary. Entry into the select group of attorneys depends in part on mastery of an esoteric vocabulary with all its nuances. And it is helpful to the profession that the general population cannot understand real estate agreements and other contracts written by attorneys. Most of us are compelled to pay for the specialized knowledge of an attorney to interpret important documents. And, as you might have noticed, college professors, when acting out their professional roles, usually use words, sentence constructions, and speech styles that have distinctive characteristics. (Even textbook authors sometimes do the same thing with their word choices and writing styles.) This is partly to increase the precision of communication, but it also serves to distinguish them from other people with less (or different forms of) formal education.

In sum, in a diverse and complex society, occupational or other kinds of groups may develop specialized speech to facilitate communication, to mark themselves off from everyone else, to help ensure the continuation of their privileges and records, and so on. What about differences *between* whole languages, spoken by members of *different* cultures? Similar ideas apply. To understand them, the concept of **semantic domain** is useful. A semantic domain is a set of words that belongs to an inclusive class. For example, *chair, table, ottoman,* and *china cabinet* belong to the semantic domain of "furniture." "Color" is another semantic domain, with members such as *violet, red,* and *yellow.*

Semantic domains typically have a hierarchical structure, meaning that they have several levels of inclusiveness. For instance, two colors the English language distinguishes can be further broken down:

Blue	Green
aqua	kelly
sky	mint
royal	forest
navy	avocado
teal	lime

We divide the semantic domain of color into specific colors (e.g., blue, green), each of which in turn is divided into "kinds of blue" and "kinds of green," and even into—for some of us—"shades of sky blue" or "tones of forest green."

By now you can see where this discussion is headed: Different languages, spoken by members of different cultures, vary in the semantic domains they identify, in how finely they carve up these domains, and in how they

make distinctions between different members of a domain. Some of these differences are rather obvious. For instance, the semantic domain of "fish" is unlikely to be as elaborate among desert dwellers as among coastal or riverine peoples. Tropical lowland peoples are not likely to have the semantic domain we call "snow" in their native language, whereas some Arctic peoples discuss it so much that they have an elaborate vocabulary to facilitate communication about snow conditions. Further, the degree to which some semantic domain has a multilevel hierarchical structure depends on the importance of the objects or actions in peoples' lives: Island, coastal, or riverine people dependent on fish are likely to have many categories and subcategories of aquatic life, fishing methods, and flood and tide stages, for instance. Can we go beyond such fairly obvious statements?

For some semantic domains we can. There are some things or qualities that seem to be "natural domains," meaning that the differences between their members seem to be obvious to anyone. In fact, they seem to be inherent in the things themselves. We therefore would expect that people everywhere would carve up these domains in similar ways. For instance, color is an inherent (natural) quality of things, which can be measured by instruments that determine the wavelength of light reflected from an object. Surely anyone can recognize that blue and green are different colors, and surely this recognition is reflected in separate terms for the two colors? Likewise, biological kinship is a natural relationship, in the sense that who an infant's parents are determines who will and will not be his or her closest genetic relatives. What human cannot recognize that his or her aunts and uncles are fundamentally different kinds of relatives than parents?

Although blue and green are objectively different colors, and aunts are objectively different relatives from mothers, people are not obliged to recognize these differences and make them culturally significant. The semantic domains of color and relatives are in fact divided up differently by different cultures, and these divisions are not at all self-evident.

The domain of "relatives" or "kinfolk" is an excellent example of how members of different cultural traditions divide up an apparently natural domain according to different principles. Because we return to this subject in Chapter 8, here we want only to show that different cultures do not in fact make the same distinctions between relatives as we do; that is, the way relatives are culturally distinguished is variable.

Consider the relatives that English-speaking people call *aunt, first cousin,* and *brother.* An aunt is a sister of your mother or father; a first cousin is a child of any of your aunts and uncles; and a brother is a male child of your parents. These individuals are all biologically related to you differently, so you place them in different categories and call them by different terms.

But notice that other distinctions are possible that you do not recognize as distinctions and are not reflected in the kinship lexicon of English. Your aunts are not related to you in the same way: One is the sister of your mother, one is the sister of your father. Why not recognize them by giving them different terms? Similarly, your first cousins could be subdivided into finer categories and given special terms, such as *child of my father's sister, child of my mother's brother,* and so on. And since we distinguish most other categories of relatives by whether they are male or female, (e.g., brother versus sister, aunt versus uncle), why does sex not matter for any of our cousins?

How do we know that the way a culture divides up the domain of relatives into different categories is not entirely natural? Because different cultures divide up the domain in different ways. People in many societies, for instance, call their mother's sister by one term and their father's sister by another term (although we collapse both into one term, *aunt*). It is also common for people to distinguish between the children of their father's sister and their father's brother, calling the first by a term we translate as "cousin," the second by the same term as they use for their own brothers and sisters. Even stranger—to those of us who think that relatives are a purely biological category—are cultures who call the daughters of their maternal uncles by the term "mother" (just like their "real mother"), but not the daughters of the paternal uncles, whom they call "sister"! (These various ways of categorizing kin, by the way, are not random, for anthropologists have discovered that such labels are related to other aspects of a people's kinship system—see Chapter 8.) Obviously, the way various peoples divide up the seemingly "natural domain" of biological relatives is not the same the world over.

The same applies to color, our other example. Brent Berlin and Paul Kay found diversity in color terms among various human populations. Some had only two terms for, roughly, "light" and "dark." Others had terms for other wavelengths of the color spectrum, which, however, do not always translate neatly as our words *red, blue, green,* and so forth. This does not mean that members of other cultural traditions are unable to see differences between what we call, for example, "green" and "yellow." It does mean that any differences they perceive are not linguistically encoded, presumably because people do not need to communicate precise information about colors.

Other examples could be cited, but the overall point is clear. Cultures divide up the world differently, forming different categories and classifications of natural and social reality out of the objective properties of things. These differences are reflected in the language of the bearers of the culture.

Language and World Views

As we have just seen, some aspects of a language reflect the culture of the people who speak it. Is the converse also true? Is it possible that knowing a given language predisposes its speakers to view the world in certain ways? Could it be that the categories and rules of their language condition people's perceptions of reality and perhaps even their world view (see Chapter 2)?

Language could shape perceptions and world views both by its lexicon and by the way it leads people to communicate about subjects such as space and time. Any language's lexicon assigns labels to only certain things, qualities, and actions. It is easy to see how this might encourage people to perceive the real world selectively. For instance, as we grow up, we learn that some plants are "trees." So we come to think of *tree* as a real thing, although there are so many kinds of trees that there is no necessary reason to collapse all this variety into a single label. But we might perceive the plants our language calls *trees* as more similar than do people who speak a language that makes finer distinctions between these plants.

Further, language might force people to communicate about time, space, relations between individuals and between people and nature, and so forth in a certain kind of way. Potentially, this constraint on the way people must speak to be understood by others can shape their views of what the world is like.

The idea that language influences the perceptions and thought patterns of those who speak it, and thus conditions their world view, is known as the **Whorf-Sapir hypothesis,** after two anthropological linguists who proposed it. One of the most widely quoted of all anthropological passages is Edward Sapir's statement, originally written in 1929:

> [Language] powerfully conditions all our thinking about social problems and processes. Human beings do not live in the objective world alone, nor alone in the world of social activity as ordinarily understood but are very much at the mercy of the particular language which has become the medium of expression for their society. . . The fact of the matter is that the "real world" is to a large extent unconsciously built up on the language habits of the group. . . The worlds in which different societies live are distinct worlds, not merely the same world with different labels attached (Sapir 1964, 68-69).

Sapir and Benjamin Whorf believed that language helps define the world view of its speakers. It does so, in part, by providing labels for certain kinds of phenomena (things, concepts, qualities, and actions), which different languages define according to different criteria. Some phenomena are therefore made easier to think about than others. The attributes that define them as different from other, similar things become more important than other attributes. So the lexicon of our language provides a filter that biases our perceptions. It digs grooves in which our thought patterns tend to roll along.

But the Whorf-Sapir hypothesis is subtler than this. In the 1930s and 1940s, Whorf suggested that language conditions a people's conceptions of time and space. Whorf noted that English encourages its speakers to think about time in spatial metaphors (e.g., "a long time" and "a long distance"), although time cannot really be "long" or "short" in the same sense as distance. Also, English-speaking people talk about units of time using the same concepts with which they talk about numbers of objects (e.g., "four days" and "four apples"), although it is possible to see four objects at once but not four units of time. Finally, English-speaking people classify events by when they occurred: those that have happened, those that are happening, and those that will happen.

Because they share a different language, however, the Native American Hopi must speak about time and events differently. With no tenses exactly equivalent to our past, present, and future and no way to express time in terms of spatial metaphors, Hopi speak of events as continuously unfolding, rather that happening in so many days or weeks. Whorf argued that the Hopi language led the Hopi people into a different perception of the passage of time.

What shall we make of the Whorf-Sapir hypothesis? None of us as individuals create the labels our language assigns to reality, nor do we create the constraints our grammar places on the way we talk about time and space. We must adhere to certain rules if we are to be understood. Surely this necessity biases our perceptions to some degree. It is, therefore, likely that language does affect ways of perceiving, thinking about, classifying, and acting in the world. To some degree, then, language does "create" views of reality. The question is, how much? More precisely, how important is language as opposed to other influence perceptions and views of reality?

Although intriguing, the Whorf-Sapir hypothesis is not widely accepted, for several reasons. First, if a language greatly shapes the way its speakers perceive and think about the world, then we would expect a people's world view to change only at a rate roughly comparable to the rate at which their language changes. Yet there is no doubt that world views are capable of changing much more rapidly than language. How else can we explain the fact that the English language has changed little in the past 150 years compared with the dramatic alteration in the world views of most speakers of English? How else can we explain the spread of religious traditions such as Islam and Christianity out of their original linguistic homes among people with enormously diverse languages? (This is not to suggest that these traditions have remained unchanged as they diffused.)

Second, if language strongly conditions perceptions, thought patterns, and entire world views, we should find that the speakers of languages with a common ancestor show marked cultural similarities. More precisely, we would expect to find the cultural similarities between speakers of related languages to be consistently greater than the cultural similarities between speakers of languages that are less closely related. Sometimes we do find this; unfortunately, we often do not.

Third, many people (in fact, probably billions of people alive today) are bilingual or multilingual. In Europe, North America, and some nations of Africa and southeast Asia, many children routinely learn two languages while growing up. Yet there is no evidence that they perceive reality in different ways while speaking one or the other language.

Also, many differences in languages that would seem to affect perceptions and views of reality do not, in fact, seem to do so. For example, in some languages nouns are classified as either "feminine" or "masculine." As children learn these languages, they learn that different nouns require different articles ("the," "a") and that adjectives acquire different endings depending on whether they refer to nouns that are masculine or feminine. The Romance languages (including Spanish, French, Italian, Romanian, and Portuguese) classify objects in this way, whereas Germanic languages (including German, Dutch, and English) do not. According to the Whorf-Sapir hypothesis, the fact that Romance languages classify things into gender categories would seem to imply that the speakers of these languages somehow view gender as a more significant distinction than do speakers of other languages: Every time people speak, they use gendered terms, which should reinforce the significance of gender in their minds. But there is no evidence that speakers of Romance languages have more gendered views of reality than do speakers of Germanic languages or other languages.

For these and other reasons, the Whorf-Sapir hypothesis is not highly regarded by most scholars today. But future research may uncover unexpected effects of language on perception and, perhaps, on world views.

Social Uses of Speech

During enculturation, humans learn how to communicate and how to act appropriately in given social situations. They learn that different situations require different verbal and nonverbal behavior, for how one speaks and acts varies with whom one is addressing, who else is present, and the overall situation in which the interaction is occurring.

To speak appropriately, people must take the total context into account. First, they must know the various situations, or social scenes, of their culture: which are solemn, which are celebrations, which are formal and informal, which are argumentative, and so on. Cultural knowledge includes knowing how to alter one's total (including verbal) behavior to fit these situations. Second, individuals must recognize the kinds of interactions they are expected to have with others toward whom they have particular relations: Should they act lovingly, jokingly, contemptuously, or respectfully and deferentially toward someone else? Cultural knowledge thus also includes knowing how to act (including how to speak) toward others with whom an individual has relations of certain kinds.

These two elements—the particular situation and the specific individuals who are parties to the interaction—make up the *context* of verbal and nonverbal behavior. Enough linguists have become interested in such topics that a special field of study has been devoted to them: **sociolinguistics,** the study of how speech behavior is affected by cultural factors, especially by the social context.

How the speech of the parties to a social interaction reveals and reinforces the nature of their relationship is seen clearly by terms of address. In some parts of the United States, unless instructed otherwise, Americans usually address those of higher social rank with a respect term followed by the last name (e.g., Dr. Smith or Ms. Jones). Those with higher rank are more likely to address those with lower rank by their first name, or even by their last name used alone. This nonreciprocal use of address terms often not only expresses a social inequality; it also reinforces it each time the individuals address each other. When address terms are used reciprocally—when both individuals call each other by their first names, for example—their relation is likely to be more equal.

Spanish-speaking people have a similar understanding with polite address terms such as *Don* or *Señora*. They also have to choose between two words for you: the formal (*usted*) versus informal (*tú*). *Tú* is used between occupants of certain statuses, such as between intimate friends and relatives and to address children. In parts of Latin America, the informal *tú* is also a marker of rank, used by landlords, officials, and some employers toward their tenants, subordinates, servants, and employees. Here the fact that a social subordinate uses *usted* with a higher-ranking person, while the latter uses "*tú,*" symbolizes and reinforces the social differences between them.

Speech style and habits depend on status and rank in other ways. For example, there used to be greater differences between the speech of men and women in North America than there are today. Because of their enculturated fear of being considered "unladylike," women were less likely to use profanity, at least in public. Men, likewise, were expected to avoid profanity in the presence of women, to avoid "offending the ladies." Certain words were (and to some extent still are) regarded as more appropriate for women's use than men's, such as *charming, adorable,* and

Sociolinguists study how speech is affected by the overall social context, here exemplified by a religious service at a Lutheran seminary.

lovely. Today, as a consequence of the women's movement and the popular media, there are fewer differences between women's and men's vocabularies.

Other cultures exhibit customs in speech behavior with which most English-speaking people are unfamiliar. Here are a few examples:

• Some languages accentuate the difference between the sexes far more than English does. In languages such as Gros Ventre (of the northeastern United States) and Yukaghir (of northeastern Asia), men and women pronounced certain phonemes differently, which led to differences in the pronunciation of the words in which these phonemes appeared. In Yana, an extinct language spoken by a people who formerly lived in northern California, many words had two pronunciations, one used by men and one by women. In a few languages, the vocabularies of men and women differ, with men using one word for something and women using quite a different word. In a language spoken by the Carib, who formerly inhabited the West Indies, the vocabularies of men and women differed so much that early European explorers claimed (mistakenly) that the sexes spoke different languages! In many languages, the speech of the sexes differs in other respects, such as the degree of forcefulness of their speech, the degree to which they avoid confrontational speech, and the tone of voice.

• In parts of Polynesia and Micronesia there used to be a special language, sometimes called a *respect language,* with which common people had to address members of the noble class. On some islands this was much more than a difference in speech style because different words were used. Often there were severe penalties for commoners who erred in addressing a noble.

- On the Indonesian island of Java, there are distinct "levels" of speech, involving different pronouns, suffixes, and words. A speaker must choose between the three levels—plain, more elegant, and most elegant. The speech style the parties to the interaction use depends on their relative rank and on their degree of familiarity with one another. In choosing which style to use with a specific person, a Javanese thus communicates more than the message encoded in the utterance. He or she also imparts information about the quality of their relationship. Accordingly, changes in the relationship between two individuals are accompanied by changes in speech style.

- In Japanese, a complicated set of contextual norms (called *honorifics*) governs the degree of formality and politeness people normally use to show respect to those of higher social position. For instance, verbs and personal pronouns have several alternative forms that speakers must choose between in addressing others. The main determinant of which forms are used is the relative status of the parties. One form of the verb is used when the speaker is of higher status than the listener, another form when the two are of roughly equal status, and yet another when the speaker is a social inferior. Women, who to some extent even today are considered "beneath" men, would generally be obliged to address men with the honorific verb forms that symbolically express the superiority of the addressee. The same applies to personal pronouns (*I, you*), different forms of which are used to reflect the relative status of the parties. In fact, when a social superior is addressing an inferior, he or she often does not use the pronoun *I* as a self-reference but refers to his or her status relative to the person being addressed. For instance, a teacher says to a student, "Look at teacher" instead of "Look at me"; a father says to his son, "Listen to father" instead of "Listen to me"; and so forth. Reciprocally, one usually does not use the pronoun *you* with one of higher status but replaces it with a term denoting the superior's social position. This yields sentences like: "What would teacher like me to do next?" and "Would father like me to visit?" Confused foreigners trying to learn the subtleties of Japanese speech etiquette usually are advised to use the honorific forms to avoid giving offense unintentionally. (Fortunately for the rest of us, most Japanese are tolerant of our inability to master the nuances of their honorifics!)

- All societies have customs of taboo, meaning that some behavior is prohibited for religious reasons or because it is culturally regarded as immoral, improper, or offensive. It is fairly common to find taboos applied to language: Some words cannot be uttered by certain people. For instance, the Yąnomamö Indians of the Venezuelan rain forest have a custom known as *name taboo*. It is an insult to utter the names of important people and of deceased relatives in the presence of their living kinfolk. So the Yąnomamö use names such as "toenail of sloth" or "whisker of howler monkey" for people, so that when the person dies they will not have to watch their language so closely. Other name taboos are enforced only against specific individuals. Among the Zulu of southern Africa, for example, a woman was once forbidden to use the name of her husband's father or any of his brothers, under possible penalty of death.

As the preceding examples show, in all cultures speech is affected by the social context, including how situations are culturally defined and the particular individuals who are engaged in speaking and listening. Norms partly explain why people's use of language varies with context—you are not expected to act and speak the same way at a party as you do in church or at work, for instance, and you know intuitively and unconsciously how to adjust your behavior to these various social scenes.

The choice of speech style and the use of particular words and phrases are governed by more than just norms, however. People have personal goals, and speaking in a certain way often can help them get what they want. Nowhere is this point made so clearly as in the speech of many modern politicians which, as a rule, involves casting oneself in a favorable light while making one's opponents look bad. In the 1994 Congressional elections, the leader of one party advised its candidates to characterize their opponents using words such as "pathetic," "corrupt," "waste," "stagnation," "traitors," and "decay." Words used to portray their own party included "moral," "courage," "share," "change," "truth," "duty," and—of course—"family." The memorandum in which this advice was given referred to "Language, a Key Mechanism of Control." The next time you hear a politician give a "speech" (i.e., public address), pay attention to his or her "speech" (i.e., use of words and phrases and overall style)—how much do you let your opinions be controlled by these?

We shouldn't be too hard on politicians, however, because we all manipulate our speech to get what we want. In everyday life we strive to present the image of ourselves that we want someone else to perceive. The opinions that employers, friends, lovers and hoped-for lovers, co-workers, roommates, and even parents have of us depend partly on how we speak—our use of certain words and avoidance of others, the degree of formality of our style, whether we try to hide or to accentuate regional dialects, and so forth. In short, how we speak is an important part of what social scientists call our *presentation of self*. It is part of how we try to control other people's opinions of us. Like the jewelry we wear and where we wear it, how we sit, stand, and walk, and how we comb our hair or shave our heads, the way we speak is part of the way we tell others what kind of a person we are. Almost without knowing it, we adjust our speech style, mannerisms, and body language to manage the impressions other people have of us.

We pointed out early in this chapter that language is composed of symbols that convey conventional meanings. We can now add that the very act of speaking is itself symbolic in another way. Just as the morphemes of language communicate meaning, so do the multitude of ways in which we can say them. Like the clothes we wear, the foods we eat, and the cars we drive, the way we speak is part of the way we present ourselves to the world. Others will interpret not only our words and sentences, but will also read meanings into our speech habits and style. By adjusting our habits and style of speech, we can to some extent control the implicit messages we communicate about ourselves. The act of speaking, then, conveys messages beyond the meanings of the words and sentences themselves; consciously or unconsciously, every time we speak we tell the world the way we are.

Summary

Along with culture, language is the most important mental characteristic of humanity that distinguishes us from other animals. Five properties of language that differentiate it from other systems of communication are: its multimedia potential; the fact that it is composed of discrete units (sounds, words) that are combined in different sequences to convey different meanings; its reliance on the shared, conventional understanding of arbitrary and meaningful symbols; the ability of people to intuitively and unconsciously combine the sounds and words of language creatively to send an infinite number of messages; and the fact that language allows humans to communicate about things, events, and persons remote in time and space.

Grammar refers to the elements of language and the rules for how these elements can be combined to form an infinite number of meaningful sentences. Grammatical knowledge is enormously complex, yet it is both unconscious and intuitive. Linguists divide the study of language into several fields, including phonology, morphology, and syntax.

Phonology is the study of the sounds and sound patterns of language. Only some of the sounds humans are able to make with their vocal tracts are recognized by any specific language. The features of sounds that speakers recognize as significant—that is, as making a difference in the meanings of words in which they occur—vary from language to language. The sounds that speakers recognize as distinct from other sounds are called the *phonemes* of the language. Among many other differences, languages vary in the way they use voice pitch to convey meanings, as illustrated by tone languages.

Morphology studies meaningful sound sequences and the rules by which they are formed. Any sequence of phonemes that conveys a standardized meaning is a *morpheme*. Free morphemes can stand alone as meaningful sequences, whereas bound morphemes are not used alone but are attached to free morphemes during speech. When people learn a language they learn its free and bound morphemes and their meanings. They also learn the rules by which bound morphemes can be attached to free morphemes.

Cultural anthropologists have turned to linguistics as a source of ideas and models that might have value in the description and analysis of culture. Cognitive anthropologists have illustrated how cultural classifications of reality are built up and organized in the same way as language.

The culture of a people is related to their language. Some aspects of language, particularly lexicon, reflect the cultural importance of subjects, people, objects, and natural phenomena. The need to converse easily about some subject leads to the elaboration of semantic domains connected to the subject, as seen in the domain of color. In other domains, such as relatives, anthropologists have discovered surprising diversity in how various peoples divide kin into kinds and give them different labels according to different principles.

Some anthropologists have argued that the language a people speak predisposes them to see the world in a certain way by shaping their perceptions of reality. This idea, known as the *Whorf-Sapir hypothesis*, argues that the lexicon of a language influences perceptions by leading its speakers to filter out certain objective properties of reality in favor of other properties. The conventions of language also force individuals to talk about subjects such as time and space in a certain way if they are to be understood by others. Some anthropological linguists have argued that the way a given language (e.g., Hopi) forces people to communicate affects their perceptions of reality, and even their world view. Although language does, in some ways and to some degree, shape perceptions and world views, the Whorf-Sapir hypothesis is not highly regarded by most modern scholars.

Sociolinguistics is the study of how speech is influenced by cultural factors, including culturally defined contexts and situations, the goals of the speaker, the presence of other parties, and so forth. Speech can be used in subtle ways to mark differences in rank and status, as between ethnic groups, classes, and males and females. Because speech is part of the way we present ourselves to others, control of the way we speak is one way we influence how others perceive us.

Key Terms

grammar
dialects
phonology

morphology
phonemes
tone languages
lexicon
morpheme
free morpheme

bound morpheme
semantic domain
Whorf-Sapir hypothesis
sociolinguists

Suggested Readings

Agar, Michael. *Language Shock: Understanding the Culture of Conversation*. New York: William Morrow and Company, 1994.

* *Enjoyable description and analysis of the uses of language in society. Full of illustrative personal stories and anecdotes.*

Escholz, Paul, Alfred Rosa, and Virginia Clark, eds. *Language Awareness*. 6th ed. New York: St. Martin's Press, 1994.

* *Articles deal with various elements of English-language use. Contains sections on political speech, advertising language, jargon, prejudice, and taboos.*

Farb, Peter. *Word Play*. New York: Knopf, 1974.

* *Readable, enjoyable introduction to anthropological linguistics.*

Fromkin, Victoria, and Robert Rodman. *An Introduction to Language*. 5th ed. New York: Harcourt Brace College Publishing, 1993.

* *Excellent textbook, thorough in its coverage, readily understandable, with many excellent examples.*

Hymes, Dell, ed. *Language in Culture and Society: A Reader in Linguistics and Anthropology*. New York: Harper & Row, 1964.

* *Nearly seventy articles, many of them classics, on the subject of language and culture and the social uses of language.*

Salzmann, Zdenek. *Language, Culture, and Society: An Introduction to Linguistic Anthropology*. 2nd ed. Boulder, Colo.: Westview Press, 1998.

* *An introductory text, describing language as a system of communication as well as how language use is affected by social context, nonverbal communication, and other interconnections between language and culture.*

Tannen, Deborah. *Gender and Discourse*. New York: Oxford University Press, 1996.

Tannen, Deborah. *Talking from 9 to 5: How Women's and Men's Conversational Styles Affect Who Gets Heard, Who Gets Credit, and What Gets Done at Work*. New York: W. Morrow, 1994.

Tannen, Deborah. *You Just Don't Understand: Women and Men in Conversation*. New York: Ballantine, 1991.

* *These three popular books by linguist Deborah Tannen analyze how conversational speech style affects relationships and performance. One focus is on misunderstandings and perceptions based on language use.*

Internet Exercises

An interesting web page relating to language is "Ethnologue: Languages of the World" at (http://www.sil.org/ethnologue/ethnologue.html). This page, which is a part of the Summer Institute of Linguistics website, catalogues the more than 6,700 languages of the world. An excellent site for general linguistics is maintained by John Lawler, a professor of linguistics at The University of Michigan, at the web address (http://www-personal.umich.edu/~jlawler/). Professor Lawler's page contains many good links (not limited to linguistics), as well as numerous other creations of his own. Take a look at his Chomskybot for an interesting twist on language. There are quite a few sites devoted to specific languages, and many online language lessons. An example is "Speaking Our Language" at (http://194.35.194.1/gaidhlig/ionnsachadh/bac/), which provides Gaelic lessons with Real Audio sound clips.

Using InfoTrac College Edition you can search for articles that relate to the material covered in this chapter. Using a subject search for the term anthropological linguistics, clicking on See also 2 related subjects, and then selecting see Whorf-Sapir hypothesis, comes up with an article describing the author's test of the Whorf-Sapir hypothesis using color terminology—both of which you read about in this chapter. What was the outcome of their test? Do the results support or refute the Whorf-Sapir hypothesis?

The Development of Anthropological Thought

Nineteenth-Century Origins

Early Twentieth-Century Contributions

American Historical Particularism (ca. 1900–1940)

British Functionalism (ca. 1920–1950)

Mid-Century Evolutionary Approaches (ca. 1940–1970)

Anthropological Thought Today

Materialism

Idealism

Interpretive Anthropology

Either/Or?

Why Can't All Those Anthropologists Agree?

Anthropology arose out of the encounter of Westerners with people of other continents, such as these inhabitants of the South American Andes.
Visit http://www.wadsworth.com/humanity to learn more about the material covered in this chapter and to access activities, exercises, and tutorial quizzes.

*A*NTHROPOLOGY *began as a result of the encounter between Western Europeans and peoples of other lands—the Americas, Africa, the Middle East, Asia, and the Pacific Ocean. As Western intellectuals after about 1500 struggled to understand people who felt, thought, and acted differently from* *themselves, they did so in terms of their own conceptions of the world. Most European scholars who wrote, say, three centuries ago shared a world view that could not easily accommodate the presence of other forms of human existence. As you might expect, their perceptions and interpretations of other peoples were, from a modern perspective, quite mistaken—especially because at that time the modern concept of* culture *had not yet developed! But by the nineteenth century, some Western intellectuals began to conceptualize peoples and cultures of other continents in new ways: They explained humanity and its diverse ways of living in terms of natural processes, not divine creation. Out of their attempts to classify and make sense of human biological and cultural diversity, the field of anthropology arose.*

WE BEGIN this chapter by describing some of the historical factors that contributed to the rise of anthropology in the late 1800s. Next, we show why many nineteenth-century ideas about humanity were discarded by more recent scholars. As we briefly trace the development of anthropological thought, we focus on how each successive approach contributed to the formation of anthropology today. As we'll see, the way anthropologists in the year 2000 describe and analyze cultures is dramatically different from a century ago. But although ethnologists of today agree on certain issues, there are major divisions and disagreements in the field. One such division is between those who view the study of culture as scientific, explanatory enterprise and those who see it as a humanistic, interpretive endeavor. We conclude the chapter by discussing some of the reasons why anthropologists disagree on whether ethnology is a science.

Nineteenth-Century Origins

The discipline we now call anthropology originated as a separate field of scholarly study in the late nineteenth century. By then, most of the world's major geographic regions were known to the Western world. Indeed, much of the non-Western world had become a colony of one or another European power. As a result of centuries of contact and colonization, various Western visitors and colonists had written hundreds of descriptive accounts about the beliefs and customs of the native peoples of the Americas, Africa, Asia, and the islands of the Pacific Ocean. Who were all these people? How were they related to the more "civilized" people of the West? How could Western intellectuals make sense of them and their "savage" ways of life?

Evidence of other, earlier cultures also existed within Europe itself. In the 1800s tools made from stone were discovered in the earth, in clear association with extinct mammals. And in Germany's Neander Valley, a partial skeleton of a human-like creature was unearthed. Who made those ancient, prehistoric stone tools? Could they have been manufactured by the ancestors of modern-day Europeans? Were the Neander bones human and, if so, what did they mean?

Answers to these and many other questions about "savages" and "prehistoric" peoples varied, but until the mid-1800s the dominant interpretations were within the realm of the Judeo-Christian world view. Perhaps "savages" were the degenerated descendants of Noah's errant son, Ham. Or maybe they were remnants of one of the lost tribes of Israel. Could it be that the bones and prehistoric artifacts found in the ground were put there by the Devil to undermine our faith? Whatever the specific explanation, the customs and beliefs of distant, unfamiliar peoples generally were interpreted in terms of the biblical account of world creation and human history.

As the nineteenth century progressed, new theories about the earth and about life itself emerged. In geology, James Hutton and Charles Lyell amassed evidence showing that the earth was many millions of years old (it is even older—billions of years older—we know today), rather than the few thousands of years suggested by the Scriptures. In biology, Charles Darwin's 1859 book *On the Origin of Species* revolutionized theories about life. Rather than each plant and animal being separately made by a Creator, and reproducing "after its own kind," Darwin proposed that one species emerged out of another. The great variety of plant and animal life can be explained by a gradual, and entirely natural, process of transformation and diversification. There was great resistance in scholarly as well as religious circles to Darwin's theory of evolution. But by the closing decade of the nineteenth century, it was apparent that evolution explained so much that most scholars accepted it.

Darwin's theory had many implications for the Western understanding of humankind. Darwin himself noted the physical similarities between apes and humans in an 1871 book, arguing that humans likely were descended from African apes. Discoveries in Africa in the 1920s confirmed his hypothesis, establishing the field of paleoanthropology as a legitimate science.

But Darwin's ideas also influenced how intellectuals viewed human cultural existence, as well as human biological evolution. To many, evolutionary theory suggested that the history of life was progressive: "Lower" and simpler forms gave rise to "higher" and more complex forms. Competition—"survival of the fittest," as it came to be called—was the engine that powered this progress. In the fossil record, it was possible to find evidence of the evolutionary "stages" through which successively higher forms of life developed. The history of life on earth could be reconstructed by painstaking excavations and meticulous laboratory analysis of fossils.

Many thought that the same notions applied to human cultures. Evolution and progress provided the ideas that suggested how the "savages" of other lands were related to one another, to the early residents of Europe who left behind those prehistoric tools, and to Western civilization itself. Just as life itself had earlier, simpler forms, so did humans' various ways of life. Those prehistoric stone tool makers of Europe had been living in the early stages of cultural development, just as were the "primitives" of Africa, the Americas, Asia, and the Pacific. By studying these peoples and comparing their customs, scholars could reconstruct the stages of *cultural* progress.

This was, at any rate, the main goal of cultural anthropology in the nineteenth century. Western ethnologists aimed to use written accounts of the customs and beliefs of non-Western peoples to reconstruct the stages through which human culture progressed on its long road to the pinnacle of human cultural achievement: Western civilization. It was believed that modern evolutionary science showed that Polynesians, Africans, Indians, and the "natives" of other continents are not degenerated folk whose benighted customs prove that they are living under the Devil's iron fist. Instead, nineteenth-century intellectuals reasoned, they are merely "underdeveloped." Their thought processes are superstitious (not yet scientific), their technologies are primitive, their manners rude, their morals unenlightened. They are—in a word—precivilized. Therefore, to trace human progress, scholars must study the ancient ancestors of civilization: surviving "primitive" cultures.

To do so, nineteenth-century anthropologists devised an approach that today is known as **unilineal evolution**. The specifics of their voluminous writings are detailed and complex. But once we understand their assumption that cultural evolution proceeded from simple to complex, with the West at the apex, the basics of unilineal evolution can be stated fairly simply, as follows. First, compile accounts of other cultures written by explorers, settlers, missionaries, traders, and other (mainly Western) observers. From these descriptions, compare all the cultures to determine which are the simplest, the next most simple, . . . and the most complex. Classify the

Painting by Raphael showing the expulsion of Eve and Adam from paradise. Well into the nineteenth century, the Biblical account of history provided the dominant framework explaining the existence of "natives" in other lands and the nature of their cultures.

cultures into a series of stages of development, according to their relative complexity. Label these stages appropriately, e.g., "savagery," "barbarism," "civilization." If a new culture (or a new account of a culture) is encountered, place it in its appropriate classificatory stage, e.g., the Iroquois of North America belong in the stage of "barbarism." Finally, come up with an explanation for why people living at one stage developed into the next stage, e.g., the invention of pottery propelled some savages into barbarism, whereas some barbarians were launched into civilization once they invented writing. Using these procedures, all cultures can be arranged in a sequence of progressive stages. The "simplest" cultures found on earth today are the surviving representatives of the "earliest stages" of cultural evolution.

The concept of stages could account for why cultures differed: People with different customs and beliefs represent different stages of cultural development. So if we want to know why the Iroquois of North America have different customs from the native peoples of Australia, the basic answer is that the Australians were arrested in their development at the stage of savagery, whereas the Iroquois had progressed all the way into barbarism. Do we want to know how the very earliest humans lived? Then we should study the surviving representatives of

Unilineal evolutionists such as Morgan and Tylor believed (erroneously) that surviving tribal peoples such as the Tiwi of Australia represented the earliest stages of human cultural evolution.

live person and a dead person? (2) What is the origin of the images seen in dreams, trances, and visions? Early humans reasoned (falsely but logically, given their prescientific mentality) that (1) living people have a spiritual essence—a soul—that gives life to the physical body, and that causes death when it leaves, and (2) the things people see in their dreams and fantasies actually do exist and are not the products of their imaginations. By this logic, the fact that people sometimes see their deceased relatives in dreams means that souls live on after death. As such beings proliferated, Tylor reasoned, eventually the world was viewed as full of spirits. The earliest religions were therefore "animistic."

At a later stage of cultural evolution, some of the spirits became elevated to a higher position than others, taking on more prominence in the belief system. They ultimately became gods of the sun, moon, rain, sky, earth, animals, and other elements, thus giving rise to the next stage of religion, *polytheism*, or belief in many gods. Eventually, one god acquired dominance over the others, the rest became "false gods," and the final stage of *monotheism* (one true god) was born. Religion thus had simple origins in peoples' attempts to explain their experiences, and it evolved into its final—Western—form over many centuries. Or so Tylor believed.

From a modern perspective, the unilineal evolutionists were mistaken, as we shall see. But they did help establish one of the important hallmarks of anthropology: the comparative perspective (see Chapter 1). They also had faith that the application of scientific methods and reasoning would lead to the discovery of the natural laws that governed the development of human culture, just as science was explaining natural phenomena. The "history of mankind is part and parcel of the history of nature, . . . our thoughts, wills, and actions accord with laws as definite as those which govern the motion of waves, the combinations of acids and bases, and the growth of plants and animals," wrote Tylor (1871, 2). Many later anthropologists were not sure that these "laws of culture" existed. Still, the search for the general causes of cultural differences and of regularities in culture change remain an interest of many modern scholars.

Another legacy of the nineteenth century is the establishment of anthropology as a separate academic discipline. Scholarly fields that investigate aspects of humankind had long been represented in European and American universities as departments or schools of religion, theology, art, philosophy, classics, history, anatomy, medicine, and so forth. But a discipline whose focus was the physical and cultural diversity of humanity was not established until the last decades of the 1800s. In the United States, the first anthropology course was taught in 1879, at the University of Rochester. In 1886, the first

the stage of savagery, such as the Australian aborigines or the Polynesians. If we are curious about the immediate ancestors of civilized folk, then we must examine cultures such as the Iroquois or Fijians, who represent the barbarism stage.

As an example of this approach, consider E. B. Tylor, whose 1871 book *Primitive Culture* investigated the origins and development of religious beliefs. Tylor argued that religions had passed through three stages. The first was *animism*, defined as the belief that nature is populated by supernatural beings such as ghosts, souls, demons, and nature spirits. How can the origin of such beliefs be explained? Tylor argued that "primitive peoples" sought explanations for their experiences. Two questions puzzled the earliest cultures: (1) What is the difference between a

anthropology department was founded at the University of Pennsylvania. It was followed near the turn of the century by university departments at Columbia, Harvard, Chicago, and California.

Early Twentieth-Century Contributions

Nineteenth-century anthropologists established the study of other cultures as a legitimate subject for scholarly research and university education. It was clear that to understand humanity, we must take the great diversity of the world's cultures into account and compare cultures systematically. But by the beginning of the twentieth century, anthropologists on both sides of the Atlantic began to challenge both the methods and the conclusions of the unilineal evolutionists.

American Historical Particularism (ca. 1900–1940)

In the United States, an approach known as **historical particularism** developed. It was "historical" because its main goal was to uncover the *past* influences on a given culture that shaped its present form. It was "particularistic" because it emphasized that each people, and each culture, has its own *unique* past. Each culture, then, is unique and therefore must be studied on its own terms. More than anyone else, American anthropologist Franz Boas formulated this way of studying and analyzing culture, and his ideas revolutionized the field.

Studying each culture "on its own terms" was not something the evolutionists had done. In making their comparisons and formulating their stages, they had imposed their own "terms" (e.g., complexity, progress) on other cultures. Take the notion of relative complexity, for example. In the area of technology, most people *might* agree that spears as hunting weapons are simpler than bows and arrows, which in turn are simpler than guns and bullets. But what can "complex" mean when applied to other customs and beliefs, such as marriage, political organization, or religion? Does it have any objective meaning to say that animism is "simpler" than monotheism? Boas realized that such features are merely *different* from culture to culture. By any *objective* criterion, one form of marriage or religion does not represent "progress" over another. Only by using ethnocentric assumptions, Boas thought, could one culture be seen as more evolved than another.

This simple point seemed to mean that the unilineal evolutionists were wrong: Cultures do not develop along a single series of progressive stages, culminating in nine-

teenth-century European civilization. Instead, each culture changes along its own path, depending on the particular influences that affect it. To understand a culture, therefore, we must study it *individually*, not as a representative of some hypothetical stage which it represents only in our minds. Anthropologists must free themselves from preconceived ideas and assumptions and give up speculative schemes of evolution and ethnocentric definitions of progress.

Accompanying Boas' call for less speculation was his demand for more facts. Anthropologists simply did not know enough about human cultural differences to generalize, he felt. What was most urgently needed in his day was more information, which Boas thought could only be obtained from firsthand fieldwork. Anthropologists needed to go out and gather knowledge about other cultures themselves, rather than relying on incomplete and biased accounts written by untrained and often casual observers. This, too, was rare for scholars in the nineteenth century. The unilineal evolutionists have been called "armchair anthropologists" because (with the notable exception of the American Lewis Morgan) they carried out all their research in their offices, using documentary sources of varying reliability.

Boas was scornful of theories developed in the comfort of an armchair. He believed that to understand another culture, one must have the familiarity that can only come with long personal experience with it. Anthropologists must therefore immerse themselves in the study of other peoples. They must try to experience their customs and understand their beliefs from an insider's perspective, rather than speculate wildly about cultural progress. And Boas took his own advice. He conducted extensive fieldwork among two Native American peoples, the Eskimo and Kwakiutl, and he sent his many students out to do research on other cultures far from home. The work done on the Polynesian island of Samoa by one of Boas' students, Margaret Mead, became enormously influential in the 1920s and 1930s after the publication of the classic *Coming of Age in Samoa*.

Two other benefits would follow from lengthy, first-hand fieldwork. First, the traditional customs and beliefs of many of the world's peoples already were disappearing rapidly. Boas believed it was the duty of anthropologists to record disappearing traditions before they were gone forever. Many students of Boas did their fieldwork among Native American peoples, whose cultures were especially endangered.

Second, Boas felt that the main need of the infant field of anthropology was more factual information about other cultures, collected by unbiased fieldworkers. Facts about a given culture should be collected without preconceived notions, for preconceptions are likely to breed inaccuracies.

Fieldworkers can only become unbiased by approaching their studies relativistically (see Chapter 1)—not judging another culture's morality by our moral codes, nor evaluating the overall worth of their culture by our own standards of worthiness. More than any other single figure, Boas imparted to anthropology the doctrine of cultural relativism, which requires studying another culture on its own terms. He also did as much as anyone to show that biological differences and cultural differences are largely independent of one another; that is, the culture a human group shares is entirely learned, not explained by their genetic heritage.

In sum, historical particularism made several enduring contributions to modern anthropology: the debunking of the overly speculative schemes of the unilineal evolutionists, the insistence on fieldwork as the primary means of acquiring reliable information, the imparting of the idea that cultural relativism is essential for maximum understanding of another culture, and the demonstration that cultural differences and biological differences have little to do with one another. These contributions helped to shape modern cultural anthropology.

However, historical particularism has its own limitations. Consider the claim that each culture is unique. Certainly, if differences between cultures are what we are most interested in, we can always find them. Having discovered them, we can then go on to claim that no two cultures are alike. At some level, the claim that "each culture is unique" is surely correct. So also is the claim that no two individuals brought up within the same culture are exactly alike. Yet they *are* alike in some ways. So, *to some extent,* no culture is likely any other. But also, *in some ways,* all cultures do have things in common. There are similarities as well as differences between human ways of life. Historical particularists tended to overlook the similarities and to neglect the investigation of factors that might explain them.

Consider also the statement that, because each culture is the historical product of its particular past, one cannot generalize about the causes of cultural differences. To say (as many particularists do) that adaptation to the environment is most important in culture X, art styles in Y, political rivalries in Z, and so forth, is to say little more than that everything depends on everything else. It is also possible, however, that some influences are more important than other influences in all or most human populations—for example, it is possible that environmental adaptation is *generally* more important than art or politics in causing a people to live the way they do.

The interests of American anthropologists returned to discovering the general principles of human cultural existence in the 1940s. Meanwhile, another way of studying human diversity developed in Europe.

British Functionalism (ca. 1920–1950)

Around the same time that historical particularism dominated American anthropology, a quite different approach was popular in Great Britain. The basic tenet of **functionalism** was that the cultural features of a people should be explained by the functions they perform. By *functions,* British anthropologists meant how existing ideas and actions contribute to the well-being of individuals and/or to the persistence of the whole group or society.

A leading British functionalist was Bronislaw Malinowski. Malinowski believed that the whole purpose (function) of culture is to serve human biological and psychological needs. These basic, biologically given needs include nutrition, reproduction, shelter, protection from enemies, and maintenance of bodily health. As social animals, people also need affection and emotional security. Unlike other animals, we humans have few inborn drives or instincts that provide behavioral instructions for how to meet our needs. Instead we have culture, which provides the learned behaviors, cooperative patterns, and social institutions (e.g., families, political associations) that make need fulfillment possible. Some parts of culture (e.g., food, tools used in production) meet our needs directly. Other parts (e.g., family life, educational practices) raise and enculturate new generations of group members. Still other cultural features (e.g., religious practices, art) instill adherence to the common norms and values that make group cooperation possible. These latter features also function to fulfill needs, but they do so indirectly, by helping the society persist over many generations and encouraging individuals to conform.

Malinowski thus considered the biological needs of individuals as the starting point for explaining culture. One cannot argue with the point that culture meets human needs—although it's worth mentioning that living in a given time and place (e.g., modern Los Angeles) also creates additional perceived "needs." But notice that, *by themselves,* the biological needs of individuals cannot explain why cultures *differ.* All humans everywhere have the same kinds of needs, yet peoples vary in the types of cultures they develop to fulfill these needs. Why do different peoples living in different times, places, and circumstances meet their needs in so many different ways? For example, some people satisfy their need for protein by eating beef, whereas others—such as devout Hindus and Buddhists—not only refuse to consume cattle flesh but maintain a vegetarian diet. So the common human need for protein cannot explain the diverse cultural ways in which protein is acquired. To generalize the point: The basic needs of humans are the same everywhere and can be satisfied in so many different ways that they cannot explain cultural variation. At the least, differences in the natural environment in which people live must be taken into account to explain cultural differences.

A. R. Radcliffe-Brown was another influential British functionalist, but his approach differed greatly from that of Malinowski. Radcliffe-Brown argued that the primary function of different elements of culture is to keep the entire social system in a steady state, or to maintain social equilibrium. He used an analogy to make his point. Society is like a living organism, with individual people analogous to cells and groups of people analogous to organs. In a biological life form, cells and organs are parts of a whole, and each has a function to perform to keep the entire organism alive and reproducing. We study the physiology of the organism by analyzing how all its complementary parts work together to keep the body alive.

Analogously, for Radcliffe-Brown, the functions of the various parts of a cultural system are to maintain the entire "social body." The parts of the culture (institutions, as he called them) ordinarily function harmoniously to maintain the entire society or, as we commonly say, "to keep the system going." Occasionally, some part will disrupt the state of equilibrium, but all societies have social mechanisms (e.g., behavioral norms, means of social control) that regulate disruptions and return the social system to a steady state. In studying culture, we need to uncover the functions that different institutions perform and how they relate to one another.

But is the organic analogy valid? Most contemporary scholars would say no. Unlike cells, individual human

beings have minds and wills of their own, independent of the requirements of the social system. Also, the emphasis on steady states and equilibrium as the normal condition of society is misguided, many feel. Change—whether at slower or faster rates—is the *normal* cultural condition, yet functionalism failed to produce an adequate theory of how and why change occurs. Conflict—violent and otherwise—and disagreements between individuals and groups also is widespread in human communities. We need an approach that explains how and why conflict occurs, not just shows how it is reduced and regulated.

Despite these shortcomings, Radcliffe-Brown's emphasis on how the different aspects of culture relate to one another and to the whole system had an enduring impact on how anthropologists study culture today. More than any previous approach, functionalism emphasized the integration of culture: parts (economy, religion, family, etc.) cannot be understood in isolation from each other or from the whole system. By their insistence that culture forms an integrated system, the British functionalists greatly strengthened the holistic perspective of anthropology (see Chapter 1).

Like their American contemporary Franz Boas, the British functionalists emphasized the necessity for anthropologists to conduct firsthand fieldwork. Malinowski, especially, is well known to all anthropologists because of his ethnographic writings about the Trobriand Islanders of the western Pacific. Not only is fieldwork the best means of obtaining reliable information about a people, but it also is a necessary part of the training of anthropologists, Malinowski believed. We cannot claim to understand people, nor their diverse cultures, until we have immersed ourselves in the experience of some culture other than our own. Further, Malinowski thought the main objective of fieldwork is to see the culture as an insider to the culture sees it. In an often quoted passage from his famous 1922 ethnography of the Trobrianders, *Argonauts of the Western Pacific,* Malinowski (1922, 25) wrote:

> . . . the final goal, of which an Ethnographer [sic] should never lose sight . . . is, briefly, to grasp the native's point of view, his relation to life, to realise *his* vision of *his* world.

Finally, Malinowski thought it essential that fieldworkers take a holistic view of the culture of the communities they study and live in. In his words:

> . . . the whole area of tribal culture *in all of its aspects* has to be gone over in research. . . . An Ethnographer who sets out to study only religion, or only technology, or only social organization cuts out an artificial field of inquiry, and he will be seriously handicapped in his work. (Malinowski 1922, 11; italics in original)

Mid-century evolutionists held that how people use technology to adapt to their environments is the most important general influence on their culture. Here an Efe man of Central Africa harvests honey.

Although he said it differently, clearly Malinowski was urging fieldworkers to study the interrelationships between the various elements of a culture.

Because of the work of early twentieth-century anthropologists like Boas and Malinowski, the fieldwork experience is today an important part of the graduate training of almost all anthropologists. And both relativism and holism are perspectives that most modern fieldworkers regard as necessary for objectivity and understanding. In fact, many contemporary anthropologists half-jokingly refer to fieldwork as their *rite of passage*. More than other aspects of their training, fieldwork transforms the anthropologist as a person, giving individual anthropologists a different perspective on themselves and their own culture.

Mid-Century Evolutionary Approaches (ca. 1940–1970)

As we have discussed, Boas' attack nearly demolished the armchair speculations of the unilineal evolutionists. But one can study a subject without making the same mistakes nineteenth-century intellectuals made. Beginning around 1940, a few anthropologists renewed the study of cultural evolution shorn, they believed, of the invalid assumptions of the unilineal evolutionists. Two such American anthropologists were Leslie White and Julian Steward, whose ideas greatly influenced modern thought.

Leslie White believed that the unilineal evolutionists had been right about some things. First, the technologies available for harnessing natural resources have, in fact, improved over the centuries. Technological progress has occurred in human history. White proposed a reasonably objective measure of technological evolution: Since the main function of technology (in preindustrial times, anyway) is to capture the energy locked up in the environment, those technologies that capture the most energy per person are more evolved. Technological progress thus can be measured, at least in a rough way. Second, cultures have, in fact, grown more complex over evolutionary time. And adequate, nonethnocentric definitions of cultural complexity are possible: Societies with more territory, more occupational specialization, more functional differentiation, and more inequality can be defined as "more complex." By these criteria, for example, most hunting-gathering cultures are simple, whereas ancient civilizations such as the Egyptians, the Chinese, and the Inca are complex. The industrial societies of twentieth-century nation-states are still more complex.

Technological progress and cultural evolution are, of course, related. In a few words: As technology becomes more productive, societies become larger and more com-

In the mid-twentieth century, Julian Steward helped to make studies of cultural evolution fashionable again. He argued that the environment in which a people live greatly affects their basic adaptation, which, in turn, shapes many other aspects of their cultural existence.

plex. For this reason, White is sometimes called a *technological determinist*, meaning that he believed the technology available to a people has enormous impacts on other aspects of their culture. For instance, hunter-gatherers who exploit wild resources must live in small groups and remain mobile according to season. They tend to have little property, to share food and other products, and have weak leaders. But people with an agricultural technology are generally more sedentary, live in large villages, accumulate wealth, and develop powerful leaders.

White's contemporary, Julian Steward, agreed that technology is an important part of culture, helping to shape many other aspects of a people's way of life. But Steward felt that the local environment also is an important influence on culture. Tools, after all, must be applied to the resources available in the environment to produce food and other necessities. The abundance, seasonal availability, and spatial variability of resources affect how people apply their technology and what and how much they produce. Steward argued that environment and technology together determine the basic form of *adaptation* of a group and that their adaptation in turn shapes the rest of their culture. He therefore is sometimes called a *techno-environmental determinist*.

Despite the fact that they often are labeled as determinists, both Steward and White recognized that some parts of a people's culture are more strongly "determined" by technology and environment than are other parts. The way a people organize their productive and other economic activities is likely to be much more affected by their adaptation than the way they arrange marriages, worship deities, recite myths, or construct art. Even so, aspects of culture that are not directly tied to adaptation may be indirectly tied to it, including marriage (Chapter 8) and religion (Chapter 13).

White and Steward made the investigation of cultural evolution respectable again. Many modern anthropologists specialize in fields such as *human ecology, cultural ecology,* and *cultural evolution.* Their interests lie in long-term changes in cultures and how people adapt to their environments. Just as importantly, White and Steward felt that anthropology could and should be a *science*, in much the same way that biology or physics are sciences—indeed, White titled one of his books *The Science of Culture* (1949). On this point, a great many contemporary anthropologists disagree, as we shall now see.

Anthropological Thought Today

Contemporary cultural anthropologists adopt an enormous variety of theoretical perspectives, far more than we can cover. To organize the presentation, we classify modern approaches into two overarching categories: the *scientific approach* and the *humanistic approach.* Like any dichotomy, this one is too simple and clear-cut to portray the variety of orientations among contemporary anthropologists with complete accuracy. Particular anthropologists do not necessarily view themselves as "scientists" or "humanists"; indeed, many adopt the assumptions and methods of both approaches, depending on what aspect of culture they are studying. Nonetheless, the dichotomy does reflect some of the major divisions and controversies within the field today. (For more detail about the distinction between the sciences and humanities, see "A Closer Look.")

Those who believe that anthropology is more akin to the sciences tend to believe, like the mid-century evolutionists, that most cultural differences can be explained by the way human populations relate to their natural and social environments. Like other animals, people have material needs for food and other life-sustaining or life-enhancing resources. Acquiring these needs means that groups have to be organized in certain ways for cooperation or for successful competition with other groups. Many other elements of a people's culture are determined by or

are greatly influenced by how people organize their groups and their activities to survive and persist in their environments. Because anthropologists who adopt this view argue that it is the material resources people get out of their environment that shape culture, the approach is often called **materialism**. In essence, materialists think that how a people make their living in their environment is the most important influence on the rest of their cultural existence. (We shall see some of these effects in later chapters.)

Those who think that ethnology is a more humanistic field tend to emphasize the uniqueness of each culture, to be skeptical of any attempt to generalize about the causes of cultural differences, and to hold that cultural anthropology is a descriptive and interpretive field rather than an explanatory one. In these respects, they share many of the beliefs of the historical particularists. They obviously agree that people have material needs. But they think that humans differ from other animals in that these needs can be satisfied in such a multitude of ways that cultural differences cannot possibly be reduced to "need satisfaction." Scholars who follow this line of thinking are often called **idealists** (not to be confused with *idealistic*). In essence, idealists deny that culture has any *general* explanation, for humans and their diverse ways of living are too complex to be reduced to what idealists consider a single formula.

Materialism

Anthropologists who follow the materialist orientation point out that people face the same kinds of imperatives as all mammals: We must receive adequate intakes of food and water, regulate our body temperature (by making shelter, for example), reproduce, cope with the presence of organisms that cause disease, compete successfully, and so forth. Like all animals, human groups must adapt to the conditions in their natural environments. Materialists hold that this imperative is basic and primary.

If one thinks that adaptation to environment and the acquisition of material resources are primary, then those aspects of culture that help people adapt and get resources will strongly affect all other aspects. Humans, more than any other animal, depend on *technology* to exploit resources, compete, and cope with other problems of environmental adaptation. Technology includes not just the physical *instruments* (the tools) used to produce food, provide shelter, and generally manipulate the environment. Equally important, technology includes the *knowledge* about the environment, about resources, and about the manufacture and effective use of tools that people socially learn from previous generations (see Chapter 2).

Because humans rely on technology to acquire food and harness other resources, technology is among the

A CLOSER LOOK

Things or texts?

Within colleges and universities, anthropology is nearly always classified as a social science, along with fields like economics, psychology, and sociology. Few modern anthropologists question that two of the main subfields—physical/biological anthropology and prehistoric archaeology—can legitimately be considered sciences. (Indeed, many biological anthropologists hold that their field is a "natural," not a "social," science.) But cultural anthropologists are divided on the issue of whether their field is, or even can be, considered a science—even a "social" one.

There are many important differences between the sciences and the humanities. Sciences (physics, biology, geology, organic chemistry, and the like) investigate some aspect of the physical/material world, with the goal of understanding its structure, how it works, and what makes it the way it is. Ideally, the sciences study the world by means of systematic and replicable observation and experimentation. Here *systematic* means that facts—"data"—are observed, counted, and recorded using agreed-upon procedures and instruments of measurement. *Replicable* means that different observers—trained scientists—will obtain the same findings by using the same procedures. This implies that if two or more observers disagree on the findings, usually someone (or some instrument) has made a mistake.

In contrast, the humanities (literature, philosophy, classics, religion, art, music, drama, and the like) are concerned with the products of human intellect, emotion, creativity, and imagination. Depending on the field, the goals of humanistic fields are enjoyment and appreciation, uplifting the spirit, training the mind, pondering the meaning of life, discovering beauty, broadening horizons, and so on. Because the humanities study the products of human minds (texts, ideas, styles, creative expressions, and objects of beauty) their subject is not physical or material—although, of course, the creativity and imagination may be expressed using a material medium (a painting, a written poem, or a musical score). Scholars in the humanities themselves often create, as well as study, their subjects. Once a painting, a sculpture, a poem, a novel, or a play is publicly presented, different people are free to make what they will of it. It is to be enjoyed, interpreted, pondered, experienced, and—inevitably—critiqued. You observe it, listen to it, or read it in any way you choose. And no one expects that their discovery of it, experience of it, or opinion of it will be "replicated" by anyone else.

Now: Is cultural anthropology, which studies culture and cultural diversity, more like the sciences or more like one of the humanities? Are cultures more like "things" or more like "texts"? A culture is like a "thing" in that it is the product of (cultural) evolution and has some properties that can be observed and measured, just like a biological life form. But it is like a "text" in that its properties are the product of human thought, feeling, and creativity, much like a work of fiction or a play. If culture and cultures are similar to biological life forms, then the basic goals of anthropology can be to "explain" cultural differences and similarities. But if culture and cultures are more like texts, then the anthropologist can only "interpret" other cultures.

Connected to the science or humanity issue are methodological issues that come out of the fieldwork experience. Will two trained fieldworkers studying the same group of people at the same time come up with the same findings? When they do not, is one or the other mistaken? Since fieldworkers are human beings studying and interacting with other human beings, can we expect the ethnographies they produce to contain objective and verifiable data?

Such questions seem fundamental to an academic discipline. Students and scholars in other fields are sometimes surprised that cultural anthropologists do not agree on the answer to them. In the conclusion of this chapter, we suggest reasons why agreement on such fundamentals is so difficult to achieve for a field whose focus is describing and understanding human cultural forms in all their diversity.

---

most important aspects of culture everywhere, as White argued back in the 1940s. By "most important," materialists mean that technology strongly affects other cultural aspects, including family life, political organization, values, and even world views. Because the essential purpose of technology is to aid people in making a living in their environments, the environment itself also helps determine culture, just as Steward said. In applying their technology in their environment, over long time periods people discover that certain resources are preferable to others, and that some ways of timing and organizing their labor activities work better than others. For example, those food resources that are most productive and/or nutritious will become culturally preferred and exploited, and the best ways of scheduling and organizing the work to acquire them will become standardized.

In their emphasis on the importance of physical/biological needs, technology, and environment, modern materialists resemble earlier thinkers such as Malinowski, White, and Steward. However, in many ways modern materialists are more sophisticated than their precursors. For example, for the most part previous theories about causation were *linear,* meaning that one thing makes another thing the way it is; thus, A "causes" B, or A "determines" B. We might see technology and environment as causes, and cultures as effects. But modern materialists are more likely to view technology, environment, and culture as having *feedback* relationships to one another. That is, as people interact with their environment using their technology, they change the environment, and these changes in turn lead people to alter their technology, which then further alters the environment, and so on. For instance, as people exploit a resource, they often deplete its supply to themselves and future generations. They must then either work harder to acquire the resource in the future, develop a new method of acquiring it, or switch to an alternative resource. Other cultural changes accompany these changes in adaptation.

Following this line of argument, one leading materialist, Marvin Harris, proposes that many important changes in human cultures result from a process known as *intensification*. Although human societies develop various ways of limiting their population growth, over the long term the population in many regions increased. As population grows, people overexploit and deplete resources, which leads to degradation of their environment. This forces them to use their environment more "intensively": They turn to resources they previously ignored, which requires them to expend more labor in acquiring energy and materials, which leads them to develop new technologies to harvest and process resources. As human numbers continue to increase, people must continue to intensify their use of resources. Both population growth and intensification lead to new social relations and organizations, which develop to facilitate the new ways of exploiting nature. In turn, new social arrangements require new world views, values, and norms to reinforce them. We discuss some of these processes in later chapters.

Idealism

A great many (in the year 2000, probably most) modern ethnologists are skeptical of materialist explanations. They are often called *idealists*—not because they think the world could be a much better place (they are not necessarily *idealistic*), but because they think that the ideas and beliefs of a culture (its mental components—see Chapter 2) are fundamental in making it the way it is. Most idealists are skeptical of any effort to "explain" culture in the same way that evolutionary theory explains life or that Einstein's relativity theory explains the physical world. People, cultures, and human minds are too complex and unpredictable to be "explained" in the usual scientific sense of the word *explanation*—or so idealists believe.

Idealists believe this for many reasons, but perhaps the most important reason is their insistence on *human uniqueness*. Without denying that humans are animals,

A leading figure in modern materialist thought is Marvin Harris. Throughout his career, he has consistently championed the view that ecological, technological, and demographic forces are the main causes of cultural similarities and differences.

they think that humans are such a special kind of animal that special kinds of methods and analysis are required to understand us.

Human uniqueness, as we know, consists in our heavy dependence on social learning and in our capacity for complex communication—that is, in both culture and language. Another fundamental difference in humanity arises out of our reliance on culture and capacity for language: Other animals live in the natural world, whereas humans live, in large part, in worlds of their own making and construction. This means that people manipulate nature (with agriculture, houses, and factories) more than other animals. But more importantly, it means that the way people perceive the natural and social environment, the way they interpret events in that environment, and their view of the world itself depends on their culture.

Consider, for example, the term *resource,* one of the cornerstones of materialist theory about causation. A simple definition might be "something that people use to satisfy their needs or wants." *Resources* thus appear to be "out there," "in nature," available for a people to use or transform. For materialists, the way people acquire resources is one of the main factors that shapes other aspects of their culture, and long-term changes in the way populations acquire resources is one of the main things that leads to cultural evolution.

Idealists, though, see resources differently. To them, a *resource* is as much a cultural concept as a material thing. Further, people's "wants" and even what they think they "need" for survival are not fixed and permanent, but variable from group to group. Resources, then, are not "out there"; rather, they are *culturally defined*. What one people considers a resource is not defined as a resource for other people. Hindus do not eat cattle; Muslims and orthodox Jews refuse pork and abhor the pig; Americans shun dog meat, insects, and horse flesh; and so on. Some perfectly edible animals and plants are not culturally defined as foods because of a people's world view or classifications of reality. Likewise, wants and needs are not inherent and universal in human nature, but are culturally variable.

The same thinking applies to the way materialists and idealists view the environment. As we have seen, materialists emphasize the *objective conditions* under which people live and to which their behavior must be adapted. The natural environment is external to the group, and its characteristics are hard realities of nature to which a human group must adjust.

Idealists question whether this reality has very much significance in determining the ways in which any particular people live. They hold that the way a group of people *subjectively perceive* their environment is as important in shaping their adaptation as is the objective environment itself. Material conditions (i.e., technology, environment, and adaptation) do not "determine" the rest of culture, for cultural classifications, definitions, and conceptions shape people's perceptions of the material conditions.

Materialists and idealists also disagree on which needs and wants take priority in human life. Materialists assume that material satisfactions like shelter, nutrition, bodily comforts, wealth items, and so forth are generally the main goals and values in life. The desire for nonmaterial satisfactions are less important or are acted upon only after material needs and wants have been satisfied.

In contrast, idealists place more emphasis on what goes on in human minds than on what goes into human stomachs. They think also that human-human relationships are at least as important as human-environment relationships. Humans require more than material satisfactions for a sense of well-being and even for survival. People do not live by wheat and meat (or rice and fish) alone: We need rewarding social relationships, intellectually coherent and emotionally gratifying world views, a sense of who we are, symbols to become attached to, basic values to cling to, and other nonmaterial rewards. In brief, as *cultural beings* humans seek a meaningful as well as a prosperous existence, and our psychological need for meaning is just as important as our material needs for things. Idealists point out that some people deliberately reject material rewards in the name of cultural preservation or for religious reasons.

Finally, idealists argue that the material conditions people face impose only very broad limits on their behaviors because people can satisfy their needs in a multitude of ways. No human population adapts to its environment in a historical and cultural vacuum. Their history and traditions influence not only how they define *resource* and perceive nature, but also which of the many possible ways of adapting to nature they will adopt. There are many ways to survive and persist in a given environment.

In summary, idealists believe that the human dependence on culture and capacity for symbolic communication makes us such unique animals that attempts to explain cultural diversity in scientific terms are likely to be futile. In particular, materialist explanations fail for several reasons:

- Resources, which have such an important role in materialist theory, are culturally defined, not inherent in nature.
- A people's perceptions of the natural world are as important to their adaptation as are the objective conditions of their environment.
- Unlike other animals, material wants are not paramount among humans, who have a variety of social, emotional, intellectual, and symbolic wants as well.

Materialists claim that how people exploit and use resources is one of the main influences on their culture, but idealists counter that the very definition of resource varies from culture to culture. The sacred cattle of Hindu India, for example, are not the same kind of resource as cattle are in North America or Africa.

- Material conditions provide great leeway for a people to develop a wide diversity of behaviors and beliefs, based on their particular history and unique traditions.

If all this is true, then how is it that materialist scholars have been so wrong about the importance of environment, technology, adaptation, and so forth? Many idealists hold that materialist thinking is a product of Western cultural values and beliefs. Because the West places such a high value on material welfare and consumption, materialists mistakenly impose these values and beliefs on other cultures. They see "economic man" in cultures where he does not exist.

Some anthropologists of today go so far as to claim that the methods and assumptions of science itself are suspect. They hold that scientific thinking and methods are a product of the Enlightenment period (also called the Age of Reason) of eighteenth-century Western civilization. Because it is a product of a particular culture (the West), science is just one among hundreds of other systems of cultural knowledge. It has little more claim to Truth than do other systems of knowledge. Many scholars who adhere to the philosophical viewpoint known as **postmodernism** believe in the relativity of all knowledge, science included. Postmodernism began to penetrate anthropology in the 1980s and has gained a large number of followers. Whether it will endure remains to be seen.

There are many particular approaches within ethnology that share the basic assumptions and philosophy of idealist thought. Here we discuss only one, which we chose because it has been around for several decades and reveals especially well how idealist approaches differ from materialist ones.

Interpretive Anthropology

As much as any other single factor, the fascination with cultural variability distinguishes modern ethnology from other academic disciplines. Many anthropologists say they go into the field in search of The Other, meaning in quest of peoples and ways of life that differ from their own. They believe that the essence of anthropology is to immerse oneself deeply in another culture and, through such immersion, to come to an understanding of it on its own terms. Through such immersion they hope to better understand not only the particular culture in which they work, but themselves and the totality of the human condition as well. Through their writings, they hope to communicate their understandings and interpretations of The Other to members of their own culture, to help *them* to understand the diverse ways of being human.

This approach is often known as **interpretive anthropology**. Interpretive anthropologists emphasize the uniqueness and individuality of each human culture. Every culture has its own ways of doing things, its own world view, its own values, and so forth. Even if two or more cultures look similar, close examination shows that the meanings they attach to behaviors, objects, and concepts are different. This uniqueness makes comparisons between different cultures misleading, at best. And since science usually attempts to generalize through making comparisons between phenomena, it follows that anthropology is more of a humanistic discipline than a scientific one. It has more in common with literature and art than with biology or psychology, according to the interpretive approach.

For interpretive anthropologists, all social behavior has a symbolic component, in the sense that participants constantly must behave in ways that others will understand. All social interaction, therefore, is symbolic and meaningful. Meanings exist only by virtue of common agreement among the parties to the interaction—whether the interaction is making conversation, making change in a store, making bumpers in an auto factory, or making time at a party. Neither participant can tell an observer how he or she knows what the other participant "means" by this or that behavior. Yet participants consistently behave in ways that others understand, and they consistently interpret the behavior of others correctly.

The job of the anthropologist is not to explain elements of a culture but to explicate one element through others. That is, the anthropologist shows how one thing in a cultural system makes sense in terms of other things in the same system, because interpretation is seeing how things make sense when understood in their context. (Analogously, a dictionary explicates the meanings of words in terms of other words. Only if one knows the meaning of many words in the dictionary can one use it to decipher the meaning of unknown words.) We seek to understand a people's way of life as they understand it. In the words of one interpretivist, Clifford Geertz, we seek to grasp "the native's point of view," "to figure out what the devil they think they are up to" (Geertz 1983, 58).

According to many interpretive anthropologists, the search for generalized explanations of human ways of life is futile. So many factors contributed to the formation of a culture, and these factors interacted in such complex and unpredictable ways, that we must concentrate on understanding the unique elements of each way of life. In this respect, interpretive anthropologists exemplify the assumptions of the idealist perspective on culture.

Either/Or?

To some extent, the differences in orientation between materialists and idealists exist because of the differing interests of anthropologists. For example, scholars whose research specializations include subjects such as human

Interpretive anthropologists believe that studying culture is more of a humanistic endeavor than a scientific endeavor. Clifford Geertz was influential in formulating the view that culture is essentially a system of symbols, unique to each people, so that our primary goal is interpreting the meanings of symbols in their particular cultural context.

adaptation, economic systems, or long-term evolutionary changes in societies are likely to find a materialist approach useful. Those who study cultural aspects such as mythology, art, oral traditions, or belief systems are more likely to fall into the idealist camp. Also, in part, the diversity of modern approaches reflects the fact that human beings and their cultures are complex and multifaceted wholes, so the orientation adopted to understanding one facet (e.g., subsistence) may not prove very useful for understanding another facet (e.g., world view).

In the interest of balance, in the remainder of this book we try to avoid choosing between the two orientations by taking the following approach. We recognize (as Steward did) that different elements of a culture are influenced to different degrees by material conditions. Certainly, the way an economy is organized is greatly influenced by the local environment, by technology, and by the size and density of the human populations. But the way a people resolve their disputes, raise their children, perform their rituals, or act toward their fathers-in-law is less influenced by material conditions or is influenced by them

only indirectly. The legends they recite, the specific objects they use as religious symbols, or the way they decorate their bodies may have little to do with material conditions. Such elements of a cultural system may be only loosely tied to material forces and to desires for material things. If so, we cannot account for them without considering people's desires for a meaningful existence, for an emotionally gratifying social life, for an intellectually satisfying world view, for creative self-expression, and so forth.

So we can avoid falling into the "either/or" trap by pointing out that different orientations are useful for studying different dimensions of culture. Still, people who are new to anthropology often are puzzled by the diversity of approaches within the field. We therefore conclude this chapter by suggesting answers to the following question:

Why Can't All Those Anthropologists Agree?

Natural scientists in fields such as physics, chemistry, and geology generally agree on a set of laws or principles that govern the physical world. In geology, for example, processes such as sedimentation, plate tectonics, the mineral cycle, volcanic eruptions, fossilization, and so forth are fairly well understood and account for the main geological features of our planet. In chemistry, how atoms combine to form molecules and how molecules combine to form more complex molecules is known well enough that new chemicals can be created in predictable ways. Biologists, likewise, believe that the diversity of all life on earth was produced by the process of evolution, although the relative importance of natural selection and random events in this process remains uncertain.

Yet most social sciences—cultural anthropology included—lack a comparable set of general principles by which we understand humans and the cultural forms they create. In cultural anthropology, for example, one basic question is: "What are the important causes of the differences and similarities between the world's known cultures?" If you were to ask 100 ethnologists this question, you would get a multitude of answers. Some would mention material forces such as climate, resources, population sizes, and technology. Others would discuss how creative human minds construct new cultural forms out of previous cultural forms. Still others would say that there is no generalized explanation, because cultures are so complex and diverse that the most important causes in culture X are not at all important in culture Y. Some would say that the question itself is wrongheaded, because anthropologists should be trying to interact with and interpret other cultures, not to "explain" them. A few will say that the question is ethnocentric, and in some cases racist, because it reduces people in other cultures to the status of "objects" of our explanations.

Why don't anthropologists agree more than they do on the answer to this question and numerous other basic questions about humanity? Several factors contribute to the absence of consensus.

First, we humans are conscious and self-aware beings who state a variety of reasons for why we do what we do. The zoologist studying an animal observes and records the animal's behavior and quantifies certain aspects of it, then typically tries to identify the elements of the natural and social environment to which the behavior is adapted. But anthropologists must listen to the reasons people themselves give for their behavior. People talk back, and anthropologists must take their talk, as well as their patterns of behavior, into account.

Second, for ethical reasons anthropologists cannot set up controlled experiments to study how people respond. Suppose—following Steward's lead—we want to study how the natural environment affects human cultures. We cannot do so by holding everything constant except the food, water, or shelter supply, and then see how people react when the supply of food, water, or shelter is varied. The only way the anthropologist can "control" conditions is by choosing a sample of peoples who live in environments that appear to be similar, then seeing whether the peoples who live there have similar cultures. For example, we might compare indigenous peoples who live in the world's deserts: the Sahara of northern Africa, the Kalahari of southern Africa, the American southwest, the Gobi of central Asia, and so forth. To conduct such a comparative study, we will have to rely on the ethnographic reports written by a multitude of earlier ethnographers, whose reports resulted from their observations and discussions with peoples of the various deserts.

Suppose our comparative study finds, as it will, that the cultures are similar in some respects but different in others. Then problems arise: Natural environments are only similar, never identical. Did we fail to detect a small but critical difference in the environment that might explain the cultural differences? Or are the differences due to some nonenvironmental factor? Likewise, cultures are only similar, never identical. Shall we call customs and beliefs that differ in minor ways between the cultures the "same," or are the subtle differences between them sufficient to call them "different"? Suppose we decide that some behavior, like sharing food within a village, is the "same" behavior in the cultures. But then we discover that people in several of the cultures give different reasons for the behavior—in culture X people say they want to help one another, whereas in culture Y they say they give only because they expect to get something back later. Are both of these behaviors still "sharing food"? Or should we consider them as different because peoples' stated motivations differ? Or did the various ethnographers interpret a certain behavior as "food

sharing," when in fact it was something else? Such questions are *inherently* difficult to answer when dealing with human beings, and anthropologists cannot sort them out in laboratories or other experimental settings.

Third, anthropological fieldworkers study members of their own species. Being human, fieldworkers enter their research experience with a culture of their own. This culture inevitably affects their objectivity, and, hence, their interactions with the community, their perceptions of what is important, and so forth. Conversely, individuals in the community itself have their own perceptions, opinions, and biases about the fieldworker. Among the many factors that affect how the community responds to the research are the fieldworker's physical characteristics, sex, personality, the kinds of questions the fieldworker asks, and the historical experience of the community with individuals of the anthropologist's own society. Although most fieldworkers attempt to overcome their own cultural biases and to fit into the community, complete objectivity is impossible to achieve. (We have more to say on such difficulties in Chapter 5.) In fact, some contemporary anthropologists are writing ethnographies that focus far more on their interactions with local people than on the culture of the people themselves.

A fourth reason that anthropology lacks a common theoretical orientation and an agreed-upon set of principles is perhaps the most important of all. It is quite likely that people become anthropologists for a wider variety of reasons than people become, say, physicists. Some of us study anthropology because of our curiosity about why the human species is so diverse culturally. Others go into the field to further the cause of social justice—by educating ourselves and others about racism, ethnocentrism, or sexism, for example. Some want to immerse themselves in travel and interaction with people who are different from themselves, and they become anthropologists because the field provides them with such opportunities. The very broad scope of anthropology (see Chapter 1) helps account for the variety of reasons people choose it as a career: You can study agriculture, family life, political organization, medicine, art, religion, folklore, and almost anything else having to do with humankind. Naturally people who study topics as diverse as these are unlikely to agree on their theoretical orientations to the field as a whole. Indeed, many of them consciously reject any form of theoretical orientation, preferring to concentrate on researching particular cultures.

In sum, four major reasons that modern cultural anthropologists have such varied orientations to the study of culture are:

• Our subjects—other human beings—are themselves conscious of their own behavior and state their own reasons for why they do what they do.

- Anthropologists cannot set up experiments that allow them to control the conditions under which people live and act, so that behavior can be isolated and manipulated.
- Complete objectivity is impossible to achieve when a researcher is studying humans, both because researchers themselves are culture-bearers and because the subjects of the study react to fieldworkers in varied ways.
- The broad scope of the field itself and the enormous diversity of reasons people study anthropology make it unlikely that consensus will emerge.

Summary

Anthropology originated as a separate academic discipline in the late nineteenth century, after colonialism intensified contact between peoples of European ancestry and the indigenous peoples of Africa, Asia, the Americas, and the Pacific. Darwin's theory of evolution was one of the main notions that allowed Western intellectuals to make sense of the peoples and cultures of other lands. It seemed to imply that the history of life on earth was progressive, with simpler organisms evolving into more complex ones. Unilineal evolutionists applied this notion to cultures. Using written accounts as their main source of information about non-Western peoples, they arranged cultures into a sequence of progressive stages, from simple to complex, with Western civilization at the pinnacle. Anthropology thus began as the field that studied how humankind had progressed out of rude beginnings into a more "civilized" cultural existence.

In the early twentieth century, both American and British anthropologists developed new approaches to cultural studies. The American historical particularists, led by Boas, demolished the speculative schemes of the unilineal evolutionists by arguing that concepts such as "complexity" depend on one's point of view and thus have little objective meaning. Boas popularized the notion of cultural relativism that remains a hallmark of ethnology today. In Great Britain, functionalists such as Malinowski and Radcliffe-Brown tried to show how the various parts of a culture and its social system serve to meet the needs of individuals and society. By emphasizing the interrelatedness of cultural systems, functionalism strengthened the holistic perspective. Both the historical particularists and functionalists emphasized the importance of firsthand fieldwork as the surest path to objectivity and as essential for the training of anthropologists.

In the middle decades of the twentieth century, scholars like White and Steward returned to cultural evolution, avoiding most of the mistakes of the unilineal evolutionists. White emphasized the importance of technology, Steward of adaptation to the local environment, in making cultures the way they are. Both men thought that how a group acquires resources (energy, food, and so forth) from nature are the main influences on culture. Both also believed that anthropology was a science, whose main objective was to explain cultural differences and similarities.

In the year 2000, cultural anthropologists are enormously diverse in their assumptions and ways of studying cultures. One very broad modern division is whether one believes that ethnology is a scientific enterprise or a humanistic study. Many anthropologists who fall into the scientific camp adopt the *materialist* perspective. Essentially, materialists argue that how a given people organize their groups and activities to acquire energy and materials from their natural environment is the major explanation for other aspects of their cultural system. Thus, cultural differences and similarities ultimately can be explained by factors such as environment, technology, production, and economic organization. Idealists, in contrast, mistrust all such generalized explanations of cultural phenomena. Emphasizing the uniqueness of each culture, they favor studying, appreciating, and interpreting each culture individually and are suspicious of the validity of most comparative studies.

Contemporary anthropologists, then, do not agree among themselves on many fundamental questions, including even the major objectives of their field. Their lack of consensus, however, is understandable, given that their subjects are self-conscious and willful beings; that they cannot experiment with people's lives; that total objectivity in fieldwork is impossible; and that the field itself studies such diverse subjects that a single theoretical orientation is unlikely to be able to encompass all of them.

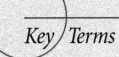

Key Terms

unilineal evolution
historical particularism
functionalism
materialism

idealism
postmodernism
interpretive anthropology

Suggested Readings

Among the volumes that discuss the history of cultural anthropology in detail are:

Harris, Marvin. *The Rise of Anthropological Theory*. New York: Crowell, 1968.

Hatch, Elvin. *Theories of Man and Culture*. New York: Columbia, 1973.

There are two excellent comprehensive readers covering the history of anthropological theory. Both include introductions by the editors as well as key original works by important anthropologists:

Bohannan, Paul, and Mark Glazer, eds. *High Points in Anthropology*. 2nd ed. New York: Knopf, 1988.

McGee, R. Jon, and Richard L. Warms, eds. *Anthropological Theory: An Introductory History*. Mountain View, Calif.: Mayfield, 1996.

To understand the contemporary divisions between materialists and idealists, consult some of the following works:

Geertz, Clifford. *The Interpretation of Cultures*. New York: Basic Books, 1973.
• *Assorted works by an idealist and interpretivist. Good place to start to understand this approach.*

Geertz, Clifford. *Negara: The Theatre State in Nineteenth-Century Bali*. Princeton: Princeton University Press, 1980.
• *Empirical, interpretive study.*

Harris, Marvin. *Cannibals and Kings*. New York: Random, 1977.
• *Intensification hypothesis of cultural evolution is explained and illustrated. Easy reading and an excellent example of materialist thought.*

Harris, Marvin. *Cultural Materialism: The Struggle for a Science of Culture*. New York: Vintage, 1980.
• *Title speaks for itself. Lays out theoretical principles of this approach and defends it from rival approaches, including dialectical materialism, structuralism, and idealism.*

Johnson, Allen W., and Timothy Earle. *The Evolution of Human Societies*. Stanford: Stanford University Press, 1987.
• *Outstanding and up-to-date theoretical and factual treatment of cultural evolution. Conceptualizes increasing complexity as shifting from family level through local level to regional level, with examples illustrating the cultures of each level.*

Marcus, George E., and Michael M. J. Fischer. *Anthropology as Cultural Critique*. Chicago and London: University of Chicago Press, 1986.
• *An influential book written from the idealist perspective. Discusses changes in anthropology and ethnography since the 1970s. Argues that the time is right for anthropologists to take on the task of critiquing their own culture.*

Internet Exercises

A good place to begin inquiring into anthropological theory is a website created for anthropology students. There are several websites that focus on theory. One is "Anthropological Theories: A Guide by Students for Students" from the Department of Anthropology at The University of Alabama (http://www.as.ua.edu/ant/murphy/anthros.htm). The discussion of the theories in this site were developed by graduate students under the direction of Dr. Michael Murphy. Another website is "Theory in Anthropology" from Indiana University at (http:www/indiana.edu/~wanthro/theory.htm).

To find out more about the major theorists in anthropology go to the "Anthropological Biographies" website at (http://kroeber.anthro.mankato.msus.edu/bio/index.htm). The biographies are part of Minnesota State University at Mankato's E-Museum at (http:kroeber.anthro.mankato.msus.edu/).

CHAPTER 5

Methods of Investigation

Ethnographic Methods

Ethnographic Fieldwork

Problems in Field Research

Fieldwork as a Rite of Passage

Ethnohistory

Comparative Methods

Cross-Cultural Comparisons

Controlled Historical Comparisons

Video · Audio · Photos
Hotlinks · Essay
http://www.wadsworth.com/humanity

Margaret Mead's highly innovative field studies in Samoa and New Guinea made her one of the most widely read anthropologists of the twentieth century.

Visit http://www.wadsworth.com/humanity to learn more about the material covered in this chapter and to access activities, exercises, and tutorial quizzes.

*A*NY SCIENCE *has a set of methods that its practitioners use to explore the reality they investigate. In cultural anthropology, our primary interest is in human ways of life— particularly the cultural differences and similarities that exist among the world's peoples. Over the decades, anthropologists have developed certain methods of investigating human cultures. These methods are the subject of this chapter.*

*A*NTHROPOLOGICAL METHODS *of investigation fall into two broad categories. The first is ethnographic methods, which involve the collection and analysis of descriptive data from a single society or several closely related societies. The end product of ethnographic research is either a case study* *describing the cultural system of some people (e.g., the way of life of the Cheyenne) or a descriptive account of some aspect of a people's cultural system (such as the Cheyenne religion). The second category is comparative methods, which involve attempts to test hypotheses about relations between certain aspects of cultural systems by using comparative ethnographic data from a number of societies. The product of comparative research usually is a monograph or article that tries to generalize about causal relations between cultural phenomena.*

So ANTHROPOLOGICAL research has two purposes: (1) the collecting and recording of new data about specific people (ethnography) and (2) the expansion of our theoretical understanding of human cultural systems in general through comparative analysis. We first discuss the methods used to describe a single people and then summarize how anthropologists use descriptive accounts to test hypotheses.

Ethnographic Methods

There are two sources of cultural data about a particular people: the living members of the society and written accounts or other records about that group of people. Collecting cultural data by studying and interviewing living members of a society is called **ethnographic fieldwork**. Studying a people's culture using written accounts and other records is termed **ethnohistoric research**.

Ethnographic Fieldwork

Ethnographic fieldwork involves the collection of cultural data from living individuals. It requires that the researcher live with or close to the people being studied so that he or she can interact with them on a day-to-day basis for a long period, usually a year or more. Not infrequently, the anthropologist has to learn the group's language and adjust his or her behavior to their social norms. By its very nature, fieldwork fosters a close personal relationship between the researcher and the members of the society being studied. This social closeness distinguishes anthropologists from other social scientists.

Fieldwork has always been the primary method used by anthropologists to collect cultural information. Over the past century the objective of fieldwork has changed, and with it, the data-gathering techniques. Today, a number of techniques are used in the course of any research project.

Interviewing is the most basic method of collecting cultural data. The anthropologist asks questions and elicits answers from members of the society being studied.

Interviews may be structured or unstructured. A *structured interview* consists of a limited number of specific questions. It may take the form of a questionnaire that the researcher fills in as the questions are answered. This type of interview is best suited for collecting general quantitative data about the group. For example, most research begins with a census of the community: the number of people in each family, their ages and relationships, and basic economic information about the family. In this manner, a demographic and an economic profile of the group can be constructed. Structured interviews are also used to create genealogies. Most research requires a clear knowledge of how everyone in the group is related to one another. Genealogies are important in understanding the social and economic behavior of individuals beyond the immediate family. There are, however, limits to the utility of structured interviews.

In *unstructured interviews* the researcher asks open-ended questions, hoping that the interviewee will elaborate on the answers. The questions may be general, about family life, marriage, a particular religious ritual, or economic activity. Most cultural data are collected through unstructured interviews. In these interviews the researcher learns the cultural explanations for information collected in the structured interviews.

Although it is the source of most cultural data, interviewing has severe limitations. The problem usually is not with the answers given by the members of the group, but rather with the questions asked by the researcher. What is relevant or irrelevant to the proper understanding of a particular cultural phenomenon depends on the culture of the individuals involved. Initially, the researcher does not understand the cultural context of the data and thus does not know what questions need to be asked and answered. The early stages of a research project often are characterized by "shotgun" questioning as the anthropologist seeks to learn enough about the culture to ask the right questions. Through interviewing, a researcher can gain a good basic knowledge of a culture's major structural features. However, no matter how knowledgeable and willing the interviewees might be, verbal descriptions in themselves are incomplete and do not enable the researcher to gain an in-depth knowledge of the people or an understanding of the true dynamics of their culture.

To understand the limitations of interviewing, ask yourself this question: If an anthropologist from another culture asked you to describe a baseball game, what would you say? How complete would your description be? Chances are, if you are an avid fan, you could relate enough information for the anthropologist to gain a basic understanding of the game. You could tell how many players there are on each side and explain the basic rules about balls, strikes, runs, errors, and innings. From memory alone, it is highly unlikely that you would explain everything that might occur during a game. What you probably would give the researcher is an idealized model of a baseball game. Certain facts would be left untold, not because you were hiding them but because they are either so commonplace or unusual that they are not part of your consciousness concerning the game. Interviews alone can give the researcher only a simplified overview of a particular cultural phenomenon, an idealized model.

If researchers want to truly understand baseball, they cannot simply talk to someone about it; they need to at least see a game. In fact, researchers should observe several games and discuss what occurred with a knowledgeable person. It would be even better for researchers to participate, at least in a minor way, in a game. Only by combining interviewing with observing and participating can one begin to understand the rules and dynamics of the game. So it is with the study of any cultural phenomenon.

During the late nineteenth and early twentieth centuries, anthropologists relied primarily on interviews to collect cultural data. This technique was well suited to the anthropological objectives of that time. Early American anthropologists were concerned with collecting general cultural information about Native American groups. These groups had already been placed on reservations, and their economies and cultures had drastically changed. Anthropologists wanted to record earlier Native American lifestyles before all knowledge of the prereservation period was lost. The only way the aboriginal culture of these peoples could be studied was by interviewing individuals who had grown to adulthood before the reservations were created. In a relatively short period, anthropologists were able to collect, and thus preserve, a vast body of general descriptive data on North American culture.

In the 1920s the interest of anthropologists began to shift from just describing the general culture of a society to attempting to understand the basic dynamics of cultural systems. In other words, anthropologists wanted to see how these systems worked and how their parts fit together. A leader in this change was Bronislaw Malinowski, mentioned earlier in the discussion of functionalism, who popularized a new data-collection technique called **participant observation**. Anthropologists no longer merely recorded and analyzed people's statements. To a greater or lesser extent, they took up residence with the people they were studying and began trying to learn about the culture by observing people in their daily lives and participating in their daily activities.

Participant observation often has been misinterpreted, even by some anthropologists who have taken it too literally. It does not mean becoming a full participant in the activities of the people—in other words, "going native."

Participant observation is the primary way in which anthropologists learn about other cultures.

The emphasis of this technique is more on observation than on participation. Participant observation usually does require that one live in the community, for only by doing so can one observe and record the behavior of individuals as they go about their daily work, visit their friends, interact with their relatives, participate in rituals, and so on. These observations of behavior serve to generate new questions. Why does a man share food with some families but not with others? Why do some men wear a particular type of hat or headdress? Does a particular color of clothing have any meaning? Some behaviors have significance, others do not. For example, variations in types of headdress may be merely the result of personal preferences, or it may reflect status differences. The color may or may not have special significance. In American society, black symbolizes mourning, but in other societies covering one's body with white clay symbolizes the same emotion. Participant observation allows the researcher to collect more detailed data than does interviewing alone, and thus it makes possible a deeper understanding of interrelations between cultural phenomena.

Firsthand observations of the members of a society also allow the researcher to see how people diverge from the culturally defined, idealized model of behavior. An incident that occurred while Malinowski was working in the Trobriand Islands illustrates the divergence between cultural norms—the way people say they ought to behave—and the way they actually behave. One day Malinowski heard a commotion in the village and discovered that a young boy in a neighboring village had committed suicide by climbing a palm tree and flinging himself onto the beach. In his earlier questioning of the islanders, Malinowski had been told that sexual relations between a man and his mother's sister's daughters were prohibited.

On inquiring into the suicide of the young boy, he found that the boy had been sexually involved with his mother's sister's daughter, and that in fact such incestuous relationships were not rare. So long as such liaisons were not mentioned in public, they were ignored. In this particular case, the girl's rejected boyfriend had become angry and publicly exposed the transgression. Although everyone in the village already knew of this incestuous relationship, by making it public the ex-boyfriend exposed his rival to ridicule, thus causing him to commit suicide. It is doubtful that such behavior could have been discovered only by interviewing individuals.

Problems in Field Research

Every fieldwork experience is, to some extent, unique. Specific problems differ, depending on the individual characteristics of the researcher, the nature of the community, and the particular questions being studied. There are, however, several difficulties that, to varying degrees, affect virtually every field-research situation: (1) stereotyping, (2) defining the fieldworker's role in the community and developing rapport, and (3) identifying and interviewing consultants.

Stereotyping   When we think of stereotypes—preconceived generalizations concerning a particular group of people—we usually think only of their effects on the perceptions of one party of a relationship. Anthropologists ask themselves how they can overcome their own stereotypes and cultural biases about the people they study. Stereotyping, however, is a two-way street. Every society has stereotypes concerning members of other societies and of ethnic and racial groups. Thus, although the goal is for an anthropologist to put aside his or her personal stereotypes sufficiently to research the cultural system of another people with some degree of objectivity, those with whom the ethnographer will be living and working will not have shelved their stereotypes. Most anthropologists are of European ancestry, yet most subjects of anthropological research are non-European peoples. Even if a particular anthropologist is of Asian, African, or Native American ancestry, a similar problem exists because anthropologists seldom belong to the local community they study and thus are outsiders. As a result, an anthropologist who enters another community must contend with local stereotypes about the ethnic group with which he or she is identified.

In the case of anthropologists of European ancestry, local stereotyping has most frequently been derived from contact with only a limited range of individuals, such as missionaries, soldiers, colonial officials, and government bureaucrats. Regardless of the nature and intensity of this contact, most non-Western peoples have a well-developed idea about the expected behavior of such individuals. The tendency of local people to fit the ethnographer into one of their stereotypical categories can at times prove a burden for fieldworkers. The behavior of anthropologists seldom conforms to the model that the local people have developed. Previous contacts with Europeans and Euro-Americans often have been structured in such a manner as to place the "native" in the position of social inferior. Thus, an anthropologist attempting to gain social acceptance in such a society typically is met with suspicion and not infrequently with hostility. The types of questions anthropologists ask about behavior and beliefs frequently arouse suspicions further and elicit guarded answers. Why does he or she want to know about our family structure, out political organization, our ritual secrets? What is the person going to do with this information? While the anthropologist is trying to understand the community, its members are attempting to understand what the anthropologist is doing. Depending on the nature of previous contacts, some types of questions may provoke more suspicion than others. For example, a minority or tribal group involved in some illegal or illicit activity—such as smuggling, poaching, or growing drugs—may wonder if the anthropologist will inform government authorities. Members of groups that have been more exposed to Western culture usually assume that the ethnographer's objective is to make money and that researchers become wealthy by publishing books.

In other cases, members of the community may be aware that Europeans and Euro-Americans do not approve of or believe in certain types of behavior, and few people will disclose information on topics they think will be met with disapproval or scorn. This reticence is particularly evident in certain types of religious beliefs and practices. As a result of extensive activities of Christian missionaries, most non-Western peoples are well aware that Westerners usually deny the validity of witchcraft and the existence of werewolves. Members of societies with these beliefs usually are hesitant about discussing such subjects with Westerners. They are understandably reluctant to talk openly about an uncle who they believe can turn himself into a deer or a snake with someone who will probably view what they say as ridiculous. Likewise, they probably would not say that their father had been killed by a witch if they thought that the outsider did not believe in witchcraft.

Developing a Role and Rapport   Often against a background of suspicion and distrust, an anthropologist has to develop a rapport with the members of the community. Rapport in this sense means acceptance to the degree that a working relationship is possible, although ethnographers are rarely, if ever, totally accepted by the people among whom they work. However, over a period of time most anthropologists succeed in gaining some degree of trust and friendship, at least with a few members of the group.

The particular role or roles that an anthropologist eventually defines for herself or himself within society vary greatly with the circumstances of the particular situation. Depending on the amount and nature of research funding, the anthropologist may be an important economic resource, paying wages to interpreters and assistants or distributing desirable goods as gifts. Anthropologists with a car or truck frequently find themselves providing needed transportation for members of the community. Ethnographers may also provide comic relief by asking silly questions, behaving in a funny manner, making childlike errors in speaking the language, and generally being amusing to have around. They may be a source of information about the outside world, disclosing information to which local people would not otherwise have access. Sometimes community members are as curious about the anthropologist's society as he is about their society. Or the anthropologist may just be considered a harmless nuisance. During the course of research, the typical field-worker at one time or another adopts all these roles plus many others.

Identifying and Interviewing Consultants Ethnographers learn a good deal about people simply by living among them and participating in many of their activities. This rather casual, informal participant observation provides a good feel for the general pattern of life.

But for most purposes, observation and participation alone are insufficient. We do not just want to know what they are doing, but why they are doing it. Because certain realms of culture are not observable (e.g., religious beliefs, myths, stories, and social values), the researcher has to interview members of the group.

An individual who supplies the ethnographer with information is called a **consultant** or **informant**. Field research involves the help of many consultants, who sometimes are paid for their services. Just as no one individual is equally well informed about every aspect of our own cultural system, so no one person in another society is equally knowledgeable about every aspect of his or her society's way of life. Women are more knowledgeable than men concerning certain things, and vice versa. Shamans and priests know more about religious rituals than other people do. The elderly members of the community usually are most knowledgeable about myths, stories, and histories. Thus, the anthropologist has to attempt to identify and interview those people who are most knowledgeable about particular subjects. Individuals

whom the local community considers to be expert in some particular area are known as **key consultants** or **key informants**.

A number of factors affect the quality and accuracy of the data collected through interviewing. The people being studied seldom understand fully what the anthropologist is trying to accomplish. In some instances, especially among minority populations, there may be a deliberate attempt to deceive the researcher. For example, collecting livestock-ownership data on the Navajo reservation can at times prove difficult. The total number of livestock on the reservation is controlled by the tribe, and each stockowner has a permit that allows him or her to keep a certain number of animals. Because some people keep more stock than their permits allow, they are reluctant to disclose the actual number in their herds. There is also the problem of humorous deception. The Osage men wear a deer tail roach on their heads during dances. During a dance, an Osage was overheard telling an inquisitive visitor that these roaches were made of horse tails, and that a young Osage male proved his manhood by cutting the hair for his roach from the tail of the meanest horse he could find. In this case, the Osage was simply having fun at the expense of a visitor, but anthropologists also encounter this problem. To get around these and other difficulties, anthropologists try to interview a number of individuals separately about specific points to gain several independent verifications.

Some societies prohibit the relating of certain kinds of cultural knowledge to outsiders. The Pueblos of the Rio Grande Valley of New Mexico are extremely secretive about their non-Christian religious beliefs and rituals. Non-Indians are not allowed to witness these ceremonies, and members of these pueblos are prohibited from talking about them to non-Indians.

Other kinds of cultural barriers also make it difficult to collect certain types of data. For example, collecting genealogies is not always as easy as it might seem because in many societies it is customary not to speak the names of the dead. Among the Yąnomamö of Venezuela and Brazil, not only is it taboo to speak the names of the dead, but it is considered discourteous to speak the names of prominent living men, for whom kinship terms are used whenever possible. When ethnographer Napoleon Chagnon persisted in his attempts to collect genealogies, the Yąnomamö responded by inventing a series of fictitious genealogical relationships. Only after five months of intensive research did he discover the hoax. When he mentioned some of the names he had collected during a visit to a neighboring village, the people responded with "uncontrollable laughter" because his informants had made up names such as "hairy rectum" and "eagle shit" to avoid speaking real names.

Fieldwork as a Rite of Passage

Fieldwork is important to cultural anthropologists not just because it is the major source of our data on human cultures, but because it is a key aspect of the education of the anthropologist. It is one thing to read ethnographies about other ways of life, but it is something quite different to live among and interact with individuals from another cultural tradition every day for a year or more. As we have seen, the anthropologist usually lives in the native community, submerging himself or herself in the social life of the people, living in native dwellings, eating local foods, learning the language, and participating as fully as an outsider is allowed in daily activities. Living as social minorities, usually for the first time in their lives, anthropologists depend on the goodwill of people whose norms and values they neither totally understand or accept. Under these conditions, the participant observer has to adjust his or her activities to fit the cultural ideas and behavior patterns of the people. This modification of the fieldworker's own behavior is a necessary part of learning about the community. Fieldworkers usually work alone and are socially and physically vulnerable to members of the community. During the course of their research, anthropologists will violate, or at least be perceived as violating, some of the societal norms of behavior. Such incidents may destroy the rapport gained with some key consultants or result in the researcher's being ostracized. In serious cases, the fieldworker may find himself or herself the target of physical violence.

When in the field, except on rare occasions, the anthropologist is there as the uninvited guest of the community. Regardless of how researchers may rationalize their work as being for the long-term good of the community or humanity, they are basically there to serve their own needs and interests. If a serious problem develops between the anthropologist and members of the community, the fieldworker must bear the primary responsibility and blame.

The fieldwork experience tests and taxes the attitude of cultural relativity that anthropologists teach in their classrooms. It is easy to discuss the concept of relativity in a university setting, but it is more difficult to apply this concept to one's own situation. Regardless of which society it is, certain cultural aspects will offend one's own cultural norms and values. For example, according to the anthropologist's own cultural standards, some local people might "abuse" certain family members or certain powerful leaders might "exploit" lower-ranking members of the society. As the fieldworker develops friendships, this "abuse" or "exploitation" frequently becomes personalized. Under what circumstances, if ever, an anthropologist should attempt to intervene and try to impose her or his cultural standards on the members of another society poses a real and personal dilemma. In theory, such intervention is never permissible, but in real-life situations the answer is not always so clear.

Many people experience a kind of psychological trauma when surrounded by people speaking a language they cannot fully understand and speak only imperfectly, eating foods that are strange, seeing architecture that is alien, and observing people using gestures and behaving in ways they either do not comprehend or do not approve of. The strange sounds, smells, tastes, sights, and behaviors result in the disorientation of many fieldworkers. Out of their normal cultural context, they do not understand what is happening around them, yet realize that their own actions often are being misunderstood. The symptoms of this **culture shock** are psychological and sometimes even physiological: paranoia, anxiety, a longing for the folks back home, nausea, hypochondria, and, frequently, diarrhea.

The attempts by ethnographers to maintain their relativistic perspective and objectivity in their daily interaction with members of the other society usually compound the normal trauma of culture shock. Socially isolated and unable to release their frustrations and anxieties through conversations with sympathetic others, they often have to cope with their psychological difficulties alone.

For many anthropologists, much of their time in the field is extremely traumatic, and as a result, most anthropologists view fieldwork as a rite of passage. More than any other aspect of their training, fieldwork transforms the individual from a student of anthropology into a professional anthropologist. Although many overemphasize the importance of fieldwork during training, it is undeniably a significant educational experience. Most individuals return from their fieldwork with a different perspective on themselves and their own culture. Fieldwork often teaches us as much about ourselves as about those we are supposed to be studying.

Ethnohistory

The study of past cultural systems through the use of written records is called **ethnohistory**. Since the late nineteenth century, anthropologists have used written materials in their studies, but the importance of this research has become widely recognized only since the 1970s. The growing interest in ethnohistory has come with the realization that non-Western societies have changed far more dramatically over the past few hundred years than had previously been thought.

Other Voices

Alice Fletcher and Francis LaFlesche

In 1911 the Smithsonian published Alice Fletcher's and Francis LaFlesche's study *The Omaha Tribe*. This study considered today to be one of the classics in American-Indian studies was the result of almost a quarter century of collaborative research by two scholars from very different backgrounds. Alice Fletcher was from a privileged east coast family, while Francis LaFlesche was the son of an Omaha Indian chief from the plains of Nebraska.

Alice Fletcher's father was a lawyer in New York City and her mother was from Boston. Her father suffered a severe illness, and soon after their marriage in 1837 they travelled the Caribbean for the winter. In Cuba, in March 1838, Alice was born. The following year her father died. Little is known of Fletcher's early life in New York City. We know that she attended the Brooklyn Female Academy/Packer Collegiate Institute, the best private school for girls in the city. We also know that her mother remarried and that Alice had a poor relationship with her stepfather. Eventually, while still in school, she moved in and lived with family friends, the Conants, who "hired" her as a governess for their younger daughters but treated her as one of the family. Even after leaving school and their "employment" Alice received financial support from the Conants which enabled her to continue life among the social elite of the city. She never married. Her early adult life centered around women's clubs and the founding of the Association for the Advancement of Women (AAW) in 1873. However, two events of the mid-1870s changed her life. A national economic panic resulted in the loss of her financial investments. After the death of Mr. Conant in 1877, she had no money and no means of support.

Well educated, articulate, and attractive she turned to giving public lectures as a means of support. Because of her abilities and social contacts she quickly became a successful paid lecturer. Travelling to cities throughout the eastern United States, she initially lectured on a wide range of topics. However, her interest became increasingly focused on American-Indian prehistory, particularly the early mound-building peoples of the Ohio and Mississippi valleys. Her interest in American archaeology soon brought her into contact with Frederic Putnam of the Peabody Museum at Harvard. Impressed by her intellectual abilities, Putnam strongly encouraged her interest in the emerging field of anthropology.

In 1881, while on a lecture tour, Susette LaFlesche, an Omaha Indian activist, and her soon-to-be husband, the journalist, Henry Tibbles, visited Boston. Fletcher had the opportunity to show them the Peabody and discuss with them the museum's research on American Indians. At the invitation of now Mr. and Mrs. Tibbles, she spent the winter of 1881–1882 in fieldwork among the Sioux and the Omahas. In the course of this research she wrote Putnam ". . . I have been nearly all the time living with the Indians, as far as possible like one of them. . . . I have worked myself round to where the Indian stands and looked at his life and ways as he does," thus hinting at the emergence of the cultural relativistic perspective which would later characterize her work and bring her into conflict with many of her anthropological colleagues. In the spring of 1882 Fletcher returned east. She returned a dedicated anthropological researcher and an ardent advocate for Indian political causes.

Born in 1857, Francis LaFlesche was the son of Joseph LaFlesche, an Omaha chief, and the younger brother of Susette LaFlesche Tibbles. Educated at a mission school on the Omaha reservation, he learned English, the Christian religion, and about the white world. However, on holidays and vacations he lived the life of an Omaha, participating in bison hunts, religious rituals, and other tribal social activities.

In 1877 the closely related Ponca tribe was forcibly moved south to Indian Territory (Oklahoma). In the south many died including the son of Standing Bear. During the winter of 1878–1879 Standing Bear and a group of his followers returned to Nebraska to bury his son. The Omahas welcomed them. However,

Standing Bear and his followers were soon arrested and plans were made to return them to their reservation. These arrests outraged many individuals in Nebraska including a newspaper editor named Henry Tibbles who nationally publicized the event. A group of attorneys representing Standing Bear took the government to federal court. Susette LaFlesche served as Standing Bear's interpreter during the trial which resulted in Standing Bear and his people being allowed to stay in Nebraska.

In 1879 Indian rights advocates organized an eastern lecture tour for Standing Bear, Henry Tibbles, and Susette LaFlesche. Francis LaFlesche accompanied them as a chaperon for his sister. Susette—"Bright Eyes" as she was also known—quickly emerged as a popular spokeswoman for Indian rights.

Francis had married an Omaha woman shortly before the tour. After his return difficulties arose between them— he later divorced her. Possibly because of his marital problems in 1881, he secured a job as copyist in the Indian Service and moved to Washington, D.C.

Returning east from her visit to the Omahas and Sioux, Fletcher went to Washington to lobby for the Omaha allotment bill pending before congress. During the summer in Washington she conferred frequently with Francis and a cooperative working relationship developed which would endure for the next forty years. The relationship was natural. She wanted to research Indian culture and he wished to create a permanent record of Indian culture. Both shared a common goal of advancing Indian rights.

The closeness of their relationship was not without problems, both social and professional. She was white and almost 20 years his senior. There was gossip about the nature of their relationship, particularly after he moved into her house in Washington, an arrangement that would continue until her death. In 1891 she had a legal document drawn up stating that she was adopting him as her son. Their relationship appears to have been that of "mother" and "son." In 1906 Francis married Rosa Bourassa in a wedding at Fletcher's home and the couple lived with Alice for the short period of their marriage.

The professional rivalry which emerged between them was more difficult to resolve. Originally Alice was the academic professional and Francis merely the native informant supplying her information on Omaha culture and acting as her interpreter. In their early collaborative studies, Francis received no professional acknowledgment. It was only at the insistence of another anthropologist, James Dorsey, that Francis finally presented his first professional paper. As long as the two were working on studies of Omaha culture there was an issue of increasing rivalry.

In the 1890s the professional interests of the two diverged. In 1890 Alice was awarded the Thaw Fellowship at Harvard which gave her the economic resources to pursue her interests. She quickly became involved in a wide range of projects, including research on the Pawnee tribe, which did not involve Francis. Francis also was free to pursue his own interests. In 1891 he received his LL.B. from the National University in Washington and in 1893 his LL.M. In 1900 he published an autobiographical work entitled *The Middle Five: Indian Boy at School*. The introduction states "the object of this book is to reveal the true nature and character of the Indian boy. . . [and it is hoped that] it may help these little Indians be judged, as are other boys, by what they say and what they do." Three years later, in a strongly worded lecture given in Philadelphia he accused not only the American public, but many of his anthropological colleagues of ethnocentrism.

It was not until 1905 that the two began collaboration on what was to be their most important and ambitious project, the writing of *The Omaha Tribe*. This time there would be no professional rivalry; both were now well-known national figures. It was the work of two equals. Although Alice's name appeared first and she wrote the foreword, plate 1 was a picture of Francis and there was no picture of Alice. The structure of the book was very different from earlier anthropological studies. Alice had noted the need for a "cultural relativistic" approach long before the term was yet coined. Francis wished to attack the ethnocentrism still prevalent in anthropolo-

gy. Thus, the book presented Omaha culture from an Omaha perspective, or as they stated it "to get close to the thoughts that underlie the ceremonies and customs of the Omaha Tribe."

The publication of *The Omaha Tribe* was not well received by many American anthropologists, particularly the students of Franz Boas. One reviewer ". . . criticized them for classifying the material in accord with 'aboriginal' rather than 'scientific' logic and for attaching historical value to the origin accounts of a primitive tribe, a 'tendency' now definitely abandoned by ethnologists." Initially, most praise for the study came from European academics.

Fletcher was 73 years old when *The Omaha Tribe* was published. It marked the end of her active career as a researcher and writer. For LaFlesche, however, it proved only the midpoint. In 1910 he was appointed as an ethnographer for the Bureau of American Ethnology at the Smithsonian and began his research on the Osage Indians of Oklahoma. This time LaFlesche conducted the fieldwork alone. Fletcher assisted LaFlesche only in transcribing the music and songs from the tapes he recorded in Oklahoma. Focusing on Osage religious rituals, his fieldwork continued until 1923 when Fletcher died.

Under the terms of Fletcher's will her estate was to be left in trust with the income going to LaFlesche. For six years following Fletcher's death LaFlesche lived in the house in Washington finishing the last volumes of his four-volume study *The Osage Tribe*. In 1929 he retired from the Smithsonian and moved back to the Omaha Reservation in Nebraska where he died in 1932. LaFlesche's monumental study of the Osages found an even less receptive audience among American anthropologists than had the Omaha study. In his obituary in the *American Anthropologist*, while his work was praised, his Osage study was called a "sentimental account."

Sources: Fletcher and LaFlesche (1911), LaFlesche (1900), Mark (1988), Ridington (1992), and Bailey (1995).

A CLOSER LOOK

Marshall Sahlins, Gananath Obeyesekere, and Captain James Cook

In January of 1778 two British ships under the command of Captain James Cook discovered the Hawaiian Islands. They stayed only three days before continuing on to the northern Pacific. In the winter of 1778–1779, they returned and for seven weeks sailed among the islands without making landfall. Finally, on January 17, 1779, they landed on the large island of Hawaii. This second landing was greeted by thousands of Hawaiians including King Kalani'opu'u. Cook was presented with a great feathered cloak and cap, and his travels were surrounded with rituals, including the multitude of people prostrating themselves before him and the chanting "Lono." On February 4, Cook and his ships departed with a spectacular send-off. However, the weather quickly turned bad, and one ship sprung its mast, forcing the expedition to return to the island for repairs. The Hawaiians did not welcome this return. Hostilities soon developed and a battle took place in which Cook was killed.

Scholars have long felt that Cook's visit was identified by the Hawaiians as the return of their god "Lono." Using ethnohistorical and ethnographic data Marshall Sahlins reexamined this interpretation in his 1981 study, *Historical Metaphors and Mythical Realities*, and reached the same conclusion.

Lono was a mythical god-king whom the Hawaiians believed periodically returned to the islands and ruled in human form, usurping power from the earthly kings who were representatives of the rival god Ku. Several earlier Hawaiian kings had been identified as Lono ruling on earth. Every year, during a period called *Makahiki*, a series of rituals were performed and dedicated to Lono. Lono symbolically returned to the islands at the beginning of Makahiki, at which time the priests of Lono took control of the temples from the priests of Ku. During the four lunar months that followed, the priests of Lono were in charge

of rituals. Makahiki ended with Lono being symbolically sacrificed and returning to the sky. With Lono gone, control returned to the king and the priests of Ku, the earthly representatives of Ku.

Sahlins found that as Cook sailed among the islands for seven weeks, the timing and direction of his movements coincidentally corresponded with the mythological movements of the god-king Lono. His landing on January 17 took place at the start of Makahiki; his departure on February 4 corresponded with the end of Makahiki. According to Sahlins, the Hawaiians identified Cook as the personification of Lono, an interpretation further strengthened by Cook when he told them during his departure that he would return the next year.

Cook's untimely return to repair one of his ships was ominously interpreted by the king and priests of Ku as Lono returning to claim earthly powers. Not surprisingly the Hawaiian priests had

---

Like historians who study their society's past, ethnohistorians make use of such materials as published books and articles, newspapers, archival documents, diaries, journals, maps, drawings, and photographs. Not surprisingly, many scholars treat history and ethnohistory as if they were synonymous. There are, however, critical—yet frequently overlooked—differences that distinguish ethnohistory from history.

- An ethnohistorian is primarily interested in reconstructing the cultural system of the people. The actual historical events themselves are of interest only because they cast light on the cultural system or changes in the system.
- Historical events have little significance outside the cultural context of the peoples involved. Ethnohistorians study nonliterate peoples. Thus, whereas historians can use accounts recorded by members of the society being studied, ethnohistorians have to use accounts recorded by members of other, literate societies. As a result, the problem of interpreting

accounts usually is more difficult for the ethnohistorian than for the historian.

The problem of interpretation raises an additional question about the validity of particular reports. Not only do we have to ask about the accuracy of the account, but we also have to ask how knowledgeable was the recorder about the cultural context of the events. Ethnohistorians use certain criteria to evaluate the potential validity of an account. How long did the individual live among these people? Did the observer speak the language? What was the role of the individual? Soldiers, missionaries, traders, and government officials have different views, biases, and access to information.

The difficulty with ethnohistory is that no hard-and-fast rules can be used in evaluating these data. The longer an individual lived among members of a particular society and the better she or he spoke the language, the more reliable the account should be; however, this cannot be automatically assumed. In some cases, the writer may have had little interest in the people, per-

him killed and viewed the killing as the ritual sacrifice of the rival god-king Lono, which they symbolically reenacted every year.

When Gananath Obeyesekere, a Sri Lankan anthropologist, first heard Sahlins present this interpretation of Cook, he was "taken aback." Why would the Hawaiians think that this European was a god? Drawing from his own knowledge of South Asian peoples, he could not think of a single example of Sri Lankans or other southern Asian peoples seeing the newly arrived Europeans as gods. To Obeyesekere this was but an example of European myth building, in which the European explorer/civilizer becomes a "god" to the natives.

In 1992 Obeyesekere published *The Apotheosis of Captain Cook: European Mythmaking in the Pacific* in which he challenged Sahlins' interpretation. In his criticism of Sahlins and other western scholars he touches on a broad range of theoretical and substantive issues. We will just cover two of the major points.

Obeyesekere argues that it was the English themselves who first mythologized Captain Cook. He had already made two successful and daring voyages into the unknown waters of the Pacific. Because of published accounts of these trips Cook had become—in the eyes of the British—the very image of the ideal explorer/civilizer. A competent, courageous, generous, decent, and human individual who understood and was well liked by the native peoples he encountered, Cook embodied all of the qualities and greatness of civilized man. His violent death at the hands of a strange and savage people to whom he had brought the prospects of civilization served only to enhance his mythic stature. In his research, however, Obeyesekere found that Cook, particularly on his third and final voyage, was not the Cook of British mythology. Cook could be brutal with both the natives and his crew, as well as arrogant and not always competent. He also found little contemporary evidence that the members of the crew thought that the Hawaiians viewed Cook as a god. The idea that Hawaiians identified Cook with Lono dates from early nineteenth-century accounts that were compiled well after the events themselves.

Obeyesekere further argues that still prevalent in Western academic thought is the idea that non-Western peoples, such as the Hawaiians, think differently.

According to Obeyesekere, "Implicit. . . is a commonplace assumption of the savage mind that is given to prelogical or mystical thought and in turn is fundamentally opposed to the logical and rational ways of thinking of modern man." Thus, the childlike natives lacked rational reflection. Even when anthropologists accept the idea that other people can act rationally, rationality is constrained by the boundaries of their own cultural beliefs, and "their thought processes are inflexible; [and] they cannot rationally weigh alternative or multiple courses of action." Thus, Obeyesekere further argues that these implicit and sometimes explicit assumptions about the nature of other peoples underlie the interpretation that Hawaiians thought that Captain Cook was a god and that that god was Lono.

In his critique of Sahlins, Obeyesekere raises a critical issue. Does anthropology reflect a western cultural bias? Are anthropological interpretations of other peoples' behavior a reflection of implicit Eurocentric beliefs about others?

Sources: Sahlins (1981), Obeyesekere (1992), and Sahlins (1995) for his response to Obeyesekere.

---

haps because the contacts were only related to a job. This attitude is evident in the accounts of many traders and government officials. In other cases, the account may be self-serving, with individuals attempting to enhance their careers. Thus, sometimes soldiers and government officials falsified their official reports. Ethnocentrism is still another factor. Missionary accounts, in particular, often demonstrate overt bias against local customs and beliefs; one has to remember that an individual becomes a missionary because he or she is an avid believer. However, some of the most objective accounts of other societies were written by missionaries, who often were scholars themselves.

Thus, in ethnohistoric research, there is no simple way to evaluate a particular document or account. At best, a single event may be recorded in several independent accounts that can each be used to verify the accuracy and interpretation of the others. Unfortunately, multiple observations are the exception, not the rule.

A final limitation on the use of ethnohistoric materials is that seldom are all aspects of a particular society evenly reported. For example, data on economic activities may be the most abundant, whereas information on religious ceremonies and beliefs may be absent or limited. As a result, ethnographic studies based on ethnohistoric research lack the depth and balance of those gleaned from research with living individuals. Despite its problems and limitations, ethnohistoric research provides us with the only clues we have to the past of many societies, as well as the key to a vast store of cultural data hitherto untapped.

Comparative Methods

So far we have discussed only how anthropologists collect cultural data on peoples, past and present, using fieldwork and historical materials. We have some cultural data available on more than 1,200 societies. As shown in the following chapters, anthropologists have used these data to demonstrate a wide range of cultural variability among human populations. However, we are not merely interested in describing particular cultural systems and the range of variability in these systems. We are also interested in attempting to explain why these differences exist. In other words, anthropologists want to make generalizations concerning cultural systems, and thus explain why differences exist between peoples. Generalizations cannot be made based on the study of a single society; we need methods by which many societies can be compared in a systematic way. The objective of comparative studies is to test hypotheses.

Cross-Cultural Comparisons

The most frequently used comparative method is cross-cultural comparison. In this method, hypotheses are tested by examining the statistical correlations between particular cultural variables, using synchronic data drawn from a number of societies. Historical changes in the societies examined are ignored; the societies are compared at whatever period they were studied. This research method involves three steps. First, the researcher must state the idea as a hypotheses—that is, state it in such a way that it can be supported or not supported ("tested") by data drawn from a large number of human populations. Second, the ethnologist chooses a sample of societies (usually randomly) and studies the ethnographies that describe their way of life. Third, the data collected from these ethnographies are classified and grouped in such a manner that the correlations between variables may be shown statistically. What the researcher is attempting to find is the pattern of association: Do two or more cultural variables consistently occur together or not? In most cases, these tasks are far more difficult than they may sound.

To illustrate how the cross-cultural method is used to test a hypothesis, we shall examine the relations between sorcery and legal systems within a group of societies. Sorcery is discussed in some detail in Chapter 13. Here it is sufficient to know that sorcery is the belief that certain people (sorcerers) have power, either supernatural or magical, to cause harm to others. Some anthropologists believe that sorcery serves as a means of social control in societies that lack a formalized legal apparatus—courts, police, and so forth—to punish wrongdoers. They argue that people will be reluctant to cause trouble if they believe that a victim of their troublemaking has the ability to use supernatural power to retaliate against them. Overall, societies without a formal legal system should have a greater need for a mechanism such as sorcery to control behavior. So if the hypothesis that sorcery is a mechanism for social control is correct, we ought to find that sorcery is more important in societies without formal means of punishment than in societies with a specialized legal system.

To see if this hypothesis is true across a variety of societies, we use the cross-cultural method. We determine for many societies (1) the relative degree of importance of sorcery, and (2) whether the society has a formal apparatus for punishing wrongdoing. We make a table in which all the possible combinations of the two cultural elements are recorded:

Sorcery	Specialized Legal Apparatus	
	ABSENT	PRESENT
Important	A	B
Unimportant	C	D

In the cells of the table we record the number of societies in which the four possible combinations are found. If the hypothesis is supported, we should find that cells A and D contain the greatest number of societies. If the hypothesis is not supported, we should find that the distribution of societies in the cells is random, or that cells B and C contain the greatest number of societies, or some other distribution.

In 1950, Beatrice Whiting conducted such a study by surveying the ethnographic literature for fifty societies. Her results were as follows (Whiting 1950, 87):

Sorcery	Specialized Legal Apparatus	
	ABSENT	PRESENT
Important	30	5
Unimportant	3	12

On the basis of this comparison, we might conclude that the hypothesis is supported, since most of the societies fall into the cells predicted by our hypothesis. We would not worry about the eight societies (the "exceptions") that appear in cells B and C. The hypothesis did not claim that social control was the *only* function of sorcery, so the importance of sorcery in the five societies in cell B might be explained by some other factor. Nor did we claim that sorcery was the *only* way that societies lacking a specialized legal apparatus had to control their members, so the three societies in cell C might have developed some alternative means of social control. (Although outside the scope of this text, statistical tests are available that show how confident a researcher can be that such associations did not occur by chance.)

Some confusions are caused by cross-cultural tabulations such as this. One of the most common is to mistake correlation for causation: Simply because two cultural elements (X and Y) usually are found together does not mean that one (X) has caused the other (Y). Y could have caused X, or both X and Y could have been caused by some third element, W. In the preceding example, it was assumed that the absence of formal legal punishments "caused" many societies to need some other social control mechanism, and that sorcery became important to meet this need. On the basis of the data in the table, we might also conclude that societies in which sorcery is important have little need for a formal legal apparatus, so they fail to develop one.

To acquire the data needed to test her hypothesis, Whiting read through ethnographic information on all fifty societies in her sample. This approach suffers from several disadvantages. It is so time-consuming that only a small number of societies can be included in the sample. There is also the problem of bias by the researcher, who must decide, for example, whether sorcery should be considered "important" or "unimportant" among some people. Borderline cases might get lumped into the category that supports the researcher's hypothesis.

Thanks largely to a lifetime of work by George Murdock, another method is available to modern researchers that partially overcomes these two problems (although it has troubles of its own, to be discussed shortly). In the *Ethnographic Atlas*, Murdock and his associates have summarized information on more than 1,200 societies in the form of coded tables. Each cultural system has codes that show its form of kinship, marriage, economy, religion, political organization, division of labor, and so forth. Contemporary cross-cultural researchers no longer need to search through ethnographies for information relevant to their investigations; rather, they use the information already coded and analyze the results by using a computer. This reduces the bias of the researcher, for whoever coded the information on a particular society had no knowledge of the hypothesis under investigation. It also allows a larger number of societies to be included in a sample because the data can be retrieved far more quickly.

Using cross-cultural methods to see if some specific hypothesis applies to a large number of societies is thus easier today than ever before, but some difficulties still exist. One seems to be inherent in the method itself, which dissects whole cultures into parts ("variables," as we called them) and assigns a value (or "state") to each part. In the preceding example, the variables were sorcery, which had two states (important, unimportant), and specialized legal apparatus, which also had two states (present, absent). To test the hypothesis that the states of these two cultural elements are consistently related, we ignored everything else about them. We also ignored everything else about the societies in the sample, such as their family systems and their economies.

A more familiar example makes the point clearly. One element of cultural systems is the number of gods in whom people believe. For purposes of some specific hypothesis, the possible states of this variable might be monotheism (belief in one god), polytheism (belief in many gods), and no gods. Any researcher who included modern North America in the sample would probably consider our primary religion—Christianity—as monotheistic. Most of the Middle East also would be considered monotheistic. The problem is, can North American monotheism be considered equivalent to the Middle Eastern monotheisms? If we consider them the same, we ignore the differences between the worship of the Christian God, the Jewish Yahweh, and the Islamic Allah. When we lump these three varieties of monotheism together into a single kind of religion, we distort them to some degree.

Cross-cultural studies examine data ahistorically, or without reference to time. In other words, the cultural system of a particular society is treated as timeless or unchanging. Thus, in cross-cultural studies and the *Ethnographic Atlas*, there is "a" cultural system coded for the Cheyenne: Cheyenne cultural system circa 1850. However, the cultural system of a society is never stable but constantly changing. For example, today the Cheyennes live in houses, drive cars and trucks, and participate in a wage-money economy. In 1850 the Cheyennes lived in hide-covered tepees, rode horses, and hunted buffalo. In 1650 the Cheyennes lived in permanent earth lodge villages, traveled by foot or canoe, and depended on farming and hunting for their subsistence. Although Cheyenne cultural systems have continuity, all aspects of their culture changed, to some degree, over the period just described. Thus, in reality, there is no stable Cheyenne culture, but an ever-changing system. The ahistorical studies used in cross-cultural research create an artificial picture of the cultural system of a society.

Controlled Historical Comparisons

Only in the past decade or two have anthropologists attempted **controlled historical comparisons**. Unlike cross-cultural studies, controlled historical comparisons use changes in particular groupings of societies over time to define general cultural patterning and test hypotheses. Controlled historical comparisons, like cross-cultural studies, usually are extremely complex. We illustrate this method by a simple example.

As we discuss in Chapter 9, people organize their family lives in various ways. Two common ways are matrilineal descent and patrilineal descent. In matrilineal societies, family group membership is inherited through your mother; you belong to your mother's family. In patrilineal societies, group membership is inherited through your father; you belong to your father's family. Anthropologists have long attempted to explain why some societies are matrilineal and others patrilineal. Cross-cultural

Christianity, Judaism, and Islam are all monotheistic and have common historical roots. But Christians and Jews do not pray by prostrating themselves toward Mecca, as these Muslims in Saudi Arabia are doing. Should cross-cultural researchers consider all of them one kind of religion, or not?

research has shown that a relation exists between matrilineality and patrilineality and the relative economic importance of males and females in the society. However, cross-cultural studies can only show us correlations between descent and other synchronic aspects of their cultural system. For example, these studies can tell us what types of economic systems are most frequently found with matrilineal or patrilineal societies. Cross-cultural studies cannot measure the long-term effects of external changes on matrilineal or patrilineal societies. Is matrilineality or patrilineality more adaptive in some situations than in others? If so, what types of situations favor matrilineal societies, and which favor patrilineal societies? To examine this question, we must turn to controlled historical comparisons.

Michael Allen (1984) has asserted that matrilineal societies in the Pacific appear to be more successful in adapting to European contact than are patrilineal societies. Is there a way to test Allen's assertion? First, we must restructure this statement as a testable hypothesis. What do we mean by success? The term *success* is rather subjective and cannot be directly measured. We have to convert this term into some measurable quantity. One quantifiable measure of the success of a particular system is the relative ability of a society to maintain or expand its population over time. Thus, our hypothesis would be that given the same degree of disruptive external pressures, matrilineal societies maintain their population levels better over time than patrilineal societies. Now we need to find a group of matrilineal societies and patrilineal societies that experienced a comparable intensity of external contact over a period of time and compare their relative populations at the beginning and end of the period. If Allen is correct, the matrilineal societies should have a relatively higher population at the end of the period than the patrilineal societies.

The farming Native American tribes of the eastern United States present an almost ideal case for testing Allen's assertion. They had similar cultural systems, except that some were matrilineal and others were patrilineal. Their collective histories of contact with Europeans were also basically the same. During the historical period, all these societies suffered the effects of epidemic diseases, warfare (with Europeans as well as intertribal), severe territorial dislocation, political domination, and social discrimination.

Now the problem is determining an appropriate time frame to examine and finding comparable population data. One problem with ethnohistoric research is that the researcher is forced to use the data available in the records. It is not until about 1775 that sufficient population data are available in missionary, military, and explorer accounts to estimate the populations of all these tribes with any accuracy. In 1910, the U.S. Bureau of the Census conducted a special Native American census, which was the first truly comprehensive census of Native American societies in the United States. Thus, the time frame we will use is from 1775 to 1910. Using ethnographic data, we can then classify particular societies as either matrilineal or patrilineal and determine their populations for the beginning and end of this period:

	1775	1910	PERCENT
Matrilineal societies	88,590	82,714	93
Patrilineal societies	36,400	13,463	37
Totals	124,990	96,177	77

From this table we can see that during this 135-year period, the matrilineal societies declined by only about 7% of their total population, whereas patrilineal societies lost 63% of their population. If maintenance of population is a measure of a society's success, then matrilineal societies in the eastern United States were more successful than patrilineal societies.

As is the case with all comparative studies, findings such as these raise more questions than they answer. Are these population figures and the historical experience of these societies truly comparable? If they are comparable, is the significant factor differences in descent form, or is it some other cultural factor we have not considered? We need to add at this point that not all matrilineal societies in this study were equally successful in maintaining their population levels, and that a few patrilineal societies studied increased in population during this period. There is room, then, for argument. If, in the final analysis, however, we decide that our findings are valid and that matrilineal societies are, under certain conditions, more adaptive than patrilineal societies, we still cannot directly say why.

Cross-cultural comparisons and controlled historical comparisons give us distinctly different measures of cultural phenomena. They address different questions and test different hypotheses. They are complementary, not competitive, methodologies.

Some anthropologists (especially idealists—see Chapter 4) believe that both kinds of comparative studies distort each cultural system in the sample so much that the whole method is invalid. They think that ripping each element out of the particular context in which it is embedded robs it of its significance because each element acquires its meaning only in its local historical and cultural context.

Despite these and other problems, comparative methods are the only practical means available for determining whether a hypothesis is valid among human cultural systems. Those who use these methods are aware of the difficulties, yet they believe that the advantage of being able to process information on large numbers of societies outweighs the problems.

Summary

Anthropological methods fall into two overall categories. Ethnographic methods involve the collection of information on a specific cultural system, whereas comparative methods are used to test hypotheses or to investigate theoretical ideas by comparing information on numerous cultural systems. The basic aims of ethnographic methods are descriptive, whereas comparative investigations aim to determine whether some hypothesis or theoretical idea is supported by the accumulated data on human cultures.

The kinds of methods used by anthropologists depend on whether they are investigating a contemporary or a past way of life. Research into the past usually involves ethnohistory (perusal of written documents). This method requires considerable interpretation by the researcher. Sometimes those who wrote the documents used in ethnohistoric reconstructions misinterpreted events because of their cultural backgrounds and ethnocentrism. The contents of documents often are affected by the private interests of their authors.

Fieldwork is the primary method of acquiring data about living people. Fieldworkers usually live among those they study for at least a year, conducting formal interviews and surveys and engaging in participant observation. Although the difficulties of conducting fieldwork vary with the personality and gender of the field-worker and with the people and specific topic being studied, three problems are common. Fieldworkers must not only fight against their own ethnocentrism and tendencies to stereotype those they study, but they must also overcome the stereotypes local people have developed about foreigners. It often is difficult to establish a rapport with local people because they may have had no previous experience with the kinds of questions field-workers ask. Identifying reliable informants and finding people willing to participate in intensive surveys may pose a serious problem. Sometimes people deliberately deceive the anthropologist, because they mistrust his or her motives, do not want certain facts to become public, or are culturally forbidden to give away secrets of their religion. Today, fieldwork is viewed as an essential part of the graduate education of anthropologists, and almost a prerequisite for professionalism. It is, in some respects, a rite of passage.

Comparative methods involve ways of systematically and reliably comparing massive amounts of information collected by previous ethnographers. The use of comparative methods presents many difficulties, including stating the research hypothesis in such a way that it is testable, reliably defining and measuring the variables of interest for many societies, deciding whether similar cultural elements from two or more societies are the "same" or "different," and contending with unintentional researcher bias. The results of comparative studies can be difficult to interpret. Correlation often is confused with causation.

Key Terms

ethnographic methods
comparative methods
ethnographic fieldwork

ethnohistoric research
interviewing
participant observation
stereotypes
consultant (informant)
key consultant (key informant)

culture shock
ethnohistory
cross-cultural comparisons
controlled historical comparisons

Suggested Readings

Works that deal with research methods and problems include:

Agar, Michael. *The Professional Stranger: An Informal Introduction to Ethnography*. New York: Academic, 1980.
  • *Quite good for the beginning student. Tells how ethnographers do their work, with lots of examples taken from the author's own field experiences.*

Martin, Calvin, ed. *The American Indian and the Problem of History*. New York: Oxford University Press, 1987.
  • *In this edited work, anthropologists, historians, and Native Americans discuss the problems in trying to objectively interpret the cultural history of Indian America. This is a critical book for any ethnohistorian studying Native American culture.*

Obeyesekere, Gananath. *The Apotheosis of Captain Cook: European Mythmaking in the Pacific*. Princeton, N.J.: Princeton University Press, 1992.
  • *In part, this study attacks Marshall Sahlin's interpretation of the Cook murder, accusing him of Eurocentric bias. Obeyesekere shows the difficulty in attempting to objectively analyze historical documents.*

Pelto, Perti J., and H. Gretal. *Anthropological Research: The Structure of Inquiry*. Cambridge: Cambridge University Press, 1978.
  • *Emphasizes importance of quantification and measurement in fieldwork.*

Sahlins, Marshall. *How "Natives" Think: About Captain Cook, For Example*. Chicago: University of Chicago Press, 1995.
  • *In this book, Sahlins replies to Obeyesekere's criticism of his work on Captain Cook.*

Spradley, James P. *The Ethnographic Interview*. New York: Holt, Rinehart and Winston, 1979.
____. *Participant Observation*. New York: Holt, Rinehart and Winston, 1980.
  • *Two books that complement each other, one focusing on structured interviewing of informants, the other on detailed observation.*

A number of books deal with the actual experiences of ethnographers in the field. They are valuable for conveying the feeling of fieldwork, of problems ethnographers encounter, of relating to local people, and so forth.

Briggs, Jean. *Never in Anger: Portrait of an Eskimo Family*. Cambridge, Mass.: Harvard University Press, 1970.
  • *A personal account of life with an Eskimo family.*

Dumont, Jean-Paul. *The Headman and I*. Prospect Heights, Ill.: Waveland Press, 1992.
  • *Account of a fieldworker's relationships with the Panare people of the Venezuelan Amazon.*

Fernea, Elizabeth. *A Street in Marrakech*. New York: Doubleday/Anchor, 1969.
  • *Journalist-author provides a lively account of her life among women in Morocco.*

Freilich, Morris, ed. *Marginal Natives: Anthropologists at Work*. New York: Harper and Row, 1970.
  • *Ten anthropologists discuss the problems of fieldwork.*

Golde, Peggy, ed. *Women in the Field: Anthropological Experiences*. Chicago: Aldine, 1970.
  • *Twelve female ethnographers discuss special difficulties they encountered because of their gender.*

Hayano, David M. *Road Through the Rain Forest*. Prospect Heights, Ill.: Waveland Press, 1990.
  • *Describes the fieldwork experiences of Hayano and his wife among the Awa, a people of the highlands of Papua New Guinea.*

Maybury-Lewis, David. *The Savage and the Innocent*. Boston: Beacon, 1968.
  • *A description of the author's fieldwork in the central Brazilian rain forest.*

Powdermaker, Hortense. *Stranger and Friend: The Way of an Anthropologist*. New York: Norton, 1966.
  • *Autobiographical work, with a description of the author's fieldwork experiences in four sociocultural settings, including Hollywood.*

Rabinow, Paul. *Reflections on Fieldwork in Morocco*. Berkeley: University of California Press, 1977.
  • *An interesting discussion of the author's experiences in Morocco.*

Ward, Martha C. *Nest in the Wind*. Prospect Heights, Ill.: Waveland Press, 1989.
  • *Wonderfully readable account of Ward's personal experiences and fieldwork difficulties on Pohnpei island of Micronesia.*

Internet Exercises

The American Anthropological Association's website (http://www.ameranthassn.org) has a section on ethics which includes the draft of the AAA Code of Ethics approved June 1998. An important part of this code of ethics is a statement of responsibility of anthropological researchers to the people they study.

The University of Kent at Canterbury's Centre for Social Anthropology and Computing has made some of its research projects available online at (http://lucy.ukc.ac.uk). Just one example is Paul Stirling's "45 Years in the Turkish Village" which includes an online version of an ethnography, photographs of the fieldsite, plus an indexed copy of his field notes.

Dr. Laura Zimmer-Tamakoshi's website "Fieldwork: The Anthropologist in the Field" (http://www.truman.edu/academics/ss/faculty/tamakoshil/index.html) presents a detailed account of all phases of anthropological research, from planning and finding funding through methodology and the fieldwork itself to the writing of an ethnography. This is a well-designed site that is quite informative about what anthropologists do.

CHAPTER 6

Adaptation: Environment and Cultures

Understanding Human Adaptation

Hunting and Gathering

Foraging and Culture

Domestication

Agriculture

Horticulture

Cultural Consequences of Horticulture

Intensive Agriculture

Cultural Consequences of Intensive Agriculture

Pastoralism

The Karimojong: An Example from East Africa

Adaptation and Culture

Video · Audio · Photos
Hotlinks · Essay
http://www.wadsworth.com/humanity

Adaptation to the natural environment is one important influence on human cultural systems. The Intuit ("Eskimo") peoples of Alaska adapted to one of earth's most inhospitable environments.
Visit http://www.wadsworth.com/humanity to learn more about the material covered in this chapter and to access activities, exercises, and tutorial quizzes.

*W*ITH THIS CHAPTER, *we begin exploring various aspects of human cultural diversity by discussing adaptation—the ways in which human groups relate to their natural environments and how these relationships affect their cultural existence. Adaptation is an appropriate topic to begin* *with because many anthropologists believe that how a people relate to their environment is the most important influence on their overall way of life. Future chapters deal with other dimensions of cultural diversity: marriage and family life, kinship systems, gender relationships, political organization, religion, and artistic expression.*

OUR FOCUS is the adaptations of preindustrial peoples— that is, those peoples whose traditional economies were based on food production, not on the extraction of resources for factory production. First, we provide some concepts that are useful in studying and comparing systems of adaptation. Then we cover the hunting and gathering adaptation, which nourished humanity for most of our existence as a species. Adaptations in most of the world were dramatically altered around 10,000 years ago, when people first domesticated plants and animals. Agriculture and herding imposed new requirements and opened up new opportunities for human groups, resulting in major changes in cultures, as we shall see.

Understanding Human Adaptation

Adaptation is the process by which organisms develop physiological and behavioral characteristics that allow them to survive and reproduce in their environment. In studying how human adaptation affects cultural systems, it is useful to pay attention to two important features. First, the environment (or *habitat*) includes *natural resources* that people harness to meet their material needs and wants: food, water, wood and leaves for shelters and fires, stones or metals for tools, and so forth. Second, the environment poses certain *problems* that people must solve or overcome: resource scarcity, excessively low or high temperatures, parasites and diseases, rainfall variability, deficient soils, and so forth. If people are to adapt to conditions in their environments, they must harness resources efficiently and cope with environmental problems effectively.

Like other species, human populations adapt to their environments physiologically and genetically. For example, bacteria, viruses, and parasites kill susceptible individuals, but those who are genetically resistant live and reproduce. By this process of natural selection, over many generations human populations will become more resistant to the life-threatening microorganisms to which they are exposed. People are part of nature, and natural selection has helped to adapt us to the environments in which we live, just as it has for other organisms.

However, one way in which humankind differs from other species is that we adapt to changes in our environ-

ments *mainly*—but not exclusively—by cultural rather than by biological/genetic means. If the climate grows colder or if a group migrates into a colder area, they cope mainly by lighting fires, constructing shelters, and making warm clothing, not mainly by evolving physiological adaptations to cold. Humans hunt animals by making weapons and mastering techniques of cooperative stalking and killing, not by biologically evolving the ability to run faster than our game. Group cooperation and technology (including both the tools themselves and the knowledge required to make and use them) allow humans to adapt to a wide range of environments without undergoing major alterations in our genes. Because cultural changes allow us to adapt to varying environments, the human species has colonized every type of terrestrial habitat on earth, from tropical rain forests to arctic tundra, from the vast grassy plains of central Asia to tiny Pacific islands. The ability to adapt to diverse habitats by means of technology and group living surely is one of the secrets of humanity's success.

People interact with their environments in many ways. One of the most important ways is the harnessing of energy (e.g., food, fuel) and raw materials (e.g., minerals for tools, wood for shelters) from nature. Acquiring energy and materials from an environment is part of *production*, meaning the patterned activities by which people transform natural resources into things (products) that satisfy their material needs and wants. Obviously, productive activities are essential for the survival and persistence of both individuals and social groups. Indeed, those modern anthropologists who follow the materialist orientation (Chapter 4) think that production is so important that many other aspects of a group's culture are shaped by it.

What does it take to transform a natural resource into a useful product? Production has three components. People apply (1) their own time and energy (*labor, work*) and (2) the tools and knowledge (*technology*) available to them to (3) the *resources* available in their environment. Labor, technology, and resources (called the *factors of production*) are combined in various ways to produce food, shelter, and other material products that people desire.

These concepts are easy to grasp, but there are a few complexities. Many such complications arise from the fact that humans are social animals (see Chapter 2), who live in groups of various sizes and compositions. Because people live in groups, they have to organize themselves to engage in production. Individuals have to know what to do and what to expect others to do, and they have to know when and where to work so they do not come into conflict or violate one another's rights. The *organization of production* solves problems such as who will do what productive tasks, when, where, and how. There are three main factors involved in the organization of production.

First, people usually prefer to spend less rather than more time in work, so they try to use their labor efficiently. Often, people can make most efficient use of their labor by dividing up tasks among themselves according to factors like sex, age, and skill. For example, young men and young women often have different productive tasks to perform, while children can do some tasks perfectly well. The allocation of productive work to different kinds of people is called the *division of labor*. Ideally, but not always in practice, tasks are allocated according to ability.

Second, using labor efficiently often requires members of a group to cooperate with one another. For example, several hunters may have a better chance of spotting, tracking, and killing large game, and net fishing may be more productive if people work together. Since cooperation is often more efficient than working alone, a group's *patterns of cooperation* are an important part of how it organizes itself to produce what its members need and want.

Third, there is the potential problem of conflict over access to natural resources: Which individuals and groups have the right to use a particular resource at a particular time and place? People have to find ways of defining their *rights to resources*. Generally, a given area of land or territory—along with its resources—is allocated to some group. Its members have the right to exploit the area's resources, whereas others are prohibited from doing so, or may do so only with permission.

In modern societies, we solve such problems by defining some people as owners of productive property, based in large part on their ability to purchase (or inherit) such property. Preindustrial cultures have property rights also, but they often differ greatly from those of modern industrialized nations. In dealing with preindustrial adaptations, anthropologists have learned that it is essential to distinguish *ownership rights* from *use rights* and *group rights* from *individual rights*. A territory and its resources are most frequently owned by some kind of group—most often a family unit of some kind or a residential group—which has collective rights to use the resources. The leader of the group (e.g., the family head, the village chief) allocates the use of the resources among the members. People in the group have the right to use the resources, so long as they do not violate the rights of other group members to use them also. Thus,

Production is usually an organized social activity. Everywhere, people cooperate in patterned ways— here illustrated by these African net fishers—to make labor more efficient.

the "property rights" of individuals are always limited by the rights of others.

In sum, one important way people interact with their environment is through production. Production involves the application of labor and technology to natural resources. Production is always an organized social activity, involving the division of labor, patterns of cooperation, and the allocation of rights to resources.

Using these concepts, we can describe and compare some of the ways in which various peoples adapt to their environments. Anthropologists generally divide preindustrial adaptations into three major categories, based largely on how people produce their food supply:

hunting and gathering (also called **foraging**), in which people exploit the *wild* plants and animals of their territory for food;

agriculture (or **cultivation**), in which people intentionally plant, care for, and harvest *crops* (domesticated plants) for food and other uses; and

herding (or **pastoralism**), in which people tend, breed, and harvest products of *livestock* (domesticated animals) for food, trade, and other uses.

The remainder of this chapter describes these three ways of exploiting the food resources of an environment and discusses some of the main ways that each adaptation affects culture.

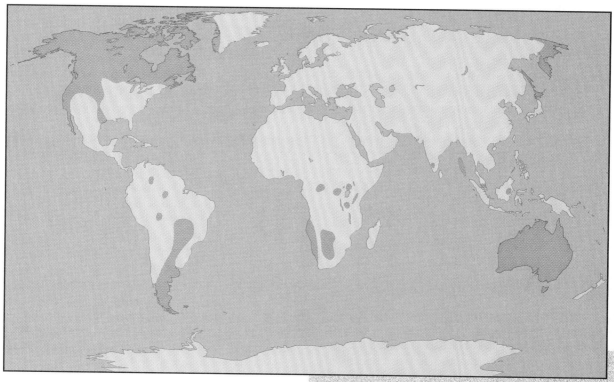

Figure 6.1 Principal Regions of Foragers at Time of First Contact with Europeans

Hunting and Gathering

Foragers, also called hunter-gatherers, get their food from collecting (gathering) the wild plants and hunting (or fishing for) the animals that live in their regions. By definition, foragers do not attempt to increase the resources found in their environments by growing crops or intentionally breeding livestock for meat and other products. But many foragers do make modest efforts to control the natural resources in their environments in other ways. For example, they may try to increase the supply of edible plants and animals by burning forests and grasslands to attract more grazing animals or to increase the supply of sun-loving wild berries or other plants.

Most physical anthropologists believe that *Homo sapiens* has existed as a species for about 100,000–200,000 years. But there was no farming of crops or herding of livestock anywhere on earth until about 10,000 years ago. The foraging adaptation thus supported humanity for the first 90 to 95 percent of our existence as a species.

However, once plant and animal domestication developed, agricultural and herding peoples began to increase in population and expand geographically. Over the millennia, cultivators and herders pushed many foraging peoples into regions that were not well suited to crops and livestock. As a result, when European contact with people of other continents intensified in the 1700s and 1800s hunters and gatherers already lived primarily in regions too cold or arid to support agriculture (see Figure 6.1). By the twentieth century, partly as a result of European colonialism and the geographical expansion of Euro-Americans over most of the New World, foragers had been further forced out of their traditional lands. In many cases, they had died out altogether.

Compared to people who live by other adaptations, hunters and gatherers exercise little control over their natural environments. If edible wild plants are available only at particular places during particular seasons, foraging groups must move to those places at those times to harvest them. If major game animals live in large migratory herds, the hunters must follow them or switch to other animals when the game has left their region. A brief statement that helps to understand both the foraging adaptation and how it affects culture is the following: To acquire resources efficiently, foragers must organize themselves to be in the right place at the right time with the right numbers of people.

Foraging and Culture

Hunter-gatherers living in different habitats differ in their cultures, partly because environments vary in the kind and quality of food resources they contain. Foraging groups of the resource-rich environment of the American Northwest Coast lived a fairly sedentary existence in large permanent settlements, whereas the Shoshone of the arid and resource-sparse American Great Basin roamed in small bands or individual families. In spite of environmental differences, most—but not all—foraging groups share certain cultural similarities. Our main goal in this section is to describe how the adaptive requirements of hunting and gathering affect the cultures of most foraging peoples.

Division of Labor by Age and Gender   The division of labor among foragers is organized largely along the lines of age and gender, although special knowledge and unusual skill also serve as a basis for assigning tasks. Among the great majority of foraging peoples, men do the bulk of the hunting and women most of the gathering of plants. However, it is not unusual for either sex to lend a hand with the activities of the other. For example, among the BaMbuti of the tropical forest of Zaire, the women and children help the men with hunting by driving game animals into nets. But in general, hunting is men's work.

Seasonal Mobility   Most foragers are seasonally mobile. None of the earth's environments offer the same kinds and quantities of resources year round. There may be seasonal differences in precipitation, and outside the tropics there usually are marked seasonal variations in temperature as well. Ordinarily, game animals are available in some places and not others at different seasons, and nuts and fruits tend to be available only at certain times of the year.

Foragers migrate to where food or water is most plentiful or easiest to acquire during a given season. For example, the Hadza people of Tanzania lived in an arid region with a marked distinction between wet and dry seasons. In rainy months the Hadza dispersed around the many temporary water holes that formed, living on the wild plants and animals in the immediate vicinity. At another time of the year, when these ponds evaporated, they congregated into camps clustered around the few relatively permanent water sources.

Seasonal Congregation and Dispersal   To exploit plants and animals efficiently, most hunters and gatherers also change the sizes of their living groups according to the seasonal availability and abundance of their food supply. At some times of the year, it is most efficient to disperse into small groups, which cooperate in the search for food.

During other seasons, these groups come together in larger congregations.

The Western Shoshone illustrate one culture in which seasonal congregation and dispersal was advantageous. Until their traditional adaptation was disrupted by white settlers in the nineteenth century, they lived in the arid American Great Basin. Most of their meat came from deer, antelope, and small mammals such as rabbits and squirrels. Plant foods included roots and seasonally available seeds, berries, pine nuts, and other wild products. For most of the year the Shoshone roamed the dry valleys and slopes of the Great Basin in tiny bands consisting of a few nuclear families, or even single families. Families occasionally gathered for cooperative hunting of antelopes and rabbits, which they drove into corrals and nets. But a more permanent aggregation of families was difficult because a local area did not have enough resources to support large numbers of people for more than a few days.

One important plant food became available in the fall and in most years was capable of supporting many families throughout the winter. Each year, around October, the cones of the piñon trees on the high mountains ripened and produced large, nourishing pine nuts. During their travels in late summer, Shoshone families noticed which specific mountain areas seemed to have the most promising pine nut harvest. They arranged their movements to arrive at these productive areas in the fall. Ten to twenty families camped in the same region, harvesting and storing pine nuts. During favorable (i.e., rainy) years, the pine nut harvest supported these large camps throughout most of the winter. Spring found the families splitting up again, to renew the pattern of dispersal into tiny groups until the next fall. No family had exclusive access to any particular territory in any season. Rights to resources were essentially on the basis of first come, first served, here meaning that whichever group arrived at an area first was free to harvest its plants and animals.

The small group size is an organizational adaptation to foraging. Over a period of days or weeks (depending mainly on the environment and its resources), groups exhaust the wild resources of a given area and must move into a fresh (actually a "recovered") environment. All else equal, the larger the group, the faster it uses up the wild plants and animals of an area and, hence, the more frequently it must relocate. One reason for the small size, then, is that smaller groups do not need to move as often as larger groups.

Bands   In most environments efficient foraging requires that people live in small, mobile groups of fifty or less. To distinguish these living groups from the settled villages, towns, and cities found in other adaptations, anthropologists call these mobile living groups **bands**. Band members cooperate in production and usually share rights to harvest the wild resources of a given territory. The size of bands is usually flexible, allowing the number of people living in the band to be adjusted according to the availability of the food supply. Further, individuals are not attached permanently to any band, but have many options about where to live and whom to live with. This way of organizing bands offers many advantages to foraging populations.

The !Kung of southern Africa illustrate these points about band organization. Living in what is now southeast Angola, northeast Namibia, and northwest Botswana, the !Kung are the most thoroughly studied of all surviving hunter-gatherers. The northern part of their environment is an arid tropical savanna, grading into the Kalahari desert toward the south. Until the twentieth century, the !Kung exploited this habitat entirely by foraging. They gathered more than one hundred species of plants and hunted over fifty kinds of animals, including mammals, birds, and reptiles. Plant foods consisted of nuts, fruits, berries, melons, roots, and greenery. A particularly important and nourishing food was the mongongo nut, which ripens around April and provided about half the people's caloric intake.

Because their habitat received so little rainfall and then only seasonally, the availability of water greatly influenced the rhythm of !Kung life. From about April to October (winter in the Southern Hemisphere), there was little precipitation, and practically no rain fell between June and September. During this dry season, water for people and animals was available only at a few permanent water holes, around which bands congregated into relatively large settlements of between twenty and fifty individuals. Between November and March—the hot and wet season—temporary water holes formed, and the bands split up to exploit the wild resources around them. But rainfall in this part of the world is not reliable, neither from year to year, nor from place to place. In some years, up to forty inches of rain falls during the wet season; in other years, as little as six inches. Drought occurs in about two out of every five years. Precipitation also is spatially unpredictable: One area frequently receives severe thunderstorms, whereas twenty miles away no rain falls.

These characteristics of their physical environment—its aridity, seasonality, and marked temporal and spatial variability in precipitation—influenced the band organization of the !Kung. Because the distribution of wild foods and water was determined by rainfall, the annual cycle of congregation and dispersal of !Kung bands followed the seasonal distinction between wet and dry. During the wet months the bands were spread out among the temporary water holes in camps numbering about ten to thirty.

When the bands first moved to a "fresh" water hole, wild resources were relatively plentiful; game was abundant and a wide variety of plant foods was easily available. But the longer a band remained around a water hole, the more the surrounding resources became exhausted. The men had to roam farther afield in their hunting, and the women had to travel longer distances in their plant collecting. After several weeks a camp reached the point at which its members judged that the costs of continuing to forage in the area were not bringing adequate returns in food. They then moved to a new wet-season camp. One ethnographer, Richard Lee, succinctly notes that the !Kung "typically occupy a camp for a period of weeks or months and eat their way out of it" (Lee 1969, 60).

As the dry season approached, !Kung bands made their way back to the area around one of the permanent water holes. These settlements, larger than the wet-season camps, commonly numbered between twenty and fifty and often even more. By the end of the dry season the supply of mongongo nuts and other preferred plant foods was exhausted and the people ate the less tasty bitter melons, roots, and gum. This was considered a relatively hard time of the year, and the !Kung waited in anticipation of the November rains, when they could again disperse into the smaller wet-season groups.

Reciprocal Sharing   It is mutually beneficial for the members of a foraging band to share food and other possessions with one another. The sharing is more or less on the basis of need: Those who have more than they can immediately use share with others. For example, among the !Kung, only some members of a band search for food on a given day. But foods brought back to camp are widely distributed, so even families who did not work that day receive a share.

In many hunting and gathering groups, reciprocal sharing especially applies to meat: Successful hunters returning to camp share the kill with other families, including those who have not participated in the day's hunt. One reason for the special emphasis on the equitable sharing of meat is the uncertain returns of hunting compared to gathering. Among the !Kung, on most days women return to camp with their carrying bags full of nuts, roots, fruits, and other wild plants. Men's chances of capturing game, however, are smaller: Richard Lee estimates that only about two out of five hunting trips capture animals large enough to take back to camp. Men who are successful one day may be unsuccessful the next, so one reason they give today is so they can receive tomorrow. Reciprocal sharing also is encouraged by the fact that all or most members of a band are close or distant relatives of some kind, and humans generally tend to share with their relatives (see Chapter 7).

Reciprocal sharing usually is *normatively expected* behavior, meaning that people who regularly fail to share are subjected to ridicule or other kinds of social pressures. Going along with the expectation of sharing is a positive cultural value placed on equality of personal possessions (property) and even of social status. Families who attempt to hoard food or other products may be ostracized. Men who try to place themselves above others socially by boasting about their hunting skills or other accomplishments are soon put in their place. The result is that there is both economic and social equality between the families of most hunting and gathering bands.

Rights to Resources   Effective adaptation requires that people have established ways of allocating natural resources between individuals and groups. Many hunters and gatherers are similar in how they determine rights to the resources that occur in their territory: who can harvest which resources, where, and when.

One way to organize rights over a territory and its resources is for each group to establish and maintain

This woman is bagging mongongo nuts, an important and nourishing food to the !Kung.

exclusive claims to particular territories. Cultural ideas about the relationship between people and territory might be, for example, that this area is *mine* or *ours* and that area is *yours* or *theirs*. In the foraging adaptation, exclusive access would mean that each band has rights to remain in a specific area during a particular season. One benefit would be that the members of each band would know they will be harvesting the foods of particular places at definite times. Another advantage is that bands would not interfere in each other's hunting and gathering activities.

Despite these (apparent) benefits, most foragers organize rights of access in quite a different way. Among the !Kung, for instance, there was a comparatively weak attachment of particular groups of people to specific territories. Particular families tended to return to the same territories year after year, according to season, and over time others came to recognize them as the "owners" of the area. Most often, the most reliable water holes together with the wild resources around them were "owned" jointly by a set of siblings. But by merely asking permission—which was seldom refused—anyone with a kinship relationship to one of the "owners" could come and visit and exploit the area's food and water. Because most !Kung had many relatives who were "owners" of different places, each !Kung had a multitude of options about where and with whom they would live, work, relax, and socialize. As a consequence of multiple options, the composition of a band fluctuated radically, for each band received visiting relatives several times a year. Far from establishing exclusive claims to particular places, !Kung were only loosely attached to territories and for the most part came and went as their preferences and circumstances allowed. Similar patterns were found among most other known hunter-gatherers.

To sum up, most hunter-gatherers develop certain ways of organizing their activities and their groups that facilitate their adaptation:

- a division of labor based mainly on gender and age
- a high degree of mobility, especially from season to season
- congregation and dispersal of groups, at least on a seasonal basis
- living groups of small bands with varying size and flexible composition
- strong values of reciprocal sharing and of equality in personal possessions and social status
- loose attachment of people to territory and flexible rights to resources

Although these statements describe most gatherer-hunters reasonably well, we must keep in mind that foragers are diverse and exhibit the aforementioned features to greater or lesser degrees.

In fact, in some environments, hunting and gathering peoples lived in quite a different way. Along the Northwest Coast of North America (roughly from Oregon into the Alaskan panhandle), food resources—especially fish—were exceptionally abundant, and the Native Americans who lived there were able to smoke and preserve food for many months. Because of abundance and storage, there was no need to maintain seasonal mobility or small living groups, so people were essentially sedentary. They lived in large, permanent villages with elaborately decorated plank houses. In addition, wild resources also were more reliable on the Northwest Coast than in most other environments lived in by foragers. Resource abundance and reliability affected property notions along the coast. If a food resource is abundant, and you can usually count on its availability, then it makes sense for you to stay close to it and defend it against other groups that might desire it as well. Northwest Coast people could count on fish being present in their rivers or coastal waters, so they developed more defined property rights: Particular groups were more definitely associated with particular locations than were people such as the Shoshone or !Kung.

Because of their adaptation, the cultures of many hunter-gatherers share certain fundamental similarities. This !Kung man butchers a small animal, which he will share with others in the band or camp.

Domestication

Domestication can be defined as the intentional planting and cultivation of selected plants and the taming and breeding of certain species of animals. It implies that people are making efforts to control the supply and distribution of the domesticated species, in order to increase their usefulness. With respect to plants, in this book we are concerned with *food crops,* or those species that people intentionally select, plant, care for, harvest, and propagate for purposes of eating. People also grow plants for other purposes, such as for fibers (cotton, hemp) or for drugs (tobacco, opium poppy). With animals we are concerned with *livestock,* or those species that people breed, raise, and control for purposes of providing food (meat, dairy products) or other useful things (hides, wool), or for performing work (pulling plows, carrying people and possessions). People keep animals for other reasons also, such as companionship (pets).

The origins of plant and animal domestication are outside the scope of this text. Suffice it to say that in the Old World, domestication occurred by around 10,000 years ago in the Middle East and by about 9,000 years ago in eastern Asia. In the next several thousand years, adaptations based on domesticated plants and/or animals developed in most African, Asian, and European environments that could support farming and/or herding. In the New World, a completely different set of plant species was domesticated in Mexico by about 5,000 years ago, and in northern Peru by 4,000 years ago. More information on plant and animal domestication is provided in this chapter's "A Closer Look."

In the Old World, several animal species were domesticated about the same time as plants. In many parts of the Old World, the availability of livestock meant that men in many regions eventually gave up hunting, putting their labor into agriculture, crafts, warfare, and other activities instead. But in the New World, except for residents of the Andes, many peoples who relied on the cultivation of crops for their food got all or most of their meat from deer, antelope, small mammals, fish, and other wild animals. Most New World peoples, then, got the bulk of their meat from wild, not domesticated, animals, even though many of them were farmers.

Plant and animal domestication probably had more long-lasting and dramatic effects on cultures than any other single set of changes in adaptation—except, perhaps, industrialization. For example, once certain plants evolved by human selection into crops, people could produce more food in a given area of land. Increased production allowed them to remain in one place for long periods—over time, groups became more *sedentary*. They also could live in much larger settlements than the bands

A CLOSER LOOK

Domesticates in the Old and New Worlds

The domestication of plants and animals occurred independently in the Old World (Europe, Asia, Africa) and the New World (North and South America). Before the age of European colonization the crops grown in the two hemispheres were completely different. A description of where some of the most familiar food crops and livestock were first domesticated follows.

Old World Crops

The first plant domestication occurred in southwest Asia (including parts of modern Iran, Iraq, and Turkey). Wheat, barley, lentils, peas, carrots, figs, almonds, pistachios, dates, and grapes were first grown in this region. Oats, cabbages, lettuce, beets, and asparagus were first domesticated in the Mediterranean. In West Africa, sorghum, finger millet, watermelons, and African rice were domesticated; sorghum and millet still feed millions of people on the African continent. Oriental rice, eggplants, cucumbers, bananas, taro, and coconuts originated in southern Asia and Southeast Asia. Soybeans, citrus fruits, and tea were domesticated in ancient China. Sugarcane was probably first cultivated in New Guinea or the islands around it. We get our morning caffeine from coffee, domesticated in the Ethiopian highlands.

New World Crops

Maize, tomato, bean, red pepper, avocado, cacao, and the squash family (squash, pumpkins, and gourds) originated in Central America and Mexico. From Peru came numerous crops that are still important to the region and to the world, including potatoes, sweet potatoes, and lima beans. From elsewhere in South America came manioc, peanuts, pineapple, and cashews.

Some plants were domesticated not just once but several times in various parts of the world. Separate species of rice were domesticated in Africa and Asia, apparently independently. Cotton was domesticated independently in three places: South America, Central America, and either in India or Africa. Three yam species were grown in West Africa, Southeast Asia, and tropical South America.

Old World Livestock

In the Old World, the earliest animal domestication occurred at about the same times and in the same places as crops were first grown. In the Middle East, the wild ancestors of the most important livestock lived in large herds, including sheep, goats, and cattle. These animals were and are kept for their hides, wool, meat, and milk. Another large mammal, the horse, was first domesticated on the Asian grasslands, around 5,000 years ago. When mounted, horses greatly increased the speed of long-distance travel and, of course, increased the fighting ability of warriors and soldiers. For thousands of years, from the Middle East to North Africa, camels have made it possible for people and products to cross vast stretches of arid land. Along with asses, donkeys, and South Asian yaks, horses and camels allowed heavy loads to be carried long distances, increasing the potential of trade. When harnessed to the plow, cattle, horses, and Asian water buffalos supplemented human labor in farming, and their dung added nutrients to agricultural fields and gardens. Finally,

of most foragers—groups came to live in *villages* and, later in some places, in *towns* and *cities*.

Agriculture

For tens of thousands of years, the hunting and gathering adaptation worked well. It allowed the human species to increase in number to several million. Further, hunting and gathering is a flexible adaptation, meaning that it can be applied to any environment with a sufficient quantity of wild, edible plants and animals. Foraging will work in rain forests, grasslands, tundras, and mountains—given, of course, adequate shelter, the right kinds of tools and skills, and appropriate ways of organizing production. Considering how quickly cultures can adapt, and how quickly new ways of doing things can be communicated and spread if circumstances warrant, one or another hunting and gathering group was able to migrate into all the major

continents except Antarctica. By around 10,000 years ago, humans were living in all the major land masses of the earth. Foraging, then, allowed humanity to be a successful species, if we measure success by species numbers and by geographical distribution.

In fact, most modern anthropologists believe that prehistoric hunter-gatherers actually enjoyed a relatively high quality of life. Richard Lee's quantitative studies of the !Kung in the 1960s show that they worked only about two and half days per week to acquire their food supply. Even adding in time spent in other kinds of work, such as making tools and housework, the !Kung worked only around 42 hours per week. Most modern-day adults would be happy to have such a short workweek! Further, the !Kung's relatively modest work efforts were sufficient to keep them well fed most of the time: Adults consumed an average of 2,355 calories and 96 grams of protein per day, more than sufficient for their bodily needs. There are, of course, exceptions, but the bulk of the evidence suggests that hunter-gatherers did not have a particularly hard life.

pigs—first brought under human control in East and Southeast Asia—are an outstanding source of protein, and today remain the major source of meat in China and non-Muslim Southeast Asia.

New World Livestock

Compared to Old World peoples, Native Americans domesticated few livestock. In the Andes, llamas and alpacas (related to camels of the Old World) were used for meat and transportation. Their thick, long hair also was woven into beautiful clothing by weavers of the ancient Andean civilizations. In South America, guinea pigs were raised for their meat. Elsewhere in the Americas, turkeys and Muscovy ducks were the only animals domesticated for food, and these only in a few areas. Dogs, present also in the Old World, were used in hunting and often as food.

Why did American Indians domesticate so few animals compared to Middle Easterners and Asians? The answer is uncertain, but one important reason may be that so many of the large herd animal species in the Americas became extinct shortly after the end of the Pleistocene epoch, about 11,000 years ago. Members of the horse and camel family, in particular, all disappeared (except in the Andes). Horses did not return to the Americas until brought by the Spanish in

the 1500s. Still, some large herd animals, such as bison and caribou, survived the extinctions. Perhaps we shall never know why Native Americans did not domesticate more animals.

What's for Dinner?

Soon after Spain, Portugal, France, Britain, and the Netherlands began exploring and establishing colonies on other continents, crops and livestock were spread from continent to continent. Many New World crops were taken to various parts of the Old World, where they became important foods for millions of people. Amazonian manioc became a staple in tropical Africa and Asia. Mexican corn spread widely, especially in Africa, Mediterranean Europe, and East Asia. After initial resistance, the Andean potato became a staple food in Russia, northern Europe, and—especially—Ireland. Imagine Italian food without the Mexican tomato! Over the centuries, Native American cultivators had become master farmers, and surely food crops are one of the greatest gifts they bestowed upon the rest of the world.

Crops and livestock moved across the Atlantic in the other direction also. European colonists took Old World wheat, oats, barley, grapes, and other crops to temperate zones of the Americas. In parts of the Americas with more tropical cli-

mates, rice, bananas, and coconuts became important foods. But livestock were the most important food import from the Old World. Pigs, cattle, sheep, and horses were introduced very soon after the European encounter with the New World. In the next couple of centuries they had multiplied wildly and spread widely. Old World livestock greatly eased the life of the European colonists, of course. But they also became integrated into Native American adaptations. The horseback riding, bison hunting, teepee dwelling Plains cultures, for instance, were affected. In the American Southwest, sheep and goats were herded alongside native maize, beans, and squash, greatly affecting the Navajo and Pueblo peoples.

Most of us do not recognize our debt to the ancient Middle Easterners, Asians, Africans, Andeans, and Mexicans who gave us our daily bread. Yet most North American dinners include foods brought to the continent from all over the world centuries ago. If you're an all-American, meat-and-potatoes kind of person, odds are that only the potatoes are truly American—and they (like another of your favorites, beans) came from south of the border!

Sources: Fagan (1986), Crosby (1972), and Diamond (1997).

Why, then, did the foraging adaptation ever change? Why did many groups shift to the agricultural adaptation over the centuries? In fact, agriculture does offer on enormous advantage over hunting and gathering: It can support far more people per unit of territory. Only in favorable environments does the population density of foragers exceed more than one or two per square mile. In contrast, agricultural peoples typically live at densities of dozens or even hundreds per square mile. The ability to support larger numbers of people on a given area of land is probably the main advantage of agriculture over foraging.

Like most benefits, however, the ability to support higher population densities entails some costs. The creation and maintenance of the artificial community of plants that make up a garden or farm requires labor, time, and energy. First, the plot must be prepared for planting by removing at least some of the vegetation that occurs naturally in the area. In some kinds of agriculture, the landscape itself must be modified by constructing furrows, dikes, ditches, terraces, or other

artificial landforms. Second, the crops must be planted, requiring more labor. Third, natural processes destroy the artificial plant community and landscape that people have created: weeds invade and compete for light and soil nutrients, animal pests are attracted to the densely growing crops, and rainfall and floods may wash away physical improvements. Cultivators, therefore, must "beat back nature" by periodically removing weeds, protecting against pests, rebuilding earthworks, and so forth. Fourth, the act of farming itself reduces the suitability of a site for future harvests, by reducing soil fertility, if nothing else. In future years the farmers must somehow restore their plots to a usable condition or their yields will fall. All these necessities require labor and other kinds of energy expenditures.

So farming is a lot of work, and much evidence suggests that people who make their living by agriculture work at least as long and hard as most foragers. Cultivation also led to other changes—in settlement size and permanence, in ownership of resources, in political organization, and in many other dimensions of life—that culminated in the evolution of whole new forms of culture, as we shall see.

So many ways of farming land exist that we cannot even mention most of them here. Commonly, preindustrial farming systems are divided into two overall forms, based partly on the energy source used in farming and on how often a garden or field is cultivated. They are usually called *horticulture* and *intensive agriculture*. Both have many, many varieties.

Horticulture

In the farming system known as **horticulture**, people use the energy (power) of only their muscles in clearing land, turning over the soil, planting the crops, weeding, and harvesting. Figure 6.2 shows the major regions where horticulture existed at the time of contact by the West. There are no plows pulled by draft animals (such as horses or oxen) to help in preparing the soil for planting. Instead, people use hand tools such as digging sticks and shovels for such tasks. Some horticultural peoples fertilize their gardens with animal or human waste, or with other kinds of organic matter. If irrigation is necessary or useful for higher

As this burning plot on the island of Tanna in Vanuatu illustrates, shifting cultivators use fire to clear the land of natural vegetation in preparation for planting.

yields, water is usually hand carried onto fields from nearby rivers or streams.

One type of horticulture is called *shifting cultivation* (or *slash and burn*). Today, it is practiced largely in the tropical rain forests of Central and South America, southeast Asia, and central Africa. Shifting cultivators farm the forest in a cycle. Using axes, knives, and other hand tools, they first cut down a small area of forest. After allowing the wood and leaves to dry out, they burn the refuse. The ashes often are spread out over the burned area, for they contain useful plant nutrients, and tropical soils are notoriously infertile. Generally, a given garden plot is cultivated for only two or three years before its fertility declines and it is gradually abandoned. Then another area of forest is cleared, a new garden is prepared, planted, tended, and harvested until it is no longer productive enough. It then is abandoned and its natural vegetation regrows over several years. The land, in other words, is left *fallow* for a long time, during which it gradually recovers its ability to produce an adequate harvest. After many years of regrowth—usually ten or more—a previously abandoned plot is fertile enough to be planted again.

Another example of horticulture is *dry land gardening*. It is defined by the main climatic factor with which cultivators have to cope: low, erratic, and unpredictable rainfall. Like all horticulture, it uses no plow, and simple hand tools—hoes, spades, and so forth—powered by human muscles are the characteristic technology. Dry land gardening occurs in the American Southwest, in parts of Mexico, in some of the Middle East, and in much of Sub-Saharan Africa. In the more arid regions of Africa it is sometimes supplemented by cattle raising, because rainfall is too erratic and unpredictable for people to depend entirely on their crops.

In this type of horticulture, low and highly variable precipitation impedes the growth of crops. Cultivation in arid lands is risky: Even if in most years rainfall and harvests are adequate, there is a good chance that in any given year not enough rain will fall. Therefore, people who cultivate in dry regions have developed various gardening techniques to cope with the possibility of drought.

The Pueblo peoples of the North American Southwest illustrate one way to cope with aridity. In this region annual rainfall averages only ten inches, concentrated in the spring. Further, in this high country the growing season for corn—the major source for food—is only about four months long. The people are faced with extreme uncertainty: If they plant too early, a spring frost may kill their crops; if they wait too long, they will lose some of the critical moisture from the spring rains.

The Pueblo therefore plant corn in those areas that are most likely to flood, where soil moisture usually lasts until harvest time. Yet in some years—they do not know

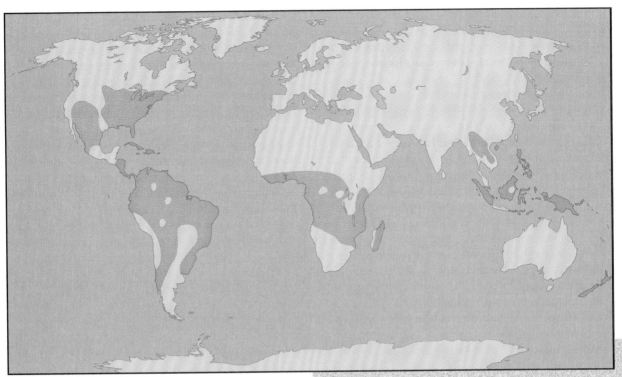

Figure 6.2   Principal Regions of Horticulture at Contact Period

in advance which years—the rains are so torrential that floods wash away the crops. The people, therefore, diversify both the place and the time of their planting. They sow the seeds of corn, squash, beans, and other crops in several locations, so that no matter what the weather, some fields produce a harvest. Gardens on the flood plains may be lost during an unusually wet year, but upland gardens still yield a crop. Staggering the time of planting likewise lowers the risk of cultivation; by planting crops weeks apart, the risk of losing all of a planting because of an untimely frost is reduced. Thus, by mixing up where and when they plant, the Pueblo peoples reduce the risk of cultivation in an arid, highly seasonal environment.

Cultural Consequences of Horticulture

Obviously, shifting cultivation and dry land gardening are quite different varieties of horticulture, practiced in distinct kinds of environments. But both methods represent successful efforts to increase the amount of food that can be produced in an area—the productivity of land is well above what would naturally be available and harvestable by foragers. And even though these kinds of methods are sometimes said to represent "simple" agriculture, both require that people remove most of the natural vegetation from the land so that crops can be planted. Finally, both require that people invest their labor in their gardens or fields (by clearing, planting, and weeding) in expectation of a later return (the harvest). Foragers, as you recall, seldom do such things.

Thus, horticulture improves the productivity of land, modifies the natural environment, and requires people to make a labor investment in their land. These facts alone affect the cultural systems of horticulturalists. How do their cultures differ from those of foragers? Subsequent chapters address this question more thoroughly. For now, we note two of the most important ways in which the horticultural adaptation shapes the cultures of people who live by it.

First, the size and permanence of settlements increase. Rather than living in bands or camps of around twenty to fifty, most horticulturalists aggregate into *villages,* often with hundreds of residents. Rather than moving every few days or weeks, people become more *sedentary,* remaining in the same location for years, decades, or even centuries. Villages are more permanent, both because effective adaptation does not require people to move frequently, and because families who have cleared and planted plots want to stay around at least long enough to recoup their labor investment.

Second, rights to resources differ from those common among most hunter-gatherers. Among horticulturalists, rights to land are better defined, meaning that particular individuals, families, and other groups are more attached to specific places where they or their ancestors have established a claim.

The main reason for a more definite claim to resources is as follows. (For now we assume that some kind of family is the group that cooperates in food production.) A horticultural family invests its labor in clearing, planting, and otherwise improving specific and relatively well-defined pieces of land (its plots or fields). This labor investment establishes a family's *claim* to the land. Their claim (their rights over the plot, minimally including the right to deny other families access to it) arises from the fact that their labor has increased the productivity of the land. Families with claims to specific plots pass their rights along to their children, most of whom will marry and transmit the rights to their own children. In any generation, any given individual or family thus has ownership rights over specific parcels, which usually include the gardens they are actually cultivating. Rights often extend to abandoned plots that they or their ancestors cultivated in the past and to which they or their children may return in future years.

Among horticultural peoples, then, ownership rights over well-defined parcels of land are usually held by families or some other kind of kinship group. In contrast, foragers most commonly have use rights over large territories with only vaguely defined boundaries. Further, horticultural families usually claim ownership over the land itself, because the soil may be made productive by planting crops on it. For foragers, use rights are typically exercised only over the wild resources of a territory, which is valuable mainly because of the wild plants and animals found there.

In sum, two of the major ways the cultures of horticulturalists differ from those of foragers are: (1) living groups (villages) are larger and more permanently settled, and (2) families have more definite rights of ownership over particular pieces of land. These two consequences, in turn, have other effects on cultures. For example, sedentism means that people can store possessions rather than having to carry them around, raising the potential for wealth accumulation. More definite land rights raises the possibility that some families will inherit or otherwise acquire more productive resources than others. These and other effects are considered in later chapters.

Intensive Agriculture

As we have seen, horticultural peoples use human muscles as the only or main source of power for tools, and they make only modest efforts to improve the soil by fertilization with natural materials. Another characteristic of the horticultural adaptation is that, compared with intensive agriculture, it takes more total land to support a single individual or family of a given size. In shifting cultivation, for every plot of land under cultivation at any given time, several ("abandoned") plots are at various stages of regrowth and recovery. For example, if for every acre of land being cultivated, ten acres are under fallow, then far fewer people could be supported per acre than if only half the land was under fallow at any one time.

Therefore, even though horticulture supports higher population densities than foraging, the number of people it can support is low relative to the farming system known as **intensive agriculture**. (Figure 6.3 shows the major regions where intensive agriculturalists lived at the time of contact with Europeans.) With the latter, fields are farmed more frequently. Indeed, some intensive agriculturalists have their lands under almost continuous cultivation—the same fields are farmed year after year, with only brief fallow. Stated differently, people use their land more *intensively*: To produce higher yields, they work the land harder. This is possible only if people take steps to maintain the long-term productivity of their land. In various regions, such steps include substantial fertilization (generally with the dung of livestock), crop rotation, careful weeding, turning of the soil prior to planting, composting, and other methods. For some of these tasks, a new tool, the plow, and a new source of energy (power), draft animals, are useful. Using plows pulled by horses, oxen, water buffalo, or other draft animals, a farmer can more quickly prepare the soil. In addition to traction for the plow, livestock provide many other useful products: meat, milk and other dairy products, manure, hides, and transportation. After harvest, livestock are turned loose to graze on the unharvested stubble, fertilizing fields in the process. In some regions, animal muscle is used to power the mechanical pumps that carry irrigation water to the fields. Livestock also were harnessed to the heavy stone wheels used to grind grains into flour.

For all these reasons, intensive agriculture is substantially more productive than horticulture. An acre of land produces greater yields and, hence, is capable of supporting far more people—five, ten, and even twenty times the number per unit of land than most horticultural adaptations. Supporting more people is probably the main advantage of intensive agriculture over horticulture.

In the Old World, especially in parts of Asia and Europe, intensive agriculture involved the use of the plow. But before the coming of Europeans, New World peoples had no domesticated animals suitable for pulling plows. Indeed, outside the Andes of South America, the only animals domesticated by Native Americans were dogs, turkeys, and muscovy ducks. Andean people also had llamas and alpacas, but these were not harnessed to plows. Despite this limitation, Native American civilizations in places such as the valley of Mexico (Aztec, for example) and the Andes found ways of increasing the

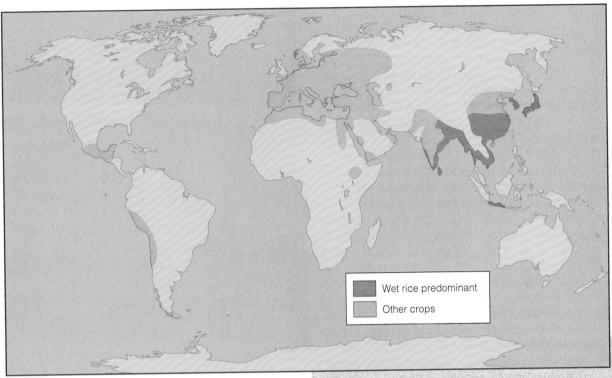

Figure 6.3 Principal Regions of Intensive Agriculture at Contact Period

Legend:
- Wet rice predominant
- Other crops

yields of their lands by intensifying their production systems. In the valley of Mexico, for example, natural swamps were reclaimed by filling in earth and constructing raised fields that were planted with crops like tomatoes, squash, and corn. By continually adding new materials to these so-called floating gardens, the people could keep them under almost continuous cultivations. In the Andes, stepped terraces were constructed to reduce erosion and an incredible variety of potatoes and other crops was grown during the summer.

Another method of increasing yields, practiced by many intensive cultivators, is the use of irrigation to cope with natural rainfall deficiencies. Various irrigation methods are used around the world. Sometimes streams are dammed to conserve runoff, and ditches are dug to transport water to the fields. In some Asian river valleys, channels are dug to transport water and fertile silt to fields during the annual monsoons, when rivers overrun their banks. In many mountainous regions of Southeast Asia, the level of water in hillside rice fields is controlled with an elaborate system of diked terraces.

In sum, compared with horticulture, intensive agriculture is more productive per unit of land. Its high productivity is due to factors such as shortened fallow periods (or having no fallow at all), preparing land more thoroughly prior to planting, removing weeds, adding manure and other organic matter to preserve fertility, and

manipulating the supply of water. These (and other) inputs give people greater control over conditions in their fields, leading to higher yields per unit of land.

Cultural Consequences of Intensive Agriculture

The development of intensive methods of farming the land eventually had dramatic cultural consequences in many regions. Some of the most important effects of this form of adaptation result from its relatively high productivity. A single farm family using intensive methods can usually feed many more people than just its own members. Far more than either foragers or horticulturalists, intensive farmers can produce a **surplus** over and above their own subsistence (food) requirements. This surplus can be used to feed other people, families, and other kinds of groups, who no longer need to produce their own food.

What happens to this surplus? Many things, depending on the circumstances. Excess food can be traded for other useful products like pottery, tools, wood, and clothing. If the community uses money (see Chapter 7), families may produce surplus food for sale, and the money is used to buy other goods. If the village or other settlement has a strong political leader, such as a chief, he can collect the surplus from his subjects and use the food to pay laborers who work on public projects such as trails, temples, and irrigation works. If the community is part of a larger, more encompassing political system, with a ruler and a governmental bureaucracy, then the government will collect part of the surplus as a tax, which it uses for public purposes (e.g., support of armies, the judiciary, and the religious hierarchy) or to further its own political interests.

All these possibilities illustrate a central fact about most peoples who depend on intensive agriculture: Most are not politically independent and economically self-sufficient communities, but are incorporated into some kind of larger organization. The villages in which most of them live are part of a more inclusive political system that dominates or rules them in some way. The surplus production of intensive farmers is traded, sold, or taxed (or all three) and supports people who do not themselves do farm work, such as rulers, aristocracies, bureaucracies, priests, armies, merchants, and craft specialists.

Intensive agriculture, then, is strongly associated with large-scale political and economic organization: Farm villages produce food and other products for people who live elsewhere and, in turn, receive things (products, services) from the larger system. The association of intensive agriculture with large-scale political organization is ancient, going back 5,000 years in parts of the Old World and more than 2,000 years in two regions of the New World.

In prehistoric times intensive agriculture peoples were incorporated into the four major civilizations of the ancient Old World: the valley formed by the Tigris and Euphrates rivers of Mesopotamia, the Nile valley of Egypt, the Indus River valley of Pakistan, and the Shang cities of China. The food supply of these civilizations was produced by intensive agriculturalists, who paid tribute or taxes to support the rulers, priests, armies, and officials who ran the government apparatus. In the New World, too, agricultural peoples were part of large-scale political units, such as the Mayans, Toltecs, and Aztecs of Mesoamerica, and the Incas of the Andean coast and highlands (Figure 6.4).

In these parts of the world, within a few centuries or millennia after the development of intensive agriculture, the socially and politically complex organization we call **civilization** (or "living in cities") emerged. All civilizations have a formal, specialized form of government known as the *state* (discussed further in Chapter 11). States are large-scale political units featuring a ruler, a governing bureaucracy, class distinctions between the elite and common people, and methods of extracting labor and surplus products from those who are responsible for farming the land. All these ancient civilizations were supported by intensive agriculture, and all involved large-scale irrigation and water control. Certainly, it appears from current evidence that intensive agriculture

Traditional wet rice agriculture—here in Thailand—is enormously productive because flooded fields offer numerous ecological benefits to growing crops.

is virtually a prerequisite for civilization. No known civilization ever developed out of a foraging or horticultural adaptation. (The Mayan civilization was once thought to have been an exception, but recent evidence shows that the Mayans, too, used intensive methods.)

In the world we live in today, virtually every human community is politically and economically incorporated into larger organizations, namely, nations and the international economic system. Rather than producing largely for their own subsistence, many modern farmers produce for sale on local or international markets. Methods of farming the land also have changed dramatically in recent decades. In most industrial nations of Europe, the Americas, and East Asia, farming the land with animal-powered plows has been replaced by mechanized agriculture, with its tractors, combines, and other machinery powered by gasoline and other kinds of energy derived from fossil fuels. Economically, most small, family-owned farms in Canada and the United States must invest heavily in machinery and other technologies to keep their farms productive, for their livelihood and standard of living is based on their yields and the prices they receive for their crops, livestock, and other products.

But intensive agricultural methods survive even today. In the developing regions of southern Asia and southeast Asia, Latin America, and Africa, millions of rural people farm the land much as their ancestors did. Economically, these rural communities often fit into their nations as **peasants**. Peasants are rural people who are integrated into a larger society politically (i.e., they are subject to laws and governments imposed from outside their communities) and economically (i.e., they exchange products of their own labor for products produced elsewhere). In many Third World countries, peasants make up the bulk of the population and produce much of the food consumed by town and nonag-city dwellers. Peasants typically subsist mainly from foods they grow themselves, although many also produce nonagricultural products for market sale. Peasant households produce goods that are sold for money, traded or bartered for goods produced by other people, paid to a landlord as rent, or rendered to a central government as taxes.

The peasantry first arose in the ancient civilizations just mentioned. The agricultural labor of prehistoric peasants fed the craft workers, the merchants, the state-sponsored priesthoods, the political elite, the warriors, and the builders. The tribute (usually paid in food, labor, or both) rendered by peasants was extracted from them by armed force or threat of force. This rendering of goods and labor by peasants to members of a more powerful social category continued into historic and modern times. The peasantry of medieval Europe, for example, eked out a meager living, paying a substantial portion of their annual harvest to their lords or working many days a year on their lord's estate.

Given this information, we might well wonder whether the development of intensive agriculture was a curse or a blessing for most of humanity. There is little doubt that it is a blessing to those who throughout history have received the surplus made possible by intensive methods. And most scholars agree that productivity of intensive agriculture allowed the specialized division of labor that led to writing, metallurgy, monumental architecture, cities, and the great religious and artistic traditions we associate with civilization.

But how about the peasants, who produced the food that made such "progress" possible? For them, writing meant that more accurate accounts could be kept of their tribute payments or of the number of days they worked for overlords. Iron and other metals meant that peasants had better agricultural tools; yet for the most part they were not allowed to use them to ease their own labor, but only to produce more surplus for others to consume. Metal also meant that weapons became more effective, so that the armies of one state could make war upon the armies of another state more effectively. Most peasant families continued to live in hovels, even while great palaces, religious structures, and walled cities and towns were constructed and the workers fed by the peasants' agricultural labor. Both prehistorically and historically, peasants around the world have been denied many of the benefits offered by technological progress, although their agricultural labor has made much of this progress possible.

Figure 6.4 Ancient Civilizations

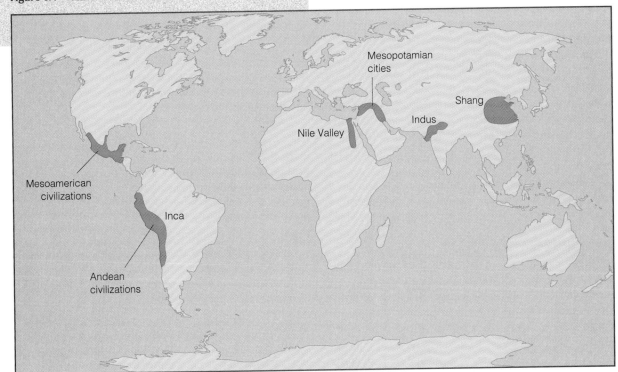

Pastoralism

Most farming people also keep domesticated animals. Southeast Asian and Pacific horticulturalists raise many pigs and chickens. Intensive agriculturalists raise horses, oxen, water buffalo, and cattle, which they use to pull their plows, fertilize their fields, and provide dairy products and meat. These livestock are not merely supplementary to the agricultural adaptation: Because of the meat, eggs, milk, hides, wool, transportation, fertilizer, and horsepower they provide, they usually are critical to the survival and nutrition of assorted farmers.

However, cultivators do not depend on their domesticated animals to the same extent or in the same way as do peoples known as *pastoralists*, or herders. Herders acquire much of their food by raising, caring for, and subsisting on the products of domesticated animals. With a few exceptions, the livestock are gregarious (herd) animals, with cattle, camels, sheep, goats, reindeer, horses, llamas, alpacas, and yaks being the common animals kept in various parts of the world.

Agriculture and pastoralism are not necessarily mutually exclusive adaptations, for a great many pastoral peoples also farm the land. When we characterize a people as "pastoral," we mean that the needs of their animals for naturally occurring food and water profoundly influence the seasonal rhythms of their lives. The key phrase here is "naturally occurring." Most farmers raise crops that they feed to their livestock or maintain fields in which their animals graze. In general, pastoralists do neither of these. Their herds graze on natural forage and therefore must be moved to where the forage naturally occurs. Some or all of the people must take their livestock to wherever the grasses or other forage is available in a given season. This high degree of mobility, known as **nomadism**, characterizes the pastoral adaptation. Most commonly, pastoralists are seasonally nomadic—they do not wander aimlessly. Their migrations often are "vertical," meaning that animals are taken to highland areas to graze during the hottest season of the year.

Although people who herd animals are found in all continents, for the most part herders live in only certain kinds of environments (see Figure 6.5, which shows where pastoralists lived prior to European expansion). The pastoral adaptation occurs mainly in deserts, grasslands, savannas, mountains, and the tundra. These environments obviously are diverse, but they do share a common feature: Cultivation is impossible, extremely difficult, or highly risky because of inadequate or great yearly fluctuations in rainfall (as in deserts or savannas) or very short growing seasons (as in mountains and tundras). As always, there are exceptions to our generalizations, but most pastoralists

Peasants make up the majority population of many modern Third World nations, including India.

live in regions that are not well suited to cultivation using preindustrial technologies.

In such arid or cold environments, the herding of livestock offers several advantages over the planting of crops. First, most of the vegetation of grasslands and arid savannas (grasses and shrubs) and of tundras (lichens, willows, and sedges) is indigestible by humans. Livestock such as cattle, sheep, and reindeer are able to eat this vegetation and transform it into milk, blood, fat, and muscle, all of which are drunk or eaten by various pastoral peoples. Thus, in some areas livestock allow people to exploit indirectly certain wild plant resources not directly available to them.

Another advantage of herding may be called *subsistence risk reduction*. Under preindustrial conditions in areas of low and unreliable rainfall, crops often fail because of drought. Livestock provide an insurance against these periodic, unpredictable droughts and accompanying crop failures. Not only do they store meat "on the hoof," but they also can be traded or sold to neighboring peoples for cultivated foods.

Finally, a big advantage of keeping livestock is their mobility: Herds can be moved to the areas of freshest or lushest pasture, to sources of water, away from neighbors who have grown too aggressive, or out of easy range of tax-seeking governments that often want the nomads to settle down so they can be better controlled.

With advantages like these you may well wonder why pastoralism was not more widespread in the preindustrial world. Why did the herding adaptation not spread to areas where cultivators lived? Part of the reason is that environmental conditions are not always conducive. For example, until recently pastoralism seldom was found in tropical forests, largely because of lack of forage. (Today, enormous tracts of tropical forest in Central and South America are cleared and replanted in grasses suitable for cattle grazing.) Livestock diseases also limit the distribution of pastoralists. For example, much of eastern and southern Africa is occupied by cattle herders (most of whom also farm, however). Herders would presumably be even more widespread on the continent were it not for the limitations imposed by the presence of the tsetse fly, which transmits the debilitating disease sleeping sickness to cattle.

But perhaps the main factor limiting the distribution of pastoralism is that herding is not the most productive way of using resources in those areas in which agriculture can be carried out reliably. The best way to understand why is to apply the ecologists' "10 percent rule." The food energy produced by photosynthetic plants lies at the base of any ecosystem except the deep oceans. In the presence of sufficient water, carbon dioxide, and minerals, plants convert the energy of sunlight into simple sugars. Herbivores (plant-eating animals) consume the

vegetation and use it to maintain their own bodies and produce offspring. Carnivores (animal-eating animals) in turn feed on herbivores. At each of these levels of the food chain, most of the energy is lost as it is carried to the next level. Thus, herbivores transform only about 10 percent of the plant energy they consume into their own flesh; and only around 10 percent of the energy carnivores acquire by eating herbivores is available to make more carnivore flesh. At each level, 90 percent of the energy consumed is lost to respiration, waste production, and other processes. The 10 percent rule says that only about 10 percent of the energy locked up in living matter at one level is available to the next level.

Now we can see why herding is not as efficient a way of exploiting an environment as agriculture: Overall, pastoralists eat higher on the food chain. More total food energy can be obtained from an environment by farming because much more energy can be gained from (cultivated) plants than from (herded) animals. People did not necessarily figure out that they could most productively exploit an environment by growing crops rather than raising animals, and then opt for cultivation. More likely, cultivation won out over herding—in areas that are suitable for both—because of its greater labor productivity. Further, the 10 percent rule also translates into higher potential (and actual) population densities for cultivators, who in the past may have outcompeted pastoralists for those territories that both could exploit.

Figure 6.5 Principal Regions of Pastoralism at Contact Period

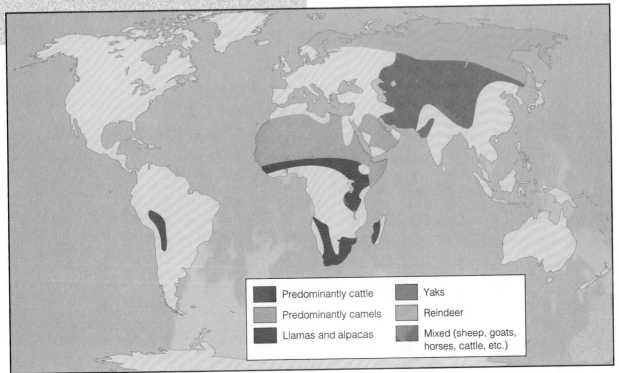

Predominantly cattle

Predominantly camels

Llamas and alpacas

Yaks

Reindeer

Mixed (sheep, goats, horses, cattle, etc.)

Aridity, temperature, short growing seasons, and other ecological and climatic factors do not totally explain the distribution of the pastoral adaptation, however. Some pastoralists live in areas where crops could be grown, and they certainly know how to cultivate, but they consciously choose not to grow crops. The cattle-herding Maasai of Kenya and Tanzania are an example. In some part of the Maasai territory cultivation is possible, and in fact most neighboring tribes combine cattle herding with cultivation of sorghum and other crops. The proud Maasai, however, look down on cultivation because their herds represent wealth and are the main symbol of their cultural identity relative to their neighbors. Maasai, therefore, live largely off the products of their cattle—blood, milk, meat, curds—and trade with their neighbors for the cultivated foods they do eat. The reasons they continue their pastoral adaptation are, therefore, as much "cultural" as "ecological."

The Karimojong: An Example from East Africa

One people who illustrate many of the aforementioned points about the pastoral adaptation are the Karimojong, who live in the modern nation of Uganda. Living on an arid savanna with marked seasonal differences in rainfall, traditionally they subsisted by a combination of horticulture and cattle herding. The 60,000 Karimojong are a fairly representative example of a cultural area known to anthropologists as the "East African cattle complex." In this complex, found throughout the East African savannas, cattle are more than an ordinary source of food. The East African man loves his cattle like some North Americans love their sports utility vehicles. Cattle represent wealth and manliness. They are the source of prestige, influence in tribal affairs, and wives (for an East African man must transfer cattle to his wife's relatives to marry her, a practice we discuss in Chapter 8). When sacrificed ritually cattle are religious symbols and are the source of blessings from the ancestors and gods. Underlying all these cultural elements of the cattle complex, according to Rada and Neville Dyson-Hudson, who studied the Karimojong, is the important role of cattle in subsistence: "First, last and always the role of cattle in Karimojong life is to transform the energy stored in the grasses, herbs and shrubs of the tribal area into a form easily available to the people" (Dyson-Hudson and Dyson-Hudson 1969, 4).

This transformation is not mainly achieved by eating the animals' flesh, as Westerners might expect. Rather, the Karimojong—and most other East Africans—consume the products of living cattle: milk and blood. Lactating cows are milked twice daily. Every three to five months, several pints of blood are taken from the jugular of some animals and drunk, usually immediately. Cattle meat is consumed mainly on religious occasions; the meat is shared among all participants.

There is a marked sexual division of labor in Karimojong subsistence activities. The central portion of the tribal territory is crossed by several rivers, and hence is relatively well watered during the rainy season. Here the women live in permanent settlements, where they cultivate sorghum (an African grain) and a few other crops. The central area,

The pastoral adaptation is based on harvesting the products of livestock, such as meat, milk, hides, and hair. This photo was taken in the Himalayas.

however, produces good grasses for the herds only during the rainy season, so for most of the year the cattle must be taken to greener pastures, often miles away from the settlements. The Karimojong therefore have another kind of settlement, the mobile "cattle camps" that are run by males, especially by young men. Rainfall is quite unpredictable, especially during the driest half of the year. But localized storms do occur, and for many days afterward grass grows well in restricted areas. The men of the cattle camps—accompanied by the cattle—move frequently in search of pasture. While living in the cattle camps, men live largely from the milk and blood of their animals, supplemented by the beer made from sorghum that the women sometimes bring when they visit.

Both cultivated crops and livestock are necessary foods for the Karimojong. Even a short three-week drought during the sorghum-growing season will seriously reduce the harvest, but the mobility of the livestock allows them to be taken to places where there is sufficient pasture. Cattle thus provide an insurance against climatic and other forces that make cultivation too risky to rely on. They also allow the Karimojong to make use of those parts of their territory that are too dry to support cultivation. The cattle transform vegetation indigestible to humans into milk, blood, and meat, which eventually are eaten by the people.

Adaptation and Culture

In this chapter, we have synthesized an enormous amount of information on the main forms of human adaptation and on how adaptation affects cultural systems. It is worth pointing out that many complications have not been covered

because of space limitations, and that many exceptions to our generalizations have been ignored in the interest of understanding broad patterns. Recognizing that there are complications and exceptions, one major point of this chapter is the following: *How a society or other group of people harness the resources and cope with the problems of living in a particular environment are important influences on many dimensions of their culture.*

Just how "important" these "influences" are, of course, is debatable, as the theoretical approaches known as materialism and idealism (see Chapter 4) illustrate. Nonetheless, few anthropologists would question certain generalizations about the relation between forms of adaptation and cultural systems:

- the foraging adaptation is most efficient when people live in small, seasonally mobile groups that maintain flexible rights to the natural resources of large territories;
- horticultural people settle in hamlets or villages in which productive land and other resources are owned by families or other kinship or residential groups;
- intensive agriculture resulted in the development of towns and cities occupied partly or largely by elites and specialists, and surrounded by rural peasant communities that contributed labor, tribute, or tax to support the government and public projects; and
- pastoral peoples are seasonally nomadic, with grazing rights to pasturelands vested in families or other kin groups or in the tribe as a whole.

In future chapters, as we cover various aspects of culture, we shall sometimes discuss the ways in which adaptation affects family life, gender relations, political organization, and other dimensions of cultural systems.

Summary

Adaptation refers to how organisms interact with their environments, acquiring characteristics that lead to their survival and reproduction. One important feature of human adaptation is that it is carried out primarily—but not exclusively—by cultural changes: Humans adapt to new habitats by means of cultural changes in technology and organization, not mainly by alteration in their genes. One of the most important ways in which human populations interact with their environments is by production, which requires labor, technology, and natural resources. To produce a product efficiently, human groups organize

themselves by the division of labor, patterns of cooperation, and defining rights to natural resources.

The earliest form of human adaptation was hunting and gathering, or foraging. Foragers live nearly exclusively from the wild plants and animals available in their habitats. All human groups acquired their food from hunting and gathering until around 10,000 years ago, when plants and animals were first domesticated. Over the next several millennia, farmers and herders grew in numbers and expanded into regions previously occupied by foragers. Only a few foraging cultures survived into the twentieth century.

The adaptive requirements of living from wild plants and animals greatly affected the cultures of most foraging peoples. People had to organize their activities so that at the proper season, they could be at the places where wild foods were naturally available. Accordingly, the majority of foraging cultures studied by anthropologists exhibited the following characteristics: (1) a division of labor based mainly on sex and age, (2) high mobility, (3) congregation and dispersal of groups, usually based on seasonal changes, (4) small living and cooperative groups called bands, (5) reciprocal sharing, and (6) loose and flexible rights to the resources of a given territory. These features are well illustrated by cultures such as the Hadza, Shoshone, and !Kung. However, in especially resource-rich environments such as the Northwest Coast, the great abundance and high reliability of natural resources allowed people to settle in large, nearly permanent villages, and to develop well-defined rights to territory.

Domestication is the attempt to increase the productivity of an environment by planting and cultivating certain plants (crops) and taming and breeding certain animals (livestock). Domestication first arose 10,000 years ago in the Old World and around 5,000 years ago in the New World. As plant and animal domestication spread into new regions over several millennia, this new way of adapting to nature greatly affected human cultures. Most modern scholars believe that the main advantage of domestication over hunting and gathering is its ability to support far greater numbers of people per unit of land.

One of many forms of agriculture is called horticulture. Horticulturalists use only hand tools in planting, cultivating, and harvesting their plots or gardens, as illustrated by shifting cultivation and dry land gardening. Horticulture produces more food per acre than foraging, and it requires that people make a labor investment in particular pieces of land (their plots). Increased productivity and labor investments alone had two important consequences for cultures: (1) people remained in one place for a long time (sedentism), and the size of their settlements increased (villages), and (2) particular families established their own claims to particular pieces of land, producing cultural beliefs that land is defined as the property of specific groups.

As populations grew in certain regions, horticultural methods were no longer sufficient to produce enough food, so land had to be worked more intensively. Intensive agriculturalists use various methods to keep yields high, including keeping a single field under production longer, with little or no fallow. In the Old World, livestock were harnessed to plows to till the fields, whereas New World intensive agriculturalists used other methods. Fertilization with animal manure and other organic matter and irrigation are common among intensive agriculturalists. These and other methods eventually raised productivity enough that a single farm family was able to produce a surplus over and above its own food needs. Out of this surplus potential, a new form of culture, called civilization, arose in several favorable regions of both the Old World and the New World. Always supported by intensive agriculture, civilization and city life changed human life profoundly, leading to new developments such as writing, specialization, huge architectural structures, roads, and familiar artistic traditions. But whether the class of peasants enjoyed very many of these benefits is questionable.

The pastoral adaptation usually occurs in regions that are unsuitable for agriculture due to aridity, extreme temperatures, or inadequate growing seasons for crops. In these kinds of habitats, herding offers several advantages. It allows people to convert, through their livestock, indigestible grasses and other vegetation into edible flesh and dairy products. It reduces the risk of living in an unreliable environment, both because livestock provide a way of storing food on the hoof and because the food supply (herds) can be moved to more favorable places when times are hard. Although herding improves humans' ability to live in cold or arid habitats, agriculture is capable of producing far more total food than herding in favorable regions. This is probably why people usually farm the land where it is possible to do so, with some exceptions such as the Maasai. The Karimojong of Uganda illustrate many of these points about the herding adaptation.

Key Terms

adaptation
hunting and gathering
  (foraging)
agriculture (cultivation)
herding (pastoralism)
band
domestication
horticulture
intensive agriculture
surplus
civilization
peasants
nomadism

Suggested Readings

The following books are fine factual and/or theoretical overviews of preindustrial human adaptations:

Bates, Daniel G. *Human Adaptive Strategies: Ecology, Culture, and Politics*. Boston: Allyn and Bacon, 1998.
- An introduction to adaptations based on foraging, subsistence-based agriculture, pastoralism, and modern mechanized agriculture. Overviews the impacts of different forms of adaptation on cultural, and especially political, systems.

Campbell, Bernard. *Human Ecology*. 2nd ed. New York: Aldine, 1995.
- Describes how humans have adapted to various environments, both prehistorically and today.

Diamond, Jared. *Guns, Germs, and Steel: The Fates of Human Societies*. New York: Norton, 1997.
- This Pulitzer-prize winning book tries to account for why some societies historically were more successful than others. Diamond, a professor of physiology, argues that differences in the natural environments in which prehistoric people lived largely explain why some human societies increased in numbers and expanded geographically at the expense of other peoples. Ultimately, this book argues, all of human prehistory and history was profoundly affected by the natural environment and how diverse peoples adapted to it.

Kelly, Robert L. *The Foraging Spectrum: Diversity in Hunter-Gatherer Lifeways*. Washington, D.C.: Smithsonian Institution Press, 1995.
- An up-to-date overview of hunter-gatherers.

Reader, John. *Man on Earth*. New York: Perennial Library, 1990.
- A photographic and textual survey of a variety of cultures and their adaptations.

Readable case studies of particular hunting and gathering peoples include:

Balikci, Asen. *The Netsilik Eskimo*. Prospect Heights, Ill.: Waveland Press, 1989.
- A study of Netsilik adaptation, technology, kinship, marriage, and religion.

Hoebel, E. Adamson. *The Cheyenne*. New York: Holt, Rinehart and Winston, 1978.
- A reconstruction of Cheyenne life during the mid-nineteenth century.

Lee, Richard B. *The Dobe Ju/'hoansi*. 2nd ed. Fort Worth: Harcourt Brace College Publishers, 1993.
- A brief but reasonably comprehensive overview of the Dobe, a local population of !Kung (San) of southern Africa.

Lee, Richard B. *The !Kung San: Men, Women, and Work in a Foraging Society*. Cambridge: Cambridge University Press, 1979.
- A detailed description of the !Kung, describing their environment, foods, working hours, nutrition, social organization, and some of the changes that have occurred since the 1960s.

Thomas, Elizabeth Marshall. *The Harmless People*. Rev. ed. New York: Vintage, 1989.
- A readable account of the !Kung written from a personal perspective.

Turnbull, Colin. *The Forest People*. New York: Simon and Schuster, 1962.
- An ethnography of the BaMbuti (pygmies) of Zaire. Good description of their hunting and organization.

Ethnographies of agricultural and pastoral adaptations include:

Barfield, Thomas J. *The Nomadic Alternative*. Englewood Cliffs, N.J.: Prentice-Hall, 1993.
- Overview of pastoral adaptation and cultures in Asia, Middle East, and Africa.

Barth, Fredrik. *Nomads of South Persia*. Prospect Heights, Ill.: Waveland Press, 1986.
- A study examining the culture of the Basseri, a pastoral, sheep- and goat-herding society of southern Iran.

Cohen, Mark Nathan. *Health and the Rise of Civilization*. New Haven: Yale University Press, 1989.
- Comprehensive overview of health and nutrition in different adaptations, using archaeological and ethnographic data. Persuasively argues that human physical well-being deteriorated with the emergence of civilization.

Critchfield, Richard. *Villages*. New York: Anchor, 1983.
- Basically a travelog of the author's visits to peasant villages on every continent; this book gives a sense of the tone and quality of peasant lives.

Critchfield, Richard. *Villagers: Changed Values, Altered Lives*. New York: Anchor, 1994.
- Similar in style to the author's 1983 book, but deals more with recent changes resulting from integration of peasants into national and global economic systems.

Lansing, Stephen J. *The Balinese*. Fort Worth: Harcourt Brace Jovanovich, 1995.
- Describes Balinese culture and the intricate relationship between Hindu temple rituals and the irrigation of wet rice fields.

Netting, Robert McC. *Smallholders, Householders: Farm Families and the Ecology of Intensive, Sustainable Agriculture*. Stanford: Stanford University Press, 1993.
- Breathtaking in geographical scope, discusses relationships between population, land use, work, cultivation methods, productivity, ownership patterns, and household organization.

Internet Exercises

At the Lawrence University's Anthropology Page (http://www.lawrence.edu/dept/anthropology) within the student Internet projects is a website created by two students, Catherine Lephoto and Jacob Yarnell. Their website has a series of pages about the !Kung people (http://www.lawrence.edu/dept/anthropology/kungsan/kungsan.html).

A site that deals with adaptation and foraging in general is the site "Hunting and Gathering" at (http://www.mc.maricopa.edu/academic/cult_sci/anthro/lost_tribes/hg_ag/hg1.html). This website has a wealth of pages and links that correlate to the material in this chapter. Go through the whole series of web pages and follow the links and you will get a great review of the chapter. This website is a part of Mesa Community College's anthropology web page (http://www.mc.maricopa.edu/academic/cult_sci/anthro). Their web page is highly recommended not only for this chapter, but as a reference resource that can be used for the whole text. Take a look at the material that goes along with their online courses.

The Department of Anthropology at the University of Georgia specializes in the study of ecological anthropology (http://julian.dac.uga.edu/home.html). Go to the research gallery to see some interesting projects, such as Dr. Nazarea's "Memory Web" which catalogues indigenous farming practices.

Another site that is replete with resources is the Center for International Earth Science Information Network at Columbia University (http://www.ciesin.org). There is a huge amount of data available at this site, but that which is most relevant to the chapter can be found under "Indigenous Agriculture and Environmental Knowledge Systems" (http://www.ciesin.org/TG/AG/iksys.html).

An excellent model that demonstrates the potential of the Internet for anthropology is the Manchester Experience Rich Anthropology Project "Peasant Social Worlds and Their Transformation" (http://nt2.ec.man.ac.uk/multimedia). This site is superb both in its presentation and content. It covers the topic of peasants thoroughly and thoughtfully, providing an introduction, history, theoretical perspectives, and case studies with video and sound.

C O N T E N T S

Reciprocity

Generalized Reciprocity

Balanced Reciprocity

Negative Reciprocity

Reciprocity and Social Distance

Redistribution

Market Exchange

Money

Peasant Marketplaces

CHAPTER 7

Exchange in Economic Systems

The exchange of products and services is part of a society's economic system. Market transactions, involving buying and selling, is only one of several forms of exchange. This is the Saquisili Market in Otavalo, Ecuador.
Visit http://www.wadsworth.com/humanity to learn more about the material covered in this chapter and to access activities, exercises, and tutorial quizzes.

*T*HE PREVIOUS CHAPTER *covered the major types of adaptations found in the preindustrial world and described some of their important effects on cultures. As people produce the food and other products they need and want, they are engaged in what we call* economic activity, *and how they allocate their labor, technology,* *and resources is part of their economic system. But producing a material product is usually only the first step towards the final use (consumption) of the product. Commonly, products are exchanged between individuals and groups between the time they are produced and consumed. In fact, in modern economic systems organized around the market principle, most products are produced explicitly for exchange (sale on the market), and once the value acquired from the exchange (money) has been gained, the producer has little further interest in the product.*

Markets, however, are only one way of organizing the exchange of products. In the subsistence-based economies found in much of the preindustrial world, families or other kinds of kinship groups produce mainly for their own needs, not for sale on the market. And rather than exchanges based on supply, demand, and prices, exchanges are organized around other principles. Economic anthropologists, who specialize in the comparative study of economic systems, often classify various forms of exchange into three major modes or types:

- **Reciprocity**, in which two individuals or groups pass products back and forth, with the aim of (1) helping someone in need by sharing with him or her; (2) creating, maintaining, or strengthening social relationships; or (3) obtaining products made by others for oneself.
- **Redistribution**, in which the members of an organized group contribute products or money into a common pool or fund; a central authority usually has the privilege and responsibility to make decisions about how the resources later will be reallocated among the group as a whole.
- **Market**, in which products are sold for money, which in turn is used to purchase other products, with the ultimate goal of acquiring more money and/or accumulating more products.

Although most products change hands through the market mode in modern industrial economies, reciprocity and redistribution also exist. Examples of reciprocity are various gifts we give and receive on holidays, birthdays, weddings, baby showers, and other culturally special occasions. If you are employed, every pay period you participate in redistribution, for federal, state, and local governments collect a portion of your wage or salary as taxes, which they expend on public purposes or transfer to other members of society. Although all these exchange forms exist in modern societies, not all preindustrial cultures have all three. Some kind of reciprocity occurs in all human populations. But redistribution implies the existence of a central authority to organize the collection of resources from the group and to make decisions about how they will be reallocated. Redistribution, therefore, is an insignificant exchange mode in societies that lack strong leaders who make decisions on behalf of the group. The market mode of exchange requires money, private property, and certain other features that are absent in many preindustrial populations.

Reciprocity

In subsistence economies such as most of those based on foraging, horticulture, and pastoralism, families and households commonly are capable of producing most of the food and other products they consume. That is, families are potentially *self-sufficient* in the sense that they own or have access to the labor, tools, and resources necessary for survival.

However, in no known society are families, households, or other kinds of social groups self-sufficient *in fact*. Everywhere, such groups are engaged in exchanging products with other groups. Most anthropologists say that this is because families and other groups need or want to maintain relationships with other families and groups, and exchange is necessary to create and sustain these relationships. Examples of why groups need such relationships include ensuring long-term economic security, acquiring spouses, maintaining political ties, and strengthening military alliances.

The common form of exchange used for such purposes is known as reciprocity. Reciprocity refers to the transaction of objects without the use of money or other media of exchange. It can take the form of sharing with those in need, hospitality, gift giving, mutual feasting, or barter. Obviously, each of these varieties of reciprocity is motivated by different considerations and values, so anthropologists distinguish three forms of reciprocity to encompass the diversity.

Generalized Reciprocity

The defining feature of **generalized reciprocity** is that those who give goods do not expect the recipient to make a return of goods at any definite time in the future. Generalized reciprocity occurs between individuals who are (or are culturally expected to be) emotionally attached to one another and, therefore, have an obligation to help one another on the basis of relative need. In North America, parents who provide their children with shelter, food, vehicles, college educations, and interest-free loans are practicing generalized reciprocity. Giving without expectation of quick return also should occur between parties to certain other kinds of social relations, such as wives and husbands, siblings, and sometimes close friends.

Because it includes various forms of sharing with relatives and other people who are defined as close by cultural norms, generalized reciprocity is found in all societies. However, among some peoples it is the dominant form of exchange, meaning that more resources are distributed using this form than any other form. For example, most hunter-gatherers expect their band mates to share food and be generous with their possessions, partly because most members of a band are relatives of some kind (see Chapter 6). Among the !Kung, for example, the band is a social group within which food sharing is culturally expected or even mandatory.

Among the !Kung and most other foraging peoples, food is shared with other members of the camp, on the principle of generalized reciprocity.

Those who are stingy with possessions or who fail to share food with others are ridiculed or socially punished in some other way. Generalized reciprocity among the !Kung and many other foraging peoples ensures an equitable—if not entirely equal—distribution of food between the band's families. It also maintains social and economic equality between the families that make up the band. In fact, the !Kung have a custom that seems designed to keep even the best hunters from becoming too proud and boastful (see "A Closer Look").

Balanced Reciprocity

In **balanced reciprocity**, products are transferred to someone and the donor expects a return in products of roughly equal value (i.e., the exchanges should "balance"). The return may be expected immediately, or whenever the donor demands it, or by some specified time in the future. With generalized reciprocity, the giver continues to provide material assistance even though the receiver is unable to return anything for a long time. With balanced reciprocity, the giver refuses to continue to transfer objects to the receiver if the latter does not reciprocate within the appropriate time period. Donors may merely be angry if the receivers fail to reciprocate, may complain or gossip to others, may try to force reciprocation, or may suspend all relations until goods of equal value are returned.

Although the value of the objects transacted is supposed to be equal (at least roughly), balanced reciprocity is characterized by the absence of bargaining between the parties. In some preindustrial economies, the exchange of objects without having to negotiate for each transaction (How much of A will you give me for my B?) frequently

is organized by a special relationship between two individuals known as a *trade partnership*. Individuals of one tribe or village pair off with specific individuals (their "partners") from other regions with whom they establish long-lasting trade relationships.

For instance, in the Trobriand Islands off the eastern tip of the island of New Guinea there was a form of balanced reciprocity called *wasi*. Residents of coastal villages traded fish for yams and other garden crops produced in the mountainous interior. The *wasi* exchange was formalized: A coastal village paired off with an interior village, and within each village individuals formed trade partnerships. The rates at which garden produce was exchanged for fish were established by custom, so there was no haggling at any particular transaction.

In *wasi*, each trade partner received foods not readily available locally, so parties to the transaction gained a material benefit. In many other cases, balanced reciprocity takes the form of mutual exchanges of gifts or invitations for social and political purposes. That is, the exchange is not motivated primarily by the desire of the parties for the objects (unlike *wasi*) but by their desire to establish and maintain good relations with one another. (On your friend's birthday, instead of giving her a CD in exchange for a gift of about equal value on your own birthday, you both could save the cost of wrapping paper and cards by buying the objects yourselves. But then the social goal of the gift—expressing and strengthening your friendly relationship—would not be attained.)

A CLOSER LOOK

"Insulting the Meat" among the !Kung

Richard B. Lee

Many gathering and hunting people have cultural mechanisms that cut proud and boastful people down to size, reminding them that they are no better than anyone else. A fascinating example of such a mechanism is found among the !Kung. They call it "insulting the meat," referring to the custom of minimizing the successful hunter's contribution. Their goal is to keep skilled hunters modest, for such modesty is an important value in their culture. In the following extract, Richard Lee describes this custom in his ethnography of the !Kung, The Dobe Ju/'hoansi ("Ju/'hoansi" refers to the !Kung).

When a hunter returns from a successful hunt, or when meat is brought into a camp, one would think that this would be met with open glee and the hunter praised for his skill. Quite the contrary: The people often display indifference or negativity at the news of a successful kill, and I was surprised to see the low-key way in which the hunters would break the news of their success. /Xashe, an excellent hunter for /Xai/xai, put it this way:

When you come home empty-handed, you sleep and you say to yourself, "Oh, what have I done? What's the matter that I haven't killed?" Then the next morning you get up and without a word you go out and hunt again. This time you *do* kill something, and you come home. My *tsu* ("older kinsman") sees me and asks: "Well what did you see today?" "Tsutsu," I reply, "I didn't see anything."

I am sitting there with my head in my hands but my *tsu* comes back to me because he is a ju/' hoan. "What do you mean you haven't killed anything? Can't you see that I'm dying of hunger?" "Well, there might be something out there. I just

might have scratched its elbow."

Then you say, as he smiles, "Why don't we go out in the morning and have a look." And so we two and others will bring home the meat together the next day.

Men are encouraged to hunt as well as they can, and the people are happy when meat is brought in, but the correct demeanor for the successful hunter is modesty and understatement. A /Xai/xai man named /Gaugo said:

Say that a man has been hunting. He must not come home and announce like a braggart, "I have killed a big one in the bush!" He must first sit down in silence until I or someone else comes up to his fire and asks, "What did you see today?" He replies quietly, "Ah, I'm no good for hunting. I saw nothing at all . . . maybe just a tiny one." Then I smile to myself because I know he has killed something big.

The theme of modesty is continued when the butchering and carrying party goes to fetch the kill the following day. Arriving at the site, the members of the carrying party loudly express their disappointment to the hunter:

You mean you have dragged us all the way out here to make us cart home your pile of bones? Oh, if I had known it was this thin I wouldn't have come.

People, to think I gave up a nice day in the shade for this. At home we may be hungry, but at least we have nice cool water to drink.

To these insults the hunter must not act offended; he should respond with self-demeaning words:

You're right, this one is not worth the effort; let's just cook the liver

for strength and leave the rest for the hyenas. It's not too late to hunt today, and even a duiker or a steenbok would be better than this mess.

The party, of course, has no intentions of abandoning the kill. The heavy joking and derision are directed toward one goal: the leveling of potentially arrogant behavior in a successful hunter. The !Kung recognize the tendency toward arrogance (≠*twi*) in young men and take definite steps to combat it. As ≠Tomazho, the famous healer from /Xai/xai, put it:

When a young man kills much meat, he comes to think of himself as a chief or a big man, and he thinks of the rest of us as his servants or inferiors. We can't accept this. We refuse one who boasts, for someday his pride will make him kill somebody. So we always speak of his meat as worthless. In this way we cool his heart and make him gentle.

Insulting the meat is one of the central practices of the Ju/'hoansi that serve to maintain egalitarianism. Even though some men are much better hunters than others, their behavior is molded by the group to minimize the tendency toward self-praise and to channel their energies into socially beneficial activities. As a result, the existence of differences in hunting prowess does not lead to a system of Big Men in which a few talented individuals tower over the others in terms of prestige.

Source: Excerpt from THE DOBE JU/'HOANSI, Second Edition by Richard B. Lee, copyright © 1993 by Holt, Rinehart and Winston, Inc., reprinted by permission of the publisher.

We all are familiar with the anger or disappointment felt at not having our gifts or dinner invitations reciprocated. Many of us also know the embarrassment of being unable to return a gift of equal value to a gift we have received. We also are familiar with the use of gift giving for social and political goals. We know that friends make gifts to one another because giving a gift to someone recreates and strengthens feelings of goodwill. Gifts are a material symbol of good relations. They sustain relations of solidarity and mutual aid between individuals and groups. This is why, cross-culturally, gift-giving ceremonies frequently are part of peacemaking between formerly hostile groups; the gifts symbolize the beginning of a new period of peaceful coexistence.

In our personal lives, too, the back-and-forth flow of tangible objects often symbolizes warm personal feelings about a relationship—perhaps better than words, since "talk is cheap." The failure to present objects of appropriate value on certain occasions also symbolizes one's personal feelings, although in a less "warm" way.

So the transaction of material symbols (gifts) is one of the ways people express positive social relationships. But gifts also are used to create social bonds that are useful to the giver, and to obligate people from whom the giver wants something. Gift giving makes someone indebted to you, and therefore can be used to create an obligation to return a favor. Lobbyists and sales representatives know this use of balanced reciprocity.

For a preindustrial example of how balanced reciprocity helps to create and sustain political alliances, we turn to the Maring of highland Papua New Guinea. These people live by a combination of shifting cultivation, pig keeping, and hunting. The Maring live in settlements composed of clusters of kin groups. Each settlement is engaged in periodic warfare with some of its neighbors. Unless a settlement is unusually large, its members form a political alliance with one or more nearby settlements. When warfare occurs, the warriors of each settlement rely on their allies for military support and, in the case of defeat, for refuge. Most Maring settlements must establish and sustain military alliances if they are not to be defeated in warfare.

An important expression of continued goodwill between allied groups is periodic invitations to feasts and exchanges of wealth objects and other goods. Every few years, whenever they accumulate sufficient pigs, the members of a settlement invite their allies to an enormous feast, appropriately called a *pig feast*. At the pig feast, which is attended by hundreds of people, allies bring large quantities of wealth objects to exchange and pay off debts; they consume enormous quantities of pork provided by their hosts; they are on the lookout for potential spouses and sexual partners; and they aid the host settlement in the ceremonial dancing that the Maring believe is ritually necessary for success in the fighting that will soon occur. The host group uses the occasion of their pig feast to gauge the amount of military support they can expect from their allies: The more people who attend the feast, the more warriors the host settlement will be able to put on the battleground. Later, the guests will have accumulated enough pigs to reciprocate by hosting a pig feast for their allies, who come with wealth objects and pledge their military support by helping the host group in their ceremonial dancing.

The Maring pig feast, and its reciprocal exchanges between the hosts and guests from various allied groups, is an important event in maintaining good relations between allies. A group sponsors a pig feast to compensate their allies for their previous military aid as well as to reciprocate previous pig feasts they have attended. The failure to organize a pig feast large enough to compensate one's allies can result in the weakening and sometimes even termination of an alliance. Thus, mutual invitations to feasts are critical to the military success and continued survival of a Maring settlement.

Negative Reciprocity

The distinguishing characteristic of the third kind of reciprocity—known as **negative reciprocity**—is that both parties attempt to gain all they can from the exchange while giving up as little as possible. Negative reciprocity usually is motivated largely by the desire to obtain material goods at minimal cost.

Insofar as it is motivated by the desire for material goods, negative reciprocity is like market exchange; it is different mainly because no money changes hands between participants. In economies that use money to purchase goods and services, market exchange partly or largely replaces negative reciprocity.

But in economies with no money, negative reciprocity is an important way for individuals and groups to acquire goods that they do not produce themselves. Few populations are entirely self-sufficient: Some foods they like to eat do not occur in their habitats; some materials they need to make tools are not found locally; or they lack the skill to produce some of the objects they use. To acquire these goods, people produce other goods to exchange for "imports."

Balanced reciprocity often is used to create and sustain relationships between groups and individuals. Reciprocal invitations to feasts is one common form of balanced reciprocity, as illustrated by this killing of a pig on the island of Tanna in the nation of Vanuatu.

This is seen clearly in North American cultural norms. We expect an individual to practice generalized reciprocity with his or her children and perhaps with siblings and elderly parents; in fact, we are likely to judge people as uncaring or selfish if they do not. But if a middle-income person repeatedly lends money to a cousin or puts a niece through college, we are likely to regard him or her as either unusually generous or a bit foolish. He or she has extended generalized reciprocity beyond the range of relatives to whom we culturally consider it appropriate.

A cultural association between exchange form and kind of relationship applies to market transactions, which, as we have seen, have largely replaced negative reciprocity in modern societies. In market exchange, individuals are supposed to be "looking out for their own personal interests," "trying to get the most for their money," and so forth. We regard this as fine—in fact, as smart shopping—with transactions between strangers in a department store or car lot. But when the seller and buyer are friends or relatives, it is difficult for them to disentangle their economic transaction from their personal feelings for each other. Kinship and friendship bonds cannot easily be mixed with market exchange, because kinship and friendship are supposed to have an element of selflessness, whereas buying and selling are assumed to have selfish motives. Therefore, although I may buy my friend's used car, I feel uneasy about the transaction: What will I do if the car is a lemon?

Further, as our social relations with other people change, so does the kind of reciprocity we practice with them. Most adults have experienced one way in which this occurs: As we grow up, our increasing independence from our parents is manifested by a change in the way we exchange goods with them. We go from being the recipients of generalized reciprocity to more of a balanced reciprocity as we become more independent, and finally—at least until the advent of Social Security—to being the provider of generalized reciprocity.

Finally, changing one form of reciprocity into another can be used as a way of changing the nature of a social relationship. Because the form of reciprocity practiced between two individuals is related to the degree of social distance between them, the social distance can be decreased or increased by one party beginning to initiate a new form of exchange. Or someone can signal his or

Negative reciprocity in the preindustrial world often takes the form of barter. In the interior highlands of Papua New Guinea, many indigenous peoples manufactured money or wealth objects by stringing shells together into long chains or belts. Because these shells did not occur naturally in the interior, they were traded from people to people until they reached their final destination. Salt also was a trade object because it occurred in only a few areas.

In western North America, the obsidian (volcanic glass) used to make stone tools occurred in only a few areas; other peoples acquired it through trade. In some cases these trade routes stretched for hundreds of miles, with the obsidian passing through the hands of numerous middlemen before finally being made into a tool.

Reciprocity and Social Distance

Each type of reciprocity tends to be associated with certain kinds of social relationships. As Marshall Sahlins, who first distinguished the three varieties, noted, the kind of reciprocity that occurs between individuals or groups depends on the **social distance** between them. By *social distance* is meant the degree to which cultural norms specify they should be intimate with or emotionally attached to one another. In other words, a given mode of reciprocal exchange is normatively appropriate with only certain kinds of social relationships.

her wish to draw another person closer (reduce the social distance between them) by tentatively initiating a relationship of balanced reciprocity. In other words, reciprocity has social uses in our culture, just as it has among preindustrial peoples.

Thus, I can let you know of my desire to become your friend by giving you an unexpected gift or invitation to dinner. In turn, you tell me whether you share my feelings by whether you return my gift on an appropriate occasion, repeatedly find reasons to refuse my dinner invitation, or come to dinner several times at my place without reciprocating. If we both use this "strategy of reciprocity," neither of us needs to be put in a potentially embarrassing position of verbalizing our feelings. I signal my wish by my initial gift or invitation, and you decline or accept my offer of friendship by your response.

In sum, forms of reciprocity are culturally associated with types of social relations, so the reciprocity practiced between people changes as their relationship changes. We can use reciprocity to achieve social goals: Reciprocating or refusing to reciprocate gifts or invitations sends messages that are too embarrassing to say outright. Finally, reciprocity can serve as a way to shorten or lengthen social distance.

Redistribution

The major difference between reciprocity and redistribution—the second major mode of exchange—is the way the transfer of products and other resources is organized. With reciprocity, goods pass back and forth between two participants, with no third party to act as intermediary. With redistribution, resources collected from many individuals or groups are taken to a central place or put into a common pool or fund. Some overarching authority (empowered to make decisions on behalf of those who contributed) later draws from this pool or fund in returning public goods and services that allegedly benefit the group as a whole.

In modern nations, redistribution takes the form of taxes on wages, profits, retail sales, property, and other income and assets. To understand redistribution it is instructive to review how our tax system is supposed to operate. Federal tax revenues, for example, are used for two main purposes. First, they are expended in such a way as to benefit the whole country. The citizens receive police protection, law enforcement, national defense, infrastructure (e.g., dams, roads, airports), regulation of polluting industries, and so forth. Resources collected from the citizenry are expended on public goods and services. Second, taxes are used to provide assistance for individuals in need. These are "transfer payments" in the form of Social Security, Medicaid and Medicare, disaster relief, and so forth. Such public expenditures are based on moral norms and cultural values about social justice, equal opportunity, and helping those in need. Redistribution systems around the world are used for similar purposes: to provide public goods and services and to provide assistance to individuals and groups in need.

But there is another side to most systems of redistribution, a side with which we also are familiar. First, there often is conflict over who should provide the public resources, how the resources should be expended, and how much of a share of them should be given to those who collect and distribute them. One common social and political problem with redistribution is political disagreement: When many individuals have contributed to the public pool or fund, not everyone is likely to agree on how the "public resources" should be spent for the "public good." Much of the conflict between political parties in modern industrial democracies is rooted in disagreements over who should be taxed and how much, and over how government revenues should be spent. Parties and various interest groups are, in many cases, quarreling over redistribution: who pays? who gets what? and how much?

Second, elected officials and other officeholders who make important decisions about redistribution sometimes use public resources to further their own interests and ambitions, rather than to benefit the entire country or to help those in greatest need. In the United States, for instance, elected officials make "pork barrel" deals with one another to allocate federal tax dollars to finance highway construction in their districts. Hours commuters spend on the road are lowered for a while, but the real purpose is to provide jobs for their constituencies or to serve special interest groups who contribute to their reelection. Speaking more generally, political interests—as well as concern for the public welfare—enter into decision making about redistribution.

A common form of redistribution in the preindustrial world is known as **tribute**. The subjects of a chief or other title-holder contribute products (usually including food) into a common pool under the control of the central authority. Often the tribute is culturally viewed as a material symbol showing that the subjects continue to acknowledge the chief's sacred authority. Some of the accumulated products are consumed by the chiefs and their relatives, some are distributed to support the work of crafts specialists (e.g., weavers and potters), and some are redistributed to the whole population at public feasts, celebrations, and ceremonies.

Examples of redistribution systems using tribute payments exist on many of the islands of Polynesia and Micronesia, in the Pacific. On many islands, the entire population was divided traditionally into two ranks or classes, noble and commoner (see Chapter 12 for more about rank and class). Members of the nobility did little agricultural or other manual work, but instead managed the political system and organized religious ceremonies. Commoners produced the food and other forms of tribute, which fed the nobility and their families and which supported other kinds of specialists. On some islands, the tribute rendered by commoners was used mainly for public purposes, such as feeding people who worked on trails and public buildings, providing relief from temporary food shortages, and publicly celebrating special events. On other islands, the nobles were sufficiently powerful to use the tribute to make themselves materially wealthy: They lived in the best houses, slept on the softest woven mats, wore special clothing, had numerous servants, and ate only the finest foods.

Market Exchange

To say that objects or services are exchanged "on the market" means that they are bought and sold at a price measured in money: Person or group A possesses goods that person B wants to acquire; B acquires the goods by giving A some quantity of money that both A and B agree on; A then uses the money to acquire more goods from other people. Market exchange thus requires (1) some object used as a medium of exchange, that is, *money*; (2) a rate at which goods and services exchange for money, that is, *prices*; and (3) parties to exchanges have alternative buyers or sellers and are free to make the best deal they can, that is, prices determined by *supply and demand*. On the third point, markets imply the absence of physical coercion: If prices are set by supply and demand, neither party to a transaction can be forced to buy or sell from the other party. This is what we mean by a "free" market—no third party (a government, for example) sets prices or forces anyone to buy or sell from anyone else, and no single supplier of a good controls enough of the market to force people to buy from him, her, or it (in the case of firms).

Because markets (as we define them in this text) require the presence of money, we begin by discussing some of the diversity in money objects and money uses.

Money

Money consists of objects that serve as media of exchange in a wide range of transactions of goods, services, or both. This facilitation of exchange is the main function of money. If an economy uses money, individual A can acquire something from individual B without having to return an object desired by B; money can be given

instead, and B can then use the money to buy an object or a service of her or his choice.

Notice that if one individual, A, sells a product (including labor) to B in return for money, then A has (as we say) "made money" off the sale. Individual A may think he or she has made a good deal, but B may turn around and sell the product to someone else, C, in return for more money than was paid to A for it. This is the simplest form of what we call *profit,* and profit making is greatly facilitated by the use of money. Notice also that, in our example, individual B has not produced anything tangible, but has merely sold a product to C that was bought from A, the producer. If B does this often enough, so long as C wants the product and is willing to pay B more than B paid A for it, then B can grow very wealthy. *Wealth accumulation,* therefore, is facilitated by markets and money, although it also exists in some economies with neither markets nor money.

Some other characteristics of money are derived from its function as a medium of exchange. For example, money serves as a standard of value: The value of the goods and services that can be exchanged for money can be compared with one another because money serves as a common measure of "how much things are worth." Money also is a store of value: Because it can be used to purchase various goods, it represents wealth in a portable form.

These characteristics mean that not just any object is suitable to be used as money. Money objects must be durable, or the value they store deteriorates over time. The supply of the money object must be controllable, because if people can get all they want of it, its value inflates and it becomes worthless as an exchange medium. The monetary supply can be controlled by a government, which manufactures the only "legal tender" in the society; or the supply can be controlled by using only imported or rare objects as money. Imported shells are especially common, partly because of their durability. The supply also can be controlled by having the money require a lot of labor to manufacture: Money remains scarce because it takes time to make it.

An enormous variety of objects serve as money in one or another region of the world. We already are familiar with currencies of modern nations, issued by governments that control the money supply. In preindustrial economies, the kinds of objects that take on the characteristics of money are surprisingly diverse. In Africa, for example, the following objects served as money in one or another part of the continent: iron, salt, beads, cowry shells, cloth, slaves, gin, gold dust, metal rods, brass bracelets, and livestock. In Melanesia the list of money objects is also diverse: assorted shells (often modified in some way and sewn into fibers to form long belts), salt, the red feathers of a certain bird (also woven into belts), and pigs.

There are nonmonetary economies in which all exchanges are based on one of the three forms of reciprocity. But even in economies that do have an exchange medium, the range of goods that can be acquired with money varies greatly. In some the range is broad: Many kinds of resources and goods can be bought and sold, including labor, land, tools, and sometimes even people (slaves). In these systems, money serves as a *generalized* medium of exchange; that is, it can be used to acquire many kinds of goods and services, including land and labor. Anthropologists call this **multipurpose money**.

Money is multipurpose in modern North America. In principle, money can buy privately owned natural resources, labor, and goods. Even money itself can be sold for a price (interest). Some preindustrial peoples also have multipurpose money. For example, the Kapauku people of Irian Jaya, which is now part of Indonesia, used imported cowrie shells and two types of necklaces as currency. Kapauku money could be used to purchase almost anything, including land, labor, crops, pigs, tools, and medical services. In fact, Kapauku money can be said to be even more multipurpose than our own. Leopold Pospisil (1963), the ethnographer, writes:

> Among the Kapauku an overwhelming amount of goods is exchanged through sales. . . . In their selling and buying most of the Kapauku are strictly profit motivated. Often they invest money in pigs, chickens, large *woti* (bailer shell), inner bark, or animal teeth, for the purpose of breeding the animals for profit, speculating on sales of the bailer shell, or for making artifacts for sale. . . . Besides the necessity of having to buy with money such commodities as land, manufactured products, labor, and services such as surgery, curing, and midwifery, the Kapauku have to pay for favors and acts for which even in our capitalistic society there is no charge. For example, one pays a bride price for a wife, the services of a foster father have to be paid for by the grown boy, a grief expressed by strangers or distantly related people over the death of a close relative has to be recompensed in money, and almost all crimes can be settled through a proper transfer of shell currency (21–22).

Kapauku sales occurred on a daily basis, much as we make purchases of one or another item regularly. Periodically, however, Kapauku political leaders (called *big men*) organized enormous ceremonies attended by hundreds of people who came to sell and buy and to make and pay off loans.

The Kapauku represent an extreme in the range of uses to which money can be put, as well as in their intense desire to accumulate wealth. More often we find the range of money uses in preindustrial economies to be narrow: Only a few categories of goods are purchased with money. For example, it may be possible to buy food, clothing, and a few other goods, but land is not available

In modern industrial capitalist economies, most products and services are exchanged through the market mechanism. Shares of publicly traded companies are bought and sold on the New York Stock Exchange, where prices are determined by the impersonal forces of supply and demand.

for sale at any price and labor is almost never sold. Here, money is called **limited-purpose money**.

A famous example of limited-purpose money comes from among the Tiv of Nigeria, studied by Paul Bohannan. Tiv money consisted of metal rods, but the rods could not be used as an exchange medium for all other goods. For one thing, land could not be sold, and labor was exchanged among relatives on the principle of generalized reciprocity. For another, among these people goods circulated in different *exchange spheres*. Certain kinds of goods could only be transacted for certain other kinds of goods. Goods were culturally classified into categories, within which they were freely exchangeable, but between which exchange was difficult.

The "subsistence sphere" category included cultivated crops, chickens and goats, and some tools and household goods. Goods within this sphere were exchangeable for one another by means of barter. The "prestige sphere" included slaves, cattle, a special kind of white cloth, and metal rods. Within the prestige sphere, metal rods functioned as an exchange medium: One could sell cattle for metal rods and then use the rods to acquire white cloth or slaves, for example, but the monetary function of metal rods normally was limited to the prestige sphere.

However, it was *possible* to acquire subsistence goods in exchange for metal rods; but these transactions were rare, for two reasons. First, few people were willing to trade their metal rods for subsistence goods. This is because goods that circulated in the prestige sphere had much greater cultural value to Tiv than subsistence goods. Second, metal rods were worth an enormous amount of subsistence goods. Yet metal rods had no denominations; that is, unlike dollars and cents, they were not divisible into fractions. So for a Tiv to try to exchange one metal rod for subsistence goods would be like an American taking a thousand-dollar bill into a grocery store to buy food, with the clerk unable to make change. As a result of these two factors, Tiv metal rods were largely limited-purpose money.

The Tiv example serves to remind us that just because we find it convenient to call some object "money" does not mean that it has all the characteristics of our own currency. Indeed, some anthropologists believe that money objects are lacking in preindustrial economies and that money is a Western concept that we should not attempt to apply to other cultures. This problem is mainly semantic, however: If we define money simply as a medium of exchange, it is found in many other economies. To avoid confusion and false impressions, we do need always to specify its uses and its cultural meaning to the local people.

As we discuss next, we also need to be careful with the term *market,* because many non-Western markets do not work the same way as ours.

Peasant Marketplaces

Those of us who live in modern, industrialized economies are accustomed to purchasing most of what we need and want in restaurants, car lots, supermarkets, and shopping malls. That is, we rely on the market to satisfy our desires—we earn money from our jobs and spend the money on goods and services. In the process, we depend on other organizations (companies) to produce and sell the products we wish to buy.

Even in the modern world, hundreds of millions of rural peasants are not nearly so dependent on market forces. Rather than selling their labor to others in return for a wage, they work the land and fish the waters to supply food for their families directly. Rather than producing goods that they turn around and sell at a price to others, families consume most of what they produce themselves. There are places in most peasant communities where goods are bought and sold—there are *marketplaces*. But people do not rely on marketplaces for most of what they consume, nor do they spend most of their working hours producing goods to sell at the marketplace.

Such peasant marketplaces are common in West Africa, southern and Southeast Asia, the Caribbean, and Central and South America. Peasant vendors sell food, cloth and clothing, pottery, leather products, livestock, and other goods produced by their families. Traveling merchants (middlemen) bring commodities imported from the developed world or from elsewhere in the region to sell to local people at the marketplace.

Although much buying and selling occurs, peasant marketplaces are not the same as modern shopping malls or department stores. Several notable differences exist between peasant markets and the markets with which people of urbanized, industrialized societies are familiar. First, the categories of products sold at the marketplace are limited, and in fact, most people produce most of their own subsistence using family labor. Most people do not acquire their livelihood from selling their labor for a wage. Rather, they rely on the marketplace for only certain kinds of products that they cannot produce for themselves efficiently. Most people are not making their living by selling something (objects, labor) on the market.

Second, producing and marketing goods for monetary profit are part-time activities for many vendors. Many marketplaces are staffed mainly by peasants, who sell small quantities of food, pottery, furniture, fibers, crafts, or other objects they have produced with family labor. Indeed, marketplaces frequently are periodic, meaning that they do not open every day, but only for a day or two a week. Peasant vendors sell their products on whatever days the market is open in their region. Traveling merchants typically visit several markets in different regions in a single week, often buying products for sale at one market and reselling them at a distant market a day or two later.

Third, peasant vendors usually sell products that they or their family members, rather than hired laborers, produce. This means that the kinds and quantities of goods offered for sale by any single vendor usually are small. Most marketplaces also feature products sold by people who specialize in buying them wholesale and selling them retail. Such people are dependent on the market—with all its insecurities and risks—for their livelihood. They therefore have developed various strategies to reduce the risks they face. We conclude this section by considering some of these strategies.

When we who live in a market economy visit a marketplace—a store or car lot, for instance—we normally buy goods from strangers. We do not expect any special treatment. We pay the same price as everyone else. If we need credit, we expect to pay the market rate of interest. We expect sellers to be looking out for themselves, just as sellers expect us to be trying to get the most for our money. This characteristic of our market exchanges is referred to as the "impersonality of the marketplace." This impersonality is expressed nicely by the old saying that "one person's money is as green as anyone else's."

In marketplaces in the small towns and villages of peasant communities, vendors sometimes develop more personal and intimate relationships with some of their customers. For example, in a Philippine marketplace studied by William Davis, vendors establish relationships called *suki* with "special customers," people who regularly buy their wares. The sellers' goal is to reduce their risks by gradually building up a steady, large clientele of customers, rather than by squeezing all the money they can out of each individual transaction. From the *suki,* the customer receives credit, favorable prices, extra quantities of goods at a given price, the best quality of goods the *suki* partner has to offer on a particular day, and certain services. The vendor benefits as well: Their *suki* are expected not to buy from any other suppliers of the goods they carry. This is helpful in calculating the quantities of goods they will be able to sell and, hence, helps prevent them from overstocking their stalls.

As *suki* in this Philippine marketplace illustrates, the impersonality of the marketplace can be modified by the

In peasant marketplaces like this one in Guatemala, many sellers produce or manufacture their wares themselves, and most buyers do not rely on market purchases for all their material needs.

formation of personal ties between buyers and sellers. Supply and demand operate to affect prices, yet people may recognize that charging as much as the market will bear on any given day is not necessarily in their long-term interest. This is not surprising in communities in which most people know most other people. Those who have things to sell often are selling them to people whom they know in other, nonmarket and noneconomic, contexts.

Summary

This chapter covers exchange, or the patterned ways in which products are transferred between the time they are produced and the time they are consumed. Economic anthropologists find it convenient to classify the variety of exchanges that exist in human economies into three major modes, or types: reciprocity, redistribution, and market.

Reciprocity is the giving and receiving of objects without the transfer of money. Generalized reciprocity usually occurs between parties who are normatively obliged to assist one another in times of need, as among relatives and sometimes close friends. With balanced reciprocity, a return of an object of equivalent value is expected within a reasonable time. The goal of balanced reciprocity may be the acquisition of goods for their utility, as in the Trobriand *wasi*. More often it is motivated by the desire to create or sustain good relations between individuals (as in gift giving) or political alliances between groups (as with the Maring pig feast). Negative reciprocity is characterized by the desire of both parties to acquire as many goods as possible while giving up as few as possible, as in barter.

The variety of reciprocity that is likely to characterize transactions between individuals and groups depends on the normative degree of social distance between them. This implies that exchange relations alter if social relationships change. Conversely, one party can initiate an attempt to alter a relationship by an offer of a good, and the other party can signal acceptance or rejection by his or her response. Therefore, varying the type of reciprocity can be used to draw people closer together or to push them further apart. In effect, a reciprocal exchange of goods (and, for that matter, services) can also serve as an exchange of messages about feelings and relationships.

In redistribution, the members of a group contribute goods or money into a pool or fund, and a central authority reallocates or uses them for public purposes. Taxes in modern nations and tribute in chiefdoms are examples. Normatively, redistribution is supposed to provide resources to increase public welfare, either to provide public goods or to support those in need. In fact, there is much conflict over collection and allocation, and those officials who do the collecting and allocating frequently use their authority for their private ambition rather than the public interest.

Market exchange involves the buying and selling of goods; it therefore requires money and prices determined by supply and demand. Money makes the exchange of goods and services more convenient, but it also facilitates the making of profit and the accumulation of wealth. Money functions as a medium of exchange, a standard of value, and a store of value. These functions mean that money objects must be durable, and their supply must be limited or controlled in some way. The range of goods and services that can be bought with money varies between economies. Money types can be characterized as multipurpose (like modern currencies) or limited purpose (like Tiv metal rods).

The affluent citizens of most modern urbanized, industrialized countries make their living by selling their labor on the market and purchasing commodities at stores and other retail establishments. Rural peasants of many countries are not so reliant on markets, for they produce most of their food themselves and shop at local marketplaces for only some of their needs and wants. In peasant marketplaces, most vendors are small-scale and part-time. In many regions they develop special relationships with sellers to reduce their risks, as illustrated by *suki* in the Philippines.

Key Terms

reciprocity
redistribution

market
generalized reciprocity
balanced reciprocity
negative reciprocity
social distance

tribute
multipurpose money
limited-purpose money

Suggested Readings

Belshaw, Cyril S. *Traditional Exchange and Modern Markets.* Englewood Cliffs, N.J.: Prentice-Hall, 1965.
• *A good, short introduction to exchange systems.*

Davis, William G. *Social Relations in a Philippine Market.* Berkeley: University of California Press, 1973.
• *An empirical study of a marketplace in a Philippine town, emphasizing market relationships.*

Douglas, Mary, and Baron Isherwood. *The World of Goods: Toward an Anthropology of Consumption.* New York: W. W. Norton, 1979.
• *An examination of cultural theories of consumption.*

Neale, Walter C. *Monies in Societies.* San Francisco: Chandler and Sharp, 1976.
• *A brief book about the uses, forms, and functions of money in a variety of economies.*

Plattner, Stuart, ed. *Economic Anthropology.* Stanford: Stanford University Press, 1989.
• *A collection of recent articles on economic systems.*

Rubel, Paula G., and Abraham Rosman. *Your Own Pigs You May Not Eat.* Chicago: University of Chicago Press, 1978.
• *Based on existing ethnographic accounts of numerous societies in Papua New Guinea, this comparative study analyzes the symbolic nature of exchange relations.*

Rutz, Henry J., and Benjamin S. Orlove, eds. *The Social Economy of Consumption.* New York: University Press of America, 1989.
• *A collection of articles focusing on consumption in various regions of the world.*

Sahlins, Marshall. *Stone Age Economics.* New York: Aldine, 1972.
• *Deals with the organization of production and modes of exchange in preindustrial economies.*

Wilk, Richard R. *Economies & Cultures: Foundations of Economic Anthropology.* Boulder: Westview Press, 1996.
• *A readable and thoughtful overview of the field of economic anthropology, focusing on major issues and debates.*

Internet Exercises

The website of The Society for Economic Anthropology (http://www.agnesscott.edu/aca/depts_prog/ info/poli_sci_soc_anthro/rees/sea/index.html) provides information about the society plus a collection of papers in economic anthropology. Be sure to use this address when looking for this site. Because the site has been moved and the server has been changed, several searches for this site were unsuccessful. Web search engines are not perfect—if at first you do not find what you are looking for, try another method.

The web can supplement your school's library as a source of data for your own research papers. As an example, searching the web for more information on economic anthropology came up with an article "Two (substantial) Cheers for Diversity: An Unfinished Intellectual History of Anthropological Economics" (http://ws.csun.edu/~ms44278/polyanyi.htm) by Mike Shupp. This article provides a good background to different approaches to economic anthropology and their proponents. Another article found on the Internet is "Social Exchange" by Peter Blau (http://wizard.ucr.edu/~bkaplan/soc/lib/bluaexch.html). A search on InfoTrac College Edition came up with an article in the *Annual Review of Sociology,* "Social Capital: Its Origins and Applications in Modern Sociology" by Alejandro Portes. These two articles provide a framework with which to build a paper. After learning which scholars address the issues that concern your topic, you can then use the bibliographies to find more material.

C H A P T E R *8*

Contents

Some Definitions

Marriage

Functions of Marriage

Nayar "Marriage"

Marriage in Comparative Perspective

Marriage Rules

How Many Spouses?

Marriage Alliances

Marital Exchanges

Kinship Diagrams

Postmarital Residence Patterns

Family and Household Forms

Marriage, Family, and Residence

Among the many functions of families is the nurturing and enculturation of children. The form and substance of family life varies significantly between cultures.
Visit http://www.wadsworth.com/humanity to learn more about the material covered in this chapter and to access activities, exercises, and tutorial quizzes.

W *HEN NORTH AMERICAN politicians proclaim solemnly that "the family is the backbone of our nation," and that their own beliefs and policies promote "family values," they can hardly go wrong. After all, how many voters see themselves as "antifamily"? Likewise, when studies show that American divorce rates hover around 50 percent and that around 30 percent of American children live in households with only one parent present, we believe that something is amiss.*

CERTAINLY, THERE IS NO DENYING *that the bonds of marriage and family are among the central social relationships of most societies. For one thing, a married couple, aided by some kind of extended family, is usually the social group that nourishes and enculturates new generations. For another, families are the basis of residential groups that not only live together but often own property together, play together, work together, and worship together. Families, we recognize, do a lot of things that are quite helpful to their members and to society at large. When too many marriages and families break down, we think a lot of harm is done to children, communities, and the whole nation.*

IN THIS CHAPTER, *we look at some of the main ways in which cultures differ in their marriage practices and in the organization of their families and households. Because in most cultures it is the marriage relationship that creates new nuclear families and that begets, nourishes, and teaches children, we begin with it. Before doing so, though, we need to define some terms that will be used in the next couple of chapters.*

Some Definitions

Reproduction is the basis of family relationships. Biologically speaking, your relatives are your relatives because they were the relatives of your parents: Your grandparents are your parents' parents, your aunts are your parents' sisters, and so forth. These kinship relationships can, in theory, serve as the basis for forming all kinds of groups: You and all your first cousins could form a group, for example, if you ever needed to cooperate in some activity. All societies do, in fact, use kinship relationships as the basis for group formation. In many societies the most important groups are defined by kinship ties. When people form a cooperative group based on their kinship relationships, anthropologists call the group a **kin group**. A North American family is a kind—but only one kind—of kin group: The members live together, share the use of property, rely on one another for emotional support, pool their labor and resources to support the family, and so on. A family is an example of a **domestic group**, a term that refers to the group of individuals who live together in a single household. Domestic groups may be very small (e.g., a parent and her/his children) or quite large (e.g., a set of siblings and all their children).

Anthropologists use the term **consanguines** to refer to "blood" relatives—people related by birth. We use the term **affines** to refer to "in-laws"—people related by marriage. So a person's *consanguineal relatives* are all of her or his blood relatives, and one's *affinal relatives* are all of one's relatives by marriage. Your parents, siblings, grandparents, parents' siblings, and cousins are examples of your consanguines. Your sister's husband, wife's mother, and father's sister's husband are some of your affines. Note that affinal relationships are always created by marriage; for instance, a woman is an affine to you because one of your consanguines married her or one of her blood relatives.

Societies everywhere have domestic groups and kin groups, and all peoples distinguish between consanguineal and affinal relatives. But the nature of these groups and relations between kin are highly variable cross-culturally. In North America and most other highly industrialized, urbanized societies, the most important domestic unit is made up of a married couple and any unmarried children they may have. We call this the **nuclear family**, and this kind of group is what Canadians and Americans ordinarily mean when they say "my family."

Like people everywhere, North Americans keep track of—and usually have social relationships with—more distant relatives who are part of our **extended family**. Cousins of various degrees, aunts and uncles, and other distant relatives may get together in large numbers for family reunions, weddings, funerals, and other such events. But by and large, middle class people do not rely on extended family members for access to resources or emotional support. In other societies, however, extended families and even larger groupings of relatives are far more important in the lives of individuals: You may live in the same household with them, you can count on them for economic support, you share access to land and other property with them, you and they have common ritual duties, and so forth. In such societies, nuclear families are important, but they are embedded in larger, more inclusive kinds of kin groups. Some of these kin groups are enormously large, consisting of hundreds of members. We discuss these large groups in Chapter 9. In this chapter, we focus on domestic groups.

Marriage

If pressed for a definition of marriage, a North American might say that:

> Marriage is a relationship between a woman and a man involving romantic love, sex, cohabitation, reproduction and childrearing, and the sharing of the joys and burdens of life.

Western assumptions about marriage may not apply to other cultural traditions. In this Taiwanese wedding procession, the bride is being ceremonially taken to her husband's home.

People trained in law might also note that marriage has legal aspects, such as joint property rights. Religious people may want to include their beliefs that marriage is a relationship sanctioned by God, a relationship that should last until the parties are separated by death.

This definition works well in North America, but it is not broad enough to include all the diversity in the marital relationship that anthropologists have uncovered. For example, we think of marriage as a *private* matter between a man and a woman, although we usually seek the "blessing" of our parents and other relatives before the wedding. In many cultures, marriage is much more likely to be a *public* matter that concerns a broad range of relatives who must consent to—and often even arrange—the marriage of a couple. Also, cohabitation in the same house is by no means universal: In many villages in Melanesia, Southeast Asia, and Africa, the men sleep and spend much of their time in a communal house (called, appropriately, the *men's house*), whereas their wives and young children live and sleep in a separate dwelling.

Similarly, as often as not romantic love between the couple is not considered necessary for marriage, and sometimes it is not even very relevant to the relationship. Couples do not marry because they "fall in love." For example, in traditional China and Japan a man and woman seldom had a chance to fall in love before they married because they usually hardly knew each other and often had not even met. Sometimes boys and girls were betrothed at birth or as children. In both Japan and China, even when couples were married as adults, the marriage was arranged by their parents with the aid of a matchmaker, usually a female relative of the groom's family or a woman hired by them. She tried to find a woman of suitable age, wealth, status, and disposition who would become a wife for the young man. The matchmaker would "match" not only the couple to each other, but also the woman to the husband's parents. Once she married, the wife would be incorporated into her husband's family; her labor would be very much under the control of her husband's parents, especially her mother-in-law; she would worship the ancestors of her husband's family, not those of her own parents; her behavior would be closely watched lest she disgrace her in-laws; and her children would become members of her husband's kin group, not her own.

The same ideas apply to most other Western cultural notions of and customs about marriage: Many things we consider normal to the marital relation are not practiced among other peoples. Sex is not always confined to the marriage bed (or mat). There may or may not be a formal ceremony (wedding) recognizing or validating a new marriage. The marital tie may be fragile or temporary, with individuals expecting to have several spouses during the course of their lives. Or the tie may be so strong that even death does not end it. In much of traditional India there used to be strict rules against the remarriage of a higher-caste widow, and such a widow often followed her husband to the grave by throwing herself onto his cremation fire (a practice now illegal in India). There are culturally legitimate marital relationships that are not between a man and a woman: Among the Nuer of the southern Sudan, sometimes an older, well-off woman pays the bridewealth needed to marry a girl; the girl takes male lovers and bears children, who are incorporated into the kin group of the older woman.

Formulating a definition of marriage that encompasses all the cross-cultural variations in the relationship is, then, a difficult task, for somewhere there will be a society that does not fit the definition. As you can imagine, numerous definitions have been offered, but there is still no agreement on the "best" one. Most anthropologists agree, however, that marriage ordinarily involves

- a culturally defined relationship between a man and woman from different families, which regulates sexual intercourse and provides for reproduction;
- a set of rights the couple and their families obtain over each other, including rights over the couple's children;
- an assignment of responsibility for enculturation to the spouses or to one or both sets of their relatives; and
- a division of labor in the domestic group.

Functions of Marriage

This conception of marriage is useful because it emphasizes the functions that marriage performs in almost all communities. Three functions are among the most important:

First, marriage forms the social bonds and creates the social relationships that provide for the material needs, social support, and enculturation of children. The creation of a (variably) stable bond between a woman and her husband is recognized in most cultures as one reason for marriage. In the human case, the tie between mothers and fathers is more important than in most other animals because of the lengthy dependence of children on adults. Until they reach ten or more years of age, human children are totally or largely dependent on adults for food, shelter, protection, and other bodily needs. Equally important, they require the presence of adults for the social learning crucial to complete their psychological and cultural development (see Chapter 2). It is theoretically possible that only one adult, the mother, is required; but almost everywhere, marriage helps to create and expand the relationships through which children receive the material support and enculturation necessary for their immediate survival, future maturity, and eventual reproduction.

Second, marriage defines the rights and obligations the couple have toward one another and toward other people. Some rights and obligations, of course, concern sex. The marriage bond reduces (but does not eliminate) potential conflicts over sexual access, by defining and limiting adult sexual access to certain individuals (normatively or legally, at any rate). Extramarital sex is not, of course, prohibited to the same degree in all cultures, but there are always limitations placed on it, and usually it is punished formally or informally. Other rights and duties concern the allocation of work and other activities. All cultures divide up work by sex and age in some way (Chapter 10 discusses the sexual division of labor): Men do some kinds of tasks, women other kinds. Although the work usually overlaps, there is enough differentiation in most communities that the products and services produced by women must somehow be made available to men, and vice versa. Marriage helps to define these rights and duties ("a good husband should . . .") and establishes the household within which family members do things for one another.

Third, marriage creates new relationships between families and other kinds of kin groups. In a few societies nuclear families are able to produce what they need to survive more or less by themselves. But in no society are the members of the same nuclear family allowed to have sex, marry, and produce children. Sexual relations between parents and children and between sisters and brothers are defined as incestuous and are prohibited normatively or legally. Violators of this prohibition—known as the **incest taboo**—usually are punished, often severely and sometimes by death. Except in a very few cultures in which members of royal families had sexual relations to produce an heir of highest possible rank, the incest taboo applies to members of one's own nuclear family. It usually is further extended to prohibit sex between some cousins, uncles and nieces, aunts and nephews, and other relatives that a culture defines as close. The near universal prohibition on sexual activity with close family members forces individuals to marry someone other than their immediate relatives. Every such marriage creates a potential new (affinal) relationship between the relatives of the couple. The importance attached to these affinal relationships varies cross-culturally. At the very least, the families of the wife and husband will have an interest in the children. In addition, a great many societies use the relationships created by intermarriage to establish important trade relationships or political alliances, as we will see later in this chapter.

Because marriage—and the new nuclear family each marriage creates—is useful to individuals and to societies in these and other ways, a relationship like marriage and a group like the family are nearly universal among the world's cultures. However, no particular *form* of marriage or *type* of family is universal. Cultures evolved various marriage and family systems to perform these functions. To show how diverse these systems can be, we now consider one of the most unusual (and now extinct) systems, that of the Nayar of southern India.

Nayar "Marriage"

Before Great Britain assumed colonial control over part of India in 1792, the Nayar were a caste (see Chapter 12) whose men specialized in warfare. A great many Nayar men were away from their villages much of the time because as a warrior caste, they served as soldiers for several surrounding kingdoms and in other parts of India. Nayar women were required to confine their sexual activity to men of their own or a higher subcaste. They suffered severe penalties—death or ostracism—if they violated this norm. The fascinating thing about the Nayar is that they almost certainly lacked nuclear families and—by the conception of marriage just described—lacked marriage as well. What alternative system did they use?

Nayar villages were composed of a number of kin groups. Children joined the kin group of their mothers. Each group was linked for certain ceremonial purposes to several other groups: some from its own village, others from neighboring villages. Any Nayar found to be having sexual relations with anyone in his or her own kin group was put to death because intragroup intercourse was regarded as incestuous. Every few years, all the girls of a given group who had not yet attained puberty gathered for a large ceremony. This ceremony was attended also by people from the linked kin groups, for the purpose of the event was to ceremonially "marry" these girls to selected men from the linked kin groups (whether these really deserve to be called "marriages" depends, as you will see, on how we define the term). At the ceremony, each "groom" tied a gold ornament around the neck of his "bride," and each couple retired to a secluded place for three days, where they may have had sexual relations if the girl was nearing puberty. After this period all the "grooms" left the village, and each had no further responsibilities to his "bride"; indeed, he might never even see her again. For her part, the "bride" and the children she would later bear had only to perform a certain ritual for her "husband" when he died. The ritual tying of the ornament by a man of a linked kin group did, however, establish a girl as an adult, able to have sexual liaisons with other men when she reached sexual maturity.

Human children are dependent on adult care for many years, as this photo of a Laotian woman and her children reminds us. Providing for the physical and emotional needs of children is everywhere a major function of families.

After her "marriage," each girl continued to live with her own kin group. When she reached sexual maturity, she began to receive nighttime male visitors from other kin groups. She established long-lasting sexual relations with some of her partners, who were expected to give her small luxury gifts periodically. None of her partners supported her or her children in any way other than these occasional gifts; indeed, they also visited other women and fathered other children. The food and clothing of a woman and her children were supplied by her brothers and other members of her kin group, who were also responsible for disciplining and providing an inheritance for her children. A woman's early "marriage," then, did not establish a nuclear family, nor did her later sexual partners live with her or support her children. There was only one other thing a Nayar woman required from her partners: When she became pregnant, one of them had to admit that he could have been the father of her child by paying the fees for the midwife who helped to deliver the baby. If none of her partners did so, it was assumed that she had had sexual intercourse with someone of a lower caste, and she, and sometimes her child, would be expelled from her kin group or killed.

We see that a Nayar girl's early prepuberty "marriage" ceremonially marked her entry into adulthood; only after she had been "married" to someone of a linked kin group should she begin (legitimately) to engage in sex. Later, when she bore a child, the infant was believed to be the product of a legitimate union if one of its mother's partners paid the birth fees. Her child then became a member of the kin group of herself, her sisters, and her brothers, who gave the child material and social support. No nuclear families existed, and in fact the Nayar had no marriage as the term is used in this book.

Marriage in Comparative Perspective

The relationship we call marriage varies enormously cross-culturally. For one thing, most cultures allow multiple spouses. For another, the nature of the marital relationship—living arrangements, what wives and husbands expect from each other, who decides who marries whom, authority patterns, how the relatives of the couple relate to one another, and so forth—differs from people to people. Some of this diversity is described in this section.

Marriage Rules

Everywhere, the choice of a spouse is governed by norms that identify members of some social groups or categories as potential spouses and specify members of other groups or categories as not eligible for marriage. One set of rules is called **exogamous rules**. Exogamy ("outmarriage") means that an individual is prohibited from marrying within her or his own family or other kin group or, less often, village or settlement. Because the incest taboo applies to those people whom the local culture defines as close relatives, members of one's own nuclear family and other close kin are almost everywhere prohibited as spouses. (Note, incidentally, that the incest taboo prohibits *sex,* whereas rules of exogamy forbid *intermarriage*.)

Other kinds of marriage rules are known as **endogamous rules**. Endogamy ("inmarriage") means that an individual must marry someone in his or her own social group. The classic example of endogamous groups is the caste in traditional Hindu India (see Chapter 12). Other kinds of endogamous categories are orthodox Jews, races in the American South during slavery and, more recently, in South Africa, and noble classes in many ancient civilizations and states.

The purpose of endogamous rules most often is to maintain social barriers between groups of people of different social rank. Rules of endogamy maintain the exclusiveness of the endogamous group in two ways. First, they reduce the social contacts and interactions between individuals of different ranks. Intermarriage creates new relationships between the families of the wife and husband and potentially is a means of raising the rank of oneself or one's offspring. Endogamy has the effect of keeping affinal relationships within the caste, class, ethnic group, race, or whatever; this reinforces ties *within* the endogamous groups and decreases interactions *between* the groups. Second, endogamy symbolically expresses and strengthens the exclusiveness of the endogamous group by preventing its "contamination" by outsiders. This is most apparent with Indian castes because the cultural rationale for caste endogamy is to avoid ritual pollution: The Hindu religion holds that physical contact with members of lower castes places high-caste individuals in a state of spiritual danger, precluding the possibility of marriage between them.

Technically, the term *endogamy* applies only to cultural rules (or even laws) about confining marriage to those within one's own group. But it is important to note the existence of de facto endogamy, meaning that although no formal rules or laws prohibit outmarriage, most people marry those they consider to be like themselves. De facto racial and social class endogamy exists in most modern nations, including North America. This is partly because opportunities for members of different classes to get to know one another often are limited. For instance, members of different classes often go to different kinds of schools and hang out with different sets of friends. Such practices decrease social interactions between classes. Hence, they reduce the possibilities for people of different classes to meet

and fall in love. De facto endogamy also exists because of powerful norms against marrying outside one's own "kind." Members of elite classes (and parents and other relatives of young people) may worry that would-be spouses of lower-class standing would not fit in with their social circle (to put their objection politely). Likewise, interracial couples are warned about the social stigma attached to their relationship and about the "problems" they and their children will encounter—problems that exist largely because many people think interracial marriages are themselves problematic!

How Many Spouses?

One way cultures vary in marriage practices is in the number of spouses an individual is allowed to have at a time. There are four logical possibilities:

- **Monogamy**, in which every individual is allowed only one spouse.
- **Polygyny**, in which one man is allowed multiple wives.
- **Polyandry**, in which one woman is allowed multiple husbands.
- **Group marriage**, in which several women and men are allowed to be married simultaneously to one another.

The last three possibilities are all varieties of **polygamy**—meaning "plural spouses." Notice that the three types of polygamy refer to the number of spouses *allowed* to a person, not necessarily to how many spouses most people have. For example, in polygynous cultures, men are permitted more than one wife, but only a minority of men actually have more than one.

It may surprise members of monogamous societies to learn that most of the world's cultures historically allowed polygamy. The most common form of plural marriage is polygyny, which is allowed in most societies of the world. Polyandry, on the other hand, is rare. There are less than a dozen societies in which it is documented—less than 1 percent of the world's cultures. Group marriage, so far as we know, has never been a characteristic form of marriage of a whole human society. Indeed, most anthropologists believe that group marriage, where it has occurred, has been a short-lived phenomenon brought about by highly unusual circumstances. ("A Closer Look" examines one well-documented case of group marriage.)

Comparisons of frequencies such as those just mentioned pose difficulties in assigning a particular people unambiguously to one of these four categories. (To appreciate this problem, answer the following question: Did the Nayar have polyandry, group marriage, or no marriage at all?) But they do give an accurate impression of how common or rare each form of marriage is in the human species.

Many Westerners misunderstand the nature of polygamous marriages, seeing them mainly as attempts, usually by men, to get access to more sexual partners. We fail to recognize the social and economic conditions that make these forms of marriage advantageous. We now look at these conditions for polygynous and polyandrous societies.

Polygyny Even though most cultures allow polygynous marriage, only a minority of men in these societies actually have more than one wife. Thus, polygyny exists as an alternative form of marriage, rather than as the predominant (most common) form. But in those societies that allow it, polygyny ordinarily is the preferred form of marriage. Men, in particular, desire to have multiple spouses, although most men are unable to achieve their goal.

Even with only a minority of men married polygynously, an obvious problem exists for some other men: If some men have two or more wives, this reduces the number of marriageable women so that some men cannot marry. This is in fact often the case. But in other cases this problem is not as acute as one might think, because in many populations there are more marriageable women than men at any one time. One reason is that in some cultures more males than females die prematurely because they engage in hazardous activities, such as warfare and hunting. Higher male death rates increase the number of men who are able to find wives, even though some men are polygynous.

Looked at from the female perspective, polygyny may have the beneficial effect of assuring that virtually all women find husbands. This is important for a woman's welfare because marriage legitimizes her children, and in many cultures children are her main or only source of social security—they are the people she depends on to support her in old age. There is another reason why a woman wants to marry in polygynous societies: to ensure that her children are well provided for. In the majority of polygynous societies, inheritance of land, livestock, and other wealth and productive property passes from fathers to sons. A woman need not marry to bear children, but she does want a husband to assure that her sons have an adequate inheritance; her married daughters usually acquire their rights to resources from their husbands. Thus, in societies in which for some reason there are more adult women than men, polygyny provides a means for almost all women to gain the benefits of husbands for both themselves and their children.

For their part, most men prefer to have two or more wives. Men usually have both social and economic incentives for marrying several women. Socially, a man's status commonly is directly related to the size of his family and, hence, to the number of his wives and children. Also, when a man marries more than one woman, he acquires a new set of affines—fathers- and brothers-in-law whom he can call on for support, trade, or political alliances. Economically, there are also short- and long-term benefits, especially in horticultural and pastoral adaptations where a woman's labor is important in providing food and wealth to her family. The more wives and children a man has, the larger the work force available to his household. In pastoral societies in Africa and elsewhere, polygyny enables a man to increase the size of his herds, since he has more herders (wives and children) to tend livestock. Similarly, in those farming societies in which female labor is important, a polygynous man has more family members to tend fields and harvest crops. As he grows older he will have more children and grandchildren to look after his herds or work his fields and care for him. Thus, as long as he has the resources to support them, a man usually tries to acquire additional wives.

What determines whether a particular man is *able* to acquire more than one wife? The answer usually is wealth: Only well-to-do men are able to afford more than one wife. "Afford," however, does not mean what North Americans might think; it is often more a matter of being able to acquire additional wives than of being able to support them. Most polygynous peoples have the custom of bridewealth (discussed later), which requires a prospective groom and

Polygyny is a permitted form of marriage in most of the world's societies. This photo shows a Bedouin man with his two wives and children, together with the wife of his brother.

Group Marriage in the United States

Most Canadians and Americans know about the communes popular with many young people in the 1960s and 1970s, which practiced free love and renounced personal property. Whether these communes represent cases of group marriage is debatable, because there are questions about whether "love" was quite as "free" in them as usually depicted. At any rate, most lasted only a few years. No doubt, many of their former members are now monogamous stock brokers and attorneys.

So "hippie" communes may or may not represent group marriage, depending on how strictly we define the term. But there is at least one well-documented case of group marriage in the United States. It occurred in an unexpected time—the nineteenth century—and among an unexpected subculture—conservative Christians.

Mainstream Christians of this time stressed premarital chastity and marital fidelity. Ever since the Reformation, however, Christian sects have sprung up that draw important elements of their doctrine from small passages of Scripture. One such passage is from Acts 4:

> [2]The host of believers were one in heart and soul; no one claimed his belongings just for himself, but everything was theirs in common. . . . [4]Not one among them suffered need; for those who owned fields of houses sold them, brought the proceeds of the sale[5] and deposited the money at the feet of the apostles. Then it was distributed to each according to his need.

This passage served as the basis of a radical utopian experiment in Oneida,

New York, initiated in 1847 by a theologian named John Humphrey Noyes. Noyes believed—not unreasonably—that the preceding scripture exhorted believers to hold property in common. He attracted some converts and founded a community based on his beliefs.

But he took the exhortation one step further. Not only were Noyes's followers required to sign over their worldly goods to the community, to eat together, to live in a single enormous house (still standing), and to work together like a giant family; "private property" in marriage and sexual matters was also forbidden. All men and women were to consider themselves husbands and wives and were allowed sexual access to one another. The tricky part was that during the first twenty years of the community, the men were not supposed to ejaculate because no children were allowed to be born, and Noyes believed that the spilling of semen was debilitating to male strength. But Noyes did make one concession to human frailty: He required young men to sleep only with postmenopausal women until they learned to control themselves. Astoundingly, in a community of around 500, only two children were born between 1848 and 1868!

The sexual aspects of group marriage in the Oneida community apparently worked as follows. A committee (no doubt under the control of Noyes, who was something of an autocrat) had the final word over who spent the night with whom. A man who wanted to sleep with a particular woman submitted a written request to the committee, who

sought the consent of the woman. The woman could refuse permission, or the committee itself could deny the request on the grounds that this man and woman were showing too much "special love" for one another rather than loving all community members equally. This rather unusual arrangement was a bit titillating to outsiders, and the community supplemented the income that it got mainly through the manufacture of steel traps by selling lunches to thrill-seekers who came up from New York City to see the community.

After 1868 children were allowed, but not just anyone could have them. Noyes thought that only the worthiest and most mentally and physically fit members should be allowed to reproduce. He set up another committee to which members could apply for a child-bearing permit. Thirty-eight men and fifty-three women were selected as parents, and they had about sixty children. Children knew their parents and had some special contact with them, but they were raised in a communal nursery; and all adults were supposed to love and nurture the children as if they were their own.

The Oneida community disbanded as such in 1879, largely because of internal discord and resentment caused by the elderly Noyes's attempt to monopolize the young women. But many former members continued to live nearby and formed a successful company, also known as Oneida. Perhaps you have some of their silverware.

Sources: Van den Berghe (1979), Whitworth (1975).

his relatives to give livestock, money, or other wealth objects to the kin of the bride. Although fathers and other relatives typically are obliged to help a young man raise bridewealth for one wife, only a minority of men can get together sufficient resources to provide bridewealth for additional wives.

There may be social and economic advantages for the co-wives of a polygynous man. Many North Americans think that no woman would want to be part of a "harem." But the most prestigious marriages for a woman are to husbands of wealth and status—the very men who are most likely to have married other women. Not only will the woman herself be better provided for, but her children may also receive larger inheritances of land, livestock, wealth, or other property. In addition, co-wives may lighten a woman's workload. Co-wives usually work together and cooperate on chores such as producing, processing, and preparing food; tending livestock; and caring for children. Thus, it is not unusual for a wife to encourage her husband to take additional wives to assist her in her chores.

Although they have advantages for both men and women, polygynous marriages also have inherent problems. A frequent problem is rivalry between co-wives and favoritism by husbands. Several strategies are used in polygynous societies to minimize friction within these families. One way is for a man to marry women who are sisters, a culturally widespread practice known as *sororal polygyny*. The rationale for sororal polygyny most often is that sisters are raised together, are used to working together, have preexisting emotional bonds, and are likely to be less jealous of one another. Sisters are, therefore, likely to be more compatible than unrelated wives. In most cultures in which a man marries a number of women who are unrelated, each wife usually has her own separate dwelling, which helps to minimize conflict with her co-wives. Also, co-wives usually are allocated different livestock to care for, and/or they will have separate gardens to tend and harvest. The effect of such practices is that each wife, together with her children, is semi-independent from the other wives. Despite such practices, rivalry and jealousy among co-wives is a problem in many polygynous marriages.

Polyandry Polyandry, the marriage of one woman simultaneously to two or more men, is a documented practice in only about a dozen societies. Much has been written about this unusual form of marriage, but ethnologists have not yet satisfactorily explained it. Some believe that female infanticide is partly responsible, arguing that the death of large numbers of girls would produce a shortage of adult women, which would lead several men to be willing to share a wife. All else being equal, female infanticide does indeed have the effect of decreasing the number of marriageable women, but far more human groups allow many of their female infants to die than practice polyandry. Female infanticide is not a *general* explanation for polyandry.

Rather than searching for such a general explanation, we begin by noting that wherever polyandry exists, it does so as an alternative form of marriage. Like polygyny, polyandry is *allowed*, but it is not the *predominant* form of marriage; most couples are monogamous even where polyandry is allowed. Therefore, to understand the reasons for polyandry, we indicate some of the special conditions that lead some people (namely, husbands and their joint wife) to choose to join in a polyandrous marriage.

The insufficiency of a family's land to support all of its heirs is one such condition. Many families in farming communities have faced the following dilemma: Our land is barely adequate, and all available farmland is already owned by another family or by a landlord, so we cannot provide all our children with enough land to support them and their families. Many European peasants faced this problem during the Middle Ages and even into the nineteenth century. In Ireland and some other parts of Europe, one solution was *primogeniture*, under which the oldest son inherited the farm and most of its property and the younger sons had to find other ways of supporting themselves. Younger sons served in the army or became priests or found some other occupation. Daughters who did not marry usually either remained at home or joined a nunnery. After the Industrial Revolution in the late 1700s, many migrated to cities and went to work in factories.

Some peoples of the Himalayas developed another solution—polyandry. The rugged topography and high altitude of Tibet and Nepal sharply limit the supply of farmland. A farm may be adequate to support only a single family, but a couple may have three or more sons. If the sons divide their inheritance by each taking his own wife, the land would become so fragmented that the brothers' families would be impoverished. To solve this problem, sometimes all the sons marry one woman. This form of polyandry, called *fraternal polyandry*, helps to keep the farm and family intact and limits the number of children in the family. Although the oldest son usually assumes primary responsibility for the wife and children, he is not supposed to be shown sexual favoritism by the wife, who has sexual relations with all her husbands. When children are born, ideally each brother treats them as if they were his own, even if he knows that a particular child was fathered by one of his brothers. To the brothers, the advantage is that polyandry preserves the family property, keeping the land, the livestock, the house, and other wealth together. Also, one brother can stay in the village and work the family land during the summer, while another brother takes the livestock to high mountain pastures and a third brother (if present) visits town in the lowlands to sell the family's products. This system also has advantages for the wife, who has multiple husbands to work for and help support her and her children. Her life usually is less physically strenuous and she usually has a higher standard of living than a woman married to only one man.

Although Himalayan polyandry has economic advantages, sometimes problems arise. A younger brother can at any time decide to end the arrangement, claim his portion of the family property, marry another woman, and estab-

Although rare compared to monogamy and polygyny, polyandry is a fairly common form of marriage in parts of the Himalayas. This is a wedding procession for a polyandrous marriage in Nepal.

lish his own family. The oldest brother does not have this option because as head of the family he bears primary responsibility for supporting their wife and children

Marriage Alliances

Cultures vary in the importance they attach to the bond between wives and husbands. In some, there is no formal wedding ceremony. Instead, a couple is recognized as "married" when they regularly live together and as "divorced" when one of them moves away (or gets thrown out!). Each partner retains her or his own separate property, so the separation or divorce is not very "messy." In the contemporary United States, the wedding ceremony is often a big and expensive affair, marriages are supposed to endure, and couples usually own houses, furniture, and other property jointly. Yet in the year 2000, about half of all new American marriages will end in divorce, many quite "messy" because of conflicts over property and custody of the children. For many Americans, monogamy is *serial monogamy*, meaning only one legal spouse at a time.

Many cultures consider the marital relationship to be far more serious. Some consider it to be so important that young people cannot be trusted to choose their spouses wisely. Marriage often establishes lasting social relation-

ships and bonds not just between the couple but also between their families and other relatives.

The affinal ties between kin groups created by the fact that one or more of their members are married to one another frequently are important not just socially but also economically, politically, and often, ritually. Marriage establishes an *alliance* between the members of two kin groups, and in many cultures **marriage alliances** are critical for the well-being and even survival of the inter-married groups. This appears to have been the case, for example, among the ancient Israelites because Moses says in Genesis (34:16): "Then we will give our daughters unto you, and we will take your daughters to us, and we will dwell with you, and we will become one people."

A good example of how intermarriage creates and maintains ties between kin groups comes from among the Yąnomamö, a horticultural and hunting tribe of the Amazon rain forest of South America. Every Yąnomamö village constantly was under threat of attack, so each had to be prepared to defend itself; likewise, the men of each village periodically went on raids intended to capture the women and resources of its enemies. It was, therefore, advantageous for villages to establish and maintain military alliances for mutual defense and offense, for the more men a village could mobilize as warriors, the more likely it was to be successful in conflicts. The smaller villages were in fact obliged to enter into military alliances or they soon would be victimized by their more numerous enemies. Having allies also was helpful in case of military defeat: A defeated group could take refuge with an allied village, whose members would feed and protect the refugees until they could establish producing gardens in a new location.

Marriage was a key strategy in creating and maintaining these alliances. When the men of a Yąnomamö village wanted to make an alliance with another village, they began by trading. For instance, one village might tell the other it needed clay pots and would be willing to trade its bows for them; or it might say that it needed hallucinogenic drugs used in shamanistic curing and would trade its hammocks for them. The people of each village were capable of making all these products for themselves, but no matter: Trade provided the excuse that villages used to visit one another to begin alliance formation. If no trouble broke out during the trading—for a Yąnomamö village did not even trust its long-time allies, much less its prospective allies—the relation might extend to mutual invitations to feasts. If the feasts did not turn violent, the men of the two villages would agree to give some of their "sisters" (female consanguines) to one another. This was considered the final stage of alliance formation; once the villages had exchanged women, the alliance was—by Yąnomamö standards—secure.

The Yąnomamö illustrate how intermarriage creates bonds and establishes important political relations between villages. In many cultures, these bonds and relations are important to families or entire settlements. If marriages are a means of establishing ties that are critical to a group's material well-being or survival, then the choice of which group to marry into may be too important to be left entirely up to the woman and man whose marriage creates the relationship. Older, wiser, and more responsible people should be making such critical decisions. This helps to explain one widespread custom—arranged marriages—that many Westerners view as an infringement on individual freedom.

The importance of the ties between kin groups created by intermarriage is also revealed by two other widespread customs. In one, called the **levirate**, if a woman's husband dies, she marries one of his close kinsmen (usually a brother). The relations between the intermarried kin groups are too valuable for a woman to be returned to her own family, because then she might marry into another kin group. Therefore, a male relative of her deceased husband takes his place. Because both her dead and her new husband belong to the same kin group, the affinal relationship remains intact. The converse custom, the **sororate**, also preserves the affinal ties between kin groups, even beyond the death of a spouse. With the sororate, if a woman dies, her kin group is obliged to replace her with another woman, for which no additional bridewealth need be transferred. The Zulu of southern Africa, as well as many other African peoples, practiced both the levirate and the sororate. In societies with these customs, marriages—and the affinal ties they create—endure even beyond death.

Marital Exchanges

In most cultures, the marriage of a man and a woman is accompanied by some kind of transfer of goods or services. These *marital exchanges* take numerous forms, including the North American custom of wedding showers and wedding gifts. In these, the presents given by relatives and friends supposedly help the newlyweds establish an independent household. We give things that are useful to the couple jointly, with food-preparation and other household utensils easily the most common type of gift. Many couples even register at stores so that their relatives and friends will provide the items they want.

From a cross-cultural perspective, the most unusual feature of North American marital exchange is that nothing is transferred between the relatives of the groom and bride: The couple treats the gifts as their private property. Like most of our other customs, this seems natural to us. Of course the gifts go to the couple—what else could happen to them?

Plenty else, as we shall see in a moment. For now, notice that the fact that the couple gets the gifts fits with several other features of Euro-American marriage. First, it usually is the bond through which new independent households are started, so the husband and wife "need their own stuff." If, in contrast, the newlyweds moved in with one of their relatives, they would not have as great a need for their own silverware, wine glasses, and other "stuff." Second, our marriage-gift customs fit with the importance our culture gives to the privacy of the marital relationship: It is a personal matter between the husband and wife, and their relatives should keep their noses out. If the in-laws like each other and socialize together, well and good, but our marriages generally do not create strong bonds between families of the bride and groom. (In fact, the two families often compete for the visits and attention of the couple and their offspring.) As we saw in Chapter 7, gifts make friends and vice versa; the fact that the affines do not exchange gifts with each other is a manifestation of the absence of a necessary relation between them after the wedding. If, in contrast, the marriage created an alliance between the two sets of relatives, some kind of an exchange would probably occur between them to symbolize and cement their new relations. Third, the gifts are presented to the couple, not to the husband or wife as individuals, and are considered to belong equally and jointly to both partners. But there are marriage systems in which the property of the wife is separate from that of her husband; if divorce should occur, there is no squabbling over who gets what.

With this background in mind, what kinds of marital exchanges occur in other cultures?

Bridewealth **Bridewealth** is the widespread custom that requires a man and his relatives to transfer wealth to the relatives of his bride. It is easily the most common of all marital exchanges, found in more than one-half the world's cultures. The term *bridewealth* is well chosen because the goods transferred usually are among the most valuable symbols of wealth in the local culture. In Sub-Saharan Africa, cattle and sometimes other livestock are the most common goods used for bridewealth. Peoples of the Pacific Islands and Southeast Asia usually give their bridewealth in pigs or shell money and ornaments.

One of the most common rights a man and his relatives acquire when they transfer bridewealth to his wife's family is rights over the woman's children. Reciprocally, one of a wife's most important obligations is to bear children for her husband. This is well exemplified by the Swazi, a traditional kingdom of southern Africa. A Swazi marriage is a union between two families as well as between the bride and groom. The payment of bridewealth—in cattle and other valuables—to a woman's relatives establishes the husband's rights over his wife. A woman's main duty to her husband is to provide him with children. If she is unable to do so, her relatives must either return the bridewealth they received for her or provide a second wife to the husband, for which he need pay no extra bridewealth. Reciprocally, a man must pay bridewealth to gain rights of fatherhood over the child of a woman, even though everyone knows he is the child's biological father. If he does not do so, the woman's relatives will keep the child; if the woman herself is later married to another man, her new husband will not receive rights over the child unless he pays bridewealth.

Brideservice   As the term implies, **brideservice** is the custom whereby a husband is required to spend a period of time working for the family of his bride. A Yąnomamö son-in-law is expected to live with his wife's parents, hunting and gardening for them until they finally release control over their daughter. Among some !Kung bands (Chapter 6), a man proves his ability as a provider by living with and hunting for his wife's parents for three to ten years, after which the couple is free to camp elsewhere.

Brideservice is the second most common form of marital exchange; it is the usual compensation given to the family of a bride in roughly one-eighth of the world's cultures. However, sometimes it occurs alongside other forms of marital exchange and occasionally can be used to reduce the amount of bridewealth owed.

Dowry   A marital exchange is called **dowry** when the families of a woman transfer a portion of their own wealth or other property to their daughter and her husband. The main thing to understand about dowry is that it is *not* simply the opposite of bridewealth; that is, it is not "groomwealth." It is, rather, ordinarily the share of a woman's inheritance that she is allowed to take into her marriage for the use of her new family, although her parents are still alive. The woman and her family do not acquire marital rights over her husband when they provide a dowry, as they would if dowry were the opposite of bridewealth; rather, the bride and her husband receive property when they marry, rather than when the bride's parents die. By doing so, parents give their female children extra years of use of the property and also publicly demonstrate their wealth.

Dowry transfers largely are confined to Europe, southern Asia, and the Middle East. Most peoples that have it are intensive agriculturalists and have significant inequalities in wealth. It is a relatively rare form of marital exchange, occurring in only about 5 percent of the societies recorded by anthropology.

Dowry is common in parts of India, where it includes jewelry, household utensils, women's clothing, and money. Much of the dowry is presented to the bride on her wedding day, but her parents and maternal uncle often provide

gifts periodically throughout the marriage. Dowry, then, is not always a one-time expense for a family but may represent a continual drain on their resources.

Kinship Diagrams

At this point we need to introduce a set of notational symbols that will be useful in the remainder of this chapter and the next. This notation allows us to express diagrammatically how any two persons are (or believe themselves to be) related by bonds of kinship. The symbols appear in Figure 8.1, along with an example of how they would be used to show a married couple with five children. By stringing a number of symbols together, it is

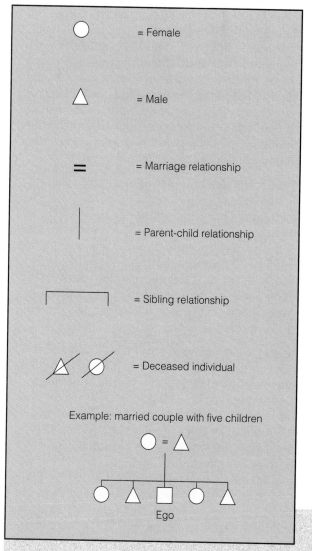

Figure 8.1   Symbols Used on Kinship Diagrams

possible to make a complete chart—called a *genealogy*—that shows all the relatives of a given individual and how they are related to that individual. In these charts, or kinship diagrams, it is useful to have a reference individual, or a person to whom everyone on the chart is related. It is customary to call this reference individual "ego." In Figure 8.1, ego is symbolized by a square to show that his or her gender is irrelevant for the purposes of the genealogy. (If ego's gender mattered, we would symbolize him or her with either a triangle or a circle.)

Postmarital Residence Patterns

In modern Euro-American societies a newly married couple usually establishes a new domestic group (household) in their own apartment, condo, or house. Couples do not always set up a new household in many other cultures. They often move into an existing household, either that of the husband or that of the wife. Where most new couples in a society establish their residence is known as the **postmarital residence pattern**. Cross-cultural research shows that our own pattern, in which couples form new households separate from their parents, is uncommon.

What are the other common patterns? By splitting enough hairs, it is possible to identify a dozen patterns, but here we present only five. In order of most frequent to least frequent, they are as follows:

Patrilocal: Couples live with or near the parents of the husband.
Matrilocal: Couples live with or near the wife's parents.
Bilocal: Postmarital residence is optional between either the wife's or the husband's kin; roughly one-half of all couples choose each.
Neolocal: Couples live apart from both parents, establishing a separate dwelling and independent household.
Avunculocal: Couples live with the maternal uncle of the husband.

Roughly 70 percent of all societies have patrilocal residence as the predominant pattern. Thirteen percent have matrilocal residence. These two patterns are easily the most widespread, accounting for about 83 percent of all societies. Bilocality, neolocality, and avunculocality together account for the remaining 17 percent.

What kinds of factors affect postmarital residence patterns? What determines whether newly married couples live separately or move in with some kind of relative? There is no simple answer, but property rights and inheritance forms are important influences on postmarital residence patterns. In societies in which the most important productive property is held by men, and in which inheritance passes from fathers to sons, brothers will

have good reasons to join their fathers (and each other) in a common household to cooperate and protect their interest in land, livestock, or other wealth. When the sons of most families in a society bring their wives and children into their father's existing household, this results in the residence pattern anthropologists call patrilocal. Where important resources are controlled or owned by women, and especially if female labor is also important in supplying food for their families, then sisters tend to live and work together, and matrilocal residence is most likely to develop.

Neolocal or bilocal patterns are most often found in societies in which inheritance of important resources passes through both sexes, rights of access to resources are ill defined, or most people rely on wage labor for their livelihood. This may be why both foragers and modern industrialized countries are usually neolocal or bilocal. Among foragers, people need to maintain access to several territories, so rights to critical resources are loose and flexible (as explained in Chapter 6). Nuclear families may live off and on with the husband's and wife's bands, depending on sentimental ties or short- or long-term availability of resources.

Modern industrialized nations usually are neolocal, for two major reasons. First, job availability forces many couples to move away from their home town. This is especially true for "upwardly mobile" couples seeking increased income, better opportunities, and the more materially rewarding lifestyle valued by many in the late twentieth century. Second, in industrialized countries most workers do not rely on their family connections for access to their livelihood but sell their labor on an impersonal market to an employer they have never met. In other words, most ordinary citizens do not inherit productive property from their parents and do not rely on their parents for their livelihood, so they establish independent domiciles free from parental control and interference. The result is neolocal residence and an emphasis on nuclear family ties.

Although control over resources and form of inheritance are important overall influences, no single factor "determines" postmarital residence. For instance, if most couples rely on the wife's family for access to the resources they need to survive and raise children, then most couples will live with the wife's family and matrilocal residence will be predominant in the society. But a multitude of other factors also affect residence choices. In fact, in some societies even though women have much control over land, residence is not matrilocal because these other factors are locally more important than keeping sisters together in a common household. The same complexities apply to the other residence patterns, so there is no single explanation.

Extended families are formed when adult siblings marry and stay together in a single household with their parents. One or another form of extended family is found among many of the world's peoples.

Family and Household Forms

The subject of postmarital residence might seem trivial. What difference does it make whether newly married couples live alone or with one set of parents? In fact, there are good reasons for being interested. Residence patterns affect all kinds of family relationships in a human community.

A moment's reflection shows that postmarital residence places a new nuclear family, which is created by a new marriage, with one set of relatives rather than the other set. In turn, who a newly married couple lives with influences who they will cooperate with, share property with, and so forth. If postmarital residence is patrilocal, for instance, then the husband lives with and works with his own consanguines (his father and brothers). The wife is likely to cooperate in household chores, gathering, gardening, and other tasks with members of her husband's family, more than with her own.

Postmarital residence also affects the relatives with whom children are most likely to develop strong emotional bonds. If residence is matrilocal, for example, then the children of sisters (who are "cousins") live together in a single household (much like biological sisters and brothers), and are likely to view their relationship as being like "real" siblings. The children of brothers, on the other hand, will live in different households, and are likely to view themselves as more distantly related.

Perhaps most important, the prevailing form of residence affects the kinds of household and family units that exist among a people. Consider neolocal residence, for example. If all or most newlyweds set up their own

households, separate from and independent of that of either of their parents, then a new household and family unit is established with each new marriage. This emphasizes the social and economic importance and independence of nuclear families because mothers and fathers—and not more distant relatives—are most likely to be the main teachers of children and "breadwinners" for the household. The couple maintains relations with their parents, siblings, and other relatives, of course, but neolocal residence tends to lead to an emphasis on nuclear families as the most culturally important and stable family unit.

(You can see this phenomenon in modern North America: When politicians worry about the decline or breakup of the American family, they usually are talking about the nuclear family, which they think is threatened by high divorce rates, unmarried couples living together, absent or deadbeat fathers, high illegitimacy rates, the gay lifestyle, and so forth. In recent years so many "families" have "split up" that family stability has become a major "social problem." The disintegration of extended family relationships is treated differently: No one worries much about the "decline" or "breakup" of relations between adult married children and their parents, or about how many married siblings seldom speak to one another or have not seen one another for years. We consider it normal—not a "social problem"—when married children move out on their parents and away from their siblings. Indeed, most view it as unfortunate if newlyweds live with either set of parents, because we think that only economic necessity could force them to do so. Many of us believe that young marrieds who visit or seek advice from their parents too often are a little strange for not making their own choices and establishing their own friendships.)

Other kinds of households and family groupings exist among the world's peoples. These extended families are made up of related nuclear families. Because the related nuclear families usually live in a single household, here we use *extended family* and *extended household* as synonyms. Extended households typically include three and often four generations of family members.

Many anthropologists think that the form of family (household) that is prevalent in a society depends on its postmarital residence pattern. For example, with patrilocal residence the married sons of an older couple remain in the household of their parents (or, often each son builds his own house on his parents' land, near their dwelling). As they grow up and marry, the daughters go to live with their husbands' parents. If all the sons and daughters of a couple do this, the resulting household is of a type called *patrilocally extended*—brothers live in a single household with their own nuclear families and parents (see Figure 8.2a). If all families in the village, town, or other settlement follow this pattern, then the settlement consists of patrilocally extended households. Notice that the residents of each household are related to one another through males. The married women of the community live scattered in the households of their husbands, or perhaps many of them have married out of the community altogether.

The converse occurs with matrilocal residence. The mature sons leave as they marry, and the daughters bring their husbands to live with them in or near their parents' households. The household type formed by the coresidence of daughters and sisters with their parents is called the *matrilocally extended household* (see Figure 8.2b). The sons of an elderly couple are scattered in the households of the women they have married, either in their own home community or in another community. If most people follow this residence pattern, then the community consists of numerous households, each of which is lived in by women related through females, plus their husbands and children.

The same relationship between residence and prevalent household form applies to the other residence patterns. With bilocal residence there is no consistency in whether households are made up of people related through males or females: Some couples live with the husband's family, others with that of the wife. The household type is *bilocally* (or *bilaterally*) *extended*

(see Figure 8.2c). The community's households are a mixture of people related through both sexes, in roughly equal frequency. With neolocal residence the settlement—be it village or modern suburb—consists of relatively small domestic units made up of nuclear families.

The avunculocal residence pattern associates nuclear families with the husband's mother's brother; if everyone in the community adopted this practice (which they usually do not), then the community would consist of households composed of older men (the household heads) and the families of their sister's sons. This is called the *avunculocally extended household* (see Figure 8.2d). It includes men (and their wives and children) who are related to one another through women (their mothers)! (Confused by this one? We shall see in the next chapter that avunculocal residence makes good sense in many societies that trace their main kinship relationships through women.)

We can now see one reason why postmarital residence patterns are important: They give rise to various household and family forms. The kinds of family and domestic groups found among a people result from where newly formed families go to live. Stated differently, the prevalent household type in a human community represents the crystallization of the pattern of postmarital residence. And who lives with whom—the household type—is important, since households so often hold property in common, cooperate in production and other economic activities, enculturate children together, and sometimes even worship the same ancestral spirits.

Figure 8.2   Household Forms

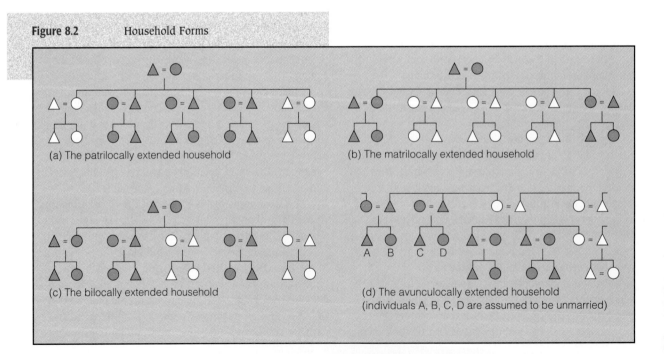

(a) The patrilocally extended household

(b) The matrilocally extended household

(c) The bilocally extended household

(d) The avunculocally extended household
(individuals A, B, C, D are assumed to be unmarried)

In this chapter we have given an overview of some variations in domestic life. If we were writing a book about industrial societies, we might stop our discussion of groupings formed on the basis of kinship relations at this point. This is because, among the industrialized portion of humanity, other kinds of relations and groupings—economic, educational, political, religious, and so on—are organized by relationships other than kinship—by specialized firms, schools, parties, governments, churches, and so on. But, as we discuss in the next chapter, in preindustrial cultures kinship principles are used to form much larger kin groups that organize and perform a range of other activities.

Summary

All human societies have some kind of family groupings to organize and facilitate child-rearing and other essential domestic activities. New nuclear families are formed by marriage, which reduces conflict over sexuality, forms social bonds that provide for children, establishes new relations between intermarrying families, and involves the exchange of goods and services between husbands and wives. Human biological characteristics make a relationship like marriage universal in human societies, although the form of marriage, the kinds of rights and duties it establishes, and many other aspects of the marital relationship vary. The Nayar illustrate an unusual form of marriage, if it is marriage at all.

Marriage is everywhere governed by rules, many of which pertain to exogamy and endogamy. Marriage systems commonly are classified by the number of spouses an individual is allowed: polygyny, monogamy, polyandry, and group marriage, in order of relative frequency in human societies. In preindustrial societies, marriage often is the cornerstone of alliance relations between families or larger kin groups. The Yąnomamö illustrate the use of strategic marriages to create and sustain military alliances, a practice quite common in the preindustrial world. The levirate and sororate are customs that preserve affinal relationships even after the death of a spouse.

New marriages ordinarily are accompanied by the exchange of goods or services between the spouses and the families of the bride and groom. The most common forms of marital exchange are bridewealth, brideservice, and dowry. These exchanges are used to create affinal relationships, compensate a family or larger kin group for the loss of one of its members, provide for the new couple's support, or provide a daughter with an inheritance that attracts a husband.

Postmarital residence patterns refers to where newly married couples establish their residence. In order of most common to least common, the patterns are patrilocal, matrilocal, bilocal, neolocal, and avunculocal. There are many influences on which of these forms will be most prevalent in a given community, including economic forces and inheritance patterns. No single factor is adequate to explain the cross-cultural variation in residence patterns.

Anthropologists are interested in postmarital residence patterns mainly because where a newly married couple go to live influences which kinship relationships will be most emphasized in a society. In particular, the prevalent forms of family and domestic groups in a community arise out of many couples living with one or another set of relatives. Patrilocally, matrilocally, bilocally, and avunculocally extended families often are interpreted as the crystallization of postmarital residence patterns.

Key Terms

kin group
domestic group
consanguines
affines
nuclear family
extended family
incest taboo

exogamous rules
endogamous rules
monogamy
polygyny
polyandry
group marriage
polygamy
marriage alliances
levirate
sororate

bridewealth
brideservice
dowry
postmarital residence pattern
patrilocal residence
matrilocal residence
bilocal residence
neolocal residence
avunculocal residence

Suggested Readings

Collier, Jane F. *Marriage and Inequality in Classless Societies.* Stanford: Stanford University Press, 1988.
- *Compares marriage systems and marriage exchanges in small-scale societies from a theoretical perspective, discussing their impact on male-female relationships.*

Goody, Jack, and S. J. Tambiah, eds. *Bridewealth and Dowry.* Cambridge: Cambridge University Press, 1973.
- *A collection of papers examining the causes and consequences of bridewealth and dowry.*

Suggs, David N., and Andrew W. Miracle, eds. *Culture and Human Sexuality: A Reader.* Pacific Grove, Calif.: Brooks/Cole, 1993.
- *An outstanding collection of articles dealing with sexuality and related topics from a cross-cultural perspective. Includes both case studies and theoretical articles.*

Most ethnographies contain a description of the domestic life of the people studied. The following are a few ethnographies specifically focused on domestic life.

Blesdoe, Caroline. *Women and Marriage in Kpelle Society.* Stanford: Stanford University Press, 1980.
- *A description of an African society.*

Hart, C. W. M., and Arnold R. Pilling. *The Tiwi of North Australia.* New York: Holt, Rinehart and Winston, 1979.
- *A brief ethnographic study of an Australian culture with a most unusual marriage system.*

Levine, Nancy. *The Dynamics of Polyandry: Kinship, Domesticity, and Population in the Tibetan Border.* Chicago: University of Chicago Press, 1988.
- *Case study of fraternal polyandry in the Himalayas.*

Malinowski, Bronislaw. *The Sexual Life of Savages.* New York: Harcourt, Brace, Jovanovich, 1929.
- *Not what you may think from its title. An ethnography that describes courtship, sexual norms, marriage, domestic relations, and love magic in the Trobriand Islands.*

Pasternak, Burton. *Kinship and Community in Two Chinese Villages.* Stanford: Stanford University Press, 1972.
- *Good empirical study of Chinese kinship at the local level.*

Shostak, Marjorie. *Nisa: The Life and Words of a !Kung Woman.* New York: Vintage Books, 1983.
- *A wonderfully readable biography of a !Kung woman, much of which focuses on her relationships with family, husbands, and children.*

Stack, Carol B. *All Our Kin: Strategies for Survival in a Black Community.* New York: Harper and Row, 1974.
- *An ethnography that shows how African-Americans in a midwestern city use family ties to cope with poverty.*

Wolf, Margery. *The House of Lim.* Englewood Cliffs, N.J.: Prentice-Hall, 1968.
- *A readable study of family life in a Taiwanese Chinese farm family.*

Internet Exercises

You can benefit from other anthropology instructors besides the one who is teaching your class. Anthony Galt at the University of Wisconsin at Green Bay has study materials for his course "Anthropology 110" posted on the World Wide Web (http://www.uwgb.edu/~galta/a100/index.htm). Go to "Study Guides, Lecture Topic Outlines, Overheads and Other Oddments." The lectures numbered five, six, and seven deal with marriage and kinship. Materials for specific courses are often sparse in information and ephemeral, but others such as this site are worth a look. This type of site is becoming more common and therefore easy to find.

From the same anthropology department that provided the website above you can find student project web pages, one of which gives more information about the Yąnomamö people (http://www.uwgb.edu/~galta/mrr/yano/yano.htm). Go back to the "Term Projects Homepage" (http://gbms01.uwgb.edu/~galta/mrr/projpage.htm) for pages about other cultures (most are discussed somewhere in this book), which each contain a section about marriage and kinship.

"Anthropology in the News" is a website maintained at Texas A&M University (http://www.tamu.edu/anthropology/news). Look at some of the current news clips. Has the knowledge you have gained from this class changed your perspective regarding any of these issues? As an example, go to the archives for sociocultural anthropology. On September 15, 1998, there is a news story titled "Chinese Matrimony Can Be Pricey." Based on what you read in this chapter about marriage, kinship, and residence, plus what you have learned about Chinese marriage practices, what other things do you think might influence Chinese couples to flout a fine for having more than one child?

Kinship

Kinship

Cultural Variations in Kinship

Unilineal Descent

Unilineal Descent Groups

Descent Groups in Action

Avunculocality Revisited

Cognatic Descent

Cognatic Descent in Polynesia

Bilateral Kinship

Influences on Kinship Systems

Classifying Relatives: Kinship Terminologies

Varieties of Kinship Terminology

Determinants of Kinship Terminology

Video · Audio · Photos
Hotlinks · Essay
http://www.wadsworth.com/humanity

Out of the biological relations between individuals created by reproduction, human societies create kinship groups and complex kinship systems. Among the Yanomamö of Amazonia, kinship relationships affect whether two groups are friends or enemies.

Visit http://www.wadsworth.com/humanity to learn more about the material covered in this chapter and to access activities, exercises, and tutorial quizzes.

*H*UMANS ARE *among the most social of all mammals. We are born into, live with, and die among other people. Children rely totally on parents and other adults for the food, shelter, protection, and learning needed to raise them to social maturity. Even as adults, we rely on cooperation with others for survival, economic well-being, and emotional gratification. When we die, many members of the groups to which we belonged in our lives mourn our passing.*

OF THE ORGANIZED *groups to which people belong, those based on kinship, or biological ties, are among the most important. In many cultures, the specific persons with whom one cooperates in everyday life are relatives of some kind. The groups that organize large-scale cooperative activities are established on the basis of kinship ties. Within those groups, the nature of the relationships that individuals have with one another depends largely on what specific kind of relatives they are.*

IN THIS CHAPTER we cover how kinship relationships are used in a variety of ways by different peoples to organize relationships and create cooperative groupings. We also describe some of the main ways that members of different cultures define and classify their relatives into labeled categories.

Kinship

Before discussing some ways societies differ in their kinship organization, we should consider why anthropologists pay so much attention to the subject. In Western cultures, kinship relations are of course important—to varying degrees—in the lives of individuals. But, compared to many other cultures that anthropologists work among, kinship is not an important organizing principle of modern society as a whole. Instead, in modern societies, different kinds of activities are organized by different kinds of institutions and groupings. We distinguish between economic, political, religious, and educational institutions, for example, meaning that different kinds of institutions specialize in different kinds of organized activities that perform different kinds of functions.

Further, each person is a member of and participates in the activities of a number of formal and informal groups. For example, you might belong to formal groups such as a nation, university, conservation organization, church, political party, and company that pays your wages. At the same time, you are active in many informal associations made up of your co-workers, fellow students, neighbors, and friends, with whom you socialize or share common interests.

Notice two important characteristics of these groups. First, they are *voluntary:* If individuals' interests change, or if they find some other group of people who better meet their goals, they are free to change jobs, churches, neighborhoods, and friends. Second, for the most part, they have *nonoverlapping membership:* Each group typically consists of a different collection of people; we cooperate and interact with different individuals in the various groups to which we belong. Members of each of these groups have varying and sometimes contradictory expectations about how we should behave because we perform different roles in each of the groups. In many ways our behavior differs according to the context of the particular group of people we are associating with at the moment— we act one way at home, another at church, and yet another at work. Our fellow church members might be surprised if they could see how we act on the job, but— probably fortunately—they ordinarily don't.

In contrast, among many indigenous peoples, one lives with, works with, socializes with, and often worships with the same people, most of whom are relatives. Kin groups and kin relationships are *multifunctional,* meaning that they organize many kinds of activities. Most of the activities organized by the firms, schools, governments, churches, and other specialized groups in a complex, industrial society are organized by one or another kind of kin group. Thus, kinship relations are far more important to the organization of preindustrial societies than they are to our own. In fact, often the organization of such societies is based on the relationships established by kinship. We can no more understand them without studying their kinship systems than we could understand the modern world without knowing about nations.

Cultural Variations in Kinship

In over a century of studying kinship systems and analyzing their role in cultures, anthropologists have discovered surprising variations. Among the most important variations are the following:

Ways of Tracing Kinship Ties   In the North American kinship system, most people believe they are related equally and in the same way to the extended families of both their mothers and their fathers. Particular individuals may develop closer ties with one or another side of their family, according to circumstances and personal preferences. For example, you may be closer to one set of grandparents because they live nearby, whereas your other grandparents live clear across the country. But there is no systematic *cultural pattern* of feeling closer to or socializing with relatives according to whether they are paternal or maternal kin.

In contrast to the American kinship pattern, many other cultures place primary importance on one side of the family—either the paternal or the maternal side—in preference to the other. For example, in many cultures most individuals become members of their father's kin group. They might live with their father's relatives, inherit property from their fathers but not their mothers, and worship their paternal but not their maternal ancestors. In such systems, relatives through one's mother usually are recognized as kin, but kin of a fundamentally different and less important kind than paternal relatives. There are also systems in which kin groups are organized around maternal relationships, and paternal kin are culturally de-emphasized.

Normative Expectations of Kin Relationships   The kinds of social relations a people believe they should have with individuals related to them in a certain way are part of the norms of a kinship system. Cross-culturally, these norms

Some cultures place primary emphasis on only one side of an individual's family, either the mother's side or the father's side. In these two men's Middle Eastern homeland, relationships traced through males are more important than those traced through females.

are surprisingly variable. There are systems in which husbands and wives do not sleep and eat in the same dwelling; in which brothers must rigidly avoid their sisters after puberty; in which sons-in-law are not supposed to speak directly to their mothers-in-law; in which a boy is allowed to appropriate the property of his maternal uncle but must show utmost restraint and respect toward his paternal uncle; and in which people are expected to marry one kind of cousin but are absolutely forbidden to marry another kind of cousin. In sum, many of the patterns of behavior toward relatives that members of one culture regard as normal are absent in other cultures.

Cultural Classifications of Relatives Kinship relationships are created through biological reproduction. When a woman gives birth, her relatives and those of her mate become the biological relatives of the child. In this sense, who your relatives are is determined for you by who your parents are. Thus, the kinship relationship between any two people depends on how these individuals are related biologically.

Despite this fact, anthropologists claim that kinship is a cultural, rather than a biologically determined, phenomenon. We make this claim mainly because societies differ in the way they use the biological facts of kinship to create groups, allocate roles, and classify the domain of relatives into various kinds. They vary in how they perceive and categorize their biological relationships. In our own kinship system, for example, whether a woman is our maternal or paternal aunt makes no difference: We still call her *aunt* and think of both our maternal and paternal aunt as the same kind of relative. But side of the family makes a difference in some other kinship systems: Father's sisters and mother's sisters are completely different kinds of relatives and are called by different terms.

Keeping this overview of kinship diversity in mind, let's look at kinship in more detail.

Unilineal Descent

If "kin" are defined in strictly biological terms, then someone is your relative because you and they share a common ancestor in a previous generation. Thus, your sister is the female child of your parents; your aunts and uncles are the children of your grandparents; your first cousins are the grandchildren of your grandparents; you and your second cousins share the same great-grandparents; and so forth. Stated differently, a man is your biological relative if you and he are *descended* from a common ancestor who lived some number of generations ago. The greater the number of generations back this ancestor lived, the more distantly you are related to the man.

Notice that you are descended from four grandparents, eight great-grandparents, sixteen great-great grandparents, and thirty-two great-great-great grandparents. Everyone alive today who is descended from these thirty-two people is related to you (the most distantly related are your fourth cousins). Because going back in time, the number of your ancestors doubles every generation, you have an enormous number of living biological relatives even if you count back only four or five generations.

Obviously, we do not keep track of all our biological kin. Nor does any other society. From the total range of potential biological kin, all cultures consider some kinds of relatives as more important than others. The reduction in the number of relatives is accomplished in two main ways: (1) forgetting or ignoring the remoter kinship relationships and (2) emphasizing some kinds of kinship relationships and de-emphasizing others. In North America we use mainly the first method: Most people forget who their kin are beyond the range of second cousin because they have little reason to keep track of their more distant relatives.

Many cultures also use the second method: They consider that some kinds of relatives are more important than others. The most common means of making some relatives more important than others is to use the sex of connecting relatives as the basis for defining which kin are close. For example, if people consider that kin relationships traced through males are most important, then individuals will think that their father's relatives are more important than their mother's relatives—for some purposes at least. Relationships through females will be de-emphasized and perhaps forgotten in two or three generations. If you lived in such a culture, some of your second cousins on your father's side would be quite important relatives, but you might not consider your second cousins through your mother as relatives at all.

Kinship relationships, then, are defined by how people trace their descent from previous generations. How people in a given culture trace their descent is called their **form of descent**. Descent can be traced through males, females, or both sexes. This section considers cultures that trace descent through only one sex.

In many cultures, relationships traced through only one sex are considered most important. Anthropologists say that such cultures have **unilineal descent**, a term that refers to the fact that people place importance on either their mother's ancestral line or their father's ancestral line, but not both. There are two categories of unilineal descent:

- **Patrilineal descent.** People trace their primary kinship connections to the ancestors and living relatives of their fathers (see Figure 9.1). In cultures with patrilineal descent, a person's father's relatives are

likely to be most important in his or her life. Individuals are likely to live among their father's kin, and most property is inherited from fathers to sons.
- **Matrilineal descent.** People trace their most important kinship relationships to the ancestors and living relatives of their mothers (see Figure 9.2). In matrilineal descent, it is the mother's relatives who are most important in a person's life. People are most likely to live with or near their mothers' relatives and usually inherit property from their mothers or mother's brothers.

Of these two forms of unilineal descent, patrilineal is the most common. There are about three times as many patrilineal as matrilineal cultures.

Let's look at each of these forms of unilineal descent more closely, to see which relatives are considered most important for an individual. In Figure 9.1, the patrilineal relatives of the person labeled *ego* are shaded in. The kinship diagram shows that ego's patrilineal kin include only those relatives related to ego through males. For instance, ego's father's brother's children are related to ego through males, whereas ego's other first cousins are not.

Looking at patrilineal descent another way, ego's patrilineal kin include all the people descended through males from the man labeled *founder* on Figure 9.1. In fact, any two individuals shaded in the diagram are related to one another through males. This includes women as well as men, but the children of these women are not related through males and, therefore, are not patrilineal kin. The children of the women have their own set of patrilineal relatives, which they take from their fathers.

How does patrilineal descent affect behavior toward different relatives? Probably the most widespread and

Figure 9.1 Patrilineal Descent

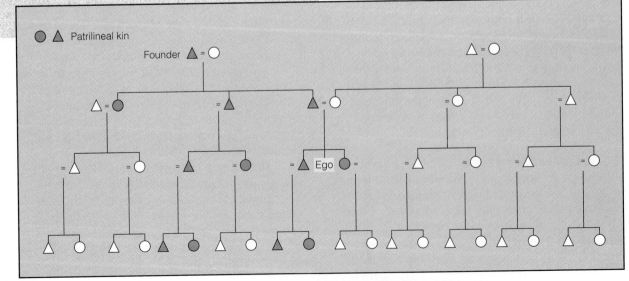

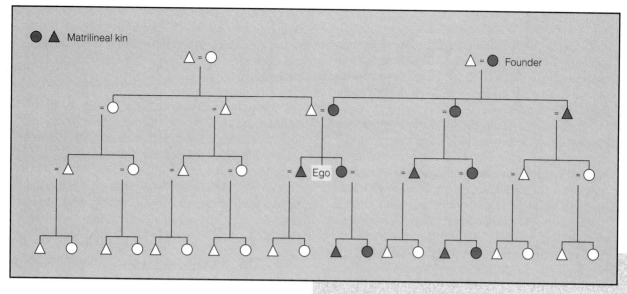

Figure 9.2 Matrilineal Descent

noticeable effect is in the inheritance of property. In patrilineal societies, property is passed down through the male line or, in other words, from fathers to sons. We can see the significance of this effect on inheritance by contrasting it with inheritance in North American society, where the dominant ethnic group makes no distinction between males and females in tracing kinship relationships. You probably do not distinguish between your two grandfathers but think of yourself as related in the same way to both. You may potentially inherit from both. But if your culture was patrilineal, your father's father would play a far more significant role in your life, and it would be from him that you would expect to inherit wealth or receive land rights. Your mother's father would pass his property on to his sons and sons' sons—not to you because you are related to him through your mother, not your father. A similar distinction exists between paternal and maternal uncles: Paternal uncles are far more important. Finally, some of your four sets of cousins are more important than others—those related to you through males, or your father's brothers' children. It is these people who would be primarily responsible for your economic and social welfare, and it is with them and your own siblings that you would probably cooperate and associate.

We can use the same logic to examine matrilineal descent. Your matrilineal kin are related to you through female links. They include your mother, mother's mother, mother's mother's mother (if she is alive), plus the daughters of all these women and their children. The sons and brothers of these women are your matrilineal kin, but their children are not. In Figure 9.2, we have shaded the people who are ego's matrilineal relatives. Note that only one set of cousins—ego's mother's sisters'

children—is shaded in the diagram. They are the individuals who are related to ego through female links, and therefore, ego is likely to have closer relationships with them than with other cousins. Property is most likely to be inherited from one's mother and maternal grandmother and from the brothers of these women. In matrilineal societies, men usually leave most of their property not to their own children but to their sister's children. As a result, maternal uncles (mother's brothers) are important figures in one's life, and in some respects they assume the role we usually associate with fathers.

As we have seen, in unilineal descent systems relations such as aunt, uncle, and cousin differ from those we are accustomed to. Some cousins, in particular, will be more important relatives than other cousins: father's brothers' children in patrilineal systems, mother's sisters' children in matrilineal systems. Recognition of the fact that not all cousins are "alike" in unilineal societies has led anthropologists to distinguish between *parallel cousins* and *cross cousins*. Two sets of cousins are parallel cousins if their parents are of the same sex, so your parallel cousins are your mother's sisters' children and your father's brothers' children. People are cross cousins if their parents are siblings of the opposite sex, so your cross cousins are your father's sisters' children and your mother's brothers' children. The significance of this distinction is that in unilineal descent systems, one set of parallel cousins always belongs to the same kin group as ego, as you can see by contrasting the cousins shaded in Figures 9.1 and 9.2. On the other hand, no cross cousin is ever in ego's kin group in a society with a unilineal descent form.

Unilineal Descent Groups

In Chapter 8, we saw how extended household groups are formed when nuclear families associate together in patterned ways. Much larger kin groups of people—also known as **descent groups**—can be established on the basis of kinship ties.

Take matrilineal descent, for example. A matrilineal descent group exists when people descended from the same woman through females recognize their group identity and cooperate for some purposes. When a matrilineal rule of descent establishes a group of people all related to one another through females, we say that the group is created using the *matrilineal principle*. We can state the matrilineal principle as "everyone joins the descent group of his or her mother." Alternatively, we can say "only children of the female members of a group become members." Looking back to Figure 9.2, all the individuals on the diagram are members of a single descent group. Check for yourself that only the female members pass their membership in the group along to their offspring. (What happens to the children of the group's men? They join the descent groups of their mothers, which usually are a different group because incest and exogamy rules usually prohibit sex and marriage between any of the group's members.)

Groups also can develop by repeated application of the *patrilineal principle*. In any given generation, only males transmit their membership in the group to their offspring. The result of applying this principle for several generations is a group of people related to one another through males. Check this on Figure 9.1: All the shaded individuals are in the same descent group, and everyone joined the group of their father. Assuming the patrilineal kin group is exogamous, the children of the group's women become members of their father's patrilineal group.

A **unilineal descent group** is a grouping of relatives, all of whom are related through only one sex. A *matrilineal descent group* is a group whose members are (or consider themselves to be) related through females, or who trace their descent through female links from a common ancestress. A *patrilineal descent group* comprises people who trace their descent through males from a common male ancestor.

Unilineal descent groups can be small or enormous, depending mainly on the genealogical depth of the group—that is, how far back in time any two members of the group must go to trace their relationships to each other. A small matrilineal group with dozens of members might consist of people descended matrilineally from a woman who lived four or five generations ago. A large matrilineal group with many hundreds of members might consist of people who trace their ancestry back to a woman who lived nine or ten generations ago. Anthropologists often use genealogical depth as a way to define different kinds of unilineal groups. From "shallowest" to "deepest," these groups are called unilineally extended families, lineages, and clans. (There are other types, but they are not discussed here.)

Unilineally Extended Families **Unilineally extended families** consist of people who cooperate and have mutual obligations based on their descent from an ancestor who lived only three or four generations ago. Extended families may be defined either patrilineally or matrilineally. Such families may or may not live in the same household (see Chapter 8), but they recognize their close ties, may hold common property, may cooperate in work, and may have shared ritual responsibilities.

Lineages A **lineage** is a unilineal group composed of several unilineally extended families whose members are able to trace their descent through males or females from a common ancestor or ancestress. By the conventional definition, the extended families that make up the group must be able to state how they are related to one another for anthropologists to call the group a lineage. Lineages may be either patrilineal (patrilineages) or matrilineal (matrilineages), depending on the form of descent prevalent among a people.

Clans **Clans** are unilineal descent groups whose members are descended from either a common ancestor through the male line (patriclans) or a common ancestress through the female line (matriclans). The major difference between a clan and a lineage is generational depth. With clans, the common ancestor or ancestress lived so far in the past that not all the members of the clan are able to state precisely how they are related to one another. Like lineages, clans usually are exogamous. Members of the clan think of themselves as relatives and frequently refer to one another as "clan brother" or "clan sister." In many societies, clans own or control land and other forms of property. Most clans are *totemic,* meaning that their members are symbolically identified with certain supernatural powers associated with particular animals, plants, and natural forces such as lightning, the sun, and the moon. Clans commonly take the name of their primary totemic symbol, and thus have names such as the bear clan, the sun clan, and the eagle clan. The association with particular supernatural powers gives specific clans control over particular religious rituals. Although the function of clans varies from one society to another, they usually are among the most significant economic, social, and political units in the society.

Whereas lineages may exist without being aggregated into clans, clans are almost always subdivided into lineages, which in turn are subdivided into extended families.

Patrilineal descent groups organize many economic, political, and ritual activities among the Maasai of Kenya and Tanzania.

Segmentary Descent Groups Often people need to be able to call upon different numbers of relatives for different purposes. A woman may need help with her gardening chores, and will ask her extended family members for help. Or a group may need to defend itself against enemies, for which purpose they need to mobilize dozens or even hundreds of men to serve as warriors, so they call upon their lineagemates or clanmates for aid. Unilineal descent is a useful organization for these and many other purposes because it allows people to mobilize varying numbers of their relatives when they need assistance. Using one of the unilineal descent principles, smaller kin groups can be nested inside larger ones.

For example, in a patrilineal society, a nuclear family is a part—a "segment"—of a patrilineally extended family. The extended family is a segment of a larger group (a small patrilineage), whereas the small patrilineage is a segment of a larger patrilineage, which in turn is a segment of a patriclan. Using this segmentary organization, dozens, hundreds, or even thousands of relatives can be mobilized, depending on the circumstances. Figure 9.3 illustrates the segmentation of a hypothetical patriclan. The flexibility of segmentary unilineal descent systems makes them useful for many economic, political, and ritual purposes (see Chapters 11 and 13).

Descent Groups in Action

The preceding description of descent forms and groupings is abstract and somewhat technical. Perhaps by now you are wondering why anthropologists bother so much with kinship.

We bother because descent groups are made up of living people who work in gardens, quarrel, conduct rituals, go to war, teach their children, construct their dwellings, and carry out innumerable other activities together. If people are to work together for common purposes, they must have ways of creating groups and ensuring their continuity over time; they must have ways of assigning group members to roles and allocating tasks to them; they must have ways of making decisions that affect the members. In short, they must be organized. More often than not, descent groups and kinship relations provide the organizational basis on which various cooperative activities are carried out.

Two examples illustrate how unilineal descent principles organize cooperative activities. One is a patrilineal people of a Pacific island who call themselves the *Tikopia.* The second is the *Hopi,* a matrilineal Native American people of the Southwest.

Tikopia: A Patrilineal Society Tikopia is a western Pacific island with six square miles of land area. In the late 1920s, when it was studied by Raymond Firth, Tikopia had a population of about 1,200. Tikopians traced their descent patrilineally and used this principle to establish groupings of people related through males. They viewed their society as composed of four patriclans, each with a name that passed from fathers to sons. Each patriclan was subdivided into several patrilineages, averaging

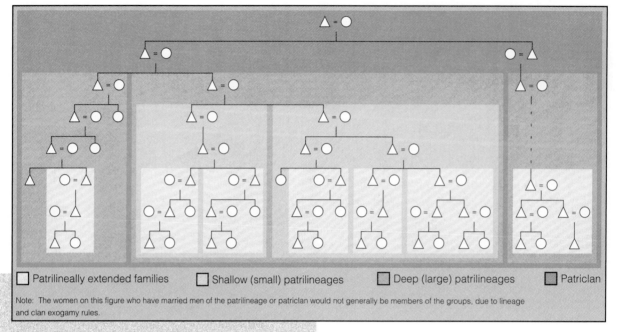

Patrilineally extended families   Shallow (small) patrilineages   Deep (large) patrilineages   Patriclan

Note: The women on this figure who have married men of the patrilineage or patriclan would not generally be members of the groups, due to lineage and clan exogamy rules.

Figure 9.3 The Segmentation of Patrilineal Descent Groups

about thirty to forty members. The members of each patrilineage traced their descent in the male line back to a common ancestor—the founder of the patrilineage—who lived four to six generations ago. Each patrilineage ordinarily considered the oldest male descendant of this founder to be its head. The women of a lineage married men of other lineages, so the children of the lineage's women did not become members of it.

What were the functions of Tikopian lineages and clans? The lineage controlled rights over land and certain other kinds of property. Each lineage owned several parcels of land that were planted in crops, including yams, taro, coconut, and breadfruit. The families that made up the lineage had the right to plant and harvest crops on lineage land; once they had planted a parcel, they had the right to continue to use it. They could not, however, sell, trade, or give it away to members of other lineages. The same rights applied to the parcels of land on which a family established their dwellings: They could live on one of the lineage's house sites but could not dispose of it to outsiders. The patrilineage, then, owned land and allocated use rights to parcels among its members, and each family acquired most of its subsistence through its members' access to the land of their lineage.

Ordinarily, each nuclear family primarily cultivated the lineage land of its husband-father. In Tikopia, the female members of a patrilineage retained their use rights to lineage land even after they married. When a woman married, a parcel of the land of her lineage was divided off for

her own and her husband's and children's use. A woman could not, however, pass any of her rights to this land along to her children; when she died, the use of the parcel reverted to the patrilineage she was born into, and her children had no more use rights to it. Thus, each patrilineage allowed its female members who had married out of it to use plots of land for subsistence during their lifetimes but not to transmit rights to the land to their offspring. (The children of the women of the patrilineage received use rights to land from their own fathers' lineage.)

The social rank of individuals also was determined largely by which kin group they belonged to and their status within it. As we have discussed, the various lineages were aggregated into four patriclans. One lineage of each clan was considered the senior lineage. Because its living members were believed to be directly descended (through males) from the founder of the clan, it was the highest ranking lineage of that clan. They received certain kinds of respect from their clanmates. The senior lineage of each clan also had the right to select one of its male members to serve as the clan chief. Just as the lineages were ranked relative to one another on the basis of genealogical closeness to the senior lineage, so families within a single lineage were ranked by their closeness to the head of the lineage. Tikopian kinship thus had a political aspect, since authority over others was granted or refused to an individual or group largely through their descent group membership and rank.

Tikopians did not live by breadfruit alone. The Tikopian world view included a belief in certain supernatural powers. These beliefs also were tied into the descent system because each descent group was allocated ritual duties to perform. Each of the four clan chiefs served as the religious leader and organizer of certain religious ceremonies. Each clan had its own ancestral spirits, which were the deceased former chiefs of the clan. Each clan also had its own gods, with whom its chief acted as intermediary.

One religious function of a clan was to carry out rituals that ensured the availability of food. Each of the four major subsistence crops was spiritually associated with one of the clans. The gods of this clan were believed to control the crop. The chief of the clan performed important rituals that ensured the continued supply and fertility of whichever crop "listened to" (as the Tikopia phrased it) the gods of his clan. Thus, each clan—in the person of its chief—had ritual responsibilities toward the other three clans.

Like clans, Tikopian patrilineages cooperated in religious contexts. Patrilineages were not residence units; rather, the members of a single patrilineage usually lived scattered among several settlements. Each patrilineage did, however, have a house that its scattered members regarded as sacred because it was believed to be the ancestral home of the entire lineage. The members of a lineage periodically held religious ceremonies at this place to honor the deceased ancestors of their kin group.

The Tikopian example exemplifies the diverse kinds of functions that often are assigned to kin groups in preindustrial populations. Patrilineages controlled use rights to land and some other kinds of property, influenced an individual's social rank, and performed joint rituals. Patriclans also had political functions, and their chiefs carried out rituals that Tikopians believed were essential for the well-being of all islanders.

Hopi: A Matrilineal Society   In northeastern Arizona live a matrilineal people known as the Hopi. The Hopi divide themselves into about fifty exogamous matriclans (some of which are now extinct). Clans are not residential groups, for most have members who live in more than one of the Hopi's nine *pueblos*. A Hopi pueblo, or village, often is a single large apartment-like building divided into many rooms in which families reside. Each clan is subdivided into several matrilineages. The female members of a Hopi matrilineage usually live in adjoining rooms within a single pueblo.

The Hopi postmarital residence pattern is matrilocal, so after marriage a man usually joins his wife, her sisters, and her other matrilineal relatives to form a matrilocally extended household. Most Hopi extended families consist of one or more older women, their daughters together with their husbands, and sometimes even their granddaughters and their husbands. Because of lineage and clan exogamy and matrilocal residence, husbands are outsiders, and—as the Hopi say—their real home is with their mothers' extended family. The residential core of a

matrilineage thus consists of its women, who live close to one another throughout most of their lives. The married men of the lineage are scattered among the households of their wives, although they frequently return to their matrilineal home for rituals and other responsibilities or in case of divorce.

Most property, both secular and ceremonial, is inherited matrilineally. Living space, for instance, is passed from mother to daughter. Farmland, on which the Hopi formerly depended for more of their subsistence, is owned by a clan, with each lineage having use rights over particular parcels at any one time. The husbands of the lineage's women do most of the farming to support their families, although they themselves do not own the land.

Membership in a matriclan not only defines one's primary social relationships but also establishes one's relationships with the supernatural world. Each clan is mystically associated with a number of supernatural powers called *wuya*. Clans usually take their name after their principal wuya, such as bear, rabbit, corn, snake, cloud, sun, and reed. The members of a matriclan pray to their wuya, asking them for protection and for bountiful harvests.

Hopi religion features a ritual calendar that includes a large number of annually required ceremonies. In most cases, each ceremony is "owned" by the members of a certain clan, meaning in Hopi culture that this clan has primary responsibility to see that the ceremony is performed on time and in the proper manner. Every clan represented in a village has a clanhouse in which the masks, fetishes, and other sacred items used in the ceremonies it owns are kept when not in use. The clanhouse usually consists of a room adjoining the dwelling of the senior female member of the clan. This woman, known as the *clan mother,* is in charge of storing ritual paraphernalia and of seeing to it that they are treated with the proper respect. The position of clan mother is passed down from a woman to either her younger sister or her daughter, depending on age and personal qualities. There is also a male head of each clan whose duties likewise are partly religious because he is in charge of the performance of ceremonies owned by his clan. A male clan head passes his position, together with the ritual knowledge required to hold it, down to either his younger brother or his sister's son. In this way, culturally important ritual knowledge is kept within the clan.

Among the Hopi, as with most other matrilineal systems, the roles of father and husband differ from those in patrilineal systems. As we have seen, a husband moves in with his wife and her relatives after marriage. A man brings little property into the marriage other than his clothing and a few personal items. Nor does he accumulate much property as a result of his marriage because the house, its furnishings, the food stored there, and other goods remain the property of his wife's family. Although a man provides food for himself and his family by working in the fields of his wife, the products of his garden labor belong to his wife. The children similarly are viewed primarily as members of their mother's lineage and clan, and indeed they have no rights to use land or any claim to ritual knowledge or property of their father's kin group.

All these factors mean that a Hopi husband has a rather anomalous position in his wife's household because each spouse owes his or her main loyalty to his or her own matrilineal relatives, and there is little common property in which they share an interest. This feature of the kinship system seems to put stress and strain on marriages because divorce rates are comparatively high. After separation or divorce, a man retires to the residence of his own mother and sisters until he remarries.

The combination of matrilineal descent and matrilocal residence profoundly affects relationships between fathers and their children. A child's relationship with his or her father usually is close and tolerant. A man seldom punishes his own children. Culturally, this is not considered his appropriate role, for—after all—children and fathers belong to different descent groups. The father's sisters and brothers likewise exhibit warm feelings for their nieces and nephews, often spoiling them with gifts and affection. The main disciplinarians of children are their mother's brother and other members of their mother's kin group. This is partly because a child's behavior reflects well or poorly on the kin group of the mother, so members of this group have the primary duty of monitoring and correcting children.

The Hopi illustrate how the matrilineal principle recruits individuals into kin groups in which they perform various economic, religious, and social roles. They also show how the form of descent found among a people influences interpersonal relationships between relatives, such as between husbands and wives and between fathers and children.

Neither the Tikopia nor the Hopi "typifies" patrilineal and matrilineal kinship. A wide range of diversity occurs in patrilineal and matrilineal systems. The Tikopia and Hopi do illustrate some of the differences between patrilineal and matrilineal peoples with respect to recruitment into groups, allocation of roles, nature of emotional attachment, and organization of common activities. They also exemplify a fundamental organizational feature of many preindustrial societies: Kin groups carry out most of the cooperative activities that more specialized groups perform in industrialized nations. If we compare ourselves with many preindustrial peoples for whom kinship ties are the organizational basis for most activities, we see that family relations are not the backbone of our nation, contrary to the statement of some politicians (see "A Closer Look").

Avunculocality Revisited

Comparatively speaking, Hopi women have a great deal of influence on domestic life and control over property—land in particular. (As we discuss in Chapter 10, Hopi women owe their relatively high status partly to their control over land and partly to matrilineality and matrilocality.) Because they are a matrilocal people, sisters live together and their husbands live apart from their matrilineal relatives for as long as the marriage lasts.

But not all matrilineal people are matrilocal. The most common pattern of postmarital residence among matrilineal peoples is avunculocality, in which married couples live with or near the husband's mother's brother (Chapter 8). More than one-third of all matrilineal societies have avunculocal residence as the predominant pattern. Most of the others are matrilocal or patrilocal. Now that we are aware of matrilineal descent groups and know that they often control property, we can understand this seemingly bizarre residence pattern.

First, the fact that a people are matrilineal does not mean that women control property and politics. That is, *matrilineality*—descent through females—should not be confused with *matriarchy*—rule by women. Even in most matrilineal societies, men control and make decisions about the use and allocation of land and other forms of wealth and have more of a say than women do in public affairs. The oldest competent man of a lineage usually has the greatest control over life-sustaining or culturally valuable property in a matrilineal society. Unlike patrilineal peoples, in a matrilineal society a lineage elder has authority over his sister's children rather than his own children because the latter are not members of his own descent group and supposedly have their property and loyalties with the group of their mothers.

How can a lineage elder have his sisters' sons living with or near him, where he can keep an eye on them, and where they can look after their own interest in land and common property? The answer is avunculocal residence. If a man's sisters' sons bring their wives to live with them in a common residence, then the elder and young male members of a single matrilineage are localized in a single place. The married women of the matrilineage are scattered among the households of their husbands' mothers' brothers. The children of the matrilineage's women are likewise scattered among the households of their fathers, so long as they are unmarried. But as they marry they return to their own mother's brother's households—the place of their own lineage. In short, avunculocal residence has the effect of localizing male matrilineal relatives who have a common interest in land, wealth, or other property. It therefore is explicable once we understand how the matrilineal

Backbone of the Nation?

How often have you heard it said that "the family is the backbone of our nation"? From a comparative perspective, our nuclear family is a rather weak and insignificant kind of group for society as a whole. You can see this in several ways now that you have some feeling for the cross-cultural diversity in marriage, family, and kinship.

First, what do we typically want to know about people as individuals? When we meet someone for the first time, do we ask "Who is your father?" or "Who is your mother?" No, we ordinarily do not. Who a stranger's kinfolk are is of no special interest to us. We are much more likely to ask "Where do you work?" or "What do you do?"—the latter being a question that could mean lots of things but (significantly) usually is a question about occupation. College-age students may instead ask "What's your major?" This last question usually means "What occupation will you perform when you've finished school?" (You can see this by answering "anthropology" and waiting for the question that often fol-

lows: "And what are you going to do with *that*?") Culturally, we identify an individual by his or her occupation; the occupational status of a person is his or her *master status*, as the sociologists call it.

Second, how do you think about and culturally categorize the organization of your society? Certainly, you do not think of it as a kinship group. You do not think of small domestic groups fitting into larger kin groups, which in turn fit into still larger kin groups, and so on. More likely, you think of it as one political and territorial unit fitting into others: cities into states, and states into the nation as a whole.

Third, what are the functions of the nuclear family—our most important kin group—in North American society, and how do they compare with the functions of kin groups in other human populations? The kinds of activities organized by the family are fewer in number than in most preindustrial societies. Even these functions are increasingly becoming alienated from the family in our society. For example, enculturation and child care,

which are among the most important "traditional functions" of a husband-father and wife-mother, increasingly are being handled by babysitters and professionals in day-care centers. Domestic chores are being farmed out to housekeepers, gardeners, and others, and not just among the elite. Restaurants cook much of our food and wash the dishes afterward. Elderly people typically live by themselves or in retirement communities and rest homes rather than with their adult children. Television shows and commercials entertain and—whether we know and like it or not—enculturate our children.

You may think that all this is for the better. But the next time you hear a politician using the cultural theme of "traditional family values" to win your vote, you might pause to consider what he or she means by the phrase. In particular, if you are a woman, you might wonder how this politician plans to arrange things so that you can enjoy these "family values" by staying at home with chores and children and still achieve the standard of living you would like.

---

principle forms kin groups that hold common property, and once we realize that men have control over wealth and public affairs among most matrilineal couples.

Cognatic Descent

In patrilineal cultures, most people become members of the kin groups of their fathers. If enough people do this over several generations, patrilineages and perhaps patriclans develop, the members of which are related through males. Conversely, in matrilineal cultures most people join the groups of their mothers, and over time matrilineal descent groups develop.

In real societies that practice either of these unilineal systems, the membership of lineages and clans is not as well defined as the descent principles make them appear. For instance, in matrilineal systems, adoptions, childless women, inability to get along with one's matrikin, insufficiency of land owned by the matrigroup, and other fac-

tors make it likely that some individuals will join a group other than that of their mothers. As a result, many matrilineages include some members who are not matrilineally related. Thus, even in unilineal systems there often is some degree of choice about which group to join, depending on personal preferences and circumstances.

Cultures with **cognatic descent** have no formal principle or rule about whether individuals join the groups of their mothers or fathers. Some people join with their fathers, others with their mothers, entirely or largely according to preferences and circumstances. A **cognatic descent group**, then, consists of all the individuals who can trace their descent back to the common ancestor (or founder) of the group, through both female and male links.

More than in unilineal systems, in cognatic descent people make choices about the groups they want to join. The choice commonly is based on factors such as one's chances of inheriting rights to land use or other forms of property or wealth; the desire to associate with a relative of high status or rank; childhood residence; and emotional ties. For example, in a cognatic system you might decide to reside and cooperate with your mother's relatives if her kin group has a lot more land available for you to cultivate than does your father's group. Or if a coveted political office or honorific title is about to become vacant in your father's group, you might decide to try to acquire it by moving in and working with his relatives.

Cognatic Descent in Polynesia

Cognatic descent is found in all continents, but it is especially prevalent among Polynesians, including the Samoans, Hawaiians, Tahitians, and New Zealand Maori. Details varied from island to island, but generally speaking, a person could join any cognatic group or groups to which he or she could trace ancestry. Membership in the group bestowed rights to agricultural land, house sites, and some other kinds of property.

In cultures with patrilineal and matrilineal descent a person ordinarily becomes a member of only one group—that of her or his father or mother, respectively. With cognatic descent, everyone potentially belongs to several groups because everyone has the opportunity to join all the groups to which their parents belong, and each parent probably is a member of at least two groups. If the kin groups intermarry, everyone potentially will belong to a great many groups—perhaps even to most of the groups that exist in their society.

Unlike unilineal systems, then, cognatic descent groups have overlapping membership. This potentially poses a problem for access to land and other culturally valued things. For example, if all members of a group have rights to the land collectively owned by this group, and if one-half or more of the entire population potentially has such rights, then the "right" does not mean much.

In some Polynesian cultures, people keep up their membership in several groups simultaneously by contributing labor and foods to feasts sponsored by the group and generally showing their interest in and commitment to the group. The islands of Samoa provide an example. Each Samoan village has a council that plans public activities, levies fines, and performs other functions for the whole community. Each village is composed of several cognatic kin groups known as *'aiga.* Although each *'aiga* has branches represented in several villages, every *'aiga* has an ancestral homeland village. In its homeland village, each *'aiga* has the right to select one or more of its men to hold titles, or *matai,* and it is these titleholders who serve as the *'aiga*'s representatives to the village council. Acquisition of a *matai* carries great honor, as

In Samoa, cognatic descent relationships make people eligible to acquire titles that bestow prestige and leadership. This is a Samoan "talking chief" making a speech.

well as authority to regulate use of the *'aiga*'s land, resolve disputes among the *'aiga*'s members, organize feasts and ceremonial gifts, and assess the members for contributions to marriages, funerals, and other events.

When a title becomes vacant because of death or some other reason, all members of the entire *'aiga* have a voice in choosing a new *matai,* whether they live in the homeland village or not. Because people belong to several *'aiga* simultaneously, they have a voice in choosing the new *matai* for several groups, although they may not exercise their rights in all the *'aiga* to which they belong. Because men belong to several groups, they have the right to compete for and gain a title in these groups. A young man might anticipate a future title vacancy in one of his *'aiga* and decide to move to the village where that *'aiga* is represented on the council to concentrate his energies on acquiring that particular *matai.* This general kinship and village-level political organization persists in rural Samoa to this day.

The Samoan *'aiga* illustrates some of the common functions of cognatic kin groups: They can hold property and regulate access to land, organize cooperative activities, and serve as the structural basis for acquiring honored and authoritative political roles. In these respects they are similar to the lineages and clans of unilineal systems. But in cognatic systems the range of individual choice about group membership is much wider than in unilineal descent.

Bilateral Kinship

Bilateral (two-sided) kinship systems differ from unilineal descent in that kinship relationships are traced through both genders. An individual regards his or her relatives through both parents as equal in importance; cousins are seen as the same kind of relative, for instance, regardless of whether they are related to ego through the mother or the father.

Bilateral kinship, as you may recognize, exists in most contemporary Western countries, but it is also common in other parts of the world. Bilateral kinship differs from both unilineal and cognatic descent in that no large, well-defined, property-holding groups exist. Rather than lineages and clans, the tracing of kinship relationships bilaterally produces associations of relatives known as the **kindred**. A kindred consists of all the people that a specific person recognizes as bilaterally related to himself or herself.

To understand bilateral kinship and the kindred, imagine a Canadian or an American woman named Liz. Liz recognizes her relatives through her father and mother as equivalent and interacts with them in much the same way (unless she has established strong bonds with someone because they live close by or for some other reason). The more distant the relationship, the less likely Liz is to interact with or even know who her relatives are. The only times she is likely to see many of her kindred in the same place are at events such as weddings, funerals, and family reunions. Many of Liz's relatives do not know one another (her cousins on her mother's side are unlikely to know her cousins through her father, for example). All the members of her kindred do not consider themselves relatives, and they certainly do not own any common property. The only thing that ever brings them together is the fact that they are related to Liz.

As this hypothetical example shows, a kindred is *ego-focused,* meaning that each individual is the center of his or her own set of relatives. Only you and your siblings share the same kindred; your mother has a different kindred, as do your father and all your cousins. Unilineal and cognatic descent groups, in contrast, are *ancestor-focused,* meaning that people are members of a descent group by virtue of the fact that they recognize descent from a common ancestor.

The Iban, a people of the tropical island of Borneo in Malaysia, provide a non-Western example of bilateral kinship. The Iban are shifting cultivators who traditionally lived in longhouses that were subdivided into numerous apartments. Each apartment was occupied by a single bilocally extended family called a *bilek.* Most *bilek* included three generations: an elderly couple, one of their

In bilateral kinship, there are no large descent groups that own common property. Rather, marriages and other important events in the lives of people provide occasions at which a person's kindred gather. This is a marriage in Hungary.

married children and his or her spouse, and their grandchildren. The *bilek* owned the section of the longhouse in which its members resided. It also formed an economically independent unit: Its members cooperated in the growing of dry rice, and it owned its own land.

The *bilek* is the main residential and property-owning group among the Iban. Compared with the unilineal and cognatic descent groups, the *bilek* is relatively small, averaging only six or seven members. When an individual Iban needs more people for some purpose, he can ask for help from his kindred, people who are related to him through bilateral ties. In organizing hunting or periodic long-distance trading or warfare expeditions, for example, a man would call out dozens of his first and second cousins to get enough people together to help him for this specific purpose. In other words, a man mobilized his kindred to help him accomplish some particular task or achieve some goal. The bilateral relatives he mobilized, however, came together and cooperated only occasionally. They did not constitute a permanent kin group and did not hold any common property because the *bilek* was the property-holding unit.

Influences on Kinship Systems

Why does a given culture develop one form of kinship rather than another? Are there any general explanations? Ethnologists have worked on this question for decades, but so far none has identified a single factor or

Most herding cultures are patrilineal, partly because men usually own and manage livestock. These are Jordanian sheep herders.

even a small number of factors that account for why different cultures develop different kinship systems. There are, however, a number of factors that seem to *influence* (as opposed to *cause*) which form of kinship a people will have.

One of the main influences is how a people adapt to their environment (see Chapter 6). For example, about 60 percent of all foraging cultures are bilateral or cognatic. These two kinship systems allow individuals and nuclear families a great deal of choice about which of their many kinship relationships they should activate at any given time. Generally, they can move to and harvest the resources of any band to which they can trace a kinship tie. Given that most foragers must adapt to seasonal, annual, and spatial fluctuations in wild food availability, keeping one's options open is advantageous.

Other descent forms are also affected by adaptation. About three-fourths of pastoral societies have patrilineal descent. According to one hypothesis, the association between nomadic herding and patrilineal descent exists because livestock most often are owned and managed by men. To conserve labor devoted to protecting and moving animals to seasonally available pastures, a group of brothers often combines their animals into a single herd. Also, inheritance of animals typically passes from fathers to sons. Brothers tend to stay together to cooperate in herd management and look after their inheritance; there-

fore, they will reside patrilocally. Patrilocal residence associates male relatives together in a single location, whereas it disperses females. Descent through males develops as a consequence.

Patrilineal descent also has been interpreted as a way to improve success in intergroup warfare. It keeps a group of related males together and thereby increases their willingness to cooperate in battles, as well as decreases the chances of male relatives becoming antagonists. Several cross-cultural studies have found a strong association between patrilineal descent and frequent intergroup warfare. But exactly why this correlation exists is a subject of much dispute.

What are some hypotheses about the causes of matrilineal descent? Some anthropologists think that it is connected to the way matrilineal peoples acquire their food. Matrilineal descent is more likely to be found among horticultural peoples (see Chapter 6) than it is with any other adaptation; nearly 60 percent of matrilineal cultures are horticultural. This association is probably related to the fact that women perform so much of the daily subsistence work in most horticultural populations.

A study by Melvin Ember and Carol Ember suggests that horticulture plus long-distance warfare or trade is likely to lead to the development of matrilineal descent. The reasoning is that if the men are far away fighting or trading much of the time, they cannot at the same time be gardening to feed their relatives; so women will have to take over most of the subsistence labor. They are unlikely to do this effectively if postmarital residence is patrilocal because then they would be working for their husbands' relatives rather than for their own. At any rate, a middle-aged or elderly couple will want to keep their daughters around after they marry, to work their land and help support them in their old age. So postmarital residence typically is matrilocal in horticultural cultures in which men are often absent. Matrilocality has the effect of localizing a group of sisters and other female matrikin in a single household or village. Their brothers move away after their marriage, and the children of these brothers develop closer relationships with their mothers' families than with their father's relatives. This ultimately leads to the tracing of descent through females (i.e., to matrilineal descent). This hypothesis is not accepted by all anthropologists, many of whom believe that there is no universal explanation. It does seem to work reasonably well for some matrilineal cultures, such as the Iroquois and the Huron of North America and the Nayar of south India. Almost certainly, no single determinant can explain all cases of matrilineality, or for that matter the other forms of kinship. It may be that cross-cultural variations in kinship are influenced by so many kinds of complex factors that no generalized explanation is possible.

The majority of matrilocal and matrilineal cultures are horticultural people, for whom women's labor is important in family subsistence. This Madagascar woman is harvesting a field.

Classifying Relatives: Kinship Terminologies

In Chapter 2 we noted that one of the major components of cultural knowledge is the way a people classify natural and social reality. As is by now apparent, kinship relationships and kinship groups are a major part of social reality in human cultures. Just as cultures differ in the ways they trace their descent and form social groupings of relatives, so do they differ in how they place relatives into types, or labeled categories. The labeled categories are called **kin terms**, and the way in which a people classify their relatives into these categories is called their **kinship terminology**.

Most people think that the kin terms they use to refer to different relatives reflect the way those relatives are related to them biologically (genetically). In fact, this is true for some English kin terms: *mother, father, sister, brother, son,* and *daughter* all define individuals related to you in distinct biological ways (setting aside considerations of adoption, foster parenting, or step relatives).

However, there are other English kin terms that do not faithfully reflect genetic relatedness. Consider the terms *uncle* and *aunt*. They refer to siblings of your parents, and they differ only by their gender. But the individuals you call *aunt* and *uncle* are related to you in four different ways: your father's siblings, your mother's siblings, your father's siblings' spouses, and your mother's siblings' spouses. Note that both consanguineal and affi-

nal relatives are included in the English terms *uncle* and *aunt*. The same idea applies to some other terms: A particular term groups together several individuals related to you in different ways. Thus, *grandfather* includes both mother's father and father's father; *grandmother* is used for both mother's mother and father's mother; and *first cousin* refers to a wide range of people who have quite different biological connections to you.

A people's kinship terminology only partly reflects the biological relationships between individuals. More fundamentally, it reflects the various norms, rights and duties, and behavioral patterns that characterize social relationships between kinfolk. Collapsing relatives of different kinds into a single term reflects the cultural fact that people think of them as the same kind of relative; in turn, people conceive of them as the same kind of relative because they have similar kinds of relations with them. Thus, the men we call *uncle* have the same general kinds of social relationships with us regardless of whether they are our mother's or our father's brothers.

Before we can discuss particular kinship terminologies, we need to understand the logic by which they are constructed. For one thing, every term has a reciprocal term. For example, the reciprocal of *grandfather* is either *granddaughter* or *grandson*. If you call a woman *mother,* she will call you *son* or *daughter.*

Kinship terminologies are constructed using several criteria. Three of the most important criteria are (1) gender of referent, (2) generation, and (3) side of the family. In the following discussion, *ego* refers to the person using the given kin term.

The gender of the individual to whom the term refers (the referent) usually is a relevant criterion for the kin term used. In English, gender matters for terms like *brother* and *sister, uncle* and *aunt,* and *grandfather* and *grandmother*. Indeed, gender is the only criterion that distinguishes the relatives just mentioned from one another. Gender is irrelevant, however, for another of our kin terms, *cousin*.

Kinship terms usually reflect whether the individual referred to is of the same or a different generation than ego's. In English, specific terms are used for relatives in ego's own generation (*cousin*), in ego's parents' generation (*aunt*), and in ego's children's generation (*niece*). In describing kinship terminologies we call ego's parents' generation the *first ascending generation* and ego's children's generation the *first descending generation*. Although the terms used in most kinship terminologies reflect generational differences, two systems of terminology use terms that transcend generations.

Side of ego's family is a third criterion by which kin terminologies are constructed. In English, side of the family is irrelevant: Relatives through the mother receive the same terms as relatives through the father. As we know, many other cultures place special emphasis on relationships through females (mothers) or males (fathers), and this emphasis is reflected in their terminological systems.

Varieties of Kinship Terminology

We shall discuss only the five most common types of kinship terminology: Eskimo, Hawaiian, Iroquois, Omaha, and Crow. Do not be misled by the names of these systems. Lewis Henry Morgan, the American anthropologist mentioned in Chapter 4, developed the basic classification system for kinship terminology in 1871. He named each system after the first people among whom he discovered it. Although four terminologies are named after Native American groups, all are found scattered around the world. To simplify our discussion, we consider only terms used for consanguineal relatives in ego's generation and in ego's first ascending (parental) generation. To make these systems easier to understand, we translate the terms into what would be their closest English equivalents. Keep in mind that these translations are only rough approximations, and that some terms have no exact English equivalents.

Eskimo   Eskimo terminology is the easiest for English speakers to understand because this is the system we use (see Figure 9.4). In this system, ego's biological mother is called *mother* and ego's biological father is called *father*. These are the only two persons to whom these terms apply. The term *aunt* is used both for ego's father's sister and ego's mother's sister, and the term *uncle* is used for father's brother and mother's brother. The terms *brother* and *sister* are used only for the children of ego's mother and father. The term *cousin* is used for all children of ego's uncles and aunts.

Hawaiian   Hawaiian kinship terminology is the simplest because it uses the fewest terms (see Figure 9.5).

All relatives in ego's first ascending generation are called either *mother* or *father*. The term *mother* is extended to include ego's mother's sister and ego's father's sister, and *father* is extended to include father's brother and mother's brother. In ego's own generation, everyone is called either *brother* or *sister*. Thus, Hawaiian terminology includes no terms equivalent to the English terms *uncle, aunt,* or *cousin*. Although the Hawaiian system extends the terms *mother* and *father,* this does not mean that individuals are unable to distinguish their biological parents from their other relatives of the parental generation.

Hawaiian often is called a generational system because only the generation of the term's referent is relevant; if Figure 9.5 showed the first descending generation, people whom English speakers called *niece* and *nephew* would be shown as ego's *daughter* and *son*.

Iroquois   Iroquois terminology categorizes relatives very differently than does either the Hawaiian or the Eskimo system (Figure 9.6). The term *father* includes father's brother but not mother's brother. *Mother* includes mother's sister but not father's sister. The term *uncle* is used only for mother's brother; *aunt* is used only for father's sister. If we look at ego's generation, we also see a difference. The children of father's brother and mother's sister are called *brother* and *sister*. The term *cousin* is used only for the children of mother's brother and father's sister. Thus, in the Iroquois system, ego differentiates cousins. Although this distinction may seem unusual to us, it also exists in the Omaha and Crow systems, so we need to understand the logic behind it.

The Iroquois system distinguishes between parallel and cross cousins. Parallel cousins are terminologically classified with ego's own brothers and sisters. Cross cousins are distinguished from parallel cousins and called by a term that we would probably translate as *cousin*. To understand the logic behind calling parallel cousins *brother* and *sister* and cross cousins *cousin,* we have to go back to the terms used for ego's parents' siblings. Ego's father's brother and mother's sister are called *father*

Figure 9.4   Eskimo Kinship Terminology

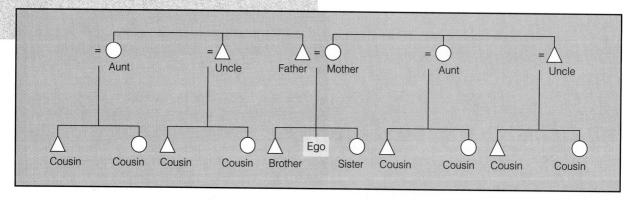

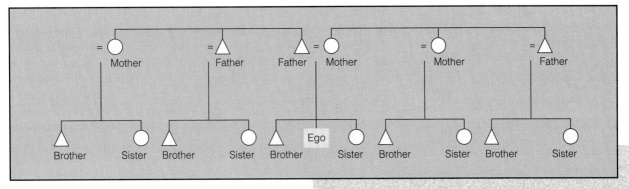

Figure 9.5 Hawaiian Kinship Terminology

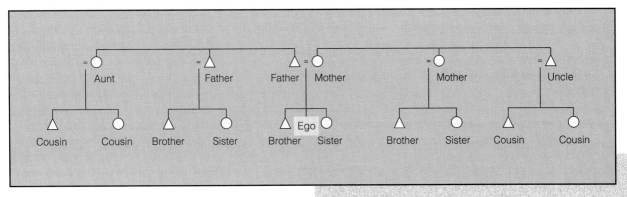

Figure 9.6 Iroquois Kinship Terminology

and *mother,* respectively. Thus, it is logical to call their children *brother* and *sister* (what do you call the children of the people you call *mother* and *father*?). Ego calls his father's sister *aunt* and his mother's brother *uncle,* so it is logical to call their children (ego's cross cousins) by a term we would translate as *cousin.*

Omaha   Omaha is a difficult kinship terminology for English speakers to understand (see Figure 9.7). The terms used in the first ascending generation are identical to the Iroquois system: parallel cousins are called *brother* and *sister.* The only difference between Iroquois and Omaha is how cross cousins are treated. Omaha terminology has no equivalent to the English term *cousin.* In addition, in Omaha terminology a distinction is made between cross cousins on the mother's side (the children of mother's brother) and cross cousins on the father's side (the children of father's sister). Mother's brothers' daughters are called *mother,* and mother's brothers' sons are called *mother's brother* (or *uncle*). Thus, ego's maternal cross cousins are grouped with individuals in ego's parents' generation. The situation appears even more confused for ego's paternal cross cousins, since the term used depends on ego's sex. If ego is a male, he calls his father's sisters' children

niece and *nephew.* If ego is a female, she calls her father's sisters' children *son* and *daughter.*

Why are there two separate terms for father's sisters' children, depending on the sex of ego? This distinction is perfectly logical. Remember that kinship terms are reciprocal and that we have only indicated the terms used by ego. To understand why the sex of ego is important in this relationship, we must ask: What would father's sisters' children call ego? In Figure 9.7, you can see that ego is their mother's brother's child. Thus, if ego is female, they would call her *mother,* and she would reciprocate by calling them *son* or *daughter.* If ego is male, they would call him *uncle,* and therefore he would call them *niece* or *nephew.*

Crow   Crow terminology is said to be the mirror image or reverse of Omaha (see Figure 9.8). First ascending generation terms are the same as in the Omaha and Iroquois systems. As in the Omaha and Iroquois systems, parallel cousins are called *brother* and *sister.* Once again the difference is in the terms used for cross cousins. In the Crow systems, father's sisters' children are called *father* and *father's sister* or *aunt.* Using the same logic

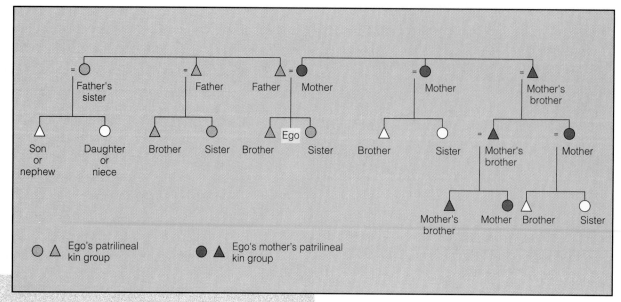

Figure 9.7 Omaha Kinship Terminology

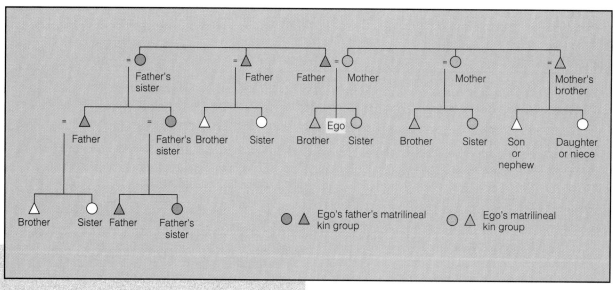

Figure 9.8 Crow Kinship Terminology

discussed for the Omaha system, in the Crow system mother's brothers' children are called *son* or *daughter* if ego is male and *niece* or *nephew* if ego is female.

There are a few other systems, but these five are the most widespread. This diversity is surprising, and some of the ways of classifying relatives are puzzling. Can we account for them?

Determinants of Kinship Terminology

In previous chapters we have emphasized that cultures are integrated: One aspects "fits" with others and sometimes makes sense only when understood in context. In kin terminology systems we have a prime example of this integration.

A good way to begin is by noting that the five terminologies described can be separated into two types. In the Eskimo and Hawaiian, the side of the family does not matter in classifying relatives; in the Iroquois, Omaha, and Crow it does. Stated another way, among the diverse peoples who use the Eskimo or Hawaiian system, the logical principle of distinguishing relatives according to side of ego's family is irrelevant; they *could* recognize the distinction between mother's and father's kin, but they do not. Among the many cultures who use the Iroquois, Crow, or Omaha system, the logical principle of distinguishing relatives according to family side is relevant. Why should the side of the family matter in some terminological systems but not in others?

You might already have guessed the answer. The side of the family matters in some terminologies because some people trace their descent through only one of their parents. The side of the family makes no difference in other systems because these populations trace their kin connections equally through both parents. *In general,* the way a people trace their descent affects the relationships between kin, which affects the terms used to refer to various kin.

Why say "in general"? Because the correlations between types of kinship terminologies and forms of descent are far from perfect. In a moment, for example, we shall show that the logical principles underlying the Omaha classification make sense for systems in which patrilineal descent is predominant; but not all patrilineal systems also have Omaha terminologies and not all Omaha terminologies occur in patrilineal systems. Here again, humankind's complexity defies our attempts to explain something totally, and we must be satisfied with general correlations that have many exceptions.

Because the Eskimo classification is most familiar, we begin with it. If we compare it with the other terminologies, it differs in two main ways: (1) it makes no distinctions between ego's father's and mother's relatives, and (2) no other relatives of any kind are lumped together with nuclear family relatives. Assume that these two features reflect people's ideas about how various kin are related. We might conclude that people think (1) that both sides of the family are of equal importance to an individual (or, rather, there is no systematic *pattern* of importance through one side over the other), and (2) that nuclear family relatives are somehow special and thought of differently than are other kinds of relatives. In the case of North America, our surnames are inherited mainly through males, but other than this, we are no more likely to have special relationships with our kin through our fathers than through our mothers. And, generally, the members of our nuclear families *are* special: We do not expect to inherit much, if anything, from other relatives; we usually do not live in extended households; kin groups larger than the nuclear family usually do not own property in common; and so on.

More generally, we ought to expect the Eskimo classification of relatives to be associated with cognatic or bilateral kinship. And usually it is: About 80 percent of all societies that use the Eskimo terminological system have either bilateral or cognatic kinship. This is because neither side of the family is consistently emphasized, so people do not think of their mother's or father's relatives as being any different. The absence of a special relation with kin through either parent is reflected in the terminological system.

What about the Hawaiian system? Like the Eskimo, family side is irrelevant. Logically, it ought, then, to be associated consistently with cognatic or bilateral kinship. The fact that it lumps other relatives with nuclear family members seems to indicate that the nuclear family is submerged or embedded in larger extended households. Ego should have important relations with the siblings of his or her parents and with their children. Despite this logic, the Hawaiian terminology is not as consistently associated with cognatic or bilateral kinship as is the Eskimo terminology; in fact, about 40 percent of societies that use the Hawaiian classification are unilineal. The Hawaiian system apparently is also compatible with unilineal descent.

And the Iroquois? Ego's father and father's brother are assigned a single term, which is different from mother's brother. Mother and mother's sister are given the same term, which is not the same term as ego uses for father's sister. Thus, ego distinguishes between maternal and paternal aunts and uncles in the first ascending generation. The fact that the side of the family matters in this generation seems to imply unilineal descent. And in fact the Iroquois system usually is found among peoples who trace their descent unilineally: Around 80 percent of all Iroquois terminologies occur in unilineal descent forms. If you look back to Figure 9.6, you will see that ego classes with his own brother and sister the children of relatives he classes with mother and father. This certainly makes logical sense—if you call someone *mother*, it is sensible to call her son *brother*. The cross cousins have a separate term because their parents are not classed with ego's own biological parents, which again is logically consistent.

The Omaha system also distinguishes between sides of the family, like the Iroquois. In fact, it carries the distinctions between the mother's and father's side "down" into ego's own generation. If you look back to Figure 9.7, you will see that the Omaha differs from the Iroquois by its splitting of cross cousins according to whether they are related to ego through ego's mother or father. Mother, mother's sister, and mother's brother's daughter are lumped, although they are members of different generations. Mother's brother and mother's brother's son likewise are lumped together under a single term.

What can explain this way of classifying relatives, which you probably find confusing? The fact that these relatives are all related to ego through ego's mother must mean something; and the fact that they are classified ("lumped") together and distinguished only by their gender must be significant. Indeed, both these features are clues to the logic behind the Omaha terminology. It is found among peoples who use the patrilineal principle to form kin groups.

How does patrilineal descent make sense of the Omaha system? In Figure 9.7, we have colored in all those relatives in the diagram who belong to ego's own patrilineal group. Notice that the cousins in ego's group are called *brother* and *sister,* to reflect the fact that they are in ego's own lineage. We have used a different color for those relatives who are members of ego's mother's patrilineal group. Notice that all the members of this latter group are assigned only two terms—one for the male members of the group and one for the female members of the group. We might translate the two kin terms that apply to them as "female member of my mother's group" and "male member of my mother's group." Their common social characteristic as members of ego's mother's kin group overrides the biological fact that they are members of three generations. If you have followed the argument, you will agree that the Omaha system makes perfect sense, provided it is associated with patrilineal descent forms. And, indeed, more than 90 percent of all cultures who use the Omaha terminological system are patrilineal.

Because the Crow system is the mirror image of the Omaha, we can make sense of it by showing how it reflects kinship relationships among matrilineal peoples. Go back to Figure 9.8 and look at the colors used for members of ego's own matrilineal descent group and for the matrilineal group of ego's father. You will see that all the male members of ego's father's group are called by the same term, as are all the female members of the same group. The underlying logic of the Crow terms is apparent, given matrilineal descent: Ego lumps together relatives who belong to the same descent group as his or her father. More than 70 percent of all people who use the Crow terms are also matrilineal.

The preceding discussion shows how terminological systems make sense once we understand that they reflect the prevalent relationships and groupings of kin produced by various ways of tracing kinship connections. The ways in which various people classify and label their relatives look mysterious until we understand these classifications and labels in the context of the kinship systems that give rise to them. The Eskimo terminology used by Americans would probably look strange to people who use, say, the Crow or Omaha terminology. Our failure to distinguish between relatives through one's mother and father would be strange because to them these relatives would be clearly differentiated, given the way their kinship systems place people into different kin groups.

Along these same lines, the various peoples who use one or another of these kinship classification systems cannot state the logic of their classifications in the same way we just did. For instance, people who use the Omaha terminology cannot tell you why they label their relatives as they do because they lack a comparative perspective on their own kinship system. To them, their mother, mother's sister, and mother's brother's daughter are called by the same term because all these women are the same kind of relative, just as aunts are all the same kind of relative to us. They do not realize that in Eskimo systems these females all have separate terms; nor are they aware that their terminology reflects the groupings and relationships of their kinship system. But then again, people who use the Eskimo system cannot account for their own classification system either unless they are aware of the diversity in human kinship systems discovered in the past century by anthropologists. The way a people classify their kinfolk seems quite natural to them until they become aware that other people do it differently.

Summary

Relationships and groups based on kinship are an especially important component of the social organization of pre-industrial peoples. Although kinship is based on biological relatedness, societies vary in their kinship systems. There is diversity in the kinds and sizes of groups formed using kinship principles, in the norms attached to kin roles, and in the way people culturally categorize their relatives.

One way cultures vary is in how people trace their relationships back to previous generations—in how they trace their descent. Cross-culturally, the most common forms of descent are patrilineal, matrilineal, and cognatic. All three kinds of descent principles place people into kinship groups and assign roles to them. In preindustrial cultures, the multifunctional groupings established on the basis of kinship usually are more important than in industrialized nations. The latter societies have groups that specialize in the performance of only a few kinds of tasks or functions, and for the most part the membership of these groups is not based on kinship.

Matrilineal and patrilineal descent are both unilineal forms of descent, meaning that a person traces his or her descent through either females or males, but not through both sexes. Unilineal descent groups may be formed using the matrilineal or patrilineal principle, yielding kin groups composed of people related through females and males, respectively. In order of increasing inclusiveness and genealogical depth, the main kinds of descent groups are extended families, lineages, and clans. All may be based on either the matrilineal or patrilineal principle. The multifunctional nature of descent groups and the diverse kinds of activities organized by such groups are illustrated by the patrilineal Tikopia and the matrilineal Hopi.

The avunculocal residence pattern is understandable once we realize that it is consistently found in matrilineal cultures. Avunculocal residence has the effect of forming households composed of men (and their families) with a common interest in the property of the matrilineal kin group.

In cognatic descent, people trace their ancestry through both males and females, depending on choice and circumstance. Kin groups whose members have use rights to common property or resources and who cooperate socially, economically, politically, and ritually are found in many parts of the world. The Samoan 'aiga illustrate the functions of cognatic descent groups.

People who trace their kinship relationships bilaterally have no true kin groups larger than extended families, because the kindreds of different people overlap so much. In most industrialized nations, kinship is bilateral, and large numbers of an individuals' relatives are likely to congregate only on certain occasions such as weddings, funerals, and family reunions. Individuals in preindustrial bilateral societies, such as the Iban, mobilize their kindreds to help them in various tasks, such as hunting, trading, and construction.

One important influence on the kinship systems of a culture is its mode of adaptation. Cognatic descent and bilateral kinship are common among foragers, who find it beneficial to maximize social contacts and access to diverse territories. Nomadic pastoralists usually are patrilineal, which is probably related to the tendency for males to own and manage herds. Patrilineal descent also is likely to be found among peoples who are heavily engaged in warfare with close neighbors. Matrilineality is most likely to occur among populations who are horticultural and whose men are absent for prolonged periods when engaged in long-distance trade, warfare, or both. These general associations have been supported by cross-cultural studies, but so many forces influence descent forms that no single explanation suffices to account for their occurrence.

People culturally classify their relatives into labeled categories by recognizing some differences between relatives and ignoring others. This classification gives rise to various systems of kin terminology. Five systems are most widespread: Eskimo, Hawaiian, Iroquois, Omaha, and Crow. With the exception of the Iroquois, each terminological system is associated with one form of descent. This is because the ideas people have about how they are related to one another are strongly influenced by how the descent form of their society sorts people into groups and establishes relations of one or another kind between kinfolk.

Key Terms

form of descent
unilineal descent
patrilineal descent
matrilineal descent
descent groups

unilineal descent group
unilineally extended families
lineage
clans
cognatic descent
cognatic descent group
bilateral
kindred

kin terms
kinship terminology
Eskimo
Hawaiian
Iroquois
Omaha
Crow

Suggested Readings

There are a number of excellent texts and collections of readings on kinship, descent groups, and the classification of relatives. The following is a list of such books.

Collier, Jane F., and J. Yanagisako, eds. *Gender and Kinship: Essays Toward a Unified Analysis*. Stanford, Calif.: Stanford University Press, 1987.
  • *Collection of recent articles focusing on relationships between the sexes and kinship.*
Fox, Robin. *Kinship and Marriage: An Anthropological Perspective*. New York: Cambridge University Press, 1984.
  • *Excellent comparative introduction to marriage forms, kinship systems, and their causes and consequences.*
Graburn, Nelson, ed. *Readings in Kinship and Social Structure*. New York: Harper and Row, 1971.
  • *Collection of about 60 essays, many of which were influential in the anthropological study of marriage, family, and kinship.*
Pasternak, Burton. *Introduction to Kinship and Social Organization*. Englewood Cliffs, N.J.: Prentice-Hall, 1976.
  • *A short, introductory text with a cross-cultural orientation.*
Radcliffe-Brown, A. R., and Daryll Forde, eds. *African Systems of Kinship and Marriage*. London: Oxford University Press, 1950.
  • *A collection of still-valuable essays by British anthropologists on kinship among nine African peoples. Radcliffe-Brown's introduction is regarded as a seminal paper.*

Schneider, David M. *American Kinship: A Cultural Account*. 2nd ed. Chicago: University of Chicago Press, 1980.
  • *A symbolic account of American kinship written by a leading idealist.*
Schneider, David M., and Kathleen Gough, eds. *Matrilineal Kinship*. Berkeley: University of California Press, 1961.
  • *Contains a description of nine matrilineal systems and an analysis of some dimensions of variation in matrilineal societies. Introductory essay by Schneider is a good overview.*

The following ethnographies include descriptions of specific kinship systems.

Chagnon, Napoleon A. *Yanomamö*. 5th ed. Fort Worth: Harcourt Brace Jovanovich, 1997.
  • *Description and interpretation of a patrilineal horticultural and hunting people of the Brazilian and Venezuelan rain forest. Shows how conflict and cooperation are based on kinship ties between individuals and lineages.*
Colson, Elizabeth. *The Plateau Tonga of Northern Rhodesia*. Manchester: University of Manchester, 1962.
  • *An ethnographic account of a southern African people.*
Eggan, Fred. *Social Organization of the Western Pueblos*. Chicago: University of Chicago Press, 1950.
  • *A study in which the author describes and compares the social organization of the Hopi, Hano, Zuni, Acoma, and Laguna pueblos.*
Evans-Pritchard, E. E. *The Nuer*. Oxford: Clarendon, 1940.
  • *An ethnography of an African society, long considered one of the classic studies in social organization.*

Internet Exercises

Brian Schwimmer of the Department of Anthropology at the University of Manitoba has developed a website specifically dealing with kinship. His "Kinship and Social Organization: An Interactive Tutorial" (http://www.umanitoba.ca/anthropology/kintitle.html) covers all the basic aspects of kinship.

Dennis O'Neill at Palomar College has also designed a series of "Anthropological Tutorials" (http://daphne.palomar.edu/anthro/tutorial.htm). "Sex and Marriage" and "The Nature of Kinship" cover the same concepts as this chapter. There are also other topics which correspond to different chapters of this text.

There are many websites that provide software and information for creating genealogies. Try making your own genealogical chart. The best place to begin is with your grandparents and other older relatives. Then use the Internet to begin researching more distant kin. Some sites to start your search are "Genealogy Resources on the Net" (http://www-personal.umich.edu/~cgaunt/gen_int1.html), "The Genealogy Home Page" (http://www.genhomepage.com/), or the National Genealogical Society (http://www.ngsgenealogy.org).

CHAPTER *10*

Gender in Comparative Perspective

Cultural Construction of Gender

The Sexual Division of Labor

Patterns and Influences

Intensive Agriculture
and Women's Labor

The Status of Women

Universal Subordination?

Influences on Women's Status

Women's Status in Industrial Societies

During enculturation, children learn that what is culturally expected of them depends partly on whether they are females or males. This Nepalese child offers a traditional greeting.

Visit http://www.wadsworth.com/humanity to learn more about the material covered in this chapter and to access activities, exercises, and tutorial quizzes.

HE KINDS of subjects we anthropologists study are influenced by our own culture. Like everyone, anthropologists live our lives in societies that are undergoing rapid and wide-reaching social, economic, and political changes. Our research and teaching interests are greatly affected by the events and movements occurring in the social environment in which we ourselves live. So it is not surprising that the feminist movement—surely one of the major social and political forces of the late twentieth century—has led to increased anthropological interest in the role of gender in human relationships. Before about 1970, only a handful of ethnologists worked on gender issues; at the close of the twentieth century, many hundreds of ethnologists make gender their primary research and teaching specialty.

IN THIS CHAPTER, *we make no pretense of covering the vast field of gender studies. Instead, we concentrate on three of the main dimensions of gender, which anthropologists have studied in some depth: (1) the cultural construction of gender, (2) the cross-cultural variations in the sexual division of labor, and (3) the influences on the overall status of women in human societies. As we shall see, each of these topics have relevance for male-female roles and relationships in contemporary industrialized nations.*

In any culture, beliefs about the nature of females and males affect most social relationships. Obviously, your own sexual identity is relevant when you interact with someone of the opposite sex. But even in same sex interactions, behavior is affected by cultural categories of persons, norms, world views, meanings, and other ideas that influence conceptions about gender. A man's behavior is influenced by his ideas about what it means to be masculine when he is talking with another man, just as when he is talking to a woman. Likewise, beliefs about gender permeate relationships in a variety of social settings and contexts: in the workplace, home, political arena, and church, to name a few. Our culture's ideas about males and females—and about masculinity and femininity—permeate most of our relationships and behaviors, whether or not we are aware of it.

From field studies of cultures around the world, anthropologists have found that gender is relevant to an individual's self-identity, roles, access to valued resources, and overall status in all known cultures. Everywhere, gender matters: It makes a difference for who you are, what you have, how you interact, and what you can become, among other things. But anthropologists have also found that in different cultures, gender matters to different degrees and in different ways. These cultural variations and the factors that affect them are the main subject of this chapter. A good way to begin our discussion is by making the point that gender is a culturally variable construct, rather than an entirely biologically determined (natural) phenomenon.

Cultural Construction of Gender

Anthropologists often say that gender is culturally constructed, not biologically determined. The **cultural construction of gender** is best introduced with a technical distinction between *sex* and *gender*. A person's sex is determined biologically, by chromosomes—your geni-

talia, predominant hormones, and secondary sexual characteristics (breasts, hair, body size and musculature, and the like) are fixed by your chromosomes. (Although not considered here, note that a person's sex is not always unambiguously female or male.) Gender, in contrast, is culturally defined. A person's sex is a physical reality, but how males and females perceive and define themselves and each other, what it means to be a woman or a man, how women and men relate to each other, what roles are appropriate for men and women—all these and most other elements of maleness and femaleness are socially learned during enculturation, not biologically fixed at birth. They are culturally variable, not constant or universal.

To say that gender is culturally constructed is to say that being biologically male or female has different implications in various cultures. Maleness among the Yąnomamö is one thing, maleness among the Maasai another thing, and maleness among the Tahitians yet something else. Likewise, womanhood in various cultures has different implications and meanings.

To exemplify the cultural construction of gender, we turn to Anna Meigs's study of the Hua, a New Guinea people. The Hua—who number about 3,500—are horticulturalists who live in villages of around 100 to 300. Each Hua village contains one or more men's houses, occupied by initiated people of the patrilineages of the village. Initiated people include men who have completed the complex "male" initiation ceremonies and women with more than two children who have passed through menopause and been initiated themselves. Other women and girls, as well as boys who have not yet been initiated, live in separate houses, away from people who have been initiated.

To describe Hua conceptions of femaleness and maleness, we focus on a puzzle. Male initiation ceremonies (discussed further in Chapter 15) occur in many cultures on all continents. Similarly, wives and husbands live in separate dwellings in many regions, especially in polygynous societies. However, the Hua practice of initiating postmenopausal women with more than two children and having them live with initiated men is unusual and, possibly, unique. The puzzle is, Why were postmenopausal women with more than two children initiated and allowed to live in the men's house? The answer takes us into how Hua culture constructs categories of gender and attributes certain characteristics to these genders.

Hua believe that bodies contain a life-giving substance (like a vital essence) that they call *nu*. *Nu* is thought of as a real, physical substance—not a mystical or magical thing—that can be transferred from one person to another and gained and lost in various ways. Female bodies contain an excess of *nu,* which in Hua thought makes women grow faster and age more slowly than men but also makes them unattractively moist. On the other hand, men naturally contain a smaller amount of *nu,* so they have difficulty with growth and maintenance of vitality later in life, but they are attractively dry and hard. Hua explain many of the differences between men and women by the amount of *nu:* Men are stronger and fiercer because they are dry, for example.

Nu takes several forms. It is both gaseous (breath) and liquid (blood, sweat, semen, female sexual secretions). A transfer of *nu* between individuals may be either harmful or helpful, depending on the nature of the relationship between the giver and the recipient. Transfer of *nu* may occur during eating, sexual intercourse, and other kinds of direct and indirect contact. For example, a woman transfers *nu* to people when she serves food to them. *Nu* from her bodily secretions adheres to the food and gets ingested by her children or her husband. A woman also transfers *nu* to her husband when she has intercourse with him. But the giving of feminine *nu* to a man in the act of intercourse is harmful to the man because it pollutes and debilitates him. Intercourse is also damaging to a man because he contributes his scarce *nu* (in the form of breath and semen) to a woman during sex, so she gains strength and vitality at his expense.

Nu is what makes women polluting to males, and the greater the difference in *nu* between a woman and a man, the more dangerous that woman is to the man. But both men and women can and do lose or gain *nu,* depending on their activities, their diet, and their age. After decades of engaging in sexual intercourse with and eating foods touched by their wives and other women, middle-aged and elderly men have picked up lots of *nu.* They become invulnerable to further contamination by contact with females and therefore may eat *nu*-rich foods and participate in sexual intercourse with less anxiety than younger men. Gaining *nu* over the years makes them become "like women," Hua say.

Women lose *nu* whenever they menstruate, handle and prepare food, and have babies. Their *nu* is transferred to others by these activities and events. Over their life course women thus are drained of *nu,* and this draining means that they become less and less dangerous to males as they grow older. Women who have given birth to more than two children are considered to have lost enough *nu* that they are no longer polluting. They therefore have become "like men."

In these ways Hua culture constructs gender categories on the basis of beliefs about quantity of *nu* as influenced by a person's stage in the life cycle. If gender categories are culturally constructed using these criteria, there is no necessary reason why there are only two

highly discrete (either/or) genders. Indeed, Hua culture recognizes gender distinctions based on a person's genitals (in which case one is either male or female) and distinctions based on the quantity of *nu.* The latter criterion gives rise to two additional nondiscrete (more/less) gender categories that the Hua call *figapa* and *kakora.* Although the *figapa/kakora* distinction is relevant only in certain ritual contexts, it is significant that people who are genitally male or female can be classified with the opposite gender for certain purposes.

Figapa, which ethnographer Meigs translates as "uninitiated person," are people whose bodies contain lots of substances associated with femininity (e.g., menstrual blood, vaginal secretions, fluids associated with childbirth). *Figapa* include the following kinds of people:

- children of both sexes because they have recently been in intimate contact with a woman, their mother;
- women in their childbearing years because they are the essence of femininity and their bodies contain maximum amounts of feminine substances;
- postmenopausal women who have not had at least three children because their bodies are not sufficiently drained of feminine substances; and
- elderly men because female *nu* has been transmitted to them by their lifetime of activities that exposed them to contact with women.

These people—whether or not their genitals are female—are all "like women" because their bodies contain lots of substances symbolically considered feminine.

Kakora, translated by Meigs as "initiated person," consists of

- males in their early teens through the prime years who have been initiated (except elderly men) because during the initiation procedures they have rigorously avoided female foods and contact with women and so have minimal quantities of *nu;* and
- postmenopausal women with more than two children because three or more childbirths have drained them of most feminine substances, so they are no longer a source of danger to males.

These people are eligible to live in the men's house and to obtain the secret "male" knowledge gained during initiation ceremonies. To return to our original puzzle: Postmenopausal women are eligible to join the men's house because Hua culture constructs gender categories in such a way that they can be initiated and become *kakora,* and *kakora* live in the men's house. As Meigs (1990, 109) puts it, the feminine substances in their bodies have been "massively cleaned out three or more times," and without these substances culturally associated with femininity they are "like men."

Many North Americans believe that women are emotionally better suited to caretaker roles than are men. This belief helps to account for why women predominate in occupations dealing with the care and education of young children.

This example is presented in such detail because the Hua so clearly illustrate our point about the cultural construction of gender. The objective physical distinctions between the sexes—genitals, beards, breasts, and so on—are differences that are recognized and relevant for behavior in all known cultures. But, as the Hua show, cultures use the raw material (to speak metaphorically) of these differences to construct varying beliefs about the ways in which females and males differ. (Thus, Hua believe that men and women differ not only in the obvious physical ways but also in the quantity of *nu* each has.) These beliefs in turn affect the attitudes each sex holds about the other and the behavior each sex adopts toward each other. (Thus, Hua men in some contexts and at some ages are fearful about the possibility of feminine pollution and therefore try to minimize their contact with women, their intake of food prepared by women, and their sexual relations with women.)

The more different some culture's beliefs are from one's own, the more obvious it is that those beliefs are a cultural construct rather than a biological imperative. Therefore, because Hua beliefs pertaining to male-female

relationships seem exotic to most Westerners, the fact that gender is culturally constructed among these people is readily apparent. However, all people's ideas about gender are culturally constructed. To stimulate thought, we briefly present some ideas on the construction of gender in Euro-American culture.

Fairy tales, stories, movies, and many video and computer games reflect Western ideas about male dominance and self-reliance versus female passivity and dependence. Princesses, maidens, and other kinds of young, attractive, and usually helpless women are rescued by brave, dashing men who use their physical prowess to overcome unbeatable odds and win the fair damsel's heart and body.

Speaking more generally, many Americans see females as caring of others, emotional, socially skilled, physically fragile, family oriented, and patient. Males are taken to be more selfish, rational, tolerant of physical discomfort ("tough"), coordinated, and individualistic.

Now consider the possible effects of these cultural conceptions on the uneven distribution of occupational roles between women and men in the modern American economy. The predominant pattern is for members of each sex to move into jobs for which they are held to be best suited, given American cultural conceptions of gender. This happens for at least two reasons: (1) Individual men and women more often seek those jobs that they find appropriate for their sex or believe they have the best chance of getting or succeeding in; people apply for certain kinds of jobs according to their preferences, based in part on their beliefs about "sex roles." (2) Employers tend to hire people according to their own cultural conceptions of which sex is likely to do well in a particular job; the employment market itself allocates men and women into certain kinds of jobs.

This is changing rapidly today, but many jobs remain disproportionately female or male. Thus, women predominate in jobs that involve nurturing (e.g., nursing, day care, teaching of elementary students, pediatric medicine), routine interactions with the public (e.g., receptionists, store clerks, restaurant waitresses), repetitive and patient use of fine motor skills (word processing, sewing and stitching), and cleaning and housekeeping. A few of the jobs in which men predominate are those involving outdoor activity (equipment operation, driving, carpentry and construction), high-level decision making (management, administration), and knowledge of mathematical principles (science, engineering, computer programming). How much of the occupational difference between the sexes results from the American cultural construction of gender, which defines females as having certain inherent characteristics, males as having a contrasting set?

Women produce much or most of the food supply in a great many cultures. These women from Papua New Guinea are fishing.

To say that gender is culturally constructed is not equivalent to saying that physical differences between males and females are irrelevant. In fact, such differences are everywhere relevant in many ways, including the allocation of work activities. But, as discussed in the next section, biological differences between the sexes are relevant in diverse ways and to varying degrees in the world's cultures.

The Sexual Division of Labor

The **sexual division of labor** refers to the patterned ways in which productive and other economic activities are allocated to men and women. There is a sexual division of labor in all cultures. It implies, necessarily, that males and females share or pool some of the products of their labor. Each sex has access to the products and services produced by the other, so that the tasks of males and females are, to some extent, complementary.

In modern North America the sexual division of labor, and indeed the roles of males and females in general, is rapidly changing: Males are carrying out activities and performing roles that twenty or thirty years ago were associated with females, and vice versa. In many other societies, however, the social roles of females and males are sharply divided and the sexual

division of labor is more clearly defined. Among the Plains Indians, for instance, men and women ordinarily were engaged in different but complementary economic activities. Yet sex role "options" existed for individuals: There were culturally allowable ways in which males could assume the normal roles of females, and vice versa (see "A Closer Look").

The past 100 years of ethnographic fieldwork provide all the information needed to demolish one common idea about the sexual division of labor: that it is only natural for men to be the breadwinners for and women the caretakers of the family. Breadwinning—that is, producing the supply of food and other material needs and wants of domestic groups—is definitely not an activity of men exclusively, or even largely. As we shall see, in many societies men produce most of the food, but in others women's contribution to daily subsistence equals or exceeds that of men.

This finding of ethnographic research contradicts the opinion of those who think that the widespread domination of men over women is rooted in the "fact" that men's labor is more important to physical survival and material well-being than women's labor. Those who

A CLOSER LOOK

Alternative Sex Roles among the Plains Indians

The Plains Indians of the nineteenth century made a sharp distinction between male and female social roles and behavior. As hunters and warriors, men were aggressive and independent in their social behavior. In contrast, women were mainly involved in the domestic sphere—with activities such as cooking, working hides, making clothing, and decorating items with quill and beadwork. Women were supposed to be passive and reserved in their public behavior.

Even among Plains tribes, however, not all individuals adhered to the normatively appropriate role and behavior of their gender. There was *gender mixing* (sometimes called *gender crossing*), here meaning that some men or women adopted some of the attributes usually accorded the other gender. Particular types of gender mixing were culturally defined alternatives to normatively prescribed gender roles and behaviors. Among the Plains Indians gender crossing took three main forms: (1) berdaches, in which men took on some aspects of feminine roles; (2) manly hearted women, in which a female acted as a male normally acted; and (3) women chiefs, in which a woman assumed a role usually occupied by men.

Berdaches

A berdache was a man who dressed in women's clothes, performed women's work, and assumed the social behavior normatively appropriate for women.

Among the tribes of the plains, the Arapaho, Arikara, Assiniboine, Blackfoot, Cheyenne, Crow, Gros Ventre, Hidatsa, Iowa, Kansa, Mandan, Omaha, Osage, Oto, Pawnee, Plains, Cree, Ponca, and Sioux are known to have recognized berdaches as alternatives to the normal male role. There is little specific information about the frequency of berdaches, but early traders and explorers commonly remarked that they were "numerous" among some cultures.

Variation existed in the particular characteristics of berdaches from one plains society to the next. Sioux berdaches are the best reported in the literature. The Sioux called berdache *winkte*. Winkte dressed like women and lived in their own separate tepees at the edge of camp. They performed women's tasks such as tanning hides and working with quills and beads. In these activities, winkte were said to excel. Ceremonial and ritual items made by a winkte were especially sought after because of their fine quality. To say that a woman had "fine possessions like a winkte's" was the highest compliment to her skill.

It is not clear when a man began to exhibit the characteristics of a winkte. Some began dressing as girls quite young; others not until after they reached puberty. It was not thought that a man chose to become a winkte, but became one by dreaming about female supernatural forces. Through their visions winkte had supernatural powers, such as the ability to cure the sick. They appear to have had the right or supernatural authority to grant children special secret names, which protected the children from illness and prolonged their lives.

Although most of their activities were those normally associated with women, winkte did take part in male activities. Many were outstanding hunters. This, together with their great skills as craftspeople, made many of them wealthy. Some winkte also participated in war parties and thus engaged in the male role of warrior.

Many questions remain unanswered concerning the winkte in traditional Sioux society, such as whether they engaged in homosexuality. The degree to which they were accepted by other members of the community is also uncertain. Some say that they were well accepted and respected in the community for their skill, hard work, and supernatural powers and that they were intelligent and compassionate individuals who frequently cared for the aged and infirm. Others say that the winkte were disliked and discriminated against. Probably, different Sioux individuals had different opinions about the winkte.

Manly Hearted Women

In the northern Plains cultures, certain women adopted elements of male social behavior, acting aggressive and domineering. The Blackfoot called them *nin-auposkitzipxe*, which means literally "the manly hearted women." Women ordinarily were passive and docile, but manly hearted women were aggressive and outspoken in public affairs. At the

hold this view argue that women are everywhere dependent on men, which in turn makes women everywhere subordinate to men. But where females are subordinate to males, it is not because the things men do are somehow more important to family and group survival than the things women do. (What could be more important to group survival than bearing children?) This ethnocentric idea probably comes from the way most modern industrial economies worked until the mid-twentieth century: By and large, men earned the money

that allowed their families to purchase the goods they needed to survive. It is falsely concluded that the same economic dependence of wives on husbands characterized other peoples.

This is the anthropologist's usual warning about confusing the beliefs and practices of one's own culture with those of humanity in general. Most people's ideas about what is and is not natural for humans to think and do are products of enculturation into a specific culture at a particular time. Unless we become educated about the cultural

same time they were wives and mothers and were involved in female tasks.

Manly hearted women were invariably wealthy, due in large part to their own industry. They could tan more buffalo robes and produce better quality and greater amounts of quill and beadwork than other women. Many were also medicine women, which not only enhanced their status but brought them additional wealth. Their wealth was a key factor in their relations with men, because among the Blackfoot wealth and generosity were more highly regarded than bravery and war deeds in determining social status.

Because of their wealth and industry, manly hearted women were major economic assets to their husbands, and thus desirable wives. These same characteristics also made them independent. Within the family a manly hearted woman had an equal say, if not the dominant voice. As a Blackfoot once commented to Oscar Lewis (1941:181), "It's easy to spot a manly hearted women; the husband simply has nothing to say." Not only did they retain control of their own wealth, but they frequently controlled the property of their husbands as well. Because they were economically more self-sufficient than other women, many manly hearted women chose to divorce their husbands and support their children by their own industry.

Their public behavior also distinguished them. Their wealth made it possible for them always to dress in the finest clothes. Whereas other women modestly covered themselves with shawls and blankets, manly hearted women usually did not. Whereas most women were retiring and quiet in public discussions, manly hearted women joined in and even argued with others,

"just as though they were men." Whereas other women were shy at dances, manly hearted women aggressively chose their own partners. They were known for their sharp and cutting remarks, and it was said that a manly hearted woman would "take no lip" from either a man or another woman. Not surprisingly, they were believed to be sexually aggressive and passionate.

Women Chiefs

Among many Plains tribes, sometimes women assumed the role of chiefs. Detailed information is lacking, but an early trader (Edwin Denig) wrote a biographical account of a Crow woman, called "Woman Chief," who lived in the early nineteenth century.

Woman Chief was born into the Gros Ventre tribe. At age ten she was captured by the Crows and adopted by a Crow family. As a girl she showed a fondness for such typically male activities as riding horses, hunting, using bows and arrows, and shooting guns. She was indulged by her foster father, who made her guard of the family's horses—a responsibility usually assumed by a son. She became an excellent rider and markswoman and spent most of her time hunting deer and bighorn sheep as she grew older. She was said to be able to kill four or five bison in a single chase, to butcher the animals, and to pack the meat and hides back to camp with no assistance. When her foster father died she assumed the role of family head, hunting to feed her mother and siblings.

While Woman Chief was still a young woman, her camp was attacked by the Blackfoot. Several Crow men were killed, and the survivors took refuge in a fortified trading post nearby. After surround-

ing the post the Blackfoot asked for a parley, but fearing a trap, the Crow men refused. Finally, Woman Chief ventured out alone and was attacked by the Blackfoot. She killed one and wounded two before running back to the post. Accorded the honors of a warrior for her acts of bravery, the next year Woman Chief led a raid on the Blackfoot. Her party captured seventy horses, and she herself killed one Blackfoot and took the gun of another. In the following years she organized numerous raiding parties against the enemies of the Crow.

Accepted as a family head and warrior, Woman Chief was admitted to full participation in the council deliberations of the men. She eventually came to be ranked third out of the 160 family heads in her band. Because of her role as a frequent leader of raiding parties, she became wealthy in horses. Disdaining traditional women's tasks such as tanning, sewing, quilling, and beading, she paid the brideprice for and married four women to do these jobs for her.

Although Woman Chief was unusual, she was not unique. Women chiefs and women warriors were reported among other Plains tribes. The cases of the berdache, manly hearted women, and Woman Chief show us how individuals are not forced to conform rigidly to the normal social roles and activities of their gender in many cultures. Alternatives frequently are available to both sexes, even in those preindustrial societies in which sex role "deviance" is—according to our stereotypes—supposedly not allowed.

Sources: Benedict (1934), Callender and Kochems (1983), DeMallie (1983), Denig (1961), Hassrick (1964), Lewis (1941), Medicine (1983).

diversity of humanity, we consistently—and usually mistakenly—conclude that the ideas and practices of our own society are universal or even inherent in human nature.

So Man the Breadwinner and Woman the Homemaker does not accurately describe the sexual division of labor in other cultures. Humanity is too diverse for that. But despite cultural variation, there are some cross-cultural regularities and patterns in the sexual division of labor. What are these patterns, and what sorts of factors influence them?

Patterns and Influences

Table 10.1 summarizes a vast amount of comparative work on the sexual division of labor. It lists some specific tasks and whether they are most likely to be performed by females or males. Those tasks toward the left of the table are more likely to be performed by males; those to the right are more likely to be done by females. The nearer an activity is to the left, the more likely it is to be performed by males, and vice versa for females.

Table 10.1   Patterns in the Sexual Division of Labor

	Tasks Performed by Gender				
	Exclusively Males	Predominantly Males	Either or Both Sexes	Predominantly Females	
Extracting food and other products	Hunting	Fishing	Gathering small land animals	Gathering shellfish, mollusks	Gathering wild plant foods
	Trapping	Clearing land	Planting crops		
		Preparing soil	Tending crops		
			Harvesting crops		
		Tending large animals	Milking animals	Tending small animals	
	Woodworking			Gathering fuel	Fetching water
	Mining				
	Lumbering				
Manufacturing, processing, and preparing goods for consumption	Butchering				Processing plant foods
					Cooking
	Boat building	House building	Preparing skins	Making clothing	
	Working with stone, horn, bone, shell	Making rope, cordage, nets	Making leather products	Matmaking Loom weaving	
	Smelting ore				
	Metalworking			Making pottery	

Source: Adapted from Murdock and Provost (1973).

A few comments are needed to clarify Table 10.1. First, the table does not portray the sexual division of labor in any specific society. Rather, it represents a kind of composite or aggregate of information drawn from hundreds of societies in various parts of the world. For example, the tasks listed as "Predominantly Females" should be interpreted as those that are done by women in most societies, although in some specific societies one or another of the tasks are performed mainly by men. Tasks listed as "Exclusively Males" are accomplished by men in all or almost all societies, with very few exceptions.

Also, for convenience, Table 10.1 includes only those activities that produce some kind of material product. Left out of the table are other activities that are predominantly or exclusively male, such as holding political office and fighting wars. Also omitted are some activities, such as caring for infants, that are predominantly or exclusively women's work in all cultures. Of course, there is a sense in which all activities are "productive" (of social order or of children, for example), but here our discussion is limited to activities usually considered to be "economic tasks."

Anthropologists would like to explain two things. First, Table 10.1 shows that all human groups divide *some* kinds of labor by sex in similar ways. Some tasks are done mainly or nearly exclusively by one sex in most societies. For instance, hunting, land clearing, soil preparation, working with hard materials, and cutting down trees are exclusively or predominantly men's work in just about all cultures. Gathering wild plants, processing plant foods, and cooking are mainly the work of females in most cultures. In short, although cultures certainly vary in the kinds of tasks allocated to women and men, there are widespread (although not universal) *patterns;* consistently, some tasks are likely to be done by men, others by women. The first thing to explain is: Why are some tasks done mostly by women, whereas others are performed mainly or entirely by men?

Second, notice the tasks listed under the column labelled "Either or Both Sexes." These tasks are not sex-specific—that is, they are about equally likely to be performed by men or women. Members of either sex may do them, or both may work together on them. For example, whether men or women plant crops, milk animals, or work with skins or leather varies from people to people, with no clear pattern apparent. In sum, which sex performs these kinds of tasks is so culturally variable that we cannot predict who will do them; whether they are done by women, men, or both depends entirely on local circumstances. The second thing to explain is: What determines the *cultural variability* in the sexual division of labor? Why are women more heavily involved in agriculture (planting, tending, and harvesting crops) in some societies than in others, for example?

This section focuses on hypotheses that deal with the first question. We put off discussion of the second question until the next section.

What can explain why some tasks are nearly always done by men, whereas others are performed by women in most cultures? Biological differences between the sexes provide one possible explanation. Perhaps men are physically well equipped to handle certain kinds of tasks, and women to perform others. In most cultures, tasks are assigned in such a way that the members of each sex do what they are physically able to do most efficiently. The result is that biologically based differences between males and females are manifested behaviorally in the sexual division of labor in all or most cultures.

This hypothesis is not simple (or potentially sexist) biological determination. Those who believe that physical differences have a role in explaining cross-cultural similarities in the sexual division of labor claim only that these differences are *relevant*. They do not say that biological differences *alone* account for the similarities. Because of biological factors, they contend, men can perform certain kinds of tasks more efficiently than women, and vice versa, and these sexual differences are reflected in the widespread cross-cultural similarities in the division of labor.

For example, anthropologists used to say that there was at least one task that was everywhere done by men: hunting. Hunting seems to require certain biological capabilities—such as speed, strength, and endurance—that men have more of than women. It also was thought to be incompatible with certain responsibilities universally borne by women for biological reasons: pregnancy, lactation (breastfeeding), and child care. Pregnant women would have a hard time chasing game; lactating mothers would have to quit the hunt several times a day to nurse their infants; and the risk of injury to both mother and child would be high. Because men could hunt more effectively than women, foraging populations allocated hunting to men. Gathering, in contrast, required less strength and ability to run fast and long, so gathering is allocated largely to women.

These arguments are probably correct, but female and male biological differences do not make it *mandatory* that males are the hunters and females are the gatherers in foraging populations. For one thing, not all kinds of hunting and not all tasks connected to hunting require strength, speed, and endurance. For another,

Despite the cross-cultural variation in the sexual division of labor, certain tasks are done largely or exclusively by men in all cultures, including cutting wood.

there are questions about whether males have more endurance than females. Finally, there is no necessary *biological* reason why a woman could not give up hunting only during her pregnancy and lactation and leave her older children in camp under the care of someone else.

In fact, it is just not true that hunting is *universally* an exclusively male activity. When the BaMbuti pygmies of the Zaire rain forest hunt animals with nets, the women help by driving game into the nets held by men. In another part of the world, Agnes Estioko-Griffin has reported on hunting by women among the Agta, a mountain tribe of the Philippines who live on the island of Luzon. Agta men do most of the hunting, but women often accompany them in teamwork efforts, and women frequently hunt together without the company of men. Interestingly, sometimes women take their infants with them on the hunt, carrying the children on their backs. There are some differences between the methods used and types of game hunted by women versus men. Still, cases such as the Agta and BaMbuti show that the "man the hunter" image is oversimplified.

It is not, however, wrong. The great majority of cultures in which hunting is a significant means of acquiring food are foragers or horticulturalists. There is no question

In most cultures, loom weaving is a predominantly female task. This woman is from Guatemala.

that in most of these cultures women do most of the gathering of wild plants or the planting, weeding, and harvesting of cultivated plants, whereas men hunt to provide meat. The male hunting/female gathering pattern is not quite universal, but it is clearly the predominant pattern. The images of "woman the gatherer" (or gardener) and "man the hunter" do not apply to all people everywhere, but they are common enough that most anthropologists believe that there must be some physical differences between men and women that are relevant to the division of labor.

What kinds of physical differences seem to be most important? Comparative research suggests that several factors are important and interact to influence how female-male tasks are divided up. Three of the main factors are: (1) the relative strength of the sexes, (2) the possibility that regular, very heavy exercise depresses female fertility, and (3) the fact that only women give birth to and nurse infants and young children. Although all three of these factors interact, for now we consider each separately.

Relative Strength   One biological difference is the relative strength of males and females (some people believe that "relative stamina" also is relevant). On average, adult men are able to more efficiently perform tasks that require great strength, so such work is usually allocated to males. In Table 10.1, superior male strength is *relevant*—no one claims it is "all important"—in many of the tasks under the column headed "Exclusively Males": mining, tree cutting, and working with hard materials. Relative strength also helps to explain some tasks listed as "Predominantly Males," such as clearing land for cultivation, preparing soil for planting, and perhaps tending for large animals. On the other hand, greater male strength has no obvious relation to other exclusively or predominantly male tasks, such as trapping, butchering, and working with fibers. It is also worth noting that many tasks usually performed by women require significant strength, such as gathering fuel and fetching water. So relative strength does influence the sexual division of labor, but other physical differences also matter.

Fertility Maintenance   Women have another physical characteristic that might explain why some activities are allocated to males. Modern female athletes—especially long-distance runners—often do not menstruate and ovulate monthly. Apparently, this is because of a low ratio of body fat and complex hormonal changes in women who engage in prolonged and strenuous physical exercise. It has been suggested that productive activities that require comparable exertion—notably hunting—would depress a woman's fertility, and thus help to explain why most hunting is done by men. Possibly female reproduction would be so decreased by the strenuous exercise involved in hunting that the population might not be able to maintain its numbers over the course of many generations. But it is difficult to know whether this adequately accounts for why women so rarely hunt (or cut down trees). For instance, we do not know how much (or even if) the exertion involved in hunting would affect women's ability to bear children. This is because we must locate and study several cases of women hunting in the same way as men before we can measure hunting's effects on female fertility, but no one has yet done so.

Compatibility with Child Care   A third sexual difference affecting the sexual division of labor is that women are the bearers, nursers, and primary caretakers of infants and young children. This biological fact means that families and larger human groups tend to assign females those tasks that women can perform effectively even while caring for children, that is, tasks that are easily compatible with child care. In 1970, Judith Brown argued that such tasks usually have several characteristics:

- They are fairly routine and repetitive, so they do not require much concentration.
- They can be interrupted and resumed without significantly lowering their efficient performance.
- They do not place the children who accompany their mothers to the site of the task in potential danger.
- They do not require women to travel very far away from home.

The gathering of various products and the domestic work listed in Table 10.1 is highly compatible with child care. In addition, among horticultural people, garden tasks such as planting, weeding and tending crops, and harvesting usually are done by women; these activities, too, seem to be highly compatible with caring for children. The degree to which various tasks are compatible with caring for infants and young children, then, is relevant in determining whether women are likely to perform them effectively.

Even if all three hypotheses in combination are able to account for the widespread similar patterns in the sexual division of labor, none of them can explain the *differences*. In fact, no biological difference alone can explain

the cross-cultural diversity in the sexual division of labor. The biological differences between females and males in strength, reproductive physiology, and ability to care for infants are constant in all human populations. But a condition that is constant in all groups cannot, by itself, account for things that vary between the groups. Constants cannot explain variability and diversity. We need other hypotheses to account for the cultural variability in the sexual division of labor.

Intensive Agriculture and Women's Labor

Anthropologists have given considerable attention to one cross-cultural variation in the sexual division of labor: that between women's relative importance to subsistence production in horticultural versus intensive agricultural populations. (See Chapter 6 for a discussion of the distinction between these two systems of cultivation.)

It is fairly well established that women usually do most of the everyday garden work in horticultural populations. Of the major tasks involved in growing food using horticultural methods, only two—clearing land for cultivation and preparing the plot for planting by removing natural vegetation and turning over the soil—seem to be almost always done by men (see Table 10.1). Other tasks, including planting, weeding, and harvesting, are most often carried out by women in horticultural societies.

Why do women contribute a relatively large amount of garden labor in horticultural adaptations? Whether a people practice shifting cultivation, dry land gardening, or some other variety of horticulture, most female gardening tasks do not require great strength and are compatible with child-care demands. But this statement merely says that women (or, rather, mothers) *can* contribute effectively to subsistence; it does not say why they *will*.

No satisfactory answer has been offered. One suggestion is that in horticultural populations, men frequently are absent in trading expeditions or hunting, so women do most gardening by default. For instance, among Native American horticultural peoples (before contact with the West) most of the meat supply came from men's hunting because no large animals had been domesticated outside the Andes. Because men were so occupied with hunting, one of the nearly exclusively male tasks, women were left to garden. Yet we do not know how much of male time hunting usually required, so this suggestion is difficult to evaluate.

Similarly, in many horticultural societies men were so heavily involved in offensive warfare and guarding the settlement against attack that they had little time for cultivation. Among some horticulturalists most able-bodied

One important influence on the sexual division of labor is that tasks allocated mainly to adult women are compatible with child care. This is a !Kung woman with her children.

men were expected to be active in defensive and offensive warfare, so most garden work falls to women. Another possibility is simply that gardening is not much fun—remember the "routine, repetitive" nature of so many women's tasks noted in the preceding section. Essentially, males exploit females by making them do the "drudge work," some argue.

Whatever the reason why females do so much of the gardening among horticulturalists, the importance of women's labor relative to men's usually declines as cultivation systems become more intensive. ("Intensity" increases as cultivators increase the amount of food they harvest from a given amount of land by putting in more hours of work per acre, by plowing with animal power, by digging irrigation wells and ditches, by gathering dung and spreading it over the fields as fertilizer, and so on— see Chapter 6.) Women usually contribute much less agricultural labor than men in intensive agricultural systems. Why should this be?

A number of anthropologists have proposed a fairly complicated hypothesis. Their ideas are based on studies suggesting that, as cultivation becomes more intensive, two changes occur in women's domestic work loads. First, domestic tasks that women perform in almost all cultures require more of women's time in intensive systems. Second, in intensive systems, new kinds of tasks emerge that are generally done by women. Both sets of changes—the increased time required for old domestic tasks and the addition of new kinds of work—divert women's time away from cultivation, so they work relatively less than men in supplying food.

In 1983, Carol Ember compared how much time men and women spend in food production versus domestic work in horticultural and intensive agricultural societies. She suggested that women typically have significantly more domestic work to perform in intensive agricultural societies. There are several reasons that women's domestic work load generally increases with increasing intensity. For one thing, about one-half of all horticulturalists concentrate on root crops (such as yams, potatoes, manioc, taro, and sweet potatoes) rather than cereal crops. In contrast, about 90 percent of all intensive agriculturalists subsist mainly from cereals (such as wheat, rice, corn, oats, barley, and millet).

How could this general difference in the kinds of crops grown affect the kinds of tasks women perform in the two systems? In 1975, Kay Martin and Barbara Voorhies suggested an important implication of this seemingly insignificant difference—showing us how subtle differences can have major effects on cultural patterns of behavior. The root crops grown more often by horticultural peoples tend to be harvested continuously rather than seasonally. Edible roots can be stored in the ground for relatively long periods, allowing cultivators to harvest them more or less at will (within limits, of course). Cereals (grains), however, are the seeds of cultivated plants, so they mature at about the same time every year. The seeds will fall off and rot (or sprout) unless harvested at the proper time. Therefore, cereals typically are harvested seasonally, dried, and stored for processing and eating the rest of the year. This increases both cooking and processing time—picture the Mexican peasant woman grinding corn to make tortillas, or the Greek woman winnowing, grinding, making flour, and baking bread from wheat. Because, overall, cereals require more labor to process and prepare for eating than roots, and because in almost all societies such domestic tasks are done by females, women tend to devote more hours to domestic work in intensive agricultural societies. They therefore have relatively less time to spend in the fields, so men pick up the slack.

Douglas White, Michael Burton, and Malcomb Dow pursue this line of reasoning. In a 1981 cross-cultural study they noticed a fairly consistent relation between crop type and the average length of the dry season: The longer the dry season, the more likely cereals rather than roots are to be the main crops of a people. They also found a relation between crop type and the importance of animal husbandry: Domesticated animals are more important to people who grow cereals, since so many cereal-growers are intensive agriculturalists who use animals to pull plows.

In summary, and in general, most intensive agriculturalists live in regions with a long dry season, grow cereals as an important part of their diet, and keep domesticated animals for both traction and food. How might the association between these factors explain the lower involvement of women in intensive agriculture than in horticulture?

First, consider the possible effects of a long dry season. Because of the lack of rain for many months of the year, the timing of crop planting needs to be adjusted so that the growing plants will have adequate water. Therefore, planting tends to be concentrated during a few weeks of the year; harvesting is later concentrated into a small time period as a result. So the seasonality of agricultural tasks usually is greater than that of horticultural tasks. There is an increased need for agricultural laborers who can do a lot of hot, heavy work in a short period that cannot be interrupted by other tasks, that is, for men's rather than women's labor (see previous section).

In contrast, root-growing horticultural peoples living in regions with a short or no dry season, or in which the time of planting is relatively unaffected by climate, spread cultivation tasks out more evenly over the entire year. Gardening is a day-in, day-out activity but also requires less muscle power and is relatively interruptible. So women are able to do it effectively.

Now consider the possible effects on women's work of the keeping of large numbers of domesticated animals used to pull plows, supply meat and dairy products, and fertilize fields in intensive systems. Burton and White cite some evidence that many of the labor burdens involved in keeping domesticated animals are borne by women (as well as children). Women do most of the work of collecting fodder for the animals to eat, of gathering dung, of watering livestock, and of milking cows, as well as several other animal husbandry tasks. This also tends to divert their labor from direct involvement in agricultural chores, Burton and White believe. (Their evidence that women do most of the care of domesticated animals is questionable, however.)

In summary, some cross-cultural researchers suggest that a combination of the following factors explains why women contribute less labor to cultivation in intensive agricultural than in horticultural adaptations:

- The cereals grown using intensive cultivation methods require more of women's processing time than the root crops of horticultural peoples.
- Cereal-growing intensive agriculturalists tend to live in parts of the world with a long dry season, which increases the efficiency of using men's rather than women's labor in the fields.
- Intensive agriculturalists tend to keep more domesticated animals, which directly or indirectly increases the nonagricultural work load of women.

It is important to note that these associations are *generalized*. Intensive agriculturalists "tend to" live in regions with a long dry season; domesticated animals are "generally" cared for more by women than by men; and so on. Further, there are numerous exceptions to the general patterns discovered by comparative work. In many cultures, the sexual division of labor is not associated with the kind of cultivation that cross-cultural research says it is "supposed" to be associated with.

For example, the Kofyar of Nigeria are intensive agriculturalists who use terraces, manuring from stall-fed goats, composting, and other means of raising the productivity of their fields. Using the hoe as their main tool, Kofyar grow a mixture of root crops (yams and cocoyams), cereals (millet, sorghum, rice), and groundnuts (peanuts). The comparative research summarized above suggests that Kofyar women should be less involved in various cultivation tasks than men, based on the degree of intensification of their land use. Yet quantitative studies of working hours published in a 1995 article by M. P. Stone, G. D. Stone, and R. McC. Netting reveal that the two sexes work nearly equal hours in their fields. Further—contrary to the general pattern—there is surprisingly little difference in the kinds of tasks done and in the crops grown by women and men (with the exception of groundnuts, grown mainly by women). The researchers suggest that one reason for the Kofyar "exception" is that these people have intensified their use of the land mainly by means of increasing labor inputs, rather than by technological changes such as plows. Therefore, high labor inputs by both sexes are needed to maintain sufficient yields.

We mention the Kofyar exception to make two points. First, the existence of general patterns uncovered by comparative research does not predict what any particular group of people will be doing. The culture of any human society is a product of a complex interaction between its history, adaptation, beliefs, and other factors. In any particular group, factors *unique* to that group may be more important than factors that are *generally* important.

In preindustrial, subsistence-oriented cultures, biological factors such as relative strength and compatibility with child care are important influences on the sexual division of labor. Given the kinds of tasks (jobs) most people in industrial, wage-labor countries now do, biological factors matter less and less for effective job performance.

machinery has greatly reduced the need for strength and stamina to perform tasks; so there is less of a biological basis for allocating some tasks ("jobs," they have become) exclusively to males. It matters, second, because the economies of Japan, Western Europe, and North America are increasingly service- and high tech-oriented; so the biological differences that once mattered need not matter so much (if at all) today. It matters, third, because the birthrate of industrialized nations is lower than that of most preindustrial peoples; so child-care burdens are lower for modern women. It matters, fourth, because one reason some tasks were allocated to women in preindustrial societies was their compatibility with women's child-care duties; but today these duties are carried out during work hours to child-care specialists and elementary schools.

A more general implication arises from the fact that the sexual division of labor shows great, but not unlimited, variability in human populations. Much of this variability results from the interaction between female-male biological differences and the overall economic conditions of a people. The sexual division of labor responds to other changes in a people's way of life—particularly to changes in their adaptive, productive, and economic systems. That the sexual division of labor in industrialized nations is responding and will continue to respond to similar changes is not surprising. That the long-term development will be toward a decreasing emphasis on gender as a basis for allocating tasks and roles is consistent with many anthropological ideas about the sexual division of labor. As technological, economic, and demographic changes reduce the importance of male-female differences in the ability to perform most jobs, the sex of the job holder will come to matter less and less.

The Status of Women

Another main issue in the anthropological study of gender is how and why the status of women varies cross-culturally. Women's status is difficult to define precisely, because it includes so many components that interact in complex ways. In this book, the phrase **status of women** will encompass the following factors, which vary from culture to culture.

- the kinds of roles men and women perform, with their associated rights and duties;
- the cultural value attached to women's contributions to their nuclear and extended families and to society at large;
- whether or how much women defer socially to their husbands, male relatives, and other men with whom they have important relationships;
- female access to positions of power and influence;

Second, the mere fact that there are exceptions does not invalidate a general pattern, provided, of course, that the generalization is well established. If we want to know the factors that affect the sexual division of labor in human societies generally, then we must do comparative work to look for *general patterns*. The fact that *particular cases* do not fit the general pattern does not invalidate the generalization—at least not until the number of exceptions becomes large enough to lead us to become suspicious of the existence of the general pattern!

Does this general pattern have any relevance for the relation between sex and occupational roles in a modern, industrialized society? If it is true that the sexual division of labor in preindustrial populations is mainly affected by factors such as (1) male strength (and perhaps the ability to run fast or long) and (2) the fact that only women bear and nurse children, then this matters for modern employment patterns. It matters, first, because automated

- the degree to which women control their own lives by making marital, sexual, childbearing, work and leisure, and other important decisions for themselves; and
- general cultural beliefs and ideas about the relative equality or superiority/inferiority of women and men.

Think of the previous list as some of the main features or dimensions that constitute the overall status of women in particular cultures. Obviously, women's status is multidimensional. The complexity of these features means that it is difficult to categorize the status of women in terms such as "high" or "low," even within a single culture.

Comparative research on variations in the status of women is relevant for the present and future of female-male relations in modern society for two reasons. First, if women's status is low to the same degree and in the same ways in most societies, then it may be more difficult to improve women's status in modern nations. Conversely, if there are preindustrial cultures in which women have status higher than or equal to men, then our confidence that modern societies can reach the same state is increased.

Second, assuming the status of women varies significantly across cultures, comparative research can perhaps suggest why. Perhaps there are one or two economic, political, familial, or religious factors that determine women's status in all or most societies. If so, and if modern nations are now (or should later become) committed to sexual equality, then government policies might focus on these key factors. Feminists, too, might concentrate more of their political attention on these factors.

Before proceeding, we need to acknowledge the difficulties of determining "the" status of women in a given society. As mentioned, women's status is multidimensional, and often some dimensions seem to contradict others. For example, studies of family life often report that women have a great deal of control in making decisions about childrearing and about the allocation of domestic resources, even though they have little independence outside the domestic context. In two Andalusian towns of south Spain, David Gilmore's fieldwork showed that wives have great autonomy in managing household affairs. He believes this is because many women are able to live near their own mothers, so that wives and their mothers frequently "gang up" on a husband. Even in male-dominated societies like traditional Japan and China, the eldest female in a household usually had the right to manage household affairs with a fair degree of autonomy. Yet in China, Japan, and many other societies, women were not allowed to participate in public affairs, had hardly any property of their own, had little say over whom they married, and were clearly subordinate to their fathers and husbands socially and even legally.

Added to the fact that specific aspects of women's status vary according to social context and situation is the fact that distinctions of rank or class (considered in Chapter 12) or of ethnic affiliation (Chapter 17) often override male-female distinctions. In modern North America, most professional white women enjoy higher living standards and achieve more of what their culture values than do working class black men—what shall we say about their "overall status in society"?

A final factor complicating the concept of women's status is that in most cultures, a woman's status changes over the course of her life. For example, most scholars agree that "the" status of women was comparatively low in traditional China, Japan, and India. In all three regions, most families were patrilocally extended (Chapter 8), so when women married they left their own families and moved into or near the house of their husband's parents. A young wife was subjected to the authority of her husband's mother and was duty-bound to work extremely hard. But as a woman settled into the household, had a son, and aged, her status improved and she gradually took over control from her mother-in-law. When the latter died, she became the everyday manager of the household and became an authority figure over her own daughters-in-law after her sons married.

The same pattern of women's status improving with age appears in numerous other cultures. As Judith Brown points out, the cross-cultural evidence clearly indicates positive changes in the status of women as they become middle-aged. Brown suggests that an important reason for the widespread tendency for female status to rise with age is that an older mother in most cultures has the affection and deference of her grown children, who look after their mother's interests and support her decisions. Also, older women in many cultures have fewer restrictions placed on their behavior because their sexual reputation is secure.

So we must not think of women's status as a unitary phenomenon: The way men regard and treat women and the rights of women have many dimensions, and the factors that constitute women's status are not always consistent with one another. Like other kinds of relations, male-female relations are complex. We should not be surprised by this complexity. People of other cultures did not invent the notion of "status of women." Nor are women's lives so simple that modern anthropologists can characterize them easily by statements like "women have low status in culture X."

In spite of its difficulties, we shall continue to use "status of women" as a useful shorthand. Specifically, the concept is a meaningful one for discussing the degree to which women are subordinate to men, a subject to which we now turn.

Universal Subordination?

A main question asked by anthropologists interested in gender is whether females are everywhere subordinate to males. Are there societies in which women and men are equal? Are there societies in which women dominate men?

The answer to the second question is no. Despite the stories we sometimes read or the occasional old adventure movie in which the hero is captured by "amazons," not a single instance of clear female domination over men has ever been found by ethnographers. Matriarchy—rule by women over men—does not exist, nor has it ever existed, to the best of our knowledge. Certainly there have been and are individual women who hold great power, control great wealth, and are held in high esteem. Certainly there are queens, female chiefs, and individual *matriarchs* of families and kin groups. But no instance of *matriarchy*—women as a social category holding power over men as a social category—has been documented.

The first question, of whether cultures exist in which men and women are equal, has a more uncertain and complex answer. Even anthropologists who have devoted their careers to studying gender cannot agree. Some scholars believe that women are never considered to be fully equal to men. They interpret the ethnographic record as showing that an asymmetry always exists between the sexes in one or more areas of life.

Those who believe that male dominance/female subordination is a cultural universal point to two fairly well established ethnographic generalizations. One applies to political institutions (see Chapter 11). In no known society are the primary political authority roles restricted to or even regularly performed by females; but in many societies all women are denied the right to succeed to political offices. In the majority of cases even kin-group leadership roles are dominated by men. Male elders of the lineage or clan decide how the group's land and other resources are to be used and allocated, how the group's wealth objects are to be disposed of, whether the group is to engage in a battle to avenge a wrong, and so on. (But as we shall soon see, women often do have significant influence over these matters, especially in matrilineal societies.)

The other realm of life in which sexual asymmetry is found is religion. In many societies women are excluded from performing major religious leadership roles and are forbidden to participate in the most important rituals. For example, sometimes the death of a man is blamed on the witchcraft of his wife, and she is cruelly punished for her alleged "homicide." In many New Guinea societies—the Hua, for instance—men believe that their health or masculinity is jeopardized if they come into contact with women's menstrual discharges, so women must seclude themselves during their periods to avoid harming the men.

According to some scholars, then, the activities of males are everywhere regarded as more important than those of females. Women as a social category are everywhere culturally devalued relative to men as a social category. Women are universally subordinate to men.

But the ethnographic record can be interpreted differently. Many scholars note that most fieldworkers—and hence most of the ethnographic data available to shed light on the issue of universal female subordination—have been biased in two ways. The first is the *androcentric* (male) bias. Most of the fieldwork until the 1970s was done by males, who usually were uninterested in the females of the cultures they studied. At any rate, simply because they were themselves males, fieldworkers had little access to women's points of view, so they often unwittingly took the men's values, attitudes, and opinions of the culture. Female points of view were largely unreported.

The second source of fieldwork bias in the study of gender is *Eurocentric* bias. Because of the inequalities in wealth, power, and status in Western (European-derived) societies, Western anthropologists might perceive relations of inequality, hierarchy, and domination/subordination even among cultures where they are less developed. For instance, when a wife greets her husband by bowing her head or stays behind him while walking, Western fieldworkers may interpret such behaviors as indications of female subordination, when in fact they are merely public demonstrations of politeness.

In short, some scholars think that many fieldworkers have been sexually and culturally biased. Because of this bias, the ethnographic record is not objective; it "records" a universal female subordination not justified by the real world. Note, however, that even those who accuse others of bias may be biased themselves, albeit perhaps in another direction!

Anthropologists who believe that female-male equality does exist in some cultures can point to particular peoples whom they believe document their belief. The Iroquois, a matrilineal and matrilocal people of northeastern North America, are the most famous ethnographic example of women achieving equality (or is it only relative equality?) with men. Iroquois women produced the corn and other cultivated foods, put them in storage, and largely controlled how they were distributed from the storehouses. Iroquois men were away from their apartments in the longhouse much of the time, engaged in warfare or cooperative hunting expeditions. After the introduction of the fur trade into northeastern North America in the seventeenth century, men often were away searching for beaver pelts or raiding their neighbors for pelts. The matrilineally related women of a longhouse influenced their inmarried husbands' behavior by withholding provisions from their hunting trips and war parties. Only men had the right to hold the most powerful political leadership offices because only males could be elected to the great council of chiefs. But representatives to the council were selected by the older women of the various matrilineages, and these women also had the right to remove and replace men who did not adequately represent the group's interests. Also, women had a voice in the deliberations of the council itself: They could veto declarations of war and introduce peace-making resolutions.

Iroquois women's control over cultivated foods and their distribution gave them relatively high status.

So who is right? Are women subordinate to men in all societies or not? Certainly, some male ethnographers have been biased—but does this bias explain their reports of female subordination? Certainly, the Iroquois and many other peoples demonstrate that women in some cultures have achieved considerable control over their own lives and over public decision making—but do such cases represent full equality of males and females? Indeed, would we know "total equality" if we saw it in a society? What would it look like? Would men and women have to carry out the same kinds of economic tasks before we could say they are equal? Is monogamy necessary, or can a society be polygynous and still qualify? Shall we require that women occupy 50 percent of all leadership roles before we say they have equal rights? How should family life be organized before we can say that husbands in culture X do not dominate their wives?

As you can see, many questions must be answered before we can say whether women are everywhere subordinate—not the least of which is how we would know complete gender equality if we were to encounter it!

But perhaps too much weight is given to the issue of universal male dominance. Many anthropologists mistakenly think their discipline must ferret out human cultures in which women and men are equal for ethnographic data to lend support for the feminist cause. Feminist psychologists, sociologists, historians, biologists, and other scholars likewise have examined ethnographic accounts. Their reasoning is that if numerous cultures can be found in which women have achieved equality, then women will be more likely to achieve equality in the future. Their hope is that there are many such cultures. Conversely, their fear is that the ethnographic record shows few or no such cultures.

But how much does it matter for the cause of sexual equality today if women are universally or nearly univer-

sally subordinate? Perhaps it does not matter as much as some think it does. What matters most is that women and men are a good deal more equal in some societies than in others, which allows us to study the conditions under which future equality is likely to be possible. To argue that because women have always been subordinate they are forever doomed to be subordinate is analogous to many pre-twentieth-century arguments that humans will never be able to fly. Just because no human society has achieved some state in the past does not mean that none will achieve it in the future. It does not mean that we should give up trying to achieve it today. And it certainly does not mean that women alive in the year 2000 have achieved about all the equality they are likely to achieve.

Influences on Women's Status

What influences the status of women in a society? Women's status is affected by such a multitude of factors that thus far no one has shown that any small number of forces are the primary determinants of women's status in all times and places. Here we discuss only a few influences that are most widespread and important.

Women's Contributions to Material Welfare Many scholars argue that women's role in production strongly influences their property rights, their role in public affairs, their degree of personal freedom, and other dimensions of their overall status. Possibly, where women produce a sizable proportion of the food, shelter, clothing, and other necessities of existence, their contributions will be recognized and rewarded with influence, property, prestige, dignity, and other benefits. In other words, the sexual division of labor, together with the proportion of valued goods women produce, are strong influences on women's overall status.

Such ideas might apply to some foraging and horticultural people, among whom women's gathering or gardening contributes a sizable amount of resources to their domestic groups. Women's productive labor might give them a status that is closer to equality with men than they have in other forms of adaptation in which their subsistence contributions are not as great. For example, among the BaMbuti and Aka, two foraging groups of the central African rain forest, women's labor is critical for success in net hunting, and ethnographic reports on both these "pygmy" peoples report male-female equality or near equality.

But everyone's status is "closer to equality" in most hunter-gatherer and many horticultural populations (see Chapters 6 and 12). So perhaps the relative equality of women in these two systems of adaptation results not from their importance as food providers but from something else that "levels out" social inequalities of all kinds.

Women's Control over Key Resources   A more complex proposal is that women's contribution to production, by itself, is not enough to "earn" them relative equality. It is necessary for women to contribute heavily to material welfare to gain resources, rights, and respect, but this alone is not sufficient. (After all, enslaved Africans contributed a lot to production in the Americas and the Caribbean in the eighteenth and nineteenth centuries, but they were not rewarded with social equality!) One specific hypothesis is that women must also own productive resources (land, tools), or have considerable control over the distribution of the products of their labor, or both. If women own productive resources and have a great deal of say over what happens to the goods they produce, then they can have some influence on the activities of men. Overall, this gives them more equality. Peggy Sanday found some support for this hypothesis in a cross-cultural study (1973).

This hypothesis seems to account reasonably well for some specific cases. For instance, Iroquois women controlled the production and distribution of important resources. They used this control to nominate their kinsmen to chiefly positions and to influence the public decision making from which they were formally excluded. Likewise, Hopi (see Chapter 9) women owned land and had considerable control over the distribution of its products. Women had relatively high status in both these societies.

Along the same lines, in many West African and Caribbean societies, women are more active than men in market trade in foodstuffs, handicrafts, textiles, and other goods produced by themselves. Sometimes market-trading women are able to transform their independent control over exchangeable resources into more equitable relations with men. Wives commonly maintain separate income from their husbands, which they are free to expend on themselves and their children. One such culture is the Yoruba, who make up most of the population of many towns in Nigeria. Yoruba women are active in market trade and in craft production, which gives them access to income and economic security independent of their husbands and other men. Many women purchase houses in urban areas and use the rent to improve their and their children's economic well-being and social autonomy. According to ethnographer Sandra Barnes (1990, 275):

> Property frees the owner from subordinating herself to the authority of another person in domestic matters. It places her in a position of authority over others and in a position to form social relationships in the wider community that are politically significant. Property owning legitimates her entry into the public domain.

The economic independence that some Yoruba women are able to acquire translates into increased participation in neighborhood associations and other public affairs and allows them much freedom from male authority.

Thus, many ethnographic and comparative studies suggest that controlling resources is one way for women to get respect and independence from their husbands, brothers, and other men. This ability to acquire some measure of control over family resources helps to account for why many late-twentieth-century wives are demanding and receiving more help from their husbands in housework and child care. In recent decades, married women in increasing numbers have acquired wage- and salary-earning jobs by selling their labor and skills to the private or public sector. Between 1960 and 1990, in the United States, the percentage of all married women who were employed doubled, from around 30 percent to 60 percent. Even the presence of young children does not keep most American women from entering the workforce: Between 1960 and 1990, the percentage of employed women with preschool-aged children tripled, from about 20 percent to about 60 percent. Among the reasons why so many married women have entered the workforce since the 1960s are the insufficiency of one person's (formerly, the husband's) income to support the family at an acceptable living standard; structural changes to a more service-oriented (less goods-producing) economy; the increasing value women place on personal fulfillment

Where women commonly earn income for themselves by marketing products, as in Jamaica, their overall status tends to be relatively high.

through career advancement (partly because of the feminist movement); and high divorce rates. Even more recently, increasing numbers of couples are "role-reversed": Husbands/fathers stay home with the kids while wives/mothers bring home the family income.

As a result of entering the workforce as wage- and salary-earners, many American women (married and unmarried) have gained considerable economic independence from their husbands and other men. Husbands have, therefore, lost considerable economic leverage in the household relative to their wives. Not only do working wives now have psychological ammunition against their husbands' domestic incompetence or laziness, but they also have the wherewithal to back up their demands. With most women now out in the world of work, and with the families of married women now virtually dependent on their income to pay the bills, more women are demanding equal pay for equal work, equal treatment and opportunity in the workplace, equal legal rights, and equal respect.

Descent and Postmarital Residence   The form of descent and postmarital residence also influences women's overall status. Women in matrilineal and matrilocal societies have greater equality in many areas of life than their counterparts in patrilineal societies. What is it, specifically, about matrilineality and matrilocality that gives relatively high status to females? It is *not* that "females rule" in these societies. Men hold positions of both political and domestic authority in most matrilineal societies (see

Chapter 9). The main difference is whom among their relatives men have authority *over:* their sisters and sisters' children in matrilineal systems, versus their sons, unmarried daughters, and sons' children in patrilineal systems.

But other elements of matrilineality and matrilocality benefit females. In a cross-cultural study Martin Whyte found that women enjoy more authority in domestic matters, have more sexual freedom, and have more worth placed on their lives in these societies. Two factors contribute to their equality. First, because it is husbands who go to live with the families of their wives, sisters remain with or close to one another throughout their lives. Husbands who marry into a family face a relatively cohesive and enduring group of related women. A typical wife thus has her mother, sisters, and perhaps other female relatives around to support her in domestic quarrels. Second, in many matrilineal and matrilocal societies, domestic authority over a married woman is divided between her husband and her brother. Alice Schlegel suggests that this arrangement increases her freedom because each man acts as a check on the other's attempts to dominate her.

Contrast this situation to patrilineal and patrilocal China before the mid-twentieth century. When a Chinese woman married she was incorporated as a member of her husband's household. This was symbolized by the fact that she began to pay homage to his deceased patrilineal ancestors rather than to her own. A woman's relationships with her own parents and siblings were sharply curtailed when she married. Her main duties were to work for her husband and his parents, to obey them in all things, and to bear them male heirs. In many respects a new wife was treated as a domestic servant to her father- and mother-in-law: She was given arduous household tasks to perform for most of her waking hours, and she could be berated and even beaten with impunity. Only when she herself bore sons and heirs to her husband's family did her status improve, and only when she herself became a mother-in-law to her sons' wives could she relax a bit. The Confucian social and moral philosophy, which held that women must always be submissive to men, affected the way wives and daughters-in-law were treated. But also important were the social facts that wives were fully incorporated into the households of their husbands' parents, and the lines of authority over them were clearly and legally redrawn on their marriage. A Chinese wife had few viable alternatives to submission to her husband's family and few sources of social support when she was treated poorly. In contrast, in most matrilocal and matrilineal cultures women do have alternatives to suffering the dominance of their husbands, and they likewise receive support from their own relatives.

Overall Social Complexity So far, we have discussed ideas that try to account for the variations in women's status synchronically. That is, we have treated societies as if they are frozen in time, and we have looked at what kinds of cultural factors might be associated with variations in women's status. Another approach considers women's status in general evolutionary terms (Chapter 4). That approach largely ignores specific societies with their specific variations and asks instead what has happened to women's overall status in the very long term.

Rather than present an overview of existing evolutionary hypotheses, here we concentrate on one. It holds that women's overall status has decreased as social complexity has increased (at least until the industrial revolution of the late 1700s and the profound cultural changes that resulted from it in the next two centuries). This idea comes mainly from the work of Jack Goody, Alice Schlegel, Ester Boserup, and Martin Whyte, whose ideas we shall sketch and integrate. The following argument is complex, but it is worth the effort to understand it. Not only is it a fascinating attempt to show how women's place in societies has changed throughout history, but it is an example of how alterations in one cultural subsystem affect other subsystems in subtle and unexpected ways.

Recall the strong relation between cultivation systems and the relative degree of importance of women's labor to subsistence. As the intensity of cultivation increases, women participate less and less in agricultural tasks, for reasons suggested earlier in this chapter. Recall also (from Chapter 6) that intensive agriculture is associated with societies that are highly stratified, with economies featuring much centralized control, with well-developed craft and other specializations, with marked distinctions between rulers and ruled, and so on. Such large-scale hierarchically organized societies are called **complex societies** by anthropologists. How does increasing agricultural intensity, together with these other features of complexity, affect the status of women?

Jack Goody made a connection between increasing complexity and the (seemingly unrelated) overall status of women. He compared the predominantly horticultural societies of sub-Saharan Africa with the mainly intensive agricultural societies of Eurasia (Europe, the Middle East, and Asia). In Eurasia, land is relatively scarcer because of higher population densities. It is also more intensively exploited, with plows, irrigation, and fertilization with animal manure used to increase yields. Because land is scarcer and more productive in Eurasia, there is more competition for it, family wealth and prestige depend more on access to it, and a family has a greater chance of losing it to someone else. Finally, because Eurasian societies are more stratified than African societies, in the former there is a real danger of downward mobility for one's children and grandchildren unless access to resources is maintained through generations. Therefore, in Eurasia, parents are concerned about maintaining their male and female children's access to land, since so much else depends on it.

Goody argues that these differences between Africa and Eurasia have important cultural consequences. In most of Africa, land and other property is transmitted through males. An African man passes land rights down to his sons; his daughters receive little or no inheritance but rely largely on their husbands to supply them with access to land, cattle, and other productive resources. In Eurasia it is relatively more important that parents make a "good match" for their daughters, meaning that their daughters marry someone of at least equal wealth. So in most Eurasian societies, parents give property to their daughters as well as their sons, to maintain their daughters' and daughters' children's access to adequate resources. By giving property to their daughter, parents improve her chances of attracting "the right kind of husband," one with sufficient resources to maintain the social and economic standing of her and her children. Bilateral inheritance thus is typical of Eurasia.

Eurasian daughters often receive their inheritance when they marry—that is, as a dowry (Chapter 8). Dowries usually include money, jewelry, and household goods rather than land itself. The purpose of a dowry is

According to one theory, as societal complexity increases, it becomes more and more important for families to control the sexual behavior and marital choices of their unmarried female members. Towards this end, restrictions are placed on female behavior and female modesty is strictly enforced. These are women from Afghanistan.

not just to provide a daughter and her children with resources but also to attract a husband with a sizable inheritance of land and other property. Therefore, dowry is part of the marital transaction in European and Asian societies. In contrast, dowry is practically nonexistent in sub-Saharan Africa, where bridewealth is the predominant form of marital exchange.

All these factors influence patterns of marriage. In horticultural Africa, where female labor is so important to subsistence, men who can pay bridewealth for several wives acquire a critical resource: their wives' labor. But more wives mean more children, which in turn means the need to find spouses for all these children. In a bridewealth society a man acquires wives for his sons partly out of the bridewealth he receives for his daughters. So, unlike dowry, bridewealth "circulates" in a single generation as well as "passes down" to the next. If, in contrast, an African man had to provide all his daughters with dowries, the daughters would become more of an economic liability than an asset to him. So we see how the importance of female labor to subsistence, polygyny, and bridewealth all go together in most African populations; they form a system, each reinforcing the other.

In contrast, Eurasian societies with bilateral inheritance tend to be monogamous. This is because (1) women's labor has less value in accumulating wealth

in intensive agricultural systems and (2) it would be difficult for all but the very rich to provide an adequate dowry for the daughters of more than one wife. It is relatively more important for parents to control who their daughters marry because a bad match could impoverish her and her offspring and lower the wealth and honor of the whole family. As Alice Schlegel points out in a comparative study, in such complex societies it is common for a high cultural value to be placed on virginity for unmarried women, to minimize the possibility of families being taken advantage of by some young man of lower wealth and status who hopes to gain access to the family's resources by seducing its daughter. A woman therefore has little say about whom she marries. As part of their effort to control whom their daughters marry, parents place restrictions on their unmarried daughters' relations with males. In the Islamic Middle East and northern India a woman's virtue strongly reflected on the honor of her whole family, so extreme steps (to Western eyes) were taken to ensure that no question could arise about her virtue: Daughters lived secluded lives in the houses of their fathers and had to veil their faces and cover their heads when out in public. In some societies, women who had premarital or extramarital sex—sometimes even including women who were raped—were beaten or killed by their fathers, brothers, or husbands. All these cultural effects have negative impacts on the overall status of women, since they reduce women's ability to control their own bodies and make their own choices, and since in some cultures they lead to violence against women who are believed not to have conformed to the restrictions placed on their behavior.

Women's Status in Industrial Societies

We conclude by bringing together some of the information and ideas covered in this chapter and suggesting how they might be relevant to women living in industrialized, modernized nations. Some anthropological scholars have tried to show what has happened to the overall status of women throughout the long course of cultural evolution. Generally, they believe that women in many foraging and horticultural populations had relatively high status, especially in matrilineal and matrilocal societies. But as agricultural methods and land use systems became more intensive, the sexual division of labor was affected: Women's labor was pulled out of agricultural work and allocated more into domestic tasks.

A large number of cultural changes accompanied agricultural intensification, as discussed in Chapter 6. Population densities grew; the size of political units increased; urbanization and occupational specialization developed; class systems based largely on heredity emerged; and vastly unequal access to land, property, and other culturally valuable resources arose. These changes, which led to the evolution of "complex societies," did not occur in all regions, and even where they did occur they took many centuries. But one important end result was that the ability of individuals and families to acquire social and economic rewards came to depend largely on acquiring and sustaining long-term access to more resources than their peers.

Under such circumstances, many families would move downward in the social and economic ladder unless control over productive resources was passed along to the next generation. But families competed with one another over resources, in part by bilateral inheritance, monogamous marriages, and providing dowry to improve their daughters' marriage prospects, as Jack Goody argues for Eurasian soci-

eties. As a result of changes in inheritance, marriage, and marital exchanges, in many respects women's overall status deteriorated as societies grew more complex. Women had little control over their marriage partners; a double standard of sexual morality became pronounced; women had little public presence and almost no role in public decision making but were more confined to their households; restrictions (in the form of modest dress and demeanor) were placed on women's behavior to maintain family honor; divorce at the wife's initiative became difficult or impossible; and women often suffered from violence and threats of violence by members of their own family or their husbands'. Specifics vary between particular complex societies, and there are—as always—numerous exceptions. But much evidence suggests that women's overall status tended to decrease as societal complexity increased, for preindustrial cultures.

This evolutionary trend has reversed in some industrialized countries in the twentieth century, in spite of the fact that complexity is greater than ever. Perhaps this reversal occurred because industrial technology increasingly substitutes for labor and muscle power, reducing the relevance of female-male biological differences in performing economic tasks ("jobs"). Perhaps modern social scientists have been partly successful in debunking previous cultural beliefs about sexual differences in emotional responses, intellectual capacity, psychological propensities, and the like. Perhaps—as materialists might argue—increased female access to money and wealth has given them power in their relationships with males.

Whatever the reason, anthropological research on women's status provides today's women with a hope and a warning. The hope derives from the fact that women's roles and rights, and the restrictions placed upon them, vary from place to place and from time to time. Although we cannot decide whether women and men have "equal status" in any culture, we certainly know that sexual equality varies significantly. So there is reason to think that modern societies can move further toward eliminating barriers to female opportunity and achievement.

If the hypotheses we have covered here are at least broadly correct, then any change that improves women's independent access to material resources and to social support will have positive impacts on their status in other realms of life. If married women have their own source of income independent of their husbands, then they are better able to become empowered within their families and to get out of relationships with men who are physically or psychologically abusive. If, as in matrilineal and matrilocal societies, women are able to maintain relationships of "sisterhood" (i.e., support from other women), and/or of extended family ties (i.e., aid from their kin), then they can mobilize these supportive relationships in times of hardship. If women have legal recourse to sue discriminating employers and would-be employers, then their opportunities and compensation on the job will be improved by the threat of monetary damages.

The warning? Cross-cultural studies have not yet discovered the key that unlocks the door leading to equality between the sexes. Comparative anthropological work—like most work dealing with human behavior and beliefs—is highly suggestive, but it is not conclusive. Thus far we cannot identify the one or two or three things that women can do that will lead to equal treat-ment in the workplace, in the household, in the bedroom, and in the political arena. No one or two or three male-dominated institutions could be changed that will radically improve the position of women in various realms of their lives. For example, outlawing sexual discrimination in the workplace and making comparable pay for comparable work legally mandatory might not be realized in greater female-male equality in other contexts such as family life or politics. Therefore, feminists—of both sexes—need to continue to work on a broad front to achieve their objectives.

Summary

Physical differences between females and males are recognized and relevant to social behavior in all known cultures. Although whether one is male or female matters to all peoples, it matters in different ways and to different degrees.

A person's *sex* is determined biologically by chromosomes, but *gender* is a cultural construct. The cultural construction of gender means that cultures vary in how they perceive the physical differences between the sexes, in the significance they attribute to those differences, and in the ways those differences are made relevant for self-identity, task and role allocation, access to property and power, and so forth. The Hua of New Guinea illustrate how one culture constructs gender categories and interprets the meaning of those categories.

Much attention has been given to how and why the sexual division of labor varies cross-culturally. One firm conclusion of this research is that sexual stereotypes that men are breadwinners and women are caretakers are not based on natural differences between the sexes. Male domination is not rooted in men's supplying the material necessities of existence because women's labor frequently produces much or most of the food supply.

There are certain widespread patterns in the sexual division of labor, as shown in Table 10.1. Three major influences on the broad cross-cultural similarities in the allocation of economic tasks are: superior male strength; the depression of fertility that seems to occur when a woman engages in heavy exercise; and the compatibility of a task with care of infants and young children, which is everywhere primarily a female responsibility.

But no biological difference between the sexes can account for the cross-cultural variations in the sexual divi-sion of labor. A difference to which much attention has been given is the higher importance of female labor in horticultural populations relative to intensive agriculturalists. Credible hypotheses explain why women's contributions to subsistence decline as intensity increases. The cereal grains grown by most intensive agriculturalists require seasonally heavy work at planting and harvest (done by males), more processing of food before it is eaten (done by females), and more time spent in caring for domesticated animals (done by females). As a result, males spend more time in cultivation, and females experience a greater domestic workload. Although much comparative research supports these generalizations, specific cultures, such as the Kofyar, vary greatly from the general pattern. As technology reduces the importance of biological differences in task performance and as birthrates decline, gender will matter less for occupational recruitment in industrialized nations.

Another issue in gender studies is the nature and causes of cultural diversity in the status of women. Even specialists in this subject cannot agree whether ethnographic studies reveal that females are universally subordinate to males. This is mainly because no explicit criteria can be used to judge whether there are populations in which males and females are fully equal. It does seem to be true that females as a social category are never dominant over males as a social category.

A multitude of forces influence women's overall status in a culture, including their relative contributions to subsistence, their control over key resources, the prevalent pattern of descent and postmarital residence, and overall societal complexity. Studies that document the variability in women's status suggest that greater sexual equality is an achievable goal for modern women, but there may be no single attitude or institution that feminists can alter that will give women equality in all realms of life.

Key Terms

cultural construction of gender   status of women
sexual division of labor   complex societies

Suggested Readings

Books that are excellent brief introductions to the anthropological study of gender include:

Friedl, Ernestine. *Women and Men: An Anthropologist's View*. New York: Holt, Rinehart and Winston, 1975.
Tiffany, Sharon W. *Women, Work, and Motherhood*. Madison, Wisc.: Four Seasons Press, 1982.

The following books investigate some particular dimension of gender from a comparative perspective:

Buckley, Thomas, and Alma Gottlieb, eds. *Blood Magic: The Anthropology of Menstruation*. Berkeley: University of California Press, 1988.
Collier, Jane. *Marriage and Inequality in Classless Societies*. Stanford, Calif.: Stanford University Press, 1987.
Dahlberg, F., ed. *Woman the Gatherer*. New Haven, Conn.: Yale University Press, 1981.
Gilmore, David D. *Manhood in the Making: Cultural Concepts of Masculinity*. New Haven, Conn.: Yale University Press, 1990.
Margolis, M. *Mothers and Such: American Views of Women and How They Changed*. Berkeley: University of California Press, 1984.
Sanday, Peggy R. *Female Power and Male Dominance*. Cambridge: Cambridge University Press, 1981.

A number of edited volumes are useful. On the list below the best single resource for both students and professionals is the 1989 volume edited by Morgen. In addition to an excellent introductory essay, it covers gender studies in all four anthropological subfields. It also contains chapters on gender relations in the major world regions: Africa, Middle East, Latin America, and so forth.

Collier, Jane, and Sylvia Yanagisako, eds. *Gender and Kinship: Essays Toward a Unified Analysis*. Stanford, Calif.: Stanford University Press, 1984.
di Leonardo, Micaela, ed. *Gender at the Crossroads of Knowledge: Feminist Anthropology in the Postmodern Era*. Berkeley: University of California Press, 1991.
MacCormack, Carol, and Marilyn Strathern, eds. *Nature, Culture, and Gender*. Cambridge: Cambridge University Press, 1980.

Morgen, Sandra, ed. *Gender and Anthropology: Critical Reviews for Research and Teaching*. Washington, D.C.: American Anthropological Association, 1989.
Ortner, Sherry B., and Harriet Whitehead, eds. *Sexual Meanings: The Cultural Construction of Gender and Sexuality*. Cambridge: Cambridge University Press, 1981.
Reiter, Rayna R., ed. *Toward an Anthropology of Women*. New York: Monthly Review Press, 1975.
Rosaldo, M. Z., and Louise Lamphere, eds. *Women, Culture, and Society*. Stanford, Calif.: Stanford University Press, 1974.
Sanday, Peggy Reeves, and Ruth Gallagher Goodenough, eds. *Beyond the Second Sex: New Directions in the Anthropology of Gender*. Philadelphia: University of Pennsylvania Press, 1990.

Readable case studies of gender relations in particular cultures include:

Abu-Lughod, Lila. *Writing Women's Worlds: Bedouin Stories*. Berkeley: University of California Press, 1992.
Fernea, Elizabeth W. *Guests of the Sheik: An Ethnography of an Iraqi Village*. Garden City, N.Y.: Anchor, 1965.
Friedl, Erika. *Women of Deh Koh: Lives in an Iranian Village*. New York: Penguin, 1991.
Fujimura-Fanselow, Kumiko, and Atsuko Kameda, eds. *Japanese Women: New Perspectives on the Past, Present, and Future*. New York: The Feminist Press, 1995.
Goodale, Jane. *Tiwi Wives*. Seattle: University of Washington Press, 1971.
Lepowsky, Maria. *Fruit of the Motherland: Gender in an Egalitarian Society*. New York: Columbia University Press, 1993.
Mead, Margaret. *Sex and Temperament in Three Primitive Societies*. New York: William Morrow, 1963.
Mitter, Sara S. *Dharma's Daughters: Contemporary Indian Women and Hindu Culture*. New Brunswick, N.J.: Rutgers University Press, 1991.
Nanda, Serena. *Neither Man nor Woman: The Hijras of India*. Belmont, Calif.: Wadsworth Publishing Co., 1990.
Roscoe, Will. *The Zuni Man-Woman*. Albuquerque: University of New Mexico Press, 1991.
Saitoti, Tepilit Ole. *The Worlds of a Maasai Warrior: An Autobiography*. Berkeley: University of California Press, 1988.
Shostak, Marjorie. *Nisa: The Life and Words of a !Kung Woman*. Cambridge, Mass.: Harvard University Press, 1981.
Wolf, Margery. *Women in China*. Stanford, Calif.: Stanford University Press, 1975.

Internet Exercises

The United Nations Development Programme-Gender in Development Programme has a site devoted to "Gender Equality and the Advancement of Women" (http:www.undp.org/undp/gender/). This site has a lot of information on gender and development issues worldwide.

Recently the *Washington Post* ran a series about contemporary issues in the United States (http://www.washingtonpost.com/wp-srv/national/longtem/gender/gender22a.htm). This series of articles is informative on its own, but should be even more so with the anthropological knowledge that you now have. An interesting facet of anthropology is that by studying other societies you gain a deeper perspective on your own.

"Reflections on Fieldwork Among the Sinai Bedouin Women" is a webpage by Ann Gardner (http://www.sherryart.com/women/bedouin.html). This page has many links to gender- and women's studies-related sites.

The website "The Female Genital Mutilation Research Homepage" (http:/www.hollyfeld.org/fgm/) concerns the topic of "female circumcision," although the operations performed often involve more serious procedures. You can link to topics such as an overview of female genital mutilation, references (books and films), eradication efforts, and a discussion forum. One set of links connects to human rights issues. This is a nice place to start investigating these controversial cultural practices.

CHAPTER *11*

The Organization of Political Life

C O N T E N T S

Forms of Political Organization

Bands

Tribes

Chiefdoms

States

Social Control and Law

Social Control

Law

Legal Systems

Self-Help Systems

Court Systems

*In modern urban societies such as England, uniformed police
are an important part of the legal system.*

Visit http://www.wadsworth.com/humanity to learn more about the material covered
in this chapter and to access activities, exercises, and tutorial quizzes.

*E*VERY SOCIETY *has some form of political system, meaning those
institutions that organize and direct the collective actions of the
population. In small societies, political leadership and organization may be informal and even ad hoc. Only when a specific need
for leadership arises does some individual assume an overt leadership
role. In general, the larger the population, the more formalized the leadership and the more complex the political organization.*

LIKEWISE, AS MENTIONED *in Chapter 2, all societies demand some minimal
degree of conformity from their members. All, therefore, develop mechanisms of social control by which the behaviors of individuals are constrained and directed into acceptable channels. There are always
behavioral patterns that are approved or acceptable and patterns that are
disapproved or unacceptable. By means of social control, a society
encourages normatively proper behavior and discourages unacceptable*

actions, the objective being the maintenance of harmony and cooperation. The most serious deviations from acceptable behavior, which threaten the cohesiveness of the group, fall under that aspect of social control known as law, also discussed in this chapter. In the least organized societies, law and political organization exist independently of each other. As political organization becomes increasingly formalized and structured, governmental institutions take over legal institutions, until legal institutions become part of the formal political structure.

Forms of Political Organization

When we speak of the political organization of a particular cultural system, we frequently are left with the impression that political boundaries and cultural boundaries are the same. But the boundaries of a *polity,* or politically organized unit, may or may not correspond with the boundaries of a particular way of life. For example, the Comanche of the Great Plains shared a common language, customs, and ethnic identity, yet politically, they were never organized above the local group. Thus, the term *Comanche* refers to a people with a common language and culture who never united to carry out common political activities.

At the other extreme we find highly centralized polities that incorporate several culturally distinct peoples. In these instances, the political boundary is suprasocietal and multicultural. The United States is unusual in this regard only in the degree of cultural heterogeneity that exists in the population. France, although predominantly "French," also includes Bretons and Basques. India has several hundred different ethnic groups. Russia, China, Indonesia, and the Philippines also integrate highly diversified populations into a single polity. In fact, every large and most small countries in the world today politically integrate several ethnic groups (see Chapter 17).

Political organization falls into four basic forms. From the least to the most complex, these forms are **bands** (**simple** and **composite**), **tribes**, **chiefdoms**, and **states**. Today, few societies exist that are not integrated into state-level political systems. Thus, to understand societies organized at less complex levels, we have to reconstruct the structure of such societies at an earlier period.

Bands

As the least complex form, bands were probably the earliest form of human political structure (see Chapter 6). As more complex political systems developed, band-level societies were unable to compete for resources. Thus, bands survived until the modern period only in regions of the world with limited natural resources. Most known band-level societies were found in the deserts and grasslands of Australia, Africa, and the Americas. A few others lived in the tropical forests of Africa, Asia, and South America and in the boreal forest and tundra regions of North America and Asia.

Bands consist of a number of families living together and cooperating in economic activities throughout the year. Band-level organization most frequently was found among peoples with foraging economies, which usually dictated low population densities and high seasonal mobility. As a result, only a relatively small number of people could stay together throughout the year. Bands ranged in size from only a dozen to several hundred individuals. The adaptive significance of the band's size and seasonal mobility is described in Chapter 6. In this chapter we are concerned with leadership statuses and political organization of bands.

The smallest bands, called *simple bands,* usually were no larger than an extended family and were structured as such. Leadership was informal, with the oldest or one of the older male members of the family serving as leader. Decision making was reached through consensus and involved both adult males and adult females; simple bands operated as families. Because all members of the band were related either through descent or by marriage, they were exogamous units, and members of the band had to seek spouses from other bands. Thus, although an autonomous economic and political unit, every band was, by social necessity, allied through intermarriage with other bands, usually territorially adjacent ones. Simple bands usually had names, although names may have been informal and may have simply referred to some prominent geographical feature associated with the band's usual territory.

Resource availability influenced the formation of such small groups. Simple bands often were associated with the hunting of nonmigratory game animals, such as deer, guanaco, moose, or small mammals, which occupy a limited territory on a year-round basis and are found either singly or in small herds. The foraging activities of simple bands usually did not generate any significant surpluses of food, which necessitated the year-round hunting of game animals. Effective hunting required only a few male hunters who had intimate knowledge of the seasonal shifts in range of these animals within their territory. The game resources of such areas could be exploited most effectively by a small and highly mobile population. In addition, such bands depended on the seasonal collection of wild roots, berries, nuts, and other edible plants, as well as on limited fishing and shellfish collection.

Composite bands consisted of a larger aggregation of families, sometimes numbering in the hundreds. In contrast to simple bands, composite bands encompassed unrelated extended families. Although leadership in composite bands was informal, it was more defined. Such leaders frequently have been called **big men**. Big men did not hold formal offices, and leadership was based on influence rather than authority over band members. **Influence** is merely the ability to convince people that they should act as you suggest. **Authority** is the recognized right of an individual to command another person to act in a particular way. Thus, a big-man leader could not, by virtue of his position, make demands or impose rules on the members of the band, and his decisions were not binding on others. Because big-man status did not involve a formal office, no prescribed process for attaining leadership status existed. A man might emerge as the leader through a variety of personal accomplishments or qualities, such as his proven ability in hunting or warfare, the supernatural powers he possessed, or merely his charisma. There was no set tenure in the position, which was filled by a man until he was informally replaced by some other leader.

Like simple bands, many composite bands were nomadic groups that moved within a relatively well-defined range. Because of their greater size, composite bands were not as cohesive as simple bands and were politically more volatile. Disputes between families could result in some members joining another band or even the band splitting into two or more bands.

The formation of composite bands resulted from economic pressures that facilitated or necessitated the cooperation of a larger number of individuals than found in a single extended family. As in the case of simple bands, the behavior of the principal game animals was an important influence. Composite bands were associated with the seasonal hunting of migratory animals that form large herds, such as bison and caribou. Migratory herd animals usually appeared only seasonally in the range of a particular composite band as the herd moved between its summer and winter ranges. Because bison and caribou migrated in herds that sometimes numbered in the tens of thousands, there was no difficulty in locating the herds on the open grasslands and tundra. Unlike the nonmigratory-animal hunters, who secured game steadily throughout the year, hunters of migratory animals took most of their game only twice a year, as the herds passed through their territories during migrations.

Hunting large herds of animals effectively required directing the movements of the herd into situations where large numbers could be slaughtered. Herds might be run over a cliff, into a holding pen, or into a lake, where hunters in boats could kill them. Regardless of the method used, all these strategies required the presence of a larger group of hunters than was available in a simple band. Thus, composite bands were formed to bring together a sufficiently large number of hunters to control the movements of large herds of animals.

The Comanche of the southern Great Plains of the United States illustrate the nature of composite bands. These horse-raising, bison-hunting people were politically autonomous until the Red River War of 1875. During the early and middle years of the nineteenth century, the Comanche numbered about 6,000 to 7,000, divided between five and thirteen main bands. Comanche bands had only vaguely defined territories, and two or more bands frequently occupied the same general area or had overlapping ranges. Membership in Comanche bands was fluid: Both individuals and families could and did shift from one band to another, or a number of families might join together to establish a new band. Some anthropologists have theorized that there were only five major bands, with a varying number of secondary bands appearing and disappearing from time to time.

A band consisted of a number of families, each headed by an older male member who was "peace chief" or "headman." One of these family heads also served as the peace chief for the entire band. There was no formalized method of selecting either the family heads or the head of the band. As the Comanche say, "No one made him such; he just got that way." A Comanche peace chief usually was a man known for his kindness, wisdom, and ability to lead by influencing other men. Although a war record was important, peace chiefs were not chosen from among the most aggressive or ambitious men. Such men usually remained war chiefs—great warriors who periodically recruited men to raid neighbors—but frequently had little influence outside war and raiding.

A band peace chief was responsible for the well-being of the band. Through a consensus of the family heads, he directed the seasonal movement of the band and the bison hunts. He did have men who voluntarily assisted him. In the morning the peace chief usually sent out two men to scout the area around the camp for the presence of enemy raiding parties. He also sent a crier through the camp periodically to announce plans for the movement of the camp, an upcoming hunt, or some other cooperative activities. During the bison hunts, the peace chief called on a number of men from the camp to police the hunt and restrain overly eager hunters from scattering the herd and thus spoiling the hunt for others.

In an extraordinarily individualistic and egalitarian society, Comanche band leaders had to strive for and maintain consensus. If a dispute arose and a consensus could not be reached, individuals and families were free either to shift residence to another band or even to form a new band under another leader.

Comanche bands were economically and politically autonomous units. Only seldom did two or more bands come together for any unified action, and never did leaders of the bands come together to discuss issues. At the same time, there was a strong consciousness of common identity, of being Comanche. Comanches freely traveled between bands to visit, marry, and even shift residence. There was an informally reached general consensus on whether relations with a particular neighboring group were friendly or hostile. Comanche bands also usually refrained from attacking other Comanche bands, although on occasion some did ally themselves with foreign groups.

Thus, on the band level of political organization, populations are fragmented into numerous independent political units that operate only at the local-group level. These various communities share a common cultural identity and usually attempt to maintain harmonious relations with one another, but they lack any political structure capable of organizing all the various communities into a single unit for collective actions.

Tribes

Tribes differ from bands in that they have formally organized institutions that unite the scattered residential communities, give the society greater cohesiveness, and make possible a more united response to external threats. These institutions are called **sodalities**. Sodalities take various forms: They may be based on large kin groups, such as clans and lineages; on nonkinship units, such as age sets (see Chapter 15); or on voluntary associations, such as warrior societies. Regardless of their exact nature, sodalities unify geographically dispersed communities into political units. Although tribal-level societies usually are egalitarian, with leadership dependent in part on the persuasive abilities of individuals, formalized political offices with institutionalized authority exist. Although tribes vary greatly in structure, here we can examine only one tribal-level society.

The Cheyenne of the Great Plains numbered between 3,000 and 3,500 during the early 1800s. The Cheyenne, like the neighboring Comanche, were horse-mounted bison hunters. They were divided into ten main nomadic villages, which averaged between 300 and 350 persons. Village membership was not based on kinship, although the members of a particular village usually were related either by blood or by marriage. Village membership was relatively stable, and marriages between villagers were common. Despite this stability, myths concerning village origins were not well developed, and band names were only nicknames (e.g., Grayhairs, Hair-rope Men, Ridge

Men, or some other trivial characteristic). Although a particular village usually frequented a certain range, there was no sense of village territoriality. Periodically and seasonally, family camps and subvillage camps broke off from the main village.

The only time the entire tribe came together was in early summer, when all the widely scattered villages gathered into a single camp at a predetermined location. This crescent-shaped encampment stretched for several miles from end to end, with the open portion facing east. Within the tribal encampment every village had a designated location; and while camped together, they performed the great tribal ceremonies (e.g., the Arrow Renewal, the Sun Dance, or the Animal Dance). At least one and possibly two of these rituals were performed, depending on the particular ritual needs of the tribe at that time. After the performance of the ritual, the tribe as a unit staged the great summer bison hunt. After the hunt, the tribe again scattered into smaller village camps.

Politically, the tribe was controlled by the Council of Forty-four and the warrior societies. The Council of Forty-four, which had both political and religious duties, was headed by the Sweet Medicine chief, who was responsible for keeping the Sweet Medicine bundle, a sacred package of sweet grass. Second to him in importance were four other sacred chiefs, each representative of specific supernatural beings. Under these five sacred chiefs were thirty-nine ordinary chiefs.

Chiefs served in their positions for ten years and could not be removed for any reason. Serving as a chief placed a burden on the individuals. Chiefs usually were selected from among the older men, all of whom had war records. When an individual was chosen as a chief, he was to act like a chief, not an aggressive warrior. If the man was an officer in one of the warrior societies, he had to resign his position, although he remained a member of the society. A chief was to be generous, kindly, even tempered, and aloof from everyday disputes. In short, he was expected to display ideal human behavior at all times: He was to take care of the poor, settle disputes between individuals, and be responsible for the ritual performances that protected the tribe.

The major sodalities were the warrior societies, of which there were five. These were formal voluntary associations of men, each with its own style of dress, dances, songs, and set of four leaders. As young warriors, men were recruited by the different societies until all had joined one or another. The term *warrior societies* is slightly misleading. The heads of the various societies constituted what some call the *tribal war chiefs*. Although this group planned and led attacks on their enemies, the different societies did not fight or operate as

Political authority is frequently indicated by differences in dress, as in the case of American Indian peoples on the northwest coast of North America.

military units in battles. In battles men fought as individuals, and members of several societies may have been present in a particular raiding party.

Subordinate to the council of chiefs, the warrior societies cooperated as a group only in the policing of the camps. During the summer tribal encampment, the Council of Forty-four appointed one of the societies as camp police. Later, when the village scattered into separate camps, the members of the council resident in the village appointed one of the warrior societies to police the camp. After being appointed, the warrior society usually carried out its function with little direction from the chiefs. Its members scouted the area around the camp to check for the presence of any enemy raiding parties, and intervened in any serious disputes between village members.

There are two points to be emphasized about the political organization of tribal societies. First, although there were some formalized political and religious offices that bequeathed some limited authority and prerogatives, on the whole, tribal societies were basically egalitarian (see Chapter 12). Few positions were hereditary, and

most leaders were selected on the basis of personal qualities and individual merit.

Second, there was little economic specialization, either individual or regional, among tribes. Except for cooperation in communal hunts, families produced their own food and manufactured their own clothes and other material goods. From an economic perspective, each band or village was capable of sustaining itself without support from other communities; therefore, it was not economic necessity, convenience, or efficiency that led to the supracommunity political organization of tribes. Although sodalities unite tribes at a higher level of cohesiveness than bands, the mere existence of sodalities is not sufficient to generate or maintain the cohesiveness of a tribe. It is likely that external threats, either real or perceived, necessitated the cooperation in warfare of a large group of people and was the major factor that united geographically dispersed communities. Thus, warfare—the existence and activities of hostile human neighbors—was an important force in creating the political integration of separate communities.

Chiefdoms

Like tribes, chiefdoms were multicommunity political units. Unlike tribes, chiefdoms had a formalized and centralized political system. A chiefdom (see Chapter 7) was governed by a single chief, who usually served as both political and religious head of the polity. The chief had authority over members of the chiefdom, and the position often was hereditary within a single kin group, which based its rights chiefly on supernatural powers. Thus, a chiefdom was not an egalitarian society but a ranked or stratified society (see Chapter 12) with access to resources based on inherited status. With authority and power conferred by supernatural beings, governing was not by consensus but by decree.

Most chiefdoms were associated with horticultural societies in which craft or regional specialization in production had emerged. There was a need for regularized exchanges of goods either between geographically dispersed communities or, at times, within a single community. This economic exchange was managed through redistribution, with the chief occupying the central position in the flow of goods (see Chapter 7).

In earlier historic periods, chiefdoms probably were found throughout much of the Old World. During more recent periods, such political systems were primarily concentrated in Oceania (Polynesia, Micronesia, and Melanesia) and in the Americas (the circum-Caribbean and coastal portions of South America and the northwestern coast of North America).

The Polynesian-speaking people of Tahiti, an island in the southeastern Pacific, illustrate many characteristics typical of a chiefdom. This relatively large, mountainous, volcanic island had a population of about 100,000 at the time of European discovery. Tahiti was divided among about twenty rival chiefs. Although most of these chiefdoms were about the size of the average tribe and significantly smaller than the largest tribes, their political organization differed significantly.

The economy of Tahiti was based largely on farming. Taro, breadfruit, coconuts, and yams were the main crops; pigs and chickens were also raised, and fish and other seafoods supplemented the food supply. Food production was sufficient not only to meet the needs of the population but also to produce surpluses for export to other islands. Although sufficient food was produced in all regions, there were significant regional differences in types of food produced because Tahiti varied ecologically.

Tahitian society had at least three, and possibly four, distinct classes, depending on how finely one wants to divide the units. *Arii,* or chiefs, and their close relatives formed the ruling elite. The arii were divided into two groups: the *arii rahi,* or sacred chiefs, and the *arii rii,* or small chiefs. Under these chiefs were the *raatira,* or subchiefs, and the *manahune,* or commoners. The sacred chiefs were viewed as descended from the gods, whereas the commoners were merely created by the gods for their use. The subchiefs were the offspring of intermarriage between the sacred chiefs and commoners, whereas the small chiefs were the products of still later intermarriages between sacred chiefs and subchiefs. Once these four classes were established, class endogamy became the rule.

The sacred chiefs, viewed as gods on earth, evoked both reverence and fear. Whatever the highest-ranking sacred chiefs touched became *tabu,* or sacred, and could not be used for fear of supernatural punishment. Such a chief had to be carried on the back of a servant, lest the ground be touched by his feet became tabu. He could not enter the house of another individual, for the same reason. The lifestyle of the chief's family differed from that of other individuals: They had larger and more elaborate houses, the largest canoes, insignia of their rank, and particular clothing.

Unlike band and tribal-level societies, resources in chiefdoms were individually owned. Land was owned mainly by the chiefs and subchiefs, but ultimate authority rested with the sacred chiefs within the polity. Although sacred chiefs could not withhold the title to lands from the families of subchiefs, they could banish an individual subchief. Crafts were specialized, and craftspeople were attached to particular sacred chiefs and produced goods for them. Thus, the sacred chiefs directly controlled craft production and communal fishing. The chiefs could make any demands on the property of the subchiefs and commoners. If someone refused, the chief could have the recalcitrant banished or make him or her a sacrificial vic-

tim. Theoretically, the sacred chief was the head judicial figure in the polity, but some believe that the chief seldom intervened in disputes between individuals; the chief usually used these powers only against people who challenged his authority.

The sacred chief in each polity was the focal point for redistributive exchanges. The chief periodically demanded surplus production from all his subjects for a public redistribution. Such events were associated with a number of occasions: a rite of passage for a member of the chief's family, the organizing of a military attack, religious ceremonies, or the start of the breadfruit harvest. During such ceremonies, the chief distributed the goods collected to all his subjects.

States

Although they had a centralized political system, chiefdoms were still kinship-based structures. Even in Tahiti, the sacred chief's authority rested in large part on his control over families of subchiefs, each of whom had his own inalienable rights to lands—and thus families—of commoners. As a result, the number of people who could be effectively integrated into a chiefdom was limited. In Polynesia, most chiefdoms ranged from only a few thousand to 30,000 persons. Polities with larger populations require a political structure based on institutions other than kinship.

States, like chiefdoms, have a centralized political structure. States are distinguished from chiefdoms by the presence of a bureaucracy. A chiefdom is basically a two-level system: (1) the chiefs (which in Tahiti included the subchiefs), who have varying levels of authority and power, and (2) the commoners, or great mass of the populace. A state has three levels: (1) the ruling elite, (2) a bureaucracy, and (3) the populace.

In states, as in chiefdoms, highest authority and power reside in the ruling elite, the formal political head or heads of the polity. States vary greatly in the types of political leaders present and in the basis for the leaders' authority and power. Leaders in the earliest states frequently were considered to be the descendants of gods, and thus themselves gods on earth. The Inca of Peru and the pharaohs of Egypt were leaders who ruled as gods. Other political leaders, although not claiming to be gods, have legitimated their positions with claims of having been chosen by God. Early European kings legitimated their claims to leadership on such a basis; and as English coins still proclaim, the queen rules *Dei gratia*—by the "grace of God." Other states have evolved political leadership that uses strictly secular ideas to justify its power. In countries where leaders are elected by a vote of the populace, rule is legitimated by the internalized acceptance of such ascendence to office. Even strictly secular kingdoms, dictatorships,

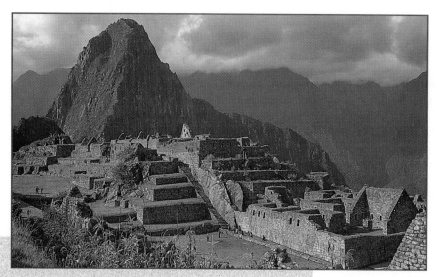

The Inca were able to construct cities such as Machu Picchu despite mountainous terrain.

and oligarchies can, if in power for a sufficient time, have their rule accepted by the populace as "legitimate." We have more to say about legitimation in Chapter 12.

Although they differ greatly in political leadership, states all share one characteristic: the presence of a bureaucracy that carries out the day-to-day governing of the polity. In simple terms, a bureaucrat is a person to whom a political leader delegates certain authority and powers. The bureaucrat thus acts on behalf of the political leader. Lacking any inherent authority or powers personally, bureaucrats depend on the continued support of political leaders. Using bureaucrats as intermediaries, political leaders could expand the size of their polities both geographically and demographically, while strengthening their political control over the population. Bureaucrats could engineer such expansion without threat of revolution and political fragmentation because they lacked any personal claims to independent political legitimacy.

Inca Empire   The Inca Empire of ancient Peru was typical of a state-level organization. From the capital of Cuzco, the ruler, or Sapa Inca, controlled a multiethnic empire of between six and twelve million subjects speaking dozens of different languages and extending over 2,500 miles from modern-day Ecuador to central Chile. Dissected by some of the highest mountain ranges and most inhospitable deserts in the world, the Inca Empire also existed without a writing system for communication, a monetary system for exchange, or wheeled vehicles for the transporting of goods. In spite of this limited technology and hostile terrain, the central government was able to

organize human labor for massive public works projects, ranging from the construction of buildings and terraced fields to a 9,500-mile highway network that stretched the length and breadth of the country.

The Sapa Inca was also able to mobilize and supply armies numbering in the tens of thousands for extended periods of time. The Inca Empire was a conquest state created through the military conquest and incorporation of smaller neighboring states. However, it was the administrative abilities of its leaders, more than their military might, that gave the empire its political cohesiveness.

The Sapa Inca was believed to be the direct descendant of the Sun God. Thus, the Sapa Inca was a divine being, with absolute authority over and control of all the people and resources of the empire. Succession was not clearly defined. Any son of the Sapa Inca had a legitimate claim to his father's position. To avoid conflict, the Sapa Inca usually chose one of his sons as his successor before his death, but the death of the Sapa Inca usually resulted in conflicts between potential heirs.

The empire was administratively divided into four geographical regions, each with its own head. The regions were divided into provinces, with governors and regional capitals. The provinces were in turn organized on the basis of what some have called a "decimal administration" of hierarchically nested administrative units based on population size. The largest was a Huno, with a population of 10,000 households. A Huno was divided into units of 5,000, 1,000, 500, 100, 50, and finally 10 households. Each unit had an official head responsible to the person above him. Periodically, a census was conducted and adjustments made. This was of course the ideal administrative model. The actual structure varied somewhat from province to province due to local demographic and ethnic factors.

Regional heads were members of the Incan royal family. In some provinces, relatives of the Sapa Inca also filled the position of governor. However, in most cases provincial governors and other provincial officials were drawn from local elite families, and these families even held hereditary rights to these offices. Beneath these officials and their families was the great mass of people, the commoners.

Land was divided into plots used by individual families and households, and land used for the support of public functions. Every household in the empire was given sufficient land to meet its economic needs. Households and local communities were basically self-sufficient. Food and other goods produced on their land and within the family belonged to the family.

The government of the empire was supported by a labor tax, not a tax on production. Every household was required to supply labor for state purposes. Some assignments were for only a number of days per years, others were yearlong, and still others lifelong. The major function of provincial officials was to assign tasks, organize work parties, and oversee the work.

The majority of commoners paid their labor tax by working part of the year farming public fields, tending herds of state-owned animals, weaving cloth, making pottery, repairing public buildings, working on public roads, or performing some other local task. In every province, food, clothes, and other utilitarian goods produced by state tax labor were stored in public buildings. State-owned food, clothes, and other goods were used to support the army, visiting government officials, and commoners who had been assigned long-term labor tasks that made it impossible for them to be self-supporting. In return for their services, all provincial officials in charge of 100 households or more were allowed to use tax laborers to farm their fields, tend their herds, build their houses, and make their clothes and other goods.

In the 1530s, the Spanish conquered the Inca Empire and murdered the last Sapa Inca. However, the provincial governmental structure and the "decimal administrative" system were incorporated into the government of colonial Peru.

The emergence of states increased the complexity of political units, and bureaucracies not only allowed for specialization in governmental functions but also made possible the effective integration of large land areas and populations into political units. For example, chiefdoms seldom exceeded 30,000 persons, whereas modern states such as China may have populations of one billion people.

Social Control and Law

All societies have clearly defined rules that govern the relationships between members. Not all individuals in any society will conform to these rules. There will always be some who behave in a socially unacceptable manner. Thus, among all peoples there exist formal and informal ways to correct the behavior of individuals. In general, we call these mechanisms social control. One form of social control is called law.

Social Control

Social control refers to the diverse ways in which the behaviors of the members of a society are constrained into socially approved channels. All cultures have certain behavioral norms that most people learn and begin to conform to during enculturation. But all societies have individuals who, to one degree or another, deviate also from those norms. Violations of norms usually result in sanctions or punishments for the offender, which serve both to correct the behavior of particular people and to show others the penalties for such deviance. The severity of sanctions and the process by which sanctions are imposed differ greatly, depending on the seriousness culturally attached to the violated norm, the perceived severity of the violation, and the overall political and legal system of the people.

Children who get into mischief usually are corrected by their parents. In our own society, parents may impose sanctions ranging from scolding to spanking to withdrawing privileges. The correcting of children trains individuals in proper behavior at an early age.

The community also applies informal sanctions against individuals—both children and adults—who are not behaving properly. Gossip, or fear of gossip, serves as an important method of social control in most societies. Most people fear the contempt or ridicule of their peers, so most individuals try to conform to acceptable behavioral norms. People attempt to hide behavior that would be the subject of gossip, scandal, and ridicule. Individuals whose known behavior consistently violates social norms may even find themselves ostracized by friends and relatives (the severest of informal punishments). Informal economic penalties also may be imposed. A family may withdraw economic support in attempts to modify errant behavior of a member.

A wide variety of supernatural sanctions may assist in controlling individual behavior, and in some cases these supernatural sanctions are automatically imposed on particular types of behavior. Whether the commission of these acts becomes public knowledge or not, and thus regardless of whether other punishments are inflicted on the individual, the commission still endangers one's immortal soul. Supernatural sanctions can be more specifically directed. In many societies, including some Christian ones, an individual may place a curse on another person by calling on a supernatural being. Fear of sorcery or witchcraft (see Chapter 13) frequently serves as another important form of social control. Most victims are people who in some way offended a witch or sorcerer, often through a breach of social norms.

Law

Law is the highest level of social control, and legal punishments usually are reserved for the most serious breaches of norms. The question of how law can be distinguished from other forms of social control is not easy to answer. In societies with court systems the distinction

Gossip is one of the primary means of social control.

is formalized, but in societies without such formalized legal systems the division is not as clear.

E. Adamson Hoebel (1954, 28) defined law in the following way: "A social norm is legal if its neglect or infraction is regularly met, in threat or in fact, by the application of physical force by an individual or group possessing the socially recognized privilege of so acting." Law so defined was and is present in virtually every society.

In a legal action, some individual or group must have publicly recognized authority to settle a case or punish a violation. In societies with courts the authority is obvious, but in societies that lack courts the authority becomes less clear. What emerges frequently is an ad hoc authority; that is, because of the peculiarities of the case, a particular individual or group becomes recognized by the community as the authority responsible for its resolution. In some cases, the victim may be the recognized authority. In the victim's absence (as in the case of murder), the victim's family, clan, or kin group may be placed in the role of authority. Such ad hoc authority is discussed later in some of the examples.

Implicit in all legal actions is the intention of universal application, which means that in identical cases the sanction imposed is the same. Although one might argue that no two legal cases have been or will ever be identical, the notion of universal application requires that the law be consistent and thus predictable; the arbitrary impositions of sanctions is not law.

Hoebel limited legal sanctions to physical sanctions. However, other scholars have argued that this definition is too narrow. A legal sanction does not have to be some form of corporal punishment, nor does it have to involve the loss of property. Based on his work with the Kapauku of New Guinea, Leopold Pospisil contended that the impact of psychological sanctions can be severer than that of actual physical punishment. For this reason he stated, "We can define a legal sanction as either the negative behavior of withdrawing some rewards or favors that otherwise (if the law had not been violated) would have been granted, or the positive behavior of inflicting some painful experience, be it physical or psychological" (Pospisil 1958, 268).

The legal institutions of a society consist of two distinct components: (1) **procedural law** and (2) **substantive law**. Procedural law refers to the manner in which a breach of the law is adjudicated or resolved, and it focuses on questions such as the following: Who assumes the role of authority? How is it determined that a breach of the law has taken place? How is the proper sanction determined? Who imposes the sanction on the offending party? Substantive law, on the other hand, is concerned with defining the types of behavior that are categorized as illegal—in other words, violations of the rights and duties of individuals and the appropriate sanctions to be imposed. Substantive laws—or at least the relative significance of such laws—differ greatly. For example, some societies have laws against witchcraft. Witchcraft, however, is not illegal under American law because we deny the existence of true witchcraft. In many societies, adultery is considered a crime punishable by death, whereas in other societies, adultery is of little consequence.

Although substantive laws vary widely in particulars, they do fall into two main categories: (1) criminal laws and (2) civil laws or torts. Criminal law is concerned with breaches of social norms that are considered to be crimes against the state or against society as a whole. They are handled by the society acting in a collective manner through its legal institutions, such as courts, prosecutors, judges, and police. In contrast, civil laws or torts are breaches of social norms that are considered to affect only an individual or groups of individuals. The society may or may not have formal organized institutions to adjudicate such cases. Not all societies make a distinction between criminal and civil law. In some societies there are only civil laws or torts, even for the more serious breaches of norms, such as murder.

Legal Systems

On the basis of procedural characteristics two main levels of complexity and formality can be defined: (1) **self-help legal systems** and (2) **court legal systems**.

Self-Help Systems

Self-help systems, also called *ad hoc systems,* are informal and exist in the absence of any centralized or formalized legal institutions capable of settling disputes. Such systems are associated with band-level societies and most tribal-level societies. In such systems there is only civil law. All legal actions concern only the principal parties and/or their families. The reason for terming the legal procedure in these societies *self-help* will become clear.

Self-help legal systems fall into two main forms: (1) *familial* and (2) *mediator*. In familial systems, all actions and decisions are initiated and executed by the families or larger kin groups involved. Mediator systems add the formal presence of a neutral third party—the mediator—who attempts to negotiate and resolve the dispute peacefully.

In familial systems, legal actions are handled by the families involved. A legal offense only indirectly concerns the community as a whole. When an individual and/or family determines that its rights have been violated, the imposition of the proper sanction falls to the plaintiffs; in other words, the offended party assumes the role of authority. Such a system in which the redress of a legal grievance falls to the victim, or in the case of murder to the victim's family, has some problems in implementation but not as many as one might anticipate. This is not a system of "might makes right." Certainly cases arise in such societies in which the physically (or militarily) weak are victimized by the strong. However, in cases of legal redress there is a community consensus in support of the victim and usually a recognized means by which even the weakest members of the community can gather support adequate to impose appropriate sanctions on the strongest.

The Comanche exemplify how a familial legal system operated and how victims weaker than their opponents could nonetheless obtain redress. One of the most frequent Comanche offenses was "wife stealing." Most older Comanche men were polygynous, and some of their wives were significantly younger than their husbands. Among young Comanche men it was considered prestigious, although illegal, to steal the wife of another man. Under Comanche law the injured husband could demand either his wife back or some property, usually horses, in compensation. The husband had the responsibility of imposing these sanctions. In such actions the community played no direct role, but a husband could not ignore the loss of a wife. If he did ignore it, the community would ridicule him, and his prestige would decline. Thus, not only did the community support the husband in pressing his claim, but they informally pressured him to act.

In imposing these sanctions the husband was allowed to use whatever physical force was needed, short of killing the individual. In cases in which the men involved were physically about equal, the two met to negotiate and discuss the husband's demands. Behind these negotiations was the potential threat that the husband might physically assault the defendant.

In cases where the husband presented little or no personal threat to the defendant, institutionalized means existed whereby the husband could gain the physical backing needed. Although it lowered his prestige in the community, he could call on his relatives for support; the husband, with his male relatives present and prepared to support his demands physically, could then negotiate with the defendant. The defendant always had to stand alone. Even if he had asked his kinsmen for support, they would not have responded for fear of community ridicule.

In cases where the husband was an orphan or lacked kinsmen to negotiate successfully, the aggrieved man could call on any other man he wanted to prosecute his case. He usually called on the assistance of one of the powerful war leaders in the band. Such a request was so prestigious that a war leader could not refuse. At the same time, such a request was demeaning to the man asking for help and greatly lowered his prestige. As a result, it usually required a great deal of social pressure to force a man to ask for assistance; once the request was made, the issue was between the defendant and the war leader alone. On approaching the defendant the war leader would call out, "You have stolen my wife," and then proceed to exact whatever demands the husband had requested. For his action the war leader received nothing in payment other than the admiration of the community; the husband received the settlement. Although this process most commonly was used in wife-stealing cases, it could be used for other issues as well. Thus, Comanche legal institutions gave any individual the means to marshal overwhelming physical force in the protection of his rights.

As the Comanche example shows, familial systems often work relatively well in protecting individual rights. There are exceptions, and in some situations this system can fail. The Caribou Inuit illustrate one of the inherent problems. In cases of murder, the authority and responsibility for imposing the sanction—execution—fell to the family of the victim. Execution of the murderer was not always immediate. The family might wait years until the opportunity presented itself to kill the murderer with impunity; shooting the man in the back while he was working was considered an ideal situation. For the system to work, a relative of the victim had to be left alive to impose the sanction. To prevent being killed himself, a murderer might not stop with the killing of his intended victim but proceed to kill the entire family as well. For example, a Caribou Inuit man was rebuffed by the family of a woman he wanted to marry. He killed the woman's father, mother, brothers, and sister—a total of seven or eight persons—and then took the woman as his wife. Such massacres were thought by many Inuit to be prudent behavior and sometimes enhanced the prestige of the individual.

The cloak of this Nuer man indicates that he is a leopard-skin chief. As such, he is in charge of mediating disputes.

The Caribou Inuit case illustrates the problems with familial systems of law; yet we must remember that all legal systems have defects, and manipulative individuals escape sanctions in all societies. Under the American legal system, murderers sometimes escape punishment because of legal technicalities. Also, the fact that an individual may enhance his prestige by committing a particular illegal act does not necessarily reflect on the law—after all, American folk heroes include Jesse James and Pretty Boy Floyd.

A more formalized type of legal procedure is found in the mediator system. Under this system, disputes are still between individuals and families. The offended party and/or his or her family fills the position of authority. However, a third party is called on, usually by the offending individual or his or her family, to attempt to negotiate a mutually agreeable solution. The mediator has no authority to impose a settlement. The aggrieved party and/or family must agree to accept the compensation negotiated.

The Nuer, a pastoral tribal society of the Sudan, provide an example of how mediator systems operate. The Nuer live in small villages of related families. Although villages are tied together through lineages and clans,

there is no effective leadership above the village level. The only formalized leaders who transcend the local units are *leopard-skin chiefs,* whose position is indicated by the wearing of a leopard-skin cloak. These men have no secular authority to enforce their judgments but only limited ritual powers to bless and curse.

The most important function of leopard-skin chiefs is mediating feuds between local groups. The Nuer are an egalitarian, warrior-oriented people. Disputes between individuals frequently result in physical violence, and men occasionally are killed. The killing of a Nuer requires that his kinsmen exact retribution. Any close patrilineal kinsman of the murderer may be killed in retaliation, but at least initially the kinsmen of the victim attempt to kill the murderer himself. Immediately after committing a murder the killer flees to the house of a leopard-skin chief. This dwelling is a sanctuary, and as long as the man stays in the chief's house he is safe. The victim's kinsmen usually keep the house under surveillance to try to kill the murderer if he ventures out.

The leopard-skin chief keeps the murderer in his house until a settlement is arranged. The chief will wait until tempers have cooled, which usually requires several weeks, before he begins to negotiate the case. First, he goes to the family of the murderer to see if they are willing to pay cattle to the victim's family in compensation. Seldom do they refuse because one of them might be killed in retaliation. After the murderer's family has agreed to pay, the chief proceeds to the family of the victim, offering so many cattle in compensation. Initially the victim's family invariably refuses, saying that they want blood, that cattle cannot compensate them for the death of their beloved kinsman. The leopard-skin chief persists, usually gaining support of more distant relatives of the victim who also pressure the family to settle. The leopard-skin chief may even threaten to place a curse on the family if they continue to refuse to settle for a payment rather than blood. The family finally agrees and accepts cattle, usually about forty head, as compensation. Even though the matter is formally settled, the killer and his close patrilineal kinsmen will avoid the family of the victim for some years so as not to provoke spontaneous retaliation.

Up to this point we have examined legal systems that operate without formalized or centralized political structure capable of resolving disputes. In many of these societies law, not subordination to a common set of formal political institutions, defines boundaries. To see what we mean, consider the Nuer. The Nuer distinguish among a *ter,* or a feud within a tribe that is a legal action subject to arbitration; a *kur,* or a fight between members of two tribes that cannot be arbitrated; and a *pec,* or a war with non-Nuer people. Nuer believe that disputes within a tribe should be

resolved by legal means (that is, peacefully), whereas disputes between individuals
who are not members of the same tribe
should be resolved by extralegal means,
including organized warfare. Legal
processes serve to repair and maintain
social relations between families; thus, law
serves both to maintain the cohesiveness
and define the boundaries of the society.

The Jivaro, a horticultural and foraging people of eastern Ecuador, illustrate
how law defines social boundaries. By
the 1950s, the Jivaro had been reduced
to slightly more than 2,000 persons settled in more than 200 scattered family
households. Such households usually
consist of a man, his wife or wives, their
children, and, possibly, a son-in-law or other relatives.
Households are grouped into "neighborhoods," which
consist of a number of households living within a few
miles of one another; the membership of a neighborhood
is fluid. Poor hunting, a dispute with other households, or
other factors might result in a family's moving away. Neither corporate kin groups nor formalized leadership positions exist. Except for household heads, only a few men
are called *unta,* or "big," but their informal leadership
role is limited and transitory. Politically, the Jivaro are
organized at a band level. Although they have only limited political institutions, the Jivaro have a strong sense of
common cultural identity and territorial boundaries. Living in adjacent or nearby territories are four other
"Jivaroan" groups, who speak mutually intelligible
dialects, share the same basic customs, and at times trade
with Jivaro households. Despite their minimal political
integration, there is little question about which households are Jivaro and which belong to the other four
groups.

With this political organization, the methods used to
settle disputes define the effective boundaries of the society. Disputes between Jivaros are resolved by legal
means, whereas disputes with members of other societies
are resolved through extralegal means. Like the Nuer, the
Jivaro make a sharp distinction between a **feud** and a
war. A feud is the legal means by which a sanction is
imposed on another family for the murder of a kinsman.
As a legal procedure, a feud proceeds in a manner quite
different from a war.

As in most societies, murder is the most serious
offense. According to Jivaro beliefs, few deaths are attributable to natural causes; most are the result of physical
violence, sorcery, or avenging spirits. Deaths caused by
physical violence and witchcraft are considered murders,
which have to be avenged by the kinsmen of the

In New Guinea, as elsewhere in the world, the threat of
physical force is an important component of law.

deceased. In most cases of physical violence, the murderer is readily identifiable. In cases of poisoning and witchcraft, divination is used to determine the guilty party.

Determination of the guilty party and whether they
are Jivaro or non-Jivaro affect how the victim's kinfolk
avenge the death. If the guilty party is Jivaro, the kinsmen
of the victim attack the household of the murderer with
the goal of killing the man himself. If they are not successful in finding him, they may kill a male relative of his,
even a young boy. They normally will not harm women
or little children, except in cases in which the victim was a
woman or a child. Even if they have the opportunity to
kill more, only one individual will be killed. This is a legal
action, and Jivaro law allows only a life for a life.

If, on the other hand, the guilty party is determined
to be a non-Jivaro, the relatives of the murdered person
attack the household of the guilty party, trying to kill as
many people as possible. They attempt to massacre the
entire family, with no regard for either sex or age. In
some cases they attack nearby households as well,
attempting to kill even more members of the group. This
is a war, not a legal action.

The Jivaro, the Nuer, and other peoples who lack
centralized and formal political structure nonetheless have
definite means of maintaining social control. To those of
us who have formal governmental institutions that are
supposed to handle our grievances and right the wrongs
done to us, self-help systems look rather anarchic. However, rules govern such systems. Some anthropologists
believe in fact that the best definition of *society* in self-
help systems is those individuals whose vengeance-tak-
ing activities are constrained by procedural rules.

Court Systems

A number of factors distinguish a *court legal system* from a self-help legal system. First, authority resides not with the victim and/or his or her family but with a formalized institution, the court. The court has the authority and the power to hear disputes and to unilaterally decide cases and impose sanctions. Authority in legal matters is a component of political authority; thus, fully developed court systems can exist only in societies that have centralized formal political leadership, that is, chiefdoms or states. Second, most court systems operate with formal public hearings, presided over by a judge or judges, with formally defined defendants and plaintiffs. Grievances are stated, evidence is collected and analyzed, and, in cases of conflicting evidence, oaths or ordeals may be used to determine truthfulness. Finally, only in court systems does one find substantive law clearly divided into criminal law and civil law.

Court systems in turn may be divided into three categories: (1) **incipient courts**, (2) **courts of mediation**, and (3) **courts of regulation**. All court systems mediate disputes as well as regulate behavior; however, as societies become increasingly complex, the primary focus of the court shifts from mediating disputes to regulating behavior. This shift results in a qualitative difference not only in courts but in the nature of the law itself. Associated with this shift is an increasing codification of the laws. Laws and their associated sanctions become standardized and rigid, and civil laws are steadily transformed into criminal laws. Court systems begin to emerge with the concept of "crime against society"—the need to control individual acts that might endanger the society as a whole, as opposed to acts that threaten only individuals. Herein lies the distinction between criminal law and civil law.

Incipient Court Systems   True court systems can only be found in societies with centralized political systems—chiefdoms or states. However, some tribal societies have what might best be termed *incipient courts*. Although a tribal-level society, the Cheyenne, as described earlier in this chapter, demonstrate the development of an incipient court system. At times, both the Council of Forty-four and the warrior societies assumed the role of de facto judges and courts. The Cheyenne recognized that certain individual actions threatened the well-being of the group and thus had to be controlled. Some of these actions were purely secular, whereas others were religious. Designated warrior societies were formally empowered by the council to enforce secular laws and regulations on the camp members. For example, in preparation for a communal bison hunt, camp members would be told to refrain from independent hunting for some days. If the policing warrior society discovered someone hunting illegally, the men present became the de facto judges and court and immediately imposed sanctions on the offender. Such an offender often was beaten with whips, his horses were shot, and his tipi was slashed with knives.

Other secular criminal violations were handled just as swiftly. The Council of Forty-four was responsible for the religious, or sacred, well-being of the tribe; thus, any action that endangered the supernatural well-being of the Cheyenne was their concern. The murder of a Cheyenne by another Cheyenne was the most heinous of crimes. Such a crime was said to bloody the sacred arrows, the most sacred of Cheyenne tribal medicine bundles. The arrows were symbolic of Cheyenne success in hunting (their main economic activity) and warfare. Murder within the tribe polluted the arrows and thus made the Cheyenne vulnerable to their enemies and less successful in their hunting. When a Cheyenne died at the hands of another Cheyenne, the Council of Forty-four became a de facto court. Although there was no formal hearing, the council met and discussed the case: Was it murder? If so, then the sacred arrows had to be "renewed," or ritually purified. They also decided on the sanction to be imposed—usually exile for a period of years. With the Cheyenne there could be no capital punishment without again polluting the sacred arrows. In "A Closer Look" we have a further discussion of the Cheyenne.

Courts of Mediation   The key difference between court systems is not how the legal hearings are conducted, but the manner in which breaches of the law are determined and suitable sanctions imposed. In courts of mediation few laws are codified, and the judges follow few formalized guidelines as to what constitutes a legal violation or the sanction that should be imposed. This is not to say that judges act arbitrarily in these matters, but that they have tremendous latitude in their actions. What they apply is a **reasonable-person model**. Using prevalent norms and values, they ask the question, How should a reasonable individual have acted under these circumstances? To determine this, an individual's actions have to be examined within the social context in which the dispute occurred: What was the past and present relationship between the parties involved? What were the circumstances leading up to the event? Thus, judges attempt to examine each case as a unique occurrence. Although some sanctions are imposed as punishments, other sanctions are designed to restore as fully as possible a working, if not harmonious, relationship between the parties involved.

One difficulty in attempting to describe courts of mediation is our limited knowledge of such systems.

Murder among the Cheyenne

The killing of one Cheyenne by another Cheyenne was not only a "sin" that "polluted" the murderer and endangered the well-being of the tribe but also a crime against the society. This pollution of the sacred arrows caused the game animals that Cheyenne depended on for their subsistence to shun their hunting territory. A killing of one Cheyenne by another required the ritual purification of the sacred arrows. However, not every killing was considered a criminal act. On hearing of a killing within the band, the members of the Council of Forty-four assembled. Exactly how and what they discussed in such cases we shall never know; but the council members had to decide when a killing was to be treated as a murder. Was suicide murder? Was abortion murder? Was a killing ever justifiable? Was drunkenness a mitigating circumstance? If the council determined that a murder had taken place, the chiefs ordered the immediate banishment of the murderer. Such banishment usually included not only the murderer but his or her family, and sometimes friends who went along voluntarily. This banishment usually lasted between five and ten years. During the period of exile, the banished individual usually lived with a friendly group of Arapahos or Dakotas.

The act of a Cheyenne taking his or her own life was not typically considered murder. Several cases are known of Cheyenne women committing suicide for what were considered trivial reasons. Such cases were not considered murder, and as far as can be determined, the sacred arrows were not renewed. In other instances, however, suicide was treated as murder. For example, one mother became infuriated when her daughter eloped with a young man of whom she did not approve. The mother found the girl and beat her with a whip while dragging her home. Inside the tepee the girl seized a gun and shot herself. In another case, a young girl divorced her husband and returned to her parents' home. At some later time, her mother found the girl

participating in a young persons' dance and beat her; the girl subsequently hung herself. In both cases, the chiefs ruled that the girls were driven to suicide by their mothers, who were thus considered the murderesses. In both cases the sacred arrows were renewed, and the mothers were banished.

Was a killing ever justifiable? In one case, a man attempted to rape his daughter, who resisted and used a knife to kill her father. The sacred arrows were renewed, but the chiefs did not order the girl banished, nor did the people treat her as a murderess. In another case, a man named Winnebago took the wife of another man, who retaliated by taking one of Winnebago's wives. Winnebago was enraged and killed the second man; the murderer was then banished. After his return from banishment Winnebago argued with and killed a second man, so he was banished again. While living among the Arapaho, Winnebago became involved in a dispute with a Cheyenne named Rising Fire, who knew of Winnebago's murders and therefore shot Winnebago out of fear. Although the facts are unclear, it appears that Rising Fire was not exiled for this killing. Thus, under some circumstances, such as incestuous rape and the fear of a known murderer, the chiefs thought that killing was justifiable. In such instances the sacred arrows had to be renewed, but the killer was not exiled.

Was drunkenness a mitigating circumstance? During a drunken brawl, Cries-Yia-Eya killed Chief Eagle. In another case, during a drunken party, Porcupine Bear stabbed Little Creek and then called on his relatives to stab Little Creek as well. They did so, killing Little Creek. Cries-Yia-Eya and Porcupine Bear and his guilty relatives were banished by the chiefs; drunkenness was not a defense for murder.

The chiefs were faced with a second issue regarding Little Creek's killers. After their banishment, Porcupine Bear and his relatives had continued to stay close to the band camp. When the tribe

organized a revenge attack on the Kiowas, Porcupine Bear and his relatives kept their distance but followed along with the other Cheyenne. In the attack on the Kiowas, Porcupine Bear and his six relatives distinguished themselves by bravely attacking first and killing about thirty Kiowas. What about war honors for acts of bravery accomplished during banishment? The council ruled that exiles could not receive recognition for their military acts, not matter how courageous they might be. In a sense, during their period of banishment they were not Cheyenne.

Was abortion murder? In one case, a fetus was found near a Cheyenne camp. An investigation by a warrior society discovered that a young girl had concealed her pregnancy. The young girl was banished, but only until after the sacred arrows had been renewed. Thus, the chiefs considered abortion a less serious type of murder that required a shorter period of banishment.

The chiefs had to answer many other questions concerning murder and banishment. About 1855 one of the chiefs, a member of the Council of Forty-four, killed another Cheyenne. The sacred arrows were renewed, and the chief was banished; but what was to be done about his position on the council? The council ruled that the man could not be removed from office and that he remained a chief even though he could not participate in the council.

From the discussion of these cases emerges some of the reasoning behind Cheyenne legal decisions. The chiefs considered a range of factors in reaching their final determinations. Murder included not merely the cold-blooded killing of one Cheyenne by another, it also included abortion and acts that compelled another to commit suicide. At the same time, the chiefs thought that in particular instances killing was justifiable, but that intoxication at the time was not a mitigating factor.

Source: Llewellyn and Hoebel (1941).

In courts of regulation, the authority of judges is usually limited.

Polities having courts of this nature were some time ago brought under European colonial rule. Their courts were soon modified by and subordinated to European colonial courts, which were more regulatory in nature. The example we use is that of the Barotse judicial system, as described by Max Gluckman. The Barotse made up a multiethnic state in southern Africa that at the time of Gluckman's study in the 1940s had been under British rule for forty years. More serious offenses had been removed by the British from the jurisdiction of this court. Despite these factors, the basic Barotse legal concepts aptly illustrate a mediation type of court system.

The Barotse state had two capitals—a northern capital, where the king resided, and a subordinate southern capital, ruled by a princess. All villages in the state were attached to one or the other of these capitals. The capitals were identical in structure; each had a palace and a council house. Courts of law were held in the council house.

The titular head of the court was the ruler; in practice, the ruler seldom was present at trials. In the center at the back of the house was the dais, or raised platform, for the ruler to be seated on if present. There were three ranked groupings of judges. The highest-ranking group of judges was the **indunas**, or "councilors," who sat to the right of the dais. The second-highest-ranking group was the **likombwa**, or "stewards," who sat to the left. These two groups were divided into senior members, who sat in the front, and junior members, who sat behind. The third group consisted of princes and the husbands of the princesses, who represented their wives. This group sat at a right angle to the likombwa.

A case was introduced by a plaintiff, who was allowed to state his or her grievance at length with no interruption; the defendant was then allowed the same privilege. The statements of witnesses for both sides followed. There were no attorneys for either side; the judges questioned and cross-examined the witnesses. After all the testimony had been heard, the judges began to give their opinions, starting with the most junior indunas, followed by the others in order of increasing seniority. The last judge to speak was the senior induna, who passed judgment on the case, subject to the ruler's approval.

In judging a case, a reasonable-person model was used. With the Barotse, the reasonableness of behavior was related to the social and kinship relationships of the individuals involved. Also, a breach of the law usually did not happen in isolation, and many individuals were at fault; so one case frequently led to a number of related cases. In passing judgment and imposing sanctions, the judges considered numerous factors. One of the most important was the kinship relationship between parties. The judges attempted to restore the relationship and reconcile the parties—but not without blaming those who had committed wrongs and not without imposing sanctions. The judges' opinions frequently took the form of sermons on proper behavior. As Gluckman (1973, 22) notes:

> Implicit in the reasonable man is the upright man, and moral issues in these relationships are barely differentiated from legal issues. This is so even though . . . [they] distinguish "legal" rules, which the . . . [court] has power to enforce or protect, from "moral" rules which it has not power to enforce or protect. But the judges are reluctant to support the person who is right in law, but wrong in justice, and may seek to achieve justice by indirect . . . action.

Courts of mediation have great potential for meeting the basic social purpose of the law, which is the maintenance of group cohesiveness. There is one serious drawback: Such a system is workable only in a culturally homogeneous political unit; that is, it works only if the judges and the parties involved share the same basic norms and values.

Courts of Regulation In the second millennium B.C. the Code of Hammurabi, the earliest known set of written laws, was created in Babylon. The code covered a variety of laws. One section dealt with physicians. It set the prices to be charged for various types of operations, based on the ability of individuals to pay. It also decreed, among other things, that if a surgeon operated on an individual using a bronze knife and the patient died or lost his eyesight, the surgeon's hand was to be cut off. The laws defined in the Code of Hammurabi reflect the emergence of regulatory laws. The role of the court was no longer to merely arbitrate disputes and strive for reconciliation but to define the rights and duties of members of an increasingly heterogeneous community.

Courts of regulation were a natural outgrowth of state-level polities, which evolved socially and economically distinct classes and encompassed numerous culturally distinct peoples. As relationships between individuals in the population became depersonalized, the law, too, became increasingly depersonalized. This change in the nature of law was compounded by the political incorporation of diverse peoples who frequently had conflicting cultural norms and values. The use of a reasonable-person model is workable only as long as there is a general consensus on what is "reasonable." In increasingly complex and stratified societies, the possibility of such consensus declined. Mediation of disputes works well in small, kinship-based societies, where all parties recognize the need for reconciliation through compromise. In sharply divided societies, the need for mediation is not as great because reconciliation in itself is not seen as a gain. Compromise is viewed only in terms of what is lost. Laws were thus created to bring order and stability to the interactions between individuals who were not social equals. With law divorced from social norms and values, justice was no longer simply a moral or ethical issue, but came to be viewed in terms of consistency, or precedent.

The separation of law from social norms and values also allowed for the "politicization" of the laws.

Laws were created to serve political ends, as various groups vied with one another for the creation of laws that would protect, express, or further their own goals, interests, and values. This situation is particularly evident in multiethnic and religious and economically diverse state-level systems such as that of the United States. Given the cultural pluralism, religious diversity, and economic inequality of the United States, it would be impossible to create a code of laws that could equally protect the interests of all classes and that would be consistent with the norms and values of all groups. As a result, many people find themselves subject to laws and sanctions, many of which they judge either immoral or unethical; at times, people find that laws violate their own cultural values. We see this with groups who think that abortion is murder and thus should be made illegal. We see this with groups who oppose capital punishment on the grounds that the state does not have the right to kill individuals. During the Vietnam War, we saw it with draft resisters who argued that the state did not have the right to order men to fight in a war they considered immoral. Less obvious is the manner in which numerous ethnic minorities, notably Native Americans, subordinate their cultural norms and values to comply with the legal system. With the emergence of states and courts of regulation, law ceased to be an expression of social norms and values and became their molder.

Summary

In this chapter we discussed two distinct but overlapping cultural institutions: political organization and social control. Humans live in cooperative groups. Group action—in both economic and social activities—is a prerequisite for the survival of the population. To be effective, group activities must have leadership and organization, which are the basis for political structure. At the same time, individual differences, conflict, and competition within the group must be controlled and channeled in such a manner that the internal cohesiveness and cooperation of the individual members of the group are maintained—thus the need for social control.

Four major categories of political organization are bands, tribes, chiefdoms, and states. Found among foraging societies, the band is the simplest and least formal level of political organization. Two forms of band organization exist: simple bands and composite bands. In simple bands, the highest level of political organization is the extended family, with the highest level of political leadership being the heads of the various families. These simple bands are economically self-sufficient and politically autonomous. Because a simple band has as its core a group of related individuals, band members are forced to seek spouses from outside the band; they are exogamous units. Thus, kinship ties through marriage serve as the primary link between bands. Simple bands most commonly are found among foragers who depend on the hunting of game animals that are present in small numbers year-round.

Composite bands are larger than simple bands and include a number of distinct families. Leadership in composite bands is vested in "big men," or informal leaders, who have influence but not authority. Composite bands most often are found among foragers who depend on the hunting of migratory herd animals.

At the tribal formal level, institutions transcend local residence groups and bind the geographically scattered members of the society into a cohesive unit. The key element in tribal societies is sodalities, which may be either kinship-based, as in the case of clans, or nonkinship-based, as in the case of warrior societies or age grades. Leadership in such groups is more structured, with formal political offices.

Chiefdoms have formal, hereditary leadership, with centralized political control and authority. The associated redistributive economic exchange system focused on the chief serves to integrate economically the various communities within the political unit.

The state is the most complex level of political organization. States have centralized power and control, but the key characteristic of a state is the presence of a bureaucracy—individuals acting on behalf of the political elite, thus enabling the centralized power figures to maintain control of a greater number of individuals.

Social control consists of the various methods used to control and channel the behavior of individual members of a society into approved behavior. Law and legal systems are merely the highest level of social control. Law is defined as having three attributes: (1) authority, (2) intention of universal application, and (3) sanction. By this definition, all societies have law. All legal systems consist of two elements: Substantive law is concerned with the types of unacceptable behavior and their associated sanctions, and procedural law is concerned with handling breaches of substantive law and imposing sanctions.

In societies without centralized political systems, legal systems are self-help. In self-help systems, the responsibility and authority for determining a breach of the law and imposition of the proper sanction fall to the victim or his or her family (or both). As discussed, this system is not as arbitrary as we might think. In the case of murder or killing, the result may be a feud between families, but a feud—sharply distinguished from a war—is part of the legal process.

Law in societies with centralized political systems is handled by courts. Court systems in turn usually can be categorized as either courts of mediation or courts of regulation. In relatively homogeneous societies, most court systems take as their primary objective the mediation of disputes between individuals and the restoration of harmonious social relationships. In more heterogeneous groups, courts usually become more regulatory in nature, with formally defined laws and sanctions.

Key Terms

simple bands
composite bands
tribes
chiefdoms
states
big men

influence
indunas
authority
sodalities
social control
likombwa
law
procedural law
substantive law

self-help legal systems
court legal systems
feud
incipient courts
courts of mediation
courts of regulation
reasonable-person model

Suggested Readings

Cohen, R., and Elman Service, eds. *Origins of the State: The Anthropology of Political Evolution*. Philadelphia: Institute for the Study of Human Issues, 1978.
  • *A collection of essays from various perspectives examining the development of state-level political systems.*
Fried, Morton, *The Evolution of Political Society*. New York: Random House, 1967.
  • *A theoretical study that traces the development of political systems from egalitarian societies, through ranked, to stratified and state-level societies.*
Hoebel, E. Adamson. *The Law of Primitive Man*. Cambridge, Mass.: Harvard University Press, 1964.
  • *The first major comparative study of non-Western legal systems. Although somewhat dated, it remains a classic study.*
Mair, Lucy. *Primitive Government*. Baltimore: Penguin, 1966.
  • *Concerned exclusively with African peoples, this is an excellent introduction to preindustrial political systems.*
Newman, Katherine S. *Law and Economic Organization: A Comparative Study of Pre-Industrial Societies*. Cambridge: Cambridge University Press, 1983.
  • *A cross-cultural analysis of sixty societies to show that legal institutions systematically vary with economic organization.*
Service, Elman. *Primitive Social Organization: An Evolutionary Perspective*. New York: Random House, 1966.
  • *Traces the evolution of political systems from bands to chiefdoms.*

The following ethnographies are excellent descriptions of political and/or legal systems within particular societies.

Barth, Fredrik. *Political Leadership Among Swat Pathans.* London: Athlone, 1959.
- *A description and theoretical analysis of the political life of a people on the Pakistan and Afghanistan border.*

Fortes, M., and E. E. Evans-Pritchard, eds. *African Political Systems.* London: Oxford University Press, 1940.
- *A collection of short descriptions of the political organization of eight African societies.*

Gluckman, Max. *The Ideas in Barotse Jurisprudence.* Manchester: Manchester University Press, 1965.
———. *The Judicial Process Among the Barotse.* Manchester: Manchester University Press, 1973.
- *These two studies of the Barotse of Zambia not only describe a system in a non-Western state but also—and more important—illustrate the legal reasoning used in their court systems.*

Hoebel, E. Adamson. *The Political Organization and Law-Ways of the Comanche Indians.* American Anthropological Association, Memoir 54, 1940.
- *Good description of the political structure and legal system of a band-level society.*

Kuper, Hilda. *The Swazi: A South African Kingdom.* 2nd ed. New York: Holt, Rinehart and Winston, 1986.
- *An excellent short ethnography of Swaziland, now an independent nation. Has a good discussion of recent changes.*

Leach, Edmund. *Political Systems of Highland Burma.* Boston: Beacon Press, 1965.
- *Describes the cyclical political changes of the Kachin.*

Llewellyn, Karl, and E. Adamson Hoebel. *The Cheyenne Way.* Norman: University of Oklahoma Press, 1941.
- *One of the best descriptions of the legal system of a tribal society.*

Meggitt, Mervyn J. *Blood Is Their Argument: Warfare Among the Mae Enga Tribesmen of the New Guinea Highlands.* Palo Alto, Calif.: Mayfield, 1977.
- *Perhaps the best ethnography ever written about warfare and war-related practices among a preindustrial people.*

Internet Exercises

A good place to begin searching the Internet for material related to political institutions, international agencies, development, and law is at the site "Praxis: Resources for Social and Economic Development." This site is run by Professor Richard Estes of the School of Social Work at the University of Pennsylvania. Point your web browser to (http://caster.ssw.upenn.edu/oth.html). From there click on Other Resources, on this page click on Praxis. To find sites that deal specifically with law and legal history try the links provided by Bernard Hibbitts of the University of Pittsburgh School of Law at (http://law.pitt.edu/hibbitts/connect.htm), or "The Timetable of World Legal History" (http://www.wwlia.org/hist.htm) by the World Wide Legal Information Association.

A website with quite a bit of information about the Inca is run by Dennis E. Ogburn, an archaeologist at the University of California Santa Barbara. "Investigating Inca Strategies of Contest and Control in the Saraguro Region of Ecuador" is located at (http://www.sscf.ucsb.edu/~ogburn/).

The site "Politics, Leadership, and Social Control"(http://learnonline.micro.umn.edu/anthro/intro.html) is a course by Professor David Lipset of the University of Minnesota. It takes you through some concepts and an example of a particular culture, the Murik of Papua New Guinea, with photographs.

CHAPTER *12*

Social Inequality and Stratification

CONTENTS

Systems of Equality and Inequality

Egalitarian Societies

Ranked Societies

Stratified Societies

Castes in Traditional India

Classes in Industrial Societies: The United States

Maintaining Inequality

Ideologies

American Secular Ideologies

Theories of Inequality

Functionalist Theory

Conflict Theory

Who Benefits?

Inequality in access to possessions and other culturally valued rewards can be seen on the streets of most modern nations. The degree to which economic inequality exists and is socially tolerated varies greatly among the peoples of the world.

Visit http://www.wadsworth.com/humanity to learn more about the material covered in this chapter and to access activities, exercises, and tutorial quizzes.

"Wᴇ ʜᴏʟᴅ ᴛʜᴇsᴇ truths to be self-evident, that all men are created equal, that they are endowed by their creator with certain unalienable Rights . . ."

Aꜱ ʏᴏᴜ ᴄᴀɴ ɢᴜᴇꜱꜱ by now, whether in fact all "men" are believed to have been created equal depends on which society you happened to have been born into. Whether you have certain "unalienable rights," and the nature of these rights, also varies from people to people. In this chapter we consider another dimension of cultural diversity—the differential allocation of rewards.

Systems of Equality and Inequality

Inequality refers to the extent to which culturally valued material and social rewards are allocated disproportionately to individuals, families, and other groups.

Before discussing variations in inequality between societies, it will be helpful to consider the different kinds of rewards that exist. They are broken down into three categories. The most tangible reward is *wealth,* or ownership of valued material goods. Another kind of reward is *power,* or the ability to make others do what you want based on coercion or legitimate authority. A final type of reward is *prestige,* or the respect, esteem, and overt approval granted by others to individuals they consider meritorious. Prestige (or *honor*) is a social reward, based on judgments about an individual's personal worthiness or the contributions the individual makes to others in the group.

The distribution of each kind of reward varies between societies. Some groups allow ambitious individuals to acquire wealth, power, and prestige, whereas others make it difficult for anyone to accumulate possessions, gain control over others, or put themselves above their peers socially. For instance, many North Americans admire "self-made men" who have supposedly earned higher income (wealth) than other people by their own talents and efforts. But such men would be looked down on as self-centered and ungenerous in many other cultures.

We can classify societies by the degree to which there is inequality among their members with respect to wealth, power, and prestige. Imagine a continuum. At one end can be placed societies that feature only slight differences between individuals and groups in access to rewards. At the other end are those societies with vast differences in the allocation of rewards. In the middle are a myriad of societies that are intermediate between the two extremes: Some have contrasts in prestige but lack significant differences in wealth, for example.

In 1967, Morton Fried formulated an influential threefold classification of the kinds and degree of inequality found in diverse human cultures. He labeled the three basic types of inequality **egalitarian**, **ranked**, and **stratified**. A description and examples of each type appear later in this section. Three points need to be noted about Fried's classification.

First, Fried's three categories do not refer to access to rewards based on sex or age. When we call a society *egalitarian,* for example, we do not mean that females and males receive equal or nearly equal rewards, or that elderly people and young people are socially equal. Even in egalitarian societies there are social distinctions based on sex and age (see Chapters 10 and 15). Essentially, *egalitarian* means that there are few differences in access to rewards between families or other kinds of kin groups within a society. At the other end of the continuum, in societies we call *stratified,* there are major differences in access to rewards between families and/or kin groups, in addition to any distinctions based on sex or age.

Second, Fried's three categories are merely points along a continuous spectrum of systems of inequality. It is impossible to pigeonhole all human societies into one of these types because most fit somewhere in between the three categories. The terms *egalitarian, ranked,* and *stratified* are useful mainly as short descriptions of the kinds and range of variation in inequality found cross-culturally.

Third, it should be noted that egalitarian-ranked-stratified is the temporal order in which the three forms developed. Until about 10,000 years ago, most people on earth lived in egalitarian societies. Ranked societies developed in a few areas about then, and a few thousand years later stratification developed in the great civilizations. Over the next 4,000 to 5,000 years, stratified societies spread throughout most of the world, as some peoples and nations conquered and ruled over others.

Egalitarian Societies

Egalitarian societies are at the low end of the inequality continuum. Setting aside distinctions based on sex and age, there is little noticeable difference in received rewards between individuals and families. People who work hard, or who have attractive personalities or valuable skills, may be rewarded with respect and prestige from other members of their group. But egalitarian groups have various cultural mechanisms to prevent any individual from becoming too "big." And even people who are respected have few, if any, more possessions or power than others.

Mobile foragers such as the Inuit, !Kung, BaMbuti, and Aka are egalitarian. James Woodburn identified several reasons why access to rewards is evenly distributed among such foragers. First, and most obviously, frequent seasonal movements of the band or camp are necessary for effective adaptation. Mobility makes it difficult to transport possessions, and hence to accumulate wealth.

Second, the cultural value placed on reciprocal sharing (see Chapter 6) helps prevent individuals or family groups from becoming wealthier than their bandmates. Even should they want to, people find it difficult to accumulate because other people demand their share, and failure to adhere to norms of sharing is socially punished.

Third, among mobile foragers, families are not tied to specific territories but have the right to visit and exploit the resources of many areas, often due to bilateral kinship relations (see Chapter 9). If anyone tries to give orders or exercise control over others, people have enough options that they are free to leave and live elsewhere.

Most mobile foragers, like the !Kung, are egalitarian.

In sum, if people move around in their environments a lot, are required to share food and other possessions, and have a range of options about where to live and whom to live with, then inequality in wealth and power does not have much chance of developing. If it should develop, it does not have much chance of persisting for very long.

Not all foragers are or were egalitarian. The Native Americans of the Northwest Coast, for instance, lived in ranked societies because in their rich environment the aforementioned three conditions did not exist. Northwest Coast people were more sedentary, accumulated wealth in order to distribute it to validate and acquire rank, and formed kin groups that were mostly associated with particular territories (see Chapter 6).

Ranked Societies

In ranked societies there are a limited number of high-ranking social positions, usually titles or some kind of formal, named offices. The titles confer high honor on people who hold them. In most cases, the privilege of holding a title or occupying an office is largely or entirely hereditary within certain families, lineages, clans, or other kin groups.

In one of the most common types of ranked societies, all kin groups are ranked relative to one another: Each group has its own unique rank relative to every other kin group. Further, within each kin group, each member is ranked relative to all others, usually on the principle of genealogical seniority (elders being superior in rank to younger people). The most valued positions that bring the highest rewards in prestige, wealth, and power are held by the highest-ranking individuals of the highest-ranking kin

group. This way of ranking individuals and kin groups is most well documented for several ancient Polynesian chiefdoms.

An excellent example of such a ranked society is Tikopia, a tiny Pacific island whose kinship system is described in Chapter 9. When studied by Raymond Firth in the 1920s, Tikopia's 1,200 persons were divided into four patrilineal clans, each with its own chief who exercised authority over his clanmates. Each clan in turn was divided into several patrilineages. Every Tikopian patrilineage had a head, who was believed to be the oldest living male descendant of the man who founded the lineage about four to six generations ago. Alongside this ranking of individuals within a single lineage, the various lineages of a single clan were ranked relative to one another. One lineage of each clan, supposedly the original, "senior" lineage from which the "junior" lineages had budded off, was considered the noble lineage. Members of other lineages of the clan had to defer socially to members of the noble lineage, according to Tikopian standards of etiquette. In addition, the noble lineage of each clan selected one of its members to be the chief of the whole clan.

Chiefs and other members of the noble Tikopia lineages had little more wealth than anyone else. The nobility did receive tribute from other lineages of their clan, but they gave away most of it in the many public activities that they organized and financed through redistribution (see Chapter 7). The chief and nobility of each clan had no way to deny access to land and ocean resources to members of other lineages, for each lineage was considered to have inalienable rights to certain pieces of land. The Tikopia nobility, then, received much prestige and token tribute from other islanders, but they did not use this tribute to enrich themselves, and their sphere of power was limited. They were honored, but their wealth and power were not great. It is mainly in this respect that ranked societies contrast with stratified societies.

Stratified Societies

Stratified societies are at the high end of the inequality continuum. A society is said to be stratified if

- there are marked inequalities in access to all three kinds of rewards: wealth, power, and prestige;
- this inequality is based primarily on unequal access to productive resources such as the land and tools people need to make their living; that is, a few peo-

ple control access to the resources others need to survive at culturally acceptable levels;

• unequal access to rewards has a strong tendency to be heritable throughout the generations, regardless of the personal qualities or aptitudes of individuals.

The last point means that most individuals (and families) do not move very far up or down the social ladder during their lifetimes.

Stratified societies vary in the cultural ideas they have about the possibilities of social mobility. In some, such as North American and other contemporary Western and Western-derived democracies, upward or downward mobility is considered possible, although numerous studies have shown it to be uncommon. In others, especially in preindustrial societies, one's position is considered fixed, often because of beliefs that existing inequalities are hereditary or ordained by supernatural beings.

In stratified societies individuals, families, and other groups are differentiated on the basis of their relative access to rewards. A social group whose members share about the same degree of access to rewards is called a *social stratum*. The two major kinds of strata are **classes** and **castes**.

Two general differences between class and caste systems stand out. First, by definition, castes are endogamous groups: They have cultural norms or laws that require individuals to marry within their caste. As discussed in Chapter 8, rules that mandate marriage within one's own group have the effect of maintaining the distinctiveness of the group relative to other groups. This is because there is no possibility of upward mobility through intercaste marriage, and because there are no children who have potentially anomalous group membership. In contrast, class societies allow people to marry someone of a different class; in fact, intermarriage between classes commonly is an avenue of social mobility. It follows from the endogamous nature of caste that one's caste membership is theoretically hereditary: One is born into the caste of one's parents, one marries someone in the same caste, and one's children are likewise born into and remain members of one's own caste. (We say "theoretically" because sometimes social reality differs from cultural norms, in caste societies as in all others.)

Second, caste systems have some kind of prohibition against contact between members of different castes. High-caste members, for example, sometimes believe that they will be spiritually polluted if they should come into contact with members of other castes. Indeed, they often must perform rituals to cleanse themselves after accidental contacts.

Both of these general differences mean that castes have more permanent membership and more rigid social boundaries than classes. This does not mean that it is

easy to tell whether some particular stratified society "has" castes or classes. Some societies have elements of both. For instance, some scholars have suggested that black-white relations in the American South were more caste-like than class-like until the mid-twentieth century. There was no possibility of upward mobility into the white "caste" for blacks because no one could overcome the cultural stigma of black skin color. Interracial marriage was legally prohibited or culturally taboo, so that the two races were endogamous. Explicit laws against certain kinds of "intercaste" contacts and interactions—known as *segregation laws*—forced blacks to live apart from whites, forbade them to enter certain white business establishments and pubic restrooms, made them send their children to all-black schools, and so forth.

Castes in Traditional India

The best-known caste system is that of India. India's caste system is complex and varies from region to region, so we can present only a generalized picture. There are four main caste categories, or *varnas*. (A varna is not itself a caste.) Each varna is ranked relative to the others in honor and degree of ritual purity, and each is broadly associated with certain kinds of occupations.

The highest varna is the Brahmins, or priests and scholars; next is the varna of nobles and warriors, the Kshatriyas; third are the Vaishas, or merchants and artisans; and ranked lowest are the Shudras, or farmers, craftspeople, and certain other laborers. A fifth category—outside and ranked below the varna—are the untouchables, to whom falls work considered polluting to the varna.

The varnas (which, incidentally, first arose in the second millennium B.C. when the Aryans invaded and conquered what is now northern India) are large, inclusive categories into which specific castes are placed. The villages in which most people live are divided into much smaller and specific groupings called *jati* (castes, as the term usually is used). For example, in a particular village the Shudra varna might be represented by several jati with names such as weaver, potter, and tailor. There are thousands of these castes in India, distributed among the many thousands of villages, with each village containing a variable number of castes.

To better understand Indian castes, it is necessary to understand the basic tenets of Hinduism, the traditional religion of India. (Hinduism is incredibly diverse and complex, so here we can present only a simplified depiction of it.) Hindu religion holds that spiritual souls are reborn into different physical bodies at various stages of their existence—this is the doctrine of *reincarnation*. Souls ultimately desire an end to the cycle of earthly birth, death, and rebirth, but to achieve this end each soul must be

Hinduism regards certain substances and activities as spiritually defiling or polluting. Ritual bathing—here in the Ganges River—removes the pollution.

depends on the behavior of one's soul in previous incarnations. People are low caste either because their soul has not yet been through enough lifetimes to have reached a higher form, or because their sins in a previous lifetime merit reincarnation into a low caste. In the present life, people have what they deserve. Thus, all "men" were not created equal, in the Hindu world view; it is legitimate that some castes have more power and privilege and more status and wealth than others.

Second, caste categories are broadly associated with certain occupations. Each village contains a number of castes, most of which are named according to the occupation traditionally performed by their members. Thus, a village might include castes of priests, merchants, blacksmiths, potters, tailors, farmers, weavers, carpenters, washers, barbers, leather workers, and "sweepers" (the last refers to those who remove human waste matter from people's houses). Just as activities are ranked in Hindu beliefs according to their degree of purity and impurity, so occupations and those who perform them are ranked. Working with animal carcasses is defiling, so leather working is a defiling occupation and leather workers are so polluting as to be untouchable. The same applies to sweeping: People who remove human wastes from houses or spread excrement over village fields are polluted, and their touch pollutes those of higher castes. Therefore, members of the leather working, sweeping, and other castes associated with defiling occupations were traditionally untouchable. (Discrimination against people of untouchable ancestry is illegal in modern India, although it still occurs.) Untouchables usually live in their own special section of the village, separate from members of higher castes. Because they contaminate temples by their entry, they cannot go inside a temple. Their touch contaminates water, so they have to use separate wells. These and other restrictions on their behavior sometimes are extreme.

However, members of high-ranking castes, such as priests, landowners, warriors, and merchants, need the services of low-ranking castes. Again, this is because Hinduism defines some activities that are essential for life as polluting, so castes who would be defiled by these activities need lower castes to perform these services for them. The bullocks essential for farming die, so someone has to remove dead cattle from the village. Brahmin women give birth just as other women do, so the women

reborn many times into many bodies, both animal and human. Souls attempt to move up the "ladder" of reincarnation, from lower forms of life to higher ones: from animals to humans (of various ranked castes) to gods.

The particular body (be it human or animal) that a soul is born into depends on how closely that soul adhered to proper standards of behavior in previous lifetimes. For souls that had made it up to human forms in their previous incarnation, these standards include avoidance of activities that Hindus believe are polluting. Among the most polluting activities are handling and working with animal carcasses or human corpses; touching excrement and other waste materials; dealing with childbirth; and eating meat. People who regularly perform these activities are not only polluted themselves, but anyone of a higher caste who comes into physical contact with them likewise becomes polluted and must bathe ritually to cleanse himself or herself. One's present place in society—one's "station in life"—varies with the degree to which one is associated with pure or impure activities. In turn, because of reincarnation, whether one is associated with pure or impure activities depends on one's behavior in previous lives—such as the degree to which one has allowed oneself to become polluted or failed to cleanse oneself.

India's traditional caste hierarchy is so intimately tied up with Hindu doctrines that the two are almost inseparable. First, the caste into which one is born

of some low-ranking caste have to serve as midwives, since other Brahmin women would become polluted by so serving. Everyone passes bodily wastes, so someone must remove these wastes from the houses of high-caste members lest they pollute their occupants. Accordingly, each caste has its proper role and function in the economic, social, and religious life of the village.

Likewise, each caste has its religiously ordained duties to the other castes. In Hindu beliefs, one's soul is reincarnated into a higher or lower form partly according to how well one fulfills the obligations of his or her caste in the present life. Leather workers, for instance, cannot do much to improve their lot in this life; but by faithfully fulfilling their obligations to members of higher castes, their souls will receive higher reincarnations in future bodies.

One should not conclude that intercaste relations are harmonious, or that the complementary tasks associated with each caste are entirely mutually beneficial. A great deal of friction and outright conflict exist between individual members of different castes. In fact, local castes as a whole group sometimes organize themselves with a council to pursue their common interests. It is even possible for a caste to improve its rank in the local caste hierarchy, despite the normatively unchanging relative position of castes. This is done in several ways, including adopting the customs and prohibitions of a higher caste and "reinventing" the history of one's caste to make it seem that it originally came from a higher varna.

Classes in Industrial Societies: The United States

Class societies have strata—the classes—that have different degrees of ownership of productive property and material goods; that have different access to pubic decisions made by a government; and that are ranked in the respect or esteem accorded their position in the class hierarchy.

An important point to note about classes is that they are seldom organized *as classes*. There are no occasions on which the members of a given class come together for discussion or common action (unlike, say, an extended family or lineage). Indeed, members of a single class do not necessarily believe they have much in common with one another (unlike the members of a labor union). Many people cannot identify the class to which they belong (unlike Indian *jati* or *varna*), as when over four-fifths of Americans refer to themselves as "middle class." People cannot say how many classes exist in their societies. In fact, there is considerable debate within the social sciences over what the term *class* means, or if it has anything other than the vaguest meaning.

Whether or not the concept of class is overly vague, no one can deny the enormous differences in wealth, power, and prestige that exist in many societies. The term *class* refers to all the people in a given society who receive comparable rewards. Member of different classes have different access to the material resources (income, wealth), influential relationships (social contacts), and cultural knowledge (education, "social graces") that are valued in the culture. Unlike caste membership, people can move up or down in a class system during their lives through inter-class marriage, personal talent, hard work and effort, or good luck. More commonly, being born into a given class puts one so far ahead or behind of others that few people rise or fall very far in the hierarchy during their lifetimes.

In this section, we concentrate on the class structure of one industrialized society, the United States. In this country, the kind of work one does often is assumed to be the best single overall indication of class membership. ("What kind of work do you do?" or "Where do you work?" is one of the first questions American adults ask of new acquaintances, a question which gives a lot of information about a person very quickly.) Occupation is generally the best determinant of income, and one's income influences so much else: overall lifestyle, access of one's children to education, the kinds of people with whom one associates socially, the kind of church or club to which one belongs, and so on.

Unfortunately for our desire to make societies neat and orderly, there are problems with defining a class on the basis of occupation or any other single criterion. For one thing, different criteria used to define class membership do not always agree. For instance, people do not agree on the prestige of many occupations—attorneys are despised by some but granted high prestige by others. The same applies to politicians, physicians, academicians, police, and numerous other professionals. Further, the degree to which some occupation is respected by the population at large does not always reflect the relative wealth and/or access to power of those who practice it (see "A Closer Look").

So it often is difficult to decide to which class some individual belongs. One way around this ambiguity, favored by some sociologists, is to separate the three kinds of rewards from one another and define a separate class ranking for each reward. We can distinguish classes defined on the basis of prestige (*status groups,* as some call them) and on the basis of income or wealth (*economic classes*), for instance. The definitions and methods used for ranking the classes depend, to some extent, on the interest of the social scientist, as well as on the nature of the society under study.

In the United States, probably the most widely accepted approach to stratification uses the concept of economic class. Individuals and families are placed into

A CLOSER LOOK

Occupational Prestige in the United States

Sociological studies reveal how highly Americans regard certain occupational categories. Below is a sample of twenty-five occupations, listed from highest to lowest prestige ranking:

- physician
- college professor
- attorney
- stockbroker
- registered nurse
- high school teacher
- social worker
- electrician
- plumber
- police officer
- dental assistant
- carpenter
- welder
- mechanic
- truck driver
- hairdresser
- cashier
- assembly-line worker
- housekeeper
- coal miner
- waitress/waiter
- babysitter
- garbage collector
- janitor
- hotel chambermaid

Apparently, the main influence on how people rank occupational categories is how much formal education is required to assume the occupational role: Generally, "brain work" is ranked above "manual work."

The interesting thing about these prestige ranks is that a great many of them do not reflect income levels typical of the occupation. College professors, nurses, teachers, and dental assistants receive significantly higher prestige than plumbers, carpenters, welders, and assembly-line workers. Yet, many people employed in the latter occupations earn more yearly income than those who do "brain work." This is not a contradiction—because being in a high-prestige professional career offers other, nonmaterial rewards—but it does make it difficult to decide exactly to which "class" some individuals and families belong.

Source: Tischler (1990).

classes based on their wealth. Using wealth as the primary basis of class ranking has four major advantages. First, it is more measurable than other indications of class membership (although cash income alone does not measure it adequately).

Second, wealth is the best single indication of the overall benefits individuals and families are receiving from their citizenship in the nation. Money cannot buy you love, happiness, or many other things, but it can buy you much of what Americans value.

Third, extremely high wealth is generally correlated with ownership of productive resources such as factories, financial institutions, and income-producing real estate. By and large, the very wealthy people in the country own the nation's large businesses. They either built their companies themselves, or their ancestors made fortunes through business activity and passed their ownership along to the current generation.

Fourth, wealth levels broadly determine people's access to political power. Through campaign contributions, the wealthy have a greater say in who gets nominated and elected to important offices. Through lobbying efforts, the rich enjoy greater influence on the laws and policies of the nation than their numbers warrant. By providing much of the funding for think tanks and other public advisory groups, the wealthy subsidize the expertise of many economists, political scientists, sociologists, and other social scientists who advise government. Many appointed

officials in the executive branch of the federal government are members of the elite. Some appointees move back and forth between business and government service regularly.

For these and other reasons, we can learn most about class inequalities in the United States by focusing our discussion on the distribution of wealth. We begin with the distribution of annual income, summarized for the year 1997 in Table 12.1. (These data—the latest available—were published in 1998 by the U.S. Bureau of the Census.) In the table, American families are divided into fifths based on their 1997 cash income. For example, the richest one-fifth (or the wealthiest 20 percent) of American families earned 49.4 percent of the total income earned by all American families in 1997. The poorest one-fifth of families earned only 3.6 percent of all family income. The table also shows that the richest 5 percent of American families earned 21 percent of the total family income.

The size of the gap between rich and poor has grown considerably in the last 30 years, according to a study released in 1996 by the U.S. Bureau of the Census. Since 1968, the average income of the poorest fifth of American households rose only 8 percent, while the average income of the wealthiest fifth grew 44 percent. Furthermore, the average yearly income of the richest 5 percent of American families rose by 60 percent between 1968 and the mid-1990s. The benefits of economic growth over the last three decades have been distributed quite unequally, going far more to the affluent than to the poor.

Census Bureau data over the past couple of decades also shows that inequality in the distribution of yearly income has increased in the United States. In 1977, the bottom three-fifths (the "poorest" 60 percent) of American households earned 31.7 percent of all cash income, but by 1997 their share had fallen to 27.5 percent—a *loss* of 4.2 percent. In 1977, the richest one-fifth earned 43.6 percent of all cash income, but by 1997 their share had increased to 49.4 percent—a *gain* of 5.8 percent for the most affluent 20 percent of American households. Thus, the most well-off families in 1997 had an even greater share of the total income than the most well-off families in 1977.

So inequality in the distribution of yearly income has increased in the past 30 years. But the distribution of income does not accurately reflect the extent of economic inequality in the United States, because figures on annual *income* do not show how much *wealth* is owned by families of different classes. Yearly income figures such as those given in Table 12.1 greatly underestimate the degree of economic inequality in the United States. If we consider the distribution of wealth, we see that middle income families, and even families who are generally considered affluent, own little in comparison with the truly wealthy.

People's material standards of living are not determined in any simple way by their income, nor is their influence over local, state, and national political decision making. Living standards and political influence are more greatly determined by a person's or family's net worth, that is, by all assets (property) minus all indebtedness. There are two kinds of assets: *financial* and *tangible*. Financial assets include property such as savings and checking accounts, stocks, bonds, money-market funds, and trusts. Tangible assets include material property such as real estate, houses, automobiles, and other personal property. Like financial assets, tangible assets can be assigned a dollar value equal to what they would be worth if they were sold on the market. The assets a particular family owns are a better measure of its wealth than its annual income. Tangible assets directly affect material standards of living, and both tangible and financial assets represent stored-up purchasing power, since by selling them families can acquire additional money.

In 1983 the Federal Reserve Board conducted a study of the assets and liabilities of a random sample of more than 4,000 American households. The findings of the 1983 study revealed the remarkable inequality in net worth between the wealthiest families and everyone else. The Economic Policy Institute, a private think tank, updated this study in its 1994 report titled *The State of Working America: 1994–5*, written by Lawrence Mishel and Jared Bernstein. The following data are taken from this 1994 report, which summarizes the latest reliable figures on the distribution of wealth (net worth) for the year 1989.

To summarize the information in the report, we divide American families into one of three categories:

- Very rich: the richest 1 percent of American families.
- Rich: the next richest 9 percent of American families.
- Everyone else: the rest of America's families, or 90 percent of all families.

How much of the nation's privately owned wealth is owned by these three categories of families?

- The very rich families own 39 percent of all assets.
- The rich families own 33 percent of all assets.
- Everyone else (the "bottom" 90 percent) owns 28 percent of all assets.

Together, the very rich and rich families (the wealthiest 10 percent) own 72 percent of all wealth under private ownership. Thus, the distribution of wealth in 1989 was much more concentrated than the distribution of annual income.

Just as important as the fact that wealth is unequally distributed is the nature of the assets owned by the most affluent families, compared to everyone else. Financial assets represent wealth that produces future income for their owners in the form of interest, dividends, and other returns on savings and investments. What percentage of financial assets is owned by the three categories of families?

- The very rich families own 47 percent of all stocks, 54 percent of all bonds, 54 percent of all trusts, and 41 percent of all real estate not used as the owner's residence.
- The rich families own 43 percent of stocks, 34 percent of bonds, 35 percent of trusts, and 40 percent of real estate not occupied by the owner.
- Everyone else owns 10 percent of stocks, 12 percent of bonds, 11 percent of trusts, and 19 percent of nonowner-occupied real property.

Putting this same information together a little differently, the richest 10 percent of American families own 90 percent of stocks, 88 percent of bonds, 89 percent of trusts, and 81 percent of real estate not used as the residence of the owner.

Table 12.1   DISTRIBUTION OF FAMILY ANNUAL INCOME IN THE UNITED STATES, 1997

PERCENTAGE OF INCOME EARNED BY		AMOUNT EARNED, 1997
Poorest fifth	3.6	Less than $15,400
Second fifth	8.9	Between $15,401 and $29,200
Third fifth	15.0	Between $29,201 and $46,000
Fourth fifth	23.2	Between $46,001 and $71,500
Richest fifth	49.4	Over $71,500
Richest 5%	21.0	Over $126,550

SOURCE: U.S. Bureau of the Census (1998 Table B and Appendix B-6)

In the contemporary United States, homelessness is only one manifestation of extreme economic inequality. In the past two or three decades, the distribution of annual income and wealth has grown more uneven.

Barring economic collapse, and excepting short-term market fluctuations, assets such as stocks, bonds, trusts, and investment real estate produce continuous income for their owners. Further, possession of such assets enormously increases a family's economic security.

Maintaining Inequality

How is it that such high degrees of inequality in stratified societies persist? As the United States illustrates, a small percentage of the population typically controls most of the wealth and wields a great deal of influence over public affairs. Why does the relatively underprivileged majority allow them this power and privilege?

One possible answer is that the question itself is ethnocentric: Even to ask it assumes that the cultural value North Americans supposedly place on human equality is universal, which, of course, it is not. One might argue that we find high degrees of inequality puzzling, especially if wealth and power are largely inherited, because we believe that all people are created equal. But people brought up in other cultural traditions accept inherited inequalities as a normal part of human life.

This response will not suffice. First, it is no response: It says merely that not everyone in the world has the same beliefs about inequality that we do, but it explains neither our beliefs nor why others lack them. Second, there is evidence of widespread conflict between strata in a wide range of stratified societies. Resentment, rebellion, and occasional attempts at revolution occur in stratified societies from all parts of the world (which is not to say that they are universally present). A great many powerless and poor people do not simply accept their place in the social hierarchy, so we need some understanding of why so many others do. Finally, although our knowledge of the history of preindustrial stratification systems is scanty, we know that in a great many societies a conquering militaristic group imposed their rule over the indigenous population of a region. This was true in African states such as Bunyoro and Zulu, in the ancient civilizations of the Americas such as the Aztec and Inca, in China and India, and in many other regions. In many and probably most stratified societies, the lower classes did not consent to their low standing but had it forced on them.

Another possible explanation of how inequality persists is that members of the highest stratum (hereafter called the *elite*) use their wealth and power to organize an armed force stronger than that of their opposition. If the elite somehow manage to monopolize control over weapons or to organize a loyal army, then they can use coercion and threat to maintain their access to rewards and resources. Sometimes armed force is used by the elite to put down rebellions, and no doubt the ever-present threat of coercive sanctions does deter resistance to the elite's wealth, prestige, and power.

Yet in most stratified societies, only occasionally do the elite find it necessary to actually use force. Use of actual force and the threat of force have disadvantages to the elite itself. Suppose the elite wait for rebellions to occur and then use police or armies to put them down. Even though none succeed, each time a rebellion is suppressed, more hatred and resentment and more awareness of the relative wealth and power of the elite are produced. Increased hatred and awareness caused by suppression can backfire and lead to a greater probability of future rebellion. Notice also that the elite's reliance on oppression to maintain wealth and power potentially reduces or eliminates their honor and esteem, one of the three major rewards offered by stratification, and one that they presumably covet. Further, those who supply the military might—the army, henchmen, thugs, or police—must be paid or otherwise provided for by the elite; this requires resources. The elite can either take these resources from their own wealth, thus reducing it, or they can increase their exploitation of the majority population, thus breeding more hatred and resentment toward themselves. Finally, relying entirely on the loyalty of an army is risky because this allegiance may change. In sum, reliance on threat and armed force alone is costly and risky.

This is not to deny that military might is an important reason why high degrees of inequality are maintained for many generations. Probably few elites have maintained themselves for many generations without using the deterrent value of force and periodically suppressing rebellions and dissent. Nonetheless, stratification systems that rely entirely or largely on force seem to be short-lived and unstable and have been replaced by those that use other mechanisms. What other mechanisms are available?

Ideologies

We can begin to answer this question by noting yet another reason that inequality seldom persists because of force alone. A single rebellion can have many causes, but a persistent *pattern* of rebellion is caused mainly by the lower strata's perception that they are exploited or not receiving their fair share of rewards. Putting down rebellions does nothing to change the reasons why people rebel. The instigators may be sanctioned or eliminated, but the underlying discontent that causes persistent conflict remains. Sooner or later there will be new instigators who organize new rebellions. Armed force cannot eliminate the perceptions of unfair distribution of rewards that cause rebellions.

One mechanism available to elites to maintain their privileges is to change the perceptions of the underprivileged about why they are underprivileged. For example, if poor people think it is God's will that they are poor, they are less likely to rebel than if they believe that they are poor because of exploitation. Or if they think that the elite use their property and power to benefit everyone in the society, then they are less likely to challenge the elite. Or if they think that a concentration of property and power is inevitable because that's just the way life is, they will be less likely to resist. Or if they think that they, too, can acquire property and power through their own achievements, they are likely to put their effort into improving their own position rather than into causing trouble.

If, to state the general point, members of the lower strata adopt a set of beliefs that justifies and legitimates the rewards received by the higher strata, then they are more likely to try and join the system rather than to beat it. In such beliefs the elite have a powerful and relatively cheap tool with which to reduce the amount of opposition to their power and privileges. Further, these ideas increase the prestige of the elite. If people believe that inequality is God's will, or that the activities of the elite benefit all, or that the elite became elite through intelligence and hard work, then the elite deserve the honor and respect of everyone else.

We shall call those ideas and beliefs that explain inequality as desirable or legitimate **ideologies**. The term ideology also has a broader meaning, referring to any set of ideas held by a group—as in the phrases *leftist political ideology* and *feminist ideology*. Here we use it in the narrow sense, to refer only to ideas that justify the status quo of inequality.

In many stratified societies, ideologies are based on religion. We are familiar with the notion of the "divine right of kings" from feudal Europe—certainly a handy supernatural mandate for kings and aristocracies! Similar notions are common in non-Western stratified societies. For instance, in Bunyoro, a kingdom in East Africa, the health and welfare of the ruler were mystically associated with the fertility and prosperity of the whole kingdom. Anything that threatened his life was believed a threat to everyone. In many ancient civilizations, such as the Aztec, the Inca, the Japanese, and the Egyptian, the ruler himself was believed to be a divine or semidivine being. In pre-twentieth century China, the emperor was believed to rule because he had the "Mandate of Heaven," meaning that Heaven itself had granted him secular authority over the vast Chinese empire for so long as he ruled it wisely and humanely. In traditional India, as we have seen, Hindu beliefs about reincarnation and pollution were so intertwined with the caste system that they rendered its inequities both explicable and legitimate.

In the ancient complex chiefdoms of Hawaii there was a marked social distinction between the noble and the commoner class. The nobility was believed to be endowed with a supernatural power called *mana*. *Mana* was partly hereditary, and within a single family the eldest child inherited the most *mana* from his or her parents. The highest-ranking noble, the paramount chief, was believed to be descended from one of the gods of the islands through a line of eldest sons. This descent gave him the right to rule because he had more *mana* than anyone in the chiefdom. Other nobles (lesser chiefs and their families) were relatives of the paramount and thus also were endowed with *mana*. *Mana* gave chiefs the power to curse those who were disloyal or disobedient or who violated some taboo, which further reinforced their authority. Hawaiians believed that the prosperity of a chiefdom and everyone in it depended on the performance of certain religious rituals held in grand temples. Because commoners did not have enough *mana* to enter a temple, only priests and nobles could perform the rituals needed to ensure prosperity. Everyone in the chiefdom thus relied on the social (and religious) elite for their well-being.

The preceding examples illustrate some of the ways religion serves ideological functions in some societies. In stratified societies, religion commonly gives the elite a supernatural mandate, provides them with the supernatural means to punish people, and gives them ritual functions to perform that are believed to benefit the whole population.

American Secular Ideologies

Do similar kinds of religious ideologies exist in modern industrial societies, most of which are as highly stratified as any preindustrial society? In the United States, for instance, many have claimed that the most prevalent religion (Christianity) helps preserve the status quo. But in fact, Christian teachings historically have been and still are used to support social and political movements of all kinds. Many such movements are far from supportive of the status quo, including the nineteenth-century antislavery movement and, more recently, the civil rights and liberation theology movements.

Further, most American citizens do not believe that the richest Americans have a supernatural mandate for their wealth. The wealthiest families generally do not justify their income and property by invoking religious authority. And although many powerful leaders attend church and may even bring their religious faith into their speeches, few get very far by claiming they are chosen by God. Religion does perhaps reinforce Americans' "basic values," but it is not generally used to justify the wealth and power of particular individuals and families. With regard to the issue of who has what and why, most Americans are *secularists:* They explain the unequal distribution of rewards by events here on earth, not in heaven.

In industrial societies such as the United States, then, ideologies are not based mainly on religion. But they do not have to be, for the only two essential features of ideologies are that

- they must reinforce inequality by affecting people's consciousness, not by threatening physical coercion; and
- they must be believable to large numbers of people, based on existing cultural knowledge.

On the first requirement, *consciousness* refers to cultural attitudes, values, world views, and so forth. On the second requirement, *believable* means that effective ideologies match up with people's general ideas about how their societies work. They must make sense in terms of existing cultural knowledge, or they will be ineffective and (presumably) will be replaced by other kinds of ideologies. **Secular ideologies** can meet these requirements as well as religious ideologies.

Many social scientists suggest that two major kinds of secular ideologies exist in the modern United States. One is that the whole nation benefits from inequality. Because a few people are very wealthy, people believe that "the masses" are better off than they would be if wealth were distributed more equally. After all, the chance to get rich motivates people to do their best, and we all win when our fellow citizens perform up to their potential. Besides, the accumulation and investment of wealth is necessary to create jobs, from which poor and middle-class people benefit.

The other secular ideology is that the elite have earned their rewards through their own merit and efforts.

They are believed to be more intelligent, ambitious, hard working, willing to take risks, and generally to possess more admirable qualities than other people.

To the extent that they are widely believed, these two ideas fit with Americans' other beliefs about the way people are and how their society works. They are compatible with widespread beliefs about human motivation—people need strong incentives before they will make the effort to get a good education and have a responsible career. They also fit in with many American values, such as individualism, progress, the work ethic, and private property.

Of course, many Americans do not believe these two ideas. (If you do not believe them, then they cannot be effective ideologies for you.) Others believe that these ideas are an accurate portrayal of how the whole nation benefits from economic inequality. (If you fall into this camp, you will think that these ideas are objectively true, rather than merely ideologies.) Your personal opinion depends on your class, upbringing, ideas about human nature, political views, and so forth. Can the comparative perspective of anthropology shed any light on the issue of whether stratification benefits society-at-large, or mainly members of the elite class themselves? To answer this question, we must first look at the major theories of inequality.

Theories of Inequality

To analyze inequality in human societies, sociologists have developed two sets of theories. One holds that a high degree of inequality in the distribution of rewards is necessary, socially just, and beneficial to all members of society. Unless society offers unequal rewards for unequal talents and efforts, the most talented people will have no incentive to put their talents to work for the welfare of all. This view is called the **functional theory of inequality**.

A contrary view holds that a high degree of inequality is not only socially unjust but robs the whole society of the benefits of much of its potential talent, which lies undeveloped and unrewarded in many of those at the bottom of the socioeconomic ladder. Stratification (and its ideologies) is the way elites ensure the maintenance of their access to resources, wealth, and the machinery of government. This view is known as the **conflict theory of inequality**. It holds that inequality offers few benefits to anyone except the elite and, indeed, is harmful to the whole society because of the unnecessary conflicts it creates.

Functionalist Theory

The functionalist theory holds that inequality is necessary if a society is to motivate its most talented and hard-working members to perform its most important roles. Some roles (including jobs) require more skill and training than do others. Ordinarily, the more skill and training required to perform a role, the fewer the number of people qualified to "do the job" and, all else equal, the more valuable their abilities are to the whole group. Functionalists argue that unequal rewards are effective ways to recruit the most able individuals into the most socially valuable roles. Unless there are rewards for those with the talents most of us lack, they will have no incentive to put those talents to work in activities that benefit all of us. Further, inequality is not only advantageous, it also is socially just, in the functionalist view. If society as a whole is to enjoy the fruits of the labor of its small number of well-trained, talented, and hard-working individuals, it is only fair that it reward these individuals with material goods, respect, and control over public decision making.

The functionalist analysis of inequality certainly makes sense. Functionalists claim that people who do the most valuable things get the greatest rewards. But two objections to such an analysis are possible within the framework of the functionalist theory itself.

First, there is no reason to believe that the high degree of inequality that actually exists in stratified societies is needed to ensure that those with scarce talents will work to benefit the whole society. In industrialized nations, for example, how many dollars does it take to motivate a qualified individual to manage a major company? In the United States, chief executives of manufacturing companies (e.g., auto, oil, and chemical industries) are paid about 25 times more than average workers of their companies. In Japan, chief executives earn 10 times more than average workers. Are American companies run more efficiently than Japanese companies? Two-and-a-half times more efficiently? If the compensation of American auto executives were more in line with that of the Japanese, would we have less competitive automobiles, or would auto workers simply enjoy a larger piece of the company pie and the rest of us have to pay a bit less for our cars?

Consider another example. As we have seen, in the United States, the wealthiest 1 percent of households owns 39 percent of the wealth. In Great Britain, the wealthiest 1 percent own only 18 percent of the wealth. Does this mean that low- and middle-class Americans enjoying the alleged benefits of inequality are better off than the British? Twice as well off?

As these examples illustrate, one objection to the functionalist theory is that no one knows how much inequality is needed to motivate people. Is the *high degree* of inequality actually found in some stratified society needed to realize the benefits of *some degree* of inequality? Or could the distribution of rewards be made more equal with no harm to anyone except those at the top, who would lose part of their share of the pie?

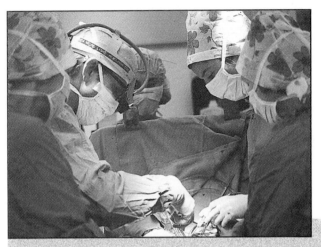

People in certain elite professions, such as medicine, earn very high incomes. The functionalist theory holds that such high rewards are necessary to motivate talented and diligent people to occupy the roles most important to society.

Second, functionalists assume that the system of stratification *effectively* places qualified individuals into important roles. But it is a large assumption that those who are best able to perform the most important roles are those who usually are recruited into them. In all systems of stratification there is a powerful element of inheritance of wealth, prestige, and power. Assume it is true (and it is not) that all those individuals who acquired their rewards in previous generations did so by performing roles that everyone else was willing to reward them for performing. There is still no guarantee that their children and children's children have the same enviable and scarce personal qualities, yet their descendants have a head start. If we think of much of economic, social, and political life as analogous to a race—like a 100-meter dash—then to ensure that the fastest runners finish first, we need to start them all off from the same place. But the tendency for rewards to be inherited is analogous to starting some runners at the starting line, others at the 40-meter mark, and a few at the 80-meter mark; who finishes first and last is not determined mainly by who is the fastest.

Only if a society were able to devise someway of beginning each generation on an equal footing, with truly equal opportunities to compete, would the functionalist theory of inequality be adequate. No stratified society has ever achieved this condition, partly because the wealthy and powerful would have to consent to such a change, and they have no incentive to do so. In sum, the second objection to functionalism is that stratification is an inefficient way to recruit talented individuals into the most valuable roles because it virtually ensures unequal opportunities in life.

Conflict Theory

The conflict theory takes off from objections to functionalism, such as the two just given; but it goes much further. Conflict theorists claim that stratification is based ultimately on control over productive resources such as land, technology, and labor. Once an elite gains control over these resources—by whatever means—they coerce other people into working for them. How this coercion is organized varies between different kinds of economic systems. In ancient preindustrial states and some chiefdoms, the noble class controlled the land and the commoners had to provide tribute and labor to the nobility in return for the privilege of using it. In parts of feudal Europe, the serfs were tied to their estate and ordinarily were not denied access to the land they worked, but they still had to contribute a certain number of days of work or a certain proportion of their harvest to their lord per year.

As for the capitalist economic system, Karl Marx—the nineteenth-century "father" of conflict theory—argued that capitalist societies include only two fundamental classes. Members of the capitalist class (or *bourgeoisie*) own the factories and tools. Members of the working class (or *proletariat*) have only one thing to sell on the market: their labor. To earn their living, workers must sell their labor to some capitalist. This seems like an equitable arrangement: The capitalists buy the labor they need to operate their capital to sell goods and make profit; the workers get the jobs they need to support their families by selling their time and skills for a wage.

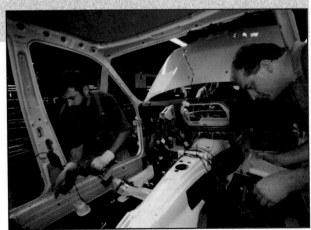

Conflict theorists hold that stratification arises out of the ability of some groups to coerce and exploit others. In a capitalist economy, for example, workers are not paid the full market value of the products they manufacture. Does this mean they are "exploited"?

But, Marx noted, the goods the workers produce must be worth more on the market than the workers themselves receive in wages or there would be no profit for the capitalists. The difference between the amount the capitalists receive for the goods they sell and their costs (including the amount they pay their workers) is *profit*. Thus, although the workers are not fully aware of it, a portion of their workdays is spent in labor for the owners of the equipment they operate to make their living. Because workers do not receive the full market value of what they produce, part of their labor benefits not themselves but the capitalist (owners and/or shareholders) who employs them. For this reason, workers are exploited, Marx believed. The notion that the exchange of workers' labor for wages is mutually beneficial is merely an ideology. Sooner or later the workers will see through the ideologies and realize what the owners have been doing to them, and they will overthrow the ruling (capitalist) class. They will establish a new economic system (communism) in which the means of production are owned collectively, by workers themselves, and exploitation will disappear.

Conflict theorists have been criticized for being ideologues themselves, although of a different political persuasion than functionalists. If one wants to find exploitation in a relationship, one can always do so. Critics of conflict theory claim that the value-laden term *exploitation* does not adequately characterize relations between chiefs or kings and commoners, between lords and serfs, or between capitalists and workers. Conflict theorists ignore the valuable services that elite classes perform, such as maintaining social control, organizing the society for the provision of public goods, and accumulating productive resources (capital) put aside to increase future production.

Many conflict theorists assume that it is possible to organize a complex society without unequal rewards. This is a rather unrealistic view of human nature, according to some critics of the approach, which may be one reason "communism" has collapsed almost everywhere. Complex societies are always hierarchically organized, with centralized leadership. Many critics believe that the functions of leaders, controllers, and organizers are so valuable to society at large that they deserve the rewards they receive.

Who Benefits?

Contrasting the two theories, we see that functionalism emphasizes the positive aspects of stratification, whereas conflict theory emphasizes the negative side. Conflict theory points to the costs of stratification not just to those on the bottom of the social ladder but also to society at large. Society loses the undeveloped potential of its underprivileged members and must suffer the periodic violent conflicts (rebellions, revolutions) and/or ongoing disorder (crimes, political dissent) caused by a high degree of unjust inequality and inherited privilege.

In addition, conflict theorists argue that many of the problems that have afflicted modern North America in the last couple of decades are caused (or at least made worse) by increasing inequality. Much resentment towards "the system" comes out of peoples' sense that their lives will not get better or are getting worse. Unable to identify the causes of their frustrations, some white conservative groups find scapegoats in welfare mothers, African Americans and Jews, immigrants, and overseas laborers. Unable to make a personally acceptable living in a socially acceptable manner, inner city youths turn to dealing drugs. Economic hardship contributes to family breakup. Poorer people need more social programs, funded by taxpayers, who revolt and elect representatives who demand *fewer* services—for the poor, at least. More generally, the sense of national unity and social responsibility is undermined by worsening inequality.

The functionalist and conflict theories imply different philosophical and moral views of inequality, views that have contemporary relevance for industrial societies. The first implies that inequality is socially useful; the second that it should be reduced or even eliminated. The first argues that the best and the brightest naturally gravitate to the top; the second that much goodness and brightness never have a chance to reveal themselves. The first suggests that government get out of the business of redistributing wealth; the second proposes an active government policy to redistribute wealth to maximize the chances that hidden genius will have a chance to manifest itself. Profound issues of social policy are involved.

Does the comparative perspective of anthropology have anything to offer to a solution of this issue? Who does benefit from inequality? In preindustrial stratified societies, elites did indeed perform some vital roles for the whole population, just as functionalists claim. For example, elites often organized labor for the construction and maintenance of public works projects, provided relief to regions struck by famine, and raised a military force to provide for the defense of the political unit (see Chapter 11). Some kind of central authority may indeed be necessary for such tasks to be coordinated effectively. Cooperative activities require organization; organization requires leaders and controllers; leaders and controllers deserve to be rewarded.

On the other hand, preindustrial elites performed some roles that probably were created mainly to maintain their positions as rulers. Thus, their religious functions often were viewed as indispensable to the general welfare by ordinary people, but in fact the rituals they sponsored did not ensure rain or the fertility of land or women. Their regulation of access to land and other resources might have

been necessary, but it was partly because they themselves controlled so many resources that other people's access to them had to be "regulated." The social order they helped to maintain benefited everyone, but the elite's power, wealth, and internal political rivalries produced violent conflicts that otherwise would not have existed.

We see, then, that some functions of nobles, lords, and other elite classes in the preindustrial world are useful for the whole population. Other "functions" are imaginary and exist only because of prevailing (usually religious) ideologies. Still other "benefits" that the population receives from the elite are beneficial only because of the control of the elite itself over society. The existence of inequality itself produces some societal "needs" that the elite help to meet, and then they claim to deserve rewards for fulfilling the so-called needs.

With the insight gained from this comparative perspective, we can be fairly certain that some of the "functions" carried out by the elite in industrialized nations likewise are imaginary. We also can imagine that some of the "benefits" the rest of the people receive from the roles performed by the elite exist only because the past and present elite class itself has set up society's institutions in such a way that their roles are popularly perceived as necessary or beneficial. (To take a provocative example, if there were no such occupation as lawyer, how often do you think you would need one?) It is difficult for insiders to pick out which functions of an elite are and are not needed—most people are enculturated to see these functions as necessary for the general welfare. But with a comparative view of humanity we can see that much of what is needed for the general welfare is relative to time, place, and cultural conditions. In turn, such conditions are influenced by those with wealth and power.

Along these same lines, note that many of the institutions we regard as beneficial to all in fact do not benefit everyone to the same degree. A good example of this is our laws regarding the government's protection of private property. Most Americans are enculturated to believe that private property is a basic human right and that the general welfare requires laws to protect everyone's property. But, as shown previously, the bulk of the private property is owned by a small percentage of citizens. It may be true that we all benefit somewhat from the legal safeguarding of our private property, but we do not all benefit equally. For one thing, we differ vastly in the amount of property that needs to be protected. For another, because the rich live in more protected neighborhoods than the poor, the property of the poor is less secure than that of the rich.

So who does benefit from the inequality found in stratified societies? The functionalists probably are correct in their assumption that some degree of inequality is needed for motivation. We might also agree that unequal rewards for unequal efforts is a fair and just standard. But we do not know now much inequality is necessary to provide incentives, much less whether some particular stratified society—including our own—has just the right amount. We do know that power and privilege are partly—and usually largely—inherited in stratified societies and that therefore the current members of the elite class are not automatically more talented and diligent than everyone else. By comparing stratified societies, we see that elites do provide some useful services for the population at large. But we also see that many popular ideas about their functions are ideologies, and that many of their roles are useful only under circumstances that they themselves had a hand in creating.

Probably most of us would benefit from some degree of inequality, if only there were some way to find out what the optimum amount of inequality is for some given society, if only there were some way to achieve this optimum initially, and if only there were some way to ensure that opportunities to succeed and achieve are equal for all children. But no known human society has ever achieved this utopia.

Summary

Inequality refers to the degree to which individuals and groups enjoy differential access to socially valuable rewards of wealth, power, and prestige. Fried's typology of egalitarian, ranked, and stratified societies provides a useful description of the range of cross-cultural diversity in inequality.

Most foragers are egalitarian. This is largely because their adaptation makes it difficult for anyone to exercise control over productive resources and the behavior of others. Such adaptive features include high rates of mobility, ability of individuals to choose their band affiliation, a cultural value placed on sharing and the social pressure against making oneself stand out, and the difficulties of maintaining exclusive access to a territory.

In ranked societies there are a set number of honored positions (chiefs, titles, offices) to which only a small number of people are eligible to succeed. Succession may be determined by genealogical ascription, or membership in a particular kin group may establish a pool of candidates from which one will emerge or be selected. Tikopia illustrates one form of ranking.

Stratified societies are defined by three characteristics: They have marked inequalities in access to all three kinds of rewards; this inequality is based largely on unequal access to productive resources; and the inequality is strongly heritable. One system of stratification is the caste system. Castes are best known from India, where they were intimately associated with the Hindu doctrines of reincarnation and pollution.

Class systems are more common in the preindustrial world and are characteristic of all modern nations. In modern nations, in theory interclass mobility is possible. Assigning a particular family to a particular class is not always easy, but in the United States the best criterion of class membership is wealth. Studies conducted by scholars and by the federal government reveal an enormous disparity in the distribution of wealth, especially if net worth rather than annual cash income is used to measure a family's wealth.

How such highly unequal distribution of rewards persists in stratified societies is puzzling. The mobilization of armed force by the elite is an insufficient explanation. Cultural beliefs that inequality is inevitable, divinely ordained, legitimate, and/or beneficial to society as a whole provide ideologies that justify and reinforce the power and privilege of elite classes. Among preindustrial peoples, religious beliefs were the main form of ideology, as exemplified by ancient Hawaii. In modern countries, ideologies are more secular in orientation, because effective ideologies must be compatible with a peoples' overall cultural ideas about how their society works. In the United States, Americans' ideas about the social and economic usefulness of inequality, about the fairness of unequal rewards for unequal talents and efforts, and about how the well-to-do achieved their wealth may be interpreted as secular ideologies.

The two major theories about inequality are the functional and the conflict theories. Functionalists hold that societies offer unequal rewards to those individuals who have the scarcest talents and who use them to perform the most socially valuable roles. Conflict theorists claim that inequality is based ultimately on control over productive resources. The two theories imply contrasting views of the nature of inequality. Anthropology's comparative perspective suggests that although elites often do perform valuable services for society at large, many of their "functions" are illusory. Others exist only because past elites have set up the structure of society so that their "services" are necessary. Although functionalists are correct that some degree of inequality is necessary for incentive, we have no way of knowing whether any society has the amount it "needs," nor has any society ever succeeded in establishing the equal opportunity required for the functionalist theory to be correct.

Key Terms

inequality
egalitarian

ranked
stratified
class
caste
ideology

secular ideology
functional theory of inequality
conflict theory of inequality

Suggested Readings

Bendix, Reinhard, and Seymour M. Lipset, eds. *Class, Status, and Power: Social Stratification in Comparative Perspective*. 2nd ed. New York: The Free Press, 1966.
  • *A reader intended primarily for sociologists. Contains many seminal articles, although now dated.*

Berreman, Gerald D., and Kathleen M. Zaretsky. *Social Inequality: Comparative and Development Approaches*. New York: Academic Press, 1981.
  • *A collection of papers discussing social inequality in a number of societies.*

Fried, Morton. *The Evolution of Political Society*. New York: Random-House, 1967.
  • *A well-known book with an extensive discussion of ranking and stratification and how they relate to political organization.*

Lenski, G. *Power and Privilege*. New York: McGraw-Hill, 1966.
  • *A treatment of stratification comparing the range of inequality in preindustrial and industrial societies. Best known as an attempt to reconcile the functionalist and the conflict perspectives.*

Scheper-Hughes, Nancy. *Death Without Weeping*. Berkeley: University of California Press, 1992.
  • *How poor northeast Brazilian families cope psychologically with high rates of infant and child mortality.*

Several studies treat the concentration of power and wealth in the United States in great detail.

Danziger, Sheldon, and Peter Gottschalk. *America Unequal*. New York: Russel Sage, 1995.
  • *Two economists analyze the reasons for the growing inequality in the United States and propose solutions using government policies.*

Domhoff, G. William. *Who Rules America: Power and Politics in the Year 2000*. 3rd ed. Mayfield, 1998.

Gilbert, Dennis. *The American Class Structure In an Age of Growing Inequality*. 5th ed. Belmont, Calif.: Wadsworth.
  • *Sociological textbook containing factual information on various aspects of class differentiation in the contemporary United States, as well as conceptual and theoretical issues surrounding inequality.*

Newman, Katherine. *Falling from Grace: The Experience of Downward Mobility in the American Middle Class*. New York: Vintage, 1988.

Newman, Katherine. *Declining Fortunes: The Withering of the American Dream*. New York: Basic, 1993.
  • *Written by an anthropologist, the interview and observational data in these two books show the impacts of job loss or declining income on former members of the American middle class and how they cope with downward mobility.*

Internet Exercises

"Explorations in Social Inequality" (http://www.trinity.edu/~mkearl/strat.html) is a site by Michael Kearl at Trinity University in Texas. This site addresses social inequalities in the United States and throughout the world. There are many links to social class, theory (including functionalism and conflict theory), and much more.

Another site that examines social stratification in the United States is Edward N. Wolff's Internet article "How the Pie is Sliced: America's Growing Concentration of Wealth" from *The American Prospect,* no. 22 (http://epn.org/prospect/22/22wolf.html).

Relations with the Supernatural

Defining Religion

Supernatural Powers: Beings and Forces

Myths

Rituals

Theories of Religion

Intellectual/Cognitive Functions

Psychological Functions

Social Functions

Sphere of Supernatural Intervention

Supernatural Explanations of Misfortune

Sorcery

Witchcraft

Interpretations of Sorcery and Witchcraft

Varieties of Religious Organization

Individualistic Cults

Shamanism

Communal Cults

Ecclesiastical Cults

Revitalization Movements

Prophets and Revelations

Melanesian Cargo Cults

Native American Movements

The religion of a people includes their traditional ways of communicating and interacting with supernatural powers. These Buddhist monks are praying at a temple in Thailand.
Visit http://www.wadsworth.com/humanity to learn more about the material covered in this chapter and to access activities, exercises, and tutorial quizzes.

*A*LL KNOWN *cultures have some form of religion—beliefs in the existence of supernatural powers and attempts to influence or control these powers by the organized performance of rituals. Like the other dimensions of culture we have covered, religion varies greatly among the world's diverse peoples. In this chapter, we introduce this diversity. We begin with an extended definition of religion. Then we cover some of the main theories social scientists use to understand religious beliefs and rituals. Next we look at some of the major forms of religion that have most interested anthropologists. We conclude by discussing religious movements, which often occur when a society is undergoing rapid change and foreign domination.*

Defining Religion

What is religion? How can we best define it so as to encompass all the diversity of religion found among humanity? It is ethnocentric to define religion simply as "belief in God," for the same reason it is ethnocentric to define politics as "the activities and organization of a government." Just as some societies have no formal government, so are there societies that lack a belief in any kind of deity, much less in the Judeo-Christian God. We need a definition that can be applied cross-culturally.

A nineteenth-century definition that many scholars still use is E. B. Tylor's **animism**, or "belief in spiritual beings." Most modern conceptions follow Tylor's lead: They specify that, at the least, all religions include beliefs that some kind of spiritual or supernatural powers exist. But Tylor's definition leaves out much about religion. By expanding on it we can present an overview of religion in cross-cultural perspective.

Supernatural Powers: Beings and Forces

"Beings" are not the only kind of spiritual powers that people believe in. Many religions posit the existence of other kinds of powers that are more like "forces" than "beings." For example, in aboriginal times the peoples of Polynesia believed in *mana,* a diffuse, impersonal, incorporeal power. Mana lent supernatural potency to things, which explained unusual qualities; or to people, which explained unusual success. People and objects could be infused with greater or lesser amounts of mana. Having a lot of mana explained why some chiefs always won battles, why some fishing equipment seemed to work so well, why certain gardens produced such fine crops, and so forth.

The widespread belief in powers such as mana make it useful to divide supernatural powers into beings and forces. Spiritual *beings* usually have qualities such as a bodily form, some way of appearing before people, a personality, and a fairly predictable way of responding to human actions. The characteristics people attribute to supernatural beings vary enormously: They can be capricious or consistent, stubborn or reasonable, vengeful or forgiving, amoral or just. Some beings have human origins, such as souls or ancestral ghosts, which reside in or resided in a specific individual. Other kinds of beings have nonhuman origins, such as many gods or demons.

Supernatural *forces* likewise have definite properties, which vary from people to people. Because forces usually have no will of their own—no power to refuse humans who know how to command or manipulate them in the proper manner—they often can be used for either good or evil purposes. In most cases, people believe that supernatural forces can be manipulated by humans who know the proper rites and spells. The manipulation of forces by means of rites and spells, known as *magic,* is discussed later in this chapter.

Myths

Belief in the existence of supernatural powers (beings and forces) is only part of religion. Religion also includes **myths**—oral or written stories about the actions and deeds of supernatural powers. Myths commonly tell of the actions of cultural heroes and supernatural powers of long ago. Sometimes they explain how the entire universe was created. They may recount how and why people, animals, plants, and natural features originated. Myths explain how a people acquired their tools and customs and how they came to live where they do. They often tell why people should or should not act in certain ways and what happened to someone in the past who did something people are forbidden to do.

North Americans mostly learn their mythology in formal settings: Myths are taught at church and, to a lesser extent, at home. (Here we need to emphasize that calling Bible stories "myths" does *not* mean that we regard them as false.) In many societies, people learn the mythology of their religion as an ordinary part of enculturation. Elders recount myths in moments of leisure. Myths are repeated regularly on days set aside for religious performances. They are sung or chanted while one is doing daily tasks. The fact that myths sometimes are recounted rather casually does not mean that their importance in a people's way of life is negligible. A people's world view is greatly affected by their mythology.

It has been argued, for example, that the Judeo-Christian mythology makes it easy for North Americans to view nature as something to be conquered and used for their own profit and gratification. God gave humans "dominion" over nature and told us to "subdue" the earth and its living creatures (see Genesis 1:26–30). Because of the Biblical account of creation, when it suits our purposes and interests we have no divine prohibitions against polluting the air and water, ruining the habitats of other creatures, destroying the landscape with strip mines and highways, and so forth. According to this argument, because of the religious heritage of Western civilization—which influences the world view of Europeans and peoples culturally derived from Europe—Westerners are more likely to believe that God gave the earth to humans to conquer and exploit than to preserve and protect.

In contrast, Westerners might show more respect for other living things if (as in some cultures) the sacred myths of our religious heritage recounted how some of us came from bears, some from coyotes, some from whales, and so forth. We might hesitate to destroy a forest if the scriptures told us explicitly that trees are just as precious to God as are humans. In short, if Western mythology emphasized the importance of living in harmony with nature rather than subduing nature, perhaps the modern "ecological crisis" would be less of a crisis.

However, Judeo-Christian scriptures can be interpreted in many ways and used for many purposes, not all of which involve the uncontrolled exploitation of resources for profit or material self-gratification. The Amish communities of North America, for example, are thoroughly Christian, but they reject much of the materialism of modern society. Amish have retained many of their beliefs and worship practices intact by restricting interactions with outsiders, even as they have adapted to modern economic realities.

A people's myths—and this is the general point we are trying to make—are more than stories they tell after dark or recite on appropriate occasions. They do more than satisfy curiosity and help pass the time. Myths are part and parcel of a people's world view: their fundamental conceptions of nature and society and how people ought to relate to the world and to one another. They therefore affect how people behave in their everyday lives.

Rituals

Religions include behaviors as well as beliefs and myths. People everywhere believe that gods, ghosts, demons, devils, and other supernatural beings take an active interest in worldly affairs, particularly in the lives of human beings. Such beings can be asked for blessings or aid, or sometimes they can be commanded to do things for or to people. Similarly, people can use supernatural forces to cause helpful or harmful effects. Because people believe that supernatural beings and forces can make natural events occur and can intervene in human affairs, all cultures prescribe certain behaviors that are used to interact with and influence various powers.

The organized performance of behaviors intended to influence spiritual powers is known as **ritual**. Rituals are always stereotyped: There are definite patterns of speech or movement, or definite sequences of events, that occur in much the same way in performance after performance. In general, people performing rituals want supernatural powers to do things on their behalf: to make someone (or everyone) healthy or fertile, to bring rain, to make the crops grow, to save their souls, to bring back the game, to provide blessings, and so forth. People may pray, worship, make sacrifices, and follow ritual procedures scrupulously to ensure that their gods, their personal spirits, or the ghosts of their dead ancestors intervene favorably in their lives.

In some cultures, the performers of ritual often want supernatural powers to harm their enemies in some way: to make them sick or barren, to bring floods or pestilence to their land, to drive the animals out of their territory, to make their spears fly crooked in the upcoming battle, and so forth. If we can ask supernatural powers to harm our enemies, our enemies may have the same ability; they can cause supernatural harm to us, making us sick or prone to misfortune. So ethnographers commonly report that members of some society believe that many or all illnesses, deaths, and accidents are caused by the supernatural powers of evil or enemy humans. And many kinds of rituals exist whose explicit purpose is to counteract the harm caused by other rituals performed by enemies.

Rituals the world over have symbolic aspects. They often occur in *places* that have symbolic significance to the performers. For example, they may be held where some mythological event occurred, or where the women who founded a matrilineage were born. Rituals often involve the display and manipulation of *objects* that symbolize an event (e.g., the cross), a holy person (statues of Jesus and Mary), a relationship (wedding rings, the symbol of holy matrimony), and a variety of other things. Symbolic significance usually is attached to the *language* and *behavior* of ritual, as in the Christian rituals of worship, hymn singing, prayer, baptism, communion, and confession. (The symbolic places, objects, language, and behaviors used in rituals are sometimes said to be sacred, but the Judeo-Christian distinction between sacred and profane must be applied with great care in describing non-Western religions, as shown in this chapter's "Other Voices.")

Anthropologists classify rituals on two bases. The first basis is their conscious purposes—the reasons people themselves give for performing them. For example, there are divination rituals, which are performed to acquire information from a supernatural power about the future or about some past event. There are also curing, sorcery, sacrificial, and exorcism rituals. There are rituals to renew the world, to make a man out of a boy and a woman out of a girl, and to free the soul from a dead person's body. There are rituals held for single individuals, for kin groups, for people of similar age, for whole societies, and so forth.

The second basis of classification is when rituals occur—whether they are held on a regular schedule (like Sunday church services) or simply whenever some individual or group wants or needs them (like funerals or prayers for a sick person). If rituals are held regularly (seasonally, annually, daily, monthly, etc.) they are called *calendrical rituals*. *Crisis rituals* are organized and performed whenever some individual or group needs, wants, or asks for them—for purposes of curing, ensuring good hunting or fishing, or other events that happen sporadically or unpredictably.

Other Voices

Understanding the Sacred

The concept of the sacred is one of the most difficult aspects of another culture to understand. An early American-Indian anthropologist, Francis LaFlesche, on numerous occasions voiced his concern over the misinterpretation of Indian religious beliefs by his colleagues. In an attempt to correct some of these misconceptions he spent over a decade recording Osage Indian beliefs and rituals. He had an advantage over most of his colleagues. His native Omaha language was mutually intelligible with Osage, and his field research was conducted almost entirely in Osage. In his publications he revealed a number of characteristics of Osage religious beliefs that have received little attention.

What do we mean by sacred? In Osage the word *wa-xo'-be* referred to anything made sacred. By made sacred they meant something that had been consecrated for ritual use. There was a wide range of *wa-xo'-be*. The most important were those ritual items commonly referred to as medicine bundles. There were three types of bundles: (1) *wa-xo'-be zhin-ga* or "little sacred object," (2) *wa-xo'-be ton-ga*, or "great sacred object," and (3) *mon-kon ton-ga wa-xo'-be* or "great sacred medicine object." The little sacred objects were clan bundles and each of their twenty-four patrilineal clans had its own bundles which were controlled by the clan priesthood. The great sacred object and the great sacred medicine object were controlled by two tribal priesthoods. In addition to these sacred objects there was a wide range of secondary sacred objects: pipes, hides, war standards, rattles, and clubs to name just a few. Virtually any object could be made *wa-xo'-be* or sacred by being smoked and prayed over by the priests. It was neither form nor even use in rituals that made an object *wa-xo'-be*. The war standard is a good example of this distinction

The war standard was a wooden staff about six feet long and curved at the top—some call this a *shepherd's staff*. The whole staff was encased in buckskin and then covered with swanskin. Twelve feathers, in four groups of three, were attached and a deerskin was tied to the top. As part of their war ceremony, which preceded the sending of a war party against their enemies, the priests of the Bow and Bear clans constructed two war standards. These two standards were consecrated during the ceremony to make them *wa-xo'-be* or sacred and were carried by the warriors in their attack. The war standards also appeared in other religious ceremonies. These standards were also made by the priests of the Bow and Bear clans, and were identical in construction to those made in the war ceremony and carried by the warriors. However, for these rituals only one standard would be made; it would not be consecrated and it would only be used in the ritual. This single war standard was not a sacred object; it was what the priest called a *wa-zhin-wa-a-thin-bi-kshe* or "those carried to excite enthusiasm."

LaFlesche thought that there was some confusion over the relationship between sacred objects and supernatural power. It is sometimes assumed that supernatural power is embodied within sacred objects. The Osage priests made clear that their rituals and ritual objects, including the *wa-xo'-be*, were the conscious creations of humans, and not the creations of *wa-kon-da*, the mysterious force that created and controlled the universe. Rituals and their sacred objects were used to ask for *wa-kon-da*'s blessings, by showing respect for *wa-kon-da*. A *wa-xo'-be* was nothing more than wood, hides, feathers, stone, and other objects. There was no supernatural power inherent in these objects. They were merely the symbols of this power. One treated these sacred objects with respect, not for what they were, but rather for what they symbolized.

However, LaFlesche also noted that not all Osages saw their rituals and sacred objects as merely symbolic. Many Osages, including some of the priests, had "drifted hopelessly into a literal belief that articles declared by the 'Holy Men' to be sacred and to be treated with reverent regard had . . . become possessed of a mystical power which the articles themselves could exercise for good or for evil" (LaFlesche 1925:91). Thus, while all Osages agreed as to which objects were sacred and which were not, they differed greatly as to those qualities that made an object *wa-xo'-be*. However, all treated these sacred objects with the same reverence, whether out of fear of the power embodied in the object, or out of respect for the power which it symbolized.

Sources: LaFlesche (1925) and Bailey (1995).

The three components of all religions, then, are (1) beliefs about the nature of supernatural powers, (2) mythologies about the historical deeds of these powers, and (3) rituals intended to influence these powers to intervene favorably on behalf of the performers. With this conception of religion we can glimpse at the ways in which cultures vary in their religious dimension.

There is diversity in beliefs about the nature of supernatural beings and forces, in what spheres or realms of life their powers extend to, in how they can be requested or commanded to intervene in human affairs, and in who can organize the rituals that make such requests or demands. We consider some of these variations in this chapter.

Rituals, usually involving stereotyped behaviors and the use of symbolic objects, are a part of all religions. These are Guatemalan Catholics in a ritual procession.

With this brief and broad overview of religion in mind, we now look at a few aspects of the anthropological study of religion. A good place to start is with some of the major theoretical orientations offered to understand or explain religion.

Theories of Religion

So far as we know, every culture has religion. The fact that religion is universal is a bit surprising, for two reasons. First—with regard to beliefs and myths—it can never be proved that supernatural powers such as ghosts, gods, devils, demons, angels, souls, mana, and so forth exist, much less that myths about them are true. Indeed, from an outsider's ("nonbeliever's") perspective, other people's religious beliefs and myths often seem merely superstitious. Yet in every culture we know about, many, most, or all people believe in supernatural powers and recite myths about them. Why?

Second—with regard to rituals—religious behavior may not be effective at achieving the goals the performers have in mind. From an outsider's perspective, many rituals seem to be a huge waste of time and resources. For example, when a Trobriand Islander plans a yam garden, he does

some things that "work" in the way he thinks they do: He clears the land, removes the weeds, and so forth, just as anyone should for success. But a Trobriander believes that acts that many outsiders consider superfluous are also necessary for success in gardening. He hires a magician to perform rites and spells that will keep his yams from leaving his garden at night and roaming around, because he knows that other people are performing magic to steal his yams by luring them into their own gardens. We—meaning those outside the culture's belief system—easily understand what the Trobriand gardener gets out of the first kind of activity: a yam harvest, if nature cooperates. But what does he get out of the magical rites and spells? How did Trobrianders come to believe that magic is needed?

We can state this second problem another way to see the major puzzling thing about rituals. When the Trobriander clears land, plants a crop, and weeds his garden, his actions are effective in attaining the goal he has in mind—they work in more or less the way he thinks that they do. But when the garden magician performs rites and spells to keep his client's yams from being stolen by a neighbor during their nightly wanderings, his actions do not achieve the result he has in mind. Yams do not "really" roam around; the magic does not "really" work. (Again, remember that these statements are made from an outsider's perspective.) How, then, did the Trobrianders get the idea that they do?

Speaking generally, rituals do not work the way the performers imagine they do—the rain does not fall because of the rain dance; the crazy woman is not made sane by exorcizing the devil within her; no spirits enter the body of the medicine man; there were no witches in Salem, Massachusetts, in 1692. Why, then, do so many people believe in the power of ritual?

You may already have thought of possible answers. If rituals do not work in the way performers believe that they do, perhaps they work in some other way. If they do not have the effects people believe that they have, they may have other effects that people find useful or satisfying. As for myths, if they are not accurate historical accounts, perhaps they are symbolic statements that help people make sense of reality and give meaning to real-world things and events.

We have all heard people who consider themselves sophisticated and educated say that religious beliefs rest on simple ignorance and superstition. This non-answer to the question "Why religion?" is (or should be) rejected by all anthropologists. Its ethnocentrism is apparent: Superstition is something that someone else believes in but you do not. Yet many of your own beliefs seem superstitious to others, and probably many of the accepted truths of the year 2000 will be considered superstitious in the year 2100. Besides, even if we admit that such beliefs and practices are superstitious, we have not explained them. Why does one form of superstition develop in one place and another form in another place?

Few, if any, modern anthropologists believe that religious beliefs and rituals can be explained as simple delusions. That is, few of us claim that religion results from ignorant folk making mistakes in logic that lead them to perform ritual activities that are a total waste of energy and resources. Practically all of us believe that religion has some kind of positive value to individuals, society, or both. It is difficult to explain its universality in any other way: How could something that is totally worthless be found among all humanity?

We do not, however, agree on what this positive value is. This leads us to the functions of religion—its benefits to individuals, to society as a whole, or to some social group within a society. Broadly, social scientists have proposed three types of functions of religion: the **intellectual** (or **cognitive**), the **psychological**, and the **social**.

Intellectual/Cognitive Functions

Scholars who focus on cognitive functions of religion begin with the assumption that humans want explanations for the world around them. Religious beliefs help satisfy the uniquely human desire to understand and explain things and events. Without religion, much of the world would be incomprehensible and inexplicable, which (these scholars argue) would be intolerable to the mind of a conscious, reasoning, problem-solving species like *Homo sapiens*. For example, religion satisfies human curiosity by providing explanations for the movements of the sun, moon, and stars. *Origin myths* explain things like the creation of the sky, land, and water; where animals and plants come from; and where people got their language, tools, rituals, and other customs and beliefs. The essential purpose of religion, in the intellectual view, is to provide people with explanations.

A very influential scholar who followed the intellectual approach was Sir James Frazer. His most famous work was the twelve-volumes *The Golden Bough,* which became known in the fields of classics and religion as well as in anthropology. Frazer claimed that "savages"— as he called peoples whom he imagined were living representatives of the earliest cultures—usually believe in some kind of magical power that can be manipulated by people who perform the proper rites and spells. He saw this belief as a prescientific one: People wanted to influence natural occurrences and other people, but they did not understand true scientific cause-and-effect relations. Believers in magic thought, for example, that a magician could cause harm to people by performing rites and spells on things that were once in contact with their victims, such as hair, nails, feces, or even footprints. Such beliefs had a kind of logic—by doing something to things once in contact with a man, you can do something to him— but the logic was based on false premises. Frazer thought that people gradually realized their logical errors and eventually gained knowledge of true scientific cause and effect. Frazer thus believed that magic and science are alternative world views: Each provides people with an intellectual model of the way the world works and a means to manipulate events and people. But whereas magical beliefs are false, scientific theories are objectively correct—in Frazer's view. Because science is a superior system of knowledge, Frazer thought it is in the process of replacing magical and religious beliefs.

The idea of Frazer and others that religious beliefs provide people with explanations for things and events is correct, as far as it goes, but it is an incomplete explanation for religion. Religion does satisfy curiosity about the world, but this is not its only function. "Savages" possess and use practical knowledge just as we do—a Trobriander knows that he must care for his yams as well as perform garden magic. Conversely, many "civilized" and "scientific" folk believe in and practice religion—even many of those who make their living practicing the science for which religion supposedly substitutes. Religious beliefs do not take the place of practical or scientific knowledge; in some way that we do not fully understand, they supplement it.

Although few modern scholars believe that religion functions solely or even mainly to provide "prescientific" people with explanations their culture would otherwise lack, the intellectual approach is by no means passé.

Clifford Geertz, a leading modern cultural theorist, holds that religion provides its believers with the assurance that the world is meaningful—that events have a place in the grand scheme of things, natural phenomena have causes, suffering and evil happen to specific individuals for a good reason, and injustices are corrected. Cultural beings (i.e., humans) cannot tolerate events that contradict the basic premises, categories, and world view of their cultural tradition. Yet such events do occur periodically. Because of religion, people are able to maintain their world view in spite of events that seem to contradict it. Religion, Geertz believes, reassures believers that the world is orderly rather than chaotic, all within the framework of their existing cultural knowledge.

Psychological Functions

The notion that religion helps people cope psychologically with times of trouble, stress, and anxiety is a common one. Sicknesses, accidents, misfortunes, injustices, deaths, and other trials and tribulations of life can be better handled emotionally if one believes that there is a reason and meaning to them or that one's troubles can be controlled or alleviated by means of ritual.

In anthropology a well-known psychological theory of religion is that of Bronislaw Malinowski, whom we

introduced in Chapter 4. Malinowski thought that religion (including magic) serves the valuable function of giving people confidence when they are likely to be unsuccessful despite their best efforts. There are always natural phenomena that people cannot control and that constantly threaten to ruin their plans and efforts. Belief in the power of ritual to control these (otherwise uncontrollable) elements instills confidence and removes some of the anxiety that results from the uncertainties of life.

Another specific psychological theory of religion holds that, as self-conscious beings, we humans are aware of our own mortality. Knowing that we will eventually die causes us great anxiety and leads us to worry about our own death. Experiencing the serious illness or death of one's parent or other relative likewise produces grief and psychological stress for most people. We must have some way of coping emotionally with the grief over the death of our loved ones, and with the anxiety caused by the knowledge of our own mortality. Religion helps us cope by denying the finality of death, that is, by inculcating beliefs about the existence of a pleasant afterlife, in which our immortal souls live forever.

The notion that beliefs in life after death helps to calm our fears and alleviate our anxieties seems reasonable. However, this theory is tainted by an ethnocentric assumption: Although most religions do include beliefs abut some kind of afterlife, in a great many cultures the afterlife is far from pleasant. The Dobu people of Melanesia believe that human bodies also have a ghostly form, seen as a shadow or a reflection. During life, the ghostly self goes out at night and appears in the dreams of other people. Once the corpse rots after death, the ghosts of people go to a place called the Hill of the Dead, where they have a "thin and shadowy" existence and mourn for their homeland. How are such beliefs about the afterlife "comforting"?

Religion is psychologically useful. For some people some of the time, it relieves anxieties, calms fears, and helps one cope emotionally with life's uncertainties and hardships. That religion serves such functions is not subject to dispute. On the other hand, sometimes religious beliefs actually increase our anxieties, fears, and stress levels. Consider the Kwaio, a people of the Solomon Islands. Kwaio believe that women are spiritually dangerous to men, so Kwaio wives are expected to take elaborate precautions to avoid polluting their husbands when preparing food for them. If a man dies of an illness, his wife is likely to be blamed,

Psychological approaches hold that religion helps people cope with personal emotional traumas, such as the death of a loved one and fear of one's own death. These people from Surinam are hoisting a coffin at a funeral.

These people are gathered for a ritual in Irian Jaya, Indonesia. French sociologist Emile Durkheim proposed that communal rituals enhance social solidarity by enhancing a group's sense of unity and reliance on society.

and perhaps killed, for her "offense." Just whose anxieties and fears are "relieved" by this belief?

The general point of the Dobu and Kwaio examples is that, from a psychological perspective, religion has two "faces." On the one hand, it does—for some people, some of the time, in some respects—help us to cope emotionally with times of trouble and hardships. On the other hand, beliefs about the supernatural often create fears and anxieties that would not otherwise exist. Pleasant afterlifes ("Heaven") offer us comfort and hope. But what *psychological* benefit does the threat of eternal damnation ("Hell") offer?

Social Functions

"Societies need religion to keep people in line," you may have heard people say. The idea here is that religion instills and maintains common values, leads to increased conformity to cultural norms, promotes cohesion and cooperation, promises eternal rewards for good deeds and eternal damnation for evil acts, and so forth. Those who champion the social function (also called the *sociological*) theory hold that religion exists because of the useful effects it has on human societies. Rather than helping individuals cope emotionally, religion helps societies maintain harmonious social relationships between individuals and groups. It encourages people to respect the rights of others and to perform their proper duties.

Consider the Ten Commandments, for example, which serve as a moral code for Christians and Jews. Two prescribe how people ought to feel and act toward God and other people, and eight proscribe actions, including the five "thou shalt nots" (see Exodus 20:3–17). Note that five of the divinely ordered prohibitions are against the commission of acts that could result in harm to others, such as killing and stealing. God gave us commandments that will, if obeyed, lead to good relations with others and therefore promote earthly social order. More general Judeo-Christian moral guidelines are the Golden Rule ("do unto others as you would have them do unto you") and love of one's neighbor (Matthew 19:19), both of which are useful prescriptions for harmonious social life.

Another social function of religion is to enhance the cohesion of society by making people feel their interdependence on one another and on their traditions. Emile Durkheim, a French sociologist of the early twentieth century, was influential in formulating this perspective. Durkheim's view was that the main function of religion in human society is to promote *social solidarity,* meaning that religion has the effect of bringing people together and enhancing their sense of unity, cohesion, and reliance on their society's customs. Groups of people who share the same beliefs and who gather periodically to perform common rituals experience a feeling of oneness and harmony. Religion exists, Durkheim believed, because it is socially useful or—stated differently—functional for society as a whole.

Numerous social scientists have championed the sociological interpretation of religion. (In fact, if any interpretation can be said to be *the* most popular, this is it.) We present several examples of sociological approaches to specific religious phenomena later in this chapter.

Sphere of Supernatural Intervention

One way religions differ is the sphere—or the range of human activities and natural occurrences—in which spiritual powers are believed to have an influence. A religious person in modern North America is likely to have a relatively narrow conception of the realms of personal and public life in which God intervenes. (This varies with denomination and personal belief.) Most of us do not use divine action to explain the failure of a company, car wrecks, illnesses, great wealth, poverty, or the outcome of elections. We are more likely to blame poor business practices, carelessness, coincidence, poor eating or drinking or exercise habits, and personal skill or laziness for misfortune or success. The same is true for natural occurrences: Most of us do not blame God for earthquakes, floods, hurricanes, volcanoes, and other natural disasters, which we attribute to natural forces.

In contrast, in most religions of the preindustrial world, people believe that spiritual powers actively intervene in a wide range of human activities and natural events. Rituals are performed to request or command that their future intervention be favorable or that they remove the effects of their previous malevolent interference. A few examples will illustrate.

- The matrilineal Ndembu of Zambia attribute various female health problems to the actions of ancestral spirits. Infertility, frequent miscarriages, stillbirths, and other reproductive disorders are explained by the actions of one of the victim's ancestresses, who is punishing the woman for "forgetting her ancestress" or for doing something of which her ancestress disapproves. The cure for the affliction consists of a lengthy ritual that makes the victim "remember" her dead relative.
- Some central Canadian Inuit believe that prolonged inability to find game may be caused by a goddess who is angry over the misconduct of members of the camp. They persuade the goddess to release the game by performing a ritual in which camp members publicly confess their violations.

- To help them locate caribou, the Naskapi foragers of eastern Canada used divination. They heated a caribou shoulder blade over a fire until it cracked. The pattern of cracks in the scapula told them the direction in which to look for game.
- The Trobriand Islanders periodically go on long overseas voyages to acquire the shell valuables that are symbols of status and wealth in their culture. They perform magic to induce their trading partner to give a certain valuable to them rather than to someone else. The ocean trip is hazardous because of the possibility of sudden storms, so before they depart the voyagers also perform magic to ensure favorable weather.
- The Hopi of the American Southwest believe that rainfall is brought by supernatural beings. These beings, called *kachinas,* live in the peaks of mountains to the southwest of Hopi villages. In the spring and summer, Hopi believe that kachinas dwell in the villages. During this period men wearing masks of the kachinas perform ritual dances. The spirit enters the body of the dancer, who thus becomes the kachina. Rain is brought to the Hopi's cornfields by the dances.

These examples illustrate three areas of human life in which the supernatural commonly is believed to intervene. First, various peoples believe that supernatural powers are responsible for success or failure of many group activities, such as hunting and trading. Second, spiritual beings or forces frequently must be asked to bring about some desired natural event, such as good weather and the return of game. Finally, supernatural powers are believed to interfere in the personal lives of individuals, making them ill or poor, or healthy and wealthy. This last kind of intervention is universal, or nearly so. We now consider how religion helps people account for and deal with misfortunes.

Supernatural Explanations of Misfortune

One occurrence that many cultures attribute to the action of spiritual powers is personal misfortune, including death, illness, and events that many Westerners consider accidents. Many beliefs and rituals of various societies are concerned with explaining, preventing, and curing illness and disease. Cross-culturally, two major complexes of beliefs about illness are most common.

First, many people believe that sickness is caused by the action of some spiritual power. Sickness often is thought to be brought on by a taboo violation, which some supernatural being or force is punishing. Other societies believe that the ancestral spirits of kin groups cause their members to become ill because of conflict or bad feelings within the group. (We consider ancestral cults later in this chapter.) The same kinds of beliefs may apply to accidents that many Westerners attribute to bad luck or carelessness. Drownings, falls, snakebites, prolonged failure to succeed at some activity—such events are likely to be seen as evidence of unfavorable supernatural intervention. The victim has offended a god or spirit, who brings an "accident" as punishment.

Second, many people think that illnesses or other misfortunes are caused by the action of some evil human who is using special supernatural powers against the afflicted person. Belief that certain people, called *sorcerers* and *witches,* have powers to harm others by mystical means is enormously widespread among humanity. Sometimes witches and sorcerers are thought to strike randomly and maliciously against people who are innocent of any wrongdoing. More commonly they direct their evil magic or thoughts toward those against whom they have a grudge. Sorcery and witchcraft are worth considering in more detail.

Sorcery

Sorcery is the performance of rites and spells intended to cause supernatural harm to others. In come cultures, almost everyone learns to harm their enemies by sorcery as an ordinary part of enculturation. Among other peoples, sorcery is a more specialized practice: Only certain people inherit or acquire the knowledge of how to recite spells and perform the rites correctly.

In 1890, Sir James Frazer proposed that magic (including sorcery) is based on two kinds of logical principles or assumptions. Both involve a symbolic identification of something (e.g., an object or action) with something else (e.g., an event or a person).

One kind of logical principle on which magic is based is called the *imitative principle,* often stated as the premise that like produces like. That is, if an object resembles a person and the sorcerer mutilates the object, then the same effect will happen to the person. The so-called voodoo doll is a familiar example of the imitative principle: An image or effigy is made of the enemy; some act is performed on the effigy; and the enemy supposedly experiences the same fate. The effigy symbolically represents the person, so to mutilate the effigy is believed to harm the person. In another kind of imitative magic, the magician or sorcerer mimics the effects she or he wants to produce. For example, sorcerers among the Dobu of Melanesia cast spells by imitating the symptoms of the disease they want to afflict on their victims.

The second kind of logical premise underlying magic and sorcery is called the *contagious principle of magic,* which is the assumption that power comes from contact. That is, things that were once in contact with someone can be used in rites and spells to make things happen to that person. By performing the correct rites and spells on such objects as hair clippings, bodily excretions, nail parings, infant umbilical cords, or jewelry and clothing, harm can be done to one's enemies. In societies in which sorcery rests on the contagious principle, people must be careful to dispose of objects they have been in contact with, lest one of their enemies use them for sorcery. As with the imitative principle, a symbolic identification is made between the objects and the victim. But in the case of the contagious principle, the symbolic equation comes from previous contact rather than from resemblance: By acquiring possession of something once belonging to a person, supernatural power is acquired over that person.

Whether based on the imitative or contagious principle, beliefs about sorcery are affected by the patterned relationships between individuals and groups. In all societies, certain kinds of social relationships are especially likely to be fraught with built-in conflicts. Co-wives of a polygynous man may be jealous over their husband's favors or be in competition over an inheritance for their children. People who have married into a kin group or village may be viewed as outsiders who retain loyalty to their own natal families. Two men who want the same woman, or two women who want the same man, have reasons to hate one another. Men who are rivals for a political office have conflicts of interest.

These and other kinds of relationships are sources of strain and conflict. Which relationships are likely to cause strain and conflict vary with the way the society is organized: Brothers-in-law are allies in one society, but their interests regularly conflict in another society, for instance. In any case, the relationships most likely to be troublesome are *patterned.*

If you were brought up in a culture that explained illness or accident by sorcery, and if you or a relative became ill or suffered misfortune, you would not suspect just anyone of harming you. You would ask who has a motive to perform evil magic against you? Who envies you? Who would profit from your sickness or death? Who harbors a grudge against you? With whom have you recently quarreled? These people are your prime suspects, and they are the ones you or your family are most likely to accuse.

Members of most cultures reason in much the same way. They believe that sorcerers do not strike randomly, but harm only their enemies or people towards whom they feel anger, envy, or ill-will. But bad feelings are more likely to exist in certain kinds of relationships than in others, within a single society. Accusations of sorcery, therefore, usually follow the prevalent lines of conflict: Because people who stand in the same kinds of relationships are likely to accuse one another again and again, sorcery accusations are patterned.

Witchcraft

Witchcraft is another explanation that people in many societies give for misfortune. There is no universally applicable distinction between sorcery and witchcraft. Whereas sorcery usually involves the use of rites and spells to commit a foul deed, here we define **witchcraft** as the use of psychic power alone to cause harm to others. Sorcerers manipulate objects; witches need only think malevolent thoughts to turn their anger, envy, or hatred into evil deeds. (Our own language's distinction between the two—witches are female, sorcerers usually male—is not useful cross-culturally.) Many cultures believe in the existence of both kinds of malevolent power, so sorcery and witchcraft often are found among the same people. Like sorcery accusations, accusations of witchcraft are likely to be patterned, for people most often believe that both witches and sorcerers harm only people they dislike, hate, envy, or have a conflict with.

Cultures vary in the characteristics they attribute to witches and in how witches cause harm. A few examples illustrate some of the diversity.

- The Navajo associate witches with the worst imaginable sins—witches commit incest, bestiality (sex with animals), and necrophilia (sex with corpses); they change themselves into animals; they cannibalize infants; and so on.
- The Nyakyusa of Tanzania hold that witches are motivated mainly by their lust for food; accordingly, they suck dry the udders of people's cattle and devour the internal organs of their human neighbors while they sleep.
- The Azande of the southern Sudan believe that witches possess an inherited substance that leaves their bodies at night and gradually eats away at the flesh and internal organs of their victims. Witches, as well as their victims, are considered to be unfortunate, because the Azande believe that a person can be a witch without even knowing it. Witches can do nothing to rid themselves permanently of their power, although they can be forced to stop bewitching some particular individual by ridding themselves of bad feelings against their victim.
- The Ibibio of Nigeria believe that witches operate by removing the spiritual essence (soul) of their enemies and placing it into an animal; this makes the victim sick, and he dies when the witches

slaughter and consume the animal. Sometimes Ibibio witches decide to torture, rather than kill, a person. In that case they remove the victim's soul and put it in water or hang it over a fireplace or flog it in the evenings; the afflicted person will remain sick until the witches get what they want out of him or her.

- The Lugbara, a people of Uganda, claim that witches—who are always men—walk around at night disguised as rats or other nocturnal animals. Sometimes they defecate blood around the household of their victims, who wake up sick the next morning.

Such beliefs, it might appear to someone who does not share them, are logically outrageous; no one's soul leaves his or her body at night to cavort with other witches, for example. It might seem that these beliefs are socially harmful as well; beliefs in witchcraft, fear of witchcraft, and accusations of witchcraft engender conflict and aggression among a people. Finally, the treatment many suspected and "proven" witches receive offends our notions of social justice. As we know from the witch hunts of European and American history, the truly innocent victims of witchcraft often are the accused witches, who sometimes are cruelly executed for crimes they could not have committed.

Interpretations of Sorcery and Witchcraft

Anthropologists wonder why beliefs in witches and sorcery are so widespread, given their seemingly harmful effects and the injustices that frequently result from them. Why should so many cultures independently have developed such beliefs? Why should most of the world's peoples think that some or all of their misfortunes are caused by the supernatural powers of their enemies? What use or value could a human society possibly derive from accusations of witchcraft or sorcery?

Many answers have been offered to these questions. In line with the overall theoretical approaches discussed earlier, the answers fall into two categories: cognitive and sociological. (In the following discussion, for simplicity, we use the term *witchcraft* to refer to both witchcraft and sorcery because the ideas presented have been applied to both kinds of beliefs.)

Cognitive Interpretations   The most influential of the various cognitive approaches is that witchcraft explains unfortunate events. The argument is that most people find the idea of coincidence or accident intellectually unsatisfying when some misfortune happens to them or their loved ones, so they search for other causes. Their logic is something like this: I have enemies who wish me harm, and harm just came to me, so my enemies are responsible.

The classic example of how people account for misfortune by reference to the actions of witches comes from among the Azande, an African people. The Azande attribute prolonged serious illnesses and many other personal misfortunes to witchcraft. Ethnographer E. E. Evans-Pritchard (1976) describes their beliefs:

> Witchcraft is ubiquitous. . . . There is no niche or corner of Zande culture into which it does not twist itself. If blight seizes the groundnut crop it is witchcraft; if the bush is vainly scoured for game it is witchcraft; if women laboriously bail water out of a pool and are rewarded by but a few small fish it is witchcraft; . . . if a wife is sulky and unresponsive to her husband it is witchcraft; if a prince is cold and distant with his subject it is witchcraft; if a magical rite fails to achieve its purpose it is witchcraft; if, in fact, any failure or misfortune falls upon any one at any time and in relation to any of the manifold activities of his life it may be due to witchcraft (18).

All this does not mean that the Azande are ignorant of cause and effect and therefore attribute every misfortune to some witch who is out to get them. When a Zande man seeks shelter in a granary and its roof falls and injures him, he blames witchcraft. But Zande know very well that granary roofs collapse because termites eat the wood that supports them. They do not attribute the collapse of granaries in general to witchcraft; it is the collapse of this particular granary at this particular time with this particular person inside that is caused by witchcraft. Do not granaries sometimes fall with no one sitting inside them? And do not people often relax in granaries without the roof falling? It is the coincidence between the collapse and the presence of a particular person—a coincidence that many other peoples consider bad luck—that witchcraft explains.

Another benefit people gain is that witches serve as scapegoats. When things are going poorly, people do not always know why. Witchcraft provides an explanation. It also provides people with a means to do something about the situation: identify, accuse, and punish the witch responsible. If, as often is the case, things still do not improve, there are always other yet-to-be-identified witches! People can blame many of their troubles on witches—evil enemies conspiring against them—rather than on their personal inadequacies or on bad luck.

Sociological Interpretations One sociological hypothesis is that witchcraft reinforces the cultural norms and values that help individuals live harmoniously with one another. Every culture has notions of how individuals ideally ought to act toward others (see Chapter 2). Witches typically are the antithesis of these cultural ideals. They act like animals, or actually change themselves into animals. They mate with relatives. They often put on a false front, pretending to be your friend by day while they eat your liver

by night. They have no respect for age or authority. They are in league with the forces of evil (in the Judeo-Christian tradition, witches made compacts with the Devil, agreeing to be his servant in return for worldly pleasures.) All the most despicable personal characteristics of people are wrapped up in the personality of witches, whom everyone is supposed to hate. So witches symbolize all that is undesirable, wicked, and hateful. Just as one should despise witches, so should one hate all that they stand for. In short, by providing a hated symbol of the abnormal and the antisocial, the witch strengthens cultural conceptions of normatively approved social behavior.

Another argument is that witches provide an outlet for repressed aggression, and thus beliefs about witches lower the overall amount of conflict in a society. Writing about the Navajo in 1944, Clyde Kluckhohn argued that Navajo culture emphasizes cooperation and maintenance of good relationships between members of the same extended household. When bad feelings do develop within the household, Navajo culture leads people not to express them. But pent-up hostilities have an outlet in the form of witches, whom people are allowed to hate and gossip about. Because most people the Navajo believe to be witches are members of distant groups, usually little action is taken against them. Solidarity between relatives of the in-group is preserved by displacing hostility to people of the out-group.

Another hypothesis is that witchcraft beliefs serve as a mechanism of social control. This might work in two ways. First, many people believe in the existence of witchcraft but do not know which specific members of their community are witches. This leads individuals to be careful not to make anyone angry, since the offended party may be a witch. Second, individuals who fail to conform to local cultural norms of behavior are most likely to be suspected and accused of being witches. People who are always mad at somebody; who carry grudges for prolonged periods; who are known to be envious and resentful of the success of others; who have achieved wealth but selfishly refuse to share it in the culturally accepted manner—such violators of these and other standards for behavior frequently are believed to be the likely perpetrators of witchcraft. Fear of being accused and punished presumably increases adherence to norms and ideals of behavior.

These are some of the major ideas that anthropologists have proposed about the benefits people derive from beliefs that witches and sorcerers cause many of their misfortunes. But notice that none of them explain the origin of such beliefs. They all state: "Assuming a people believe in witches or sorcerers (or both), individuals or groups derive positive benefits from these beliefs." Like other functionalist approaches (see Chapter 4), these theories specify the rewards the individual or society gains as a *consequence* of beliefs in witches and sorcerers. They do not answer the *causal* question: "Why do some cultures develop a belief that misfortune is caused by the supernatural powers of enemies?" For not all cultures have such beliefs: some hold, for example, that illness is attributable to punishment by ancestors, or violations of a taboo, or divine retribution, or invasion of their bodies by invisible microorganisms that they themselves have never seen but that experts assure them exist.

Varieties of Religious Organization

There is no way to present an overview of the diversity of human religions without distortion. Just as we oversimplify a given culture when we classify it as (for example) horticultural, polygynous, patrilineal, tribal, and egalitarian, so do we simplify when we pigeonhole its religion as (for example) shamanistic or monotheistic. Nonetheless, a typology of religion is useful, because it gives a general picture of religious diversity among humanity.

In the 1960s, an anthropologist named Anthony Wallace proposed a classification of religious diversity that is influential and quite useful for our purposes. His typology is based on the concept of *cult*. As we use the term here, *cult* does not refer to some exotic, offbeat, irrational, and (usually) short-lived set of beliefs that grow up around a "cult leader." Rather, we use the term in a neutral way to refer to an organized system of beliefs and practices pertaining to the control or worship of specific supernatural powers. Thus, rituals intended to help sick people get well might be called *curing cults;* rituals believed to bring precipitation might be called *rain cults;* and so forth.

Defined in this way, cults have diverse and sometimes quite specific purposes. It is important to understand that the members of a given society can participate in many different kinds of cults, each with a specific orientation such as hunting, rain, war, agriculture, salvation, protection, initiation, divination, and so forth. Therefore, a *cult* is not the same as the *religion* of a given culture. Rather, religion is a more inclusive concept: A society's total religion may include many different cults devoted to different purposes like curing illness, controlling weather, worshipping gods, foretelling the future, renewing nature, protecting people from enemies, and keeping ancestral spirits happy.

Wallace's classification distinguishes four kinds of cults.

- **Individualistic cults**. Each individual has a personal relationship with one or more supernatural powers, who serve as his or her guardians and protectors. The aid of the powers is solicited when needed for personal goals.
- **Shamanistic cults**. Some individuals—shamans—are believed to have relationships with the supernatural that ordinary people lack. They use these powers primarily for socially valuable purposes, to help (especially cure) others in need. They may also act on behalf of their band or village to cause supernatural harm to the group's enemies.
- **Communal cults**. The members of a particular group gather periodically for the performance of rituals that are believed to benefit the group as a whole, or some individual in it. There are no full-time religious specialists, as is also true of individualistic and shamanistic cults.
- **Ecclesiastical cults**. The hallmark of ecclesiastical cults is the presence of full-time religious practitioners who form a religious bureaucracy. The practice of religion is carried out by formal, specialized officials—priests—who perform rituals that are believed to benefit the society as a whole. The priesthood usually is materially supported by institutionalized governmental authorities through taxation or redistributive tribute (see Chapter 7).

Although any given culture usually has more than one of these kinds of cults, the cults are not randomly distributed among the peoples of the world. Rather, there is a rough evolutionary sequence to their occurrence. For example, in many foraging bands and horticultural tribes—such as the Netsilik, !Kung, and Yąnomamö—shamanistic cults are common, whereas ecclesiastical cults occur mainly in stratified chiefdoms and states. If we consider the religion of a people to be composed of some number of cults, more kinds of cults are found in states than in tribes.

But the evolutionary matching of kinds of cults with kinds of economic and political organizations is only very rough and general. For instance, the aboriginal peoples of Australia had communal cults, although they were foragers and lived in bands. Many tribes of the North American Great Plains had individualistic, shamanistic, and communal cults, although they were primarily foragers.

Further frustrating our desire to "pigeonhole" religions is the fact that in many societies there are several religions, sometimes at odds with one another. In the Caribbean nation of Haiti, voudon ("voodoo") persists even though the official hierarchy of the Catholic church has tried to eliminate it for over a century. Multiethnic nations also have a variety of religions within their borders (see Chapter 17).

But these complications should not obscure the general pattern. The religions of hunter-gatherer bands do differ generally and significantly from those of complex chiefdoms and states. We now discuss these varieties of religious organization and how they relate to economic and political organization.

Individualistic Cults

The defining characteristic of individualistic cults is that individuals intentionally seek out particular spirits or other supernatural powers to protect and help them. Individualistic cults emphasize direct, personal interactions between people and the supernatural.

The most well-known example of individualistic cults is the **vision quest**. It is widespread among Native American peoples but is especially important for the Great Plains tribes. To the Plains Indians, the world is charged with spiritual energy and supernatural power. Power exists in inanimate objects such as rocks or mountains and in living animals and plants. Human beings require the aid of the supernatural in many activities—in hunting, warfare, and times of sickness or other troubles.

Spiritual power comes to individuals in visions. These visions play an important role in the religious life of the people because it is through them that people achieve the personal contact with the supernatural that is essential in various endeavors. Spiritual powers occasionally make contact with individuals for no apparent reason, coming to them as they sleep or even as they are walking or riding alone.

More often humans—especially young men—have to seek out these powers through an active search, or quest, whose purpose is to acquire a vision. There are places that supernatural powers are believed to frequent: certain hills, mountains, or bluffs. A young man goes to such a location alone. There he smokes and fasts, appealing to a power to take pity on him. Among one tribe, the Crow, sometimes a man will even amputate part of a finger or cut his body to arouse pity. The vision commonly appears on the fourth day, since four is a sacred number to the Crow. Many young men fail at their quest, but others do achieve visions.

The supernatural power that contacts a man and the manner in which it manifests itself vary. Sometimes he only hears the spirit speak to him. Sometimes it comes in the form of a dream-like story. In other instances it simply materializes before his eyes, taking the form of a bear, a bison, an eagle, or some other large animal. Sometimes small animals like rabbits, field mice, and dogs also appear.

The power tells the man how it will help him. It might give him the ability to predict the future, locate enemies, find game, become a powerful warrior, or cure illness. It tells him the things he will have to do to keep his power—what songs to sing, how to paint his war shield, how to wear his hair, and so forth. It also tells the man some things he cannot do; for example, if the power comes from the eagle, the man might be prohibited from killing "his brother," the eagle. As long as he continues to behave in the prescribed manner, the power will be his supernatural protector, or guardian spirit. It aids him in his endeavors and gives him special powers other men do not have.

There is no known culture in which individualistic cults constitute the entire religion. Even among Plains Indians, in which this kind of cult is unusually well developed, shamanistic and communal cults also exist.

Shamanism

A **shaman**, or **medicine man**, is a person with a culturally defined special relationship to supernatural powers, which he frequently uses to cure sickness. In many societies (especially among many foraging peoples), the shaman is the only kind of religious practitioner; that is, he practices the only kind of ritual and possesses the only kind of abilities not available to ordinary people. Shamans seldom are specialized practitioners. They carry out their tasks whenever their services are needed, usually in return for a gift or fee; but otherwise they live much as everyone else.

Shamans are believed to possess several qualities. They have access to the power of spiritual beings, called *spirit helpers*. The effectiveness of a shaman in curing (or causing harm) is believed to derive from the potency of his spirit helpers and from his ability to contact them and get them to do his bidding. Contact with one's spirit helpers commonly is made by achieving an altered state of consciousness. This altered state (referred to as a *trance*) is reached in various ways: through intake of drugs, ritual chanting, or participation in percussive or rhythmic music. People quite often believe that one of a shaman's spirit helpers has physically entered (possessed) the shaman's body. The spirit takes over his body and speaks to the assembled audience through his mouth. When possessed, the shaman becomes a *medium,* or mouthpiece for the spirits—he may lose control over his actions and his voice changes its quality because a spirit is speaking through him.

The way in which a person becomes a shaman varies from people to people. Shamans usually are considered to have knowledge and powers lacking among other people. They acquire these in three major ways. In some societies they undergo a period of special training as an apprentice to a practicing shaman, who teaches the novice chants and songs and how to achieve the trance state. Many shamans must have endured difficult

Curing is a main responsibility of shamans. Healing often involves the removal of foreign substances believed to be the source of illness. This Amazonian shaman sucks on the patient's body to remove the object causing sickness.

deprivations, such as prolonged fasting, the consumption of foods culturally considered disgusting, or years of sexual abstinence. Finally, in many societies shamans are people who have experienced some unusual event. For example, they have miraculously recovered from a serious illness or injury, or they claim to have had an unusual dream or vision in which some spirit called them to be its mouthpiece.

In most cultures, the shaman's major role is curing. Again, how the shaman performs this role varies. By considering an ethnographic example of sickness and curing, we can see shamans in action. We also can use the case to suggest an answer to one of the questions frequently asked about shamanism: How does the belief that shamans have the power to make people well persist, even though many of their clients die?

The Jívaro are a rain forest people of Ecuador. Jívaro believe that most sickness is caused by the actions of their human enemies (rather than by natural causes). Jívaro shamans acquire their power from their control over their personal spirit helpers, which live in their bellies in the form of tiny magical darts. A man becomes a shaman by presenting a gift to an existing shaman, who regurgitates some of his spirit helpers, which the novice swallows. If the novice drinks a hallu-

cinogenic drug nightly for ten days and abstains from sexual intercourse for at least three months—the longer the better—he will acquire the power to transform any small objects (insects, worms, plants, etc.) he ingests into magical darts.

The Jívaro recognize two kinds of shamans: bewitching shamans, who have the ability to make people sick, and curing shamans, who try to make people well by counteracting the evil deeds of bewitching shamans. By ingesting and storing many magical darts in his body, a bewitching shaman can later harm his enemies. He causes illness by propelling one or more magical darts into the body of his victim; unless the darts are removed by a curing shaman, the victim will die. To effect the cure, a curing shaman first drinks tobacco juice and other drugs, which give him the power to see into the body of the victim. Once he locates them, the curer sucks out and captures the magical darts; if the cure is successful, the darts return to their owner and the patient recovers.

Many patients die, which means that the curing shamans often are ineffective. How, then, does the belief in curing abilities of shamans persist? The answer is that the Jívaro believe that a supernatural battle is waged between the bewitching and the curing shamans. Bewitching shamans have two special spirit helpers. One, called a *pasuk,* looks like an ordinary tarantula to people who are not shamans; the other takes the form of a bird. A bewitching shaman can order his pasuk or spirit bird to remain near the house of the victim, shooting additional magic darts into him as the curing shaman sucks them out. If the victim dies, Jívaro believe it may be because the darts shot by the pasuk and spirit bird were too many for the curing shaman to remove. Or, it may be because the bewitching shaman has more power than the curing shaman.

Aside from serving as an example of shamanism, the Jívaro show how beliefs about supernatural causes and shamanistic cures for illness form a logically coherent system. If the patient recovers, as usually happens, the ability of the shaman to cure is confirmed. If the victim dies, Jívaro believe this event, too, is explained in terms that are consistent with existing beliefs. Events in the real world—getting better or getting worse, living or dying—do not disprove the beliefs because the belief system itself covers such events and contingencies.

Faith healers, those shamans of modern times, use similar premises. God's power to heal is unquestionable, and faith healers seldom publicly doubt their own calling. If the cancer is not cured, if the blind do not see, if the disabled do not walk away, if the heart patient does not recover, the fault often is with themselves: They had too little faith.

Communal Cults

Like shamanism, communal cults have no full-time religious specialists. Rituals organized communally frequently have leaders—often an elderly person or someone with a special interest in the outcome of some ritual—who manipulate the symbolic objects or who address the supernatural. But the cult leaders are unspecialized—they do not make their living as religious practitioners.

Communal rituals are held to intercede with the supernatural on behalf of some group of people, such as a descent group, an age group, a village, or a caste. To illustrate, we consider two widespread kinds of communal rituals organized by descent groups: **ancestral cults** and **totemism**.

Ancestral Cults   Practically all religions hold that people have a spiritual dimension—what we call a *soul*—that lives on after the physical body has perished. Beliefs about the fate of the soul after death vary widely. Some religions—such as Hinduism—believe that it is reincarnated into another person or animal. Others hold that the soul passes into a spiritual plane, where it exists eternally with a community of other souls and has no further effects on the living. Still others believe that souls become malevolent after death, turning into ghosts that cause accidents or sickness or that terrify the living.

One of the most common beliefs about the fate of souls after death is that they interact with and affect their living descendants. A great many peoples hold such beliefs. They usually practice rituals to induce the spirits of their deceased ancestors to do favors for them or simply to leave them alone. Beliefs and rituals surrounding the interactions between the living and their departed relatives are called *ancestral cults,* or *ancestor worship.*

The Lugbara, a people of Uganda, illustrate ancestral cults. The patrilineage is an important social group to Lugbara. Its members are subject to the authority of lineage elders. As the most important member of the lineage, elders are expected to oversee the interests and harmony of the entire group. They serve as the guardians of the lineage's morality, although they have no power to punish violations physically.

Lugbara believe that the spirit of a deceased person may become an ancestral ghost of her or his lineage. The ghost punishes living descendants who violate Lugbara ideals of behavior toward lineage mates. People who fight with their kinsmen (especially a relative older than oneself), who deceive or steal from their lineage mates, or who fail to carry out their duties toward others are liable to be punished by an ancestral ghost. Sometimes this happens because a ghost sees an offense committed and causes illness to the offender. More commonly, the ghosts do not act on their own initiative to make someone sick. Rather, the ghosts act on the thoughts of an elder who is indignant because of the actions of some member of the lineage. John Middleton (1965) describes Lugbara beliefs about the power of lineage elders to cause illness by invoking ghosts.

> [The elder] sits near his shrines in his compound and thinks about the sinner's behavior. His thoughts are known by the ghosts and they then send sickness to the offender. He "thinks these words in his heart"; he does not threaten or curse the offender. For a senior man to do this is part of his expected role. It is part of his "work," to "cleanse the lineage home." Indeed, an elder who does not do so when justified would be lacking in sense of duty toward his lineage. (76).

In the Lugbara example we see how elders maintain harmony and cooperation in the lineage. This is a common feature of ancestral cults.

Why do some societies have ancestral cults in which ghosts are believed to punish their descendants who violate cultural prescriptions of right behavior? Like most "why" questions, this one is controversial. But many anthropologists agree that such beliefs are related to the degree of importance of large kin groups in a society. The greater the importance of kin groups such as lineages and clans in making public decisions, regulating access to resources, allocating roles, controlling behavior, and so on, the more likely a society is to develop an ancestral cult.

Totemism   Totemism, another widespread form of communal cult, is the cultural belief that human groups have a special mystical relationship with natural objects such as animals, plants, and, sometimes, nonliving things. The object (or objects) with which a group is associated is known as its *totem*. The group most often is a unilineal kin group, such as a clan. The totem frequently serves as a name of the group, for example, the Bear clan, the Eagle clan.

The nature of the relationship between the members of the group and its totem varies widely. Sometimes the totem is used simply for identification of the group and its members, much like our surnames. Often there is a mystical association between the group and its totem object: People believe they are like their totem in some respects.

Members of other groups also resemble their totems. In many populations—most notably among some of the aboriginal peoples of Australia—the members of a clan treat their totem like a clanmate, believing that the totem gave birth to their ancestors in a mythical period. The welfare of the clan is mystically associated with the welfare of the totem, so periodically the clan gathers for rituals that ensure the reproduction of its totem.

Ecclesiastical Cults

In Chapters 6 and 11, we saw that a high degree of specialization accompanied the development of civilization. Among New World peoples such as the ancient Incas, Aztecs, and Mayans, and in the Old World cities of ancient Mesopotamia, Egypt, China, Japan, and India, this specialization extended into the religious dimension of cultural systems. Rather than organizing rituals on a communal basis—in which a wide range of people controlled and participated in the performance—a formal bureaucracy of religious specialists controlled most public rituals. The religious bureaucracy probably also had a large voice in formulation of the religious laws, which prescribed certain kinds of punishments for those who violated them.

These religious specialists are known as **priests**. It is instructive to compare priests with shamans. In addition to their more specialized status, priests differ from shamans in several respects. First, most shamans perform their ritual functions without aid from other shamans; indeed, as we have seen, many peoples believe that enemy shamans engage in supernatural battles with one another. In contrast, priests are organized into a hierarchical priesthood under the sponsorship of a formal government, the state. Second, priests undergo a lengthy period of special training because they must master the complex rituals needed to perform their role. Third, the priesthood was at or near the top of the social ladder in ancient civilizations, so individual priests lived much better than the population at large. Fourth, shamans typically perform mainly crisis rituals, whenever some person requires their services. The rituals at which priests officiate tend to be calendrical—they occur at regular intervals because the gods that the rituals are intended to appease demand regular praise or sacrifice.

A final difference is especially revealing. With the development of a *priesthood* comes a strong distinction between priest and layperson. The layperson has little control over the timing of religious performances or the content of myths. The population at large relies on the priesthood to keep it in proper relation to supernatural powers. This creates a sense of spiritual dependence on the priesthood and on the state apparatus that sponsors

it, a dependence that reinforces the high degree of stratification found in states.

These state-sponsored cults are called *ecclesiastical* (meaning "of or pertaining to the church") because their priesthood was highly organized and their rituals usually were held in grandiose buildings that served as temples. The entire ecclesiastical cult was under the control of the government. Officials exacted tribute or taxes to finance the construction of temples, the livelihood of the priesthood, the sacrifices that often accompanied state rituals, and other expenses needed to support and organize religious activities on a fantastically large scale.

There is little question that ecclesiastical cults provided a body of myth and belief that supported the domination of the ruling dynasty. (This is not to say that this function totally explains these cults or that it constitutes their entire significance.) This is seen by the content of the cults' beliefs, myths, and rituals, which almost invariably express the dependence of the entire population on the ruler's well-being and on the periodic performance of rituals. A common belief of official state religions is that the ruler is a god-king: He not only rules by divine mandate but is himself a god or somehow partakes of divine qualities. This was true of most of the ancient civilizations and of the states that developed in sub-Saharan Africa.

Many official rituals of ecclesiastical cults are held to keep the entire polity in beneficial relationship with supernatural beings. For example, the state religion of the ancient Aztec taught that the gods had to be periodically appeased or they would cause the world to end in a cataclysm. To keep the gods' goodwill, the priesthood periodically performed human sacrifice at temples, offering the heart of the victim (usually a war captive) to the deities. The ancient Egyptians believed that their pharaoh would rule in the afterlife—just as in the present world—so when he died, he took much of his wealth, his wives, and his servants into the next world with him.

Ecclesiastical cults everywhere consumed enormous resources, but they did not wipe out other kinds of cults. Common people usually continued to rely on local shamans for curing, to practice magic, to believe in witches and sorcerers, and to worship their ancestors. In China, for example, each household and lineage continued to revere its own ancestors.

Most Christian denominations—Catholic and the diverse Protestant sects—have an ecclesiastical character. In medieval Europe, the authority of the Catholic Church was tightly interwoven with the exercise of secular power, although there often was conflict between pope and king. Only in the past few centuries has the formal alliance between the power of government and the power of the gods been broken for any length of time. (Informally and unofficially, religion continues to prop up political systems—

God seems always to be on "our side," according to many religious people in our own and other modern nations.) We should not assume that even this official separation between church and state will necessarily be permanent. As the recent history of Iran and Afghanistan suggests, the intermingling of political and ecclesiastical authorities can be reborn even in the modern world.

Revitalization Movements

So far we have discussed religions in cultures that are changing only slowly. Under conditions of rapid change, many peoples have turned to supernatural beings for aid and protection when their way of life or their lives themselves are threatened by contact with powerful outsiders. To preserve their way of life or to cope with changing conditions, large numbers of people join organized movements, usually called **revitalization movements**.

Revitalization movements are most likely to occur in a society when three conditions coalesce: (1) rapid change, often caused by exposure to unfamiliar people, customs, and objects; (2) foreign domination, which leads to a sense of cultural inferiority, especially common in colonial situations; and (3) the perception of relative deprivation, meaning that people see themselves as lacking wealth, power, and esteem relative to those who dominate them. The movements are especially common in situations of colonialism, but colonialism does not always produce them.

Prophets and Revelations

Revitalization movements usually originate with an individual—a **prophet**—who claims to have had a dream or vision. Sometimes the prophet says that he or she is a messiah, or savior, sent by a spiritual being to save the world from destruction. In the dream or vision the prophet received a message—a **revelation**—from a god, an ancestor, or another spiritual power.

Revelations typically include two kinds of information given by the spirit. The first is a statement about what has gone wrong with the world, about why people's lives have changed for the worse. The introduction of corrupting foreign objects and habits—such as tobacco, alcohol, money, religions, or formal schooling—commonly are blamed for the troubles of today.

Members of the John Frum cargo cult in Tanna, Vanuatu, perform a ritual march. They await the return of their messiah, John Frum, who will bring wealth and a new life. This movement, which has also become a political party, has existed on the island of Tanna since the 1940s.

Second, prophets' revelations usually include a vision of a new world and a prescription for how to bring it about. In some cases the message is vague and secular, the prophet claiming that earthly lives will improve if people do (or stop doing) certain things. The message often is *apocalyptic:* The prophet says that the present world will end at a certain time, and only those who heed his message will be saved. The expulsion or death of foreigners is a frequent theme of apocalyptic visions: Foreigners will be drowned in a flood, burned in a fire, swallowed up by an earthquake, or killed by deities or ancestors. Another common theme is the reversal of existing political and economic dominance relations: Foreigners will work for us, we will have the wealth instead of them, we will tax them and make laws that they must obey, or some other inversion of the existing structure. Nearly always, the prophets' revelations are *syncretic;* that is, they combine elements of traditional myths, beliefs, and rituals with introduced elements.

Examples from two regions illustrate prophets, revelations, and the syncretism of revitalization movements.

Melanesian Cargo Cults

The area called *Melanesia* in the southwest Pacific has experienced numerous revitalization movements in the twentieth century. Melanesians placed great cultural emphasis on wealth—and the manipulation of the flow of wealth—as the route to becoming a big man or powerful leader. It is therefore not surprising that they were most interested in the material possessions of German, English, French, and Australian colonial powers. Because European wealth was brought to the islands by ship or plane, it became known as *cargo,* and the various movements that sprang up with the aim of acquiring it through ritual means became known as **cargo cults**.

To Melanesians, all Europeans were fantastically wealthy; yet the Melanesians seldom saw them do any work to earn their possessions. The whites who lived in the islands certainly did not know how to make tanks, cars, canned foods, radios, stoves, and so forth. In many traditional religions, technology was believed to have been made by deities or spirits, so it followed that European objects likewise were made by their God. Further, when the whites living in Melanesia wanted some new object, they simply made marks on papers and placed them in an envelope or asked for the object by speaking into metal things. Some weeks later, the object was delivered in ships or airplanes. It seemed to appear from nowhere. Surely the goods were made by spirits, and the meaningless acts the whites did to get their spirits to send cargo were rituals. Melanesians therefore believed that they, too, could acquire this wealth through the correct ritual procedure, which they frequently believed the whites were selfishly withholding from them.

Numerous prophets sprang up among diverse Melanesian peoples, each with his own vision or dream, each with his own story for why the Europeans had cargo and the Melanesians had none, and each claiming to know the secret ritual that would deliver the goods. The prophet often claimed to have received a visit from one of his ancestors or a native deity, who told him that the whites had been lying to people about how to get cargo.

The Garia, of the north coast of Papua New Guinea, illustrate some common themes of cargo cults. Like most other indigenous peoples, the Garia were visited by missionaries. Also, like many other peoples, the Garia initially adopted Christianity for reasons other than those the missionaries had in mind. They assumed that the whites knew the ritual that was the "road to cargo." The missionaries would give it to the Garia if only they practiced what the missionaries preached: church attendance, monogamy, worship of the true God, cessation of pagan practices such as sorcery and dancing, and so forth. Based on their belief that the missionary lifestyle and Christian rituals held the secret of cargo, many Garia converted to Christianity early in the twentieth century.

But the cargo did not arrive. The Garia grew angry with the missions because they concluded that the missionaries and other Europeans were withholding the true ritual secret of how to get cargo to keep all the wealth for themselves. In the 1930s and 1940s, two Garia prophets arose. They told the people that the missionaries had been telling them to worship the wrong gods! God and Jesus both were really deities of the Garia, not of whites. The Europeans knew the secret names of God and Jesus and asked them for the cargo with secret prayers. All along, Jesus had been trying to deliver the goods to the Garia, but the Jews were holding him captive in heaven. To free him, the Garia had to perform sacrificial rituals. To show him how poor they were and to make him feel sorry for them, they had to destroy all their native wealth objects. If they did these things, Jesus would give the cargo to the ancestral spirits of the Garia, who would in turn deliver it to the living.

Native American Movements

Revitalization movements occurred among American Indians, whose tragic sufferings at the hands of white traders, settlers, armies, and administrators are known to all twentieth-century Americans. Two movements were especially important, both of which were precipitated by a deterioration of tribal economic, social, and religious life.

Handsome Lake　By 1800 the Seneca of New York had lost most of their land to the state, settlers, and land speculators. Whites committed many atrocities against the Seneca in the 1780s and 1790s, partly because many Seneca supported the British during the American Revolutionary War. There were also the usual diseases—such as smallpox and measles, which wiped out millions of Native Americans all over the continent—that reduced the tribe to a fraction of its former numbers. Seneca men had been proud warriors, hunters, and fur traders, but all these activities became more difficult because of the loss of land and the presence of whites. The American government waged psychological warfare against them, intentionally corrupting their leaders with bribes and liquor and generally attempting to dehumanize and demoralize them.

Seneca men became victims of alcoholism and drank up most of what little money they could still earn from the fur trade. Neighboring peoples, once subject to the authority of the Seneca and other members of the League of the Iroquois, ridiculed them. A growth in witchcraft accusations increased the internal conflict and divisions of their communities. Many women lost their desire for children and took medicines that caused them to abort or become sterile altogether. A way of life—and indeed a people themselves—was dying.

In 1799 a Seneca man named Handsome Lake lay sick. He was cured by three angels, who gave him a message from the Creator. Handsome Lake reported that the Creator was saddened by the life of the people and angry because of their drunkenness, witchcraft, and taking of abortion medicines. The Seneca must repent of such deeds. Handsome Lake had two more visions within the next year. There would be an apocalypse in which the world would be destroyed by great drops of fire, consuming those who did not heed Handsome Lake's teachings. People could save themselves and delay the apocalypse by publicly confessing their wrongs, giving up sins such as witchcraft and drinking, and returning to the performance of certain traditional rituals.

The apocalypse did not occur, but Handsome Lake was able to give his teachings a new, more secular twist between 1803 and his death in 1815. He continued to preach temperance because the Creator had never intended whiskey to be used by Indians. He taught peace with both whites and other Indians. He urged that the scattered reservations of the Seneca be consolidated, so that the people could live together as one community. Family morality must be impeccable: Sons were to obey their fathers; divorce (commonplace among the Seneca in aboriginal times) was no longer to be allowed; adultery and domestic quarreling were to cease. Most important, Handsome Lake succeeded in changing the traditional division of labor, in which cultivation of crops was done by women and garden work by men was considered effeminate. Seneca men took up farming and animal husbandry and even fenced their fields and added new crops to their inventory.

Peyote Religion   Peyote is a small cactus that grows in the Rio Grande valley of Texas and northern Mexico. It produces a mild narcotic effect when eaten. The ritual use of peyote among Mexican Indians predated European conquest. However, its consumption as the central element in a revitalization movement dates only from the last two decades of the nineteenth century.

In 1875 the Southern Plains tribes, the Kiowa and Comanche, lost their land after they were defeated militarily. During their confinement to reservations in southwestern Oklahoma, the Lipan-Apache introduced them to peyote. By the 1880s the two tribes had made the cactus the center of a revitalization movement. Like many movements, peyotism subsequently spread, reaching about nineteen Indian groups in Oklahoma by 1899. It

ultimately was incorporated as an official church in 1914, with the name Koshiway's First Born Church of Christ. During the early twentieth century, the church spread rapidly to other Indian communities throughout the western United States and Canada. It exists today as the Native American Church.

The peyote movement had no single prophet or leader. Local churches developed their own versions of services and rituals. One early leader was John Wilson, a Caddo/Delaware from western Oklahoma who had learned to use peyote from the Comanche. While eating dinner in the early 1890s, Wilson collapsed. Thinking him dead, his family began preparations for the burial. But Enoch Parker, a Caddo, told the family that he had learned in a vision that Wilson was not dead. Indeed, Wilson revived three days later. He reported that a great Water Bird had sucked the breath and sin out of his body, causing his collapse. Jesus brought him back to life three days later, telling him that his sins had been removed and that he was to teach the Indian people to believe in God and to use peyote to communicate with him.

Until his death in 1901, Wilson proselytized the peyote religion among the Osage, Delaware, Quapaw, and other groups. He preached that they needed to believe in God and Jesus, work hard, act morally, and abstain from alcohol consumption. They were to abandon their traditional religious practices because the spirits that formerly had aided them could be used for evil as well as good purposes. Wilson attracted the greatest number of adherents among the Osage, who combined the use of peyote in worship services with the Christian teachings they had learned in mission schools.

Peyote was not integrated into Christian teachings among all Native Americans who adopted it for ritual use. It did, however, provide meaning and moral direction to Indian life during a period of rapid and harmful change.

What is the fate of revitalization movements? Many with apocalyptic messages simply disappear when the end of the world does not occur. Other movements were remarkably tenacious. In Melanesia, certain areas saw the rise and fall of numerous prophets, each claiming to have the cargo secret. People followed again and again because they had no other acceptable explanation for the existence of cargo, for why whites had it and they lacked it, or for how they could acquire it. Certainly their own worldly efforts—working for Europeans in mines and plantations, growing and selling coffee, copra, cocoa, and so forth—showed no signs of rewarding them with the fantastic wealth that whites enjoyed with virtually no effort. Cargo cults did not exactly disappear in some regions; instead, they transformed into a political movement or party. This was the fate of cargo cults among the Garia, Manus, Tannese, and some Malaitans.

Other movements do not wither away or transform into a more secular, political movement. They retain their religious character, frequently teaching that contentment is to be found within oneself rather than in worldly material things. After his death in 1815, Handsome Lake's exhortations on how to live became codified and still persist as a Native American church—the Old Way of Handsome Lake, also known as the Longhouse religion.

Peyotism also became formally organized. Like many other revitalization movements that give birth to new religions, the adherents of peyotism are thus far largely confined to a single ethnic category: Native Americans. Other movements, however, grow in scale over the centuries. From humble beginnings they eventually attract millions of believers. They develop a formal organization complete with priests rather than prophets. Revelations become sacred writings. Beliefs become formal doctrines. Followers and disciples become organized into a church. Most of the major religions of the modern world began as revitalization movements, including Islam, Judaism, and Christianity.

Summary

In comparing religions, it is useful to identify three components that all share: beliefs about the nature of supernatural powers (beings and forces), myths about the past deeds of these powers, and rituals intended to influence them. All known human societies have such beliefs and myths and practice such rituals, so all have religion.

Religion is universal despite the facts that beliefs and myths can never be proved true or false and that rituals are not effective in achieving the goals people have in mind when they perform them. One puzzling thing about religion is what it does for people as individuals or for society as a whole. Various social scientists have proposed that religion performs intellectual/cognitive, psychological, and social functions. No consensus exists about which of these functions is most important. Religion probably fulfills all these "needs," but none seems able to explain religion itself or the great diversity of human religions.

Religions vary in the range of human activities and natural occurrences in which spiritual powers are believed to intervene. Most religions include a belief that supernatural beings or forces cause or influence group or personal misfortune, such as deaths, illnesses, and "accidents." The malevolent powers of sorcerers and witches are blamed for misfortune in a great many societies. Accusations of sorcery and witchcraft tend to be patterned and to reflect prevalent conflicts and tensions in the organization of society. Although beliefs in sorcery and witchcraft might seem to be harmful, anthropologists have argued that they have psychological and social functions.

Religions may be classified according to the types of cults they include, although any such classification is inadequate to depict the diversity of the world's religions. Cults may be characterized as individualistic, shamanistic, communal, and ecclesiastical. In a generalized way, there is an evolutionary sequence to cults, in that they tend to be associated with different degrees of cultural complexity.

Revitalization refers to religious movements that aim to create a new way of life to replace current conditions that are intolerable. Most revitalization movements originate with prophets who claim to have received a revelation, which usually is syncretic and often apocalyptic. Twentieth-century Melanesian cargo cults are among the best studied movements. The Handsome Lake religion among the Seneca of New York and the peyote religion are two of the many North American revitalization movements.

Key Terms

animism
myths
ritual
intellectual/cognitive functions
    of religion
psychological functions of religion

social functions of religion
sorcery
witchcraft
individualistic cults
shamanistic cults
communal cults
ecclesiastical cults
vision quest
shaman (medicine man)

ancestral cults
totemism
priests
revitalization movement
prophet
revelation
cargo cults

Suggested Readings

Numerous books are available that provide basic introductions to the anthropological study of religion, including the following.

Child, Alice B., and Irvin L. Child. *Religion and Magic in the Life of Traditional Peoples*. Englewood Cliffs, N.J.: Prentice-Hall, 1993.
- *A comparative study of religion and magic, intended mainly as a textbook.*

Guthrie, Stewart. *Faces in the Clouds: A New Theory of Religion*. Oxford: Oxford University Press, 1993.
- *Theoretical treatment of religion and other topics. Argues that humans everywhere tend to attribute humanlike qualities to natural phenomena (to "anthropomorphize" nature and other things), and that this tendency helps to explain religion. Also applies the idea of anthropomorphism to topics such as art, science, and advertising. Readable and thoughtful.*

Howells, William. *The Heathens: Primitive Man and His Religions*. Salem, Wisc.: Sheffield, 1986.
- *This book was originally written in 1948. Interpreted with the date of its first publication in mind, it is a good place to start for an overview of human religious diversity.*

Klass, Morton. *Ordered Universes: Approaches to the Anthropology of Religion*. Boulder, Colo.: Westview, 1995.
- *An introductory textbook in the anthropological study of religion and religious diversity. Although some definitions and concepts are nonstandard, this book is generally quite user-friendly.*

Lehman, Arthur C., and James E. Myers, eds. *Magic, Witchcraft, and Religion*. 4th ed. Palo Alto, Calif.: Mayfield, 1997.
- *A reader prepared mainly for undergraduates.*

Levack, Brian P., ed. *Anthropological Studies of Witchcraft, Magic and Religion*. New York: Garland, 1992.
- *Reprints of twenty-one influential articles published at various times in the twentieth century. Especially good on witchcraft and religion.*

Mair, Lucy. *Witchcraft*. New York: McGraw-Hill, 1969.
- *Excellent introduction to witchcraft and its analysis.*

The following ethnographies examine religion and religious movements.

Anderson, Edward F. *Peyote: The Divine Cactus*. 2nd ed. Tucson: University of Arizona, 1996.
- *An excellent description of peyote and its religious uses among Native Americans.*

Boyer, Dave, and Stephen Nissenbaum. *Salem Possessed*. Cambridge, Mass.: Harvard University Press, 1974.
- *Historical study of the witchcraft outbreak in 1692 in Salem, Massachusetts. Shows that the accusations closely reflected long-standing lines of conflict in the community.*

Brown, Michael Fobes. *Tsewa's Gift: Magic and Meaning in an Amazonian Society*. Washington, D.C.: Smithsonian, 1986.
- *Detailed study of shamanism among the Aguaruna of Peru.*

Geertz, Clifford. *The Religion of Java*. Glencoe, Ill.: The Free Press, 1960.
- *One of the great case studies of non-Western religions.*

Grim, John A. *The Shaman: Patterns of Religious Healing Among the Ojibway Indians*. Norman: University of Oklahoma, 1983.
- *Empirical study of Ojibway shamans that also compares Ojibway with shamanism in other parts of the world.*

Keesing, Roger. *Kwaio Religion*. New York: Columbia University Press, 1982.
- *Study of the religion of a Solomon Island society.*

Kehoe, Alice Beck. *The Ghost Dance: Ethnohistory and Revitalization*. Fort Worth: Holt, Rinehart, and Winston, 1989.
- *Descriptive account of the 1890 Ghost Dance that began among the Nevada Paiute and spread to the Lakota and other peoples of the plains. Shows the impact of the religious movement on Native American cultures today.*

Luhrman, T. M. *Persuasions of the Witch's Craft: Ritual Magic in Contemporary England*. Cambridge, Mass.: Harvard University Press, 1989.
- *Detailed and lengthy ethnographic study of witchcraft and the use of magic in England. One focus is how people maintain beliefs in the powers of magical rituals.*

Malinowski, Bronislaw. *Coral Gardens and Their Magic*. New York: American Book Company, 1935.
- *A detailed description of garden magic and horticultural practices in the Trobriand Islands.*

Myerhoff, Barbara. *Peyote Hunt: The Sacred Journey of the Huichol Indians*. Ithaca, N.Y.: Cornell University Press, 1976.
- *An ethnography describing how the Huichol Indians of northern Mexico locate and acquire peyote, which they use in their rituals.*

Neihardt, John G. *Black Elk Speaks*. 2nd ed. Lincoln: University of Nebraska Press, 1961.
- *A very popular and readable account of an Ogalala Sioux holy man and an excellent introduction to the religious beliefs and practices of this American Indian people.*

Sandner, Donald. *Navaho Symbols of Healing*. Rochester, Vermont: Healing Arts Press, 1991.
- *The author, a psychiatrist, presents an informative and readable description and interpretation of Navajo-curing ceremonials and myths.*

Stewart, Omer. *Peyote Religion*. Norman: University of Oklahoma Press, 1987.
- *Detailed study of the peyote religion.*

Stoller, Paul, and Cheryl Olkes. *In Sorcery's Shadow: A Memoir of Apprenticeship Among the Songhay of Niger*. Chicago: University of Chicago Press, 1987.
- *Personal and adventurous account of Stoller's efforts to learn sorcery techniques from a famous Songhay sorcerer.*

Turner, Victor. *The Forest of Symbols*. Ithaca, N.Y.: Cornell
University Press, 1967.
  • *Collection of papers on the religion of the Ndembu of
  Zambia. Turner's descriptions are rich in detail, and his
  analysis of the meaning of symbols used in rituals has
  been influential.*

Wallace, Anthony F. C. *The Death and Rebirth of the
Seneca*. New York: Vintage, 1969.
  • *A highly readable and interesting account of the Longhouse religion, a revitalization movement that first appeared
  among the Seneca of New York State in the early 1800s.*

Internet Exercises

The Anthropology of Religion Section of the American Anthropological Association has compiled an
extensive list of websites, links, discussion groups, and journals that they judge to be useful to scholars interested in the anthropology of religion at (http://www.uwgb.edu/~sar/links.htm).

An interesting site with many links to sites dealing with cargo cults is the "Jon Frum Home Page"
at (http://altnews.com.au/cargocult/jonfrum/). This site describes the Jon Frum Movement, a cargo
cult located on the island of Tanna, Vanuatu, and also provides background information on Melanesia
and cargo cults in general. InfoTrac College Edition also contains an article about this movement. See
if you can locate it. (Hint: In this article the name is given as John Prumm.)

CHAPTER *14*

Art and the Aesthetic

The Pervasiveness of Art

Forms of Artistic Expression

Body Arts

Visual Arts

Performance Arts

Art and Culture

Secular and Religious Art

Art and Gender

Social Functions of Art

Video · Audio · Photos
Houihaka · Essay
https://www.wadsworth.com/humanity

All known peoples appreciate the aesthetic value of certain objects, actions, images, and sounds. This Latin American man makes fine musical instruments.
Visit http://www.wadsworth.com/humanity to learn more about the material covered in this chapter and to access activities, exercises, and tutorial quizzes.

*T*HERE IS MUCH *more to human life than the acquisition of food and other necessities like clothing and shelter. There is also more to living than the production and use of things for their utilitarian value. In all societies there is both a sense of and a desire for the aesthetic: those things that appeal to the eye, the ear, the taste, the touch, the emotions, and the imagination. Such sensory experiences are important not only for their functional value, but because their color, form, design, sound, taste, or feel are pleasurable in their own right. Commonly, these experiences are sought after to stimulate our imaginations and emotions through the creation of feelings of happiness, fear, and even anger. These expressions of the aesthetic are what we generally call art—the subject of this chapter.*

The Shakers of the nineteenth century emphasized simplicity and utility, not ornamentation and aesthetics, in the objects they manufactured. Yet today many of their products are considered works of art. Shaker chairs such as those hanging from the walls of this house are highly prized by collectors.

Art is one of those elusive terms which we all know and use, and think we understand, but is difficult to define. Some scholars have attempted to define art by saying what it is not, that it is not utilitarian. The difficulty is: When does something stop being utilitarian and become art? Richard Anderson uses a Tikopean wooden headrest as an example. Any block of wood, even a log of proper size, might serve one as a headrest. A person might go further by cutting away portions of the block or log to form legs, which Anderson argues still serve a utilitarian purpose of lightening the weight of the block. If, however, the person goes further and carves designs on the headrest, this carving becomes its artistic component, and the object becomes art. According to Anderson, it is this artistic component, the designs, that transforms the object from the realm of the utilitarian to the realm of art. Thus, it is ornamentation placed on the object—not the functional design of the object—that defines it as art.

If this way of defining art seems simple enough, consider the Shakers. The Shakers were a religious communal group that reached its height in the early nineteenth century in the United States. As "plain folk" they emphasized the utilitarian. The qualities of simplicity and function were incorporated into everything they made and used in their communities. Their wooden furniture was simple, delicate, and superbly crafted, but unpretentious with stark straight lines or gentle curves. Veneering of wood was considered "deception," and paint was never used.

There were no accessories, carvings, extravagant turning, or inlays. In keeping with their idea of natural purity, only light stains and varnishes were used on the wood. Their furnishings were very different from those of their neighbors, and some Shakers said that their deigns came from heaven, having been communicated to them by angels. Extremely functional and utilitarian, the beauty of Shaker furniture is in its masterful simplicity of form. Collected today as art, Shaker furniture is among the most highly prized and priced form of American furniture. Form and superb craftsmanship, not ornamentation, makes Shaker furniture art.

So at what point is a piece of wood, stone, or ivory transformed into a work of art? When does noise become music, body movements become dance, and words become poetry, literature, or song lyrics? When does a building or shelter become an architecture? Are there any limitations on what can be considered art? Can the preparation and serving of food be considered art? Is the painting or alteration of the human body art?

In this chapter we use a broad definition of art. Something becomes **art** when its purely utilitarian or functional nature is modified for the purpose of enhancing its aesthetic qualities and thus making it more pleasurable for our senses. Artists can produce art objects that only they themselves will see or hear, but most of the time art is displayed publicly or used in social events such as gatherings or ceremonies. In such contexts, art objects sometimes take on an additional function: They become material means of communication. Thus, Western artists often claim that they are trying to "make a statement" through their artwork, although we all recognize that the artistic message is in the eye of the beholder. In other cultures, too, artistic creations communicate messages, which have both religious and secular meanings.

Obviously, art is inseparable from the **aesthetic,** and the aesthetic is an elusive quality since it is subjective. Anthropologists since Franz Boas have argued that there are no universal standards as to what is considered beautiful or pleasurable. Something that members of one society might find beautiful or pleasing, others might consider ugly, disgusting, or even repulsive. As we frequently hear, "There is no accounting for taste." Aesthetics cannot be separated from culture. Just as we learn other aspects of our culture, so we also learn what is beautiful. Beauty is culturally determined. Aesthetics is unrelated to complexity, difficulty, or skill in the creation or performance of what is considered art. While we might appreciate the craftsmanship that went into the making of a piece of pottery, or the difficulty in the performance of a particular piece of music, we may or may not find them aesthetically pleasing. During a visit to Scotland, the English writer Samuel Johnson complained about bagpipe music. On being informed that bagpipes were an extremely difficult instrument to play, Johnson replied, "I wish it was impossible."

Not only does every culture, as well as every individual, have its own ideas as to what is aesthetically pleasing, but aesthetics change within a culture over time. For example, if one examines European or Chinese art over the past 2,000 years, there are dramatic changes in both the nature and the complexity of designs. Thus, not only is the idea of what is beautiful subjective, but it is also volatile and ever changing.

The Pervasiveness of Art

In the urban, industrial world, we usually think of artistic creation as a separate and distinct kind of activity and artistic objects as a special set of things. We also most commonly think of art only in terms of "fine art": painting, sculpture, music, and dance. If pressed further, we might add great architecture, literature, and even poetry. We tend to categorize as art only those things whose sole or basic value is aesthetic. Artists, in turn, are those painters, sculptors, composers, writers, architects, performers, and others who produce these things of aesthetic value. Individuals who are not directly involved in the production of "art" commonly are seen as merely the audience or consumers—people who buy, see, and hear art.

The notion that art is a conceptually separate realm of social and cultural existence is not found among all peoples. As anthropologists have long noted, American-Indian peoples had no word for art in their languages. Similarly other traditional peoples in other parts of the world also frequently lack words for art. The basic reason for this is that art is integrated into virtually every aspect of their lives and is so pervasive that they do not think of it as something separate and distinct. The idea of "art for art's sake" is a recent Western cultural phenomenon that in some ways both distracts and diminishes the reality of human creative expressions. If we define art broadly, then it permeates virtually every aspect of our lives. All of us search for and attempt to create that which is aesthetically pleasing and, thus, we are all "artists." Creative artistic expressions are found in even the most mundane and commonplace acts of the daily lives of all peoples. Consider, for example, three behaviors that most of us think of as "mundane" rather than "artistic": dressing for the day, residing in a particular place, and eating.

We begin the day by ornamenting our bodies. From among our clothes we make choices as to what to wear based on colors and styles appropriate for the day's events. We make choices on how to wear our hair and even the color of our hair. We may paint our faces and further adorn our bodies with jewelry of varying kinds, worn on our fingers and arms, around our necks, in our ears, noses, and—in recent years—other parts of our bodies. Some of us have our bodies permanently decorated with tattoos. By these everyday acts we are artists, attempting to enhance the aesthetic qualities of our persons by making ourselves a work of art. In these acts we also are adept communicators of messages about ourselves, for through hair, makeup, dress, jewelry, and other ways of adorning our bodies we present to the public certain kinds of images of ourselves.

Consider also your living space. In finding or building a place to live, we don't just look for something that will meet our physical needs; aesthetic appeal also plays an important role. Not infrequently we will alter our homes by changing walls, adding rooms, remodeling the bathroom or the kitchen, and repainting everything in different colors inside and outside. We decorate the inside with furniture, rugs, paintings, posters, mirrors, and a host of knickknacks and smaller things. If we have a yard, we may relandscape by removing or adding trees, shrubs, flower beds, and fences. Even temporary apartment and college dormitory dwellers try to make a place their own. Although some of these additions and changes may be of utilitarian value or need, most serve to enhance the aesthetic appeal of the place we live.

Finally, think about mealtimes. Whether we eat food raw or cooked, boiled, baked, fried, hot or cold, and whether we season it with salt, pepper, garlic, or other herbs and spices, we are attempting to create something that is pleasing to our sense of taste. Our quest for new and exciting ways of preparing food seems endless, giving rise to the steady flow of new cookbooks from publishers. Nor is eating food a purely utilitarian act. We set the table and arrange the repast in bowls and on plates, which have usually been purchased for their aesthetic appeal. In our food preparation and serving we attempt, not always successfully, to create something that is appealing to both the palate and the eye. (Chinese, incidentally, are far more conscious of this artistic quality of food than are most North Americans.)

Even in our daily lives, then, we attempt to surround and immerse ourselves in the aesthetic. The search for the aesthetic is reflected in the appearance of our persons, our homes, and our meals, as well as in our places of worship, recreation, and work. Much of our day is filled with music, song, dance, drama, comedy, literature, and sports, which we listen to, participate in, and sometimes

We often do not appreciate that aesthetic considerations pervade our everyday lives. Notice the ways this woman's clothing and jewelry both enhance her appearance and seem to present the world with an image of herself.

create. Art, anthropologists recognize, is a cultural universal. But beyond this the artistic impulse is seen in the everyday lives of individual human beings, for we are all both producers and consumers of art.

Forms of Artistic Expression

Although art permeates most aspects of human activity, from clothing and furniture to music and theater, space constraints do not permit us to discuss all these diverse forms of artistic expression. For this reason we limit our discussion to certain categories: body arts, visual arts, and performance arts.

Body Arts

Humans in all societies are concerned with their physical appearance and attempt to enhance it in a variety of ways. People around the world are highly creative in altering their physical appearance. Almost anything that can be done to the body is probably being done or has been done in the past. In Euro-American societies, for example, parts of the body are now being pierced that few people even thought of as pierceable a decade or two ago. For convenience, we focus on physical alterations, body painting, and tattooing and scarification.

Physical Alterations   In almost all societies people attempt to physically alter their bodies. Head and body hair is treated in many different ways. In western societies hair is styled and often artificially colored. Some people shave their heads, their beards, and even their legs and armpits. Others let their beards and/or mustaches grow and style them in various ways. Still others, particularly middle-aged males, attempt vainly to have replacement hair grown on the tops of their heads. In most western societies these actions are mainly a matter of fashion or personal taste; in other societies such actions may have deeper cultural meanings.

In parts of Africa the status of a woman—e.g., whether she is unmarried or married, or is a mother or a widow—is indicated by hairstyle. Among the Hopis, adolescent girls of marriageable age wear their hair in a large whorl on each side of the head, creating the so-called "butterfly" hairstyle. After marriage they will wear their hair long and parted in the middle. Children among the Omahas and many other tribes of central United States had their hair cut in patterns indicative of their clan membership.

The wearing of beards is not always a matter of personal taste and fashion. In many societies, such as among Hasidic Jews, Mennonites, Amish, some Muslim sects, and Sikhs, the wearing of a beard is an act of religious belief. In the ancient world social status was frequently associated with beards. In Egypt only the nobility were allowed to wear beards. Not only did noblemen wear beards, but women of the nobility frequently wore artificial beards as well to indicate their social rank. In contrast, in ancient Greece only the nobility were allowed to be clean shaven; men of commoner status had to let their beards grow.

Hair alterations usually are reversible, for hair will grow back. Other parts of the body, though, frequently are altered on a permanent basis. Cranial deformation or head shaping has been and is widely practiced among the peoples of the world. The skull of a baby is soft and if the baby's head is bound the shape of the skull can be permanently changed, flattening the back and the forehead, or lengthening the head. In parts of France cranial deformation was virtually universal until the eighteenth century. The face of a baby was tightly wrapped in linen, resulting in a flattened skull and ears. In the Netherlands, babies once wore tight-fitting caps which depressed the frontal portion of the skull. The elite classes of the ancient Andean civilizations elongated the skull, as did the ancient Egyptians. For the first year of its life a Chinook baby in Oregon was wrapped on a hard board, with another board bound against the top and front of the head. This technique resulted in a head with additional breadth. Some peoples of central Africa bound the heads of female babies to create elongated skulls that came to a point on the back.

Some peoples permanently altered other parts of the body as well. In China the feet of female children of high-status families were bound at the age of five or six to deform the feet and keep them small. This was not only considered attractive, but was practiced as a visible indication of the fact that the family was sufficiently wealthy that its women did not have to do much physical labor. In parts of Africa and among some Native American peoples holes were cut in earlobes or the lower and upper lips were expanded so that ear plugs and large lip plugs could be inserted. Some of these plugs were up to three inches in diameter. Some central African pygmy peoples file their front teeth into points, which in their culture enhances their attractiveness. In parts of Africa, a series of rings was placed around a girl's neck over a period or time, so that when womanhood was achieved the shoulders were pressed down, making the neck appear longer and making it possible to wear multiple neck rings.

Such alterations continue in modern nations. Much of the lucrative work of plastic surgeons in contemporary Western nations is concerned with altering physical appearance by changing the shapes of the eyes, nose, mouth and jowls, or increasing or decreasing the size of breasts, lips, thighs, hips, or waistlines.

Body Painting Painting is a less drastic and temporary manner of changing an individual's appearance. Some peoples paint only their faces, while others paint almost their entire bodies. Face painting is more common than body painting. When face painting is mentioned, most people think first of American Indians and "war paint." American-Indian peoples did commonly paint their faces for war. Among the Osages, before attacking their enemy, the men would blacken their faces with charcoal, symbolic of the merciless fire and their ferocity. With other Native American groups the designs and meaning varied. Among some, face painting was individualized, each man using different colors and designs to create a ferocious appearance. Among others, the manner in which a man might paint his face depended upon a vision and his spiritual helpers (see Chapter 13). However, not all face painting was associated with war. Faces were commonly painted for religious rituals as well. In ritual face painting the painted symbols usually had some form of religious significance. In addition, many Native American peoples simply painted their faces to enhance

their social appearance. Thus, Native Americans painted their faces for a variety of reasons—warfare, religious rituals, and social appearance. The same range of reasons was and is true for other peoples in the world as well.

Body painting refers to painting the entire body, or most of it. Like face painting, body painting is widely distributed among the world's peoples. In some cases, body painting has religious significance and meaning; in other cases, it is purely secular, designed to enhance the physical appearance of the person. Many peoples in Papua New Guinea cover their faces and limbs with white clay when a relative or important person dies, as a sign of mourning and respect for the deceased. Among the aboriginal peoples of Australia, bodies were painted with red and yellow ocher, white clay, charcoal, and other pigments. During rituals individuals were painted, at times with elaborate designs covering most of the body. The colors and designs were standardized and had symbolic meaning. Ritual specialists who knew these designs were charged with the actual painting for religious ceremonies. Outside of ritual contexts, for many Australian peoples, body painting was a secular and daily activity, performed by family members on one another. Here individuals were free to use whatever colors and designs pleased them, so long as they were not ritual designs.

Tattooing and Scarification Tattooing and the related practice of scarification are widespread practices. Tattoo designs, achieved by etching and placing a colored pigment under the skin, have been practiced by diverse peoples. When the skin is too dark for tattooing designs to be seen, then people may use scarification, the deliberate scarring of the skin to produce designs on the body.

Tattooing has a long history as an art form. Tattooing was practiced in ancient Egypt, as well as by the ancient Scythians, Thracians, and Romans in Europe. The ancient Bretons, at the time of the Roman conquest, were reported to have had their bodies elaborately tattooed with the images of animals. In the fourth century A.D., when Christianity became the official religion of the Roman Empire, tattooing was forbidden on religious grounds. Tattooing virtually disappeared among European peoples until the eighteenth century when it was discovered in the Pacific and Asia by sailors and reintroduced to European peoples as purely secular art.

Robert Brain noted an important difference between body painting and tattooing and scarification: Paint is removable; tattooing and scarification are indelible and permanent. As a result, tattooing and scarification are usually associated with societies in which there are permanent differences in social status. In complexity of designs and parts of the body tattooed, peoples differed. Among some people, tattooing was limited to a few lines

These Australian aborigine boys have their bodies painted for a dance. Body painting is commonly used in many cultures for ceremonial and ritual occasions.

enteenth and later centuries. Tongans, Samoans, Marquesans, Tahitians, the Maori of New Zealand, and most other Polynesian peoples practiced tattooing, which everywhere was connected to social distinctions such as class or rank, sex, religious roles, and specialization. Polynesian peoples are all historically related, so it is not surprising that marking the body with tattoos is found on almost all islands, albeit to different degrees and with somewhat different styles.

Many Maori had large parts of their bodies covered with tattoos, which could be placed on the torso, thighs, buttocks, calves, and, most notably, the face. Several instruments were used by skilled tattoo artists to incise the curvilinear patterns characteristic of most Maori tattoos. One was a small chisel made of bone and etched into the skin with a hammer. Apparently, no anesthetic was used to relieve the pain and, in fact, tolerating the pain of the procedure may have been part of its cultural significance. To make pigment, several kinds of wood were burned for their ashes. After the artist made the cuts, pigment was rubbed into the wounds to leave permanent markings. The most skilled tattoo artists were rewarded with high prestige and chiefly patronage, and their craft was in such high demand that they traveled widely over New Zealand's two huge islands.

Both Maori men and women wore tattoos, although men's bodies were more thoroughly covered. For both sexes, tattoos were seen not merely as body ornamentation or expression of one's personal identity. Having tattoos brought certain privileges. Men who did not undergo tattooing could not build canoe houses, carve wood, make weapons, or weave nets. Untattooed women could not help in the gardens with sweet potatoes, the Maori staple vegetable crop.

Maori facial tattoos, called *moko,* have special importance. Women were tattooed on the lips and chin, often near the time of their marriage. Male facial tattoos were designed by splitting the face into four fields—left versus right of the nose and upper versus lower at roughly eye level. Moko were basically symmetrical on the vertical axis, with curvilinear designs on the forehead and eyebrows, cheeks, and mouth regions. In many cases, virtually the whole male face was tattooed. Not just any moko design could be worn by just any male, for designs were related to factors such as hereditary status, locale of birth, and achievement in battle. Social restrictions thus were placed on the wearing of facial tattoos, suggesting that they were important symbols of both group identity and personal achievement. North Americans might see echoes of their own wearing of styles of clothing, jewelry, hairstyle, and other personal ornamentations in Maori and other Polynesian tattoos. (See "Other Voices" for an indigenous view of Maori art.)

on the face, chest, or arms. Among others, complex designs covered most of the body from the face to the legs. In some cases, every adult had some tattoos; in other societies, only certain individuals had tattoos. While the significance and meaning of tattoos varied, most had socioreligious significance and the more fully tattooed an individual was, the greater the social status.

Among the Osages of North America, only men who had earned thirteen war honors in battle were entitled to be tattooed. These tattoos, consisting of thirteen elongated triangles, were placed on the chest, radiating out from the neck like a necklace. These men were also entitled to have their wives and daughters tattooed on the chest, back, arms, and hands. For the women these tattoos were considered prayers for long life, children, and good health.

The adornment of the body by tattoos is most highly elaborated in the scattered islands of Polynesia. In fact, the word *tattoo* itself is Polynesian. The word, like the practice of tattooing sailors, came into use as a result of the voyages of Western explorers and whalers in the sev-

Other Voices

A Native View of Maori Art

In terms of complexity of designs and craftsmanship, Maori art from New Zealand ranks among the finest in the world. Wood carving was their primary medium, and their houses, ceremonial buildings, and even storage houses were literally covered with either carved or painted designs. Similar intricate designs were carved on the prows and sterns of canoes, storage boxes, bowls, clubs, flutes, canoe bailers, paddles, adzes, weaving tools, fishhooks, combs, and ceremonial items. The desire to decorate extended to the human body as well. Not only were the chest, back, arms, and legs frequently covered with intricate tattoos, but sometimes the face was fully covered as well. Art was and is still a central and important part of their life. In a discussion on the meaning and significance of Maori art objects, Sidney Moko Mead, a Maori anthropologist, has shown some differences between Maori and Western artistic concepts.

In understanding the Maori concept of art or art objects, two terms are important, *taonga* and *whakairo*. *Taonga* can be translated as "property" or as something that is "highly prized." It is something inherited from the ancestors. Implicit in the concept of *taonga* is the idea of *korero* (text or words); it might also be seen as history or the past. Some types of *taonga* are called *taonga whakairo*.

Whakairo is the closest word in Maori to the English word for art and refers to something that is decorated—carving, tattooing, painting, or a weaving. It refers to something more than the mere form or shape of an object. Decoration incorporates into the object something of the human spirit and, therefore, something of the world of the gods. Thus, through decoration an object is transformed from the natural world to the cultural world. As Mead expressed it, *"Whakairo* represents the triumph of man Maori (power) over the environment and represents a gift from ancestors to their descendants born and yet unborn."

The very act of placing designs on an object gives the object *korero,* and thus makes it *taonga.* As Mead stated, ". . . the form and size selected by the artist are already clothed in a thousand words." The talent to decorate comes from the gods. And "thus it follows that an artist is merely a vehicle used by the gods, to express their artistry and their genius." Still other things are said to have *korero tuamaha* (heavy). Rituals may have been performed over it and speeches said about it. It may have been that the artists made errors in creating the object and died because of them. Such histories make the object *tuamaha* (heavy), meaning that they are extraordinary objects.

In judging art, the Maori people saw beauty not in the sense of harmony, color, craftsmanship, or originality. The Maori artists attempted to incorporate into the object *ihi* (power), *wehi* (fear), and *wana* (authority). If the object or even the performance of dance inspired these feelings of power, fear, and authority in the viewer, then the object was beautiful. *Taonga* were not inanimate things; one should sense the presence of power, even though the person may be unaware of its *korero* and history. Thus, Maori people show respect for *taonga,* at times even fear and awe of such objects.

Source: Mead (1984).

In other Polynesian islands tattooing was similar to the Maori in broad pattern, but varied in detail. In Samoa, for instance, a group of boys was tattooed together on the hips and thighs in their early teens, accompanied by much ceremony. The primary recipient of the tattoo was the son of a high-ranking chief, and other boys participated to share his pain and, therefore, publicly show their respect and loyalty. Supposedly, Samoan women disdained men as sexual partners if they did not have tattoos. Traditionally, Samoan girls received tattoos only on the backs of their knees, which they were not supposed to reveal to others. It is interesting that in Samoa greater and more elaborate male tattoos were connected to different sexually-based biological functions. There was a saying:

The man grows up and is tattooed.

The woman grows up and she gives birth. (Milner, 1969: 20)

According to one interpretation, voluntary tattooing gives pain to men just as childbirth causes pain to women. Perhaps the male experience of pain by tattooing is connected to Samoan women's contempt for tattoo-less men.

In all of Polynesia, it was the people of the Marquesas whose bodies were most covered by tattoos. The highest ranking chiefs even had tattoos on the soles of their feet. Alfred Gell argues that this relative thorough covering of the body in the Marquesas was necessary to wrap the body in images in order to protect it from spiritual dangers. Gods and spirits were not tattooed; tattoo images protected the human body from spiritual harm.

Decorating the body by cutting and creating scars, or scarification, is more limited among the world's peoples than tattooing. As in tattooing, scarification is practiced for numerous reasons. Depending on the culture, both men and women may be scarred. Sometimes the scarred design is on the face; in other cases, the chest, breast, back, and even the legs and arms may be elaborately covered with such designs. Sometimes scarification forms part of the puberty rite or some other initiation rite. Among the Nuer of the southern Sudan, a series of horizontal cuts is made on the foreheads of men who have completed male initiation rituals. On young men, these cuts symbolically mark and communicate their maturity and courage. After they scarify, these cuts become permanent symbols of Nuer manhood.

Visual Arts

Visual arts are produced out of material, tangible objects, so they are part of the material culture of a people. They may be religious or secular in meaning and use. Usually they are permanent in that they are meant for long-term use, but sometimes they are created for a one-time use only and then destroyed. Visual arts encompass a wide range of basketry, ceramics, textiles, clothing, jewelry, tools, paintings, masks, and sculpture, to name only a few examples. Metal, wood, stone, leather, feather, shell, paper made of fibers, pigments, and other materials are used in their creation. The two main factors which transform a material item into a visual art are form and ornamentation.

Form The physical form or shape of an object is a reflection of its utilitarian function, the materials available, the technical knowledge and skill of the person producing it, and the general lifestyle of the society. Nomadic or seminomadic foraging and pastoral people often produce items that are light in weight and easily transportable. One might think that the visual arts of nomadic or seminomadic people are "less refined" than that of more settled peoples. But Inuit peoples of northern latitudes precisely carved small art objects out of soft soapstone, and decorated many of their portable tools with figures of animals. Shields and hides were elaborately painted among many nomadic peoples of the American plains. Plains Indians heavily decorated their clothing and moccasins with shells and beadwork, thus allowing people to carry their art along with them. On the other hand, Native Americans of the western United States, especially the southwest, used pigment to paint or hard stones to etch images of animals, celestial objects, people, mythological beings, and other things on rocks. The prehistoric people who created these images might have moved on the landscape according to season, but their art was stationary and long lasting. Today we know these images as pictographs and petroglyphs, also called rock art.

Rock seems like a difficult object to use as a canvas, but the world's peoples have used other unusual materials, including sand (as we shall see later). Of course, the availability of wood, stone, clay, hides, and other natural materials does influence what people can create and how. The kinds of tools the artist uses to paint, etch, or sculpt also are important influences on the final artwork. Metal tools have advantages over stone tools in giving artistic form to a raw material. Peoples also differ in their technical knowledge of how to work stone or wood, and how to model clay or metals.

Within these natural and technical limitations, the form of an object is the result of the interplay of utilitarian function and aesthetic style. The function/style debate has long interested archaeologists. If one examines prehistoric stone tools, a bewildering variety of forms is evident. In North American archaeology, extensive typologies have been created to classify projectile point types, which differ in size, relative length and width, and shape (straight, concave, convex, or even serrated). Some are unnotched; others are notched on the bases or sides. Many of these differences are undoubtedly related

The Maori people of New Zealand are famous for their elaborate tattoos. The designs of Maori facial tattoos are important symbols of identity and achievement.

to function, but others seem to be purely stylistic. Great variability is also present in the vessel shapes and decorations of another archaeological favorite, pottery. The shapes and decorations of pottery vessel vary tremendously from one group to another, as well as within the same group of people over time.

One does not have to look at peoples remote in time or space to see that the form of an object that has utilitarian purposes is part of the artistic expression of a people. Look at something as mundane and "functional" as the legs of tables and chairs in our own culture. The legs can be straight or tapered, or round, square, or rectangular. The table may have a pedestal base. All are equally functional; they keep the seat or the top off the floor. The differences are a question of aesthetics, not of function. Thus, the physical form of an object may be part of its aesthetic appeal; however, it is difficult to always determine where function ends and the aesthetic begins.

In the American southwest, prehistoric Native Americans pecked and scraped images onto stones. This example of rock art is from Petroglyph National Monument just west of Albuquerque, New Mexico.

Ornamentation Ornamentation is design added to the physical form of an object. Humans are highly creative in developing ways of adding ornamentation to material items and a variety of techniques is utilized. Ornamental designs may be woven or carved into an object. They may be painted, incised, molded, or sewn onto an object. Or a combination of these techniques may be used to decorate.

In basketry and textiles, designs are commonly woven onto the item during its construction. For baskets, different colors of plant fibers, either natural or artificially dyed, are used for the designs. The same is true in the weaving of textiles, for which different colored yarns are used. However, not all textile designs are created using fibers of contrastive colors. By using different types of weaving techniques, designs may be created in single-color baskets and textiles.

Carving refers to the creation of a design by removing parts of the original form. Wood, stone, clay, ivory, shell, and bone may have carved designs. An object may be carved in three dimensions, such that the form itself becomes the design, as in a piece of sculpture. Or the form of the object will remain the same, with only shallow relief carving of a design on the surface.

Painting is certainly one of the easiest and most versatile methods of ornamenting an object. It is possibly the oldest method of ornamentation, being known from at least 20,000 years ago in European cave paintings. All one needs to paint is a range of colors. To make colored pigments, a variety of different materials may be mixed with water, oil, or fat, such as charcoal, plant materials,

and natural mineral pigments. Paintings can be applied to wood, stone, clay, textiles, paper, or leather. Paintings can be applied to flat surfaces, such as cave walls, exposed rocks or cliff walls, wooden furniture, or canvas. They may be made on round or irregular surfaces, such as pottery, masks, and sculpture.

Incising consists of decorating an object by scratching lines into the surface. Like painting, incising appears to be one of the earliest ways of adding designs to an item. Incising is most commonly used on ivory, bone, and shell. In these cases, the scratched lines are frequently accentuated by adding some type of colored pigment, usually black or dark in color, so one can more readily see the design itself. Incised designs are also occasionally used for decorating clay pots and leather.

Designs on ceramics and metal are commonly modeled by raising certain areas above the surface. There are two ways in which this form of ornamentation can be accomplished. One is by making additions to the object after the surface area is finished. In pottery, for example, designs may be formed by placing little balls or coils of clay on the surface after the body of the pot has been formed. A similar technique is sometimes used in adding designs to metal items, as when metal wires shaped into designs are welded to the surface. More commonly, though, molds are created with designs carved into the surface area. Clay can be forced into these molds, or metal poured into them. After the object is removed from the mold the design areas stand out as raised areas on the object surface.

Sewing is often used to add ornamentation to cloth or leather. Glass, bone, or shell beads may be sewn on an

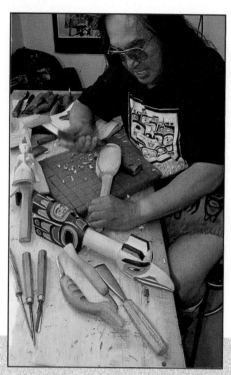

Objects can be ornamented in a variety of ways, including painting and carving. This Northwest Coast man is using both methods to create a sculpture.

item forming designs, as in moccasins or clothing. Designs may be created by sewing with various colored threads of hair, plant fiber, quills, or metal, or by sewing different colors of fabrics together, as in a patchwork quilt.

This discussion has only touched upon some of the ways in which peoples add ornamentation to and create design on objects. When it comes to ornamenting objects humans are highly creative. When most people think of artistic creativity, they think of the artist as creating a novel object (e.g., a unique drawing or sculpture) using some medium (e.g., paper or wood). Looking in broad cross-cultural perspective, we see that humanity as a whole also has been enormously creative not only in its styles, but also in its techniques of ornamentation and in some of the surprising materials used.

Art of the Northwest Coast: An Example of Style   With visual arts, some two-dimensional image (e.g., a painting or drawing) or three-dimensional form (e.g., a sculpture or mask) is created. Cultures vary in many ways in visual arts: the themes or subjects portrayed, the purposes of the artwork, the relation between the artist and the public, and so forth.

Stylistic conventions are an important variation. In visual arts, stylistic symbolism may be especially important, for artists in many cultures are not especially concerned with realistic portrayals of people or nature, but use conventional representations that are understood by themselves and the public. But even when the intention is a realistic portrayal, symbolic representation may be necessary. In a painting or drawing, for example, three-dimensional reality is portrayed on a two-dimensional surface, and the stylistic conventions of different cultures may handle this problem of representation in various ways.

The art of some of the Native Americans of the Northwest Coast, from southern Alaska to Oregon, serves as one example of stylistic variation in imagery and two-dimensional representation. Although they were hunters, gatherers, and fishers—rather than cultivators—Northwest Coast peoples were largely sedentary villagers, which was made possible by the abundance and reliability of coastal and riverine food resources, especially fish (see Chapter 6). Their social and political organization included large descent groups, chiefly roles, and hierarchical ranking. Sponsoring the creation of art objects, displaying them, and/or using them in ceremonies was one way groups and high-ranking people proclaimed their wealth and social position.

Northwest Coast art is famous for its sheer quantity, quality, and style. Most major Canadian and American museums west of the Rockies contain substantial collections of masks, wooden sculptures, incised silver jewelry, carved boxes, finely woven blankets, and sometimes larger objects such as "totem poles" and painted housefronts. Animals, humans, and spirits are the most common subjects of the art of these peoples—although many creations represent animal-human-spirit at the same time. Because of the unique style used to represent these subjects, most Northwest Coast art is easily recognizable, with only a little prior familiarity.

Animals such as beavers, ravens, hawks, frogs, bears, and killer whales were common subjects of the art, but their depiction was not intended to be realistic. Artists created animals by combining design elements representing what was culturally considered their most distinctive body parts. For example, beavers have two large incisors, a scaly (often hatched) tail, a rounded nose, and forepaws (often holding a stick). Hawks are portrayed by emphasizing their distinctive beak, which is turned backwards and often touches the face. Frogs are suggested by wide and toothless mouths. Bears usually are identified by paws with claws and a large and heavily toothed mouth. Images of killer whales have a large toothed mouth, a blowhole, and an exaggerated dorsal fin. Using such conventional design elements, Northwest Coast artists carved animals into boxes, masks used in a multitude of ceremonies, huge cedar trunks representing a group's or individual's ancestry (commonly mislabeled "totem poles"), and other three-dimensional objects.

Painters are familiar with the problem of representing the world on flat surfaces. In the Western and many other artistic traditions, three dimensions are represented on two-dimensional surfaces (canvas or paper) by such techniques as relative sizes of images, perspective, and coloration, all intended to create the visual illusion of depth. Northwest Coast artists painted on many two-dimensional surfaces, including the flat sides of boxes and communal housefronts. They also wove representations of animals into blankets and incised lines into bracelets and other metal jewelry. Most often, their work on flat surfaces tried to retain as many as possible of the design elements characteristic of each animal, so that each animal representation would be identifiable. A common technique was to split the animal down the middle and paint profiles on each half of the surface. The result was a representation that distorted the actual shapes of the body and its characteristic parts, but retained the elements that conventionally identified the animal.

Yet another stylistic characteristic of Northwest Coast art is the artists' apparent intolerance of empty spaces. The subject's body, limbs, and even hands and feet were generally filled in by design elements. Most commonly, curvilinear patterns, stylized eyes, or faces were painted or carved inside body parts. Thus, one frequently observes a face on an animal's torso or an eye pattern on a leg joint.

Although meaningful cross-cultural studies of visual arts are difficult, comparative studies have been made of stylistic elements found in ornamental designs. Working with the idea that art reflects the creator's idea of society, John Fischer studied the use of stylistic elements in twenty-eight different societies around the world. He divided the societies on the basis of their degrees of social equality and inequality (see Chapter 12), feeling that the artistic expressions of egalitarian (primarily foraging) societies would differ from those of socially stratified (primarily intensive agricultural) societies. Stylistic elements were examined in terms of relative complexity, use of space, symmetry, and boundedness. Fischer found that in egalitarian societies designs tended toward repetition of similar, symmetrical design elements, with large areas of empty space without enclosures. In more stratified societies, ornamentation was characterized by asymmetrical designs which integrated unlike elements and which more fully filled enclosed areas. Fischer interpreted these differences as symbolically reflecting the differing social realities of egalitarian and stratified

peoples. Egalitarian peoples tend to live in small, scattered isolated groups, while in stratified societies people live in crowded communities.

Performance Arts

Performance arts encompass music, song, and dance, which use voice, instruments, and/or movement to delight the senses and communicate. (Theater/drama also is a performance art, but we do not cover it here.) Music, song, and dance are closely interrelated. Dancing is usually to the accompaniment of music, especially of rhythms created partly by drumming, clapping, or other kinds of percussion. Singing often is accompanied by instrumental music. Traditional religious ceremonies and pageants commonly integrate music, song, and dance.

An interesting aspect of performance arts is not only do we watch and/or listen to such formal performances, but we also frequently perform them ourselves, in many cases for pure pleasure. We play our own pianos or guitars, we sing in the shower or as we drive, and we take part in social dances. The dual dimension of these forms of arts has been questioned by some anthropologists. Speaking only of dance, Adrienne Kaeppler has asked, "Is participation in rock and roll in any way comparable to watching ballet? Indeed, should 'dances of participation' and 'dances of presentation' be classified as the same phenomenon either in our own or other culture, let alone cross-culturally?" She further questions if dance performances for the gods should be categorized with social dancing, since their purposes are so different.

Similar questions may be asked of music and song, which so often are part and parcel of religious rituals. For example, Osage rituals integrated music, song, physical movements (including dance), and theatrical performances in such a manner as to communicate ideas that could not be expressed by words alone. In his studies of Osage religious rituals, Francis LaFlesche argued that these rituals were not merely prayers for supernatural assistance, but were educational as well. They were a manner of recording and transmitting the collective knowledge of the society, communicating social messages to the assembled participants. Thus, even within a society the purposes of performance arts may differ significantly, depending upon whether they are religious or secular in nature.

People raised in the Judeo-Christian religious tradition are quite familiar with the many functions of music in religious services. The lyrics of familiar hymns sung to praise God are an integral part of worship rituals. Music also helps to create the mood and sense of reverence for the service and is capable of altering the emotional state

This photo of a Northwest Coast house and family crest ("totem") pole was taken in the late nineteenth century. The painting on the house is identified as a bear by the prominent teeth, large central nostrils, paws, and ears protruding from the house top. Notice how the bear's image is split down the middle making a symmetrical image. Both halves of the image still contain the essential design attributes of the bear.

of the participants. The shared experience of singing in unison may help draw the congregation together, enhancing what many Christian denominations call their fellowship. In these and other ways, music is important in making the congregation receptive to the messages delivered by the sermon and prayers.

Music and other forms of performance arts are essential to the religious experience for diverse peoples from all parts of the world. The voudon ("voodoo") religion of the Caribbean heavily incorporates performance arts into religious ceremonies. Followers of voudon consider themselves to be people who "serve the spirits" (*loa*). Many *loa* originated and now live in West Africa, from where the ancestors of modern Afro-Caribbean peoples were enslaved during the era of slave trade begin-

ning about 1500. Voudon temples are elaborately decorated with sacred objects, paintings, and symbolic representations of various *loa*, which show the devotion of the worshippers and make the temple attractive to the spirits. Through drumming, music, and energetic dancing, voodoo worshippers induce the *loa* to leave their spiritual homes and take over the bodies of those who worship them. When the *loa* possess their human servants, the latter speak with the voices of the *loa*, wear the *loa*'s favorite clothing, eat their foods, drink their beverages, and generally assume their identity. Visiting petitioners with problems can ask questions of the worshipper/*loa*, who may answer with directions about what course of action to take. Voudon drumming, music, and dancing are so totally integrated into temple rituals that the religion is unimaginable without it.

Among many peoples, music, dance, and other forms of performance arts are essential elements of curing ceremonials. !Kung shamans (see Chapters 6 and 13) use percussion, song, and dance to induce the trance state they believe is necessary for curing sick people. The power to heal, !Kung believe, comes from a substance called n!um, which when heated up by dancing and trance allows shamans to draw sickness out of people. While women produce a definite rhythm by clapping and singing, the curers circle the fire in short, synchronous dance steps. The experience of music and dance causes the n!um inside their bodies to boil up into their heads, inducing trance. In this spiritually powerful state, shamans then heal by placing hands on the sick, shrieking at the same time to drive out the affliction.

Music is essential to the healing process among many other African peoples. The Tumbuka-speaking peoples of northern Malawi combine singing, drumming, and dancing in all-night curing sessions. Some kinds of illness are caused by a category of spirits called *vimbuza*. *Vimbuza* are the powerful spiritual energy of foreign peoples and wild animals (especially lions). *Vimbuza* cause various kinds of illness and even death when they possess someone. Tumbuka believe that health requires a balance between bodily cold and hot forces (similar to the bodily "humours" of old Europe). When *vimbuza* enter the bodies of people, they create an imbalance between hot and cold forces, leading to the buildup of heat that is culturally interpreted as sickness.

Tumbuka diviner-healers (curers) both diagnose illnesses and direct elaborate healing ceremonies that include drumming, music, and dance. The most essential part of the curing ritual is a shared musical experience in the context of a group gathering, with every individual present expected to contribute to the music making. Even patients themselves participate in the total experience by singing, clapping, and dancing. As the sick person dances to the accompanying rhythm of drums and music, the heat inside her or his body increases. This leads the possessing spirit to expend excess energy and cool off. By thus restoring the balance between hot and cold, the individual is cured, at least temporarily.

Steven Friedson, who worked among the Tumbuka, briefly summarizes the importance of music and performance to healing among just a few African cultures:

> . . . Africans approach healing through music and dance. Azande "witch doctors" eat special divinatory medicines, activated by drumming, singing, and dancing. In northern Nigeria among the Hausa, the sounds of the *garaya* (two-stringed plucked lute) and *buta* (gourd rattle) call the divine horsemen of the sacred city of Jangare to descend in to the heads of *boorii* adepts, thus healing the people they have made sick. Similarly, the various *orisha* and *vodoun* spirits of the Guinea Coast, called by their drum motto, mount their horses (possess their devotees). The resultant spirit-possession dance, though religious in nature, is in the first instance often a therapy for those afflicted by the same spirits. Spirit affliction is healed through music and dance in Ethiopia and Sudan, wherever *zar* cults occur. . . . Central, southern, and parts of Equatorial Africa have examples of

Percussive music often is part of curing ceremonials, where it helps healers and shamans to achieve the state of trance that makes them spiritually powerful. This San healer in a trance shrieks to drive out the patient's illness.

the *ng'oma* type of healing complex, whose name . . . points to the centrality of music in curative rites. (Friedson, 1998: 273–4; references in the original deleted)

In the early 1980s, the authors of this book first heard about a medical field that involves integrating music into the treatment of both biomedical and psychological disorders. At the time, we thought the field now called music therapy was a new mode of treatment and a new occupation. As the previous examples illustrate, many other cultures have long recognized the connection between music and healing and have integrated the performance arts into their treatments.

As with other forms of aesthetic expression, comparative studies of performance arts are difficult and few. Alan Lomax's comparative studies of dance and song rank with the most ambitious. Lomax and his collaborators analyzed film footage of peoples from around the world comparing body movements in everyday activities with their dance movements. What they found was that dance movements were formalized repetitions of the movements found in daily life. Lomax further argued that the form of dance was correlated with the relative complexity of the society.

In his comparative study of songs, Lomax found that differences in song styles were also correlated with societal complexity. The songs of less complex peoples, such as egalitarian foragers, included more vocables (sounds not words). Words were not enunciated as clearly in their songs and there was greater repetition of vocables and words. The songs of most complex peoples included fewer vocables, less repetition, and more words which were more clearly enunciated. While Lomax's conclusions concerning the correlation between dance and song and relative cultural complexity have been questioned, there are some interesting parallels between his findings and those of Fischer on stylistic elements in ornamental designs.

Art and Culture

Anthropologists are not interested in art simply for art's sake. As we have already seen with the examples of body, visual, and performance arts, art is embedded in a cultural context. Three of many features of this context are religion, gender, and identity.

Secular and Religious Art

In our discussions of the various forms of art, we mentioned that certain artistic products are sacred and others are not. There are both sacred and secular designs, forms, dances, songs, music, and literature. This division between secular and sacred cuts across many forms of art and across most cultures.

In contemporary industrial society, the greatest artistic energies are expended in the creation of secular art, although such art may at times include religious themes. If, for example, you examine the works of the greatest Western painters, architects, and composers of the last century, you will find that most of their work is secular. This was not always true. The great art of earlier periods was for the most part concerned with religion, partly because religious and political authorities so often sponsored artists and their creations. The pyramids and great temples of ancient Egypt were related to conceptions of the afterlife and other dimensions of the supernatural world. While visiting pyramids and great statues carved of the pharaohs, one must remember that the pharaohs were gods on earth.

In classical Greece, the cradle of Western European artistic traditions, religion was a central focus for most of their greatest artistic accomplishments. The Parthenon in Athens was the temple of Athena, while most of their greatest public statuary depicted gods such as Poseidon, Zeus, Apollo, and Venus. Much Greek drama had strong religious overtones and was associated with the god Dionysus. In Rome, secular art became more prominent: The great buildings were usually palaces and theaters, while public monuments honoring the triumphs of living or recently dead heroes filled Roman cities. With the advent of the Middle Ages religion regained preeminence. The great buildings of the Medieval and the Renaissance period were cathedrals, while the greatest artists of the time labored to fill these buildings with frescos, mosaics, paintings, statuary, and other artistic works, as well as music, song, and pageantry dedicated to the worship of God.

The 1700s began the emphasis on reason and science, the industrial revolution, the rise of capitalism, and the beginnings of modern political democracy. Ever since, Western art has become increasingly secular. The largest buildings in our cities are no longer dedicated to religion, but to government, commerce, or athletics. Contemporary painters choose secular subjects, from realistic landscapes and buildings to abstract designs and cans of Campbell's soup. The most illustrious composers and performers today seldom produce or perform religious music, but focus on secular and, at times, even irreligious themes. For those of us who learned our culture in a society dominated by secular art, it is important to remember that for most peoples and for most of human history, religion and religious art have been preeminent. The most elaborate artistic achievements of a great many peoples are associated with religious ceremonies: visual arts, music, dances, ornamentations, architecture, and their associated mythologies.

We have already discussed examples of the integration of performance arts like music and dance into African healing practices. Another people for whom art—both visual and verbal arts in this case—is part and parcel of curing rituals is the Navajo of the American southwest. In Navajo belief, the most common cause of peoples' illness is the loss of harmony with their environment, often caused by the person's violation of a taboo or other transgression. When illness strikes and a diagnosis is made, a Navajo "singer" (curer or medicine man) is called upon to organize a complex curing ceremony.

In curing ceremonies (and there were traditionally hundreds of such ceremonies), the singer addresses and calls on the Holy People, who are spiritual beings believed by Navajo to have the power to restore sick people to harmony and beauty. Ceremonies usually occur in a hogan (house) at night, and in theory the procedures must be executed perfectly for the cure to work.

For the ceremony, the singer creates images of the Holy People out of sand, called sandpaintings. Navajo sandpaintings are visual and sacred representations that are created, used in a single ceremony, and then destroyed. Most sandpaintings are stylized scenes of events involving various Holy People that occurred in the mythological past. Each sandpainting is part of a ceremony that also includes other sacred objects (such as rattles and prayer sticks) and lengthy songs or chants recited by the singer. The songs/chants that are recited over the sandpainting and the patient may last for hours. Most songs/chants tell of the myths depicted in the specific sandpainting. Thus, each curing ceremony calls to mind the Navajo world view to the patient and the audience present.

In their years of learning to become singers, Navajo singers must memorize the lengthy songs and chants that they recite over sick people to restore their harmony with the world. Singers also learn to make precise sandpaintings that represent specific mythical scenes and events. To make the images, a singer, usually with the help of his family members and/or apprentices, collects and mixes sand and other materials of various colors. The colors, including white, red, yellow, black, and blue, come from mixing different colors of sand with charcoal, corn pollen, and various plant materials. Pictures are created by carefully dribbling fine grains of sand through the fingers onto the prepared floor of the hogan.

There are, literally, hundreds of sandpaintings. Most ceremonies involve a combination of many sandpaintings used in association with particular chants. Because some are quite large and enormously detailed, they often take hours to create. But all must be exact representations of the ideal model of the mythical scene or event depicted. The images are stylized drawings of the Holy People, many of whom are depicted with weapons and armor. Most scenes represented in the sandpaintings are from particular myths familiar to the patient and audience.

Sandpaintings are made for the express purpose of inducing the Holy People to come to the hogan where the ceremony is held. The Holy People are attracted by the beauty of the sandpainting, the compelling chants recited by the singer, and the manipulation of powerful ritual objects. During the ceremony, the patient usually is sitting on the sandpainting itself, which contains drawings of the Holy People whose presence in the hogan imbues the images with power. The singer completes transfer of power to the patient when he rubs the patient's body with the sand of the images of the Holy People. After each phase of the ceremony is finished, the sandpainting is destroyed, for the Holy People commanded the Navajo not to make permanent images of them.

Navajo sandpaintings certainly are works of art. Some Anglos who have seen them think it is a "shame" to destroy such beautiful images that singers and their helpers have worked so hard to create. But in the context of Navajo beliefs, sandpaintings are made for specific curing ceremonials held for particular patients. That purpose—not expressing the singer's creativity, making an artistic statement, celebrating Navajo culture, or publicly displaying the singer's talents—is their objective. For Navajo, fulfilling that purpose requires that they not be permanent.

Navajo sandpaintings and the singing of curers clearly have strong religious overtones, but the division between secular and religious purposes is not always clear. The kachina dolls of the Hopis are small figures carved out of cottonwood root and painted to look like one of the kachina or supernatural beings which are a central focus of their religious life (see Chapters 9 and 13). Traditionally, these dolls were given to girls at ceremonial dances by people wearing kachina costumes and masks. The dolls themselves were not ritual items, but

A Navajo singer creates an image of the Holy People out of colored sand. Most sandpaintings represent scenes from the Navajo mythological past. When patients come into contact with them, they are imbued with the power of Holy People, and thus restored to harmony and beauty.

rather a way to help the children learn about and recognize the 500 or so different kachina spirits.

Similarly, the Hispanic peoples of New Mexico have a tradition of producing *bultos,* which are carved wooden crucifixes and figures of saints, and *retablos,* which are flat wooden boards, painted with images of Christ or saints. Today, in New Mexico there are dozens of artists who produce and sell *bultos* and *retablos.* Some of these paintings and figures of saints find their way into churches or family chapels and altars, but the majority are used in a more secular context, as decorative art for the home. Religious symbolism is often used to decorate clothing and other items of everyday use, blurring the distinction between secular and sacred art.

Religious considerations have other effects on secular art as well. The use of certain types of motifs or themes may be religiously forbidden. The Koran prohibits the use of human images, which are viewed as idolatry. Thus, many Islamic peoples extended this ban to include any pictorial representation of humans or animals. As a result, much of the art of Islamic peoples is devoid of naturalistic representations, focusing instead on elaborate geometric or curvilinear designs. The Shakers emphasized singing and dancing as important parts of their religious services, but prohibited the use of musical instruments. Religious beliefs frequently place limits on even secular artistic expressions.

Art and Gender

Gender differences often are reflected in body, visual, performance, and verbal arts. Colors and designs sometimes are considered male or female, as most familiarly reflected in clothing and body decoration. Gender also influences who creates and/or performs certain types of visual, performance, or verbal arts. The BaMbuti pygmies of the African rain forest have a ritual performance involving dance and music they call *molimo.* They view the forest as like their parent and, like any parent, the forest looks after its children—themselves. Therefore, when misfortune strikes, it must be due to the fact that the forest is asleep. To wake up the forest, at nighttime the women and children retire to their huts while the men make *molimo* music. Women are not supposed to know that the *molimo* is just a long, flutelike instrument stored in a local stream, but to believe it to be some kind of forest animal. (In fact, women seem to know all about the *molimo.*)

As discussed in Chapter 10, men and women are usually involved in the production of different types of durable items, and usually the individuals involved in production decorate the items as well. In many cases, the aesthetic qualities of the items are an integral part of the production process itself, as with the shape of a pottery vessel or metal tool, or the design in a blanket or a basket. However, in other instances, decorative arts are separate and distinct from the production of the basic item itself, and decorative artists may be defined by gender.

Among the Plains Indians, beadwork and quillwork were produced by women. The only men who produced beadwork and quillwork were berdaches, men who dressed and acted as women. While women and men painted hides, there were distinct differences in subject matter. Women painted only geometric designs. The hide containers, called parafleches, used for the storage of food and clothing were made by women and were only painted in geometric designs. Representational designs of people, horses, and other animals and supernatural beings were only painted by men. Tepees and buffalo robes, though made by women, were painted by either men or women depending upon whether the design was to be geometric (by women) or representational (by men).

Some visual art objects are made for specific rituals or ceremonies. Initiation rites are usually held for only one sex (see Chapter 15). The art produced for them, therefore, is sometimes "sex-specific." In many cultures of the highlands of Papua New Guinea, long bamboo flutes are played at male initiation ceremonies. Women are not supposed to know about the existence of flutes. Many initiation ceremonies also include carved and painted masks, supposedly kept secret from women and uninitiated boys.

Performance arts often are carried out during religious ceremonies. Men have historically played the dominant role in most religions. Not surprisingly, in most societies men dominate the performance arts associated with religion. For example, even though many of the Hopi kachinas are female, in traditional kachina dances all dancers, even those impersonating female spirits, are men. In ancient Greek drama, the roles of women were played by men. In the West, women were not allowed to participate in certain performance arts long after they had become secularized. The role of Juliet, in the original production of Shakespeare's play, was performed by a young boy, for women could not be actors in Shakespeare's time. It was not until the late seventeenth century that women could perform in the English theater.

Social Functions of Art

Does art exist solely to satisfy the human desire for the aesthetic? Perhaps, but if so why have humans expended such incredible energy in its creation? Perhaps art also has a critical role and function in human social life and cultural existence. Through the use of art people can simultaneously express their identities as members of particular groups, while at the same time demonstrating their unique individuality.

Through the production, consumption, and use of art, we can express our personal individuality, our group identities (including ethnic affiliation), and even our social status.

Individuality   Many of us attempt to express our individuality by creating art or displaying art, as shown by the widespread appeal of handmade goods produced by skilled craftspeople. The attraction of handmade over machine made goods has been, since the advent of the industrial revolution in the nineteenth century, their individuality. This individuality is not solely the result of the differing technical skill of the makers, but rather that the makers have consciously tried to make every item unique by varying colors and designs. Thus, if one looks at oriental rugs, American-Indian jewelry, pottery and baskets, Maya textiles from Guatemala, or wood carvings from New Guinea, rarely are two items identical. If they are, it is probably because they were produced for the commercial market.

Similarly, our clothing and houses express our individuality. Even though we usually conform to the norms of our society in clothing styles, most of us abhor uniforms, and thus we enhance them in some manner so as to make them uniquely ours. Similarly in dwellings or buildings people attempt to express individuality. While all Maori dwellings were carved and painted, different designs and images were used. Today in suburban North America builders of subdivisions usually vary the houses by using a range of floor plans, building materials, and colors. Many residents of older neighborhoods, though, still consider the new subdivisions as lacking in character, style, and individuality.

Social Identity   As well as displaying our individuality, art is a means of expressing social identity, publicly displaying what kind of person you are or which group of people you identify with. In the 1960s and early 1970s, many young individuals wore long hair, beads, and baggy clothes decorated with peace signs and upside-down flags. Some traveled the country in old Volkswagen minibuses or school buses that were hand painted in strange colors and designs. The minute you saw them you knew they were "hippies." Clothing styles, hairstyles, and other art forms are commonly used to indicate social group identity, from

Multiculturalism in the United States has led to the acceptance of graffiti and other forms of artistic expression as "legitimate art." Too many of us, though, seem to think that appreciating such artistic alternatives is all it takes to make us sensitive to issues of multicultural diversity.

the black leather jackets painted with club emblems of motorcycle gangs to the shepherd crook spears and red sashes of the Cheyenne Dog Soldier society.

A widespread use of art to express social membership has to do with ethnic affiliation. In Chapter 17 we discuss ethnic boundary markers in more detail, but here it is important to note that art is one of the common expressions of ethnic identity. Clothing styles and decoration are important visual markers of ethnic identity. Plaid kilts are markers of Scots, as much as beaded clothing and feather headdresses are of American Indians. A woman in Guatemala wearing a huipuli is a Maya. If you see a man wearing a cowboy hat and boots in Europe, you can guess that he is an American tourist, even though he has probably never ridden a horse or seen many cows.

Ethnicity is expressed in more than clothing. The full range of artistic forms—body, visual, performance, and verbal arts—is employed to display one's ethnic identity. Thus, we speak of ethnic art, ethnic dance, ethnic music, ethnic songs, ethnic literature, and ethnic foods. Despite our use of the word *ethnic* in such contexts, ultimately, of course, all art is ethnic art, since it is associated with a specific ethnic group and everyone is a part of some ethnic group. For various reasons, people value and pay

A CLOSER LOOK

The Ethnic Art Market

The development of the ethnic market is one of those peculiarities of contemporary urban society. Produced by smaller indigenous ethnic groups, these are ethnically distinctive items, produced not for domestic use of the community, but made for sale to members of other dominant groups. Although the items may have functional forms—baskets, pots, rugs, and so on—they are not purchased for use, but for ornamental or decorative purposes. Thus, value is not the result of their utility, but rather that they represent, or at least are thought to represent, an authentic artistic expression of the people who made the items.

In North America, native indigenous peoples began producing pottery, basketry, and other craft items for sale to white settlers during the colonial period. However, these items were purchased for their utilitarian value, not because they were made by native peoples. The market for indigenous ethnic art evolved out of what some have called the "curio trade." As early as the 1840s Niagara Falls, on the New York/Ontario border, had developed as a tourist mecca. As with all tourists, visitors wished to purchase souvenirs as tangible mementos. Native groups on both sides of the border quickly responded by producing "Indian curios" for sale. Initially, these curios were items which these communities also made for their own use; but native craftspeople quickly developed novelty items specifically made for the tourist market.

The market for Indian art remained small and localized in North America until the 1890s. At the turn of the twentieth century, many affluent families began creating "Indian dens" in their homes, rooms decorated with Indian craft items. The market for Indian crafts peaked about the time of World War I, waned during the 1920s, and collapsed during the great economic depression of the 1930s. During the 1960s the market for Indian crafts began to revive in the United States. Individuals throughout the country once again began to collect and decorate their homes with historic and contemporary Indian produced items: rugs, baskets, pots, and beadwork. In the late 1970s major auction houses on the east coast began holding special Indian art auctions. By the 1990s the demand and prices paid for Indian art had risen dramatically. Many Indian art items that had sold for $10 to $50 in the mid-1960s today command prices in the thousands of dollars. The growth in the market for Indian art in the United States is paralleled by the growth in Canada for indigenous art. In the 1950s some of the Inuit communities in northern Canada began producing and marketing stone sculptures and prints of native life.

Today, Inuit art is widely collected not only in Canada, but in the United States and other countries as well. As a result, even more Inuit communities are producing sculpture and prints for the growing and lucrative ethnic art market.

When does a curio become art? Why do people collect ethnic art? These are difficult questions to answer. The answer to the first question may be price. Curios are inexpensive, while many art objects are or can be expensive. Thus, when Maria Martinez of San Ildefonso Pueblo in New Mexico was selling her pottery for a few dollars a piece they were or could be considered curios. Today the same pots can sell for thousands of dollars, and thus they are art. As the prices have escalated the old Indian curio stores have all but disappeared, replaced by Indian art galleries. The reasons why people buy and collect ethnic art are varied. Many individuals collect ethnic art out of a deep aesthetic appreciation of the objects themselves. Others purchase them as status symbols, because they are expensive and not everyone can afford them. Even though they may be expensive there is still a memento or souvenir dimension to the ethnic art market. A visitor to Canada might purchase an Inuit carving or a Northwest Coast mask as something that is uniquely Canadian. Similarly, a visitor to New Mexico might buy

premium prices for the art produced by ethnic groups other than their own (see "A Closer Look").

From an anthropological perspective, much of the multicultural movement in contemporary North America—and particularly in colleges and universities—is really about understanding and appreciating "ethnic" forms of artistic expression. When Anglo-Americans talk about "other cultures," as often as not they are referring to African-, Hispanic-, Asian-, and other "non-Anglo-" Americans. When they "celebrate diversity," as often as not they are celebrating differences in literature and other forms of verbal art, interpreting graffiti as a legitimate art form, listening to African or Mexican music, eating South Asian or Vietnamese foods, and so forth. Overall the multicultural movement has had a positive influence on intercultural tolerance and understanding. In fact, multiculturalism is part of what anthropologists have been trying to get across to their students for nearly a century. But perhaps more people ought to realize that appreciating "multicultural" diversity should mean far more than celebrating diversity in forms of artistic expression.

Social Status Finally, relative social status within societies is reflected in the use of art. As discussed earlier, body

an Acoma pot or a Navajo rug as something uniquely Southwestern or American. Thus, indigenous ethnic art serves as a reminder of place.

There is, however, still another dimension to ethnic art. An American, living in England, purchased a Navajo rug in Jackson Hole, Wyoming. She wanted something uniquely American to have in her home in England. The rug was symbolic of her homeland and a tangible reminder of her ethnic identity. Art is or can be an expression of national/ethnic identity. One of the problems which has confronted the people of European ancestry in Canada and the United States is identity. The peoples of Europe have distinct ethnic identities that are expressed not only with their languages, but with their art traditions. Both Americans and Canadians have faced a similar problem of attempting to establish identities separate from that of Europe. While we may have distinct histories, we are lacking in more tangible expressions of national identity. In our traditional art, we are but extensions of a generic European tradition. Not surprisingly, there have been attempts to establish separate art traditions. In painting, during the early nineteenth century the so-called Hudson River School emerged in the United States, while in Canada the Group of Seven attempted to establish a distinctive Canadian school in the early twentieth century. Interestingly, both groups focused on landscape paintings, emphasizing the distinctiveness of the land itself. The difficulty was and is that the

Native Americans sell silver and turquoise jewelry to tourists on the plaza in Santa Fe, New Mexico. Anglos pay high prices for "authentic" Indian objects for a variety of reasons, ranging from acquiring souvenirs from a rare trip to Indian Country to expressing their own identities as Americans.

differences between Canadian, American, and European art traditions are, in most cases, so subtle that only experts can really distinguish between them.

To Americans and Canadians the art of indigenous peoples has become important because native art is clearly and uniquely identifiable as American or Canadian. Ethnic art is not only identified with people, but, more importantly, with specific geographical places as well. It is this identification with place that has allowed indigenous ethnic art to be transformed from merely symbols of an indigenous community to broader symbols of a national identity.

arts are frequently an indicator of social status. Other art forms also indicate status. In many ranked and stratified societies the rights to make use of certain art forms may be the property of families or status groups. Only certain individuals will have the right to wear or use particular colors or designs, sing particular songs, dance particular dances, and even tell particular stories. This control over the use or performance of particular artistic expression is a symbolic indicator of individual social status.

Similarly in contemporary society we use art to demonstrate our relative status. We display our status in our homes, automobiles, furnishings, and clothing, com-municating to the world "Look what we can afford to buy." We also demonstrate our status in what we hang on our walls, read, listen to, and watch. In our consumption of visual, performance, and verbal arts the evaluation, of course, is more subjective and difficult to measure. But for many people opera, ballet, and classical music have higher status than comedy, square dancing, and country-western or rap music. Classical literature has higher status than romance novels, science fiction, and comic books. Personal taste obviously still plays a significant role in our artistic choices, but when is the last time you heard of a really rich person endowing a dance hall?

Summary

All cultures have artistic objects, designs, songs, dances, and other ways of expressing their appreciation of the aesthetic. The aesthetic impulse therefore is universal, although cultures vary in their ways of expressing it and the social functions and cultural meanings they make of it. People raised in the Western tradition are inclined to think of art as something set apart from everyday life—as when we use the phrase "fine arts"—yet we all express ourselves aesthetically in many ways, including how we dress, decorate our houses, and eat our meals. In addition to allowing people to express themselves aesthetically, art serves communicative functions by encoding meanings and messages in symbolic forms.

Art takes a multitude of forms, including at minimum body, visual, and performance arts. People around the world change their bodily appearance by such means as physical alterations, application of body paints, tattoos, and scarification. These decorations of the body are used for a variety of purposes, including beautification, expression of individual or group identity, display of privilege or social position, and symbolic indication of social maturity. The tattooing practices of the Maori of New Zealand and other Polynesians exemplify some of these functions.

In the visual arts, humankind as a whole has shown enormous creativity in form, style, design, techniques, materials, and many other features. Ornamentation of tools, clothing, basketry, houses, and practically all other material objects is a universal practice. The Northwest Coast peoples illustrate one way in which art varies in style and two-dimensional representation.

Performance arts include the use of sound and movement for both aesthetic and communicative purposes. In preindustrial cultures, performances of music (including song and percussion), dance, and theater often involve heavy audience participation, as they often do in the everyday lives of people everywhere. Often, performance art is tightly integrated into a people's spiritual and religious life, from Judeo-Christian worship services to possession trances in the *voudon* religion of the Caribbean. The integration of music and dance into the healing practices of the Tumbuka of Malawi and many other African peoples shows that using music to help cure both physical and psychological ills is not a recent, Western innovation.

Perhaps many forms of art began as "sacred" in that they were connected to the appeal to or worship of spiritual beings. Certainly, the religious elements of artistic expression are important not only in the history of Western art, but in the artistic traditions of people the world over. In their complex curing ceremonies, Navajo singers used both visual arts (sandpaintings) and performance arts (chants/songs) in appealing to the Holy People. Distinguishing "sacred" and "secular" art seems like a simple thing, but in real cases objects with religious significance are used for practical purposes. Art is connected to other social and cultural elements such as gender, identity, and status.

Key Terms

art
aesthetic
body arts

visual arts
performance arts

Suggested Readings

Boas, Franz. *Primitive Art*. New York: Dover Publications, Inc., 1955 (original 1927).
  • *The first systematic treatment of the subject by an anthropologist. Despite its original publication date nearly 75 years ago, this book remains insightful today.*
Brain, Robert. *The Decorated Body*. New York: Harper & Row, 1979.

Faris, James C. *Nuba Personal Art*. London: 1972.
Mead, Sidney Moko. *Te Maori: Maori Art from New Zealand Collections*. New York: Harry N. Abrams, 1984.
The Garland Encyclopedia of World Music.
  • *This very useful reference includes large volumes dedicated to the music of particular world regions, such as Australia and the Pacific, Africa, and North America. Not all volumes are yet available. Each volume has dozens of articles written by experts on various specific cultures of the region, or on various topics about the region's music.*

Internet Exercises

The "Ur-List: Web Resources for Visual Anthropology" from the University of Southern California (http://www.usc.edu/dept/elab/urlist/index.html) has many links to sites related to culture and the creative experience. Some of the categories are museums and archives, art collections, and multimedia collections.

"Ethnomusicology Online" maintains a peer-reviewed, multimedia web journal. This site is provided by the University of Maryland, Baltimore County (http://research.umbc.edu/eol). A peer-reviewed journal usually assures articles of high quality, since those that do not live up to an academic standard do not make it through the review. One of the concerns about information on the Internet is that there is more quantity than quality. Be careful to investigate the source of information you find on the Internet.

CHAPTER 15

Personality, Culture, and the Life Cycle

CONTENTS

Personality and Culture

Child-Rearing Practices and the Formation of Personality

Cultural Consequences of Modal Personality

Age Categories and Age Sets

Life Cycle

Childhood

Becoming an Adult

Initiation Rites

Adulthood

Old Age

By interacting with others while growing up in a particular society, individuals acquire certain ways of thinking and feeling, which affects how they react to events, people, and life's experiences.
Visit http://www.wadsworth.com/humanity to learn more about the material covered in this chapter and to access activities, exercises, and tutorial quizzes.

*T*HE PATTERNED *ways infants and children interact with their parents and other adults vary from culture to culture. Ethnologists are interested in how the process of nurturing and enculturating children affects the development of an individual's motivations, emotional reactions, behavioral predispositions, and other elements of what* *people commonly call personality. As we shall see, although growing up in a culture does affect the kind of personality people tend to develop, culture does not determine personality, for personality characteristics vary greatly between the members of a culture. How personality and culture affect each other is one topic of this chapter.*

PEOPLE CHANGE as they pass through childhood into puberty, become married, have children, reach middle age, and grow old. In all cultures, the movement of people through the various stages of life brings new roles and responsibilities, which are often marked off by rites of passage. Such life cycle changes also are considered in this chapter.

Personality and Culture

A child learns how to think, feel, speak, and behave while growing up in a social environment made up of other people and the cultural traditions they live by. No two children experience the same social and cultural environments during their childhood, but people brought up in similar environments do develop similarities in their emotions and reactions to people and events. The specialization known as *psychological anthropology* studies the relation between individuals and their cultural systems. One major interest of psychological anthropology is the relation between personality and culture.

What do we mean by **personality**? A concise definition appears in the 1991 *Dictionary of Concepts in Cultural Anthropology:* "The characteristic modes of thought, motivation, and feeling, conscious and unconscious, which guide the behavior of an individual" (Winthrop, 1991, 213). This definition implies that to the extent that two individuals share a similar personality, their behavioral reactions to events and situations will be similar.

The type of personality an individual develops is a product of the complex interaction between that individual's unique biological make up and total life experiences. A discussion of how these two forces interact to fashion a unique human individual is outside the scope of this book. Psychological anthropologists have focused much more on life experiences than on biological influences on personality. They are especially concerned with the effects of how children are cared for and enculturated on the type of personality they are likely to develop. If nurturing and enculturation practices differ from culture to culture, then these differences might be reflected in the personalities of the members of these cultures.

Child-Rearing Practices and the Formation of Personality

Child-rearing practices refers to a culture's consistent and widespread behavioral patterns involved in caring for and enculturating children. These include practices such as how children are nursed, weaned, and toilet trained; how adults and people their own age interact with children; the kinds of behaviors that are punished and rewarded; how much time children spend with their mothers, fathers, and other caretakers; how much attention and love they receive from adults and other family members; and the like. Child-rearing practices are important influences on the type of personality people acquire. All else equal (and all else never is equal), children exposed to similar child-rearing practices tend to develop common elements of personality.

Although scholars find it convenient to speak of "the" way the members of a culture raise children, it is important to note that there is always variability in how families interact with their young, even within a single cultural tradition. Nonetheless, people share much in common by virtue of the fact that they were raised in the same culture, and the cultural knowledge they share has at least some impact on how they rear their children. They may broadly agree, for instance, on the proper age and methods for nursing and weaning infants, on appropriate physical punishment, and on other practices. Likewise, in culturally homogeneous societies families may be subject to similar kinds of economic or social pressures that lead to similar child-rearing practices. For example, if men frequently are away on hunts or wars, then fathers and other male relatives may not be as active in child care as are women, and this may impact their children's personality formation.

Significant differences exist between cultures in behavioral patterns related to child-rearing. To illustrate this diversity we use two examples: weaning and discipline methods.

Cultures differ in their ideas about whether infants should be allowed to nurse whenever they desire or only at certain times. There are culturally variable norms about the proper age of weaning and how it should be accomplished. Many !Kung mothers breastfeed their children for about four years. Reportedly, some Inuit allowed children to nurse as long as they desired; even ten-year-olds might occasionally be given the breast. Weaning methods likewise vary: Some people believe that infants should be allowed to wean themselves, whereas other mothers coat their nipples with bitter substances to discourage nursing after a certain age.

Norms about disciplining children likewise vary from people to people. In some societies, people believe that physical punishment is an integral and necessary part of childhood discipline (as in the saying "spare the rod and spoil the child"). In other societies, correcting children's behavior by slapping or beating them is rare. Parents and siblings may ridicule a child for misbehaving, or children may be indulged until they reach a certain age, after which they are punished severely for their misdeeds. In many Micronesian and Polynesian islands, an infant of either gender is caressed, fondled, played with, and generally the center of interest of the whole family. Such indulgence and attention continue until a younger sibling is born. Then attention shifts to the newborn, and the child finds herself or himself just another member of a (usually large) family. Prolonged tantrums often result.

In some cultures children are threatened by animals, ghosts, spirit beings, and the like (the equivalent of "the boogey man will get you if you act like that"). Among the Hopi, children are threatened by *kachinas,* or masked dancers impersonating spiritual beings whom Hopi believe live in the mountains near their villages. When a Hopi child seriously misbehaves, parents often get someone to put on a costume (including a frightening mask) of an "ogre" kachina believed to eat children. When the kachina tries to steal the child for misbehaving, the parents come to his or her rescue. Children are so grateful to their parents for saving them that they accede to their wishes—for a while, anyway. Kachinas also reward "deserving" children by passing out gifts during their dances. Boys often are given a small bow and arrow, whereas girls receive carved wooden figures shaped and painted like the spirits.

Numerous other differences in child-rearing norms and practices exist between societies. Age and methods of toilet training are diverse. The kinds of social interaction with adults vary widely—children are constantly fussed over among one people, left alone more to amuse themselves among others. Youngsters are punished for playing with their genitals in one society but are fondled playfully by adults in another. Pubescent boys and girls are allowed to associate freely with one another in some societies but are discouraged or forbidden from doing so in others. Fathers often are hardly involved with their children and in fact are absent much of the time, but sometimes men are more equal partners in child care. Caretaking roles vary: In some cases, virtually all the care is the responsibility of the mother, but in others, relatives of the child (e.g., grandparents, uncles, aunts, older siblings) share the duties.

These are only a few of the many ways cultures vary in child-rearing norms and practices. Partly as a result of these variations, members of different cultures develop some differences in adult personality. A major question of psychological anthropology is: How are differences in adult personality related to different child-rearing practices? More broadly phrased: How do cultural systems affect the personalities of their members?

The answer is not simple. Early studies often assumed a one-to-one relationship between personality and culture. That is, largely through its child-rearing practices, each culture was seen as molding the personalities of its members into a certain basic type. It commonly was believed that "a" culture fashioned the individual personalities of its members into the kinds of persons "it" needed to persist.

The most famous exponent of this approach was Ruth Benedict, whose 1934 book *Patterns of Culture* was enormously influential. Benedict argued that, from the vast array of humanly possible cultures, each develops only a limited number of "themes," "patterns," or "configurations" that come to dominate the thinking and responses of its members. These patterns are essentially emotional: Each people develop a unique set of feelings and motivations that govern their behavior. Each culture has a conception of an ideal personality type, and these ideas vary from culture to culture. The essence of both the culture and the personality of a people could be described in simple terms—sometimes even by a single word. Behavior that one people considered crazy or otherwise abnormal would be acceptable, normal, and even ideal among another people.

For instance, Benedict wrote that the Kwakiutl of the northwest coast of North America are individualistic, competitive, intemperate, and egoistic. This culture (or is it a personality?) affects Kwakiutl customary behaviors. They stage ceremonies known as *potlatches* in which one kin group gives away enormous quantities of goods to another. The aim is to shame the rival group because if the rival is unable to return the presentations on certain occasions, it suffers a loss of prestige. In fact, to avoid losing prestige the recipient group is obliged to return gifts of even greater value. Over time the presentations often snowball until the members of one group, in their ceaseless quest for prestige, are left destitute (or so Benedict imagined). The whole complex of behavior connected to the potlatch reflects the cultural configuration of the Kwakiutl—so caught up is Kwakiutl culture by the prestige motivation that groups impoverish themselves to achieve this goal. Benedict used the term "Dionysian" to describe the Kwakiutl, after the Greek god known for his excesses.

Benedict contrasted this configuration to the Zuni villagers of the North American Southwest. Zuni control their emotions; they are moderate, modest, stoical, orderly, and restrained in their behavior; they do not boast or attempt to rise above their fellows but are social and cooperative. This "Apollonian" cultural theme, as Benedict called it, penetrates all of Zuni life. Unlike a Kwakiutl leader, a Zuni man does not seek status; indeed, a leadership role practically has to be forced on him.

So, according to Benedict, each culture has its unique patterns and themes, which produce images of the ideal personality that vary from culture to culture. One culture's crazed megalomaniac is another culture's ideal person. And culture programs personality more or less completely.

Benedict's approach is not highly regarded today by most psychological anthropologists. The notion that whole cultures can be described, compared, and contrasted with fairly simple labels that depict their basic emotional patterns is simplistic. It is invalid to apply single labels to *the* personality type of the members of a culture, such as that Kwakiutl are Dionysian (given to excesses), whereas the Zuni are Apollonian (moderate in all things). Yet labels comparable to those used by Benedict are common even today. They often take the form of stereotypes that one people have about the "personality" or "national character" of another. For example, the Japanese are popularly said to have "authoritarian" personalities because they seem to submit to instituted authority more than some other people. Italians are "excitable" to North American perceptions because they seem to be so enthusiastic about love, food, and family and so quick to take offense. Similarly, according to common American stereotypical labels, French are passionate, Irish have bad tempers, Swiss are humorless, and Swedes are sensual.

In fact, wherever researchers have tried to measure the personality "type" of a people, they have found considerable variability. Individuals do not share the same personality just because they belong to the same culture and have experienced similar child-rearing practices and other influences. There is always variability, due to hormonal and other biological differences between individuals, to idiosyncratic practices of parents, and to other factors. The best we can do is to identify and describe those major elements of personality that many or most members of a culture share. Such elements are known as **modal personality,** meaning that they are elements that are most common, or that are shared by many or most members of a group. Thus, although not all Yąnomamö are alike, as a people their personalities do seem to differ from the Semai (see Chapter 2). Yąnomamö are more likely to behave aggressively to an offense, to demand things of others, and so forth. These differences are connected to how the two people nurture and enculturate children.

To illustrate some of these connections, we briefly consider one of the historically most influential case studies in culture and personality, *The People of Alor* (1944), written by Cora DuBois. The Alorese live on the island of Timor in eastern Indonesia. DuBois was concerned partly with Alorese child-rearing practices and their effects on

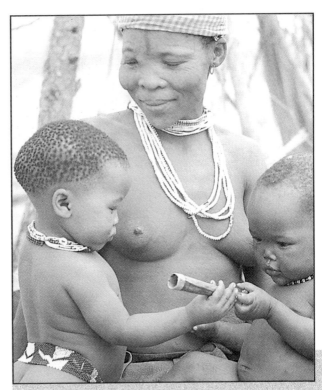

!Kung woman with her children. How parents and other adults interact with children is one of the multitude of influences on personality formation.

personality formation. She gave the people psychological tests and had them interpreted by a psychologist when she returned from the field.

The Alorese are a horticultural people who acquire most of their food by gardening. Women are responsible for most food production. When a woman gives birth, she devotes most of her attention for several weeks to her newborn, nursing the baby whenever he or she cries and generally nurturing the infant. After only two or three weeks the mother returns to work almost daily in the family gardens. From early morning until late afternoon the child is left with grandparents, siblings, or other relatives. The father often is absent, engaged in the borrowing and lending of pigs and other wealth objects that are so important to Alorese.

During the long hours his or her mother is away the infant is not suckled, although attempts are made by caretakers to offer premasticated foods to quiet the infant's crying. As the child matures, his or her emotional demands are met only irregularly and by various individuals. Children are not often caressed or praised, and they frequently are teased and lied to. Their demands for attention often are ignored by their caretakers. Weaning is accomplished by pushing the child away from the breast; sometimes a mother will deliberately provoke a recently weaned child by nursing another child because adults find the child's reaction humorous. All in all, the Alorese child lives in an uncertain, insecure, and, to some degree, hostile social environment.

As a result of these childhood experiences, many Alorese develop a personality described (by DuBois) as suspicious, antagonistic, uncooperative, prone to violent outbursts of jealousy, and lacking in self-confidence and social responsibility. These features of Alorese modal personality affect adult interpersonal relationships. Relations between husbands and wives, for instance, usually lack intimacy and often are downright hostile.

Child-rearing practices seem to be the major link between culture and the personalities people are most likely to develop. The cultural system influences how adults raise their children, and child-rearing practices in turn influence modal personality. The Alorese case illustrates how these influences might operate in one society. (It is worth emphasizing, again, that not all Alorese share these modal personality characteristics, any more than all Anglo-derived North Americans have the same personalities.) Note that the fact that so many Alorese mothers work long in gardens, and that fathers are absent much of the time, affects how children are raised. Mothers and fathers probably do not intend to mold their offspring in these ways, but it is a by-product of their behavior.

Cultural Consequences of Modal Personality

So far we have considered only one-half of the relation between personality and culture: how culture (particularly, child-rearing practices) affects modal personality. The other half of the relation is the impact of personality "type" on culture, that is, how the common elements of people's personalities affect culture. We would like to have a framework to analyze how personalities and cultures interact and *mutually* affect each other.

Such a framework is available. Clearly, certain subsystems of a people's overall culture have greater impact on child-rearing practices than other subsystems; that is, some aspects of a culture affect the kinds of personalities individuals develop more than other aspects. In turn, because many individuals share certain personality elements, they relate in certain patterned ways to other individuals, and they find certain kinds of behaviors and ideas more psychologically appealing than others. Modal personality, therefore, influences other subsystems of the culture.

According to this approach, then, for purposes of relating cultural elements to personality, we divide a cultural system into two parts: (1) those subsystems that importantly affect child rearing and hence influence the

kind of personality many or most individuals develop and (2) those subsystems that are partly determined by this modal personality.

What, specifically, about a people's overall way of life is most likely to have important effects on how they raise their children? The norms, values, attitudes, world views, and other kinds of shared cultural ideas are important. For instance, parents who view the world as a hostile place with many dangers may impart feelings of insecurity to their children. Adults who mistrust other people may have children who grow up suspicious of others.

But some psychological anthropologists believe that they can make conclusions more important than to simply say that "it all depends on a culture's ideas and beliefs." They can conclude more than this because child-rearing *practices* are affected by more than people's *ideas*. People's norms, values, world views, attitudes, and beliefs about the proper way to raise children affect how they actually raise children, but they do not entirely determine how they do so. For example, in the case of the Alorese we saw how the sexual division of labor leads mothers to leave their children for many hours a day, forcing other relatives to assume the role of caretaker. In modern North America, parents with jobs make child-care arrangements for their children, leaving them with relatives, baby-sitters, or day-care centers. Alorese or North American parents may believe that they *ought* to spend more time with their children. But their *actual* child-rearing practices are affected by more than just their beliefs and ideals. Economic and social conditions impact what parents do. And parents themselves have other values and goals that may conflict with their desire to bring up their children the way they or others think they should.

One sophisticated and realistic model recognizes that child-rearing practices are affected by more than just people's ideas about the proper way to care for and rear children. The relation between modal personality and culture is suggested by the social systems model, developed by John Whiting and Irvin Child. The model is diagrammed in Figure 15.1.

In the figure, the *maintenance system* essentially is those specific aspects of cultures we have discussed in Chapters 5 through 12. It includes how people acquire energy and materials from their environment; the organization of production and exchange; the prevalent forms of family and domestic groups; the kinds and sizes of kin groups and the strength and breadth of kinship relations; inequalities in access to resources and to social rewards; and the organization of political life, legal systems, and warfare. A maintenance system, in short, consists of a people's basic adaptation to nature and how their society is organized to persist, cooperate, allocate rewards, defend itself, and maintain internal

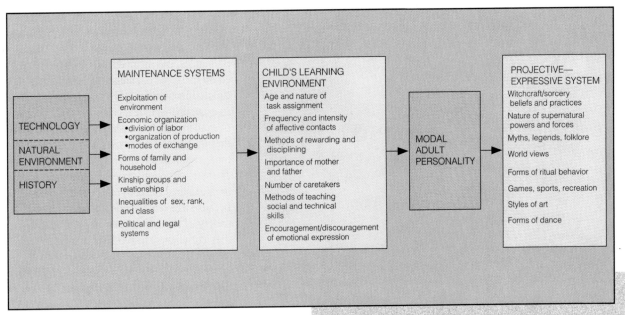

Figure15.1   The Social Systems Model

Source: Adapted from "A Model for Psychocultural Research," by John Whiting in *Culture and Infancy*, P. Herbert Leiderman, Steven R. Tulkin, and Anne Rosenfeld, eds. Orlando, Fla.: Academic Press, 1977. Reprinted by permission.

order. It is influenced by technology, natural environment, and historical forces.

The maintenance system affects how adults enculturate and raise children, which provides the *child's learning environment:* how soon children take on household chores, how they are punished and rewarded, how they interact with caretakers, whether their fathers are often present, whether their mothers defer to their fathers, whether they experience social or economic deprivation, and so forth. The kind of personality children tend to develop depends on the total learning environment to which they are exposed (as the Alorese example illustrates). To the extent that most or many children experience the same learning environment, they tend to develop similar *modal adult personalities*.

Thus, the social systems model suggests that the basic way a society maintains itself by adapting to its environment, organizing its family life and kinship relationships, structuring inequality, and maintaining social control affects the environment in which new generations of children are raised. This learning environment, in turn, leads to some similarities in the personalities of adults.

The social systems model also suggests how modal personality influences culture as well as being influenced by it. Those parts of culture that are strongly influenced by modal personality—typical ways of feeling and reacting—are called the *projective-expressive system*. The idea is that, because many people have similar personalities, they tend to find some kinds of beliefs about the world more plausible than others. For example, depending partly on their personality, people may believe that supernatural beings are benevolent or vengeful, or that nature

should be respected or conquered. People with a certain type of personality also tend to find certain kinds of recreational activities, styles, and objects more pleasurable than others. For example, they find some kinds of games, art styles, dances, and stories more enjoyable to play, view, participate in, and hear than others (see Chapter 14).

One important suggestion of the social systems model is that economic, social, and political factors outside the control of parents and other caretakers are *universally* important influences on how parents rear their children. Employed parents in modern industrial nations often think that there is something unique about their failure to spend as much time with their children as they would like, or as much as they believe is necessary for their children's emotional well-being or intellectual development. To make up for the hours spent on the job instead of at home with the kids, modern parents have adopted the idea of devoting quality time to one's children. The implication is that in the past no one had to worry about such things. But parents everywhere face conditions (such as those identified by the social systems model) that affect how they rear children. Societies have adjusted to these conditions, and they have readjusted as these conditions have changed. Thus far in the United States, working parents themselves have had to make most of the familial rearrangements needed to find child care. Perhaps it is time for more employers to find ways of accommodating their employees' familial needs.

Age sets often occur among people who lack a highly centralized political system, yet need to mobilize young men for warfare or raiding. These Maasai warriors, here braiding one another's hair, belong to the same age set and are likely to remain close throughout their lives.

Given the alleged concern for family values in the United States, perhaps it is time to change "an occupational system that operates 'as if' the family did not exist." (T. Cohen 1987, 72).

Age Categories and Age Sets

In all societies, chronological age makes a difference in the kinds of roles people adopt and in the activities people perform. Everywhere, individuals are culturally classified on the basis of their age: infant, child, adult, elderly person, and so forth. Although all peoples have such age categories, societies vary in the number of recognized categories, the sharpness with which they are defined, their importance relative to other distinctions such as gender and class, and the roles members of the category are expected to adopt.

Like other people, Westerners classify people on the basis of their age. In the United States we make subdivisions of age categories as needed by the context (e.g., the age category "child" may be divided into infant, toddler, preschooler, first-grader, and so on). Many cultures establish more formal and highly organized groups of individuals of similar age. These age groupings assume definite and important rights in and duties to the society as a whole.

One such grouping common in the pre-industrial world is the **age set association**—a formally organized, named group of males or females, the members of which are recruited on the basis of similar age. (Modern educational institutions have analogous associations—grade levels—in which people of similar age enter a class together and pass through successive classes as a cohort.) It is more common for males to be organized into age sets, although some societies have such organizations for both males and females. Because age sets include all members of a society of a particular sex and age cohort, they cut across kinship lines and often serve as pantribal sodalities (see Chapter 11). In many societies, age sets take over functions usually assigned to kin groups and frequently surpass the kin group in relative importance for the individual. If a society has age sets, people usually enter them about or a little after the time they reach sexual maturity. Although age sets are found among peoples in North and South America, Melanesia, and Asia, they are especially common in Africa. There are two distinct types of age sets: *cyclical age sets* and *lineal age sets*.

Societies with *cyclical age sets* have a limited number of named associations based on age. Although the same people continue to associate with one another throughout their lives, the members move as a group from one association to another in rank or age order. The Hidatsa of the Great Plains are an example of this type of system. About every four to six years, all adolescent Hidatsa boys banded together. With the help of their parents they purchased the lowest ranking of the ten age set associations from the members of that association. This lowest-ranking association was called the *Kit-Foxes*. The purchase of the age set gave the new members the sole rights to wear the insignias of this group, as well as to perform its dances and songs. Many rights and duties of individual members were defined by the association of which they were members. After they themselves sold the lowest-ranking age set to a younger age group, the former members of the Kit-Foxes association purchased the rights and privileges of the next highest association, and within a short period all the groups had moved up a step to the next age set. The few surviving old men in the highest-ranking association withdrew from the system after selling their age set because there was no higher place for them to go within the system. Among the Hidatsa, age sets were primarily men's social clubs, with limited economic and political significance. Among the Cheyenne and other Great Plains peoples these organizations frequently filled the role of camp police.

In contrast, in a *lineal age-set* system an individual remains a member of the same association throughout his or her life. The Swazi of southern Africa provide an example of lineal age sets. Every five to seven years, the king of the Swazi announced that a new age set would be created to include all the adolescent boys in the kingdom. This announcement coincided with the proclamation that the members of what had up to then been the youngest set were now free to marry. The role of the youngest set was to serve as active warriors, so its members could not be married. Many of them moved to barracks near the royal family, and even those who remained in their home communities were organized into military units. Every association had its own leaders and insignias, and a man belonged to the same age set for his entire life. All sets participated in wars, each as a separate and distinct military unit. Indeed, after English contact, age sets commonly were called regiments.

Loyalty was expected between members of a given Swazi age set, who referred to one another as *brother* or *age mate*. Whether living in a royal barracks or at home, the members of an age set worked together. Some ethnographers suggest that a man's identity was more closely linked with his age set than with his family. Intense rivalries developed between members of different age sets, and the fighting that occasionally broke out sometimes pitted close relatives against one another.

Age sets illustrate how different societies use the principle of age to allocate roles to individuals and to place them into cooperative groups. In a sense, age sets represent one extreme in the use of age as a principle—age differences are sharply defined, and they become the organizational basis of many common economic and political activities. One African people, the Nyakyusa, even used age together with sex to establish residence. Male members of the same age set lived in the same age-based village, bringing their wives to live with them.

Why do some societies have age sets, whereas most do not? Age sets most commonly are found among peoples who lack a centralized political system yet frequently are engaged in warfare. This correlation has led some anthropologists to suggest that age sets are a means of organizing males for warfare among people who lack formal political leadership and specialized armies.

Life Cycle

A person's **life cycle** consists of the culturally defined age categories through which he or she passes between birth and death. It includes stages such as birth, childhood, sexual maturation (puberty), marriage, adulthood, old age, and death. Each stage in the life cycle carries certain cultural expectations; as individuals move through these stages, their overall role in society changes. All societies recognize at least three major distinctions in the life cycle: childhood, adulthood, and old age. These stages serve as a convenient way to organize our discussion of the life cycle, but it is important to recognize that cultures vary in how they conceive of these stages and in how transitions from one to the other are recognized and marked.

Transitions between stages may take place gradually and not be the object of any particular notice. In some cultures, though, they are sharply and formally defined by a rite of passage. A **rite of passage** is a public ceremony or ritual that marks a change in status, usually brought about or related to increasing age. Examples of rites of passage in North America include baptisms, conferrals, bar mitzvahs, graduation ceremonies, weddings, and funerals.

Childhood

Intuitively, childhood begins at birth. But actually the question is more complex, for people and cultures do not agree on when life begins. Like other phases of the life cycle, "child" is a culturally defined category of person in addition to being a stage of physical and mental development. Does one become a human person at the time of conception, at some later phase in the mother's pregnancy, at birth, or at some time after birth? Because cultures differ in their conceptions of when a person becomes fully "human," the time when childhood begins varies.

One important implication of this variation is when a person is accorded legal protection. The American legal system has struggled with this issue for years, for people of different religious beliefs, ethnic affiliations, and political persuasions do not agree on when human life begins. Members of the pro-life (antiabortion) movement believe that human life, and thus legal protection, begins at the time of conception. Abortion, to them, is murder, unless the mother's own life is at stake. Pro-choice forces believe that human life begins only late in pregnancy, or even only at birth itself, so that a woman's right to choose takes precedence over the right of a child yet unformed or yet unborn.

Information from other cultures reveals a diversity of conceptions of when human life and legal protection begins. The Cheyenne of the American Great Plains considered the murder of one Cheyenne by another as the most serious of crimes. A woman who aborted her child was considered a murderer (see "A Closer Look" in Chapter 11).

In other cultures, though, even birth itself does not automatically confer human status. Infanticide is a widespread (though almost always sorrowful) practice in some cultures. Among some Canadian Inuit a child, particularly a female child born during the winter, could be placed outside immediately after birth to die of exposure. No stigma was attached to such an act. In ancient Greece parents of sickly or unwanted newborn babies could abandon them along the road to die. Any passerby was free to adopt such an infant or to raise it as a slave to be sold, as in the famous story of Oedipus, the Greek king who unknowingly married his mother. In preindustrial societies with a high infant mortality rate, the conferring of full human status sometimes is delayed until infancy has passed; thus, the responsibility for providing formal burials for the large numbers of children who die in infancy is avoided. Even where infanticide is not practiced, the bestowal of full human status sometimes is delayed for some period after the birth of a child.

The formal naming of a child frequently is associated with the conferral of human status and often is the first rite of passage. For the Osage, a Native American people, the naming rite was the most important rite of passage, for it bestowed human status on the individual. Osage parents often waited several months—in the case of a sickly child, possibly more than a year—before naming a child. If the child died before acquiring a name, he or she was quietly buried and the family did not have to observe a year of mourning. After they were convinced the infant was going to survive, parents began to prepare for a naming ritual. A ritual specialist called a "little-old-man" from the child's father's clan was chosen to organize and direct the ceremony. Little-old-men representing all twenty-four Osage patrilineal clans gathered in the "lodge of mystery," a ritual structure in the village, to hold the ceremony. One at a time the leader gave a trade blanket to all the little-old-men, each of whom recited a long and complex ritual prayer asking God's blessing for the child and outlining the supernatural powers associated with his particular clan. After all twenty-four clan prayers had been recited, the child was handed to each of the little-old-men, who in turn blessed the child. Some anointed the baby with water, others rubbed the child with cedar or touched the child with ground corn. Then the baby was seated on a specially prepared robe in the center of the lodge and given a name belonging to his or her clan by the leader. The giving of this name symbolized the acceptance of the child as a member of a particular clan. The ritual participation of members of the other twenty-three clans indicated the acceptance of the child as an Osage. The ritual ended with the father of the child giving horses and blankets to the main little-old-men and lesser gifts to the other little-old-men. Only after the naming ritual occurred did Osage childhood truly begin.

Childhood is the period when people begin to acquire technical and mechanical skills. In most societies, the learning of technical skills begins early by Western standards, by about age five or six. Simple tasks not demanding great strength are done even earlier—three-year-olds may sweep the house, feed the animals, wash the baby, pick up the yard, run errands, deliver messages, and so forth. In industrial societies, much technical learning takes place in schools, where children are instructed by trained specialists. Elsewhere, children learn most skills informally by watching and imitating adults and following their instructions. Among cultivators, children begin going to the fields with their parents and performing minor tasks that are suited to their physical abilities. In herding societies, children begin caring for the herds at a young age. For example, among the Navajo, six- and seven-year-old boys and girls begin helping with the herds of sheep and goats. While Navajo boys learn the technical skills needed by men, girls learn the skills of women by imitating their mothers and playing with toy animals. As they become older they help their mothers by preparing wool for weaving, preparing foods, making clothing, and caring for their younger brothers and sisters.

Becoming an Adult

A person usually reaches puberty between ages twelve and fifteen. In most societies, sexual maturation alone does not convey full adult status, with all its rights and responsibilities. Biologically determined sexual maturation usually precedes culturally defined social maturation, especially for males. This intermediate stage of transition from childhood to adulthood is what we call *adolescence*.

In American society, adolescence often is a troubled period of life, filled with conflict, experimentation, rebellion against parental authority, moodiness, and the like. Some researchers attribute the problems that arise during this period primarily to physiological changes, but others consider cultural factors to be the major causes. In the 1920s Margaret Mead examined adolescence in a Pacific culture in her classic study *Coming of Age in Samoa*. Mead found that adolescence was not a particularly traumatic time in the life of Samoan girls, and she argued that the problems associated with adolescence were the result of cultural factors, not physiological changes. In 1983 Derek Freeman challenged Mead's Samoa findings in his book *Margaret Mead in Samoa*, arguing that Samoan adolescents have about as much trouble and conflict as do American teenagers. He went on to suggest that the physiological changes that occur during adolescence have similar effects among all peoples, so this stage of the life cycle is always stressful despite the cultural context. Most modern anthropologists probably would contend that the universal physiological changes do create problems for adolescents everywhere, but that these problems are manifested in various ways, depending on the cultural context.

Changes in culturally expected behavior also occur during adolescence. Although adolescents begin to take on many of the social and legal responsibilities of adulthood, they usually are not accorded the full prerogatives of adults. For example, in the United States adolescents frequently can be tried and sentenced in an adult court for a criminal offense, yet cannot vote in local, state, or national elections; purchase liquor; marry without parental consent; or get a bank loan without a cosigner. Until the voting age was lowered to eighteen in 1971, a male could be drafted in the army before he could vote. Thus, in the United States an adolescent has some of the legal obligations of an adult but lacks full adult privileges. There are similar disparities in many other societies. Among the Cheyenne, older adolescent boys were expected to join war parties and to be daring and aggressive warriors and raiders. Along with adult males, they were expected to take part in hunts and help supply food for their family. At the same time, they could not hold an official position within the tribe and had to remain silent in the presence of elders.

Initiation Rites

The manner in which individuals are incorporated into adulthood and into adult rights and responsibilities varies from people to people. In the United States, the transition to the adult stage of life is marked by rites of passage we call graduation ceremonies (from high school or college): One leaves the status of "student" and (we hope!) becomes an independent, wage-earning adult. In many societies, the transition from childhood to adulthood is marked by an elaborate set of ceremonies known as **initiation rites**.

Initiation rites often occur around puberty, so sometimes they are called *puberty rites,* although they do far more than simply mark off a person's sexual maturation. During many rituals, the initiates are educated in the intricate responsibilities of adulthood, being told of the changes that will from then on be expected in their behavior and often being let in on ritual secrets.

Some societies have initiation rituals for males only, others for females only, and still others for both sexes. But even those societies that hold initiation rites for both males and females almost always have separate ceremonies for each sex. This generalization suggests that an important function of initiation rituals is to incorporate children not just into adulthood but also into the adult roles and responsibilities culturally appropriate for their sex (see Chapter 10). In fact, the most common theme of initiation rituals is to make girls into women and boys into men.

Some of the most interesting male initiation rituals occur in the highlands of New Guinea. Before describing

an example we must point out that in many of these societies (and there are many hundreds of them) people believe that females can pollute males. Above all else, men fear contact with women's menstrual discharges, which they believe can cause them to sicken and die. Ethnographer Mervyn Meggitt (1970) describes the beliefs of one New Guinea people, called the *Enga,* about women's pollution:

> Men regard menstrual blood as truly dangerous. They believe that contact with it or a menstruating woman will, in the absence of counter-magic, sicken a man and cause persistent vomiting, turn his blood black, corrupt his vital juices so that his skin darkens and wrinkles as his flesh wastes, permanently dull his wits, and eventually lead to a slow decline and death. Menstrual blood introduced into a man's food, they say, quickly kills him, and young women crossed in love sometimes seek their revenge in this way. Menstrual blood dropped on the bog-iris plants . . . that men use in wealth-, pig-, and war-magic destroys them; and a man would divorce, and perhaps kill, the wife concerned. (p. 129)

Because of such beliefs, among many New Guinea peoples women must remain in seclusion during their periods, either in a menstrual hut away from the main settlement or in a special place in their houses, which men never enter.

These beliefs about feminine contamination have many implications for women's lives. Women must take precautions to avoid accidentally causing injury to their husbands by polluting the food they serve. In some New Guinea societies, women must travel on separate paths from men, lest a man unknowingly step on a female secretion and become polluted. Sometimes a wife is believed to "murder" her husband by introducing her bodily fluids into his food; a woman occasionally is killed in retaliation if her husband dies suspiciously. Women have to suffer through having their young sons taken away from them by force because, according to beliefs, the sons are endangered by continued association with their mothers once they reach a certain age.

Finally, it is common in these societies for husbands and wives to live in separate dwellings. A man's wife or wives have their own house, where they live with their children. Their husband lives in a separate men's house, together with all the older boys and men of the hamlet or village. By the time they are around ten, boys usually are taken away from their mothers—because even contact with one's own mother is dangerous for a boy—and brought to live in the men's house. Male initiation rituals usually begin when a boy is dissociated from the company of his mother and other women and inducted into the men's house.

Beginning in their early teens, Awa boys participate in a prolonged series of rituals intended to strengthen, protect, and instruct them. This second-stage initiate is having his nose bled to remove harmful substances from his body.

The details of male initiation vary from people to people in New Guinea. One common cultural rationale of the rituals is to transform a boy into a man: Boys do not grow up naturally but must go through a lengthy series of rituals to give them masculine qualities. Masculine courage, strength, aggressiveness, and independence are desirable not only for the boys themselves but for the group as a whole, because most New Guinea peoples traditionally were heavily involved in warfare with their neighbors and so needed warriors to survive. Another goal of the rituals is to protect boys from feminine contamination: Initiates learn ritual procedures that will allow them to have sexual relations in relative safety.

The Awa, a New Guinea people numbering about 1,500 who were studied by Philip Newman and David Boyd, illustrate both themes: "maturation" and "protection." Like many of their neighbors, Awa men believe that if female substances penetrate male bodies, the men will become sick or old before their time. Beginning in their early teens boys go through a series of rituals that have five stages and last well into their twenties. When several boys in a region have reached the appropriate age of twelve to fourteen they are taken from their mothers' houses. They are inducted as a group into the men's house during an intimidating ritual involving food and

water restrictions, beating with stinging nettles to toughen them, and rubbing the inside of their thighs with a coarse vine. This is the first stage of their initiation.

In the second stage, about one year later, the boys experience the first cleansing of their bodies from female pollution. At a secluded site in the forest they are forceably bled and made to vomit. The purpose of these acts is to protect their general well-being and promote their physiological maturity by removing female substances from the boys' bodies. Small bundles of sharp-edged swordgrass are jabbed into their nostrils and two small cuts are made in the glans of their penises to bleed out contamination. A vine is looped and thrust down their throats, inducing the vomiting that also cleanses and helps dry out their bodies—for the Awa believe that desiccation is necessary for boys to achieve maturity.

The third ritual stage occurs when the males are between eighteen and twenty. They again are purged of female contamination by nose bleeding, penis cutting, and induced vomiting. They also are let in on certain ritual knowledge, known to all adult men but kept secret from women and boys. After they have been through the third stage, the young men are taught why too much contact with women is so dangerous. They learn how menstrual pollution can overstimulate their growth and age them prematurely. Because they have not yet learned to protect themselves from female substances, they are warned to avoid sexual intercourse altogether until they are married.

About five years later, when the men are in their mid-twenties, they go through the "sweat ceremony," which is the fourth stage of initiation. They sit together next to the fire in the men's house and sweat profusely for a week or more. The older men lecture to them about their upcoming responsibilities as husbands and fathers. They are told about how to protect themselves from the dangers of sexual intercourse and are emphatically warned about the evils of adultery. When the men emerge from the men's house after the sweat ceremony they receive new clothes and body ornaments, including a pair of boar's tusks that they wear in their pierced noses as a symbol of their adult status. After this stage, young women chosen as brides are brought to the hamlet of their future husbands.

The fifth stage—appropriately called the "severe penis cutting"—occurs only a few days later. The young men are again subjected to food and water taboos, to nosebleeding and vomiting, and to penis cutting. This time, however, canes are driven deep into their noses to cause severe bleeding. Small wedges of flesh are cut from either side of their penises, producing deep gashes in the glans. In fact, at the final stage of initiation, all the adult men present line up and expose their penises to puncture wounds made by tiny stone-tipped arrows. This treatment is held to be necessary periodically to remove harmful female substances that have entered the body through the penis during sexual intercourse. Once a man has been through the fifth stage, Awa believe that he has been sufficiently strengthened by the hardships of initiation that he is capable of withstanding feminine pollution, although he must continue to undergo ritual bloodletting to maintain his strength.

The Awa illustrate several themes common in male initiation rituals: inducing physical maturation, strengthening and protecting, imparting secret knowledge, and learning the importance of masculine responsibilities. Awa initiation also exemplifies another practice, common not just in New Guinea but around the world: The rituals are almost always painful and traumatic to the boys. They frequently involve scarification, beatings, genital mutilation, tattooing, intimidation by threats and frightful stories, social seclusion, fasting, going without water, and so forth. These pains and traumas usually are considered necessary to strengthen the boys and prepare them for the rigors of adulthood (see "A Closer Look" for one mildly comparable ritual in the United States). Certainly such ordeals indelibly mark the transition from boy to man in the minds and usually the bodies of the males.

Initiation rites for females most often emphasize attainment of physical maturity, instruction in sexual matters and childbearing, and reminders of adult duties as wives and mothers.

Mescalero Apache are one people who have puberty ceremonies for girls. Each year, around the Fourth of July, the people celebrate the attainment of womanhood in a ceremony that lasts four days and four nights. Apache girls in the region who have had their first menses in the last year go to a place where a large tipi is erected. During the ceremony, the girls are regarded as reincarnations of White Painted Woman, a spiritual being who gave many good things to the people. During the ceremony, the girls are blessed by singers (specialists who have gone through lengthy training to learn the stories and chants) and by their relatives and friends. Those attending participate in traditional songs and dances dedicated to the four directions and to spirits associated with them. The Apache ceremony places a lot of emphasis on the girls becoming the "Mothers of the Tribe," perhaps because the Apache are a matrilineal people. On the fourth day, singers recount the history of the Apache and the girls are reminded of their ancestry and obligations. The ceremony honors the girls as individuals, reaffirms their commitment to the community and vice-versa, urges them to act responsibly, and

Mescalero Apache girls undergo an initiation ceremony that celebrates their attainment of womanhood. These young women are dressed for the four-day ceremony, which seems to help them assume the responsibilities of adulthood.

upholds and re-creates Apache traditions annually. According to ethnographer Claire Farrer (1996, 89), "almost invariably, the girls report having been changed, not only into social women but also at a very basic level. They are ready to put aside their childhoods and become full members of their tribe and community." The ceremony thus helps the girls make the social transition to adulthood, with all its rights and responsibilities.

Among Apache, there are no painful ordeals. But female ceremonies in some other cultures do involve pain. When a girl among the Tucuna Indians of the Amazon has her first menstruation, she is immediately placed in the loft of the large communal dwelling where she lives. She remains there until a special seclusion room next to the dwelling is constructed for her. She stays isolated in this room while preparations for her puberty rite are made. During this period the older women tell her about the danger from various spirits to which she as a woman is now subject, and they also inform her of what will be expected from her as a wife and mother. The ritual itself involves the presence of forty to fifty masked dancers who imitate spirits that both terrify and instruct her. Toward the end of the ceremony the girl is placed on a tapir hide in the middle of the house, and a group of elderly women slowly pull all the hair out of her head to the sound of a drum and rattle. The girl has to endure this pain without crying out. Although the Tucuna have an elaborate puberty rite for females, they have no such rite for males.

A CLOSER LOOK

Liminality and Becoming a Soldier

The late anthropologist Victor Turner pioneered the modern study of rites of passage. In his study of initiation rites among the Ndembu of Zambia, Turner noted that the rites have three phases: separation, liminality, and incorporation. These phases correspond to the basic nature of rites of passage: Individuals who go through them are separated from their former statuses in society, go through a transition ("liminal") period during which they are "betwixt and between" normal roles and social categories, and finally are reincorporated into society as a new person with new rights and obligations.

These phases are seen clearly in common cultural themes and behaviors involved in male initiation rituals among numerous peoples. The boys often are forcibly removed from their homes, a frequent practice being to separate them from the company of women (especially their mothers, who sometimes are expected to mourn as if their sons had died) so they can become real men. The boys often are secluded during the rituals and subjected to tests of their ability to endure pain without crying out. They may have to fast or go without drink for days. Nearly always, some painful operations are performed on their genitals; they may be circumcised or have their penises mutilated in other ways. Scarification of face and body is common because it is a visible symbol that a male has gone through the proceedings and is entitled to the privileges of manhood. Although sometimes the proceedings last for years, the initiates may have to refrain from eating certain foods or from coming into contact with females or female things because the period of transition into manhood is regarded as a dangerous time. A simple social structure characterizes the liminal period: The initiates are equal in status and utterly subordinate to the control of the men who are in charge of the proceedings. The boys typically are stripped of all possessions, their faces or bodies are painted in an identical way, they are dressed alike, and their heads are shaved, all to make them look alike and to emphasize their common identity.

Western industrial societies have rites of passage that serve similar functions: births, graduations, marriages, and deaths are marked by some kind of public ceremony signifying the social transitions involved. Baptisms, betrothals, promotions, installations of new public officials, birthdays, and many other ceremonial gatherings also are rites of passage.

But one of our most interesting rites of passage—because of its similarity to the initiation rituals just discussed—is entering military service. Many of the behaviors involved in entering the military are reminiscent of so-called puberty rites. Basic training is a liminal period—recruits have been separated from civilian life but have not acquired the knowledge and skills needed to become a soldier. Recruits are stripped of possessions, their hair is cut, they are issued identical uniforms, they are secluded from most contact with the outside, they all have identical (low) rank that requires complete subordination to sergeants and superior officers, they must undergo arduous trials and perform daring physical feats (such as getting up before sunrise), and they live in a common barracks where they have identical sleeping and eating facilities. In the military, too, the aim is to grind down a boy so that he can be rebuilt into a man (as the Marines used to say). Masculine qualities of courage, toughness, dedication, discipline, and determination are supposed to be instilled. When the recruit has successfully completed his training he is incorporated into a new group, the military, and acquires a new status (rank and job).

We should not carry the analogy too far—recruits are not operated on (but note that voluntary tattooing used to be fairly common), nor is it necessary for a boy to enter the military to be a real man (although many men who were not in the military are looked down on by many of those who were). Still, the similarities are striking enough for us once again to see our common humanity with pre-industrial peoples. Other behaviors and beliefs may seem strange to us, but we often engage in similar activities that only seem perfectly natural because we are used to them.

Adulthood

At what point is a person considered an adult? In most societies, adult status is assumed with marriage. When people marry there is at least the implicit assumption that both people are sufficiently mature socially and physically to assume the responsibilities required of spouses and parents. Thus, marriage in most societies is marked ceremonially with a rite of passage—a wedding. Women marry shortly after puberty in many societies, at twelve to fifteen years of age, whereas males in the same societies usually do not marry until their early twenties or even later in many polygynous societies (see Chapter 8). This difference in age at marriage means that males usually experience a considerably longer period of adolescence than do females.

The importance of marrying and having a family has lessened in Western industrialized societies. In most pre-industrial societies, however, the eventual marriage of nearly every individual is expected, and there are relatively few unmarried people. Why should marriage be so important for the attainment of adulthood in so many preindustrial societies?

There are several reasons. For one thing, bearing and rearing children is everywhere one of the central functions of marriage. People in most preindustrial cultures enjoy enhanced prestige from marrying and having many children, for large families are more valued. Also, marriage is essential because children provide the only form of economic security available for elderly people in most preindustrial societies. Establishment of economic and social independence is another reason for high marriage rates in these cultures. Some kind of family is usually responsible for producing and processing the food and other products required. Because of the sexual division of labor (see Chapter 10), each sex requires the goods and services provided by the other, and most people who do not marry remain dependent (and typically low-status) members of someone else's household.

More than among industrialized people, then, marriage established a person's prestige, security, and social and economic independence. That modern industrial nations have relatively high percentages of never-married people, as well as high rates of separation and divorce, is partly explained by the fact that marriage has lost many other economic and security-providing functions it so often performs in preindustrial cultures.

Old Age

Gerontology, the study of elderly people, has only recently become an important interest of anthropologists. Part of our interest stems from conditions in our own society, in which elderly people so often are seen as a burden, both to their children and to those of us who pay Social Security taxes. One popular notion is that the neglect of and contempt for elderly people in modern American society is something recent. Sometimes we hear or read statements like "The elderly were respected and admired for their wisdom in primitive societies." As we have so often emphasized, however, "primitive" people are enormously diverse in all respects, including the way they regard and treat elderly people.

Among some preindustrial peoples, adults who can no longer economically contribute to the family because of age, physical injury, or severe illness become burdens to their families. As they become dependent on the goodwill of others, their prestige declines rapidly. Among the Comanche, old men often were the victims of pranks by young boys, who sometimes slashed the prized painted buffalo robes of the old men. As elderly people became increasingly helpless, they frequently were "thrown away" or abandoned by their relatives and friends. Little time was spent mourning the death of

an old or "useless" person. Intense mourning was reserved for people who died while still physically in their prime because only their death constituted a true loss to their community.

Among the Inuit of Canada, conditions for survival were even more tenuous, and parricide (the killing of close relatives) was common. The old or infirm who could no longer keep up with the migratory movements of the group were abandoned by their families. In some Inuit groups, an elderly person who was no longer able to travel would be abandoned in a sealed igloo with a little food and a seal-oil lamp for warmth. Further south, in the subarctic forests, the Athabaskan tribes sometimes abandoned elderly people. Animals, particularly wolves, were likely to find the helpless individual before death and attack and kill him or her. To avoid leaving relatives to such a fate, a family member frequently killed them. Such ethnographic cases are not "typical"—there is no generalization that can be made about *the* treatment of elderly people among preindustrial cultures. They do suffice to show that modern attitudes toward the elderly are not unique.

Other preindustrial peoples come closer to the romantic ideals some of us have about all such peoples: Authority over family and community, control of resources, and the respect one receives increase with advancing age. Senior members of the family and community are elevated to positions of leadership. Knowledge and wisdom gained from experience replace physical strength and stamina as the elderly person's contribution to the well-being of the family and community.

Old age does not depend solely on chronological age but varies with an individual's health and with cultural conceptions. In many societies, physically fit people continue to work well beyond the normal age of retirement in American society. Among the Navajo, for example, it is common to find men and women in their seventies and eighties still tending herds of sheep and goats and working alongside their children and grandchildren.

In industrialized societies, retired individuals frequently surrender most of their authority and control over economic resources and withdraw from extended family decision making. Most are supported partly or entirely through investments, retirement funds, and/or government programs. In many instances, individuals physically withdraw from daily contact with their families, moving to retirement communities or to areas of the country with warm climates, such as California, Arizona, and Florida. Thus, many individuals culturally classified as elderly are segregated and isolated (sometimes by their own wishes) from younger adults and children, living in their own relatively closed communities. In industrialized societies in general, and in the United States in particular, old age

In many societies advanced age brings increasing prestige and authority, as in these elders' homeland in Xinjiang, China.

Some anthropologists argue that the explanation lies not in economic control per se but in the contrast between literate and nonliterate people. In societies without writing, elderly people become the major repositories of historical, religious, and technical knowledge, functioning as the de facto libraries of these societies. Their control of knowledge makes them indispensable to the community and gives them power over its members, enhancing their social value and the respect they receive. This might be termed the "knowledge is power" explanation.

Another contributing factor is the rate of change a people is experiencing. In slowly changing societies with relatively stable technologies, knowledge is seen as cumulative and wisdom as the product of experience. Thus, wisdom is thought to increase with age. The older individuals within the group are viewed as the repositories of community wisdom and cultural knowledge, so they are the individuals most capable of making important political and economic decisions. In contrast, industrialization has unleashed rapid and profound changes in the technologies of modern societies, and existing technologies quickly become obsolete. Therefore, we view knowledge not as cumulative but as ever changing and transitory; and in our view, experience alone does not generate the wisdom necessary for effective decision making. Like yesterday's technology, elderly people often are viewed as obsolete and out of step with today's realities. Their ideas and knowledge are thought by many to be antiquated and thus of limited value in decision making. From this perspective, it is not surprising that older individuals are frequently forced out of positions of authority and replaced by younger individuals thought more capable of making the critical decisions.

often is associated with the inability to maintain a meaningful economic or social role in the community. This in turn frequently results in a loss in self-esteem.

Why do cultures vary in their regard for and treatment of elderly people? One argument is that the elderly receive the greatest respect and authority in those societies in which they control the land, livestock, and other resources of their kin group. Younger members rely on them for use rights to land, and their children (or sister's children in matrilineal societies) may increase their chance for a large inheritance by acceding to their wishes and deferring to their judgments. Almost everyone who lives long enough will gain the status of elder and the esteem and authority it brings.

Summary

Personality refers to those mental processes that affect a person's behavioral reactions to events and situations. The kind of personality an individual develops is influenced by the way he or she is reared, as the Alorese case illustrates. Cultures differ in their child-rearing practices—in nursing and weaning norms, the degree and methods of discipline, toilet-training practices, nurturing, sexual permissiveness, caretaking roles, and so forth. Therefore, differences in the modal (i.e., typical, or most common) personality found among different peoples are expected. But in any society a wide range of personality types exist, so we cannot accurately characterize "the" personality of a people in any simple way.

The relation between modal personality and culture is complex, but several attempts have been made to order this complexity. One such attempt is the social systems model. In this model, the maintenance systems of a people affect the overall learning environment of children, which results in a tendency for children to develop some important similarities in personality. In turn, individuals with similar personalities develop or find attractive other cultural elements, known as the *projective-expressive system*.

The changes that occur in people's lives as they mature and age are referred to as *life cycle changes*. In some populations, relative age serves as the recruitment principle for formal groups known as *age sets,* two forms of which are illustrated by the Hidatsa and the Swazi. Most societies lack age sets, but age is everywhere a relevant social characteristic used to allocate roles. This is shown by the fact that transitions from one age category to another so often are marked by formal public ceremonies called *rites of passage.*

Exactly when childhood begins and ends is culturally, not biologically, determined. Often, as among the Osage, a naming ritual confers human status to an infant. Childhood is universally a period of intense social learning and of personality formation. Among preindustrial peoples it is typical for children to begin contributing to the support of their families at a much younger age than among ourselves.

The passage from childhood to adolescence often is accomplished and marked by an initiation ritual, which can involve severe physical and psychological trauma, as illustrated by the Awa. In preindustrial societies, marriage frequently is necessary to attain full adulthood.

Human societies vary enormously in their regard for and treatment of the elderly. The chronological age at which an individual is considered elderly likewise varies. The degree to which elderly people exercise control over important property and its inheritance seems to be important in how they are regarded. Other influences include the degree of literacy—for among preliterate peoples, elderly people serve as a repository of knowledge—and the rate of technological change a people is experiencing.

Key Terms

personality
child-rearing practices

modal personality
age set association
life cycle
rite of passage
initiation rite

Suggested Readings

Bernardi, Bernardo. *Age Class Systems, Social Institutions and Policies Based on Age.* New York: Cambridge University Press, 1985.
 • *A comparative study of the significance of age in social institutions.*

Erchak, Gerald M. *The Anthropology of Self and Behavior.* New Brunswick, N.J.: Rutgers University Press, 1992.
 • *A recent introduction to the field of psychological anthropology. Despite its brevity, this book gives a thorough overview of the subject.*

Farrer, Claire R. *Thunder Rides a Black Horse: Mescalero Apaches and the Mythic Present.* 2nd ed. Prospect Heights, Ill.: Waveland, 1996.
 • *A brief and readable description of the author's experiences with the Apache girl's initiation ceremony. Focuses on the ceremony itself, the roles surrounding it, the symbolism, and the place of the ceremony in the people's culture.*

Freeman, Derek. *Margaret Mead and Samoa: The Making and Unmaking of an Anthropological Myth.* Cambridge, Mass.: Harvard University Press, 1983.
 • *A critique of Margaret Mead's description and analysis of Samoan adolescence. Freeman argues that Mead's findings were erroneous and that Samoan girls experience the same kinds of psychological processes as Western girls during their adolescence.*

Hewlett, Barry S. *Intimate Fathers: The Nature and Context of Aka Pygmy Paternal Infant Care.* Ann Arbor: University of Michigan Press, 1991.
 • *Fathers among the Aka pygmies of Central Africa are more involved in the care and nurturing of infants than in any other known culture. An excellent study of Aka paternal care and how the case relates to wider issues of adaptation and gender egalitarianism.*

Leiderman, P. Herbert, Steven R. Tulkin, and Anne Rosenfeld, eds. *Culture and Infancy: Variations in the Human Experience.* New York: Academic, 1977.
 • *A volume of twenty-three articles, mostly dealing with infancy in various cultural settings.*

LeVine, Robert A., Suzanne Dixon, Sarah Levine, and Amy Richman. *Child Care and Culture: Lessons from Africa.* Cambridge: Cambridge University Press, 1996.
 • *Examines parenthood, infancy, and childhood among the Gusii of Kenya and compares it to child care and parent-child relations in the American middle class.*

Marsella, Anthony J., George DeVos, and Francis L. K. Hsu, eds. *Culture and Self: Asian and Western Perspectives.* New York: Tavistock, 1985.

- *Nine articles on cultural conceptions of selfhood in the West, Japan, and China, and in Hinduism and Confucianism. First two chapters are quite good.*

Mead, Margaret. *Coming of Age in Samoa*. New York: Morrow, 1928.
- *Account of adolescent girls in Samoa and one of anthropology's great classics. Few anthropological studies have been more widely read by the general public.*

Scheper-Hughes, Nancy. *Death Without Weeping: The Violence of Everyday Life in Brazil*. Berkeley: University of California Press, 1992.
- *An account of women's lives in a poor region of Brazil, showing that many women are forced into heartbreaking choices about their children's survival and welfare.*

Turnbull, Colin. *The Human Cycle*. New York: Simon & Schuster, 1983.
- *A readable summary of life cycle changes in various populations from all parts of the world.*

Whiting, Beatrice B., and John W. Whiting. *Children of Six Cultures: A Psycho-Cultural Analysis*. Cambridge, Mass.: Harvard University Press, 1974.
- *A comparative psychocultural analysis of children from six societies around the world, discussing the influence of culture on personality and vice versa.*

Wilson, M. *Good Company: A Study of Nyakyusa Age-Villages*. Boston: Beacon, 1963.
- *An interesting and readable account of the unusual age set village organization of the Nyakyusa of East Africa.*

Internet Exercises

"Rites of Passage in America" (http://www.libertynet.org/balch/rites.html) is a multimedia site based on a traveling exhibition organized by the Balch Institute for Ethnic Studies. There are several essays dealing with rites of passage, plus ten case studies. Some examples of the case studies include "'Doing the Month' and the "Full Month' Party: Chinese Birth Traditions in America," "Quinceanera: Latino Sweet Sixteen," and "Kiddushin: An Interracial Lesbian Wedding."

Though it is a commercial site (it contains advertising), the "Weddings Net" site from Hong Kong (http://www.weddingsnet.com.hk/traditions/eng/etradit.html) provides a large amount of data on Chinese marriage customs.

CHAPTER 16

The Changing Human World

Culture Change

History and Anthropology

The World in 1500

The World Since 1500

Initial Expansion of Europe

The World and the Industrial Revolution

European Impact on World Cultural Systems

The World Since 1945

The Global Economy

Demographic Changes

Political Fragmentation

Consequences of an Interdependent World

European expansion and conquest has drastically changed the peoples of the world over the last 500 years. In this mural, Diego Rivera presents a reconstruction of life in Mexico City under the Aztecs.
Visit http://www.wadsworth.com/humanity to learn more about the material covered in this chapter and to access activities, exercises, and tutorial quizzes.

*T*HE *PAST* five hundred years have been a time of monumental changes for the world's peoples. These changes are most readily apparent in the cities. Although the faces and languages of the people may differ, whether the city is Miami, Seattle, Tokyo, Singapore, or Lagos, in architecture and technology we find a basic sameness *about modern cities. It is the rural peoples who most frequently deceived us. When we see photographs of a farming village in China or India, or view a film about Maasai cattle herding or Pygmy hunters of the Ituri forest, we think of these peoples as unchanged for centuries, if not millennia. In their actions, dress, and technology they differ greatly from us, and so we conclude they have yet to be affected by change. In reality, no people are caught in a cultural time warp. While the changes may not be as apparent, all peoples' lives have changed dramatically over the past five centuries.*

So far we have presented a static picture of culture, discussing the range of known variability without reference to time. In this chapter we will look at world culture in its dynamic dimension. Only by examining culture within its broad historical context can we understand how the present global economy evolved and led to the challenges that confront all of us.

Culture Change

Since the late nineteenth century, anthropologists have been aware that culture is never stable—that it is in constant flux. Although the process of culture change has been extensively studied by anthropologists, here we only briefly discuss how and why a system changes over time. There are two main processes by which a culture changes: *innovation* and *diffusion*.

An **innovation** may be anything—from new religious beliefs to a technological change—that is internally generated by members of the society. People are constantly changing what they do and how they do it. In most cases these changes are minor, imperceptible, and unconscious. In the telling of a myth a person may delete some part while elaborating another. Individuals may wear their hair differently or paint their faces with a new design. Most innovations consist of the recombining of two or more existing ideas or objects to produce something new. This factor is evident in technology, since most technological advancements are the result of such recombinations. In North America, Fulton took a paddle wheel, a steam engine, and a boat and put them together to create a steamboat. Still later, several individuals succeeded in powering a wagon by the use of a gasoline internal combustion engine, and thus the automobile was born.

Diffusion is a second way in which new elements are introduced into a culture. Diffusion consists of "borrowing" or adopting a cultural trait from another society. Any category of customs, beliefs, or objects, from religious beliefs and practices to technology, may be diffused from one people to another. The adoption of new traits requires that these traits be integrated into the existing culture of the recipient population. In many cases, the form may remain the same while the meaning and function of the trait change.

Why a group of people adopts or rejects a particular new custom or belief is extraordinarily complex. As a rule, people are receptive to new traits that enhance either their economic well-being or their social survival. Thus, farming peoples often are receptive to new crops that complement their existing crops and new technology that increases their harvest. Societies involved in warfare readily accept more advanced military technology. Still other factors stimulate changes in culture. Political and economic domination usually result in the forced introduction of new traits from the dominant society as it restructures the culture of dependent peoples to meet new needs and objectives. The displacement and relocation of a people into a different natural environment generate changes in the existing culture. Demographic changes—rapid increases or decreases in population—and their associated changes in relative population densities also necessitate changes in the culture.

History and Anthropology

Frederick Maitland, a historian, commented during the late nineteenth century that anthropology had to be history or it was nothing. Although few, if any, anthropologists would totally agree with Maitland, they have for some time realized that history has played an important role in shaping culture. Until recently, anthropologists have treated non-Western societies as if they were static. The importance of change among these peoples was either ignored or minimized. During the early part of this century, ethnographers wrote descriptions of nineteenth-century culture using the "ethnographic present," indicative of the "timeless" or static concept of these societies. If any changes had taken place, they were seen as very recent.

Only during the past three decades have anthropologists begun to see the magnitude of the changes that have occurred among even the most technologically unsophisticated peoples over the past few hundred years. Virtually every group of people in the world, no matter how geographically isolated, has directly or indirectly had its culture altered to some degree as a result of European expansion and industrialization. In turn, the Europeans were also changed by borrowing and adopting ideas and technology from other peoples. There is not now, nor has there been, a truly pristine society.

The World in 1500

Keeping in mind how and why changes occur in cultures, we can now briefly outline world history over the past 500 years. In this summary we have two objectives: (1) to provide the reader with some idea of the magnitude and pervasiveness of change, and (2) to demonstrate the main patterns and directions of change.

The world has experienced phenomenal changes over the past 500 years. Foremost among these changes have been technological advancements and the harnessing of new sources of energy: coal, petroleum, electricity, and nuclear power. Associated with these advancements has been an explosion in the human population of the earth—from only about 500 to 600 million in A.D. 1500 to more than 5.5 billion today. Not only has the population of the world grown, but there have been major intraregional and interregional population shifts. In the period since 1500, profound cultural changes have affected virtually all peoples in the world.

The major catalyst for these changes has been the economic and political expansion of European populations that began toward the end of the fifteenth century. To understand world cultural history during this period, we have to trace the history of European expansion and determine how and when it affected various regions and peoples.

European expansion took place in two rather distinct stages. The first can be called the *mercantile phase*. During this period, European traders brought most of the continents of the world into direct trade contact with one another. Some migration and colonization and limited political conquest occurred during the mercantile phase, which began during the 1490s and lasted until the latter half of the eighteenth century. The second stage, called the *industrial phase,* encompassed the period when European peoples politically conquered almost every region of the world and established a global economic system that they dominated.

Before A.D. 1500 the major world regions were relatively isolated from one another. Most contact was limited to societies that occupied adjacent territories. Trade was minimal, and long-distance trade that existed between Europe and China or Africa seldom involved direct exchange between members of those societies. Trade was managed by intervening groups whose members acted as middlemen. Thus, although Europeans were aware of the existence of places like China, India, and Ethiopia, their knowledge was extremely limited and seldom based on firsthand accounts. Although innovations in technology and cultural institutions did diffuse from one center to another, diffusion was slow because direct contact was lacking.

Although the terms *Old World* and *New World* are ethnocentric, this distinction is useful from a cultural-historical perspective. The Old World—Europe, Africa, and Asia—did form a unit within which trade and contact, however tenuous and limited, allowed for the spread of technology and institutions. The *New World* is a term usually applied only to the Americas, but could just as well be applied to Australia and most of Oceania because both of these regions were outside this exchange network before 1500. Thus, before European expansion the world consisted of two broad geographical regions with peoples who had for much of their history developed technologies and lifeways in isolation from one another.

The World Since 1500

Initial Expansion of Europe

With the "discovery" of the Americas by Christopher Columbus in 1492, the age of European expansion began. In population and technological achievement, Europe was not the most developed region of the world during the fifteenth century. Asia had a total population four to five times that of Europe, and in overall technology Asia was ahead of Europe. Compared with the states of Asia, European countries were small. The populations of such soon-to-be-imperial powers as England, Portugal, Spain, and the Netherlands were insignificant in comparison with those of China or the Mogul (Islamic) states of India. Even the Aztec Empire in the Americas may have had a population equal to the total of these four European countries. The major advantage of European societies was in military technology. Guns, crossbows, iron weapons, armor, and horses gave them significant advantages over the stone-tool military technologies of the peoples of the Americas and Oceania. To a lesser degree, they also enjoyed a military advantage over most peoples of Africa. The same was not true in Asia: On land, European armies enjoyed no technological advantage. Only in naval warfare were the European technologically superior to the Asian states. These factors influenced European expansionist policies during the early period and caused the history of contact with Asia, Africa, the Americas, and Oceania to differ significantly. With some exceptions, principally in the Americas, the expansion of Europe during the sixteenth, seventeenth, and eighteenth centuries consisted of the development of maritime mercantile empires, as opposed to actual overseas colonies and territorial empires.

Because European contact took such different forms from one region to the next, it is necessary to examine the history of contact region by region.

Conquest of the Americas In 1492, Columbus found a new world inhabited by numerous people, who still had only an advanced stone-tool technology. Initially, the Spaniards were disappointed in their new discoveries because they failed to find the immense treasures of the Indies they were expecting. On the island of Hispaniola, where they first settled, there were some gold deposits, but most Spanish settlers quickly turned their attention to the development of sugarcane plantations and cattle ranches.

During the first quarter century after its discovery, the New World attracted only a few thousand Spaniards, but they quickly spread over the major islands of the West Indies: Cuba, Jamaica, and Puerto Rico. In 1519, Hernando Cortez landed on the coast of Mexico and by 1521 had completed the conquest of Tenochtitlán, the capital of the Aztec Empire. Cortez sent gold and silver back to Spain in quantities beyond belief. The discovery of such vast treasures encouraged the migration of others to search for still more wealth and plunder. Between 1532 and 1534, a military expedition led by Francisco Pizarro conquered the Inca Empire and took the wealth of Peru for Spain. By the late 1500s, Spanish expeditions had explored much of the Americas and had located and conquered every major Native American state. In little more than half a century, the Spaniards had conquered the richest and most populous portions of the Americas: the West Indies, Mesoamerica, and Peru. More than half the native population of the Americas had fallen under Spanish domination.

The Treaty of Tordesillas, signed in 1494, divided the non-Christian world between Spain and Portugal. The easternmost part of South America, Brazil, fell into the Portuguese portion. Although Portugal's area lacked rich gold and silver deposits, the coastal regions of Brazil were well suited for sugarcane plantations. Starting in 1500, Portuguese settlers began colonizing Brazil, and by 1550 small settlements were scattered along most of the coast.

The Spanish and Portuguese were able to conquer large portions of the Americas in a surprisingly short time. As the Spanish demonstrated in their conquests of the Aztecs and Incas, their military superiority was so pronounced that small armies numbering in the hundreds were able to vanquish well-organized native armies whose troops numbered in the thousands. Small groups of European troops could move about with near impunity throughout the length of the Americas. Only lack of manpower limited Spanish and Portuguese expansion and kept them from subjugating all of the Americas. The populations of Spain and Portugal were relatively small, and there were never enough troops or civilians to control such a vast and populous region. Although the conquests of Mexico and Peru stimulated Spanish migration to the New World, the number of immigrants remained relatively small, averaging between 1,000 and 2,000 a year during the 1500s.

The main period of conquest and territorial expansion had virtually ended by 1600, and Spanish settlers turned their attention to exploitation of the West Indies, Mesoamerica, and Peru, where they developed silver and gold mines, ranches, and plantations. The Portuguese contented themselves with coastal Brazil and worked to expand their plantations.

Conversion of native peoples to Christianity was one of the primary interests of the Spanish in the Americas.

The cultural impact of the Spanish and Portuguese was most pronounced in those regions directly under their control. Existing native political organization was either replaced or modified and integrated into a colonial government. European technology was introduced— iron tools, plows, cattle, horses, sheep, and so forth—as existing economic systems were altered to meet European needs. Indian labor was used in the mines and on the plantations and ranches that were developed. Missionaries flooded the Americas seeking converts. Temples were replaced by Christian churches. In some regions, such as Mexico and Peru, native peoples managed to maintain their languages and Indian

social and ethnic identity, but even these societies were given a veneer of Christian customs and beliefs. Even Native American peoples beyond direct European control were affected. Old World crops, domesticated animals, and metal tools in limited numbers were diffused to these autonomous peoples. In some regions the introduction of European items had revolutionary effects. The horse in particular revolutionized many native societies. On the Great Plains of North America the introduction of the horse resulted in a cultural florescence, and a whole new way of life evolved as we discuss in "A Closer Look." The horse had an equally profound effect on native life on the Gran Chaco and pampas of South America.

As important as these material elements were in altering Native American culture, they were not the only causes of change. Old World diseases such as small pox, measles, influenza, bubonic plague, diphtheria, typhus, cholera, malaria, and scarlet fever were the most pervasive agents of change introduced by early Europeans. Isolated as they had been, the peoples of the Americas had no natural immunities to these diseases. Because they frequently spread well in advance of European contact, it is impossible to estimate with any exactness the size of native populations before that contact. The massive population decline caused by European diseases is best documented in regions under direct Spanish and Portuguese control. Father Bartolome de las Casas reported that there were 1,100,000 Indians fourteen years of age or older on Hispaniola in 1496. Even the most conservative estimate of the Indian population for the island is 100,000. Regardless of the original figure, we do know that the native population underwent rapid decline and that by 1535 there were only 500 Indians left on Hispaniola. By the 1550s, the Taino and Ciguayo Indians were extinct. Similar declines were reported on the other major islands of the Caribbean: Cuba, Puerto Rico, and Jamaica. In Mexico the decline was also severe, but not as devastating. One study places the contact population at 25,200,000 in 1519, with a decline to 16,800,000 by 1532, 2,650,000 by 1568, and 1,075,000 by 1605. Although these estimates are open to question, there is no doubt that Native American societies suffered severe population declines after European contact.

Disease was the major factor in the population decline, but other factors also contributed. As the native populations under their control decreased, the Europeans faced a shortage of available laborers. One answer to this problem was to "recruit" new labor by raiding other Native American groups for slaves. Thus, peoples who were not under direct Spanish or Portuguese control suffered heavy losses from slave raiders during the sixteenth and seventeenth centuries. During the first half of the sixteenth century, more than 200,000 Indian slaves were captured in Central America and sold in the West Indies. Similar decreases in population caused by slave raiders were common in coastal regions and interior areas beyond European political control. Enslavement of Native Americans proved to be only a stopgap measure because these new recruits also died off rapidly from European diseases. New sources of human labor had to be found to fill the expanding vacuum.

Awareness of the rapid and dramatic decline in Native American population is critical to understanding the history of the Americas during the past 500 years. If the Native American societies had maintained their populations, there is little doubt that they would have eventually been able to absorb the relatively small numbers of Europeans who initially conquered them. The history of the Americas could have been similar to the histories of European contact with Africa and Asia, which we discuss later in this chapter. The population decline created a vacuum that was filled by the massive resettling of Old World peoples in the Americas. However, neither Spain nor Portugal sent sufficient emigrants to offset the declining Native American population and meet the increasing labor demands of their American colonies. Another source of labor had to be found. This was the genesis of the African slave trade. As early as the 1490s, African slaves had been sent to the island of Hispaniola. During the 1500s and 1600s, ever-increasing numbers of African slaves were sent to the Spanish and Portuguese colonies. By the eighteenth century, these colonies had more individuals of African ancestry than of European ancestry.

During the late sixteenth and early seventeenth centuries other European powers—England, France, and the Netherlands—began contesting Spanish and Portuguese dominance of the Americas. For the most part, these countries occupied portions of the Americas outside the limits of Spanish and Portuguese control. There were some exceptions. The French, English, and Dutch were able to gain control over some of the small islands in the West Indies, but the major region of occupation by these European powers became the Atlantic Coast of North America. During the early 1600s the French, English, and Dutch were able to successfully establish colonies along this coast. The Native American populations in this region had already suffered the devastating effects of Old World disease and were of little interest to northern Europeans as a source of labor. Unlike the Spanish and Portuguese to the south, these settlers were primarily interested in the land the Indians occupied, and they considered Native Americans to be a hindrance and danger to their settlements, not an economic resource. As these northern European settlers pushed their frontiers into the interior, Native American populations were evicted and forced west. Although there was some enslavement of

A CLOSER LOOK

Importance of the Horse to Plains Indians

To the white American public, no group of Indians typifies what Native American life was like more than the Plains Indians: the Cheyenne, Dakota, Crow, and Comanche. Thanks in large part to Hollywood, these tipi-dwelling, buffalo-hunting, horse-mounted warriors of the grasslands have come to represent the very essence of "Indianness." When we visualize Indian ways of life of the past, we picture Red Cloud, Black Kettle, Sitting Bull, or some other plains leader dressed in beaded buckskin clothing, wearing a feather "war bonnet," and seated on a horse. What we fail to realize is that Plains Indians in particular, and American Indians in general as we view them, were in large part a product of European contact.

In the nineteenth century, horses were the primary means of transportation and as such were an integral part of Plains Indian culture. The modern horse, however, was not native to the Americas, but was first brought by the Spanish. It was not until the late 1600s and early 1700s that horses in any numbers became available to the tribes of the Great Plains.

Before horses were available, the open grasslands of the Great Plains held little attraction for American Indians. Not only were bison difficult to hunt for people on foot and armed with only a bow and arrow or spear, but transporting of game any distance over the vast grasslands was physically arduous. Whether food or other material goods, all the possessions of these people had to be carried either on their own backs or those of their dogs. For these reasons, the plains were inhabited year round only by widely scattered small bands of nomadic foragers. People probably depended more on the collecting of wild food plants than on the vast herds of bison for subsistence. Compared with

the farming peoples who lived along the eastern and southwestern margins of the plains, these tribes were materially impoverished and militarily weak. Thus, not surprisingly, before acquiring horses, only a few tribes lived the nomadic life on the plains: the Comanche, Kiowa, Shoshone, a few groups of Apache, possibly the Blackfoot, and a few other, smaller tribes. Many of the major tribes later associated with the plains were still farming people.

The horse truly revolutionized life among the Plains tribes. The horse drastically altered the economic base and changed the lifestyle of these peoples. On horseback a hunter armed with bow and arrow could find and kill enough bison within a few months to feed his family for the year. Not only could he kill larger numbers of game animals, but he could pack the meat onto horses and readily transport it vast distances. Horses also allowed for the transporting of increased quantities of material goods. Tipis increased in size, and clothing and other material items became increasingly abundant and elaborate in decoration. For the first time these widely scattered groups could gather together in large camps, sometimes numbering in the thousands, for at least a portion of the year. In short, the horse quickly elevated the Plains tribes to relative prosperity.

The horse also sharply altered the relationship between these peoples and the neighboring farming tribes. The once relatively inoffensive nomads were now transformed into aggressive, predatory raiders. The Plains tribes were now capable of quickly assembling large parties of horse-mounted warriors who could raid the sedentary farming villages with impunity. The military balance of power had shifted.

In the decades immediately after the acquisition of the horse, the original Plains tribes flourished. Attacks on the neighboring farming peoples had a devastating effect, and many villages were abandoned. It was not long, however, before many cultivators saw both the economic and the military advantages derived from being horse-mounted nomadic bison hunters. The Cheyenne and some of the Dakota abandoned the life of settled farmers and moved westward to the plains to become nomadic, tipi-dwelling, bison hunters themselves. As they moved onto the plains, they came to challenge directly the original Plains tribes for dominance over critical hunting resources, which intensified warfare. As a result, warfare and the warrior tradition became an integral part of Plains Indian values, social organization, and behavior.

The Plains Indian culture as we think of it emerged during the first half of the nineteenth century. Given the diverse origins of the various Plains tribes, they developed a remarkably homogeneous way of life within a short period: elaborately equipped tipis, beaded (with European trade beads) clothing, the Sun Dance, and the emphasis on the male's role as a warrior. It was not until the latter half of the nineteenth century that Euro-Americans seriously challenged the Plains Indians for control of the Great Plains, 300 years after they had first begun acquiring horses. Because the Plains peoples were the last major group of tribes to resist Euro-American dominance, militarily, it is not surprising that we mistakenly think of them as the "essence of Indianness."

Sources: Ewers (1955), Lowie (1954), and Oliver (1962).

Native Americans by these colonists, it was not as significant as in the Spanish and Portuguese colonies. Native American slaves usually were sold or traded in the West Indies for African slaves; few were kept in mainland

North America. As early as 1619, English colonists in Virginia were purchasing African slaves. The number of African slaves in the French, English, and Dutch West Indies and in English North America steadily increased during the 1600s and 1700s, paralleling the pattern in the Spanish and Portuguese colonies.

Although Native Americans seldom were enslaved in the northern European colonies, their labor was used indirectly. Unlike the Spanish and Portuguese, the French, English, and Dutch quickly established trading networks in the interior regions, exchanging cloth, metal tools, guns, and other items of European manufacture for hides and furs. By the late 1700s most of the Native American societies in North America were in regular trade contact with these Europeans and dependent on this fur trade. By the end of the eighteenth century, virtually every Native American society had been affected by European expansion. Many had already become extinct. Others were under the direct political and economic control of European colonial governments. Even those societies that had been able to retain their autonomy had seen their populations sharply reduced through disease or warfare and their lifestyles changed by the introduction of European material goods and technology. No "pristine" societies were left in the New World.

Sub-Saharan Africa Portuguese explorers first made contact with sub-Saharan Africans in 1444 and 1445. Trade quickly followed, and Portuguese explorer-traders steadily expanded farther south down the west coast of Africa. In the 1470s they reached the Gold Coast and found the area so rich in gold that in 1482 they erected a fort at Elmina to protect their trading interest. This fortification was the first of a series of coastal forts that the Portuguese established to exclude other European powers from the region. By 1488, Portuguese explorers had reached the Cape of Good Hope, the southern extremity of the African continent. Between 1497 and 1499, Vasco da Gama successfully sailed to India and back by way of the Cape. By the beginning of the fifteenth century, the Portuguese had established the basis for a trading empire that stretched along the coast of Africa and all the way to Asia. The problem confronting the Portuguese was strengthening and maintaining their hold against European and Islamic rivals. Trading ports were created along the African coast not only to acquire gold and ivory but also to serve as way stations for ships bound to and from Asia. The major Portuguese centers in Africa became what are today Angola (on the west coast) and Mozambique (on the east coast).

In 1482 the Portuguese discovered one of the largest states in Africa, the Kongo kingdom, near the mouth of the Congo. The Portuguese developed friendly relations with the Kongo, and in 1490 missionaries and various artisans were sent there. The missionaries soon converted the king and many of the people, and the capital of the kingdom was rebuilt on a European model and renamed Sao Salvador. Many younger Kongo were voluntarily sent to Portugal for formal education.

In 1505, the Portuguese attacked, looted, and virtually destroyed the Omani city of Kilwa. Shortly afterward they occupied the Kilwa port town of Sofala, which became their main base in Mozambique. From this base they usurped the trade with the Monomatapa Empire formerly led by Kilwa.

Although gold and ivory were the primary trade items, early Portuguese traders dealt in other commodities as well: slaves, sea lion oil, hides, cotton cloth, and beeswax. Slaves eventually emerged as the most valuable trade item of the African coast, and this factor led other European countries to challenge Portuguese control.

Slavery and the slave trade existed in portions of Europe before European expansion. On the Iberian Peninsula in Spain and Portugal, slavery knew no racial or religious boundaries: Slaves could be black or white, Christian, Jewish, or Muslim. However, the number of slaves in Europe was limited, and African slaves were transported to Hispaniola as early as the 1490s. During the early 1500s, the market for African slaves in the New World expanded rapidly, not only in the Spanish colonies but also in the Portuguese colony of Brazil.

The magnitude of the African slave trade cannot be determined with any exactness. We know that the slave trade grew steadily during the sixteenth and seventeenth centuries, reached its zenith during the last decades of the eighteenth century, and ended about 1870. Estimates of the number of African slaves shipped to the Americas range from about 10 million to about 50 million, but the actual number was probably closer to the 10 million estimate. Likewise, estimates of the number of slaves taken to the Americas during particular centuries vary: Estimates for the sixteenth century range from 250,000 to 900,000; for the seventeenth century from 1,341,000 to 2,750,000; and for the eighteenth and nineteenth centuries from 6 million to 11 million.

The Portuguese became the first major traders of African slaves in the Americas. In the earliest period of the trade, slaves brought to America had already been slaves in Africa. However, the number of such people was limited, and as the demand for slaves increased the Portuguese turned to other methods—in particular, raiding—to acquire them. The expanding demand for slaves changed the relationship of the Portuguese with African societies. The kings of Kongo allowed their subjects to trade slaves to the Portuguese, but they refused to permit them to raid for additional slaves. As a result, in 1575, Portuguese mercenaries and African "allies" began systematically to stage slave raids throughout much of central Africa. Finally, in 1660, the Portuguese virtually destroyed the Kongo kingdom in a short war.

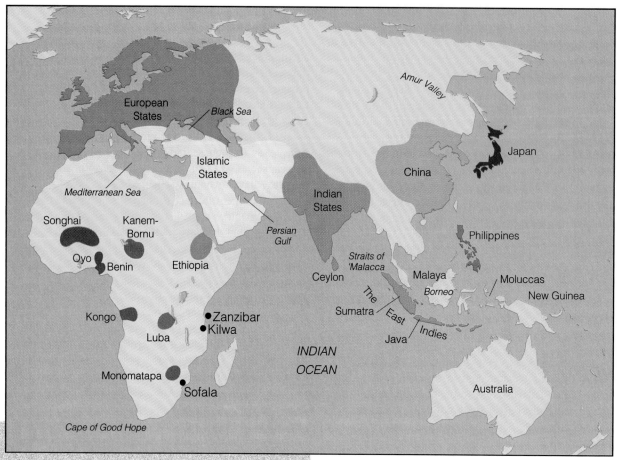

Figure 16.1 Major States and Regions of Europe, Asia, and Africa (ca. 1500).

In Mozambique, the Portuguese also increased their control over trade. Trading posts were built along the Zambezi River, which led to war with the Monomatapa Empire and the subsequent disintegration of that power. In 1629, the king of Monomatapa declared himself a vassal of the king of Portugal.

In the late 1500s, the English and French began competing for a share of the African slave trade by marketing slaves in the Spanish colonies. During the early 1600s, with the establishment of French, English, and Dutch colonies in the West Indies, even more traders attempted to tap this lucrative trade. French, English, Dutch, Swedes, and Danes obtained slaves along the west coast of Africa. For the most part, these new traders concentrated on West Africa, where they established their own fortified trading stations and drove the Portuguese out of many posts. The French, English, and Dutch were not just challenging the Portuguese in Africa; they were also competing for the Asian trade. To reach Asia, they

also had to circumnavigate Africa, and they needed ports. In 1652, the Dutch East India Company established a colony of Dutch farmers at the Cape of Good Hope to supply their ships.

By the late 1700s, the French, English, Dutch, Portuguese, and Spanish controlled ports scattered along the western coast and much of the eastern coast of Africa. Most of these posts were manned by only a handful of Europeans. Actual European settlements were few and small; the main settlements were the Portuguese colonies in Angola and Mozambique, and the Dutch colony at the Cape. Few Europeans had ever penetrated the interior, and little was known of the inland peoples of Africa. Yet at the same time, the European presence in Africa had produced far-reaching effects on the lives of all Africans through the slave trade and through the introduction of New World food crops.

Slaves were acquired through raiding and warfare, usually in exchange for guns supplied by the Europeans.

In Africa, the gun trade and the slave trade were inextricably linked. By the early eighteenth century, about 180,000 guns were being traded annually, and by the end of the century that figure had climbed to between 300,000 and 400,000.

The slave-for-gun trade shifted trade networks and disrupted the existing balance of power among African societies. Some groups, primarily coastal peoples in contact with Europeans, faced the choice of becoming slave raiders and acquiring guns or falling victim to those who opted for raiding. As slave-related warfare escalated, new states sprang up, and there was a concurrent decline in many older states.

In West Africa, there was a decline in the power and influence of the old states of Sudan. The Songhai Empire disintegrated, and Kanem-Bornu weakened considerably. At the same time, along the coast of West Africa, many small kingdoms and city-states—such as Oyo, Aboney, Ashanti, and Benin—were undergoing rapid expansion that was traceable to the slave traffic. In west-central Africa the Kongo kingdom refused to be involved in the slave trade and disintegrated because the Portuguese supported and encouraged the development of slave-raiding states. Lunda was the largest and most important of these new states.

At the same time that Africa was undergoing this dramatic escalation in warfare, New World crops brought to the continent by Europeans dramatically changed African farming. During the early 1500s, the Portuguese introduced corn, manioc, sweet potatoes, pineapples, peanuts, papayas, and some lesser crops. The introduction of these new crops, particularly corn and manioc, greatly increased the productivity of farming in Africa. In the savannas and grasslands, corn produced higher yields than native cereal crops, and in the tropical forest regions, manioc was superior to existing starchy crops. In portions of West Africa, central Angola, and the northern and southern extremes of the Congo basin, as well as in portions of eastern Africa, corn became the dominant staple in the diet. Manioc, which was not introduced in portions of the Congo basin until the late 1800s, spread more slowly than corn. Few details are known about exactly how these New World crops affected African populations. Some researchers have suggested that the introduction of corn resulted in a population explosion that minimized the demographic impact of the slave trade. It is also clear that corn and manioc allowed for the expansion of populations into regions that had hitherto been only sparsely occupied.

Thus, on the one hand, the Europeans' quest for slaves had caused an escalation in warfare that had resulted in major losses in population and significant restructuring of African political power. However, the Europeans also introduced new crops that increased and expanded African farming. Although we cannot describe exactly what happened, we can say with certainty that the population of Africa underwent major changes. Basil Davidson (1969, 235) provides an excellent summary of the situation in Africa at the end of the eighteenth century: "By 1800 or soon after there were few regions where many polities, large or small, old or new, had not clearly felt and reacted to strong pressures of transition. Widely varying in form and power though it certainly was, the impact of change had been constantly and pervasively at work."

Europeans in Asia The Portuguese were the first Europeans to reach Asia by sea: In 1498, Vasco da Gama landed on the coast of India. The Europeans soon learned that Asia offered a situation quite different from what confronted them in the Americas and Africa. The population of Asia far surpassed that of Europe, and Asia was divided into numerous highly developed and militarily powerful states. In economic terms Asia was a self-sufficient region with only limited interest in outside trade. Although Asia offered such desirable goods as silk, cotton textiles, spices, coffee, tea, porcelain, and so forth for trade, the Europeans had little to offer Asia in exchange other than gold and silver bullion. The Europeans had only one major advantage over Asia: In naval warfare, European technology was superior to that of Asia.

Da Gama encountered difficulty trading Portuguese goods in India, but he managed to trade his cargo and returned home. From the outset, the Portuguese realized that the only significant role they could play in the Asian trade was as middlemen in the inter-Asian trade, particularly between the Far East (China) and India. In 1509 they defeated the Egyptian fleet and effectively wrested control of the Indian Ocean trade from Islamic traders. Although they were militarily inferior to the Asians on land, the Portuguese were able, by entering into agreements with local rulers, to establish fortified trading ports. During the early and mid-1500s they established a series of these ports from India to China. Asian goods flowed through these ports to Europe in exchange for silver and gold coming from the Americas. This trade was extremely limited; during the 1500s, the trade between Europe and Asia averaged only ten ships annually. Of greater economic importance was the fact that an ever-increasing percentage of the lucrative trade between Asian peoples themselves was being carried by Portuguese merchant ships.

The same treaty that gave Portugal a portion of the Americas (Brazil) gave Spain a portion of Asia (the Philippines). In 1564 the Spanish founded Manila (Philippines). Unlike the Portuguese trade that flowed westward around Africa, the Spanish ships (called *Manila Galleons*)

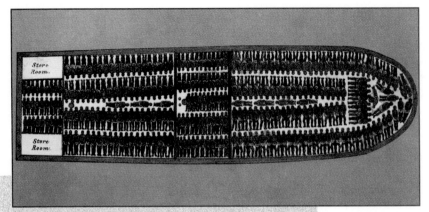

Between 1500 and 1870, millions of Africans were packed into the holes of slave ships and transported to the Americas for labor.

holdings and populations under direct control were small, usually little more than port cities. The regions most strongly affected by Europeans were the Philippines and the areas in the Indies under Dutch political control. But such regions constituted only a small portion of Asia. Europeans had little effect on Asian economic life; they were little more than a small, parasitic group attached to an Asian economic system. The most significant influence on the Asian economy during this period was the introduction of New World crops, the most important of which were corn and sweet potatoes.

sailed between Manila and Acapulco, Mexico. From Acapulco goods were transported over land to Vera Cruz, and from there shipped to Spain.

It was not until after 1600 that other European powers began to compete for the trade with Asia. The earliest of these new competitors were the Dutch, who in 1602 organized the Dutch East India Company. By 1605 they had established themselves in a portion of the Moluccas, despite Portuguese opposition. In 1619 they established a base at Batavia (modern Jakarta) on the island of Java. Between 1638 and 1658 they were able to dislodge the Portuguese from Ceylon, and in 1641 they seized Malacca from the Portuguese. With fewer ships and less capital, the English were at a disadvantage relative to the Dutch during the first half of the seventeenth century. Early English attempts to establish trading bases in Asia failed. Their first success came in India (Madras) in 1639. By 1665 they had Bombay, and in 1691, Calcutta.

While western European maritime powers were active on the southern and eastern coasts of Asia, Russia was expanding by land across northern Asia. Ivan the Terrible fused the Russians into a single centralized state during the 1550s, which allowed them to challenge the powerful Tartar groups to the east. Russian frontier people, the Cossacks, were able to sweep eastward quickly and conquer the small nomadic tribal groups of Siberia. By 1637 the Russians had reached the Pacific Coast of Asia. In the 1640s they invaded the Chinese settlements in the Amur valley, only to be defeated by the Chinese Imperial Army in the 1650s. In 1689 Russia and China signed a treaty that permitted trade: The Russians exchanged gold and furs for Chinese tea.

On the whole, the initial European influence on Asian society was not significant. European territorial

Oceania Oceania was the region of the world least affected by the rise of European mercantilism. In 1520, Ferdinand Magellan crossed the Pacific from east to west and in the process discovered some of the islands. Starting in 1565, the Manila Galleon annually sailed between Acapulco and Manila. The galleons stopped only at Guam; other islands were either avoided or unknown to Spanish navigators, who held to the same course for 250 years. As a result, only Guam came under European domination and had any significant direct European contact.

European expansion indirectly exerted an influence on other Oceanic peoples during this period. By some unknown means, the sweet potato, a Native American crop, was introduced into Melanesia sometime during this period. Capable of being grown at a higher altitude than yams, the sweet potato made possible the growth of native populations in the highlands of New Guinea.

Although Europeans had limited effects on Micronesia (mainly Guam) and Melanesia, Polynesia and Australia appear to have experienced no significant contact with Europeans and few indirect cultural influences during this period.

The World and the Industrial Revolution

The industrial revolution began during the waning decades of the eighteenth century with the production of machine-woven cotton textiles in England. By the early nineteenth century, the industrial revolution included the production of steel and was spreading to other European countries and the former English colonies in North America, now the United States. The industrial revolution dramatically changed the relationship between European peoples and the other peoples of the world. The technological advances that were associated with industrialization rapidly elevated European peoples to a position of military, political, and economic dominance in the world.

As a result, European peoples redrew the political map and restructured the world economy to meet the needs of their new industrial economy. This new European economic system required overseas sources of raw materials, as well as markets for finished goods. Technological advancements resulted in the construction of larger and faster ships, which meant that maritime commerce was no longer limited to high-cost luxury goods. Sharply lower shipping costs made possible the transportation of massive shipments of basic foodstuffs and raw materials on a global scale. The development of railroads opened the interiors of the continents by lowering the cost of transporting goods to the coastal ports.

During the sixteenth, seventeenth, and eighteenth centuries, global trade and cultural exchange had developed. In the nineteenth century there was the incipient evolution of a global economy based on regional economic specialization and the production of commodities for export. As in the earlier period, the effects of this change varied from one portion of the world to another.

The Americas   The Americas were the first region to experience this changed relationship because the Americas were more closely tied politically and economically to Europe. Just as the industrial revolution was beginning in Europe, a political revolution was starting in the Americas. From the English-speaking colonies this revolution spread to the Spanish-speaking portions of the Americas. By the third decade of the nineteenth century, most areas of mainland America were independent of European political domination. These independence movements did not change the status of Native Americans because the new countries were dominated by Euro-Americans, or, in the case of Haiti, African-Americans.

Although these new countries had achieved political independence, they maintained economic ties to Europe and quickly became the major sources of raw materials as well as markets for industrializing Europe. The West Indies and the United States supplied cotton for the textile mills of England, and the Americas—both the English- and the Spanish-speaking countries—served as the earliest major market for finished cotton textiles. The expanding European market for raw

materials stimulated economic development and territorial expansion of Euro-American and African-American settlements throughout the Americas. With the initial emphasis of the industrial revolution on the production of plantation crops, such as cotton and sugar, the African slave trade escalated to unprecedented proportions. Of the estimated 10 million-plus African slaves brought to the Americas, the vast majority were relocated between 1750 and 1850.

As industrial centers developed in the northeastern United States and as mining, grain farming, and ranching expanded throughout the Americas during the nineteenth century, the need for slave labor declined. In 1833 slavery was abolished in the British West Indies, and by the 1880s slavery had been abolished throughout the Americas. As the importation of African slaves declined, the migration of Europeans to the Americas increased. In 1835 there were about 18.6 million individuals of European ancestry in the Americas, compared with 9.8 million people of African ancestry. By 1935 the population of Euro-Americans had jumped to 172 million, whereas the number of African-Americans had risen to only 36.5 million.

In 1775 the area of Euro-American and African-American settlement in North America was, for the most part, limited to the region east of the Appalachian Mountains. Within a century, however, the territorial limits of these settlements had been pushed across the continent to the Pacific Ocean. During the period of expansion, Native American populations had been quickly defeated militarily

The introduction of New World crops greatly changed the lives of many of Africa's farming peoples.

In the Congo Free State natives were forcibly conscripted to work on the plantations and in the mines. Working under armed guards the labor conditions in the Congo were some of the most brutal and exploitative in world history.

and confined to small reservations. A similar pattern of territorial expansion occurred in South America. The grasslands of Argentina had initially attracted few European settlers. In 1880 the territorial limits of Euro-American settlements were about the same as they had been in 1590. In the late 1800s, however, Euro-American ranchers swept through the pampas and Patagonia, virtually eliminating the Indian population. By the early 1900s, autonomous or semiautonomous Native American societies were found only in the Amazon basin and in a few scattered and isolated pockets in other portions of the Americas.

Sub-Saharan Africa   The initial impact of European industrialization on Africa was an intensification of the slave trade. During the mid-nineteenth century, as the slave trade declined, European economic interest in Africa changed. Africa had potential as both a supplier of raw materials for industrial Europe and a market for finished goods. This economic potential could not be realized under existing conditions because the slave trade and resulting warfare had destroyed the political stability of

the entire region. If the economic potential of Africa was to be realized, political stability had to be reestablished, transportation systems developed, and the economies restructured to meet European needs. These goals were accomplished through direct military and political intervention by European countries, primarily England, France, Germany, Belgium, and Portugal, who proceeded unilaterally to divide up the peoples and resources of Africa. As late as 1879, European powers claimed only small portions of Africa. The Portuguese had the coastal areas of Angola, Mozambique, and Guinea. The British had Cape Colony, Lagos, Gold Coast, Sierra Leone, and Gambia. The French had only Gabon, Senegal, and a few coastal ports. Twenty years later, virtually all of sub-Saharan Africa, with the exception of Liberia and Ethiopia, was under direct European rule.

With Africa divided, the European countries concentrated on bringing the peoples of their new territories under political control. Colonial administrations supported by European soldiers and native troops soon established their authority. With some exceptions, the imposition of colonial control was accomplished with relatively little bloodshed.

As colonial authority was established, the usual policy was to institute a tax system. Taxation of native populations served a dual purpose. The revenues generated were frequently sufficient to cover the cost of the colonial administration and troops. In addition, native populations were forced either to produce marketable exports or to work for European-owned plantations or mines to raise the money for taxes. Thus, taxation forced Africans into the European economic network.

Although exploitation of native populations characterized all European colonies in Africa, it reached its height in the Congo basin. In 1885, King Leopold of Belgium claimed the Congo as "Crown lands" and organized it as the Congo Free State. He then sold concessions to companies, which received sole rights to all land and labor within given tracts. These companies then were able to ruthlessly exploit the resources and native populations within their concessions. Africans were forced to work for the companies, and any resistance was crushed. Murder and mutilation were common. Between 1885 and 1908, when protests from other European powers caused the Belgian government to assume control, as many as 8 million Africans were killed, or about half the total population of Congo.

By the early part of the twentieth century, the authority of Europeans had been established throughout Africa. The economy of the region was being developed and integrated into the European system. Gold, silver, copper, diamonds, palm oil, rubber, cacao, and other raw materials were flowing back to Europe, while Africa became an expanding market for European manufactured goods. Few Europeans immigrated to Africa, except to South Africa, although Africa had been divided into European colonies. In most regions, the presence of Europeans was limited to a handful of government administrators, soldiers, missionaries, and entrepreneurs.

Asia The basic pattern of European political and economic expansion in Asia was similar to that of Africa. However, the magnitude of the population and the presence of an already highly developed economic system tempered much of the European impact. The industrial revolution had resulted in major advances in European military technology, which shifted the balance of power in favor of the Europeans. For the first time they could successfully challenge even the largest and most powerful Asian states. This change became evident during the mid-1800s. China had successfully resisted making trade concessions to European powers. In the Opium War (1839–1842) with England, and in a second war with England and France between 1856 and 1858, China saw its navy and army badly defeated and was forced to make humiliating land and trading concessions. During the late 1700s and early 1800s, the British East India Company steadily expanded its territorial control in India through manipulation of internal political rivalries and

limited localized wars. The crushing of the Sepoy Mutiny (1857–1858) ended any question about English political dominance of India.

By the end of the nineteenth century, most of Asia had been brought under the control of European colonial governments. England had India, Burma, Malaya, Sarawak, Hong Kong, and Ceylon. The French held Indochina, and the Dutch had extended their control over the Dutch East Indies. Although still politically independent, China, Nepal, Afghanistan, Thailand, Persia (Iran), and most of the Middle Eastern countries were so strongly dominated by various European powers that some historians have called them *semicolonial regions*. Japan stood alone as the only Asian state that truly retained its autonomy.

During the late nineteenth century, as European political control spread over Asia, the economy of the area was steadily modified by various means to meet the needs of industrial Europe. Although Europeans owned and operated plantations, mines, and various industries in some areas, the principal instruments for changing the existing economies were taxes and duties. Taxation encouraged the production of cash crops for export, whereas import and export duties encouraged the production of some goods and commodities and discouraged the production of others. Native industries that would directly compete with European goods were discouraged.

The degree to which the local economy was changed differed greatly from region to region. In some regions there were large-scale developments for the production of critical cash crops, and massive relocations of populations to supply labor often were associated with these developments. Such changes were most characteristic of, but not limited to, territories within the British Empire. Ceylon became a tea-producing colony, whereas Malaya focused on rubber, Burma on rice, and Bengal (India) on jute (hemp for rope). To increase production, additional labor frequently was needed. Indians and Chinese were recruited to work on the rubber plantations in Malaya. Tamil speakers from southern India provided the labor on the tea plantations of Ceylon. Rubber, tea, and hemp flowed to Europe, and Indian immigrants in Burma increased rice production ninefold, a surplus that was in turn shipped to India, Malaya, Ceylon, and other plantation regions within the empire to feed the workers.

These comprehensive changes in the political and economic life of Asia were accomplished despite the relatively small number of Europeans present in Asia. For example, in India during the mid-1920s, Europeans numbered only about 200,000 administrators, soldiers, and civilians, as opposed to a native population of about 320 million—a ratio of 1:1,500.

Oceania   During the latter half of the eighteenth century, French, Russian, and English naval expeditions explored the Pacific, charting and describing the major islands and island groups. These men were soon followed by merchants, colonists, and whalers. In one way, the history of Oceania during the nineteenth century parallels the history of the Americas during the first three centuries after European discovery. The total population of Melanesia, Micronesia, Polynesia, and Australia was estimated at several million at the time of contact. Disease and warfare quickly reduced the population of much of Oceania during the nineteenth century.

In 1785 the English established a penal colony at Botany Bay in Australia and laid the foundation for the Europeanization of portions of Oceania. The pattern of white settlement expansion in Australia, Tasmania, and New Zealand during this period closely followed that of European settlement and occupation of the United States and Canada. The initially small colony of Europeans grew through continued migrations of European settlers. Native populations declined because of disease and warfare, whereas European settlements expanded, occupying an ever-increasing portion of the land. Surviving native populations were eventually limited to small reserve areas. Numbering about 5,000 at the time of contact, the Tasmanians were extinct within fifty years. During the nineteenth century the population of native Australians declined from about 300,000 to only 60,000. Tasmania and Australia had become European regions. In New Zealand the native Maori were only slightly more successful in resisting. Numbering only about 100,000 in 1800, by the 1840s the surviving 40,000 Maori were a minority population confined on small reserves.

Aside from Tasmania and Australia, Polynesia (including New Zealand) was the region most affected by Europeans. During the nineteenth century, the indigenous population of these islands declined from 1,100,000 to only 180,000. The causes varied significantly from one island to another. Easter Island was depopulated by Peruvian slave raiders who raided the island in 1842, taking about 1,000 slaves and killing numerous others. Fifteen of these slaves, who were suffering from smallpox, eventually were returned home; this had a deadly effect on the remaining islanders. Among a population that had formerly numbered between 4,000 and 7,000, decline set in, until only 111 Easter Islanders were left by the late nineteenth century. Captain Cook in 1779 estimated the native population of Hawaii at between 300,000 and 400,000. By 1857, only 70,000 native Hawaiians remained. Missionary-entrepreneurs from the United States were able to secure lands for plantations, and as the native population declined, they began importing laborers from Asia to work

the fields. This influx of Europeans and Asians reduced the native Hawaiians to a minority population before the end of the nineteenth century. There were major exceptions to these patterns. Although the native populations of Samoa and Tonga declined, there was no significant influx of Europeans, and the native populations of these islands eventually recovered.

The islands of Micronesia also suffered from a population drop during the nineteenth century, declining from about 200,000 to about 83,000. However, these small, scattered islands had little to attract large numbers of Europeans. For the most part, Europeans contented themselves with asserting their political dominance and claiming these islands as possessions. Micronesians were mostly left on their own.

The pattern of contact differed significantly from island to island in Melanesia. Although the Germans, English, and Dutch politically divided New Guinea and established plantations along the coast, the indigenous population of the island was too vast to be displaced by Europeans. The same was not true in Fiji and New Caledonia. The native population of Fiji decreased from 300,000 to 85,000, and New Caledonia's native population declined from 100,000 to a low of 27,000. In Fiji, English entrepreneurs secured land for sugar plantations and began importing laborers from India, until by the twentieth century the Indians constituted a majority of the population. Mineral wealth attracted European settlers to New Caledonia, which came under French administration. By the twentieth century, the population of the island was about equally native and nonnative.

European Impact on World Cultural Systems

In the four-hundred-year period following 1492, the world had been dramatically changed. The Columbian Exchange, as the historian Alfred Crosby termed the flow of plants, animals, and technology between the Old and New Worlds, had altered the lives and cultures of virtually every people in the world. This exchange in turn made possible the global population explosion and dramatic advancements in technology that came with the industrial revolution during the nineteenth century.

In terms of peoples, there were winners and losers. Certainly the biggest losers in the New World were the American Indians, the Australian aborigines, and some of the peoples of Polynesia. Not only had these peoples lost most of their population, but most of their lands had been taken by peoples from Europe or Africa. Politically, economically, and culturally, they were dominated by the Neo-European and Neo-African peoples. Among Old World peoples, the sub-Saharan Africans were the greatest losers. As slaves, their labor materially contributed to the rise of European power. In return, however, sub-Saharan Africa received little other than the pain and chaos that accompanied the destructive slave wars. The only real winners had been the Europeans, both in Europe as well as in the Neo-Europes of the Americas and the Pacific. By 1900, economically and politically, they exercised virtually total control over the world and its resources, a situation that allowed them to impose Western cultural norms, values, ideas, and institutions on the world's peoples.

The World Since 1945

The four decades from the turn of the twentieth century until the start of World War II were, for the relationship between European and non-Western peoples, a period of stability and consolidation.

Political dominance served to enhance European feelings of racial and cultural superiority. Non-Western peoples and their cultures were looked on as inherently inferior. Non-Western cultures, if studied at all, were looked at only out of curiosity for the strange and the exotic. For the most part, the attitude was that there was nothing of significance that non-Western peoples could teach Europeans. The unilineal evolutionary ideas of Lewis Henry Morgan and Edward Tylor were, in part, a response to this thinking. There were more advanced and less advanced cultures, and the Europeans were at the top. Thus, they were the only people whose ideas and cultural systems mattered, and colonialism was morally justified on the basis of European superiority.

So complete was European dominance that many non-Western peoples began to question the worth of their own cultural institutions and to adopt and emulate the European lifestyle. There was, however, one major non-Western people who successfully resisted European domination—the Japanese. Having adopted European military technology beginning in the 1870s, the Japanese defeated the imperial Russian forces in Manchuria during the Russo-Japanese War of 1904–1905. This defeat marked the first time a major European power had been decisively beaten by a non-Western people, and the inherent superiority of Europeans was brought into question. At the time, other Europeans dismissed the war as being of little consequence, which in fact was true. It did, however, set the stage for later events. More than any other event, the Russo-Japanese War encouraged the development of nationalist independence movements in the colonial world. Between World War I and World War II, nationalist movements had taken root in many colonial possessions. The best known of these movements was the one led by Gandhi in India.

World War II was a major watershed in world history in that it created the conditions necessary for the success of nationalist movements and the collapse of the colonial world. In Asia, the Japanese army quickly overran a number of important European colonies: the Dutch East Indies, Hong Kong, Indo-China, Malaya, North Borneo, Sarawak, Burma, and the Philippines. In the wake of their eventual defeat, the Japanese left behind not only a destroyed colonial infrastructure, but numerous well-organized and well-armed nationalist groups as well. Meanwhile, in Europe, the war with Germany had destroyed the home economies and industrial bases of the major colonial powers. Their own cities and factories damaged or destroyed, they could not resist the rising forces of nationalism. One by one, their former colonies gained independence; by the late-1960s, the colonial world had almost vanished.

The past half-century has been a time of far-reaching and profound changes in the lives of the world's peoples. The collapse of the colonial world signaled the beginning of a decline in the power and influence of European peoples. No longer can European leaders alone dictate the course of world events. The centers of political, economic, and cultural power and influence are increasingly dispersed and ethnically diverse. At the same time, technological changes have increased industrial and agricultural production and greatly intensified the social contacts between an economic interdependence of the various countries and peoples of the world. A highly integrated global economy has evolved. Concurrent with these changes, a population explosion has more than doubled the earth's population. Virtually every country in the world has, since 1945, experienced major internal economic and demographic shifts, as well as significant changes in external relations with other countries. As a result, there have been fundamental changes in the economic, demographic, and political structure of the world.

The Global Economy

For better or worse, the market principle increasingly integrates the economies of the world into a global economy in which manufactured goods, foodstuffs, and raw materials are marketed worldwide. Thus, the price we pay for a sack of flour in Kansas or a gallon of gasoline in Texas is determined in large part by the world price for wheat and oil. The price we pay for a Ford made in Detroit is no longer solely influenced by competition from General Motors, but also by auto manufacturers in Japan, Scandinavia, and Germany. Foreign imports not only place American auto companies and dealers in competition with foreign companies, but also put American auto workers in direct competition with their foreign

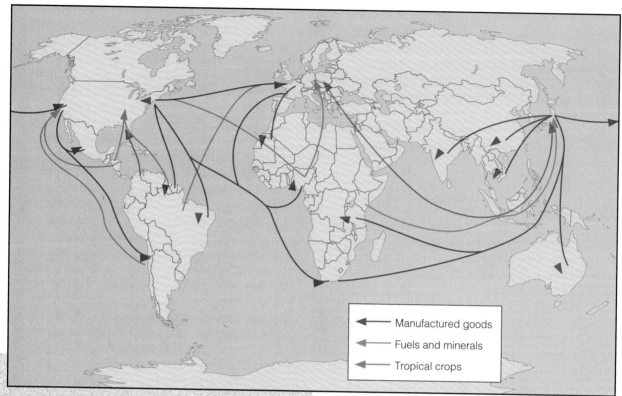

Figure 16.2 Map of Commodities and Manufacturing Flow
The modern world is linked together by the flow of materials and manufactured goods, creating a global economy.

counterparts. American farmers, oil producers, business-people, and workers are now finding that they have to compete on a global level for the prices they can charge for their goods and labor.

Three main factors have been instrumental in the development of this global economic system. First, the colonial powers economically monopolized their colonies, using them as protected sources of raw materials as well as markets for their manufactured goods. With the end of colonialism, the export products of these regions could be sold on the world market and imported goods could be purchased in the same competitive world marketplace. Second, technological improvements in transportation have resulted in a drastic lowering of the cost of transporting ores, metals, manufactured goods, and foodstuffs. Supertankers have been developed for the shipping of oil. The use of containers in transporting and loading has greatly reduced the cost of shipping manufactured goods. Larger and faster cargo planes have revolutionized the international transportation of lightweight, high-value goods. Geography no longer protects markets or limits the products produced by a region. Third, international bank-

ing and financial institutions have evolved and loaned money to capital-poor Third World nations for economic development, ultimately increasing both the exports and the imports of these countries (see Figure 16.2).

These and other changes have stimulated and expanded the volume of world trade. World trade stagnated between World War I and World War II. After World War II, the volume of world trade began once again to expand, until by the mid-1990s it was more than ten times the level it had been just before and after the war (see Figure 16.3).

Until the 1950s, the industrialized regions of the world were concentrated in Europe and North America, with Japan being the only non-Western country that had industrialized to any significant degree. The rest of the world served basically as a source of raw materials and a market for the manufactured goods of these regions. Starting in the 1960s, other countries in the Far East and Southeast Asia, such as Hong Kong, Taiwan, South Korea, and Singapore, began emulating Japan's success. At first they used their low labor costs to produce textiles, clothing, footwear, and other labor-intensive products that undercut the prices and invaded the markets of the established "first-wave" industrial countries. At the same time, Japan was expanding its heavy industry (steel making, ship building, and automobiles), as well as its electronic industries. In recent years, industrialization has spread to the adjoining countries: Thailand, Malaysia, Indonesia, and China. Not only are these countries now competing with Western Europe and North America in heavy industry, but in high-tech industries as well. The countries of the Far East and Southeast Asia have the fastest growing economies in the world. If the present growth rates continue, in a generation or two the Far East and Southeast Asia will equal, if not surpass, Western Europe and North America in both industrial production and technological sophistication.

The changing economic relation between the United States and the rest of the world over the past forty years illustrates the increasing degree of global interdependence. Just before World War II, the United States was what geographer L. Dudley Stamp characterized as a "young nation," meaning that more than 50 percent of U.S. exports consisted of foodstuffs and raw materials such as oil, raw cotton, wheat and other grains, and tobacco. Imports were dominated by products that did not occur naturally or grow well domestically, notably tropical foodstuffs and raw materials such as rubber, sugar, coffee, and silk. The United States was self-sufficient in most minerals critical for industry, including iron, copper, potassium, coal, and petroleum. Indeed, the United States was an exporter of these items. In turn, American industrial output was more than sufficient to meet domestic needs for most categories of manufactured goods.

The postwar era has seen major shifts in both the kinds and the quantities of goods that the United States imports and exports. As the volume of trade has increased, the nature of American imports and exports has changed. From a strategic perspective, the most significant change is that the United States now has to rely on other countries for many of the critical raw materials for industries and fuels that it once produced. The increasing dependence of Americans on the importation of metals, petroleum, and other raw materials is the result of several factors. The expanding economy of the United States has resulted in an increased consumption of energy fuels and raw materials. At the same time, either domestic energy and raw-material reserves have declined in production or production cannot be increased to meet demands.

While the United States has become increasingly dependent on foreign sources for basic energy needs and raw materials, the nature of American industry itself has been changing. The American shoe industry is almost gone, replaced by factories in Brazil, Italy, Taiwan, South Korea, Indonesia, and Vietnam. Segments of the American electronics industry have lost out to foreign competi-

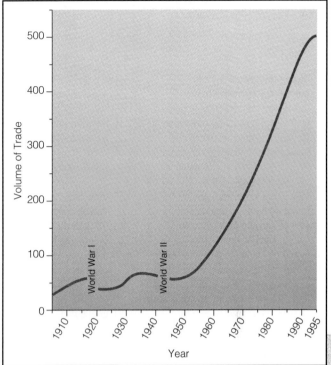

Figure 16.3   Growth of World Trade: 1905–1990

tion; most television sets, radios, and videocassette recorders are now produced in Japan, Hong Kong, Singapore, and Thailand. The American garment industry is rapidly losing its domestic market to clothing imported from South Korea, Hong Kong, Taiwan, China, and Malaysia. The American automobile industry, traditionally the bulwark of the manufacturing economy, has lost a significant portion of both its domestic and its world markets to Europe, Japan, and South Korea. In 1950, American factories produced 75 percent of all motor vehicles manufactured in the world, dominating not just their own domestic market but most of the world market as well. By 1991, American production had dropped to only 18 percent of the world's total, and almost 25 percent of the automobiles sold in the United States were imported. A similar loss of the domestic market has occurred for the American steel industry. Today the United States depends on foreign sources for much of its basic needs in manufactured goods. To pay for these increased imports, the United States has shifted from being primarily an exporter of raw materials to being an exporter of specialized manufactured goods. In 1990, the Japanese Ministry of International Trade and Industry targeted several industries for expansion. These targeted industries included aircraft, machine tools, microelectronics, telecommunications, and

A CLOSER LOOK

The Bankers and the Sheiks

During the Middle Ages in Europe, the Catholic Church through its canon courts declared usury, or the charging of interest on loans, to be un-Christian. Thus, Christians were prohibited from charging interest, and banking in medieval Europe was in the hands of Jews. During the late Middle Ages, Italian Catholics began founding banking houses and by clever semantics were able to circumvent the church laws against usury. An individual would be loaned money, interest free, for an unrealistically short period. When the loan was not repaid within this stated time, which it seldom was, the bankers charged "damages."

The Islamic religion also prohibits usury. However, Islam differs in a number of significant ways from Christianity. The Koran is not merely a book of religious teachings but also a codified legal system called the sharia. Courts in traditional Islamic countries use the Koran as the basis for legal rulings, functioning as what are sometimes called *Islamic courts*.

The law courts in much of the Arab world—Saudi Arabia, Kuwait, Bahrain, and the United Arab Emirates—are Islamic courts. Thirty years ago, this fact had little international significance. Relatively poor, these countries had little need for financial transactions and banking institutions. With the discovery of oil and the rapid development of this region starting in the 1960s, a need for such institutions quickly developed. A number of European and American banking houses, such as Citibank and Chase Manhattan, opened Middle Eastern branches. Not only did they manage the vast flow of dollars changing hands through the sale of oil and the purchase of imports, but they also began loaning money to local Arab entrepreneurs who organized companies to profit from this economic boom.

Like the medieval Italian bankers, they developed semantic ways of circumventing the Islamic prohibition against usury. The word *interest* was never used in loaning money. Instead, these banks charged Islamic borrowers "administrative fees" or "loan initiation discounts." By 1986 it was estimated that the various world banks had between $8 and $9 billion in loans to Saudi Arabian companies alone. This system worked well as long as oil income kept rising and all parties made handsome profits. In the 1980s the price of oil began to decline, and in early 1986 the price collapsed, falling from $28 a barrel to (at one point) under $10 a barrel.

As their income from oil plunged, governments began to slow payments to government contractors and suppliers. Arab companies with a cash flow problem quickly fell behind on loan payments to banks. Many Arab businessmen suddenly rediscovered their religion. A flood of Arab companies and individuals quickly took the banks to court, charging them with usury. These courts correctly found the bank guilty of usury under Islamic law.

In the summer of 1986, a number of international banks cut back on their Middle Eastern operations. Citibank reduced its offices in Bahrain and the United Arab Emirates; Chase Manhattan closed its Jordanian branch. International and Middle Eastern bankers quickly proved themselves to be as adaptive as the medieval Italians. There was a rapid growth of "Islamic banks." While most Islamic banks were local, some were branches of large international banks, while others were associated with international banking houses. By scrupulously avoiding the charging of "riba," or "interest," and operating as "modarebs," or "money managers," Islamic banks are able to provide a handsome profit for their investors while meeting the banking needs of the region.

---

computers, industries which are critical to American export trade. The competition for markets between industrialized countries is only going to intensify.

The emergence of a global economy has also resulted in the emergence of multinational corporations. Unlike earlier companies, these corporations are not economically tied to or dependent on any single country. Having manufacturing plants located in several countries and worldwide sales and distribution facilities, not infrequently these companies produce and sell most of their goods in countries other than the one in which their corporate headquarters is located. Unconstrained by national political boundaries, these corporations can and do move their facilities from country to country in search of cheaper labor, lower taxes, and less demanding governmental regulations.

International corporate mergers and buyouts have made national identities of companies and products even more ambiguous. CITGO, formerly Cities Service, the largest gasoline retailer in the United States, is now totally owned by Petroleos de Venezuela, S.A., the national oil company of Venezuela. Chrysler has merged with Daimler-Benz to form Daimler-Chrysler, a German-based corporation.

These recent changes in the world economic system would not have been possible without the development of international financing, which has made money available to capital-poor nations for economic development. In 1945, the World Bank and the International Monetary Fund were created to help war-ravaged Europe and Japan reestablish their industrial plants. These two institutions have played a pivotal role in the creation of the existing global economic system. The

World Bank has been a major conduit for economic development loans to Third World nations. The World Bank's role in making loan money available to Third World countries has now been supplemented by numerous European, American, and Japanese banking houses that have become international financiers. Some banking practices have adapted to foreign traditions in interesting ways, such as in the Middle East as we discuss in "A Closer Look."

Loans provided to these capital-poor countries have allowed them to adopt high-cost technology more quickly and increase their economic productivity. With these funds, Third World countries have constructed irrigation projects, expanded and modernized their transportation and communication systems, developed or expanded port facilities, and, in some cases, developed their own manufacturing industries. In the past decade alone, these loans have amounted to hundreds of billions of dollars. An underappreciated consequence of these loans is a stimulation of the exports of industrialized nations because most of these funds are used to purchase needed technology and equipment from Japan, Europe, and the United States. At the same time, most of the economic development projects funded by these loans have focused on increased production of raw materials needed by these same industrialized countries.

International financing adds another dimension to the increasing interdependence of nations. With Third World countries owing hundreds of billions of dollars in loans to industrial nations through international banks, the citizens of the industrial nations have a direct vested interest in the economic prosperity of these countries.

As discussed in this overview, neither the United States nor any other country in the world even approaches economic self-sufficiency. Virtually all peoples are integrated into the global economy. We depend on one another for critical energy fuels, raw materials, and particular categories of foodstuffs and manufactured goods. Without these imports we could not sustain our economy or even adequately provide food, clothing, and shelter for our population. In turn, other countries depend on us, both as a source for particular manufactured goods and foodstuffs, and as a market for their products. Although some countries and regions may be more critical than others because they provide some particular essential goods or resources, all are important in maintaining the current global economic system. In the future, the integration and interdependence certainly will become significantly greater. Given that we are all part of the single global system that evolved as a consequence of the expansion of European peoples and ideas, enlightened

Most of the clothes now sold in the United States are made elsewhere.

self-interest as well as humanitarianism demand that we understand and respect those with cultural heritages different from our own.

Demographic Changes

The postwar period has also been a time of rapid population growth. Since 1950 the world population has jumped from slightly more than 2.5 billion to almost 6 billion. This population growth has not been equally as pronounced among all the world's peoples. The greatest increase has been in Africa, Asia, and Latin America. The population growth rate in Europe, North America, and the former Soviet Union during this period was well below the world rate. As a result, European peoples have declined from about 30 percent of the world's total population in 1950 to only about 20 percent, a factor that has contributed to the waning of European influence and power in the world.

The highest rates of population growth—those of Latin America, Asia, and Africa—are in the least industrialized regions of the world. Although the economic development of many of these regions has been significant, economic expansion has not kept pace with population growth. Thus, this population explosion has created extreme economic and population pressures in many of the less developed rural regions of the Third World, contributing to outmigrations of peoples. (Chapter 18 discusses some anthropological insights

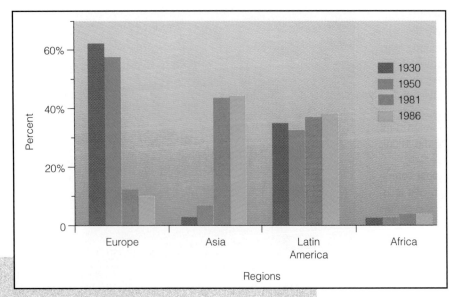

Figure 16.4 Immigrants to the United States

In fact, the world's most rapidly growing cities are located in nonindustrialized nations. In some of these cities the growth rate has been phenomenal. In the 1950s, Bogotá, Columbia, had a population of only about 650,000; by 1995 its population was over 5 million. Similar increases are common in many Latin American, Asian, and African nations. Most Third World cities lack the large industrial complexes capable of employing the great masses of people migrating into them, but their small-scale industries, transportation services, and government jobs, although limited, offer greater economic opportunities than do the overcrowded rural regions.

Most migration has been within countries, but a growing trend has been toward international migration. Most evident has been the migration from the nations of Latin America, Asia, and Africa to the highly industrialized countries of North America and Europe. As their industrial economies expanded during the 1950s and 1960s, many Western European countries began experiencing labor shortages. West Germany initiated a "guest-worker" program to actively recruit foreign laborers, first in southern Europe, Italy, and Spain, and later in Yugoslavia and Turkey. Concurrently, French factories began recruiting Arab workers from their then North African colonies, particularly Algeria. In the 1950s, England began experiencing an influx of West Indians from its possessions in the Caribbean. In the 1960s, a wave of Pakistani and Indian immigrants also settled in England. Other Western European countries experienced a similar phenomenon, although usually on a smaller scale.

By the early 1970s, when the economic growth of Western Europe began to slow, large non-European communities were well established in most of the major cities. When West Germany ended its guest-worker program in 1974, it had hosted 2.5 million foreign workers, a number equal to over 10 percent of its total labor force. Through various means the West German government tried to repatriate these guest workers and their families, but failed. France, England, and other Western European countries have considered stricter immigration laws to stop the continuing influx of African and Asian workers, but the number of new immigrants is increasing despite tighter controls. Today almost 10 percent of the popula-

on population growth.) As we have noted, mass movements of people are not new in history. However, both the nature and the geographical direction of population movements since World War II differ from those of earlier periods. Earlier migrations were primarily movements of European and African peoples to the Americas, with secondary waves of European immigrants settling in portions of Oceania, Africa, and Asia, and Asian immigrants being relocated in Asia or resettled in portions of Africa and Oceania. Since 1945, there have been two main patterns of human migration: (1) a worldwide phenomenon of rural-to-urban migration and (2) a migration of Third World peoples to the industrialized countries of Europe and North America.

During the nineteenth and early twentieth centuries, the development of major urban centers was associated with industrial economies. Increasing demand for industrial workers had been the primary factor in the growth of cities. In industrialized societies this trend toward urbanization has continued. In addition, major urban centers have emerged in nonindustrialized Third World countries. Just before World War II, about 50 percent of the total population of the United States and Europe was urban, compared with only about 8 to 10 percent for Africa and Asia and 25 percent for Latin America. Today, about 75 percent of Americans and 70 percent of Europeans are city dwellers. However, the urban populations of Asia and Africa have jumped to between 25 and 30 percent, and in Latin America the urban population has increased to more than 60 percent. The growth rate of urbanization has thus been highest outside Europe and North America.

tion of Western Europe are recent immigrants. As a result, Western European countries, which once had relatively homogeneous populations, are now home to a number of culturally and ethnically diverse peoples.

This change in patterns of human migration is equally evident in the United States, a country peopled primarily by Old World immigrants and their descendants. Since World War II, about 25 percent of American population growth has been the result of immigration.

Migration patterns to the United States have changed dramatically in the postwar period (see Figure 16.4). In the 1950s, well over one-half the immigrants to the United States were still coming from Europe; the second largest group, about one-third, were coming from Latin America. In the 1960s, the flood of immigrants began to increase. From only about 300,000 persons per year in the 1960s, the number of immigrants jumped to more than 400,000 per year in the 1970s and to more than 700,000 per year in the 1980s. As the number of immigrants increased, the origin of the immigrants shifted markedly. Proportionally, the number of Latin-American immigrants remained about the same, and European immigration declined. The major increase change was in the number of Asian arrivals, from less than 10 percent of all immigrants in 1950 to more than 40 percent by the 1980s. As a result, between 1980 and 1990 the number of Asian Americans more than doubled, from 3.5 million (1.5 percent) to almost 7.3 million (2.9 percent), whereas the number of Latin Americans increased almost 50 percent, from 14.5 million (6.4 percent) to more than 22 million (9 percent). These figures are only for legal immigrants; if the number of illegal immigrants could be added, the shift would have been much greater, since most of these immigrants are Asian or Latin Americans. Large and ever-growing communities of Chinese, Vietnamese, Cambodian, Laotian, Korean, Asian Indian, Arab, Iranian, Mexican, Guatemalan, Colombian, Salvadoran, and Peruvian immigrants—to name just some—are appearing in the cities of the United States. Thus, the ethnic diversity of the U.S. population is increasing.

Although Europe and North America have been the primary destinations for most international migrants, other regions with high income, labor shortages, or both have experienced major influxes of immigrants. Many of the oil-rich Arab countries—Libya, Saudi Arabia, Kuwait, Quatar, Oman, and the United Arab Emirates—have recruited foreign workers from India, Pakistan, Bangladesh, and Egypt, and from among Palestinian refugees. Indeed, in some of the smaller of these countries foreign workers outnumber native Arabs. Thus, the population of the world is in constant flux.

In the not too distant past, white missionaries took Christianity and European culture to the peoples of the Americas, Africa, Asia, and Oceania. Although Christian missionary work continues, today we also find Islamic mosques in such cities as Berlin, Paris, London, and New York, and Hindu gurus find converts among European peoples in both Europe and North America. Before World War II, small pockets of European peoples were found scattered throughout the cities of Africa and Asia. Today, enclaves of newly arrived Turks, Arabs, Africans, Asians, and Latin Americans are scattered throughout the cities of Western Europe and North America.

This massive migration of peoples has alleviated some of the economic and population pressures in many Third World countries. At the same time, like it or not, it is bringing peoples from extremely diverse cultural backgrounds into direct daily contact with one another.

The Hare Krishna movement and many other non-Western religions have found converts in the United States and Western Europe during the past few decades.

Other Voices

Orientalism and the Western View of the Arab/Islamic World

In Western culture one of the strongest and most pervasive images of others is that of the Orient, more specifically the Arab/Islamic world. This is not surprising when we consider the history of these regions. The division between the West (Europe) and the East (Asia) is not geographical, but cultural. The boundary that separates the two was and is the frontier between Christianity and Islam. In the ancient period, under the Romans, the Mediterranean world, Europe, North Africa, and the Middle East were united. By the seventh century A.D., when the Islamic religion emerged, most of this world was Christian, or rapidly becoming Christian. Relations between the two competing religious traditions quickly became hostile as Islam spread throughout the Middle East and North Africa. In the eighth century A.D., Islamic armies crossed into southern Europe, invading Spain, Portugal, and even France. By the eleventh century A.D., the Christian princes of Europe were becoming increasingly united against

Islam. In Spain and Portugal Christian armies were making progress against Islamic domination, when the first of the Crusades to free the Holy Land of Islamic control was launched. Although they ultimately failed, the Crusades, more than any other factor, served to create the image of Europe, versus the Orient, and define the division between the two. To be European (Western) was to be Christian, while to be Oriental (Eastern) was to be Muslim. For the Europeans, the Muslims were the "Others" who served to give them a higher level of identity, as European, as opposed to just French, German, English or Polish, or just Catholic, Protestant, or Orthodox.

The identity as European or Western was thus forged in war with and opposition to the Islamic world. Over the past thirteen hundred years, the boundary has fluctuated, but it has been and remains the bloodiest and most contested division between the world's peoples. Even today the conflict continues—in

Bosnia, between the Moslems and Christians; in Kosovo, between Serbs (Christians) and Albanians (Moslems); and in Nagora Koraba, between Armenians (Christians) and Ageri (Moslems). In a recent study, the eminent political scientist, Samuel Huntington, described this "fault line" between the Christian and Muslim worlds as the most potentially dangerous and volatile of all the divisions among the world's peoples.

What makes this conflict between the Western and Islamic worlds so dangerous are the misconceptions which exist. Edward Said, an Arab-American scholar, born in Palestine, became concerned over the negative stereotypes of Arabs and Islams which he found pervasive in American culture. In American popular culture, television, movies, and the news, the Islamic world and Arabs in particular were described in negative terms. The Arab "appears as an over-sexed degenerate, capable . . . of cleverly devious intrigues, but essentially sadistic, treacherous, low." Not shown with individual or personal characteristics or dif-

Political Fragmentation

The postwar era has been characterized by increased political fragmentation. Although the precise number varies, depending on how one defines an "independent" or "autonomous" country, at the beginning of World War II there were about sixty countries in the world. Most of Asia, Africa, and Oceania was divided between European colonial empires. As the era of colonialism came to an end after the war, the number of politically independent countries increased rapidly. Between 1946 and 1980, eighty-eight new countries were carved out of the colonial empires of Europe. The recent collapse of the Soviet Union and Yugoslavia has resulted in the creation of eighteen new countries. From only about 80 countries in 1945, the number of independent countries has grown to almost 200.

The emergence of these new countries has forever changed the face of global politics. Before the war,

European leaders, consulting only among themselves, controlled the political destiny of the world's peoples. Even Japan was considered a second-level power. As non-European countries have increasingly emerged as economic and even military powers, non-European leaders have come to play an ever-expanding role in world politics.

Consequences of an Interdependent World

As stated earlier, the world we live in today is not the world of our grandparents. This is true at both the individual level and the national level.

For the individual, the consequences of recent changes are both direct and indirect. Urbanization is resulting in increased daily contact between individuals

ferences, they are presented as "masses" of peoples in either "rage" or "misery." However, what was even more disturbing to Said was that members of the academic community, the scholars who were "experts" and specialists on the Arab and Islamic worlds, presented the Arab world in much the same way. In response to these anti-Arab and anti-Islamic stereotypes Said researched the origins of such stereotypes. He found that the basic anti-Islamic stereotype prevalent among the American academic community started evolving in Europe during the Middle Ages and the Renaissance.

By the late eighteenth century, Orientalism or the academic study of the Orient, emerged in European universities. During the nineteenth century as European powers, principally England and France, extended their empires into North Africa and the Middle East, academic interest increased. However, increasing the academic study did not challenge the preexisting Western stereotypes but rather reinforced and modified them in such a way as to justify imperial political designs. Thus, the Western academic community marched in locked step with the armies of the empire, providing them the moral rationalization for domination. They—the Islamic peoples of the East—

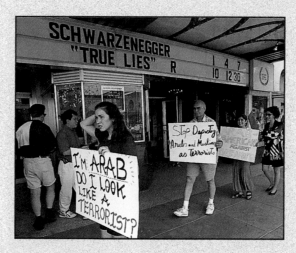

Arab-Americans protest the depiction of Arabs in the movie *True Lies*.

were the ultimate "Others," inferior to Westerners in their intellectual potential and achievements. Inheritant in their religious beliefs and language were qualities which made them irrational and unable to control and develop themselves. But most of all they were dangerous to themselves and others. The Arab/Islamic world had to be controlled and this control had to come from the outside; i.e., the Western world.

These ideas to which the British, French, and other European academic communities gave voice were the justifi-

cations for colonial policies. With the collapse of the colonial world after World War II, and ascendence of the United States in world affairs, these same ideas were adopted in the United States. Whether academics or politicians, whether studying history or anthropology or developing political policies, Westerners today basically see and judge the Arab/Islamic world through the eyes of a Medieval Crusader.

Sources: Huntington (1993) and Said (1978).

from diverse ethnic and cultural backgrounds. In cities throughout the world, people are finding that employers and employees, customers and vendors, landlords and tenants, doctors and patients—in other words, individuals whose actions affect the quality of their everyday lives—are increasingly individuals with whom they do not share a common cultural heritage. Certainly there has always been diversity in American cities; but when our grandparents thought of ethnic diversity, they thought primarily about the differences between Irish, Italians, Poles, Germans, Russians, Swedes, and so forth. Although there were some cultural differences between these groups, they shared a basically common cultural tradition. Today these new immigrant groups are from Asia, Africa, Latin America, and the Middle East, people with whom most Americans do not share a common cultural tradition. Thus, greater awareness of and tolerance for cultural differences are increasingly necessary parts of our lives.

These changes have important consequences at the individual level, but it is at the national level where the consequences become greatest. First, the economic interdependence of the world's peoples requires a steady flow of manufactured goods, foodstuffs, and raw materials from other countries. Because virtually no region of the world is economically self-sufficient, disruption in the steady flow of this exchange could conceivably have catastrophic economic repercussions. The vulnerability of the United States and its dependence on other countries for critical resources were made clear in 1973 when the Arab oil-producing countries embargoed shipments of oil to the United States for six months in retaliation for American support of Israel. The result was a major shortage of petroleum products that created lines at gasoline stations throughout the country. The primary threat to this global trade network is political conflict that has the potential to cut trade in particular items. Population pressures and related economic pressures

Many recent immigrants to North America from Vietnam, Korea, India, and elsewhere have started small businesses where the entire family is employed.

In the United Nations and other international organizations, the political influence of non-European leaders is increasing.

increase the possibilities for political conflict. Whether we want to view the existing and potential problems of the world in a humanistic way or with pragmatic self-

interest, the answers are the same. The turning to desert of portions of Africa and the resulting problems of starvation are not simply African problems; these are problems of the world community. Economic development projects in Latin America or Africa and Asia serve the needs not only of the peoples of these particular regions but also of the global economy.

What is the value of anthropology to me? Why should I study the cultural institutions of people from some other region of the world? The reason is simple. These "strange and exotic" people no longer live half a world away; they live in your city, your neighborhood, and maybe next door. They may soon be your schoolmates, your colleagues, your customers, or your employer—if they are not already. You depend on these people, directly or indirectly, for much of the food you eat, the clothes you wear, the tools you use, the gasoline that powers your car, and, possibly, the car itself. You in turn have to sell, either directly or indirectly, to these same people goods or services so that you can afford to buy what they produce. In the modern world there is no escape from other people. In the highly interdependent world that is rapidly evolving, the understanding of and toleration for other people's cultural values, norms, and traditions will be a necessity for living.

In the world today there are two dangerously contradictory trends in the directions of human history. One is the global economy and the ever-increasing economic interdependence of the world's peoples that we have just discussed. The other is toward political fragmentation, which we have only mentioned. Nationalism and ethnic conflict are escalating rapidly. If nationalism continues unchecked, there is the very real possibility that it will destroy the global economy and with it the economic well-being of every people in the world. In the next two chapters we examine the nature of ethnic conflict and the factors that serve to inflame these conflicts.

Summary

The past 500 years have been a period of tremendous change for the peoples of the world. The purpose of this chapter has been to show the magnitude, pervasiveness, and general patterns of this change.

This period in history can be divided into three main time periods: the mercantile phase which lasted from about 1500 to 1800; the industrial phase which began about 1800 and lasted until the end of World War II; and the post-World War II phase, the modern period.

The discovery of the Americas by Columbus in 1492 initiated this time of rapid change, as European contact allowed for the transferring of Old World technology, food crops, domesticated animals, diseases, and people to the New World, and vice versa. Although the region most profoundly affected during this phase was the Americas, the effects of these changes were global. By the late 1700s, the culture of virtually every people in the world had been either directly or indirectly affected.

With the advent of the industrial revolution, starting about 1800, the nature of European contact with non-Western peoples changed primarily from trade to colonialism and political domination. During the nineteenth century, European domination over the non-Western peoples of the Americas, Africa, Asia, and Oceania spread rapidly until by 1900 it was complete. The European powers restructured the economies of their possessions to meet European needs. The period of Europe's ever-increasing political and economic control continued until World War II.

The post-World War II period has been a time of continued economic, political, demographic, and sociocultural growth and change. The two important features of this period have been the emergence of a highly interdependent global economic system and the political fragmentation that ensued as colonial empires were dismantled and "new" countries were created.

During the past half century, a rapidly growing world economic interdependence and a shift in world economic and political power have taken place. Before World War II, with the exception of Japan, the world was both economically and politically controlled by individuals of European ancestry—people from the United States, England, Germany, France, and so forth. Thus, important decisions were made by a relatively small group of leaders who shared basically common sets of values, norms, and beliefs. With European political and economic dominance rapidly waning, this is no longer the situation. In today's increasingly complex global political and economic climate, important decisions now frequently involve agreements between leaders with quite different sets of cultural values, norms, and beliefs. The economic and political conditions of the world necessitate a far greater degree of cross-cultural understanding and tolerance than ever before in human history.

Certainly we would not argue that tolerance and understanding of cultural differences can solve all the world's difficulties. However, many problems in the world today are the result of cultural intolerance and misunderstandings. Anthropologists and anthropological theory are well suited to understanding and arbitrating these problems and to showing why we all ought to show more respect for one another's rights and opinions.

Key Terms

innovation
diffusion
assimilation

global economy
demographic changes

Suggested Readings

There are numerous excellent historical studies of world history since 1500. The following list includes only studies of more general interest.

Abu-Lughod, Janet L. *Before European Hegemony: The World System A.D. 1250–1350*. New York: Oxford University Press, 1989.
• *An excellent introduction to the economy and trade of Europe, the Middle East, India, the Far East, and Southeast Asia just before the European expansion.*

Crosby, Alfred W. *The Columbian Exchange*. Westport, Conn.: Greenwood, 1972.
• *An important and readable study by a historian, showing some of the major cultural and demographic effects of contact between the Old World and the New World. The study emphasizes the exchange of food plants, animals, and diseases.*

Crosby, Alfred W. *Ecological Imperialism: The Biological Expansion of Europe, 900–1900*. Cambridge: Cambridge University Press, 1986.
• *A companion work to his earlier study, Crosby shows that European expansion was not just of people but of plants and animals as well.*

Mintz, Sidney W. *Sweetness and Power*. New York: Penguin, 1986.
• *An interesting study examines the effect of sugar and its production on the course of world history.*

Stavrianos, L. S. *The World Since 1500: A Global History*. 4th ed. Englewood Cliffs, N.J.: Prentice-Hall, 1982.
• *A history textbook that is the best and most readable general description available of world history over the past 500 years.*

Wolf, Eric. *Europe and the People Without History*. Berkeley: University of California Press, 1982.
• *A study that should become one of the great classics in anthropology, this is the first attempt by an anthropologist to describe and analyze global history since 1400.*

In recent decades, a host of studies have considered historical changes within the cultural systems of particular societies or regions of the world. The following studies are recommended.

Hemming, John. *Red Gold: The Conquest of the Brazilian Indians, 1500–1760*. Cambridge, Mass.: Harvard University Press, 1978.
• *Few books so well illustrate the destruction of Native American peoples as this study of European settlement of Brazil.*

Kelly, Raymond. *The Nuer Conquest*. Ann Arbor: University of Michigan Press, 1985.
• *An important study of the Nuer from a historical perspective that challenges many of the earlier ahistorical explanations for the development of Nuer cultural institutions.*

Klien, Martin A., ed. *Peasants in Africa: Historical and Contemporary Perspectives*. Sage Series on African Modernization and Development, vol. 4. Beverly Hills, Calif.: Sage, 1980.
• *A group of essays in which some of the effects of colonialism on native African populations are discussed and analyzed.*

Leacock, Eleanor, and Nancy Lurie, eds. *North American Indians in Historical Perspective*. New York: Random House, 1971.
• *A collection of fourteen essays on various North American Indian societies that directly challenges the static notion of American Indian culture.*

Sahlins, Marshall. *Islands of History*. Chicago: University of Chicago Press, 1985.
• *An important but not very readable theoretical study of historical anthropology in which the author analyzes a series of historical events in Hawaii, Fiji, and New Zealand. The focus of the study is how native populations interpreted and responded to events of European contact.*

Schieffelin, Edward, and Robert Crittenden, eds. *Like People You See in a Dream: First Contact in Six Papuan Societies*. Stanford: Stanford University Press, 1991.
• *In this edited work, the nature and effects of the first contact with Europeans on six New Guinean peoples are examined. With this contact in the 1930s one could say that the period of expansion had come to an end.*

White, Richard. *The Roots of Dependency: Subsistence, Environment, and Social Change among the Choctaws, Pawnees, and Navajos*. Lincoln: University of Nebraska Press, 1983.
• *A study by a historian who, by using a dependence model, examines the effects of white contact on three Native American societies.*

Wolf, Eric. *Sons of the Shaking Earth*. Chicago: University of Chicago Press, 1939.
• *A very readable sociocultural history of Mexico and Guatemala from prehistoric times to the present.*

There is a growing literature on the sociocultural adjustments of specific immigrant groups in North America and Europe. The following is a list of some of those studies.

Donnelly, Nancy D. *Changing Lives of Refugee Hmong Women*. Seattle: University of Washington Press, 1994.

Haslip-Viera, Gabriel, and Sherrie L. Baver, eds. *Latinos in New York: Communities in Transition*. Notre Dame, Ind.: University of Notre Dame Press, 1996.

Hopkins, Mary Carol. *Braving a New World: Cambodian (Khmer) Refugees in an American City*. Westport, Conn.: Bergin and Garvey, 1996.

Metcalf, Barbara Daly, ed. *Making Muslim Space in North America and Europe*. Berkeley: University of California Press, 1996.

Internet Exercises

The "Fernand Braudel Center for the Study of Economies, Historical Systems, and Civilizations" (http://fbc.binghamton.edu/) at Binghamton University, State University New York, has journals, papers, and links related to the materials presented in this chapter. One of the links that you may want to try is The Journal of World Systems Research. Another site is the Library of Congress with an online exhibit titled "1492: An Ongoing Voyage" (http://sunsite.unc.edu/expo/1492.exhibit/ Intro.html).

A great deal of information relevant to the global economy and international issues can be found at the following sites run by large international agencies:

The United Nations   (http://www.un.org)
The World Bank   (http://www.worldbank.org)
United States Agency for International Development (http://info.usaid.gov)

CHAPTER *17*

Ethnicity in the Modern World

CONTENTS

Ethnic Groups

Situational Nature of Ethnic Identity

Attributes of Ethnic Groups

Fluidity of Ethnic Groups

Types of Ethnic Groups

The Problem of Stateless Nationalities

Resolving Ethnic Conflict

Homogenization

Accommodation

Resolution

Ethnic conflict is increasing throughout the world. Here, Sikh separatists demonstrate in British Columbia against Indian domination.
Visit http://www.wadsworth.com/humanity to learn more about the material covered in this chapter and to access activities, exercises, and tutorial quizzes.

*W*ITH THE *collapse of the Soviet Union and the end of the Cold War, many people thought we had entered a new, more peaceful era. Instead, we have found that ideological conflicts (capitalist vs. communist) have been replaced by ethnic conflicts. It is not that ethnic conflicts are something new in human affairs, far from it. Ethnic hostilities and hatreds are the oldest and most basic source of conflicts among peoples. It was simply that ideological rivalries between the superpowers served to obscure and suppress these differences.*

So INSTEAD *of living in peace, we now find ourselves in a time of growing ethnic conflicts which are becoming ever more violent and destructive. In the past few years, over a million people have fallen victim to genocidal wars, while millions more have joined the ranks of political refugees. Central governments have ceased to exist in Liberia, Somalia, and Afghanistan, while several others verge on disintegration. Terrorist bombs have exploded in New York, London, Paris, and Jerusalem. Concerns increase about nuclear proliferation: Does, or will, Iran, Iraq, India, Pakistan, or North Korea have the bomb? New phrases like "ethnic cleansing" and "failed state" have become part of our vocabulary. As the level of ethnic violence escalates, no place in the world appears immune; the differences lie only in the groups involved and their methods and objectives.*

As we discussed in Chapter 16, the emergence of global trade has resulted in an ever-increasing economic interdependence among the peoples of the world. At the same time, ethnic conflicts have escalated and seem likely to increase. One could argue that ethnic conflict is the most potent political force in the modern world. It threatens not only the political stability of many nations, but possibly the global economy as well.

In this chapter we address several questions: (1) What is an ethnic group? (2) Why is ethnicity such a powerful political force in the modern world? and (3) What has been and can be done to try to resolve ethnic conflicts?

Ethnic Groups

Over the past few decades, the terms *ethnic* and *ethnicity* have become part of our everyday vocabulary. We frequently hear and use the terms *ethnic food, ethnic vote, ethnic conflict, ethnic clothes, ethnic neighborhood,* and *ethnic studies*. In the 1960s, anthropologists began studying ethnicity as a distinct social phenomenon, and since that time literature on ethnicity has proliferated. Part of the increased scholarly interest in ethnic groups came as a result of Nathan Glazer and Daniel Moynihan's study (1963) of ethnic groups in New York City. They found that "in the third generation, the descendants of the immigrants confronted each other, and knew they were both Americans, in the same dress, with the same language, using the same artifacts, troubled by the same thing, but they voted differently, had different ideas about education and sex, and were still, in many essential ways, as different from one another as their grandfathers had been" (13). These findings contradicted the idea of the American melting pot. Ethnic differences were far more resilient and significant than had been believed.

What is an ethnic group? First, it is necessary to realize that all peoples, not just minority populations, have an ethnic group identity. In essence, an **ethnic group** is a named social category of people based on perceptions of shared social experience or ancestry. Members of the ethnic group see themselves as sharing cultural traditions and history that distinguish them from other groups. There is in ethnic group identity a strong psycho-

logical or emotional component that divides the social world into the categories of "us" and "them." In contrast to social stratification (discussed in Chapter 12), which divides and unifies people along a series of horizontal axes on the basis of socioeconomic factors, ethnic identities divide and unify people along a series of vertical axes. Thus, ethnic groups, at least theoretically, crosscut socioeconomic class differences, drawing members from all strata of the population.

Before discussing the significance of ethnic differences and conflicts in the modern world, we need to examine the varying dimensions of ethnic group identity, including (1) the situational nature of ethnic group identity, (2) the attributes of ethnic groups, (3) the fluidity of ethnic group identity, and (4) the types of ethnic groups.

Situational Nature of Ethnic Identity

One of the more complicating aspects of ethnicity is that an individual's ethnic group identity seldom is absolute. A particular individual may assume a number of different ethnic identities, depending on the social situation. For example, in the United States an individual may simultaneously be an American, a Euro-American, an Italian American, and a Sicilian American. The particular ethnic identity chosen varies with the social context. When in Europe or among Europeans, he or she would assume an ethnic identity of American, in contrast to German, French, or Italian. In the United States the same individual might assume an identity of Euro-American, as opposed to African-American or Native American. Among Euro-Americans, the person might take the ethnic identity of Italian American, as opposed to Irish American or Polish American. When among Italian Americans, the individual might identify himself or herself as Sicilian American, as opposed to an Italian American whose family came from Rome, Naples, or some other region of Italy.

The situational nature of ethnic identity demonstrates what some have called the **hierarchical nesting** quality of identity. A particular ethnic group forms part of a larger collection of ethnic groups of like magnitude or social significance. In turn, these ethnic groups may collectively form still another, higher level of ethnic identity, which may in turn be nested in still another, higher level. Thus, ethnic identity does not simply divide the world into categories of "us" and "them," but into varying, hierarchically ranked categories of "us" and "them."

Attributes of Ethnic Groups

Two main attributes help to define and identify an ethnic group: (1) an origin myth or history and (2) various ethnic boundary markers.

Carrying a Mexican flag, Hispanics in Los Angeles protest the treatment of illegal aliens.

Origin Myth Each ethnic group is the product of a unique set of social and historical events. The common or shared historical experiences that serve to unite and distinguish the group from other groups and give it a distinct social identity constitutes the group's **origin myth**. By *myth* we do not mean to imply that the historical events did not really happen, or that the group is not what it claims to be. We mean only that these particular experiences serve as the ideological charter for the group's common identity and provide the members with a sense of being different from other people. Origin myths play an integral part in creating and maintaining ethnic group identity: They define and describe the origin and collective historical experiences of the group.

Not all historical events are equally important; origin myths make selective references. Wars and conflicts frequently are emphasized, since they clearly distinguish "us" from "them." The origin myth imbues the group's members with feelings of distinctiveness and, often, superiority in relation to other groups. What makes an origin myth so powerful is that mythic themes and concepts are embedded in virtually every aspect of the people's popular culture: stories (written and oral), songs, dances, games, music, theater, film, and art. So pervasive are these mythic images in everyday life that they are learned passively rather than consciously. Thus, all members of the group

are well versed in the basic tenets of the group myth, and in the minds of most, these ideas become an unquestioned "truth." In larger, more sophisticated groups, the origin myth also takes the form of a written, purportedly objective history that is formally taught in schools. American history as taught in elementary and high school is not merely the objective, factual history of a geographical reason; it is also the story of the American people. Thus, it serves as the officially sanctioned origin myth of the American ethnic group. Similarly, English, French, Japanese, and Russian history as taught in their schools is the "authorized" origin myth of those groups.

When you realize that history as taught in schools is in fact the collective origin myth of the group, then you realize the significance of including or excluding a particular subgroup of the population. Using American history as an example, we can see how historical events play a critical role in the emergence and definition of a distinctively American ethnic identity. Among these events are the landing of the *Mayflower*, the American Revolution, the Civil War, the westward expansion, and the world wars. Certain historical groups, such as cowboys and cavalry, are used as embodiments of American ideals and identity. Americans are the descendants of the various peoples who collectively participated in these and other group-defining events. Thus, it is not surprising that every American subgroup is sensitive to its portrayal in these events. To African-Americans, it is important that American history, as taught in the public schools, acknowledge that the first man to die in the American Revolution was an African-American, that African-Americans fought as soldiers in the Revolutionary and Civil Wars, that a high percentage of cowboys were African-Americans, and that African-American cavalrymen played an important part in winning the West. Similarly, public acknowledgment and recognition that their groups were active participants in some, if not all, of the major events of American history are equally important for Polish-Americans, Italian-Americans, Irish-Americans, Chinese-Americans, and other immigrants in a nation of immigrants. It is inclusion in the collective origin myth that truly legitimates a people's status as members of the group.

Ethnic Boundary Markers Every ethnic group has a way of determining or expressing membership. Overt factors used to demonstrate or denote group membership are called **ethnic boundary markers**. Ethnic boundary markers are important not only to identify the members to one another, but also to demonstrate identity to and distinctiveness from nonmembers. Because they serve to distinguish members from all other groups, a single boundary marker seldom is sufficient. A marker that might distinguish one ethnic group from a second group may not distinguish it from still another group. Thus, combinations of markers commonly are used. Differences in language, religion, physical appearance, or particular cultural traits serve as ethnic boundary markers.

As we saw at the end of Chapter 4, speech style and language use serve as symbols of personal identity: We send covert messages about the kind of person we are by how we speak. Language, therefore, frequently serves as an ethnic boundary marker. The native language of an individual is the primary indicator of ethnic group identity in many areas of the world. In the southwestern United States, Hopi and Navajo members are readily distinguished by their language alone. However, just because two populations share a common language does not mean they share a common identity, any more than the fact that two populations speak different languages means that they have two distinct identities. For example, the Serbs and Croats of what was Yugoslavia speak Serbo-Croatian. They are, however, distinct and historically antagonistic ethnic groups. Conversely, a person may be Irish and speak either Gaelic or English as his or her native language. The German government grants automatic citizenship to all ethnic German refugees from Eastern Europe. A difficulty in assimilating these refugees is that many speak only Polish or Russian. Thus, one does not have to speak German to be an ethnic German.

Like language, religion may serve as an ethnic boundary marker. The major world religions such as Christianity, Islam, and Buddhism encompass numerous distinct ethnic groups, so that religious affiliation does not always indicate ethnic affiliation. But in many cases religion and ethnic group more or less correspond. The Jews may be categorized as either a religious or an ethnic group. Similarly, the Sikhs in India constitute both a religious and an ethnic group. In still other situations, religious differences may be the most important marker of ethnic identity. As we mentioned earlier, the Serbs and Croats speak the same language; the most important distinction between these two groups is that the Serbs are Eastern Orthodox and the Croats are Catholic. Conversely, the Chinese ethnic identity transcends religious differences: A person is still Chinese whether he or she is a Muslim, Christian, Taoist, Buddhist, or Marxist atheist.

Physical characteristics, or phenotypes, can also (at times) indicate ethnic identity. It is impossible to identify Germans, Dutch, Danes, and other northern European ethnic groups by their physical characteristics. A similar situation is found in those regions of the world in which populations have been in long association with one another. Thus, physical characteristics do not distinguish a Zulu from a Swazi, a Chinese from a Korean, or a Choctaw from a Chickasaw. However, with the massive movements of people, particularly over the past few hundred years, physical characteristics have increasingly emerged as a marker

The dress of this woman not only identifies her as a Maya Indian, but also that she is from the town of Nabaj, in Guatemala.

of ethnic identity. Members of the three major ethnic groups in Malaysia—Malays, East Indians, and Chinese—are readily distinguishable by their physical appearance. The significance or lack of significance of physical characteristics in ethnic identity may also vary with the level of ethnic identity. The American identity includes almost the full range of human physical types. However, at a lower level of identity—Euro-American, African-American, and Native American—physical characteristics do serve as one marker of ethnic identity. Yet within these groups, physical characteristics alone cannot be the only marker. Some Native Americans physically appear to be Euro-Americans or African-Americans, and some African-Americans would be identified as Euro-Americans or Native Americans on the basis of physical appearance alone.

A wide variety of cultural traits, clothing, house types, personal adornment, food, technology, economic activities, or general lifestyle may also serve as ethnic boundary markers. Over the past 100 years, a rapid homogenization of world material culture, food habits, and technology has erased many of the more overt cultural markers. Today you do not have to be Mexican to enjoy tacos, Italian to eat pizza, or Japanese to have sushi for lunch. Similarly, you can dine on hamburgers, the all-American food, in Japan, Oman, Russia, Mexico, and most other countries. Cultural traits remain, however, the most important, diverse, and complex category of ethnic boundary markers. For the sake of brevity, we will limit our discussion to one trait—clothing (see Chapter 14).

Clothing styles have historically served as the most overt single indicator of ethnic identity. In the not too distant past, almost every ethnic group had its own unique style of dress. Even today, a Scottish-American who wants to overtly indicate his ethnic identity wears a kilt, and a German American may wear his *lederhosen*. Similarly, on special occasions Native Americans wear "Indian clothes" decorated with beadwork and ribbonwork. These are not everyday clothing, and they are worn only in social situations in which people want to emphasize their ethnic identity. In many regions of the world, however, ethnic clothes are still worn every day. In highland Guatemala, clothing, particular women's clothing, serves to readily identify the ethnic affiliation of the wearer. Guatemalan clothing styles actually indicate two levels of ethnic identity. If a woman wears a *huipil*, a loose-fitting blouse that slips over the head, she is a Native American. Non-Native American women, called *Ladinas*, dress in Western-style clothes. The style, colors, and designs on the huipil further identify the particular Native American ethnic group the woman is from: Nahuala, Chichicastenango, Solola, or one of the other hundred or so Native American groups in highland Guatemala.

Fluidity of Ethnic Groups

Ethnic groups are not stable groupings, since (1) ethnic groups vanish, (2) people move between ethnic groups, and (3) new ethnic groups come into existence.

During the past 500 years, numerous ethnic groups have vanished. Massachusetts, Erie, Susquehannock, and Biloxi were not originally place names but the names of now-extinct Native American ethnic groups. Still other ethnic groups in Asia, Africa, Oceania, Europe, and the Americas have vanished as well. Extinction of an ethnic group seldom is biological extinction. In most cases, the members of one group are merely absorbed into the population of a larger ethnic group. The Tasmanians of Australia are typical of what happened to many smaller ethnic groups. Numbering at most 5,000 when the British began colonizing the island of Tasmania in 1802, the population was so ravaged by wars and massacres that only a handful existed by 1850; and the Tasmanians as a viable ethnic group had ceased to exist. In 1869 the last full-blooded Tasmanian man died, and in 1888 the last full-blooded Tasmanian woman died. However, even today, mixed-blood descendants of the Tasmanians can be found among the Australian population.

Both individuals and communities can and do move between ethnic groups. During the sixteenth and seventeenth centuries French Protestants, called *Huguenots*, fled persecution in France and settled in large numbers in England and the English colonies in North America. These people quickly became absorbed into the English population. Over the past 200 years, Americans have absorbed numerous immigrant populations.

Ethnogenesis refers to the emergence of a new ethnic group. Ethnogenesis usually occurs in one of two ways: (1) a portion of an existing ethnic group splits away and forms a new ethnic group, or (2) members of two or more existing ethnic groups fuse, forming a new ethnic group.

Probably the most common cause of ethnogenesis is the division of an existing ethnic group. At one time, the Osage, Kansa, Omaha, Ponca, and Quapaw Indians of the central United States were a single ethnic group. The origin myths of these peoples tell how at different times portions broke away, until there were five distinct groups. In the 1700s, small groups of Creek Indians began moving south into Florida, where they eventually developed a distinct identity as the Seminole. Similarly, as Bantu-speaking peoples spread through central and southern Africa, they became separated, and new ethnic groups formed. As the Spanish Empire in the Americas disintegrated during the early 1800s, new regional ethnic identities (such as Mexican, Guatemalan, Peruvian, and Chilean) began emerging among the Spanish-speaking peoples in that region. In 1652, the Dutch began settling near the Cape of Good Hope in southern Africa. These people eventually developed their own distinctive dialect of Dutch, called *Afrikaans*, and their own identity, Boers.

In other cases, members of two or more ethnic groups fuse and a new ethnic identity emerges. In England, the Angles, the Saxons, and the Jutes fused and became known as the English. The original Euro-American ethnic group was not the result of a split among the English people, but rather of a fusion of English, Dutch, German, Scots, Irish, French Huguenots, Scotch-Irish, and other European settlers residing on the coast of North America. Most African-American groups in the Americas are the result of the fusion of numerous distinct African groups. Intermarriage between French traders and Native Americans in Canada resulted in the emergence of the Metis. Similarly, in South Africa the Cape Coloured, people of mixed Dutch and Khoikhoi ancestry, are socially and politically distinct from both whites and Africans. The Cape Coloureds are an excellent example of how new ethnic categories often arise as a result of economic forces and political mobilization.

Types of Ethnic Groups

From our discussion and examples so far, it should be apparent that the term *ethnic group* covers a range of social groupings. In general, ethnic groups fall into two main categories: national and subnational.

A **nationality** is an ethnic group with a feeling of **homeland,** a geographical region over which they have exclusive rights. Implicit in this concept is the assumption of an inherent right to political autonomy and self-determination. In contrast, **subnationalities** lack a concept of a distinct and separate homeland and the associated rights to separate political sovereignty and self-determination. A subnational group sees itself as a dependent and politically subordinate subset of a nationality.

Although it is easy to define the difference between ethnic nationalities and subnationalities, sometimes it is far more difficult to classify particular groups. The ethnic groups in the United States demonstrate some of the difficulties in classification. With some ethnic groups there is no doubt about their classification. Italian-Americans, German-Americans, Polish-Americans, Scottish-Americans, and Irish-Americans are all subnational groups. At a higher level of identity, the same is true for African-Americans. None of these groups has a concept of a distinct and separate geographical homeland within the United States. Hence, they are subnational groups who, together with many other groups, collectively constitute the American ethnic nationality.

There are other ethnic groups within the United States whose status is not as clear. What is the status of Native American groups such as the Navajo, the Hopi, the Crow, the Cheyenne, the Cherokee, and the Osage, to name only a few? These groups have a concept of homelands within the United States. They also have histories quite distinct from that of other Americans. In recent years they have been asserting increased political sovereignty and self-determination within their reservations (homelands). Although there is disagreement, many Native American individuals and groups still see themselves as distinct nationalities. The U.S. government does recognize most American Indian groups as national groups with collective legal and political rights. No other ethnic groups in the United States have officially recognized governments and limited rights of self-determination. There is also some question about the ethnic status of Spanish-speaking peoples in the southwestern United States. Until the mid-nineteenth century, Texas, New Mexico, Arizona, and California were part of Mexico. The United States acquired this region through military conquest. Most of the native Spanish-speaking people in this region think of themselves as Mexican American or Spanish American, a subnational group. There is, however, a small group who see themselves as "Mexicans" living in a land that is rightfully part of Mexico, a region they call "Atzlan."

The distinction between nationality and subnationality is important because of their different political implica-

Following an attack by a Protestant paramilitary group, Catholic men stand guard in their neighborhood in Northern Ireland.

tions. As we shall see, the demands of subnational groups for equal rights and treatment have long been a source of conflict. But the demands of nationalities for independence and sovereignty in a region carved out of an existing country create a political time bomb.

The Problem of Stateless Nationalities

It is difficult for most Americans to understand the causes and bitterness of ethnic conflict in other parts of the world. We think of *nationality* and *nation* as being one and the same. An American is any person who is a citizen of the United States. Most of us think of ourselves as Americans first and secondarily as Irish, Italian, or Chinese Americans. This mind-set about the meaning and significance of ethnicity is due mainly to our history as a nation of immigrants—with the exception of Native Americans, immigrants renounced their claims to their national homelands when they came to the New World. For the most part, the ethnic groups in the United States are subnationalities, not nationalities. Thus, from our common perception, a Russian is a person from Russia, a Nigerian is a citizen from Nigeria, and so forth. Falsely equating country of origin with ethnic nationality, we view ethnic conflicts in other regions of the world as comparable to conflicts between subnational groups within the United States. Ethnic problems within a country are thought to be the result of social or economic discrimination—resolvable and reparable by reforms—and their political significance is minimized. However, the ethnic conflicts in most countries are not between subnational groups but between distinct nationalities.

A CLOSER LOOK

Acadians and Cajuns

When we think of the Acadians, we usually think of Henry Wadsworth Longfellow's poem *Evangeline,* and when we hear the word "Cajun," food usually comes to mind first. Most people, however, have only vague notions about who the Acadian and Cajun people were and are. Today, over 300,000 Acadians live in the Maritime Provinces of Canada: Nova Scotia, Prince Edward Island, and New Brunswick, while an equal if not greater number of Cajuns live in southern Louisiana. Although in their lifestyles and cultures the Acadians and Cajuns are distinct today, they are the descendants of the very same people. The word *Cajun* is the Americanized form of Acadian or *cadian.*

The Acadians/Cajuns are the descendants of the early French settlers of Nova Scotia. In 1605, the French established a small fishing-trading station at Port Royal in an area they called Acadia. It was not, however, until the 1630s when French families began arriving that the settlement took on a more permanent character. Unlike other portions of New France, Acadia had neither a wealth of fish nor furs. As a result, few families were attracted to the region; possibly no more than 40 to 50 French families actually settled there between 1630 and 1710. Although Acadia was a much colder and harsher environment than France, those that came quickly adapted their domestic architecture and farming techniques to their new environment. Although their way of life was not as idyllic as portrayed by Longfellow, they did succeed in establishing successful, self-sufficient farming communities. Having little commercial potential and military value, the relatively isolated Acadian communities were basically ignored by the French colonial authorities.

The southernmost region of New France, Acadia was occupied in 1710, when the English attacked Port Royal. In 1713, the French ceded Acadia to the English, who renamed Port Royal, Annapolis Royal, and the colony, Nova Scotia.

Although the number of French settlers was small, the climate was healthy, food was abundant, and families grew large. By 1713, the Acadian population had grown to about 3,000. In the early years of English control, the new governors did little to disrupt their lives. Although there was no new migration from France, the Acadian communities continued to grow until by the 1750s, there were over 10,000 people in their settlements.

Unfortunately for the Acadians, the wars between England and France over control of North America continued. Although the Acadians had sworn allegiance to the king of England, they refused to fight against France, adopting a position of neutrality in these conflicts. In 1754, war broke out again. Questioning the loyalty and neutrality of the Acadians, the governor of Nova Scotia ordered their deportation in 1755. Altogether, 6,000 Acadians were deported and scattered from Massachusetts to South Carolina. Others fled into the deep forests or to New France. Some went to France or to the French colonies in the West Indies.

In 1763, the war ended with the destruction of New France. France ceded Quebec to the English, while Spain took Louisiana west of the Mississippi River. No longer considered a threat, the Acadians were free to return to Nova Scotia. Impoverished by exile and widely scattered on both sides of the Atlantic, the Acadian people began separating into two groups. Some chose to return to Nova Scotia, while others, hostile to the English, began settling in Spanish Louisiana.

Since most were destitute, the return to Nova Scotia was a slow process. For several decades, Acadian families trickled back to their homes from France, the West Indies, and English colonies. Once back in Nova Scotia, they found that their farms and homes had been confiscated by English colonists and that new laws now prohibited Catholics from owning land, having their own schools, even from having priests. Although these laws were changed in 1783, the political position of the Acadians did not significantly improve. Following the American revolution, thousands of American loyalists moved to Nova Scotia. As a result, the land was divided and New Brunswick was created out of northern Nova Scotia. A minority in what had been their own land, the Acadians were subjected to political, economic, and social discrimination from their more powerful, English-speaking neighbors.

In contrast, in Louisiana the Acadian refugees were welcomed by colonial officials, and land grants were quickly made available for their resettlement. Although Louisiana was Catholic and settled primarily by French Creoles, from the very beginning the Acadians there showed a strong preference for separate communities. There was little social mixing with the other French-speaking colonists. As a separate and distinct French-speaking people in Louisiana, Acadians became Cadians and finally Cajuns. About 2,500 to 3,000 Acadians eventually settled in Louisiana during the late 1700s. By 1800, the Acadian population of Nova Scotia, New Brunswick, and Prince Edward Island had recovered to about 8,000.

Since the late 1700s, the Acadians of Canada and Louisiana have had very different histories. As a result, the two groups have culturally diverged. Once back in the Maritime Provinces, the Acadians attempted to rebuild their lives and their settlements following their pre-deportation pattern. There were some differences, however; dispossessed of their original farms, they were forced into more marginal and isolated areas. The economy and political power of the colonies were controlled by English-speaking peoples who were hostile to their Catholic religion and French language and traditions. Thus, not only did Acadians have to struggle to reestablish the economic viability of their communities, but they found themselves in a protracted political struggle with their English neighbors to maintain their language, traditions, and religious institutions.

Catholics were prohibited from voting in the Maritimes until 1810 and from holding public office until 1830. Even then, the Acadians were not a unified political force, for several reasons. They lived in widely scattered and isolated communities. Formal education was almost nonexistent in the communities, so there were few Acadian clergy, lawyers, teachers, or doctors. They were primarily a population of farmers, fishermen, and woodsmen, with few educated leaders; they were more concerned with local and personal economic needs than political or ethnic ideologies. Their strategy for ethnic survival had been to socially and geographically isolate themselves from their English-speaking neighbors, and when isolation failed they chose to ignore their neighbors as best as they could.

The self-imposed isolation of the Acadians began to change in 1864 with the establishment of St. Joseph College in New Brunswick, the first French-language college in the Maritimes. That same year, Nova Scotia passed a law making English the only language for school instruction. Language in education had emerged as a political issue. In 1867, the first French-language newspaper in the Maritimes began publication. By 1887 there were three French newspapers, indicative not only of the Acadians' growing level of education, but of their political awareness as well.

In 1881, over 5,000 Acadians met at St. Joseph's College in what was to be the first of a series of "National Conventions." At a second convention in 1884, they adopted an Acadian flag, the French tricolor with a gold star in the upper left-hand corner, and a national anthem, "Ave Maris Stella."

In contrast to the French-speaking peoples of Quebec, over the last century Acadian nationalism has taken the form of a social and cultural movement, rather than a political movement. In terms of political ideology, the Acadians have usually been fragmented. Of far greater concern has been the Acadianization of their own local institutions, particularly the Catholic church.

In Louisiana, the Acadians found a much friendlier social and political environment. Although Louisiana was a Spanish possession, French was the dominant cultural tradition and Catholicism the religion. Welcomed by both social and political leaders, the Acadians still preferred their own separate communities, and they both socially and geographically distanced themselves from the local French Creoles. In Louisiana, as in Canada, the Acadians saw themselves as distinct from other French-speaking peoples.

The hot bayous and swamps of southern Louisiana were a very different world from the cold forests of Maritime Canada. To adapt to this new environment the Acadians borrowed heavily from their new neighbors, American Indians, Africans, and French Creoles. Houses had to be raised off the ground, and walls made of mud and planks instead of logs and stone. In Louisiana, stairways to the second floor could be outside. In the swamps and bayous, pirogues (dugout canoes) became the primary means of transportation. Acadians still lived by farming, hunting, trapping, and fishing, but their crops, game, and catch were different. Thus, their diet changed: By 1800, gumbo had already become a standard fare. Other changes occurred: Their French dialect absorbed numerous new words from English and Spanish, as well as from Indian and African languages. Although staunch Catholics, Acadians saw some American Indian and African religious beliefs and practices introduced into their culture.

Even before the United States purchased Louisiana in 1803, the economy was changing. Small farmers were being displaced by plantations worked by African slaves, who cultivated first indigo and later sugarcane. As the plantation

economy spread westward, most of the Acadians were forced out of their original settlements in Louisiana. Some families stayed, enlarging their landholdings, buying slaves, and becoming part of the new plantation aristocracy of Louisiana. These families became known as the "Genteel Acadians." Wealthy and educated, they were part of the antebellum social elite. By 1860, two of these Genteel Acadians had been elected governor of the state. However, the vast majority of Acadians were relatively poor small farmers. Forced out by plantations, these families moved into the swamps or prairies where most eked out a marginal existence. Thus, by 1860 the Louisiana Acadians had split into two social classes, the wealthy and educated Genteel Acadians and the poorer and uneducated "Cajuns." Although the Genteel Acadians maintained a romanticized Acadian identity, they became increasingly Americanized and assimilated into the plantation aristocracy. Cajun was an ethnic identity as well as a social class.

The Acadian/Cajun peoples reflect the process of ethnogenesis. Isolated from the other French-speaking people of New France, they appear to have developed a separate identity by the early 1700s, as illustrated by their willingness to adopt a position of neutrality in the colonial wars between France and England. The deportation of 1755 served only to strengthen their identity and became the defining event in their ethnic origin history. In the Maritime Provinces, the political struggle over the maintenance of their language and Catholic religion against their dominant English-speaking, Protestant neighbors had served to strengthen the Acadian identity, but these ethnic differences did not create nor maintain their identity. In Louisiana, the Acadian refugees began socially and geographically segregating themselves from the local French Creole population from the time of their arrival, and have remained socially distinct from their neighbors. Few people so clearly illustrate how quickly a new ethnic identity can be established, and how, once established, how strong and persistent such an identity can be.

The ethnic conflicts in Northern Ireland and in Israel and Palestine have proved particularly bitter. In 1922, after several centuries of British colonial domination and periodic rebellions by the native Irish, the Irish Free State (now the Republic of Ireland) was established. However, not all of Ireland was given independence. In the seventeenth century, to control the Irish, the British evicted Irish farmers from the northernmost portion of the island and colonized the region with Scottish Presbyterians, who became known as the *Scotch-Irish*. The Scotch-Irish did not identify themselves as Irish and had no desire to become part of an independent Ireland. Recognizing the wishes of the Scotch-Irish, at independence the British partitioned the island. The northern six counties became Northern Ireland and remained part of the United Kingdom. Many Irish did not and do not accept the legality of this partitioning of Ireland. To them, Northern Ireland is part of the Irish homeland and thus should be part of the Republic of Ireland. Since 1968, the Irish Republican Army, a secretive guerrilla army that is illegal in the Republic of Ireland, has been actively waging a war with the object of reuniting Northern Ireland with the Republic of Ireland. Bombings, ambushes, and assassinations have claimed the lives of more than 2,200 persons. The news media frequently report the problems in Northern Ireland as conflict between the British and the Irish or between Catholic and Protestants; in reality, it is neither. The root of the problem is the conflicting claims of two rival and hostile nationalities: the Irish and the Scotch-Irish. The Scotch-Irish have emerged over the past 400 years as a distinct nationality who claim the northern part of Ireland as their homeland. In contrast, the Irish see the area as an integral and inalienable part of the Irish homeland.

After an absence of almost 2,000 years, the Jews began returning to their historic homeland in Palestine in 1882. During the early twentieth century Jewish settlements in Palestine grew, and in 1948 the state of Israel was proclaimed by the Jewish settlers. For the past fifty years, conflict between Israelis and Palestinians has been constant, varying only in the intensity and form of violence. The problem is similar to that in Northern Ireland, in that two nationalities—Israelis and Palestinians—claim the same geographical region as their legitimate homeland. While some progress has been made recently toward peaceful settlements of the conflicts in Northern Ireland and between Israelis and Palestinians, such agreements are tenuous. These situations remain extremely volatile. In Israel and Northern Ireland, it is impossible to resolve this conflict to the total satisfaction of both nationalities.

These two conflicts vividly illustrate the strength of nationalist sentiments. In both cases we see groups of educated, rational human beings who are willing to sacrifice their lives and economic well-being in unending conflicts for what they consider to be their nationality's legitimate rights.

Such conflict is more common in the modern world than most of us realize. To understand the magnitude or potential magnitude of this problem, one need only realize that the world is divided into less than 200 countries and between 3,000 and 5,000 distinct ethnic nationalities. As a result, the populations of most countries encompass a number of distinct nationalities. China officially recognizes fifty-six distinct nationalities. Some estimates are as high as 300 ethnic nationalities in Indonesia. Ethiopia has at least 70 nationalities. Only a handful of countries are peopled by members of a single nationality and are thus ethnically homogeneous.

The ethnic nationality problem is further complicated because current political boundaries frequently divide members of a nationality and their historic homeland. For example, Hungarians are found not only in Hungary but also in the adjacent portions of Romania and Serbia. Somalis live not only in Somalia but also in the adjacent Ogaden portion of Ethiopia. Thus, the world is filled with ethnic groups who do not fully recognize the legitimacy of "their" central government and who aspire or may potentially aspire to have political autonomy.

For the most part, nationality problems were not created by the nationalities themselves. The current political boundaries for most of the world are legacies of European colonialism and expansion. During the nineteenth century, the European powers divided most of the geographical regions and peoples of the world among themselves. In 1884–1885 at the Berlin Conference, European leaders sat at a table and with pens and pencils drew lines on a map of Africa, dividing the resources and peoples of that continent among themselves. Through this agreement, the English, French, Germans, Belgians, and other European powers assumed sovereignty over lands they had never traveled and over peoples who had never seen a white man. Nor was Africa the only continent to have boundaries imposed by Europeans. The national boundaries of most of the world were drawn by Europeans for their own interest, with little regard for the interest of any indigenous peoples or the boundaries of the ethnic groups affected. As a result, most European colonial possessions were a polyglot of ethnic groups, many of whom had long histories of hostilities toward one another. In other instances an ethnic group found its land and people divided between two or more European colonies. To make matters worse, colonial powers frequently moved people from one colony to another to supply labor, introducing still other ethnic groups to new areas. For example, the British settled Indian laborers in Burma (Myanmar), Malaya (Malaysia), Fiji, Sri Lanka, Kenya, Uganda, South Africa, Trinidad, and British Guiana.

The end of the colonial period did not end the ethnic conflicts in the world but only signaled the beginning of the problems. As European powers granted independence to their colonies, they made little attempt to redefine political boundaries. In most cases these newly independent countries had precisely the same boundaries and ethnic composition as the former colonies. Because these political divisions were imposed by European military power, some scholars have termed the former colonies **artificial countries** (see Figure 17.1). In most cases the basic colonial administrative and governmental structure was maintained after independence; the major departure from the colonial period was that native officials replaced European officials. However, not all ethnic groups were equally represented in these new governments, and most former colonies quickly came under the domination of one or two of the more powerful ethnic groups. Thus, in many instances European domination was replaced by domination by one or another "native" ethnic group. With this in mind, the political problems endemic in much of the Third World become more comprehensible.

India is a prime example of ethnic problems in the postcolonial period. Consisting of several hundred distinct ethnic groups as well as major religious divisions, India did not exist—and never existed—as a unified country before British domination (see Figure 17.2). As independence approached in the 1940s, hostilities between rival Muslim and Hindu factions became so intense that British officials decided that a unified, independent India was an impossibility. They decided that India had to be divided into two countries: India (predominantly Hindu) and Pakistan (predominantly Muslim). The borders of these new countries were drawn by the British. The problem was the lack of clear geographical boundaries separating these groups; in many regions the populations were mixed Hindu and Muslim. An East Pakistan and a West Pakistan were carved out on either side, separated by 1,000 miles of what was to be India. After the official announcement of the boundaries, massive migrations began as millions of Muslims and Hindus found themselves on the wrong sides. These migrations were stimulated by fanatics on both sides, who massacred Muslims living in what was to become India and Hindus in what

Hindu fundamentalists in India have become increasingly intolerant of the Muslim minority in the country. Here Hindu militants gather in Ayodhya before destroying the Muslim mosque in the background.

was to be Pakistan. Some estimate that as many as one million people were killed in these riots. The grant of actual independence to the two countries in 1947 made the situation worse because neither side was satisfied with its geographical boundaries. The new Indian army occupied the largely Muslim region of Kashmir, and war quickly broke out. The first India-Pakistan war ended in 1949, with Kashmir occupied by India.

The creation of two separate states out of British India addressed—but did not solve—only one of the region's problems. Immediately after independence, the Naga people in India's easternmost Assam province revolted and demanded an independent Nagaland. This Naga secessionist movement is still active, and for more than forty-five years periodic bloody clashes have occurred between Naga rebels and Indian authorities. More recently a Sikh separatist movement emerged, demanding an independent homeland in Punjab. The violent tactics of the Sikh nationalists resulted in the Indian army's attacking the holiest Sikh religious shrine, the Golden Temple in Amritsar, in 1984. Later that year, two Sikhs assassinated Indira Gandhi, the prime minister of India, causing more violence between Sikhs and Hindus. In 1990, violence again broke out in Kashmir. Muslim leaders are demanding either a separate nation or unification with Pakistan. As if India's problems with its religious-ethnic minorities were not sufficient, the Hindu majority is becoming increasingly hostile to non-Hindu minorities. In 1993,

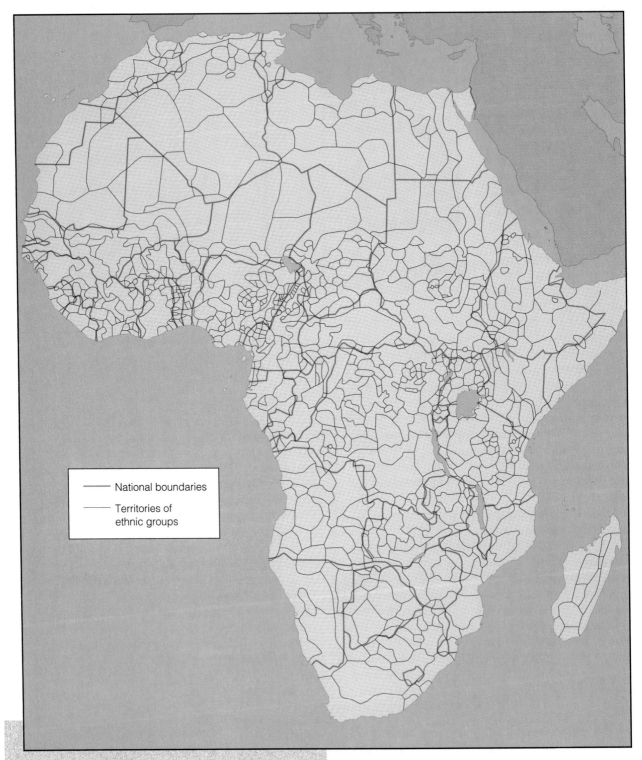

Figure 17.1 Ethnic Groups and National Boundaries
in Africa

*The boundaries of most African countries do not
correspond with the territories of ethnic groups.*

Hindu radicals destroyed a six-teenth-century Muslim mosque in northern India, claiming that it had been built on the site of an early Hindu temple. The destruction of the mosque led to a series of riots that left almost 2,000 dead. The internal religious-ethnic problems of India are increasing, not subsiding. In the past few years the problems between India and Pakistan and between Hindus and the 120-million member Muslim minority living in India have become more serious. After the Bharatiya Janata, the Hindu nationalist party, came to power, India tested its first nuclear bombs. Pakistan followed with nuclear weapons. Conflict between Hindus and Muslims within India is increasing, as members of the Bharatiya Janata party call for a Hinduization of India.

Pakistan has also experienced ethnic difficulties. Although both Pakistans were Muslim, there were major ethnic differences between the two. East Pakistanis were predominantly Bengalis. West Pakistan was more heterogeneous ethnically but dominated by Urdu-speaking peoples. Although West Pakistan had a smaller population, the capital was located there after independence in 1947, and the Urdu peoples gained dominance in the government and the military. In West Pakistan, a separatist movement emerged among the Baluchi, who sought an independent Baluchistan. However, it was with the Bengalis in East Pakistan that the major conflict emerged. Although the Bengalis were economically exploited and discriminated against by the Urdu, it was not until the government attempted to impose the Urdu language in the schools of East Pakistan that the situation came to a head. In 1971 the East Pakistanis revolted and, after a short but bloody war aided by India, succeeded in establishing the state of Bangladesh.

Bangladesh is experiencing its own internal ethnic problems. Even before independence from Pakistan, Bengali settlers had begun occupying land in the Chittagong hills, displacing the indigenous tribal peoples. After independence, with official encouragement, the flow of Bengali settlers increased, causing the tribal peoples to rebel

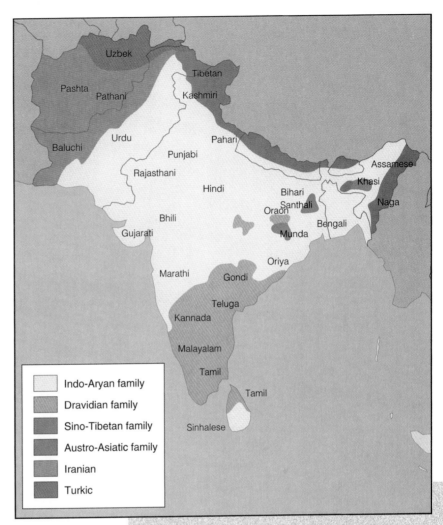

Figure 17.2   Language Regions of South Asia
Some of the ethnic boundaries of India are reflected by these language regions.

and demand local autonomy. The government has refused to halt the settlements, and periodic killings and massacres are continuing. In the realm of ethnic conflict today's victims can quickly become tomorrow's villains.

Similar secessionist movements have occurred and are still occurring throughout the old colonial world.

• Burma includes a dozen or more distinct ethnic groups. Immediately after independence from Britain in 1948, Karen and Shan peoples declared their freedom from Burma and revolted. Other ethnic groups soon followed. Today, more than fifty years later, the Burmese army is involved in an inconclusive war with secessionist armies of ten different ethnic groups.

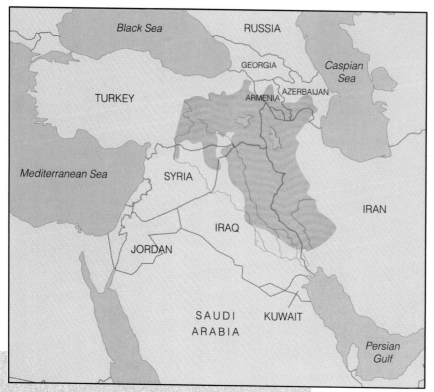

Figure 17.3 Kurdistan

The Kurdish area and the proposed boundaries of an independent state of Kurdistan.

1960s (see Figure 17.3). At different times they have fought the Turks, the Iraqis, and the Iranians. In 1950 China invaded and occupied Tibet, a region that the Chinese consider part of China. A Tibetan revolt in 1959 was crushed, but conflict is again escalating as Tibetan Buddhists seek political autonomy under the Dalai Lama, their spiritual leader.

Today some of the most violent ethnic conflicts are in Europe and the former Soviet Union. In the early 1990s, Yugoslavia disintegrated as the republics of Slovenia, Croatia, Bosnia, and Macedonia proclaimed their independence. Yugoslavia was reduced to only two of the former six republics: Serbia and Montenegro. Hundreds of thousands of ethnic Serbs found themselves living in Croatia and Bosnia. Supported by the Serb-controlled Yugoslavian army, Serb nationalists in Croatia and Bosnia rebelled, took control of regions in both republics, and demanded unification with Serbia. With more than 100,000 dead and more than one million homeless, the war in Bosnia has been the bloodiest and most destructive war in Europe since World War II.

In 1995 an agreement was reached between the Bosnia Muslims, Croats, and Serbs. Fighting stopped, and NATO troops occupied zones between the warring factions. The question remains whether a workable political solution can be found to the Bosnian problem before NATO troops are withdrawn.

Many fear that the war in Bosnia might spread to the Kosovo province of Serbia and the republic of Macedonia. Conflict is already developing in Kosovo and the problem is even more difficult than the one in Bosnia. Although today between 80 and 90 percent of the population of Kosovo is Albania Muslims, historically Kosovo was the heartland of Serbia. The Albanian Liberation Army is calling for a free and independent Kosovo, but Serb political leaders are in position to surrender what their people consider the core region of their historic homeland. Open war in Kosovo could serve to ignite a wider war that could spread throughout the Balkans and involve Greece, Albania, Bulgaria, and Turkey on competing sides.

This is only a sampling of armed nationalist conflicts. Nationalist movements are difficult to defuse. In most cases the recognized national governments lack the

- In 1960, Nigeria became independent. In 1967, the Ibos, seeing Nigeria increasingly controlled by the Yoruba and Hausa peoples, seceded and established the Republic of Biafra. Three years of bloody war followed before the Ibos were militarily overwhelmed.
- Burundi became independent in 1962, and political conflict developed between the Tutsi and the Hutu; in 1972 this conflict culminated in the slaughter of about 200,000 Hutu.

Nationalist separatist movements are also active in the southern Sudan, the island of Mindanao in the Philippines, and in Sri Lanka—just to name a few of the most important. Certainly, it is facile to lay all the blame on colonialism for these and other conflicts in the postcolonial era. But it is undeniable that violence between ethnic nationalities, each believing its political and territorial claims are legitimate, is one of colonialism's most unfortunate and long-lasting legacies.

Not all ethnic conflicts have been or are confined to the old colonial world. For example, the Kurds (who live in the mountainous regions of Turkey, Iraq, Iran, and Syria) have had an active separatist movement since the

military resources to totally defeat them. Even when a government has overwhelming resources, such as the British in Northern Ireland, guerrilla wars are difficult to win decisively. As a result, few separatist movements have been extinguished. In some cases, the central governments have either disintegrated or lost control over most of the country, as in Liberia and Afghanistan. In other cases, the central governments have adopted policies of geographical containment and lessening of direct conflict. A graphic example of this approach is in Western Sahara, formerly Spanish Sahara. In the early 1970s, Spain committed itself to a policy of independence and self-determination for its colony. However, in 1976, before independence was achieved Morocco occupied the northern portion of the region, claiming it was historically part of Morocco. In 1979, Morocco occupied the southern portion of the region. The Spanish did not resist the Moroccan occupation. However, the local Sahrawi population rejected Moroccan domination, formed by Polisaria Front, and initiated a guerrilla war. Unable to defeat the guerrillas but yet unwilling to withdraw, the Moroccan government partitioned the region with a 2,500-kilometer-long sand "wall" equipped with electronic devices to detect movements; the purpose of the wall was to separate the portion Morocco controlled from the area they did not control. In 1989 the Moroccan government agreed to a referendum sponsored by the United Nations, but the status of Western Sahara has yet to be resolved. Almost yearly the number of unresolved ethnic conflicts increases and the number of peoples and regions affected widens. There are about 150 ongoing armed conflicts in the world today, and 80 to 90 percent of these conflicts would be classified as nationalist movements.

Central governments as a whole have been unsuccessful in achieving total military victories over separatist groups, but nationalist separatist groups themselves seldom have been successful in achieving political victories.

Bangladesh was recognized by the United Nations only because it was a *fait accompli,* backed by the overwhelming military support of India. In contrast, the United Nations was extremely slow to extend recognition to Slovenia and Croatia. Only when it appeared that Yugoslavia might militarily intervene did the United Nations act, and then only in hopes of preventing a war. Under the military protection of the United Nations, the Kurdish people in northern Iraq have proclaimed their independence and organized their own republic. However, while protecting them from the Iraq military, neither the United Nations nor any other country has formally recognized the new Kurdish state. The reason is simple. If an independent Kurdish state is created in northern Iraq, it would encourage Kurdish nationalists in Turkey, Iran, and Syria. With an active Kurdish separatist movement in its

country, Turkey is adamantly opposed to the creation of any Kurdish state, and neither the United States nor the United Nations will challenge Turkey on this issue. The recent problems of chaos and starvation in Somalia have been limited to the southern portion of the country. When the central government of Somalia disintegrated in 1991, the leaders in the north declared their independence and established their state of Somaliland. Although Somaliland is politically stable, it has yet to be granted recognition by any country. The United Nations and the Organization of African Unity have taken the position that northern and southern Somalia will "remain" united, and act as if no government exists in the north.

One may well ask why separatist movements seldom are extended official recognition. In Chapter 1, Article 1, of the Charter of the United Nations, the right of a people to self-determination is recognized. The United Nations also recognizes the sovereignty and territorial integrity of existing states. Thus, recognition of a secessionist group would be considered intervention in affairs of a sovereign state. Other governments have also pledged themselves not to recognize separatist states. In

In Rwanda the recovery and identification of victims of the recent genocide is a long and ongoing process.

A CLOSER LOOK

Collapse of the Soviet Union

The most significant political event of the early 1990s was the collapse of the Soviet Union and its division into fifteen countries (see Figure 17.4). In many ways the Soviet Union serves as a microcosm of the ethno-political problems besetting the world. Just before its collapse the Soviet Union encompassed almost 290 million people and more than 100 distinct ethnic nationalities. Although ethnic Russians constituted a slight majority (about 52 percent), there were more than twenty-three minority nationalities with populations in excess of one million people.

The Soviet Union was, politically speaking, nothing more than the Russian Empire under a new name, with Lenin, Stalin, and other Communist leaders being the political heirs of Czar Ivan IV. It was Ivan, also known as "the Terrible," who laid the foundations of the empire in the sixteenth century by solidifying the political hold of the czar over the Russian people. In the centuries that followed, subsequent czars and their armies extended their political control beyond the lands of Russian people. In the seventeenth century Russian frontiersmen known as Cossacks overran and conquered the tribal peoples of Siberia, extending the boundaries of the empire all the way to the Pacific Ocean. During the same period, Russian armies began extending the boundaries of the empire west and south, incorporating other Slavic and non-Slavic peoples—Finns, Latvians, Estonians, Lithuanians, Poles, Ukrainians, Bylorussians, and others. The ethnic composition of the empire was further diversified during the eighteenth century when the czar invited German farmers to settle on some of the newly won lands. Finally, during the nineteenth century, Russian armies pushed into central Asia, bringing numerous Muslim peoples into the empire.

In March of 1917, the revolt against the czar began. The three years that followed were a period of internal wars and political chaos. It was not until 1920 that the Communists eliminated the counter-revolutionaries and solidified their control. During this period, numerous ethnic nationalities had taken the opportunity to escape Russian domination. The Finns, Estonians, Latvians, Lithuanians, Georgians, Armenians, Azeris, and Bylorussians established their own countries. The Moldavians seceded and politically united with their close kin, the Romanians. With the support of the allied powers, the Polish regions of Russia, Germany, and Austria were joined to create a new Poland.

The new Communist rulers of Russia worked feverishly to rebuild the "empire." Soon they were able to reestablish control over Georgia, Armenia, Bylorussia, and Azerbaijan and group them into what was now called the Soviet Union. In 1939 the Soviets signed a secret nonaggression pact with Nazi Germany, and in September they joined the Germans in attacking and partitioning Poland. In November 1939 they invaded Finland, but the Finns were successful in halting their advance. In March of 1940 they militarily occupied the Moldavian portion of Romania and quickly reintegrated it into the Soviet Union. In June 1940 they invaded and annexed Estonia, Latvia, and Lithuania. Thus, by the end of June 1940, the Communists had reannexed to the Soviet Union all the lands of the czar with the exception of Finland. The invasion of the Soviet Union by Germany in 1941 proved only a temporary reversal, since Soviet troops "liberated" these regions near the end of World War II, and their reannexation was not questioned. The other allied powers even agreed to the redrawing of the boundaries of postwar Poland to correspond with Soviet territorial claims.

The Soviets created a political structure that superficially gave political recognition and "autonomy" to at least the major national minorities within the Union. The Soviet Union was divided into fifteen "union republics," one for each of the major ethnic nationalities: Russia, Byelorussia, Ukraine, Georgia, Armenia, Estonia, Latvia, Lithuania, Moldavia, Azerbaijan, Kazakhstan, Uzbekistan, Kirghizia, Tajikistan, and Turkmenistan. Five of these "union republics" included regions called "autonomous republics" for smaller nationalities. Altogether there were twenty "autonomous republics." Sixteen were in the Russian Republic, those for the Ossetians, Tatars, Yakut, Chechen-Ingush, and twelve other groups. Five of the union republics had still other, smaller ethnic political units called "autonomous oblasts." The best known of the eight oblasts are Nagorno-Karabakh (an Armenian ethnic region in the Azeri republic of Azerbaijan) and Yugo Ossetian (an Ossetian ethnic region in the Georgian Republic). In addition, the Russian Republic had six very small ethnic regions called "nationality okrugs." Thus, about forty-five of the largest nationalities within the Soviet Union had some form of political recognition.

Although every level of ethnopolitical unit had its own formal government, there was no meaningful local autonomy. Nor were these various regions the exclusive homes for the designated ethnic group. Members of different ethnic groups moved or were moved between ethnic regions. This was particularly true for Russians. Large Russian minorities were found in most of the fourteen other union republics. In fact, it was not uncommon for resident Russians to control the political bureaucracy of other republics.

Political recognition did not mean that the Soviet government encouraged ethnic differences. Any overt demonstration of ethnic pride or nationalism was ruthlessly crushed. The Russian language was taught in the schools, and local cultural traditions were suppressed. This suppression was particularly marked in the Islamic regions of central Asia, where Islamic schools and mosques were closed and many religious leaders were shot or imprisoned. This intolerance toward cultural and religious dissidents was not limited to larger, potentially dangerous nationalities. For example, the Yokuts, a

Figure 17.4 Republics and Divisions of the Former Soviet Union

—— International boundaries	1. Karel'skaya A.S.S.R.	8. Bashkirskaya A.S.S.R.	15. Abhazskaya A.S.S.R.
	2. Komi A.S.S.R.	9. Kalmytskaya A.S.S.R.	16. Nakhichevanskaya A.S.S.R.
	3. Mordovskaya A.S.S.R.	10. Dagenstanskaya A.S.S.R.	17. Karakalpakskaya A.S.S.R.
—— A.S.S.R. boundaries	4. Chuvashskaya A.S.S.R.	11. Checheno-Ingushskaya A.S.S.R.	18. Tuvinskaya A.S.S.R.
	5. Mariyskaya A.S.S.R.	12. Severo-Osetinskaya A.S.S.R.	19. Buryetskaya A.S.S.R.
	6. Tatarskaya A.S.S.R.	13. Kabardino-Balkarskaya A.S.S.R.	20. Yakutskaya A.S.S.R.
	7. Udmurtskaya A.S.S.R.	14. Yugo-Osentinskaya A.O.	

reindeer-herding people of Siberia who numbered only a few hundred thousand, also suffered. In the 1920s and 1930s their herds were collectivized, their language and cultural activities suppressed, and their religious leaders shot.

The Soviet Union was the "Russian Empire" under a new name, and regardless of what was publicly stated by political leaders in Moscow, members of the other nationalities recognized that they were under Russian domination. Given this, the events of the past few years should not have surprised us. The political chaos in the Soviet Union in the early 1990s once again gave the minority nationalities the opportunity to regain their independence, and thus there was a repeat of what happened in 1917 and 1918.

The disintegration of the Soviet Union into fifteen new nation-states has

not ended the ethnic problems of the region but rather intensified them. Ethnic problems exist both within and between the new states. More than eighty of the smaller nationalities have yet to achieve political independence. In other cases, a portion of the population of one of the fifteen nationalities who do have their own nation-state resides within the boundaries of another state. Fully 25 percent of the total population within the fifteen republics belongs to a minority national group.

The disintegration of the Soviet Union has increased the nationalist aspirations of many of the eighty or so smaller national groups. In Russia itself, separatist movements have already emerged among the Tartar and Chechen peoples. By declaring their independence, the Chechens have placed the Russian government in an awkward position. Fearing

that an independent Chetnya will encourage other minorities to follow suit, Russia appears committed to suppressing the Chechen separatists, regardless of the cost in lives and property. The Ossetian peoples (Yugo Ossetia) in Georgia have also rebelled, seeking to be politically reunited with the Ossetian peoples in Russia. Thus, we see a second wave of nationalist movements emerging.

The most potentially dangerous ethnic problems are between, not within, the fifteen new states. A destructive war is already raging between the Armenians and the Azeris over Nagorno-Karabakh. However, it is the twenty-five million Russians living in the fourteen non-Russian republics who may create the greatest threat to peace. In some countries, ethnic Russians constitute 30 to 40 percent of the population. What is going

Continued

Continued

to happen to these Russian minorities? Local nationalists are openly hostile to Russian residents and want them to return to Russia. In Estonia, nationalists have tried to deny resident Russians any political rights by imposing stringent residency and language (ability to speak Estonian) requirements for citizenship. Fearing reunification with Romania, the Russian and Ukraine residents of Moldavia have rebelled and proclaimed the independent Dniester Republic. In Tajikistan and some of the other central Asian republics, Russian residents have been attacked and murdered. In Kazakhstan, militarily the most powerful of these republics, 37 percent of the population (more than six million people) is Russian, and the northern portion of the republic is almost exclusively occupied by Russians. Russian and Kazakh are both official languages of the republic. Some believe that the Kazakh leaders are trying to strengthen their positions before moving against the Russian minority. The fear is that the Russians might succeed and unite northern Kazakhstan with Russia.

The leaders of the Russian Republic have recognized the problem facing the Russian minorities in the other republics and proclaimed that their rights will be protected. On a limited scale, the Russian army has already intervened to protect the Russian residents of Moldavia and Tajikistan, as well as the Ossetians in Georgia. The complicating factor is the rebirth of the Cossacks. The Cossacks were free Russian peasants who lived on the borders of the empire. Organized as paramilitary communities under their own leaders, they saw themselves as the protectors of the Russian people and the Eastern Orthodox Church. Disbanded by the Communists, military units are being reorganized in many of the Cossack communities. Cossack volunteers have already joined the Russian secessionists in the fighting in Moldavia, and several hundred other Cossacks have joined the Serbs (also Eastern Orthodox) in Bosnia fighting the Muslims. What would happen if an "ethnic cleansing" program against Russians occurs in Kazakhstan, Uzbekistan, or some other former Soviet republic? There can be little doubt that the Russian army would be forced to intervene.

We have mentioned only a few examples of ethnic conflicts within the former Soviet Union. The *Moscow News* in 1992 compiled a list of seventy-nine existing or potential ethnic conflicts. What makes the situation more dangerous than in most similar regions of the world is the presence of vast quantities of not only modern conventional weapons, but also nuclear weapons at military bases throughout the republics. The potential exists for ethnic conflict and bloodshed on a massive scale. You might as well ask, Other than for humanitarian reasons, why should we be concerned about our former enemies? The answer is simple. It is doubtful that large-scale ethnic wars could be confined within the boundaries of the fifteen republics. These wars would quickly spill over into the Middle East and Eastern and Western Europe. Even if these wars could be contained, the republics of the former Soviet Union are the world's largest producers of oil, producing 20 percent of the total world supply. These same republics supply the peoples and industries of Western Europe with most of their natural gas. Thus, large-scale conflicts in this region would have a devastating effect on the global economy.

1964 the Organization of African Unity adopted the policy that "the borders of African States on the day of independence constitute a tangible reality," and thus they firmly oppose any changes in the political boundaries of Africa. The real, unstated reason is that almost every country in the world has one or more minority nationalities that either have or potentially may develop an independence movement. Thus, both formal and informal agreements are made among the existing countries to maintain the current political status quo.

Resolving Ethnic Conflict

How can such deep-rooted conflicts be resolved? The most obvious solution is to divide the country, giving the dissatisfied nationality their land and independence and allowing them to establish their own country or merge with another country. However, central governments have always been highly reluctant to surrender their territorial claims. As Burma, the Sudan, and many other countries have shown, they would rather fight a long, destructive, and inclusive war than officially recognize the independence of a rebellious nationality. This stance is taken partly because governments fear setting a precedent. As a result, most ethnic conflicts have been resolved—and future solutions will probably have to be sought—within the existing political structure.

Historically, such internal solutions to ethnic issues have taken two forms: (1) ethnic homogenization of the population through the elimination of rival ethnic groups and (2) the political accommodation of ethnic groups.

Homogenization

Ethnic homogenization is the process by which one ethnic group attempts to eliminate rival ethnic groups within a particular region or country. Historically, ethnic homogenization has taken one of two main forms: (1) **ethnic cleansing** or (2) **assimilation**.

The term *ethnic cleansing* entered our vocabulary in reference to the warfare in the republics of what was formerly Yugoslavia. Ethnic cleansing is the physical elimination of an unwanted ethnic group or groups from particular geographical areas. It involves the use of genocide and/or relocation.

Genocide is the deliberate and systematic attempt to physically destroy the members of the rival population. The objective may be the total destruction of the group, the reduction of their numbers, or a stimulus for the surviving members of the group to migrate. Regardless of the actual objective, the process is the same: the indiscriminate slaughter of men, women, and children of the targeted ethnic group.

Today, when we think of genocide, we think of the recent events in Bosnia or of the killing of millions of Jews and Gypsies by the Germans during World War II, but genocide has been a recurrent event in human history. Only the magnitude of the killing has varied. In the late 1970s and early 1980s, thousands of Native Americans were massacred by the Guatemalan army. The Turks instituted a policy of systematic killing of Armenians during the early years of this century. During the colonial period, the English, Dutch, French, Spanish, Portuguese, Belgians, and Germans were periodically guilty of genocide. Incidents of genocide are found even in American history, beginning with the slaughter of the Pequots in Connecticut in 1637 and ending with the massacre of more than 150 Sioux at Wounded Knee, South Dakota, in 1890. Genocide has been and still is a far too common response to ethnic conflict and rivalry.

Relocation is the forced resettlement of an unwanted ethnic group in a new geographical location. The forced relocation of the target population may be in conjunction with genocide, as in Bosnia, or separate from it. Sometimes the unwanted group is forced outside the boundaries of the country, becoming what today we term *refugees*. In other cases, an ethnic group is forcibly moved to a new area within the boundaries of the state, where it is assumed that they will pose less of a problem.

At the outbreak of World War II, the Soviet Union was home to several million ethnic Germans who had settled in Russia at the invitation of Empress Catherine the Great in the 1760s. In 1924, a separate German autonomous republic within Russia was established along the Volga River, for the so-called Volga Germans. When Germany attacked the Soviet Union in 1941, Stalin, fearing that the ethnic Germans might join the invaders, ordered all of them moved from Russia and Ukrania to Kazakhstan, Siberia, and other remote areas.

After World War II, the boundaries of much of Eastern Europe were redrawn. That portion of Germany locat-

Following World War II, millions of ethnic Germans, such as these from Czechoslovakia, had their family property confiscated and were deported.

ed east of the Oder River was given to Poland, and seven million German residents were forcibly evicted. At the same time, Czechoslovakia evicted almost three million resident Germans from their homes (see Figure 17.5). After independence, many East African countries expelled many East Indians who had settled there during the colonial period. In American history, Native Americans were regularly relocated as the frontier moved west, thus "solving" the Indian problem for white settlers and the U.S. government. The largest and best known of these relocations occurred in the 1830s, when the Five Civilized Tribes were forced to move (along the so-called Trail of Tears) from their homes in the southeastern states to what is today Oklahoma. Most indigenous tribes of the United States experienced similar resettlement programs. In Bosnia and Croatia, the main objective of the Serbs is the relocation of the Croats and Muslims. The killings, rapes, and destruction are the tactics used to cause them to abandon their homes. In this case there is no designated place for these people to go, and thus hundreds of thousands of refugees are attempting to find refuge in Western Europe and Turkey.

Assimilation is the social absorption of one ethnic group by another, dominant one. Assimilation may be total, in which the ethnic identity of one group is lost, or

group. The ultimate objective usually is the total absorption of the group into the dominant ethnic group. A key target of forced assimilation policy is the elimination of ethnic boundary markers: language, religion, modes of dress, and any cultural institution that readily distinguishes the population. If these boundary markers are destroyed, the group loses much of its social cohesiveness. For example, until recently the Bulgarian government pursued a policy designed to assimilate its Turkish population. Turks were not free to practice their Islamic religion, and they were forced to speak Bulgarian in public and adopt Bulgarian names.

One of the best examples of forced assimilation was the United States' Indian policy in the latter part of the nineteenth and early twentieth centuries. Federal Indian policy attacked Native American ethnic identity from several directions. Reservation lands, which were owned communally, were broken up, and the land was allotted (deeded) to individual members of the tribe. The objective was to destroy community or village life. Many ceremonies, such as the Sun Dance and peyote religion, were made illegal. Traditional or hereditary tribal leaders were not recognized, and tribal governments were either dissolved or reorganized along an American political model. People who worked for the government commonly were forced to cut their hair and wear "citizens" (western-style) clothes. Native American children were taken from their families and placed in boarding schools, where they were forbidden to speak their native language, had their hair cut, were made to dress in citizens' clothes, were taught Euro-American technical skills, and were indoctrinated with Euro-American Christian values and attitudes. As the head of the Carlisle Indian School said, "You have to destroy the Indian to save the man."

Assimilation need not be the result of a conscious official policy to solve an "ethnic problem" by incorporat-

Figure 17.5   Relocation of Ethnic Germans after World War II
Direction arrows indicate the transfer, eviction, or flight of ethnic Germans. Figures are in thousands of people.

partial, in which one ethnic group assumes a subordinate identity. Assimilation may be either forced or passive.

Forced assimilation occurs when the government adopts policies designed to deliberately and systematically destroy or change the ethnic identity of a particular

ing the population into the cultural mainstream. Another form, called **passive assimilation,** occurs without any formal planning or political coercion. Unless strong social barriers prevent assimilation, social and economic forces frequently result in more dominant ethnic groups absorbing members of less powerful groups with whom they are in contact. The dominant ethnic group does not necessarily have to be the larger, but it must be the most socially prestigious and economically powerful group. Many of the governments in Latin America have historically followed a laissez-faire policy toward Native American groups. Guatemala has not had a policy of forced assimilation. In Guatemala the primary differences between Ladinos and Native Americans are not biological but social and cultural, and people who are technically identified as Native Americans are socially and economically discriminated against. As a result, more ambitious and educated Native Americans frequently have abandoned their native languages, dress, and lifestyles (ethnic boundary markers) and reidentified themselves as Ladinos. During the past 100 years, the Native American population in Guatemala has decreased from about 75 percent of the total population to less than 50 percent; passive assimilation is the primary cause of this decrease.

Accommodation

An alternative to ethnic homogenization is some form of political **accommodation** that formally recognizes and supports the ethnic and cultural differences of the population. A number of multinationality countries have adopted this strategy of formalized ethnic pluralism. For instance, Canada has two main nationalities: Anglo-Canadians (English-speaking) and French-Canadians (French-speaking). Both English and French are formally acknowledged as official languages. Although Quebec is the only province in which French-Canadians are the majority, French speakers are found throughout the other, predominantly Anglo-Canadian provinces. Belgium also has two major national groups: the Flemish (Dutch speakers) and the Walloons (French speakers). Both Flemish and Walloon are official languages of Belgium, and although internal political boundaries closely correspond to ethnic boundaries, neither group is recognized politically. Spain has four main linguistic ethnic groups: Spanish, Galitian, Catalinian, and Basque. Although Spanish is still the official language of Spain, since 1980 both the Basques and the Catalonians have had local political autonomy.

In the cases of Canada, Belgium, and Spain, the number of distinct nationalities is limited. Other countries have confronted far more complex ethnic mixes. The two most ambitious attempts to create functioning multinational states have been those of the Soviet Union and Yugoslavia. The Soviet Union, as we discussed in "A Closer Look," encompassed more than 100 national groups.

Yugoslavia had eight major nationalities: Serbs, Croats, Muslims, Slovenians, Montenegrins, Macedonians, Hungarians, and Albanians. Separate republics were established for the Serbs, Croats, Montenegrins, and Macedonians. Although no separate republic was created for the Muslims, they were the largest group in the ethnically mixed republic of Bosnia. The Albanians and Hungarians were given autonomous provinces within the republic of Serbia. Yugoslavia was organized as a confederacy, and a great deal of local autonomy was given each of the republics.

Resolution

Having looked at the various means by which people have attempted to resolve ethnic differences, we can now examine the results. What are the results of ethnic cleansing? No American can deny that ethnic cleansing does not work. You need only look about you. How many Native American faces do you see? Yet America was once entirely Native American. American Indian peoples were massacred and the defeated survivors driven steadily westward to lands considered less desirable. Today, most Native Americans survive in small, scattered communities in the western states.

Setting aside the moral issues, ethnic cleansing seldom is a permanent solution. Except for very small groups, rarely has one ethnic nationality been successful in destroying another. Even though it may be greatly reduced in number, the targeted group usually survives. The history of genocidal attacks by the other group becomes an integral part of the origin myth of the victimized group and thus serves to strengthen—not weaken—their identity. Genocide also creates hatred and distrust between groups that can persist for generations after the actual event and make future political cooperation difficult, if not impossible.

Relocation also produces mixed results. As in the case of genocide, the forced removal of a people becomes part of their origin myth and serves to strengthen their cohesion and identity. Removal of a people from their homeland in no way negates their claims to the lands they lost. Four hundred years after the Irish were evicted from Northern Ireland, the Irish Republican Army is fighting to reclaim this portion of the lost Irish homeland. The Jews were expelled from Jerusalem in the first century A.D. and dispersed over Europe, North Africa, and the Middle East. Yet the past century has seen their return to Israel and the reclaiming of their homeland. The collective memory of a nationality is long. Old wrongs seldom are forgotten, and lost homelands are never truly relinquished.

Overt ethnic boundary markers usually are the main targets of forced assimilation policies. This is the same Native American before and after attending an Indian school founded by the government.

So genocide, relocation, and forced or passive assimilation may be effective to a greater or lesser degree, but each, under most circumstances, does not truly resolve ethnic problems. More often they postpone the formulation of workable policies and are even counterproductive—they worsen rather than alleviate conflicts. Besides these "pragmatic" considerations, genocide and forced assimilation are so morally abhorrent that few modern governments would admit to pursuing such policies. Relocation, likewise, poses ethical dilemmas; most groups are moved against their will, and some other nationality must be relocated to make room for the migrants. In the modern world, there is nowhere to relocate to without violating some other group's rights. Finally, as we have seen, passive assimilation usually is slow and its result is uncertain: Many nationalities want to maintain their traditions and refuse to give up their identity.

Political accommodation is the only practical and morally acceptable solution. But how well does it work, and what are the problems in maintaining a multinationality state? Although the vast majority of countries encompass two or more national groups, few have attempted to politically accommodate multiple nationalities. Most countries are controlled by a single nationality that politically and economically dominates the other nationalities and holds the country together by force or the implied threat of force.

In an effort to understand the problems of political accommodation, we are going to examine the recent history of three such states: Canada, Czechoslovakia, and Yugoslavia. Canada remains a united country as the leaders of both English- and French-speaking Canadians struggle to find a political solution to their ethnic problem. Czechoslovakia peacefully split into the Czech Republic and Slovakia in January 1993. The disintegration of Yugoslavia into six republics in 1991 and 1992 has resulted in a series of bloody ethnic wars. Each of these three cases tells us something about the volatility and problems inherent in multinationality states.

Canada originally was settled by French colonists during the seventeenth century. The British gained control of portions of eastern Canada in 1713, after Queen Anne's War. French settlers were expelled and replaced by British colonists. In 1763, after the French and Indian

Assimilation—whether passive or forced—is not always effective. There is no question that throughout history, smaller groups have been absorbed by larger groups, but assimilation usually is a slow and uncertain process. As we discussed, in Guatemala, Native Americans have slowly declined over the past 100 years as a percentage of the total population. We might therefore assume that passive assimilation has proved effective in this case. However, considering absolute rather than relative population, we find that the Native American population actually increased from one million to about four million during the same period. The main problem with passive assimilation, then, is that population growth often creates new members as fast as or faster than former members become assimilated. Another problem is that many people do not want to give up their ethnic identity; if they did, forced assimilation would not be necessary. The forced assimilation policies in the United States were equally unsuccessful in regard to Native Americans. Loss of language, material culture, and other cultural institutions that functioned as ethnic boundary markers did not destroy ethnic identity or group cohesiveness because new cultural institutions and ethnic boundary markers soon emerged to replace the old. From a population of only about 250,000 in 1890, the Native American population of the United States has risen to more than 1.5 million today, and their major political demands are for greater tribal sovereignty and self-determination on Native American lands.

War, the British took control of the rest of French Canada. Under the Quebec Act of 1774, French settlers were granted the right to have their own language, religion, and civil laws. After the American Revolution, large numbers of American loyalists settled in Canada, which greatly increased the resident English-speaking population. In 1867, the Dominion of Canada was created and the policy of accommodation continued, with both French and English being recognized as official languages.

In the 1960s, a separatist movement emerged among the French-Canadians in Quebec. The main catalyst for this movement was demographic changes. Originally a small minority, the English-speaking population in Canada grew rapidly during the nineteenth century. The twentieth century has seen an acceleration of this trend. Most immigrants to Canada during the twentieth century chose to adopt English, not French, as their language, thus adding to the English-Canadian population. At the same time, the birthrate of French-Canadians has declined. Thus, the French-Canadians see themselves as constituting an ever-smaller percentage of the total population. French-Canadian separatism is not the result of personal animosity toward English-Canadians, but rather the collective fear of being overwhelmed by the sheer number of English speakers, the loss of their language, and the erosion of their cultural distinctiveness. In the 1976 elections, the Parti Québécois, the separatist party, won control of the government of Quebec and the next year made French the official language of the province. However, in a 1980 referendum in Quebec, voters rejected separation from Canada. Although 60 percent of the people in Quebec voted against separation in 1980, the issue was not resolved.

Although opposing separation from Canada, the majority of French-Canadians remained concerned about the potential loss of French culture and identity. In 1987, the Meech Lake Agreement was negotiated. This agreement would have given Quebec constitutional rights that could be used to preserve the French language and culture. The agreement had to receive the unanimous approval of all the provinces. Two English-speaking provinces rejected the agreement in 1990. In another attempt at reaching a political compromise, a new agreement, called the Charlottetown Accord, was reached in 1992. This new agreement would have weakened the powers of the central government and recognized Quebec as a "distinct society." It also would have permanently given Quebec 25 percent of the members of the House of Commons. Submitted to a national referendum in October 1992, the Charlottetown Accord was soundly rejected, even by the people of Quebec. As a result, in 1995 another referendum was held on Quebec separation, and this time it failed by less than 1 percent.

Feeling that it is now only a matter of time before they succeed, Quebec separatists are already planning to call for a third referendum.

The early 1990s saw the demise of two multinationality states: Czechoslovakia and Yugoslavia. Both had similar histories: They had been created by the Allied Powers after World War I; they had attempted political accommodation for their different nationalities and were controlled by Communists since the end of World War II; they disintegrated once democratic institutions evolved.

Czechoslovakia was created in 1919 out of a portion of what had been the Austro-Hungarian Empire. It was a two-nationality state that combined both the Czech ethnic regions of Bohemia and Moravia and the Slovak ethnic region of Slovakia. Linguistically, culturally, and socially, the Czechs and Slovaks are closely related peoples. Although rivalry exists, there was no history of any major hostilities or wars between them. Yet in January of 1993, by mutual agreement, the country peacefully split into the Czech Republic and the Republic of Slovakia. It was the smaller nationality, the Slovaks, who initiated the division, despite the fact that separation would be to their economic disadvantage. The industrial heart of Czechoslovakia was always in Bohemia. In terms of political and economic power as well as education, the Czechs had always dominated the country. Not surprisingly, many Slovaks thought that the Czechs treated them like poor country cousins. It was ethnic pride, not ethnic hostility, that led to the breakup of the country.

In the dismantling of the Austro-Hungarian Empire after World War I, a new country was also created in the Balkans. Yugoslavia was to be the most ethnically diverse of the central European countries and included within its boundaries Slovenians, Croats, Serbs, Bosnian Muslims, Macedonians, Montenegrins, Hungarians, and Albanians. Unlike other European countries, Yugoslavia had no ethnic majority group. Originally a kingdom, the country was overrun by the Germans during World War II. The local Communist partisan forces under Marshal Tito were able to liberate the country with little direct outside assistance. After the war, Tito created a new political structure for the country in which every ethnic would have at least some local autonomy. The country was divided into six republics: Slovenia, Croatia, Serbia, Bosnia, Montenegro, and Macedonia. Within the republic of Serbia, two autonomous provinces were created: Kosovo, in which the majority of people were Albanians, and Vojvodina, which had a large Hungarian population. The national capital, Belgrade, was also the capital of Serbia. The army was also dominated by Serbs. With 36 percent of the total population, the Serbs were the largest national

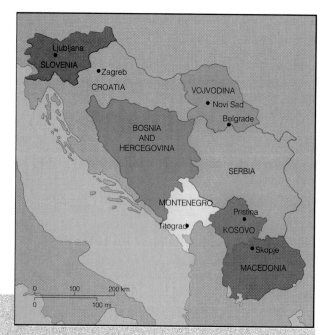

Figure 17.6 Republics and Autonomous Provinces of Yugoslavia

The individual republics and autonomous provinces more or less correspond with the territories of major ethnic groups.

group, followed by the Croats (20 percent), the Bosnian Muslims (9 percent), the Slovenes (8 percent), the Albanians (8 percent), the Macedonians (6 percent), and the Montenegrins (3 percent). Members of the other ethnic groups complained that the Serbs acted as if Yugoslavia was "their" country. After Tito's death in 1980, the office of president rotated among the presidents of the six republics (see Figure 17.6).

The history of the Balkans is a history of long and bloody wars between the various ethnic groups. A particularly deep hatred exists between the Croats (Catholics), the Serbs (Eastern Orthodox), and the Bosnian Muslims. Genocide has been common, and at one time or another each has massacred members of the other group. During World War II almost two million Yugoslavians died, and more were killed by members of rival ethnic groups than by Germans.

In June 1991, Slovenia and Croatia declared their independence, with Slovenia leading the way. The wealthiest and best educated of the nationalities, the Slovenians believed that the poorer republics of the country were inhibiting their economic development. The Croats seceded for both economic and nationalistic reasons. With Slovenia and Croatia gone, the ethnic balance in the remainder of Yugoslavia shifted. Serbs now consti-

tuted a majority in what remained of Yugoslavia—the country was now a de facto Serb state. In the fall of 1991 Macedonia declared independence, and in early 1992 the Bosnians voted for independence.

So far there has been major fighting only in Croatia and Bosnia. Croatia has an 18 percent Serbian minority population. Unable to tolerate political domination by the Croats, the Croatian Serbs rebelled, demanding that the areas in which they lived be politically joined to Serbia. The situation in Bosnia was different. With a population consisting of 43 percent Muslims, 31 percent Serbs, and 17 percent Croats, Bosnia had no ethnic majority. Once again the resident Serbs rebelled. Historic hatreds aside, there were two main reasons for the rebellion of the Bosnian Serbs. The Bosnian Muslims as a group are more prosperous than the local Serbs, creating economic jealousy. In addition, the birthrate among the Muslims is higher than that of the Serbs. Thus, there was the expectation that in the future the Bosnian Muslims would become the majority, and Bosnia would become an Islamic country.

By examining these three cases we can see some of the problems that exist in multinationality states, even under the best of conditions. The very presence of two or more nationalities within a country creates the potential for political volatility. Historic hatreds between groups increase the potential for conflict and political division. To be successful, political accommodation requires the creation and maintenance of a social, political, and economic balance between the groups. Members of all groups have to feel a collective social equality with members of other groups. They cannot think that their language or cultural institutions are being threatened or eroded by those of another group. Politically, they have to believe that their collective political rights are secure. Finally, no group can feel that their collective economic well-being is inhibited or that they are collectively being exploited by other groups. No country has ever existed with a perfect social, political, and economic balance between nationalities. Some social, political, and economic differences and inequalities between nationalities always exist. However, these differences and inequalities must not be of such magnitude as to threaten any particular ethnic group, and all must believe that political unity is to their mutual benefit. The problems faced by multinationality countries are not in their initial creation but in their maintenance over time.

The factors that most seriously threaten the political stability of multinationality countries are (1) differential rates of population growth and (2) relative differences in economic development between the constituent nationalities. If the population of one nationality grows more rapidly than that of another, it threatens the existing social and political balance of the country. The nationality or nationalities whose relative populations are declining may think that their social and cultural institutions are being threatened. They may also think that their collective political influence will decline. Regional differences in resources may result in significant changes in the relative economic status of the different nationalities. Changes in relative economic power can be translated into shifts in relative political power. Attempts to redistribute or divide the new wealth of one nationality among the other nationalities within the country can result in a feeling of exploitation.

The evolving global economy requires close cooperation between countries and nationalities. Rising nationalism directly threatens the global economy. Although we cannot change our basic human feelings, we can more clearly understand those factors that serve to unleash ethnic emotions, and attempt to minimize them. In the next chapter we discuss the critical issues of population growth and world hunger.

Summary

In this chapter we have discussed the nature of ethnic groups and their significance in the world. Every individual, not just members of minority populations, belongs to an ethnic group and has an ethnic identity. An ethnic group is a named social grouping of people based on what is perceived as shared ancestry, cultural traditions, and history. Ethnic group identity divides the world into categories of "us" and "them."

An individual's ethnic group identity seldom is absolute, but changes with social context. An individual may assume various hierarchically ranked identities. This characteristic is called the *hierarchical nesting quality* of identity.

There are two main attributes of an ethnic group. Every ethnic group has an origin myth or "history" that describes the common or shared historical experiences that created the group. Every ethnic group also has ethnic boundary markers that make its members identifiable. Ethnic boundary markers may include language, religion, physical characteristics, and other cultural traits such as clothing, house types, personal adornment, food, and so on.

There are two distinct types of ethnic groups. An ethnic nationality is an ethnic group with a feeling of homeland and the inherent right to political autonomy. An ethnic minority does not have a feeling of a separate homeland or of an inherent right to political autonomy.

Much of the conflict in the world today is between ethnic nationalities. There are between 3,000 and 5,000 ethnic nationalities in the world, but only about 200 separate countries. Most countries are multinationality countries, and much conflict is the result of nationalities wanting to establish their own independent countries.

There is no simple or easy solution to ethnic conflict. Genocide, relocation, and forced assimilation are not only immoral, but history shows that they seldom solve ethnic problems. Passive assimilation is a slow and uncertain process. Attempts by governments of multinationality states to accommodate cultural differences and nationalistic aspirations are not always successful. Ethnic conflict is and will be a major destabilizing factor in world politics for some time to come. So far, the citizens and even governments of militarily powerful Western nations have not come to grips with the threat of nationalism.

Key Terms

ethnic group
hierarchical nesting
origin myth
ethnic boundary markers

ethnogenesis
nationality
homeland
subnationalities
artificial countries
ethnic homogenization
ethnic cleansing

assimilation
genocide
relocation
forced assimilation
passive assimilation
accommodation

Suggested Readings

Bodley, John. *Victims of Progress*. 4th ed. Palo Alto: May-field Publishing, 1998.
- *A very readable book that is a good overview of tribal peoples in the modern world, with emphasis on how they are being destroyed by industrial civilization.*

Burger, Julian. *Report from the Frontier: The State of the World's Indigenous Peoples*. Cambridge, Mass.: Cultural Survival, 1987.
- *A general survey of the plight of indigenous peoples of the world.*

Carmack, Robert, ed. *Harvest of Violence*. Norman: University of Oklahoma Press, 1988.
- *This collection of twelve original essays is concerned with the war in Guatemala during the late 1970s and early 1980s, and how the war affected and involved the native Maya communities.*

Danforth, Loring M. *The Macedonian Conflict: Ethnic Nationalism in a Transnational World*. Princeton: Princeton University Press, 1995.
- *An interesting look at one of the most critical countries in the Balkans.*

Eicher, Joanne B., ed. *Dress and Ethnicity: Changes Across Space and Time*. Oxford: Berg, 1995.
- *In this edited volume dress and changes in dress are examined in a series of case studies of different peoples from throughout the world.*

Horowitz, Donald L. *Ethnic Groups in Conflict*. Berkeley: University of California Press, 1985.
- *The best and most comprehensive study of global ethnic conflict. Published in 1985 some of the materials are dated.*

Moynihan, Daniel Patrick. *Pandaemonium: Ethnicity in International Politics*. New York: Oxford University Press, 1993.
- *A good introduction to the problem of increasing nationalism and conflict.*

Internet Exercises

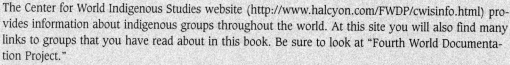

The Center for World Indigenous Studies website (http://www.halcyon.com/FWDP/cwisinfo.html) provides information about indigenous groups throughout the world. At this site you will also find many links to groups that you have read about in this book. Be sure to look at "Fourth World Documentation Project."

The site "Homelands: Autonomy, Secession, Independence and Nationalist Movements" (http://www.wavefront.com/~homelands/) contains numerous links, one near the bottom of the page will take you to a list of Internet readings. The "Ethnic World Survey" (http://www.partal.com/ciemen/-ethnic.html) has information on ethnicity, nationalism, and nationalist movements worldwide. Within these two sites see if you can discover any links that pertain to your local area. I found several webpages where groups have declared their states independent from the United States.

To find out more about the different ethnic groups found within the United States you can use any Internet search engine (Yahoo was used to find the sites listed here). Try searching on several different search engines and you will discover that the same terms will often come up with different results. Most search engines have instructions, and with a little practice you will get a feel for finding the information you want. A tip is to start with a broad category and then narrow down the categories from within the original results. Searching the term Gullah came up with quite a few sites. "Gullah Geechee Sea Island Coalition" (http://users.aol.queenmut/GullGeeco.html) and "The Gullah Islands" (http//dune.srhs.k12.nj.us/GullahWP.html) are good starting points for learning more about the Gullah people. Searching the term Amish will give you some practice narrowing down a search. There are many sites that are related to the Amish people, but most of them are advertisements. How many sites can you find that provide you with more information on the Amish? Some sites that are more factually oriented include (http:www.poopets.com/amishhist.html), (http:www.religioustolerance.org/amish.htm), and (http://goshen.edu/~lonhs/GCPUBLICATIONS/Tom_Meyers_Amish/meyers-amish.html).

An enormous amount of websites related to Native Americans is available. One of the best places to go for information is the Smithsonian Institution (htp://www.si.edu). There you will find the "National Museum of the American Indian" and other Native American resources. Also check out the Smithsonian Institution's African-American, Asian Pacific American, and Hispanic/Latino American resources.

CHAPTER 18

Applied Anthropology and World Problems

Applied Anthropology

Population Growth

Anthropological Perspectives on Population Growth

Consequences of Population Growth

Costs and Benefits of Children in North America

Costs and Benefits of Children in the LDCs

World Hunger

Scarcity or Inequality?

Is Technology Transfer the Answer?

Agricultural Alternatives

The Uses of Fieldwork: Two Studies

Planting Trees in Haiti

Delivering Health Care Services in Swaziland

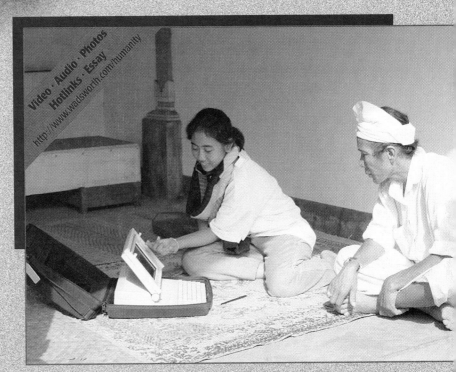

Video · Audio · Photos
Hotlinks · Essay
http://www.wadsworth.com/humanity

Many modern anthropologists use their skills and knowledge to help in local development and other ways of improving human lives. Using computer simulations, anthropologist Stephen Lansing found that traditional wet rice irrigation in the Indonesian island of Bali is regulated by a complex system of rituals held at water temples, which determine when irrigation water is released to farmers' fields. Like that of applied anthropologists, Lansing's research has practical value.

Visit http://www.wadsworth.com/humanity to learn more about the material covered in this chapter and to access activities, exercises, and tutorial quizzes.

*I*NCREASING NUMBERS *of anthropologists today are using their training to help solve human problems. In the private sector, for example, anthropologists work in a variety of roles, from training international businesspeople to become culturally sensitive when dealing with people from other countries to observing how humans interact with machines. Government agencies and international organizations employ anthropological expertise in problems connected to development, health, education, social services, and ethnic relations. This chapter covers the field of applied anthropology, showing some of the specific contributions anthropologists have made to problem solving.*

Applied Anthropology

Applied anthropology is most simply defined as the application of anthropological perspectives, theory, empirical knowledge of cultures, and methods to help assess and solve human problems. The subfield has grown dramatically since the early 1970s, partly because the number of new Ph.D.s has outstripped the number of academic jobs available, and partly because larger numbers of anthropologists want to use their expertise to help people and organizations.

What special talents or insights do applied anthropologists bring to problem solving? What unique contributions can anthropologists make to programs and agencies? One way to answer this question is to think of cultural anthropologists as sharing a certain world view (see Chapter 2), which differs somewhat from that of other professional people. This world view includes how we think about people and groups: the assumptions we share, the categories we use to describe and analyze ideas and behavior, the kinds of information we think is important to collect for understanding of a human group, how we believe this information can best be collected, and so forth. Anthropologists learn this world view through our graduate training, our fieldwork and other experiences involving members of other cultures, our interactions with one another, our readings of ethnographies and theoretical studies, and so forth. Not all ethnologists share this exact world view, of course, and (like all world views) this one changes over time. Nonetheless, its basic features are well-engrained in most anthropologists, and the *uniquely and distinctively* anthropological contributions to problem solving come out of this world view more than anything else. For applied work, five consequences of this world view are most relevant.

Attention to small-scale communities. Ethnologists pay attention to peoples and cultures too often ignored or—what is sometimes worse—known to others mainly by inaccurate or simplistic stereotypes. In applied work, an anthropologist who has worked in a particular small-scale community often is the only outsider who knows enough to provide information about it. Commonly, because of our training in fieldwork methodologies, we are the professionals most qualified to acquire new information relevant to some project about some local community. Through field research, anthropologists provide outside agencies and organizations with information about specific people and cultures.

Insistence on prior detailed knowledge. Because of anthropology's long-standing emphasis on firsthand fieldwork, we believe it is important to devote the time and resources necessary *prior* to the planning of a project or program to determine what the people affected are doing and thinking. Whatever their goals, almost all projects introduce some kind of change to a group, and prior knowledge of the culture is essential to plan and implement the changes. Many projects fail because those who design them know too little about the "target population" (those whose lives will be affected by the project).

Sensitivity to cultural differences. Anthropologists try to make themselves aware of the customs and beliefs of a community, to interact with members of the community in culturally appropriate ways, and to treat community traditions with respect. This cultural sensitivity derives partly from anthropology's relativistic, anti-ethnocentric perspective (see Chapter 1).

Appreciation of alternatives. Anthropologists believe that no one culture's experts know all the answers and solutions. Different people with different histories and traditions have worked out varying solutions to similar problems. What works well in one place and time and among one group may not work well elsewhere. Indeed, local people themselves often know the solutions to their problems, but do not have the resources to implement them. More than most other professionals, anthropologists listen to local voices.

Recognition of systematic complexity. Even the smallest and most homogeneous human groups are enormously complicated. But this complexity is ordered and patterned, and ethnographers have long recognized the importance of trying to determine how the parts of a complex system relate to one another and to the whole. A recognition of systematic complexity allows applied anthropologists to realize that changes introduced into a community may have unforeseen, unintended, and often undesirable consequences. Sometimes making small modifications in a program can avoid some of the potential negative impacts.

In the remainder of this chapter, we describe some examples of how these five emphases of anthropological thinking lead to new insights on human problems. Two of our cases deal with major global problems: population growth and world hunger. We show how anthropological work has contributed new insights on these problems. We hope to challenge your conceptions of population growth and hunger and to lead you to think about them in new ways or—at the very least—to question much of what you read and hear in the popular media. We also hope you will think about alternative solutions to these problems.

We shall also describe two studies done by applied anthropologists working in specific communities: planting trees in Haiti and delivering health care services in Swaziland. In these two cases, the problems are local-level rather than global in scope. Anthropologists used the knowledge gained through firsthand research in the communities to help the projects succeed.

Quite often, applied anthropologists work in the lesser developed countries (LDCs), which are often collectively known as the Third World. Terms such as "developed," "lesser developed," "First World," and "Third World" imply a certain level of prejudice resulting from a Western view (e.g., "Third World" to whom?). However, because they are familiar we continue to use them as shorthand descriptions of major world regions.

Population Growth

One of the most important worldwide problems of modern times is the phenomenal increase in the earth's population. Contrary to the beliefs of many, high population growth rates are a recent phenomenon, on a global scale. Around the time of Christ there were 250 to 300 million people on earth. By the mid-nineteenth century there were one billion. By 1930 human numbers had reached 2 billion; by 1960, 3 billion; by 1974, 4 billion; by 1986, 5 billion; by 2000, over 6 billion. What has changed in the past century or two that accounts for this increase?

If we exclude the effects of migration, the rate of growth of a population depends on its excess of births over deaths. Population growth is caused by some combination of falling death rates and rising birthrates. (See the following list for definitions of terms used in this section.)

POPULATION TERMINOLOGY (all rates are per year)

- birthrate (crude birthrate): number of births per 1,000 persons
- child mortality rate: number of deaths of children under the age of five per 1,000 children under the age of five
- infant mortality rate: number of deaths of children under the age of one per 1,000 children under the age of one
- total fertility rate: number of children born to an average female during her entire reproductive life.

Most demographers (experts who describe and analyze human populations) agree that improvements in public health and medical care are the main reason for twentieth-century population growth. Vaccinations against smallpox, typhoid, yellow fever, and other diseases have lowered death rates significantly. The transmission of diseases such as dysentery, cholera, and tuberculosis has been reduced by drugs and public health measures. Pesticide sprayings have reduced the numbers of mosquitoes and other insects that carry malaria and bubonic plague. Physicians and other medical personnel carry scientific

Because of anthropology's emphasis on fieldwork, ethnographers often become intimately involved with people they work among, which makes them more likely than most outsiders to listen to local voices.

treatments for illness into most parts of the world. The recent development of new treatments for AIDS leads its victims and the medical community to hope that this most recent killer will soon be brought under control.

These and other improvements in public health and medical care affect population growth by reducing death rates: more children survive into adulthood, or more adults live longer, or both. The former is the most important way in which public health and medical science has reduced death rates, for the infant mortality and child death rates in almost all LDCs began to decline significantly in the mid-twentieth century. They continue to fall today. For example, in the low-income countries of sub-Saharan Africa and southeast and south Asia, child mortality rates fell from 175 to 113 between 1980 and 1996. Two countries, China and India, together contain nearly 40 percent of the earth's people, so what happens to their mortality and birthrates has a large effect on the total world rates. In China, the child mortality rate fell from 60 to 39 between 1980 and 1996. In India, it fell from 173 to 85 over the same period. Crude death rates likewise have fallen significantly in most Third World countries over the past two decades. The result of such powerful trends is that more children are surviving into adulthood and into their reproductive years in the vast majority of poorer countries.

In Third World countries, birthrates and total fertility rates likewise have declined and continue to fall, but not so dramatically as mortality rates. Between 1980 and 1996, the total average fertility rate in the low income countries fell from 5.6 to 4.1, meaning that in 1996 an average Third World woman bore over four children during her lifetime. In contrast, an average Canadian woman had only 1.7 children, an American woman had 2.1, a Japanese woman had 1.4, and an Italian woman had only 1.2. So fertility rates in the LDCs are generally two or three times higher than in the developed nations at the close of the twentieth century.

Many countries generally considered as "overpopulated" have participated in national and international programs that have greatly lowered fertility recently. In some of the most densely populated countries of South Asia and sub-Saharan Africa, total fertility rates fell significantly between 1980 and 1996: in Bangladesh, from 6.1 to 3.4; in Pakistan, from 7.0 to 5.1; in India, from 5.0 to 3.1; in Nigeria, from 6.9 to 5.4; and in Kenya, from 7.8 to 4.6. Obviously, Third World couples are having significantly fewer children than a couple of decades ago, but their fertility rates are still high compared to those of high income countries.

The result of quickly declining mortality rates combined with not-as-quickly declining fertility rates is that population growth rates in the low income countries continue to be relatively high. Between 1990 and 1997, the low income countries increased their populations at an annual rate of around 2.1 percent, compared to around 0.7 percent for the high income countries.

In summary, progress in public health and medicine since around 1900 is the main cause of worldwide population growth. Although global population growth accelerated rapidly in the twentieth century, the rate of population increase has steadily declined in most countries over the past two or three decades. Most population growth today is occurring in the Third World countries of south Asia, southeast Asia, and sub-Saharan Africa because mortality rates have fallen faster than fertility rates. But birthrates have declined significantly in most Third World countries in the past twenty or thirty years, a hopeful sign for the new millennium.

Anthropological Perspectives on Population Growth

What contributions have anthropologists made to the analysis of worldwide population growth? Anthropological insight on this issue is twofold. First, anthropologists study human reproductive behavior—including the choices couples make about how many children to have—holistically, meaning in terms of the total system in which people live their everyday lives. By understanding the overall context of behavior, we can understand how the birthrates of a region result from local conditions—especially economic conditions faced by many rural poor. Second, anthropologists have conducted detailed fieldwork in local communities to uncover the major causes of high birthrates in Third World settings. To understand these anthropological perspectives, we begin by considering some of the negative effects of population growth on the world and on countries with high fertility rates.

Consequences of Population Growth

High population growth rates have many undesirable consequences. Some consequences are *global*—they affect everyone on earth, even citizens of nations that are not experiencing high rates of growth. The cutting of large amounts of tropical forest to feed growing numbers of people in the Americas and Africa may significantly contribute to global warming, with detrimental impacts on coastal regions and unpredictable impacts on agricultural yields. Migration from poorer to richer countries is increased by population growth in the former, which cannot provide enough jobs at living wages for their growing numbers of people. Population growth is a threat to the whole world, so the whole world should care about it for practical as well as for humanitarian reasons.

Other consequences of population growth are *local*—they negatively affect those very people who are "having too many children." These effects are harmful to the nation as a whole, to regions within the nation, to villages, and even—or so many people think—to the couples who are having the children. What are some of these adverse consequences?

Population growth contributes to environmental problems. More people consume more resources of all kinds, so the production of food, wood, minerals, and energy will have to grow. In turn, this increased exploitation of nature means environmental deterioration—pollution, soil erosion caused by overgrazing and more intensive land use, habitat destruction for other living things, deforestation, urban sprawl, and so forth are accelerated by increasing numbers of people.

Economic problems also are magnified in countries with growing populations. The higher the population growth rate, the more children as a proportion of the total population will be alive, so the country must devote more of its resources to education and other things that "unproductive" children require. Further, when all these children grow up and become potentially productive adults, some of them will enter the labor force. Many will be unemployed, and even those who find work will suffer low wages because there will be so much competition for jobs.

Finally, many social and political problems are related to overpopulation. To escape rural poverty, many people born on farms migrate to cities, where they may add to crime rates, increase housing shortage, worsen problems of sewage disposal and water supply, and so on. Increases in human numbers contribute to political conflicts, insurrections, and even civil wars as different ethnic groups, regions, classes, and parties compete for their slice of a shrinking pie. Resource scarcities—caused in part by dense and growing populations—have contributed to serious armed conflicts in Central America, Peru, Bolivia, Colombia, Somalia, Rwanda, Burundi, and eastern Europe, to name only a few recent and familiar examples.

Enough has been said to make the point: Population growth is harmful to most LDCs. Most governments have policies designed to curb fertility through educating couples in family planning and providing them with contraceptive devices. For example, realizing the probable disastrous long-term effects of continued population growth, in the late 1970s the Chinese government initiated a policy of allowing a family to have only two children. In the 1980s, a controversial one-child policy was instituted. Women apply for a childbearing permit for the right to bear their only child, and those who become pregnant for a second time are subjected to intense social, political, and economic pressure to have abortions. In the 1980s and 1990s, a tragic consequence of the one-child policy in China became apparent: Due to the preference for sons, female children suffered high mortality due to adult neglect and infanticide, and hundreds of thousands of girls were abandoned and placed in orphanages.

There is an apparent paradox about the comparatively high birthrates of many LDCs. An average North American family is able to afford more children than an average Nigerian family. Canadians and Americans have more money to house, feed, clothe, educate, and otherwise provide for their children. Yet they have only two or three, whereas the Nigerian family averages six or seven. And this is the most puzzling thing about high fertility: It continues despite its adverse consequences for those very nations that are experiencing it and whose citizens are causing it—the LDCs.

Why do these people continue to have so many children? Are Indians, Nigerians, and El Salvadorans too ignorant to realize that they cannot afford to support so many children? Can't they see the strain that all these children put on their nations' educational, health, and agricultural systems? Isn't the refusal of couples in these countries to practice birth control even when condoms and pills are available a perfect example of their backwardness and ignorance?

Not at all.

Costs and Benefits of Children in North America

The March 30, 1998, cover story of the weekly newsmagazine *U.S. News & World Report* was titled "Cost of Children." The article reported on the high monetary expenses of raising an American child born in 1997. Middle-income parents (defined in the article as couples who earn between $35,000 to $60,000 a year) can anticipate paying around $300,000 for their daughter's or son's day care and education, food and clothing, housing, transportation, health care, and other expenses, between birth and the age of eighteen. If parents also finance their child's college degree (not including graduate school), the cost of caring for and educating each new member of a middle-income family rises to around $460,000—close to a half million dollars!

Canadians, Japanese, Americans, Europeans, and parents living in other modernized, highly urbanized, industrial, or postindustrial nations are well aware of these monetary costs. Of course, parents in such societies do not have children because we expect our children to bring us future material rewards. For the most part, we do not have children because we expect them to help with chores around the house and yard, or that they will share their income with us when they (finally!) get jobs, or that our kids will support us in our old age. Most of us realize all too well that children are an *economic* liability—however *emotionally* gratifying they might be.

Children certainly do cost a lot of money to wage-earning working-class and middle-class couples of an urbanized, industrialized, developed country. Bills for food, housing, doctors, clothing, insurance, and transportation are higher with children—not to mention the costs of day care, baby-sitting, and education. Nor do most children contribute much economically to their parents as they grow older—retirement plans, Social Security, 401(K)s, and IRAs provide most of the income of the elderly. No wonder that when a young couple read in a newsmagazine that it costs a half million dollars to raise a child and finance her or his college education, they decide that one or two is quite enough!

The dollar costs of children are not the only factor that lead North American couples to limit their family sizes. Among the other relevant factors are:

• *Cultural norms and social expectations about desirable family sizes.* Not all couples feel that one or two or three children are enough, but the majority do agree that seven or eight are too many. Enculturated

Population growth contributes to social problems in the Third World, including unemployment and overcrowding in urban areas. This is a shanty town in Rio de Janeiro, Brazil.

friends who have hardly left their house since their baby was born, and they have no desire to be so tied down.

None of this implies that North American couples always have the number of children they choose. Some have an "accident" and wind up with more children than they want or with a child sooner than they had planned. And the preceding considerations, to some extent, are class and race biased—they apply more to well-educated, middle-income whites than to blacks and Hispanics, for example. But we do make reproductive choices, and the result of them—barring infertility and so forth—is that we have about the number of children we desire.

There are other factors that North American couples consider, of course. But notice the main overall feature of the considerations just listed: They are all things that will affect the deciding couple personally. People consider the benefits and costs of having or not having children, or of having so many and not more children, to *themselves*. They do not worry much about whether their children will increase the burden on the American educational system, increase the unemployment rate twenty years in the future, contribute to society's expenditures on public waters and sewers, or overload the nation's farmlands. That is, for the most part they do not concern themselves with the *social consequences* of their reproductive decisions. They do what they think is best for themselves.

Costs and Benefits of Children in the LDCs

Curiously, although most North Americans do not weigh heavily the future societal consequences when they decide to limit their family sizes, many of them expect people in the LDCs to be more altruistic by reducing their fertility. Too often, when we learn that rural people in parts of the Third World average six, seven, or more children per couple, we think this is economically irrational. They must be having large families for other noneconomic reasons. Probably "children are highly valued in their traditional culture." Or maybe "men have higher prestige if they have lots of children." Perhaps "they are not educated enough to recognize the effects of having such large families." It could be that "they don't know how to prevent pregnancy."

Part of our error comes from our failure to put ourselves in their shoes—to grasp the conditions of their lives that lead them to bear more children than we do. Just because children are an economic liability in a highly mobile, industrialized, urbanized, monetarized society does not mean that they are a liability everywhere. Many demographers argue that rural people in the LDCs have high fertility not simply because of cultural preferences but

norms and expectations of friends and families certainly affect how many children we have. Note, however, that these norms and expectations themselves respond to other kinds of societal and economic conditions, so they alone do not explain low (or high) fertility rates.

• *Occupational and spatial mobility.* Many young couples do not know where they will be or how they will be earning a living in the next few years. They want children someday but are too unsettled and lack the income to start their family right away. If most couples postpone pregnancy until their mid-twenties or thirties, a lower completed average family size results than if most women begin childbearing earlier.

• *Women's employment.* Many women want a career and perceive that numerous children will interfere with this goal. The limited time and energy of two-earner households leads to lowered fertility rates.

• *Social burdens of children.* Modern society offers numerous social and recreational outlets, which serve as alternatives to devoting one's time and energy to children. A couple may know some

because children are economically useful. Village-level ethnographic studies suggest that children do indeed offer a variety of material benefits to their parents in the LDCs.

One such study was done in the Punjab region of northern India by anthropologist Mahmood Mamdani. He researched a family planning project that aimed to reduce the birthrate in seven villages. Mamdani found that in the village of Manupur, people accepted the birth control pills and condoms offered by the staff of the program, but most refused to use them. The reaction of the project's administrators was like that of many outsiders when local people do not behave in ways they seemingly ought to behave: They blamed the "ignorance" and "conservatism" of the villagers. To the staff, the benefits of having fewer children seemed obvious. The amount of land available to most people was barely adequate, so by reducing family size people could stop the fragmentation of land that was contributing to their poverty.

However, the village's parents interpreted their economic circumstances differently. They believed that children—especially sons—were economically beneficial, not harmful. Villagers of all castes and all economic levels reported that children were helpful to a household in many ways. They helped with everyday tasks such as washing, gathering animal dung to use as fertilizer, weeding fields, collecting firewood, and caring for livestock. Even young children supplemented family income by doing small jobs for neighbors. When they grew up, sons were the major source of support for their elderly parents, since one or more of them usually continued to live with their parents and farm the land or work in other occupations. Adult sons often went to cities, where part of the money they earned from their jobs was sent back to help their parents and siblings.

In short, Mamdani argued, the residents of Manupur recognized that the benefits of children exceeded their costs to the parents. Outsiders did not recognize this fact because they did not fully grasp the economic circumstances under which people actually were living.

But, like people everywhere, the people of this region of India proved capable of altering their behavior as their circumstances changed. In 1982, ten years after Mamdani's study, the village of Manupur was restudied by Moni Nag and Neeraj Kak. They found that couples had changed their attitudes about desirable family size: About half of all couples were now using contraception or had accepted sterilization after they had two sons. The reason was that changing economic conditions in the region had made children less valuable to families. Parents did not need as much children's labor as before. The introductions of new crops and farming methods had almost eliminated grazing land in the region, so boys were no longer useful in tending cattle. Increasing reliance on purchased chemical fertilizers reduced the value of children's labor in collecting cattle dung to spread on fields. Chemical weedkillers reduced the amount of hand work necessary for weeding. A new crop, rice, did not take as much work to grow as the old staples.

The increased value of formal education also led people to have fewer children. Because more outside skilled jobs were available than previously, parents became more interested in providing a secondary education that would increase their children's ability to acquire high paying jobs. Opportunities for women increased, and secondary school enrollment rates for girls more than doubled between 1970 and 1982. Sending more children to secondary school raised the costs of child rearing. Parents had to pay for clothing and textbooks for their children who attended school, which was a significant expense for poorer families. Accordingly, they wanted and had fewer children.

Finally, most couples believed that having lots of sons was not necessary as ten years earlier. People still desired sons for old age support, but many believed that sons were not as dependable as they used to be. Many no longer brought their wives with them to live on the family land, but left the village to live on their own. One elderly man said:

> Children are of no use any more in old age of parents. They also do not do any work while going to school. My son in the military does not keep any connection with me. My son living with me has two sons and one daughter. I have advised him to get a vasectomy. (Nag and Kak 1984, 666)

All these and other changes increased the economic costs and decreased the benefits of having large families, and couples reacted to these changes by having fewer children. In this region of northern India, then, ideas and attitudes about desirable family sizes were not fixed by tradition but changed as people adapted their family sizes to changing circumstances.

Researchers in other parts of the world also report that children offer many economic benefits to their parents, explaining why high fertility persists in most LDCs. On the densely populated Indonesian island of Java, rural parents do not have to wait for their children to grow up to acquire the benefits of their labor. Children aged six to eight spend three to four hours daily in tending livestock, gathering firewood, and caring for their younger siblings. By the time they are fourteen, girls work almost nine hours a day in child care, food preparation, household chores, handicrafts, and other activities. Most of the labor of children does not contribute directly to their family's cash income or food supply, so it is easy to see how outsiders might conclude that children are unproductive. However, children accomplish many household-maintenance tasks that require little experience and skill, which frees the labor of adult family members for activities that do bring in money or food. Ethnographer Benjamin White suggests that large families are more successful economically than small families in Java.

Similar findings have been reported by ethnographers working in rural Nepal, Bangladesh, Samoa, and the Philippines. Unlike suburban and urban North Americans, farming families in the LDCs use much of the time of even young children productively. As children grow older they are used to diversify the economic activities of a household, earning cash themselves or performing subsistence work that frees their parents for wage labor.

In many countries, the grown children of rural people migrate to a city within their own country or to a developed country. They acquire jobs—which are well paid relative to what they could earn in their own villages—and send much of the cash back to their families. Such remittances contribute half or more of the family income in Western Samoa, Tonga, and some other small nations of the Pacific, both because migrants feel a continuing sense of obligations to their parents and siblings back home and because many of them hope to return to their islands someday. Remittances also are a major source of family income (and, as a by-product, of national income) in West African countries like Nigeria and Ghana, Pakistan, India, Mexico, Central America, and parts of the Middle East.

In most parts of the world, children also serve as the major source of economic support in their parents' old age because rural villagers lack pension plans and Social Security. As Stanley Freed and Ruth Freed have pointed out, in many parts of India parents prefer to bear two or three sons to ensure themselves of having one adult son to live with them, in case one son dies or moves elsewhere.

In addition to the value of children's labor, remittances, and old age security, many other factors encourage rural families in the LDCs to have many children, including

- relatively high rates of infant mortality, which encourage parents to have "extra" children to cover possible deaths of their offspring;
- extended families, which spread out the burden of child care among other household members, thus reducing it to individual parents;
- low monetary cost of children compared with children in DCs, partly because many necessities (such as housing and food) are produced by family labor rather than purchased; and
- the fact that the tasks women commonly are assigned are not as incompatible with child care as wage employment (see Chapter 10).

Such factors mean that children are perceived (in most cases, correctly) as both more valuable and less costly than most citizens of the developed world perceive them. We should not assume that couples in the LDCs are too ignorant to understand the costs of having many children or to appreciate the benefits of small families. Nor should we think that they are prisoners of their "traditional cultural values," which have not changed fast enough to keep up with changing conditions. We should rather assume that they make reproductive decisions just as we do. Then we can begin to understand the economic and other conditions of their lives that often lead them to want more children than affluent couples in urbanized, industrialized countries want. We also can see why birthrates are falling in so many LDCs today. It is not simply the increased education due to family planning and the recent availability of contraceptive devices. Lowered fertility is also a response to the increased urbanization of most nations, to the growth in wage employment over subsistence farming, to the rising emphasis placed on education for both girls and boys, and other factors that have changed the circumstances of family lives.

As we have seen, rising human numbers contribute to the resource shortages faced by LDCs today. One of the resources in shortest supply is one of the things people cannot do without: food. Most North Americans see malnutrition and overpopulation as two sides of the same coin. In the popular view, the "fact" that there are "too many people" in the world is the major reason that there is "too little food to go around." And the solution to world hunger is "more food," that is, increased production by the application of modern agricultural technologies. In the next section we try to convince you that neither the problem ("too many people") nor the solution ("more production through better technology") is this simple.

World Hunger

The famine in Somalia in the early 1990s is only the most recent reminder of hunger in the world today. Worldwide, hundreds of millions of people are chronically undernourished to some degree. In many regions, natural or human-caused disasters can reduce production enough to cause starvation for thousands. Hunger afflicts poor people in parts of the southern Sudan, Mozambique, Ethiopia, Chad, Bolivia, Peru, Bangladesh, Pakistan, and India. Even in countries considered "moderately developed" or "rapidly developing," there are regions of extreme poverty and hunger, as in Indonesia, Egypt, Brazil, and Mexico.

Children under five are especially at risk, dying either from malnutrition itself or from illnesses and diseases that well-nourished children would survive. In 1996, the United Nations Children's Fund estimated that there are 165

Chronic hunger is especially likely to afflict children in parts of the Third World. This is a World Vision feeding center in Somalia.

million malnourished children in the world, about half of them in Bangladesh, India, and Pakistan.

In this section we discuss the conditions that contribute to hunger in the Third World. Our focus is on chronic malnutrition or undernutrition on a worldwide scale, not on short-term famine in particular countries or regions. (The reason we focus on *chronic* hunger is that the immediate causes of famine are more likely to be political upheavals and conflicts that disrupt food production or distribution than economic or demographic forces.) First we discuss two alternative explanations for hunger. Then we cover attempts to increase food supply by modern technological methods, showing why such attempts are so often unsuccessful and counterproductive. Throughout, we suggest anthropological insights on the problem.

Scarcity or Inequality?

What causes hunger? In any given region, people are hungry for a variety of reasons. On a worldwide basis, however, two explanations for hunger are most commonly offered. The first, which we call the **scarcity explanation of hunger**, is that the major cause of widespread hunger in the LDCs is *overpopulation:* In the twentieth century, populations have grown so large that available

land and technology can not produce enough food to feed them. The second, which we call the **inequality explanation of hunger,** holds that the *unequal distribution of resources* is largely responsible for chronic hunger on a worldwide basis: So many people are hungry today because they lack access to the resources (especially land) needed to produce food.

The scarcity explanation holds that there are not enough food-producing resources to provide the poor with adequate nutrition. In countries like India, Bangladesh, El Salvador, Kenya, and Ethiopia, populations have grown so large in the last century or two that there is not enough land to feed everyone. This argument holds that food-producing resources like land, water, fertilizers, and technology are absolutely scarce, meaning that there are not enough resources for the size of the population. In brief, the scarcity explanation holds that hunger is caused by *too many people*.

(Although not our focus here, the scarcity explanation accounts for starvation by saying that chronic hunger turns into outright famine when some sort of disaster strikes. With so many people chronically undernourished, anything that disrupts food production [e.g., droughts, floods, plant diseases, insect infestations, or political disturbances] will reduce food supplies enough to make hungry people into starving people.)

The inequality explanation arose, in part, as a reaction to the excesses of the scarcity explanation which (some believe) blames the victims of hunger by saying that their own (reproductive) behavior causes their hunger. The inequality explanation holds that resources are not, in fact, absolutely scarce. In fact, there is enough productive capacity in the land of practically every nation to feed its people an adequate diet, if only this productive capacity were used to meet the needs of the poor. But instead, too many productive resources are used to increase the profits of wealthy landowners and to fulfill the wants of the more affluent citizens of the world.

The inequality explanation says that poor people are hungry because of the way both the international economy and their national economies allocate productive resources. The international (global) economy allocates resources on the basis of ability to pay, not on need. For example, if affluent North American consumers want coffee and sugar, wealthy and politically powerful landowners in Central America will devote their land to coffee and sugar plantations for export, because this is how they can make the most money. If North Americans want tomatoes and other vegetables during the winter, large landowners in northwest Mexico will produce them, rather than the beans and corn that are major staples for Mexican peasants. The national economies of countries with hungry people work in a similar way. Urban elites have the money to buy luxuries, and urban middle- and working-class families pressure governments to keep food prices low. As a result, too much land is used to produce crops sold to city dwellers at prices made so low by government policy that the rural poor cannot feed themselves. In brief, according to the inequality explanation hunger is caused mainly by *the use of and unequal access to resources*.

Which explanation is correct? As is often the case, the two are not mutually exclusive. Both are correct to a certain degree, depending on time and place. The scarcity explanation is correct: All else equal, the amount of land available per person has been and is being reduced by population growth. Moreover, as population grows, land of poorer and poorer quality has to be cultivated, reducing its productivity. And as families grow poorer, they have less money to acquire new land or to buy fertilizer or other products that will raise the productivity of their land. These arguments are the kind we encounter regularly in the popular news media. It is hard to see how such conclusions can be wrong.

But they could be right and still tell only part of the story. The explanation for hunger is more complex than "too many people" combined with "low farm productivity." Hunger is created by human institutions as much as by population increase and unproductive technologies and farming methods. For example, at a growth rate of 3 percent a year a population will double in less than twenty-five years. Does this mean that in twenty-five years everybody will have only half the amount of food? Of course not. Land that formerly was underused will be brought into fuller production; more labor-intensive methods of cultivation can bring higher yields per acre; people can change their diets and eat less meat; and so on. People will adjust their cultivation methods, work patterns, eating habits, and other behaviors to the new conditions rather than tolerate hunger.

Or rather, they will adjust if they have access to the resources they need to do so. And this is a large part of the problem in many LDCs: It is not *just* that there are too few resources but that too few people own or control the resources available. In their books *Food First* and *World Hunger: Twelve Myths,* Francis Moore Lappé and Joseph Collins question what they call "the myth of scarcity." They claim that every nation could provide an adequate diet for its citizens if its productive resources were more equitably distributed.

A discussion of the evidence that inequality is as important as scarcity in explaining hunger around the world cannot be attempted here. We mention only one detailed anthropological study done in El Salvador, where William Durham analyzed in detail the relationship between population growth and resource distribution as contributing factors to hunger and other manifestations of poverty. Although Durham's study was published back in 1979, it remains one of the most convincing analyses of the scarcity and the inequality approaches to hunger and poverty. Many of its findings illustrate conditions common in the LDCs today.

Durham noted that El Salvador appears to be a perfect example of population growth outstripping the supply of land, with hunger among the rural poor as its unfortunate consequence. From about 700,000 in 1892, population rose to over five million in the 1980s, producing a population density higher than both China and India. Widespread deforestation and erosion are two of the main environmental consequences. Declining food production per capita, along with a dramatic increase in food imports since about 1950, also are apparent indicators of excessive population relative to resources.

But Durham took a closer look, concluding that population growth is only part of the reason for the hunger of El Salvador's rural poor. Briefly, he found that:

• Although the per capita production of staple foods declined, total agricultural production kept pace with population growth. Land that could be used to produce staple foods like maize, beans, and rice increasingly was planted in export crops like coffee, sugar, and cotton. In fact, by the 1960s, over 40 percent of El Salvador's cultivable land was planted in export crops.

• Most of the coffee and other export crops was not produced on land owned by peasants, notwithstanding North America's Juan Valdez images of coffee producers. Land ownership in El Salvador was and is unequally distributed. In the 1970s, less than 2 percent of farmers held nearly one half the farmland in the country. Most of the coffee and other export crops were produced on the largest farms: Only about 1 percent of farms were over 100 hectares, yet they produced about 50 percent of the coffee.

- Small farmers produced most of the country's staple foods. Farms of under five hectares made up only about 16 percent of El Salvadors' total productive land, yet the owners of these small farms produced nearly 60 percent of the country's maize.
- Large farmers underutilized their land far more than small farmers: Farms of under one hectare cultivated 80 percent of their land, whereas farms of over 50 hectares cultivated only about one-third of their land. Further, nearly half the land of these large farms was used for grazing, mainly of cattle, with the beef sold largely to affluent people.

Durham concluded his analysis of hunger and poverty in El Salvador with two points:

> First, we find that food is scarce not because the land is incapable of producing enough for the resident population, but rather because large areas have been under-utilized or dedicated to the production of export crops. Second, we find that land is scarce not because there is too little to go around, but rather because of a process of competitive exclusion by which the small farmers have been increasingly squeezed off the land—a process due as much to . . . land concentration as to population pressure. (1979, 54)

There is no denying that population growth contributes to the hunger and poverty that victimize the peasantry of El Salvador and many other LDCs. But neither should we conclude that "too many people" is *the* problem, or that the scarcity explanation is sufficient. Population growth always occurs within a political and economic context, and this context greatly influences the degree to which poor people can adjust to it.

In a similar vein, it is fascinating that many economists recognize that famines do not result mainly from an absolute scarcity of food, but from the inability of some groups—usually the poorest groups—to gain access to food. There also is increasing recognition that "development" ought to be measured by more than "income" and ought to mean more than "material affluence." (See "Other Voices.")

The combination of population growth and increasing land concentration is doubly devastating. Even if they manage to hang on to their land, the poor will get poorer if their numbers grow. If their increased poverty makes it necessary for them to borrow from the wealthy, to sell part of their land to raise cash, or to work for low wages

The inequality explanation holds that the global economy allocates food-producing resources on the basis of profit and ability to pay rather than on the needs of the poor. Where will the coffee harvested by this Colombian man go, and who will profit from its production and sale?

to make ends meet, they are likely to grow poorer still. This "double crunch" is precisely the experience of the rural poor in many LDCs.

Is Technology Transfer the Answer?

One commonly proposed solution for world hunger is to apply modern scientific know-how and technology to areas in which agriculture is still technologically underdeveloped. This solution seems simple: Thanks to agricultural machinery, plant breeding, modern fertilizers, pest control methods, advances in irrigation technology, genetic engineering, and so on, the developed countries have solved the nutrition problem for most of their people. We have developed science and technology and

Other Voices

What Is Development?

When we think of development, we almost invariably think in terms of economic development. To us economic development of a country, a state, or a region is easily measured; it is a matter of dollars and cents. We need only to look at the GNP (Gross National Product) or the per capita incomes. If we compare countries in terms of their growth of GNP, then we can determine which are the most economically successful. If we compare per capita incomes, we can determine the relative prosperity of the countries, states, or regions. However, are the gross production figures the only—or even the best—measure of development? Are per capita incomes the best measure of the standard of living of the society? Not everyone thinks so.

The Nobel prize-winning economist Amartya Sen argues that growth in the GNP alone is not a particularly good indicator of development. As a child in India he lived through the great famine of 1943 during which three million people died. Perhaps not surprisingly one of his interests as an economist is in famines. In his study of famines he discovered that famines were not solely or even primarily the result of food shortages. What he discovered was that famines are frequently the result of market forces which increase the cost of food while depressing incomes to the point that families can no longer purchase adequate food. Just as famines are not necessarily the result of food shortages, the growth in the GNP of a country does not in itself result in increased prosperity. The GNP of a country might be growing with little economic benefit to many if not most of the people.

Sen also questions how we measure the standard of living of a people. Is it merely a question of relative income? The Indian state of Kerala is an excellent example that per capita income figures alone are not always the best measure of quality of life. Covering only 24,000 square miles along the southwest coast of India, Kerala is home to thirty-three million people. Depending primarily upon agriculture, Kerala is a poor state, even by Indian standards. In terms of GDP (Gross Domestic Product), Kerala averages only about $1,000 per capita, $200 less than India as a whole, and only 1/26 of that of the United States. By such economic measures alone, residents of Kerala would appear to have a poor standard of living. However, if we look at Kerala in terms of health, education, and other social issues, Kerala presents a far different picture.

In terms of health, the people of Kerala are better off than most other peoples in India and in countries with far higher incomes. Their infant mortality rate is among the lowest in the developing world. Their life expectancy is seventy-two years, eleven years longer than the average for India, and only four years shorter than the United States.

Even more impressive are their achievements in education. Well-maintained schools are scattered throughout the state, and education is virtually universal. As a result 90 percent of the people are literate—an achievement that places Kerala on the same level as the far more prosperous peoples of Spain and Singapore.

Social discrimination is less of a problem than in other parts of India and most of the world. Protests against the caste system began in Kerala in the middle of the nineteenth century, and in no other part of India has this system been so expunged from social consciousness. Although there are sizable Muslim and Christian minorities in the state, there have not been the religious conflicts that have beset most of India.

However, possibly the major factor which distinguishes Kerala from other parts of India and most parts of the world is its relative equality in income and opportunity. In the 1960s the state government abolished landlordism, and redistributed the land to 1.5 million tenant families. Kerala also has a relatively high minimum wage. This wage has discouraged industrial development and as a result Kerala has an unemployment rate of 25 percent. However, since most families have land on which they can garden, they are shielded from destitution.

Sen argues that the purpose of development is to raise the standard of living of the people, and that standard of living cannot be measured in monetary terms alone. Thus, development must take into account not only incomes, but the relative distribution of wealth, educational levels, health standards, and the level of social discrimination. Kerala serves as an example of more balanced development; the people of Kerala are, as Akash Kapur has said, "poor but prosperous."

Sources: Sen (1984, 1987) and Kapur (1998).

---

applied it to agriculture. The LDCs need only adopt our know-how and technology to solve their hunger problems. In this view, the main thing hungry countries need is a transfer of our food production technology.

There are many problems with the **technology transfer solution**. We can touch on only a few. First, many of the methods developed for application in temperate climates fail miserably when transported to the tropics, where most hungry people live. This is largely because of the profound differences between tropical and temperate soils and climates.

Second, many experts doubt that so-called high-tech solutions to food problems are appropriate to economic conditions in the LDCs. Labor is much more available than capital in these nations, so to substitute technology (machinery, herbicides, artificial fertilizers, etc.) for labor is to waste a plentiful factor of production in favor of a scarce one. Besides, those who need to increase production the most—the poorest farmers—are those who can least afford new technology. And borrowing money for new investments involves risks because many small farmers who borrow from rich landowners lose their land if they default.

Third, new technologies often come as a package deal. For instance, new crop varieties usually require large amounts of water, pesticides, and fertilizers to do well. Small farmers must adopt the whole expensive package for success. The expense, combined with the logistics of long-term supply of each element of the package in countries with uncertain transportation and political regimes, makes many farmers wary of innovations. Further, many new high-yielding varieties of crops are hybrids, which means that farmers cannot select next year's seeds from this year's harvest. Rather, they must purchase their seeds every year from large companies, many of which operate internationally. Is it a good idea to make the world's farmers dependent on a few suppliers of genetic material for their crops?

Fourth, agricultural experts from the developed world often report problems of "resistance" by peasant farmers. Sometimes peasants cling tenaciously to their traditional crops, varieties, and methods of cultivation even when genuine improvements are made available to them. This famed cultural conservatism of peasants seems downright irrational to many technical experts.

But some anthropologists who have conducted village-level fieldwork offer an alternative interpretation of peasant resistance to change. Living in intimate contact with local people, fieldworkers sometimes are able to perceive problems the way peasants do. Subsistence farmers barely feeding their families cannot afford to drop below the minimum level of food production it takes to survive. Traditional crops and varieties give some yield even when uncontrollable environmental forces are unfavorable because over the generations they have adapted to local fluctuations of climate, disease, and pests. The new ones might not fare as well. Because the consequences of crop failure are severer for poor subsistence farmers than for well-off commercial farmers, they minimize risks by using tried and true crop varieties and methods. Peasant cultural conservatism thus may be a sound strategy, given the conditions of peasant lives.

Finally, the technology that some believe it wise to transfer to other parts of the world may not be as effective or as efficient as they think. Modern mechanized agriculture requires a large amount of energy to produce its high yields. Studies done in the 1970s suggest that on modern commercial farms in the United States, on average about one calorie of energy is required to produce about two calories of food. The "energy subsidy" to agriculture goes into producing and running tractors, harvesters, irrigation facilities, chemical fertilizers, herbicides, pesticides, and other inputs. The payoff for this energy subsidy is enormously high yields, both in terms of yields per acre and yields per farm worker. But in traditional agricultural systems, for every calorie of energy expended in agricultural production, about fifteen to fifty calories of food energy are returned (the amount depends, of course, on local conditions, cultivation methods, crop type, and a multitude of other factors). The main reason why traditional agriculture is so much more efficient in terms of energy is that human labor energy, supplemented by the muscle energy of draft animals, is the major energy input.

Many questions follow from this difference in energy subsidy. Is there enough energy for modern mechanized agricultural methods to be widely adopted around the world? If there is, can the rural poor of the Third World afford them? What will happen if the rural poor have to compete on a local level with the well-off farmers who can afford to purchase and maintain the new technologies? What will be the local and global environmental consequences of agricultural mechanization on such a large scale? The worldwide price of oil is low in the year 2000, but what will happen to it if tens or hundreds of millions of additional farmers mechanize their operations? Can such methods be used indefinitely—are they ecologically sustainable?

We raise such questions not because the answers are obvious. Some experts—mainly, economists—believe that the new problems new technologies create will be solved by even newer technologies. Others say it is too risky to count on a future of uncertain technological salvation, and the consequences of being wrong are too severe to do so. Some believe that whatever future scarcities of energy or other resources occur will stimulate the search for alternative sources, so that the free market will save us. Others claim that we are near the limits of our planet to produce affordable food and other products.

To point out that technology transfers are not economically or ecologically feasible for many regions is not to say that modern food-producing methods are always harmful or should not even be considered as solutions for world hunger. It merely points out that mechanized technologies have problems of their own and that "experts" do not have all the answers. Are there other solutions that avoid or minimize some of the problems with transfers of technology? Some agricultural scientists, anthropologists, and other scholars are researching alternative methods of boosting food production—methods that are productive and sustainable, yet avoid some of the high

Mechanical harvesters and other fuel-powered farm equipment make mechanized agriculture enormously productive in terms of land and labor. But machinery, artificial fertilizers, chemical herbicides and pesticides, and other inputs require large amounts of energy. What would be the consequences of relying on such technology on a global level?

energy requirements and the problems associated with mechanized agriculture.

Agricultural Alternatives

Since the early 1980s, increasing numbers of agricultural scientists have been taking another look at traditional farming practices, that is, methods of cultivating the soil that have been used for decades or centuries by the people living in a particular region. In the past, technical experts in agricultural development often scorned traditional farming methods, which they viewed as inefficient and overly labor intensive. But today there is increasing awareness of the benefits of traditional methods.

This awareness stems partly from the failure of so many agricultural development programs for the Third World. It also stems from the environmental movement that began in the developed countries in the 1970s, which called attention to the negative environmental impacts of mechanized agriculture. In addition to the high energy requirements of mechanized agriculture previously discussed, some farming practices commonly used in the developed countries cause environmental problems. Such problems include water pollution from fertilizer runoff, poisoning of farm workers and wildlife from agricultural chemicals, soil erosion from failure to rotate crops, and increasing resistance of insects because of exclusive reliance on pesticides.

In addition to negative environmental impacts, technologies such as machinery, pesticides, herbicides, and fungicides are too expensive for many traditional farmers.

Sometimes they are inappropriate or uneconomic to use on the small plots that are characteristic of farms in many parts of the world. They may be unfamiliar to local people, who understandably are reluctant to abandon proven cultivation methods for alternatives they perceive to be riskier.

Considerations such as these led some agricultural scientists in the 1980s to ask, Are there *viable* alternatives to mechanized agricultural technologies and practices? Some experts believe that there are. The main goals of such alternatives are minimization of negative environmental impacts, affordability to small farmers, reliance on technologies and resources that are locally available, adaptation to local environmental conditions, and long-term sustainability.

Over the centuries, traditional farming systems have evolved that meet many of these goals. Increasingly, agricultural scientists and development agencies look at traditional agriculture not as a system that should be replaced but as a set of farming techniques that they can learn from. Much research on this topic is ongoing; here we can present brief descriptions of only two traditional methods: intercropping and resource management.

Intercropping   One method used by traditional farmers in many parts of the world (in the tropics especially) is intercropping, also known as multiple cropping or polyculture. In contrast to monoculture, intercropping involves the intermingling of numerous crops in a single plot or field. It has been practiced for centuries by shifting cultivators, whose plots usually contain dozens of crops and varieties.

Although intercropped fields look untidy, this method offers several benefits, stemming from the diversity of crops growing together in a relatively small space. Many plant diseases and pests attack only one or a few crops, so if there is a diversity of crops, yields may still be good despite an outbreak. In regions where water supply is a problem and rainfall is erratic, some crops suffer during droughts but others will still produce a harvest. The varying growth patterns and root structures of diverse crops have useful ecological benefits: Erosion is low because more of the soil is covered, and sun-loving weeds are suppressed by the shade of the crops themselves.

Traditional farmers in some parts of the world have learned over the centuries that many crops grow better when planted together. Leguminous crops, such as beans, peas, and peanuts, take nitrogen (a necessary plant nutrient) from the air and store it in their roots. Intercropping legumes with crops that need lots of nitrogen can increase yields. This is done in Mexico and Central America, where traditional farmers have long intercropped corn, beans, and squash. The stout corn plants provide support for the bean vines to climb, and the ground-hugging squash plants keep the soil covered. African farmers intercrop sorghum with peanuts and millet with cowpea with similar benefits.

Traditional Resource Management Practices In many parts of the world, traditional farmers actively take steps to control the plant species growing in areas that, to outsiders, look "wild" or "abandoned." They are, in other words, managing their resources so they can continue to use them indefinitely. Two brief examples illustrate these management practices.

The Kayapó of the Xingu river basin of Brazil farm in the forest by shifting cultivation. According to anthropologist Darrell Posey, who has worked among the Kayapó for years, the Kayapó manage the forest carefully. One of their traditional practices is the creation of "islands" of forest in deforested areas. They move composted soil made from termite and ant nests and vegetation into open areas and transplant crops and other useful plants. The created and managed environment provides plant foods, medicines, and building materials and attracts some of the animals hunted by the Kayapó.

The Lacandon Maya of the state of Chiapas in southern Mexico practice slash-and-burn. Although the staple crop is corn, many other crops are planted in the cleared fields, including several tree species that yield fruits. Lacandon farmers clear and plant new plots frequently, but they do not simply abandon a plot once its main crops are harvested. Rather, they return to it for many years to harvest the long-lived fruit trees and other species they planted. Even while the natural forest is regrowing, the Lacandon continue to make use of the land. They manage their fallowing fields and thus integrate their exploitation of the land with the natural process of forest regeneration.

We have presented some of the reasons many scientists and others concerned with agricultural development are reconsidering traditional agriculture. It is all too easy to romanticize traditional farmers, to think that they really have had the answers all along and that only recently have so-called experts been forced to pay attention. This view, too, is simplistic: In all likelihood, solutions to the food crisis will require a mixture of traditional and modern technologies. It is, however, encouraging that the knowledge and methods embedded in traditional agricultural adaptations are being taken seriously by the World Bank and other institutions in a position to make critical decisions.

The Uses of Fieldwork: Two Studies

Aside from contributing insights on global problems, anthropological ways of looking at and studying people

and cultures are useful in specific projects intended to benefit particular local communities. Most commonly, the role of applied anthropologists in such projects is to provide information relevant to project design and implementation. We conduct surveys, do interviews, and use participant observation methods to find out what local people are thinking and doing. Our hope is that such information will be incorporated into the planning and application of the project.

Two case studies illustrate some of the contributions made by applied anthropologists to local-level projects.

Planting Trees in Haiti

One well-documented project that succeeded partly as a result of the involvement of anthropologists was a 1980s tree-planting program in Haiti. Haiti makes up the western third of the island of Hispaniola, a mountainous and formerly heavily forested Caribbean island. Haiti acquired its independence in 1804, after a bloody revolution by enslaved Africans against France. Haitian numbers increased over the past two centuries, and in 1995 there were nearly seven million Haitians living in a land area slightly larger than the state of Maryland. Haiti has Port-au-Prince (its capital) and several other cities, but about two-thirds of its people are peasants who make their living by a combination of subsistence farming, small-scale market sale of crops and other products, and some wage labor.

Because of population growth, the lack of alternative economic opportunities, and other factors, the Haitian landscape is severely deforested and eroded. In the 1970s, the United States Agency for International Development (USAID), a federal agency, funded a tree-planting program to reforest the countryside. The program failed to achieve its reforestation goals. Haitians refused to plant the seedlings, or they allowed their goats to eat them, or they uprooted them from their land to make room for subsistence or market crops. A report written for AID by an economist led officials to believe that the main reason for peasant "resistance" to tree planting was their lack of clear ownership over the land they were using. Haitians could not be expected to go to the work of planting and protecting trees to prevent erosion until they could be confident that the land belonged to them—or so AID officials believed.

AID asked anthropologist Gerald Murray, who had recently studied Haitian land tenure, for his views on whether lack of secure ownership was the reason Haitians did not respond to the program. Murray reported that, in fact, Haitian land ownership was more secure than AID experts believed. He went on to advise that the problems lay in the project's own defects, not in Haitian land tenure or agricultural and livestock practices. Murray joked that using his ethnographic knowledge of the Haitian peasantry, he could get more trees planted with a jeep and $50,000 than AID's multimillion-dollar project.

Ultimately, AID offered him the job of directing a new tree-planting project, funded at $4 million. Using his anthropological training and ethnographic experience with the Haitian people, Murray designed and implemented an Agroforestry Outreach Project (AOP) that avoided the flaws in previous programs and took Haitian economic and cultural conditions into account.

Murray realized that one reason previous projects failed was because they required peasants to set aside some of their scarce, valuable land for soil conservation purposes. Understandably, poor farmers were reluctant to sacrifice today's cropland in return for the uncertain future ecological benefits of forests. Murray's plan was to present the project to peasants in a different way. It would not emphasize the long-term environmental benefits of trees, but the more immediate economic advantage to individual peasants and their families. People needed to be shown that having trees on their land would enhance, not threaten, their economic welfare.

Further, from his experience in Haiti, Murray knew that many peasants thought the trees they planted in previous projects belonged to the government, not to themselves (a belief unwittingly encouraged by officials of previous projects). He realized that more trees would be planted if the program clearly identified the peasants as the exclusive owners of the trees and allowed them to choose whether to keep or uproot them. The project also allowed the farmers to receive the full economic benefits: They could sell the trees for building materials, make the wood into charcoal, or do whatever they wished with them. A program that allowed peasant control over trees and that offered cash benefits to individuals and their families would have a better chance of success.

The AOP worked in the following way. Realizing the widespread peasant mistrust of the national government, Murray bypassed the bureaucracy by setting up a network that reached into local communities. At the village level, there were local volunteers who advertised the project and explained how it would work. They compiled lists of families who wished to participate and informed project officials how many trees were needed and when they should be planted. Each farmer received 500 seedlings, which were provided and transported to their village free of charge. The farmers themselves planted the trees and were not paid for doing so, for they were told that the trees were theirs to do with as they wished: They could uproot them, cut the wood and sell it, leave them on their land for erosion control, or feed their leaves to goats. If, however, they uprooted the seedlings they would not receive any more from the project.

Careful selection of tree species was necessary for the trees to be beneficial, and hence for news of the program to spread. Their wood would have to be marketable to make the cash benefits apparent to people. The AOP distributed tree species that were useful for both charcoal and construction and could be sold to city-dwellers as cooking fuel or building materials. The trees chosen were so fast-growing that they would be ready to use after only four or five years, so peasants would not have to wait long for the rewards. The trees could be interplanted with existing crops, taking up very little space in the fields, so they would be well integrated into existing farming practices and have minimal impact on work patterns or farm productivity. Peasants who participated in the program were shown how to plant trees around field borders and to space them in such a way that other crops were not overly shaded. They were shown that the cash they could earn from selling the wood or charcoal would more than offset the small losses from reduced food production on their land.

The AOP was funded between 1981 and 1985. Near the start of the project, Murray nervously told AID officials that he expected 6,000 peasant families to plant three million trees. ("At that time I thought someone else would be directing the project," he wrote.) But peasant response exceeded what Murray feared were his overly optimistic expectations. By only the second year, the goal of three million plantings had been achieved. By the end of the fourth year (when another anthropologist had taken over as director), twenty million trees had been planted by 75,000 peasants. As expected, by the end of the fourth year, many peasants were harvesting trees to sell as wood and charcoal. But Murray was surprised at how many peasants were not cutting the wood, but leaving the trees growing on their land as a hedge against possible future crop failure. Given the high urban demand for tree products, many farmers were saving the trees so they could sell the wood in case of economic emergency.

How did anthropological involvement contribute to the success of the AOP? There are several specific contributions.

Ethnographic knowledge. From his previous experience as a fieldworker, Murray knew about peasant interest in cash-cropping, was familiar with farming and livestock practices, and was aware of the great demand for wood products in a deforested land. He writes: "Ethnographic knowledge of Haitian peasant land tenure—-which is highly individualistic—guided me away from the community forest schemes that so many development philosophers seem to delight in but that are completely inappropriate to the social reality of Caribbean peasantries" (Murray 1987:237).

Speaking more generally, anthropologists often work *firsthand* among people and in communities about which development specialists know little. The deep immersion into a community and the close personal relationships needed for effective fieldwork allow anthropologists to become aware of beliefs and behaviors that impinge on the success of projects.

Adaptation to local conditions. The AOP was designed and implemented to fit into what peasant families already were doing with their land. Rather than replacing cropland with treeland, trees were integrated into existing practices, requiring no revolutionary (and risky) changes.

The same lesson is relevant more generally. The relativist outlook of anthropologists makes them more likely to understand why people do what they do. They are less likely to dismiss people's behaviors as backwards or tradition-bound or "irrational," but will seek rational reasons for why people behave as they do. Behavior often makes sense in ways outsiders do not grasp and, at any rate, a knowledge of existing behavior can be of enormous value in a project.

Local involvement. Through the village organizers, the AOP reached into local communities, involving them in decision making about the timing of planting and allowing individual farmers to choose what to do with the trees. People invested their labor and some of their land in the project, and in return became owners of the trees and recipients of their benefits.

Delivering Health Care Services in Swaziland

Swaziland is an independent nation of about 800,000 people in southeastern Africa. As in many regions, parasitic diseases (including cholera and diarrhea) transmitted through drinking and bathing water are major health threats, especially to infants and young children. Children sometimes die from the dehydration resulting from severe diarrhea. Modern biomedicine treats dehydrated children by oral rehydration therapy, which replaces bodily fluids with a drinkable solution that promotes water retention. The treatment is cheap, effective, and easily administered.

In 1981, medical anthropologist Edward Green was hired on a two-year contract as part of a team of researchers on an AID-funded project. One goal of the project was to reduce illness due to waterborne diseases by getting more adults to seek oral rehydration therapy for their children.

Green's role originally was to carry out a survey on Swazi water use and sanitation practices. The survey would rely on structured interviews using a precoded questionnaire administered to random samples of individuals. Green's anthropological training led him to believe that such a methodology, while useful for certain purposes, had limitations when applied to local communities who had good reason to be suspicious of outsiders, espe-

cially when sensitive questions were asked. Prior to designing and administering the questionnaire, Green proposed to carry out a more informal study of Swazi health beliefs and medical practices. He used the ethnographic methods of participant observation accompanied by interviews of key informants.

Swazi communities have traditional healers to whom people turn to for treatment of illnesses. Green decided that knowing and interviewing healers would be a good way to learn about local cultural beliefs about diseases, their causes, and their treatment. He worked firsthand with 144 Swazi healers and some of their patients. He and his research assistants learned that healers believed that some diseases were "African" and therefore treatable only by indigenous African methods of healing. Most diseases were seen as caused ultimately by sorcery or loss of protection by one's ancestors. Other illnesses—a smaller number—were "foreign" and treatable by Western medicine. Healers referred their patients to modern medical clinics for treatment of diseases they considered "foreign," such as cholera.

Most healers classified diarrhea as an African disease—one for which Western medicine was inappropriate and ineffective. Swazi healers reported that most infant diarrheal diseases come from one of three causes, none of which include transmission of human fecal matter through drinking or bathing water. One of the more serious types of diarrhea is said to be caused by airborne smoke or vapors that people breathe into their bodies. In addition to traditional herbal medicines, healers administer enemas to drain out the bad air in the belly making the person sick—which further dehydrates the infant and aggravates rather than relieves the disease. Mothers—who among Swazi are the primary caregivers of infants—nearly always take their infants to traditional healers prior to going to a modern biomedical clinic. Mothers also give their babies herbal medicines and enemas, which actually promote diarrhea and add to dehydration.

At this point, most modern health professionals will bemoan the ignorance and superstition of Swazi, especially of "witch doctors" (healers). According to Green (1994:240), some local medical doctors "took the view that healers should be arrested for practicing medicine without a license."

Green recognized that the issue was far more complex. Many treatments administered by healers are medically effective. Swazi patients often sought treatment at both modern clinics and in the homestead of healers, and the latter did help relieve psychosomatic illnesses and resolve social problems. Healers were fairly influential people, and seeking their cooperation in treating diarrheal diseases would encourage others to seek oral rehydration therapy. Finally, the field study administered by Green found that there was only one physician per

10,000 Swazi, but there was a traditional healer for every 110 persons.

For these reasons, Green recommended that traditional healers be integrated into a medical program. Rather than denying the validity of Swazi beliefs—and risk alienating them—those parts of traditional knowledge that are compatible with modern biomedicine could be built upon. For example, Swazi believed that adequate intake of fluid, especially breast milk, is necessary to maintain a baby's strength. With Green's input, the Swaziland Ministry of Health organized workshops at which healers and mothers were trained to administer oral rehydration therapy as well as treatments for other illnesses.

This case study illustrates how anthropological knowledge of the customs and beliefs of a community can be used to make a program more successful. Green and his co-researchers took the trouble to find out about Swazi medical beliefs and the importance of traditional healers, using standard anthropological fieldwork methods. A way was found to deliver medical treatment working within the context of local beliefs and using indigenous healers with whom people were already familiar.

This chapter has illustrated some of the ways in which anthropological ideas and methods can aid in solving human problems. Many cultural groups in the world today are faced with the ultimate human problem: the survival of themselves as a people and of their cultural traditions. We end *Humanity* in the next chapter with a consideration of the survival of indigenous people.

Summary

This chapter summarizes some of the insights anthropologists have provided on world problems. Anthropological expertise is useful for the solution of human problems because the way anthropologists look at people and cultures (our "world view") differs somewhat from that of other professionals. Applied anthropologists have done research relevant to both global and local-level problems.

Two global problems are population growth and world hunger. Today's high rates of worldwide population growth are caused mainly by advances in medicine and vaccines and by widespread improvements in public health facilities. These advances have reduced death rates and increased life spans in most countries, but in underdeveloped regions birthrates are still relatively high.

Population growth has many unfavorable consequences. It contributes to serious environmental problems, low economic productivity, urban sprawl and shantytowns, political conflicts, and even war. This is the main paradox of population growth: The high fertility of a country's citizens is mainly responsible for it, yet their high fertility contributes to many of their nation's problems.

But having many children is not a simple product of ignorance or irrational cultural conservatism. The fertility rate is a response to the overall economic conditions in a region or country. This is shown by how North American couples choose how many children to have. Our low fertility is a rational response of couples to the conditions of their personal lives. In deciding how many children they want, most modern couples consider the personal, not the societal, costs and benefits of children.

High fertility in the LDCs likewise is a consequence of the overall economic and social environment that constrains reproductive behavior. Ethnographic studies suggest that children are a net economic asset rather than a liability in the rural areas of the Third World. Children are productive family members at a young age. They seek jobs with local people, supplementing the family income. When older, they go to the cities or to foreign countries and send money back home. They provide old-age security for their parents. Under such conditions, high fertility exists because large families are beneficial.

Population growth often is believed to be the major cause of world hunger. This is the scarcity explanation of hunger, which holds that overpopulation results in chronic malnutrition and periodic massive starvation. The alternative is the inequality explanation. It holds that land and other food-producing resources are in fact sufficient to provide an adequate diet for the whole world. Hunger is caused by the way local and world economies allocate resources—on the basis of ability to pay rather than need. Durham's study of El Salvador illustrates that the two explanations are compatible: Population growth contributes to hunger by increasing the scarcity of food production resources, yet prevalent inequalities in access to productive resources aggravate the scarcity and prevent people from adjusting to it.

Technology transfer is a viable solution to hunger in the LDCs, according to many. But there are numerous problems with this solution. Temperate agricultural methods often do not work well in tropical climates and soils. New technologies sometimes harm rather than help the poorest families. Peasants often do not adopt new technologies and crop varieties because they perceive them not worth the costs, or because they cannot afford to assume the risks of failure. Mechanized agriculture requires so much energy to produce food that it may not be affordable to Third World farmers, and may not be sustainable in the long run.

For such reasons, agricultural scientists, anthropologists, and others have been researching alternative methods that have long been used by the traditional farmers of the world. Traditional methods such as intercropping

and resource management hold promise for increasing food production sustainably. It is likely that a combination of solutions will be necessary to alleviate problems of hunger and poverty.

Besides providing insights on global problems, applied anthropologists work on local-level projects. Their main role is to provide information on local communities that is useful in designing and implementing projects. Two cases illustrating the uses of applied anthropology are a tree planting project in Haiti and a program for delivering health care services in Swaziland.

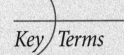

Key Terms

scarcity explanation of hunger
inequality explanation of hunger

technology transfer solution

Suggested Readings

Bodley, John H. *Anthropology and Contemporary Human Problems*. 3rd ed. Mountain View, Calif.: Mayfield, 1996.
• *A good place to start in glimpsing the relevance of anthropology to modern problems. Provides insights on war, poverty and hunger, population, and environmental destruction.*

Foster, Phillips, and Howard D. Leathers. *The World Food Problem*. 2nd ed. Boulder: Lynne Rienner Publishers, 1998.
• *Covers technical information on undernutrition and discusses some of its causes. Also has a lengthy section on policy issues.*

Franke, Richard W., and Barbara H. Chasin. *Seeds of Famine: Ecological Destruction and the Development Dilemma in the West African Sahel*. Montclair, N.J.: Allanheld, Osmun, 1980.
• *A well-documented study of the Sahelian drought and famine, arguing that planners and the international economy were as much responsible as natural disasters.*

Harris, Marvin, and Eric B. Ross. *Death, Sex, and Fertility: Population Regulation in Preindustrial and Developing Societies*. New York: Columbia, 1987.
• *Two noted anthropologists argue that fertility and other population characteristics of human groups result from material forces. People at various points in history have suc-*

cessfully controlled (regulated) their numbers. An excellent place to start for an overview of the relation between population, adaptation, and culture.

Howard, Mary, and Ann Millard. *Hunger and Shame: Childhood Malnutrition and Poverty on Mt. Kilimanjaro*. New York: Routledge, 1997.
• *Excellent, readable case study of child hunger and poverty among the Chagga, a Tanzanian people. Combines authors' analysis with original narratives of Chagga families in a particularly effective way.*

Lappé, Frances Moore, and Joseph Collins. *Food First: Beyond the Myth of Scarcity*. New York: Ballantine, 1977.

Lappé, Frances Moore, Joseph Collins, and Peter Rosset. *World Hunger: Twelve Myths*. 2nd ed. New York: Grove, 1998.
• *Two books that argue against the scarcity explanation of hunger and provide evidence and analysts in favor of the inequality explanation.*

Pimentel, David, and Marcia Pimentel. *Food, Energy and Society*. New York: Wiley, 1979.
• *A study of the energy requirements of producing various crops, livestock, and fish in the United States. Processing and transportation energy uses are also estimated.*

Podolefsky, Aaron, and Peter J. Brown. *Applying Cultural Anthropology: An Introductory Reader*. 4th ed. Mountain View, Calif.: Mayfield, 1999.
• *Contains 41 articles on the applications of cultural anthropology. A good source of case studies for students.*

Internet Exercises

The Society for Applied Anthropology's website contains information about applied anthropology, links to other sites, and a section with working papers (http://www.acs.oakland.edu/~dow/anthap.html). Another site dealing with applied anthropology is "The Bureau of Applied Research in Anthropology" from the University of Arizona (http://wacky.ccit.arizona.Edu/~bara/new0001.html).

As you read in this chapter, anthropologists have in increasing numbers begun to apply their anthropological training to solving human problems. There is little opposition within anthropology to the idea of getting involved in problem solving or in policy making, but there is much debate about exactly what roles anthropologists should play. Cultural Survival is a group formed by anthropologists at Harvard in 1972 which acts as an advocate for indigenous rights (this topic is discussed more in Chapter 19). The Cultural Survival website (http://www.cs.org) contains information on the projects the organization is involved with and also includes a section called "Active Voices," an online activist forum. This forum has articles that discuss issues related to applied anthropology.

CHAPTER 19

The Survival of Indigenous Peoples

Indigenous Peoples Today

Vanishing Knowledge

Medicines We Have Learned

Adaptive Wisdom

Cultural Alternatives

In the past, untold millions of indigenous peoples perished from their encounters with more powerful peoples. This is an 1885 photo of the Ona, a people who formerly inhabited Tierra del Fuego at the tip of South America. The last Ona died in 1974. Indigenous peoples and their cultures continue to be threatened by outside forces today.

Visit http://www.wadsworth.com/humanity to learn more about the material covered in this chapter and to access activities, exercises, and tutorial quizzes.

*I*N THIS BOOK *we have emphasized the cultural diversity of humanity, for in our view the description and analysis of such diversity is the hallmark of anthropology. Most anthropologists agree that the survival of human cultural diversity is a desirable goal, although we disagree on the terms and content of cultural survival. Certainly, there are fewer distinct cultural groups in existence today than there were in 1500, 1800, or even 1950. If these trends continue, in the twenty-first century, there will be even fewer culturally distinct human populations.*

WE CONCLUDE Humanity by discussing the survival of indigenous cultures. We cover some of the main reasons why such cultures are endangered today, and why it may be important for them to survive in the future. We end the book by advocating the rights of indigenous peoples to preserve their cultural systems—assuming, of course, that is their choice.

Indigenous Peoples Today

Indigenous may be used to refer to any people who have resided in a region for many centuries. By this definition, the Germans of Germany and the Irish of Ireland are indigenous. However, as **indigenous peoples** usually is used today, the phrase refers to "culturally distinct groups that have occupied a region longer than other immigrant or colonist groups" (*Cultural Survival Quarterly,* Spring 1992, 73). Generally, indigenous peoples are small-scale human societies who make their living by foraging, farming, and/or herding, live in roughly the same region as their ancestors, and are fairly remote from the economic and political centers of the nations which include their territory. Sometimes they are termed "tribal" peoples, or more recently "Fourth World" peoples. In most cases, they occupy the most isolated and inaccessible regions of their nation and the world. Often their territories cross modern national boundaries.

Indigenous people most often survive as ethnic enclaves within a larger nation. The government controlled by the dominant ethnic group of these nations usually claims to have ultimate control over the land and other resources of the indigenous people who live within the officially recognized national borders. For many indigenous peoples, in effect, the colonial world still exists. Lacking effective political autonomy and being too few to make physical resistance successful, their remaining lands are constantly threatened by the wider society. Too often their ways of life are destroyed because more numerous and powerful ethnic groups consider indigenous cultures barriers to national progress and development.

Altogether, there are perhaps 600 million indigenous peoples in the modern world. Among them are the Native American peoples of North, Central, and South America; the aboriginal peoples of Australia and other islands of the Pacific; the Sami (formerly known as the Lapps) and other reindeer-herding peoples of northern Europe and Asia; hundreds of "tribal" cultures of east Asia, southeast Asia, and south Asia; and numerous ethnic groups of Africa.

The legal rights of indigenous peoples became an issue with Columbus' landfall in the Americas. Questions of whether the native peoples of the Americas—or for that matter any indigenous people—had any inherent rights to their land, resources, or political autonomy were debated in Spain. Although legal particulars differed from one colonial power to another as well as over time, a basic consensus was reached early in the colonial period. An indigenous people did have some rights based on prior occupancy. However, more "civilized" peoples could unilaterally claim jurisdiction over them and make use of any land and resources that were either not utilized or underutilized. Civilized peoples had both a right and an obligation to uplift indigenous peoples and act in their "best interest." This responsibility came to be called the white man's burden. Civilized peoples also had the right to travel and trade wherever they wanted without interference from indigenous peoples. Finally, if an indigenous people resisted, then the civilized people had the right to use military force against them. These attitudes were well expressed by a colonial official in German Southwest Africa in justifying the Herero War of 1904, in which more than 100,000 Herero died:

> The native tribes must withdraw from the lands on which they have pastured their cattle and so let the White man pasture his cattle on these self-same lands. If the moral right of this standpoint is questioned, the answer is that for people of the cultural standard of the South African Natives, the loss of their free national barbarism and the development of a class of workers in the service of and dependent on the Whites is primarily a law of existence in the highest degree. For a people as for an individual, an existence appears to be justified in the degree that it is useful in the progress of general development. By no argument in the world can it be shown that the preservation of any degree of national independence, national prosperity and political organization by the races of South West Africa would be of greater or even of equal advantage for the development of mankind in general or the German people in particular than that these races should be made serviceable in the enjoyment of their former territories by the White race (quoted in Bodley 1982:55).

As this quotation illustrates, racism, ethnocentrism, and social Darwinist ideas about the inevitability and desirability of progress provided the moral justification for the treatment of indigenous peoples.

Such attitudes and policies affected the governing of most indigenous peoples in the colonial possession of European nations. When independence came to Asian and African countries in the twentieth century, the leaders and dominant ethnic groups of many of the new nations adopted similar attitudes and policies. As discussed in Chapters 16 and 17, the modern boundaries of most existing countries are legacies of European colonization in the sixteenth through the early twentieth centuries. In many cases, the political and legal systems of these countries are also Western-derived or heavily Western-influenced. Such attitudes, governmental policies, and legal concepts often are the basis for the treatment of indigenous peoples and other ethnic groups within a

"An Indian Welcome on the Charles River," reads the caption on this print. Encounters between Native Americans and Euro-Americans after Columbus' "discovery" led to the biological extinction, relocation, or cultural assimilation of most indigenous peoples of the New World.

Third World nation itself. In fact, if one wants to understand what is happening to most remaining indigenous peoples in the world today, one can start by reexamining American Indian policy during the nineteenth and early twentieth centuries. In Brazil, Indonesia, the Sudan, and elsewhere, the same introduction of new diseases, genocide, relocation, forced assimilation, and appropriation of land and resources of smaller indigenous groups by politically dominant ethnic groups is taking place.

Modern governments in parts of Latin America, Africa, and Asia face serious economic, political, and social problems. Many governments—including those democratically elected—are under pressure from their dominant ethnic group to pursue policies that lead to the displacement or assimilation of the indigenous peoples whose territories lie within their national boundaries. In many countries aspiring to modernization, indigenous people living in remote, "undeveloped" regions are forced to move aside in the interest of what the dominant ethnic group sees as the "greater good" of their nation.

Sometimes this greater good consists of opening up undeveloped areas to settlers. For example, Indonesia resettles peasants from overpopulated Java onto its outer islands, now claimed to be "underpopulated." Although often considered a modernized nation, Brazil has some of

the poorest people in the world living in its northeastern area. It also is one of the few countries left with a frontier—the vast tropical rain forest of Amazonia. In the 1970s, Brazil constructed highways intended to open up Amazonia to resettlement and to mineral, timber, grazing, and agricultural exploitation. One-third of Brazil's Native American tribes have disappeared since 1900, and many others have lost most of their lands to outsiders.

One people who are threatened by the opening up of Brazil's Amazonian frontier is the Yąnomamö, mentioned in Chapters 2 and 8. Until the early 1970s, most of the approximately 9,000 Yąnomamö were relatively isolated from outside influences. In 1974, the Brazilian government constructed a road through the southern part of Yąnomamö territory. Workers involved in forest clearing and road building introduced new diseases such as influenza and measles, and in some regions as many as one-half the Yąnomamö died during epidemics. Dirt airstrips constructed during the 1980s also made Indian

The physical and cultural survival of the Yąnomamö and other Amazonian peoples is threatened by the opening up of their traditional lands to mining, logging, ranching, and other extractive industries.

territory accessible to Brazilian gold prospectors. In the late 1980s thousands of gold seekers—most of them impoverished—poured into the area in search of wealth. By early 1990, as many as 45,000 prospectors had invaded traditional Yąnomamö lands and extracted gold worth an estimated one billion dollars.

The government's National Indian Foundation is charged to protect Brazil's Native American peoples and territories from invasion and plunder, but it has been unable to control violence against the Yąnomamö and other indigenous groups. In 1990, Brazil's former President ordered the landing strips destroyed to reduce future access, but by 1996 miners had returned to Yąnomamö lands. The Yąnomamö have already lost rights to two-thirds of their Brazilian territory, and deaths caused by violence and disease are likely to continue.

Another common justification for the neglect of the territorial rights of indigenous peoples is the desire to improve a country's balance of trade. The Philippines, Indonesia, and other countries earn foreign exchange by leasing rights to harvest timber from their tropical hardwood forests to multinational companies, although much of the "unexploited" forest is needed as fallow by indigenous shifting cultivators. Debts owed to foreign banks

and international lending agencies encourage some nations to open up their hinterlands to resource development, pushing their indigenous inhabitants aside. In countries such as Brazil and Mexico, minerals, cattle, timber, vegetables, coffee, and other exports are sold to Europe and North America to earn foreign exchange to help pay off international debts.

Many indigenous communities are affected adversely by the efforts of well-meaning people to promote environmental causes such as habitat preservation or animal conservation. For some, preservation and conservation of biological resources is interpreted to mean "no resource exploitation" or, in extreme cases, even "no people." Governments of nations with large indigenous populations sometimes react to such concerns by resettling people out of areas they have lived in for centuries. (An irony is worth pointing out here: Often the areas deemed appropriate for conservation or preservation efforts are those that are recognized as relatively undisturbed—partly because it is mainly the indigenous peoples who have been using them all along!)

Within the southern African nation of Botswana lies the Central Kalahari Game Reserve (CKGR), which is the second largest game reserve in all Africa. The CKGR was established in 1961, partly to provide the indigenous hunter-gatherers of the region—the San (see Chapter 6 for information on the !Kung, one of several local San groups)—with adequate resources for their subsistence needs. In the 1960s and 1970s, local groups of San used the territory for subsistence foraging, sometimes on horseback. In the 1980s, some environmentalists tried to persuade the European Union to pressure Botswana officials to remove the people from the CKGR and declare the area a game reserve. By the 1990s, the remaining San were encouraged to move outside the reserve by various methods, including failure to repair a needed well, intimidation by selective enforcement of game laws, and (allegedly) severe physical punishments of accused "poachers."

Then, in 1997, the government of Botswana resettled several hundred San outside the boundaries of the reserve, placing them in an environment with few trees and wild plant foods and offering them very little compensation. This action was taken partly in the name of conservation. But San argued that increasing numbers of tourists in four-wheel drive vehicles were destroying the land and that more cattle were on the reserve. According to an article by Robert Hitchcock (1999:54) in the journal *Cultural Survival Quarterly,* the San "expressed that the reason they were being removed was so that well-to-do private citizens could set up lucrative safari camps in the reserve." Perhaps environmentalists in North America and Western Europe also should give more consideration to impacts on the welfare of indigenous peoples when they propose to save wildlife or preserve ecosystems.

As these and numerous other cases show, many still consider it legitimate to take land from those who have lived on it for centuries. Racism and social Darwinism are not as fashionable official justifications as they once were. But new rationalizations exist for the forced removal and exploitation of the territories of indigenous peoples: "developing" natural resources for the benefit of the country; solving "national problems" by providing lands to peasants and making payments on debts owed to foreign banks and international lending institutions; making the country's products "competitive" in international markets; and even "preserving" animal habitats and eco-systems.

The indigenous people who remain in cultural communities are learning to protect themselves through political action. In increasing numbers, indigenous peoples around the world are fighting attempts to dispossess them of their traditional territories and resources. Many are resisting efforts to assimilate them into the cultural mainstream of their nations. They are publicly objecting to racist and ethnocentric attitudes about their beliefs and customs.

One people who are resisting are the Kayapó. In the 1980s, the government of Brazil sought World Bank funding for the construction of two enormous hydroelectric dams on Amazon River tributaries. Eighty-five percent of the land that would have been flooded belongs to one or another indigenous Indian population. Organized by leaders of the Kayapó tribe, members of twenty-nine Brazilian Indian groups protested the dams. In early 1988, two Kayapó leaders traveled to Washington with anthropologist Darrell Posey to speak against the project to officials of the World Bank and to U.S. congressional authorities. When the World Bank deferred action on the loans, Brazil brought charges against the three protesters under a law that forbids "foreigners" from engaging in political activity harmful to the nation. The courage and sophistication of the Kayapó and other members of threatened communities illustrate how indigenous peoples are organizing themselves to acquire the political power to fight various "developments."

Outside of Great Britain the entire English-speaking world was once populated by preindustrial peoples who died from disease and violence, were displaced, or became assimilated by colonists. In the past couple of decades, indigenous peoples in Australia, New Zealand, Canada, and the United States have asserted claims for territories and resources lost to Anglo settlers. In 1996, a New Zealand tribunal found in favor of the claim of the indigenous Maori that a sacred volcano was illegally taken by the British in the last century. Canada's First Nations are pressing their claims for lands and for compensation for lands illegally taken. The Nisga'a of British Columbia are one of forty-four native groups negotiating with the provincial and national governments for return of territories and compensation for past injustices. Native Americans in Alaska, Washington, and Oregon are involved in disputes with government agencies over whaling and salmon fishing rights. Indigenous people in many regions also are attempting to reclaim their past, leading to great controversies in academic circles (see "A Closer Look").

Vanishing Knowledge

Despite the increased political sophistication of indigenous peoples around the world and the protests of concerned citizens in many countries, there is no doubt that many preindustrial cultures are in danger of extinction. Even if the people themselves survive the onslaughts of lumbering, mining, damming, grazing, farming, and building, their way of life is liable to disappear. Most people would agree that genocide is a crime of the highest degree. But destruction or alteration of a culture is another matter—is it not possible that indigenous people themselves would be better off if they joined the cultural mainstream of their nations?

Yes, many peoples do want to acquire formal education, get jobs, improve their living standards, and generally "modernize" their societies. For many peoples and for many individuals within an indigenous culture,

A CLOSER LOOK

Reclaiming the Past

In November 1995, the All-Apache Culture Committee, a group representing the Apachean tribes, claimed exclusive control over all things relating to the Apachean peoples: culture, history, and all popular as well as intellectual materials. The head of the group stated that "it has implications for historians, for people who might write stories about us," since the group demands that anyone wishing to write about the Apaches will henceforth have to gain permission from the tribes.

Over the past two decades, Afrocentrism has grown in popularity in part of the American academic community. Usually involving African American scholars, Afrocentrism is a reinterpretation of history from an African perspective. Many of the historical interpretations presented by Afrocentrists contradict those accepted by the academic community in general.

The claims of the Apachean tribes and the works of Afrocentrists are reflections of one aspect of dewesternization taking place in the world today. Similar assertions are being made by indigenous and/or minority peoples throughout the Neo-Europes of the Americas and the Pacific. To understand the issue, one has first to realize that groups like Native Americans and African Americans lack cultural and intellectual autonomy. In their daily lives they see the same movies and TV programs, read the same books, magazines, and newspapers, and are exposed to the same commercial advertisements as everyone else in the society. American popular culture and its

portrayal of American Indian and African American life, past and present, help create and model these groups' view of themselves. In public schools, colleges, and universities, as children and adults, they are exposed to the same academic teaching concerning Native Americans and African Americans as are all other students. Native Americans and African Americans historically have had little influence on either American popular culture or academic teaching. As with other culturally dependent peoples, the popular and academic images and beliefs concerning them are controlled and manipulated by others, in this case by Western (Euro-American) film producers, writers, and scholars.

History is "political." People use the past to justify and rationalize the present. History is the core component in the creation of one's ethnic identity. History does not consist only of facts, but of interpretations as well. By selectively giving certain events greater importance than others, by accepting some interpretations as valid while ignoring others, ethnic groups can and do mold their past to fit the social and cultural needs of the present. These historical beliefs become disseminated through popular culture and canonized by academic scholarship.

Native Americans and African Americans are among those peoples of the world who still lack any meaningful influence over the interpretation of their past. African American and Native American identities and histories have been

and are being created and interpreted by Euro-Americans. This is not to say that these identities and histories are necessarily derogatory, demeaning, or factually inaccurate. However, they have been constructed and interpreted to conform to prevailing Euro-American beliefs. Often, they are extensions of the general Euro-American ethnic myth. No people can enhance and maintain their own feelings of self-worth and value without the freedom to construct their own past.

The recent histories of Western peoples (Europeans and Euro-Americans), Africans, African Americans, and Native Americans overlap. Western scholars dominate the academic world, and their interpretations of shared past events reflect Western beliefs. As non-Western scholars, whether African, African American, Native American, Native Australian, or others, begin to study their own pasts and interpret events from their own ethnic and cultural perspectives, contradictory interpretations are inevitable. History is one component of a peoples' cultural knowledge. As such, it is subject to the same cultural relativistic perspectives as any other aspect of culture. It is to be expected that different groups of people will have at times very different beliefs about their history and interpretations of their shared past. The critical question is whether the existing Western-dominated academic world can accept challenges to long-held beliefs about history and accommodate contradictory "truths" about the past.

contact with the wider world offers new opportunities and new choices. Young people especially are attracted by the material goods, entertainments, new experiences, and sheer variety of activities found in towns and cities. They should have these opportunities and these choices. But indigenous peoples and their ways of life often are overwhelmed by forces over which they have no control. It is not that most indigenous peoples are given the

opportunity to carefully weigh the options available to them, so that they make informed choices about whether it is best for them to preserve or to modernize their ways of life. Today, as in the past, their traditions are disappearing more often because powerful national governments want to open up their territory or because private entrepreneurs or corporations want to exploit their resources.

Anthropologists are especially concerned with the rights of indigenous peoples for several reasons. First, because of our interest in cultural diversity, we are more aware of what has happened to non-Western cultures in the past several centuries than are most people. Second, we identify with indigenous peoples partly because so many of us have worked among them. Third, our professional training gives us a relativistic outlook on the many ways of being human, so we can appreciate other peoples' customs and beliefs as viable alternatives to our own. Finally, the fieldwork experience often affects our attitudes about our own societies—deep immersion into other cultural traditions leaves some of us not so sure about our commitment to our own.

Whether one is an anthropologist or not, one can appreciate the rights of any group of people to have their lives, property, and resources secure from domination by powerful outsiders. The most important factors in considering the rights of indigenous peoples to be left alone are ethical ones. Do not people everywhere have the right to live their lives free from the unwanted interference of those more powerful and wealthy than themselves? Does any government, regardless of its "problems," have the right to dispossess people from land they have lived on and used for centuries? Is the demand of citizens in Japan, Europe, North America, or anywhere else for wood, minerals, meat, electricity, or other products a sufficient justification for relocating a people or taking land away from them? (Our American readers who follow politicians' statements about human rights violations in Iran, Iraq, China, Bosnia, Kosovo, and other countries might wonder why they have so little to say about the rights of indigenous peoples.)

Surely, most of us agree on the answers to such questions. Ethical concerns for the human rights of indigenous peoples, combined with a respect for their cultural traditions, are the primary reasons for granting their rights to survive as living communities.

But if the ethical arguments alone (based on shared values about human rights) are not compelling, there are other arguments (based on practical concerns, and even on the self-interest of the dominant majority). The long-term welfare of all humanity may be jeopardized by the loss of cultural diversity on our planet.

Think about the cultural heritage of humanity as a whole. Consider *all* the knowledge accumulated by *all* humanity over hundreds of generations. Imagine, in other words, Human Culture—here defined as the sum of all knowledge stored in the cultural traditions of all humans alive today.

Some of the knowledge existing in present-day Human Culture has been widely disseminated in the past few centuries by means of written language. We may call it *global knowledge* (not meaning to imply that it is "true" or "universally known"). Although some global knowledge will be lost or replaced, much of the knowledge stored in writing (or, more recently, on computer disks) will be preserved and added to over the coming decades and centuries.

Other knowledge comprising Human Culture is *local knowledge*—it is stored only in the heads of members of particular cultures, many of which are endangered. Most local knowledge will disappear if those cultural traditions disappear—even if the people themselves survive.

How much of this local knowledge is knowledge that may (today, tomorrow, someday) prove useful to all humanity? Of course, no one knows. But no one can doubt that the rest of the world has much to learn from indigenous cultures. (Incidentally, anthropologists have always understood the importance of learning *about* other cultures; recently, there has been increasing emphasis placed on learning *from* them.) In fact, much of what was in the past only the local knowledge of some indigenous culture has been incorporated into global knowledge, as a consequence of contact with the West and other colonizing people. We conclude this book with a small sample of some of the medical and adaptive wisdom of indigenous people, whose local knowledge has already contributed so much to the world.

Medicines We Have Learned

"The Medicine Man Will See You Now," proclaimed a headline in a 1993 edition of *Business Week*. The accompanying article described a California pharmaceutical company that sends ethnobotanists and other scientists into rain forests to learn from indigenous shamans. Companies as well as scholars are beginning understand that the traditional remedies long used by preindustrial peoples often have genuine medical value. In fact, many of the important drugs in use today were derived from indigenous knowledge.

Here we can only provide a few examples of the medicines originally discovered by indigenous peoples that now have worldwide significance. An enjoyable source of more examples is the 1993 book *Tales of a Shaman's Apprentice,* by Mark Plotkin.

Malaria remains a debilitating, although usually not fatal, sickness in tropical and subtropical regions. Its main treatment is quinine, a component of the bark of the cinchona tree. Europeans in the seventeenth century learned of the value of quinine from Peruvian Indians.

The Madagascaran periwinkle has long been used in folk medicine to treat diabetes. Researchers first became

Indigenous peoples, such as these Indonesian "medicine men," commonly have an extensive and potentially important knowledge of the curative powers of plants. How much medical knowledge of healers in indigenous cultures will be lost?

interested in the plant as a substitute for oral insulin, but it seems to have little value for this purpose. However, during the course of their investigation, scientists discovered that extracts from periwinkle yielded dramatic successes in treating childhood leukemia, Hodgkin's disease, and some other cancers. Drugs based on the plant—notably vincristine and vinblastine—remain the major treatments for these otherwise fatal diseases.

Muscle relaxants are important drugs to surgeons. A popular one is curare, made from the chondodendron tree. Taken in large amounts, curare can paralyze the respiratory organs and lead to death. This property was recognized by South American Indians, who used it as arrow poison for hunting birds, monkeys, and other game, and from whom medical science learned of the drug's value.

The ancient Greeks and several North American Indian tribes used the bark of willows for relief from pain and fever. In the nineteenth century, scientists succeeded in artificially synthesizing the compound that today we call *aspirin*.

There is no way of knowing how many plants used by surviving indigenous peoples could prove to be medically effective. The potential is great. According to pharmacologist Norman Farnsworth, about one-fourth of all prescribed drugs in the United States contain active ingredients extracted from higher plants. The world contains more than 250,000 species of higher plants. Although as many as 40,000 of these plants may have medical or nutritional values that are undiscovered by science, only about 1,100 of these have been well studied. Botanists and medical researchers are coming to realize that indigenous peoples already have discovered, through centuries of trial and error, that certain plants are effective remedies for local diseases. The future value of their medical wisdom to all of humanity is largely unknown, but probably great.

Adaptive Wisdom

Many preindustrial peoples have lived in and exploited their natural environments for centuries. Over their history, they have selected those crops and varieties that grow and yield well in the conditions of their local habitat. They have learned to control insect pests and diseases that attack the plants on which they depend, and to do so without the need for expensive and often dangerous artificial chemicals. They often have learned how to make nature work for them with minimum deterioration of their environments. They have, in short, incorporated much adaptive wisdom into their cultural traditions.

Following are a few possible benefits that all humanity might gain by preserving the ecological knowledge of indigenous peoples.

Preservation of Crop Varieties In all cultivation systems, natural selection operates in the farmers' fields. Like wild plants, crops are subject to drought, disease, insects, and other natural elements, which select for the survival of individual plants best adapted to withstand these hazards. In addition, crops are subject to human selection. For example, crop varieties most susceptible to drought or local diseases are harvested in smaller quantities than drought- and disease-resistant varieties. Perhaps without knowing it, the cultivator replants mainly those varieties best adapted to survive the onslaughts of drought and local diseases. This "tuning" of plant varieties to the local environment, with all its hazards and fluctuations, goes on automatically so long as the crops harvested from the fields are replanted in the same area. Thanks to the unintentional and intentional selection by hundreds of generations of indigenous cultivators around the world, each species of crop (e.g., beans, potatoes, wheat) evolved a large number of *land races,* or distinct varieties adapted to local conditions.

Over the course of human history, several thousand species of plants have been used for food but less than a hundred of these were ever domesticated. Of all the plants that have been domesticated, today only a handful provide significant amounts of food for the world's people. In fact, a mere four crops—wheat, rice, maize, and potato—provide almost one-half the world's total consumption of food.

Since around 1950, plant geneticists and agricultural scientists have developed new varieties of wheat, corn, rice, and potatoes that are capable of giving higher yields if they receive proper amounts of water and fertilizers. These new strains were developed by crossing and recrossing native land races collected from all over the world. The aim was to achieve a "green revolution" that would end world hunger by increasing production. Many new varieties are hybrids, which means that farmers must receive a new supply of seeds yearly from government or private sources.

Ironically, having been bred from the genetic material present in their diverse ancestors, the new strains now threaten to drive their ancestors to extinction. As the seeds of artificially bred varieties are planted by farmers in Asia, Africa, and the Americas, the traditional varieties—the land races that are the product of generations of natural and human selection—fall into disuse and many have disappeared.

Why should we care? Increasingly, agricultural experts are realizing the dangers of dependence on a few varieties. If crops that are nearly identical genetically are planted in the same area year after year, a new variety of pest or disease eventually will evolve to attack them. The famous Irish potato famine of the 1840s was directly related to the genetic uniformity of the potato because all the potatoes in Ireland were apparently descended from only a few plants. More than a million people died as a result of the potato blight, and a million more immigrated to North America. The United States has also suffered serious economic losses: The corn blight of 1970 destroyed about 15 percent of the American crop. Losses would have been less severe had most American farmers not planted a single variety of corn.

Many plant breeders are alarmed at the prospect of losing much of the genetic diversity of domesticated plants. Today they are searching remote regions for surviving land races that contain genes that one day might prove valuable. (The seeds are stored in seed banks for future study.) They have been well rewarded—although no one knows how much of the genetic diversity of crops such as wheat and corn has already disappeared.

The knowledge of indigenous peoples is an important resource in the effort to preserve land races. In many parts of the world—the Andes, Central America, Amazonia, the Middle East, and elsewhere—cultivators still grow ancient varieties of crops. They know where these varieties yield best, how to plant and care for them, how to prepare them for eating, and so on. In the Andes, for instance, hundreds of potato varieties survive among the Quechua Indians as a legacy of the Inca civilization. Many have specific ecological requirements, and some are even unique to a single valley. Research is now under way to determine how well specific land races will grow in other areas, to help solve food supply problems elsewhere. It is important to preserve the genetic information encoded in these varieties for future generations. Indigenous peoples who still retain the hard-won knowledge of their ancestors and who still use the often-maligned "traditional crop varieties" are important informational resources in the effort to save the genetic diversity of crops on which humanity depends.

"Undiscovered" Useful Species   In addition to their familiarity with local crop varieties with potential worldwide significance, many indigenous peoples cultivate or use crop species that currently are unimportant to the rest of the world. One example is amaranth, a grain native to the Americas that was of great importance to the Indians in prehistoric times. The great Mesoamerican civilizations made extensive use of the plant in their religious rituals. This led the Spanish conquerors, in their anxiety to root out heathenism, to burn fields of amaranth and prohibit its consumption. Otherwise, it—like maize, potatoes, beans, squash, and other American crops—might have diffused to other continents. Amaranth remains an important food to some indigenous peoples of highland Latin America, who retain knowledge of its properties and requirements. Its unusually high protein content might someday make it valuable to the rest of the world.

Other plants used by native peoples have the potential to become important elsewhere. Quinoa, now grown mainly in Peruvian valleys, has twice the protein content of corn and has long been recognized as a domesticate with great potential. The tepary bean, now grown mainly by the O'odham of the American Southwest, can survive and yield well under conditions of extreme drought, which might make it cultivable in other arid regions of the world. Another legume, the winged bean, has long been cultivated by the native peoples of Papua New Guinea, and it has helped nourish people in fifty other tropical countries.

Humans use plants for more than food. Indigenous peoples have discovered many other uses for the plants found in their habitats. Scientific researchers today are attesting to the validity of much native knowledge about the use of plants as sources of fuel, oils, medicines, and other beneficial substances, including poisons. Forest peoples of Southeast Asia use the toxic roots of a local woody climbing plant as a fish poison. The root is so powerful that a mixture of 1 part root to 300,000 parts water will

A CLOSER LOOK

Amish Communities in North America

Amish cultural roots lie in Switzerland, where their sect broke off from the Anabaptist movement in 1693. Persecuted and martyred in Europe because of their practices of shunning and foot-washing, many Amish migrated to the Americas in the 1700s and early 1800s. Their original settlements were in Pennsylvania, but population growth led the Amish to migrate and establish new communities in Ohio, Indiana, Illinois, Wisconsin, and adjacent states, as well as in the province of Ontario. Measured by numerical increase and geographical spread, the Amish have done well in the New World.

Amish believe they should live by certain values, four of which are most relevant here. First, their culture emphasizes humility and submission to the will of the community over individualism and personal freedom. Pride is one of their major sins. The community "will" is expressed by its religious leaders (bishops, ministers, and deacons), who often make hard decisions whether to allow or prohibit the adoption of some new technology or practice. Second, Amish prefer simplicity of living to the achievement of self-gratification by unneeded consumption. Clothing styles and jewelry that beautify personal appearance and celebrate the self are looked down on. Amish consider themselves "plain people." Third, they believe that the scriptures mandate equality in the eyes of God, and they dislike marked differences in levels of economic consumption within their communities. Farm sizes should be limited to the acreage that can be worked by a family using equipment that is (literally) horsepowered. Fourth, Amish think that work itself is virtuous. Work builds character, keeping the mind and body away from frivolous concerns, and community cooperation in projects helps tie the group together. Tools and other devices that save too much labor (that are "too handy") are unwelcome.

These and other values contrast to the individualism, self-gratification, competitiveness, materialism, future-orientation, and other values that Amish see as characteristic of the surrounding society: Like people everywhere, Amish have fun, but many activities such as dancing, joyriding, movie- and TV-watching, and alcohol drinking are too "worldly" and are considered sinful, as is divorce and the use of artificial birth control. Amish who participate in such activities or who persistently fail to uphold Amish values may be excommunicated and shunned until they repent.

Aside from shunning, two main practices of the Amish set them apart from other Christian sects. First, Amish believe that maintaining the purity of their values and religious beliefs requires that, insofar as possible, they keep themselves separate from the influence of the wider North American population (whom they often call "English"). For economic reasons alone, Amish cannot cut themselves off completely from the American "mainstream," but they do attempt to restrict interaction with the outside world. Amish do various things to maintain their separateness. They converse among themselves using an old German dialect. They forbid television and radios, out of concern that access to mass media will corrupt their values. They discourage travel outside the immediate area except for economic necessity, for fear it will expose people to worldly influences and weaken community ties. Amish children are not educated beyond the eighth grade "basics" (most communities have their own schools taught by Amish), both because this level is all Amish consider necessary for their way of life and because children will learn things that might weaken their faith.

Second, over the decades Amish leaders have decided that many new technologies threaten their "plain" way of life, and so Amish are not allowed to own and use many things the "English" consider conveniences. But, contrary to what many outsiders believe, Amish are not restricted to nineteenth-century technologies. In fact, many kinds of modern things are allowed in their communities. For discussion purposes, the restricted and allowed items may be classified into three categories: transportation, household, and farming technology.

TRANSPORTATION Amish are well known for their horse-and-buggy travel. (Indeed, in areas with large Amish populations, there are signs warning motorists of their presence on the highways.) Amish are not allowed to own or drive cars, not to have driver's licenses. However, Amish can ride in cars driven by non-Amish for certain purposes, including business necessity, visiting distant relatives, and travel to medical facilities and auctions.

HOUSEHOLD Bishops in most Amish communities have outlawed the hookup of Amish households to 110 volt electricity carried by public power lines. Leaders feel that connections to public power sources will lead to undue dependence on the outside. Also, the prohibition prevents family access to television and other mass media. Families cannot own household conveniences powered by 110 volt electrical current, such as lights, stoves, and refrigerators. On the other hand, most church districts allow access to other sources of power, including propane, kerosene, electrical current that comes from batteries, and electrical power that is generated by family-owned generators. For example, light bulbs are prohibited, but homes do have gas lanterns, and kerosene refrigerators and propane stoves are allowed and widely used.

FARMING TECHNOLOGY Some modern farm machinery is not allowed, or can only be used for certain purposes. Amish farmers are not allowed to take self-propelled tractors into their fields to plow, harvest, or do other field tasks. However, they can use tractors with gasoline engines to blow silage in the barn, to power hydraulic systems used for tools, and to spin ventilation fans. Farmers also are allowed to take mechanical corn binders, hay balers, and some other kinds of gasoline-powered equipment into their fields, provided that the equipment is pulled by horses rather than self-propelled.

These specific technologies are only a sample. Many "English" and other outsiders are puzzled by the restrictions and allowances. To the mainstream, allowing some things in while keeping similar things out seems curious, and in some cases even hypocritical. Amish can ride in cars for normatively approved visits, emergencies, and work, but cannot own or drive them. What's the reason? Their neighborhoods are likely to have a public telephone or two located in a place where several families have access to it, yet Amish cannot have private phones in their homes. Why? Amish prohibit electric stoves and refrigerators, yet propane stoves and kerosene refrigerators are okay. What's the difference? Amish can use engines in their barns and even in their fields when the equipment is pulled by horses, but the use of engines to propel farm machinery is not allowed. What's the logic?

Sociologist Donald B. Kraybill has conducted extensive research on just such questions. He found that the Amish have to reconcile two opposing objectives. First, the continued viability of their communities requires that they maintain their economic welfare in a changing world. But, second, they must do so with minimal impact on the purity of their religion, their values, and their community integrity. Amish leaders have to walk a fine line. On the one hand, continued economic viability requires that certain technologies and practices be adopted. On the other hand, wholesale adoption of the same technologies and practices might unravel their way of life. The combinations of restrictions and allowances previously discussed are explained as compromises between the need to change and the desire to stay the same.

Amish ownership of automobiles provides a good illustration. Cars are handy for transportation—too handy for the

Seeing Amish riding in their buggies, many North Americans think they reject modern technologies. In fact, they selectively incorporate technologies such as phones and certain farm equipment, which allows them to keep their living standards acceptably high while preserving their religious beliefs and community life. Do Amish provide "English" North Americans with a viable cultural alternative?

Amish. The freedom and speed of movement cars offer would take people out of the neighborhood (perhaps into cities) and expose them to worldly things (such as movies). In addition to their practical use as vehicles, car ownership has social and cultural implications. Private ownership of cars would promote individualism and independence from the community. Soon, more well-to-do families would buy and drive nicer cars and begin using them as status symbols, threatening Amish egalitarian values. Finally, car ownership threatens the use of horses and buggies, which are a key symbol of Amish identity and a visible mark of their separation.

At one time, car use as well as ownership was banned. But after World War II, Amish increasingly began using cars. Communities grew and budded off into new communities that lived too far away for horse and buggy, so non-Amish drivers were hired to take people to funerals, weddings, barn raisings, and the like. In the 1970s, more and more Amish found it impossible to make a living by farming, and some started their own businesses in carpentry, cabinet making, retailing, and, more recently, tourism. Other Amish have jobs in the dairy and

other industries (work in factories is prohibited). Transportation to and from the business or job site is required, and many businesses hire cars on a regular basis, leading to the emergence of "Amish taxis" driven by non-Amish. So, under changed economic conditions, the use of cars has become almost a necessity. But Amish avoid much of the negative impact of cars on their traditions by continuing to ban their ownership.

Similar considerations apply to farm machinery. The use of some farm machinery in fields is essential for high productivity, but making it mandatory to propel machines by horses keeps farms small-scale and family-run. It also ensures the continuance of the tradition of calling on one's neighbors to help with harvest and other labor-intensive operations. Self-propelled, rubber-wheeled tractors could be too easily used to transport people off the farm, partially substituting for the forbidden car and further undermining the horse.

Banning private telephones but allowing community phones also makes sense as a compromise. Private phones threaten the face-to-face interaction and visiting essential for community cohesion. They

Continued

Continued

allow the possibility of too-easy access to the outside, threatening worldly influences. Incoming calls—as non-Amish know all too well—disrupt family life and studies. Community phones, however, have always been allowed, for they are essential for things like medical appointments, calls to veterinarians, emergencies, placing business orders, and calling taxis. Today, neighbors often share the expense of installing a phone shanty to place and receive calls for such purposes. Kraybill

(1990, 69) writes: "The Amish have asserted their control over the phone by keeping it at a distance. . . . [They] have agreed to use the phone on their own terms, in ways that bolster their economic well-being and in collective ways that enhance the community. It is not permitted to foster individualism or indiscreet interaction with the outside world."

In these ways, Amish communities have kept most of their religious traditions intact while selectively incorporating those new technologies that are

needed to keep their living standards relatively high. Because of the compromises leaders have made with modern technologies, most people (roughly four out of five) who are born Amish choose ultimately to remain Amish. Amish culture is in little immediate danger of becoming assimilated by the "English." Indeed, perhaps the cultural mainstream can learn much from the Amish.

Sources: Hostetler and Huntington (1992); Kraybill (1989, 1990).

---

kill fish. From the indigenous tribes, scientists learned of the toxicity of these roots, which allowed them to isolate the rotenoid that now is used as an insecticide spray for plants and as dips and dusting powders for livestock.

Scientists no doubt will rediscover many other useful plants that today they know nothing about—if the tropical forests in which most endangered plant species are found last long enough. Their task will be easier if the original discoverers—indigenous peoples—are around to teach them what their ancestors learned.

Cultural Alternatives

There is another kind of practical lesson we might yet learn from surviving indigenous peoples. Industrialized humans have developed technologies that discover, extract, and transform natural resources on a scale undreamed of a century ago. To North Americans and to many other citizens of the developed world, *progress* is almost synonymous with "having more things." Yet whether our economies can continue to produce ever-increasing supplies of goods is questionable. Many of us are frightened by the thought that economic growth might not continue. The fear that we will be forced to accept a stagnation or even a decline in our levels of material consumption no doubt contributes to the interest today's undergraduates have in careers that they believe are most likely to earn high incomes for themselves and their future families.

On the other hand, some individuals and groups in the affluent, developed world have questioned the value of what most of their fellow citizens call "economic progress." They feel that the environmental and familial costs of the unceasing drive to accumulate and to succeed in a highly competitive environment are not worth the

benefits. Some of them believe that material affluence cannot bring happiness because it is gained at the high cost of the emotional gratifications that spring from community relationships, from supportive family and friendship ties, and adherence to what some call spiritual values.

Amish communities in Canada and the United States are one such people. They have thrived and expanded in the twentieth century even as they have kept the modern world at arm's length. Amish seem to be able to balance the benefits of technologies against their costs, accepting what is necessary for economic well-being while rejecting what they fear will erode their values and lead to conflict in their communities. (See "A Closer Look" for a discussion of how Amish leaders balance the costs and benefits of new technologies.) Perhaps it is the presence of a viable and satisfying cultural alternative in our very midst that explains why so many mainstream North Americans have become so interested in the Amish.

Most readers of this book are the beneficiaries of economic progress. At the same time we should be careful not to become the victims of the mentality of progress—of that unceasing desire to earn more, to have more, to succeed more. If the industrial bubble does not burst in our lifetime, most of us who live in the developed world will spend our lives in continuous effort to increase our consumption of goods. We will do so despite the fact that we can never catch up with the Joneses because there will always be other Joneses whom we have not yet caught. We will do so despite the fact that our efforts will never be sufficient to get us all we want because no one can consume goods as fast as companies can turn them out and advertisers can create new desires for them. We will do so despite the fact that many of our marriages and families will be torn apart by the effort and many of us will suffer psychologically and physically from stress-related disorders. Sadly, most of us pursue our dollars and goods unthinkingly because we remain ignorant of any alternative way of living.

The world's remaining indigenous peoples provide us with such alternatives. They do not and did not live in a primitive paradise. Subjugation of neighboring peoples, exploitation by the wealthy and powerful, degradation of women, warfare, and other ideas and practices many of us find abhorrent existed among some pre-industrial peoples, just as they do today. Yet we also find other cultural conditions that some of us long to recover: closer family ties, greater self-sufficiency, smaller communities, more personal and enduring social relations, and "more humane," "more moral" values. No anthropologist can tell you whether life is better or worse in pre-industrial communities; indeed, we cannot agree on the meaning of *better*. We do know that humanity is diverse. We know that this diversity means that human beings—ourselves included—have many alternative ways of living meaningful and satisfying lives. In the end, it is these cultural alternatives provided by indigenous peoples that might have the greatest value to humankind.

Perhaps a people themselves are the only ones qualified to judge the quality of their lives, to decide what it will take to lend meaning and dignity to their existence. We hope to have convinced you that there are many ways of being human. We hope you have learned to appreciate some of the alternative ways of living experienced by various human populations. We hope you will agree that some of these alternatives are worth preserving, both in their own right and for the long-term well-being of all humanity.

Summary

As European influences and industrial economies swept the world during the past few centuries, the lives of indigenous peoples were dramatically altered. Many groups have disappeared altogether because of deliberate genocide or introduced diseases. Many others are threatened with relocation, reduction of their traditional lands and resources, and loss of their cultural autonomy through assimilation.

As a result of these and other pressures, the cultures of many surviving preindustrial peoples are in danger of destruction. Ethical considerations alone are a sufficient reason these peoples should be allowed to remain in their communities, on their traditional lands, living in the ways of their ancestors, if that is their choice. Pragmatic considerations also are important because these people still retain a vast body of knowledge—knowledge that is of great potential value to all humanity.

Science already has adapted several important medicines and treatments from indigenous peoples. Many other plants with medical value probably will be discovered, if the tropical forests and the cultural knowledge of their indigenous inhabitants last long enough.

Adaptive wisdom is also to be found in the traditions of indigenous peoples. Land races of important crops still survive and might contain genetic materials from which useful foods might someday be bred. Crops that today are used primarily by indigenous peoples—such as amaranth, quinoa, tepary bean, and the winged bean—might eventually have worldwide significance. Nonfood plants used by indigenes are also important as insecticides, oils, fibers, and other products.

Finally, indigenous people provide us with alternative cultural models that should reduce our anxieties about the likelihood of eventual decline in our material living standards. The diversity of the human species shows that we can live meaningful and wholly satisfying lives in the future without the technologies and huge quantities of consumer goods we now consider necessary to our economic welfare. The remaining preindustrial cultures allow us to see that there is more than one narrow road to personal fulfillment, cultural health, and national dignity and prestige.

Key Term

indigenous peoples

Suggested Readings

Bodley, John. *Victims of Progress*. 4th ed. Palo Alto, Calif.: Mayfield, 1999.

- *A good overview of tribal peoples in the modern world and how they are being destroyed by industrial civilization.*

Chalk, Frank, and Kurt Jonassohn. *The History and Sociology of Genocide*. New Haven: Yale University Press, 1990.

- *Comprehensive study of genocide. Describes twenty tragic cases and contains an outstanding bibliography.*

Cultural Survival. *State of the Peoples: A Global Human Rights Report on Societies in Danger*. Boston: Beacon Press, 1993.

- *Together with other publications of the Cultural Survival organization, an excellent source on the threats to indigenous people around the world.*

Davis, Shelton H. *Victims of the Miracle: Development and the Indians of Brazil*. Cambridge: Cambridge University Press, 1977.

- *A study discussing economic development in Brazil and the resulting destruction of Indian communities.*

Denslow, Julie Sloan, and Christine Padoch, eds. *People of the Tropical Rain Forest*. Berkeley: University of California Press, 1988.

- *Written for the general public, this edited work is a broad introduction to both indigenous and recent peoples living in the tropical rain forests of Latin America, Asia, and Africa. Some articles discuss what can be learned from indigenous peoples about developing the forest in a manner that is sustainable.*

Jorgensen, Joseph, ed. *Native Americans and Energy Development II*. Washington, D.C.: Anthropology Resource Center, 1984.

- *An excellent collection of papers examining energy development and American Indian communities.*

Paine, Robert. *Dam a River, Damn a People?* Copenhagen: International Work Group for Indigenous Affairs, 1982.

- *A study discussing the effects of a hydroelectric project in Norway on the indigenous Lapp, or Sami, population.*

Plotkin, Mark J. *Tales of a Shaman's Apprentice*. New York: Penguin, 1993.

- *In part an adventure story of an ethnobotanist, this book describes the author's experiences in the Amazon forest while searching for useful medicines. An interesting place to start for an overview of the medical knowledge of indigenous peoples.*

Scudder, Thayer. *No Place to Go: Effects of Compulsory Relocation on Navajos*. Philadelphia, ISHI, 1982.

- *A study containing a short history of the Navajo-Hopi land dispute, together with a study of the effects of removal on the Navajo families.*

Sponsel, Leslie E., ed. *Indigenous Peoples and the Future of Amazonia*. Tucson: University of Arizona Press, 1995.

- *Articles discussing Amazonian culture and their prospects for survival.*

Suzuki, David, and Peter Knudtson. *Wisdom of the Elders*. New York: Bantam Books, 1992.

- *Lucid (although often romanticized) overview of how preindustrial cultures view nature and their relation to it. Sees many parallels between "scientific" and "native" knowledge of nature.*

Weyler, Rex. *Blood of the Land: The Government and Corporate War Against the American Indian Movement*. New York: Vintage, 1982.

- *A polemical attack on the U.S. and Canadian governments and corporate development of Indian resources.*

Internet Exercises

If you did not look at The Center for World Indigenous Studies website mentioned in Chapter 17, it is also relevant to this chapter (http://www.halcyon.com/FWDP/cwisinfo.html). One of its sections is the Fourth World Institute, where you can find current papers, research, and the "Fourth World Documentation Project" which includes many documents involving indigenous groups worldwide.

Native Web (http://www.nativeweb.org) provides resources on many indigenous groups and issues pertaining to such groups. Another site with information on indigenous peoples is the Australian National University (http://.www.ciolek.com/WWWVL-Aboriginal.html).

A nice site dealing with specific issues, yet that still has links to other sites on indigenous knowledge, environmental diversity, and deforestation, is "Shamanism, Indigenous Knowledge, Medical Anthropology & Borneo" (http://www.geocities.com/RainForest/Vines/7168/).

Glossary

A

accommodation The creation of social and political systems that provide for and support ethnic group differences.

acculturation The cultural changes that occur whenever members of two cultural traditions come into contact.

adaptation Process by which organisms develop physical and behavioral characteristics allowing them to survive and reproduce in their habitats.

aesthetic Qualities that make objects, actions, or language more beautiful or pleasurable, according to culturally relative and variable standards.

affines In-laws, or people related by marriage.

age set association A formally organized and named group including all males and females of about the same age.

ancestral cults A type of communal cult centered around rituals performed to worship or please a kin group's ancestors.

animism Belief in spiritual beings.

anthropological linguistics Subfield that focuses on the interrelationships between language and other aspects of a people's culture.

applied anthropology Subfield whose practitioners use anthropological methods, theories, and concepts to solve practical real-world problems; practitioners often are employed by a government agency or private organization.

archaeology The investigation of past cultures through excavation of material remains.

art Any human action that modifies the utilitarian nature of something for the primary purpose of enhancing its aesthetic qualities; or actions or words that are valued largely for their aesthetic pleasure or symbolic communication.

artificial countries Multinationality countries created by external powers; usually applied to former colonies.

assimilation The merging of the members of one ethnic group into another, with the consequent abandonment of the former group's identity.

authority The recognized right of an individual to command another to act in a particular way; legitimate power.

avunculocal residence Couples live with or near the mother's brother of the husband.

B

balanced reciprocity The exchange of goods considered to have roughly equal value; social purposes usually motivate the exchange.

band A small foraging group with flexible composition that migrates seasonally.

big men Political leaders who do not occupy formal offices and whose leadership is based on influence, not authority.

bilateral kinship Kinship system in which individuals trace their kinship relations equally through both parents.

bilocal residence Postmarital residence is with either the wife's or the husband's parents, according to choice.

biological determinism The idea that biologically (genetically) inherited differences between populations are important influences on cultural differences between them.

body arts Artificial artistic enhancement or beautification of the human body by painting, tattooing, scarification, or other means.

bound morpheme A morpheme attached to a free morpheme to alter its meaning.

brideservice Custom in which a man spends a period of time working for the family of his wife.

bridewealth Custom in which a prospective groom and his relatives are required to transfer goods to the relatives of the bride to validate the marriage.

C

cargo cults Melanesian revitalization movements in which prophets claimed to know secret rituals that would bring wealth (cargo).

caste Stratification system in which membership in a stratum is in theory hereditary, strata are endogamous, and contact or relations between members of different strata are governed by explicit laws, norms, or prohibitions.

chiefdoms Centralized political systems with authority vested in formal, usually hereditary, offices or titles; exchange in such systems is often organized by redistribution.

child-rearing practices Methods by which infants and children are nurtured, supported, and enculturated.

civilization A form of complex society in which many people live in cities.

clan A named unilineal descent group, some of whose members are unable to trace how they are related, but who still believe themselves to be kinfolk.

class System of stratification in which membership in a stratum can theoretically be altered and intermarriage between strata is allowed.

classifications of reality Ways in which the members of a culture divide up the natural and social world into named categories.

cognatic descent Form of descent in which relationships may be traced through both females and males.

cognatic descent group A group of relatives created by the tracing of relationships through both females and males.

communal cults Cults in which the members of a group cooperate in the performance of rituals intended to benefit all.

comparative methods Methods that test hypotheses by systematically comparing elements from many cultures.

comparative perspective The insistence by anthropologists that valid hypotheses and theories about humanity be tested with data from a wide range of cultures.

complex societies Large-scale societies whose features include hierarchical organization, high levels of socioeconomic stratification, crafts and/or occupational specialization, and central places (ceremonial centers, towns, cities); adaptation usually based on intensive agriculture.

composite bands Autonomous (independent) political units consisting of several extended families that live together for most or all of the year.

conflict theory of inequality Theory holding that stratification benefits mainly the upper stratum and is the cause of most social unrest and other conflicts in human societies.

consanguines "Blood" relatives, or people related by birth.

consultant (informant) A member of a society who provides information to a fieldworker, often through formal interviews or surveys.

controlled historical comparisons A methodology for testing a hypothesis using historic changes in societies.

court legal systems Systems in which authority for settling disputes and punishing crimes is formally vested in a single individual or group.

courts of regulation Court systems that use codified laws, with formally prescribed rights, duties, and sanctions.

cross-cultural comparisons A methodology for testing a hypothesis using a sample of societies drawn from around the world.

cross cousins Offspring of siblings of different sex.

Crow kinship terms Associated with matrilineal descent; in this system paternal cross cousins are called father or father's sister, while maternal cross cousins are called son or daughter if ego is a male, and niece or nephew if ego is a female.

cultivation Planting, caring for, and harvesting domesticated plants.

cultural anthropology (ethnology) The subfield that studies the way of life of contemporary and historically recent human populations.

cultural construction of gender The idea that the characteristics a people attribute to males and females are culturally, not biologically, determined.

cultural identity The cultural tradition a group of people recognize as their own; the shared customs and beliefs that define how a group sees itself as distinctive.

cultural integration The interrelationships between the various components (elements, subsystems) of a cultural system.

cultural knowledge Information, skills, attitudes, conceptions, beliefs, values, and other mental components of culture that people socially learn during enculturation.

cultural relativism The notion that one should not judge the behavior of other peoples using the standards of one's own culture.

cultural universals Elements of culture that exist in all known human groups or societies.

culture (as used in this text) The socially transmitted knowledge and behavior shared by some group of people.

culture shock The feeling of uncertainty and anxiety in individual experiences when placed in a strange cultural setting.

D

descent The tracing of kinship relationships back to previous generations.

descent group A group whose members believe themselves to be descended from a common ancestor.

dialect A regional or subcultural variant of a language.

diffusion The spread or transmission of cultural elements from one people to another.

domestic group Individuals, usually relatives, who reside together in a single household.

domestication The process by which people control the distribution, abundance, and biological features of certain plants and animals, in order to increase their usefulness to humans.

dowry Custom in which the family of a woman transfers property or wealth to her upon her marriage.

dry land gardening A type of horticulture in which aridity is the major problem that cultivators face.

E

ecclesiastical cults Highly organized cults in which a full-time priesthood performs rituals believed to benefit believers or the whole society; occur in complex societies.

egalitarian society Form of society in which there is little inequality in access to culturally valued rewards.

enculturation The transmission (by means of social learning) of cultural knowledge to the next generation.

endogamous rules Marriage rules requiring individuals to marry some member of their own social group or category.

Eskimo kinship terms In this system mother's and father's siblings are called aunt and uncle, while their children are called cousins. English kinship terminology is of the Eskimo type.

ethnic boundary markers Any overt characteristics that can be used to indicate ethnic group membership.

ethnic group A named social group based on perceptions of shared ancestry, cultural traditions, and common history that culturally distinguish that group from other groups.

ethnic homogenization The attempt to create a single ethnic group in a particular geographical region.

ethnocentrism The attitude or opinion that the morals, values, and customs of one's own culture are superior to those of other peoples.

ethnogenesis The creation of a new ethnic group identity.

ethnographic fieldwork Collection of information from living people about their way of life; see fieldwork.

ethnographic methods Research methodologies used to describe a contemporary or historically recent culture.

ethnography A written description of the way of life of some human population.

ethnohistoric research The study of past cultures using written accounts and other documents.

ethnohistory See ethnohistoric research.

ethnology The study of human cultures from a comparative perspective; often used as a synonym for cultural anthropology.

exogamous rules Marriage rules prohibiting individuals to marry a member of their own social group or category.

extended family A group of related nuclear families.

extended household A group of related nuclear families that live together in a single household.

F

feud A method of dispute settlement in self-help legal systems involving multiple but balanced killings between members of two or more kin groups.

fieldwork Ethnographic research that involves observing and interviewing the members of a culture to describe their contemporary way of life.

foragers (hunter-gatherers) Populations that rely on wild (undomesticated) plants and animals for their food supply.

forced assimilation The social absorption of one ethnic group by another ethnic group through the use of force.

forensic anthropologists Physical anthropologists who identify and analyze human skeletal remains.

form of descent How a people trace their descent from previous generations.

free morpheme A morpheme that can be used alone.

functional theory of inequality Theory holding that stratification is a way to reward individuals who contribute most to society's well-being.

functionalism Theoretical orientation that analyzes cultural elements in terms of their useful effects to individuals or to the persistence of the whole society.

G

generalized reciprocity The giving of goods without expectation of a return of equal value at any definite future time.

genocide The deliberate attempt to eliminate the members of an ethnic category or cultural tradition.

grammar Total system of linguistic knowledge that allows the speakers of a language to send meaningful messages and hearers to understand them.

group marriage Several women and several men are married to one another simultaneously.

H

Hawaiian kinship terms In this system mother's and father's siblings are called mother and father, while their children are called brother and sister.

hierarchical nesting Occurs when an ethnic group is part of a larger collection of ethnic groups, which together constitute a higher level of ethnic identity.

historic archaeology Field that investigates the past of literate peoples through excavation of sites and analysis of artifacts and other material remains.

historical particularism The theoretical orientation emphasizing that each culture is the unique product of all the influences to which it was subjected in its past, making cross-cultural generalizations questionable.

holistic perspective The assumption that any aspect of a culture is integrated with other aspects, so that no dimension of culture can be understood in isolation.

homeland A geographical region over which a particular ethnic group feels it has exclusive rights.

horticulture A method of cultivation in which hand tools powered by human muscles are used and in which land use is extensive.

human variation Refers to physical differences between human populations; an interest of physical anthropologists.

I

idealism A contemporary theoretical orientation holding that cultural knowledge and behavior patterns are largely independent of the material conditions of life; claims that each culture must be analyzed separately, on its own terms, and mistrusts cross-cultural comparisons.

ideology (narrow meaning of the term) Ideas and beliefs that legitimize and thus reinforce inequalities in stratified societies.

incest taboo Prohibition against sexual intercourse between certain kinds of relatives.

indigenous peoples Culturally distinct peoples who have occupied a region longer than peoples who have colonized or immigrated to the region.

individualistic cults Cults based on personal relations between specific individuals and specific supernatural powers.

inequality Degree to which individuals, groups, and categories differ in their access to rewards.

inequality explanation of hunger Notion that hunger is not caused by absolute scarcity but by the unequal distribution of resources and how these resources are used.

influence The ability to convince people they should act as you suggest.

initiation rite A rite held to mark the sexual maturity of an individual or a group of individuals of the same sex.

innovation The creation of a new cultural trait by combining two or more existing traits.

intellectual/cognitive functions of religion The notion that religious beliefs provide explanations for puzzling things and events.

intensive agriculture A system of cultivation in which plots are planted annually or semiannually; usually uses irrigation, natural fertilizers, and (in the Old World) plows powered by animals.

interpretive anthropology The contemporary theoretical orientation that analyzes cultural elements by explicating their meanings to people and understanding them in their local context.

interviewing Collection of cultural data by systematic questioning; may be structured (using questionnaires) or unstructured (open-ended).

Iroquois kinship terms In this system father's brother is called father, and mother's sister is called mother, while their children are called brother and sister. Father's sister is called aunt and mother's brother is called uncle, while their children are called cousins.

K

key consultant (informant) A member of a society who is especially knowledgeable about some subject, and who supplies information to a fieldworker.

kin group A group of people who culturally conceive themselves to be relatives, cooperate in certain activities, and share a sense of identity as kinfolk.

kin terms The words (labels) that an individual uses to refer to his or her relatives of various kinds.

kindred All the bilateral relatives of an individual.

kinship terminology The way a people classify their relatives into labeled categories, or into "kinds of relatives."

L

law A kind of social control characterized by the presence of authority, intention of universal application, obligation, and sanction.

levirate Custom whereby a widow marries a male relative (usually a brother) of her deceased husband.

lexicon The words that occur in a language.

life cycle The changes in expected activities, roles, rights and obligations, and social relations individuals experience as they move through culturally defined age categories.

limited-purpose money Money that may be used to purchase only a few kinds of goods.

lineage A unilineal descent group larger than an extended family whose members can actually trace how they are related.

M

market Exchange by means of buying and selling, using money.

marriage alliances The relationships created between families or kin groups by intermarriage.

materialism The theoretical orientation holding that the main influence on human ways of life is how people produce and distribute resources acquired from their environment.

matrilineal descent Form of descent in which individuals trace their primary kinship relationships through their mothers.

matrilocal residence Couples live with or near the wife's parents.

modal personality Within a single society, those personality elements that are most common.

monogamy Each individual is allowed to have only one spouse at a time.

morpheme A combination of phonemes that conveys a standardized meaning.

morphology The study of the units of meaning in language.

multipurpose money A money that can be used to purchase a very broad range of goods and services.

myths Stories that recount the deeds of supernatural powers in the past.

N

nationality An ethnic group which claims a right to a discrete homeland and to political autonomy and self-determination.

negative reciprocity Exchange motivated by the desire to obtain goods, in which the parties try to gain all the material goods they can.

neolocal residence Couples establish a separate household apart from both the husband's and wife's parents.

nomadism Seasonal mobility, often involving migration to high-altitude areas during the hottest and driest parts of the year.

norm Shared ideals and/or expectations about how certain people ought to act in given situations.

O

Omaha kinship terms Associated with patrilineal descent; in this system matrilineal cross cousins are called mother and mother's brother, while patrilineal cross cousins are called son and daughter if ego is a female and niece and nephew if ego is a male.

origin myth The collective history of an ethnic group that defines which subgroups are part of it and its relationship to other ethnic groups.

P

paleoanthropologists Physical anthropologists who specialize in the investigation of the biological evolution of the human species.

parallel cousins Offspring of siblings of the same sex.

participant observation The main technique used in conducting ethnographic fieldwork, involving living among a people and participating in their daily activities.

passive assimilation The voluntary social absorption of one ethnic group by another ethnic group.

pastoralism Adaptation in which needs of livestock for naturally occurring pasture and water greatly influence the movements of groups.

patrilineal descent Form of descent in which individuals trace their most important kinship relationships through their fathers.

patrilocal residence Couples live with or near the husband's parents.

patterns of behavior The behavior that most people perform when they are in certain culturally defined situations.

patterns of cooperation Recurrent ways in which many people coordinate their labor to make some task or activity more efficient or successful.

peasants Rural people who are integrated into a larger society politically and economically.

performance arts Forms of art such as music, percussion, song, dance, and theater/drama that involve sound and/or stylized body movements.

personality Conscious and unconscious modes of thought, motivation, and feeling that guide the behavior of a person.

phoneme The smallest unit of sound that speakers unconsciously recognize as distinctive from other sounds; when one phoneme is substituted for another in a morpheme, the meaning of the morpheme alters.

phonology The study of the sound system of language.

physical (biological) anthropology The subfield that studies the biological aspects of humankind.

polyandry One woman is allowed to have multiple husbands.

polygamy Multiple spouses.

polygyny One man is allowed to have multiple wives.

postmarital residence pattern Where a newly married couple go to live after their marriage.

postmodernism Philosophical viewpoint emphasizing the relativity of all knowledge, including that of science; focuses on how the knowledge characteristic of a particular time and place is constructed, especially on how power relations affect the creation and spread of ideas and beliefs.

prehistoric archaeology Field that uses excavation of sites and analysis of material remains to investigate cultures that existed before the development of writing.

priest A kind of religious specialist, often full-time, who officiates at rituals.

primatologists Those who study primates, including monkeys and apes.

procedural law The structured manner in which a breach of the law is adjudicated or resolved.

prophet A person who claims to have dreams or visions in which he or she received a message from a supernatural power.

psychological functions of religion The emotional satisfactions people derive from religion.

R

ranked society Society in which there are a fixed number of statuses (e.g., titles, offices) that carry prestige, and only certain individuals are eligible to attain these statuses.

reasonable person model A model used in legal reasoning that basically asks, How should a reasonable individual have acted under these circumstances?

reciprocity The transfer of goods for goods between two or more individuals or groups.

redistribution The collection of goods or money from a group, followed by a reallocation to the group by a central authority.

relocation The forced removal of the members of a particular ethnic group from one geographical region to another.

revelation A message that a prophet claims to have received from a supernatural power.

revitalization movement A religious movement explicitly intended to create a new way of life for a society or group.

rite of passage A public ceremony or ritual recognizing and making a transition from one group or status to another.

ritual Organized and stereotyped symbolic behaviors intended to influence supernatural powers.

S

scarcity explanation of hunger Holds that there is not enough land, water, and other resources to feed all the people of a country or region an adequate diet, given current technology.

secular ideology An ideology that does not rely on the will of supernatural powers but justifies inequality on the basis of its societywide benefits.

self-help legal systems Informal legal systems in societies without centralized political systems, in which authorities who settle disputes are defined by circumstances of the case.

semantic domain A class of things or properties that is perceived as alike in some fundamental respect; hierarchically organized.

sexual division of labor The kinds of productive activities (tasks) that are assigned to women versus men in a culture.

shaman (medicine man) Part-time religious specialist who uses his special relation to supernatural powers for curing members of his group and harming members of other groups.

shamanistic cults Cults in which special individuals (shamans) have relationships with supernatural powers that ordinary people lack.

shifting cultivation (slash-and-burn, swidden) Type of horticulture, most common in the tropics, in which short periods of cultivation of a plot alternate with long periods of fallow.

simple bands Autonomous or independent political units, often consisting of little more than an extended family, with informal leadership vested in one of the older family members.

social control Mechanisms by which behavior is constrained and directed into acceptable channels, thus maintaining conformity.

social distance The degree to which cultural norms specify that two individuals or groups should be helpful to, intimate with, or emotionally attached to one another.

social functions of religion The effects of religion on maintaining the institutions of society as a whole.

society A territorially distinct and largely self-perpetuating group whose members have a sense of collective identity and who share a common language and culture.

sociolinguistics Specialty within cultural anthropology that studies how language is related to culture and the social uses of speech.

sodalities Formal institutions that cross-cut communities and serve to unite geographically scattered groups; may be based on kin groups (clans or lineages) or on non-kin-based groups (age grades or warrior societies).

sorcery The performance of rites and spells for the purpose of causing harm to others by supernatural means.

sororate Custom whereby a widower marries a female relative of his deceased wife.

state A centralized, multilevel political unit characterized by the presence of a bureaucracy that acts on behalf of the ruling elite.

status of women How women are treated and regarded, particularly the degree to which females are subordinate to males, participate equally in valued activities, and are allowed access to important positions and other rewards.

stereotypes Preconceived mental images of a group that biases the way they are perceived and how their behavior is interpreted.

stratified society Society with marked and usually heritable differences in access to wealth, power, and prestige; inequality is based mainly on unequal access to productive and valued resources.

subculture Cultural differences characteristic of members of various ethnic groups, regions, religions, and so forth within a single society or country.

subnationalities A subgroup within a larger nationality, which lacks the concept of a separate homeland and makes no claim to any inherent right to political autonomy and self-determination.

substantive law Refers to the actual types of behavior that are categorized as illegal, together with the appropriate sanctions imposed.

surplus The amount of food (or other goods) a worker produces in excess of the consumption of herself or himself and her or his dependents.

symbols Objects, behaviors, and so forth whose culturally defined meanings have no necessary relation to their inherent physical qualities.

syntax The rules by which morphemes and words are combined into sequences to form meaningful sentences.

T

technology-transfer solution Notion that developing nations can best solve their hunger problems by adopting the technology and production methods of modern mechanized agriculture.

tone languages Languages in which changing voice pitch within a word alters the entire meaning of the word.

totemism A form of communal cult in which all members of a kin group have mystical relations with one or more natural objects from which they believe they are descended.

tribe Autonomous political unit encompassing a number of distinct, geographically dispersed communities that are held together by sodalities.

tribute The rendering of goods (typically including food) to an authority such as a chief.

U

unilineal descent Descent through "one line," including patrilineal and matrilineal descent.

unilineal descent group A group of relatives all of whom are related through only one sex.

unilineal evolution The nineteenth-century theoretical orientation that held that all human ways of life pass through a similar sequence of stages in their development.

universal grammar Noam Chomsky's idea that at a deep level the grammar of all languages exhibits fundamental similarities.

V

values Shared ideas or standards about the worthwhileness of goals and lifestyles.

vision quest The attempt to enlist the aid of supernatural powers by intentionally seeking a dream or vision.

visual arts Arts which are produced in a material or tangible form, including basketry, pottery, textiles, paintings, drawings, sculptures, masks, carvings, and the like. Common materials that portray visual arts include paper, bark, the human body, metal, wood, stone, shell, bone, and ivory.

W

Whorf-Sapir hypothesis The idea that language profoundly shapes the perceptions and world view of its speakers.

witchcraft The use of psychic powers to harm others by supernatural means.

world view The way a people interpret reality and events, including how they see themselves as relating to the world around them.

Notes

CHAPTER 1

Subfields of Anthropology

Information on hominid evolution is from Jurmaine, Nelson, and Kilgore (1995). Clyde Snow (1995) describes his forensic work in Argentina and northern Iraq; additional material is in McDonald (1995). Information on the percentages of anthropologists earning degrees in the five subfields in 1996–1997 is drawn from the American Anthropological Association (1997:308).

CHAPTER 2

Tylor's definition of culture is from Tylor (1871, 1).

Defining Culture

The distinction between trial and error and social learning is from Boyd and Richerson (1985) and Pulliam and Dunford (1980), who also discuss the advantages of social learning. The material on the Yąnomamö and Semai is drawn from Chagnon (1983) and Dentan (1968), respectively.

Cultural Knowledge

Edward Hall's two early books (1959, 1966) were among the first to systematically discuss the importance of nonverbal communication in everyday social interaction. The Hanunoo plant classification example is taken from Conklin (1957). Information on Navajo witchcraft comes from Kluckhohn (1967). Reichel-Dolmatoff (1971) describes shamanism among the Tukano. A wonderful recent book describing how some cultures experience and measure the passage of time is Aveni (1995).

Biology and Culture

Extended coverage of cultural universals is in D. Brown (1991).

CHAPTER 3

Some Properties of Language

Information on the five distinguishing features of human language is from Hockett's (1960) seminal discussion.

How Language Works

The examples on Thai aspiration and Nupe tones are taken from Fromkin and Rodman's (1988) textbook. The author's (J. P.) own knowledge is the basis for the discussion of the Kosraen language.

Language and Culture

The American farmers' classification of livestock is described by Tyler (1969). University of Minnesota undergraduate Toni K. Olesiak corrected an error in our presentation of this topic in previous editions, for which we are grateful. Berlin and Kay (1969) conducted the cross-cultural research on color terms. A concise description and discussion of the Whorf-Sapir hypothesis is in D. Brown (1991). See Farb (1974) and Trudgill (1983) on male and female speech and on Javanese "levels" of speech. Chagnon (1983) discusses the Yąnomamö name taboo. We thank Kathryn Meyer and Gary deCoker for help with the example of Japanese honorifics.

CHAPTER 4

Nineteenth-Century Origins

Unilineal evolutionary theory is best known from the works of Tylor (1865, 1871) and Morgan (1877). The times and places of the founding of the first anthropology programs in the United States is from Black (1991).

Early Twentieth-Century Contributions

The best single source of writings on Boas is a collection of his articles (1966). The critique of historical particularist assumptions is taken from Harris (1968). Malinowski's ideas about the functions of institutions, behaviors, and beliefs are presented in his 1944 book, reprinted in Malinowski (1960). Good sources on structural-functionalism are Radcliffe-Brown (1922, 1965) and Nadel (1951).

Mid-Century Evolutionary Theories

See L. White (1949, 1959). Steward's most influential articles appear in two volumes (1955, 1977).

Anthropological Thought Today

Marvin Harris (1977, 1979, 1985) was instrumental in the development of modern materialist thought. More recent, and more technical, sources on cultural evolution and adaptation are Johnson and Earle (1987) and Smith and Winterhalder (1992).

The text discussion barely scratches the surface on idealist approaches, which (in the way we define them) have proliferated in the last two decades. On interpretive anthropology, good sources are early works by Geertz (1973, 1980). Harris' latest book (1999) is a good introduction to his own variety of materialist theory. He also responds to the latest versions of what he considers biological determinism and responds to postmodernism.

CHAPTER 5

Ethnographic Methods

The discussion of how to evaluate a particular historical account was influenced by Naroll (1962). See also Hickerson (1970) on ethnohistoric methods. Sahlins (1981) discusses the Hawaiian interpretation of Captain Cook's visit. See Fogelson (1989) for a discussion of interpretation of historical events. The discussion of suicide in the Trobriand Islands is derived form Malinowski (1926). The problems of collecting genealogies among the Yąnomamö are recounted by Chagnon (1983).

Ethnological Methods

The cross-cultural test of the sorcery and social control hypothesis is from B. Whiting (1950). See Adams (1982 and 1988) for an excellent example of what can be done with historical data. Data on matrilineal and patrilineal societies are from Bailey (1989).

The discussion in "A Closer Look" is based in part on a series of conversations between the author and an older Kiowa Indian friend. The friend had been born and raised in a traditional Kiowa speaking household. As an adult he became a public high school teacher as well as a well-known traditional tribal singer. In speaking of his life he referred to himself as "bicultural" and drew the analogy between being "bicultural" and "bilingual." For a different perspective on this question see Obeyesekere (1992) and Sahlins (1995).

CHAPTER 6

Hunting and Gathering

Dobyns (1983) provided most of the information on the distribution of foragers in North America used in Figure 6.1. Denevan (1992) discusses the use of fire to provide habitat for game animals among prehistoric Native Americans. Information on specific foragers is taken from the following sources: BaMbuti (Turnbull 1962), Hadza (Woodburn 1968), Netsilik (Balikci 1970), Western Shoshone (Steward 1938, 1955), !Kung (Lee 1979, 1993), Northwest Coast (Ferguson 1984, Piddocke 1965, Suttles 1960, 1962, 1968).

Agriculture

On the benefits and costs of agriculture, see M. Cohen (1977). A readable book covering the origins of farming in various world regions is B. Smith (1995). Comparative information on foraging working hours are from Sahlins (1972) and M. Cohen (1977). M. Cohen (1989) overviews evidence about the health of prehistoric foragers. Sources used to draw the North American portion of the map on the distribution of horticulture are Dobyns (1983) and Doolittle (1992). See Bradfield (1971) on dry land gardening among the Western Pueblo. Material on shifting cultivation is from Conklin (1957), Freeman (1970), and Ruddle (1974). Differences between extensive and intensive agriculture are set forth in Boserup (1965) and

Grigg (1974). Material on intensive agriculture in the New World is drawn from our general knowledge and from Donkin (1979). E. Wolf (1966) is a good source on peasants. On peasant revolts, see E. Wolf (1969).

Pastoralism

Porter (1965) discusses the subsistence risk reduction benefit of pastoralism. Schneider (1981) shows the negative relation between the distribution of the tsetse fly and cattle pastoralism in Africa. A short source on the Karimojong is Dyson-Hudson and Dyson-Hudson (1969).

CHAPTER 7

Sahlins (1965) first distinguished the three forms of exchange.

Reciprocity

Malinowski (1922) describes Trobriand *wasi*. The Maring discussion is from Rappaport (1968) and Peoples (1982). Lee (1979, 1983) describes !Kung sharing, which he sees as the key to their ability to keep their work levels low and their nutritional status high. Kelly (1995) generalizes some of his points to other foragers in his excellent large-scale synthesis of the foraging adaptation.

Redistribution

Alkire (1977), Sahlins (1958), and Oliver (1989) describe tribute in Micronesia and Polynesia.

Market Exchange

See Neale (1976) on money. Schneider (1981) describes some African monies. Pospisil (1978) discusses the multiple uses of money among Kapauku. Bohannon (1955) describes Tiv exchange spheres. On Philippine *suki*, see W. Davis (1973). On Haitian *pratik,* see Mintz (1961).

CHAPTER 8

Marriage

The material on Nayar "marriage" is from Gough (1959).

Marriage in Comparative Perspective

Goldstein (1987) describes Tibetan polyandry and its advantages to husbands and the wife. Chagnon (1983) discusses the importance of marriage alliances among the Yąnomamö. Kuper (1963) describes Swazi bridewealth. See Lee (1976) on !Kung brideservice. See Goody and Tambiah (1973) and Harrell and Dickey (1985) on dowry.

Postmarital Residence Patterns

The frequencies of different residence patterns are as reported in Pasternak (1976, 44). Among those who have discussed the influences on residence patterns are Ember and Ember (1971, 1972), Goody (1976), and Pasternak (1976), but none of them should be held responsible for the ideas presented in this section.

Family and Household Forms

Murdock (1949) showed how forms of postmarital residence produce various forms of the family and household. Pasternak, Ember, and Ember (1976) suggest an economic hypothesis for why extended families exist.

CHAPTER 9

Unilineal Descent

Data on the frequencies of patrilineal and matrilineal descent are from Divale and Harris (1976). Firth (1936, 1965) describes the functions of Tikopian lineages and clans. See Eggan (1950) on Hopi matrilineal descent.

Cognatic Descent

Cognatic descent in Polynesia is discussed in Firth (1968), Howard and Kirkpatrick (1989), and Douglas Oliver (1989). The Samoan *'aiga* is described in M. Ember (1959), Holmes and Holmes (1992), and Douglas Oliver (1989).

Bilateral Kinship

Material on Iban kindred is from Freeman (1968, 1970).

Influences on Kinship Systems

Sources for this discussion are Aberle (1961), Divale (1974), Divale and Harris (1976), C. Ember (1974), Ember and Ember (1971), and Ember, Ember, and Pasternak (1974).

Classifying Relatives: Kinship Terminologies

Aberle (1961) and Pasternak (1976) provide statistical data on the correlation between forms of kinship and terminological systems.

CHAPTER 10

Cultural Construction of Gender

The Hua material is from Meigs (1988, 1990).

The Sexual Division of Labor

Table 10.1 was put together from data in Murdock and Provost (1973). On female hunting among BaMbuti pygmies and Agta, see Turnbull (1962) and Estioko-Griffin (1986), respectively. On the possibility that strenuous exercise inhibits ovulation, see Graham (1985). The influence of female child-care responsibilities on the sexual division of labor was first made forcibly by Judith Brown (1970a). The discussion of why female contributions to subsistence tend to decline with intensification uses information in C. Ember (1983), Martin and Voorhies (1975), Boserup (1970), Burton and White (1984), and White, Burton, and Dow (1981). The Kofyar material is from Stone, Stone, and McC. Netting (1995).

The Status of Women

The general discussion in this section relies on material in di Leonardo (1991), Leacock (1978), Morgen (1989), Rosaldo and Lamphere (1974), Quinn (1977), and Sacks (1982). The information about Andalusia is from Gilmore (1980, 1990). The suggestion that women's status improves with age in many cultures is from J. Brown (1988). Information on the Iroquois is from Albers (1989) and J. Brown (1970b). On BaMbuti and Aka sexual egalitarianism, see Turnbull (1962) and Hewlett (1992). The idea that women's control over key resources frequently leads to high overall status is discussed in Sanday (1973, 1981). Friedl (1975, 1978) was one of the first to argue that women's status in hunting and gathering cultures is positively related to the importance of women's labor in food production and to women's ability to control the distribution of the products they produce. Yoruba material is from Barnes (1990). Schlegel (1972) and Whyte (1978) discuss why matrilineality and matrilocality tend to give women high status, all else equal. Information on Chinese wives is from M. Wolf (1972) and our general knowledge. Materials on the effects of overall societal complexity on women's status is synthesized from Goody (1976), Boserup (1970), Whyte (1978), Sacks (1982), and Schlegel (1991).

CHAPTER 11

Forms of Political Organization

The definitions and ideas concerning political structure were influenced by Steward (1955), Service (1962), Cohen and Service (1978), Krader (1968), and Fried (1967). Ethnographic examples were taken from the following sources: Comanche from Hoebel (1940) and Wallace and Hoebel (1952), Tahiti from Goldman (1970), and Inca from D'Altroy (1987), Julien (1988), La Lone (1987), LeVine (1987), and Metraux (1969).

Social Control and Law

For the basic definition of law as well as many of the concepts about legal systems, we relied upon Hoebel (1954), Pospisil (1958), Fallers (1969), Bohannan (1968), Newman (1983), and Gluckman (1972, 1973). Ethnographic examples were taken from the following sources: Comanche from Hoebel (1940), Cheyenne from Llewellyn and Hoebel (1941), Nuer from Evans-Pritchard (1940), Jivaro from Harner (1973a), and Barotse from Gluckman (1972, 1973).

CHAPTER 12

Systems of Equality and Inequality

The classification of societies into egalitarian, ranked, and stratified was proposed by Fried (1967). Woodburn (1982) discusses the reasons for the egalitarianism among foragers. The material on Tikopia is from Firth (1936). Berreman (1959) noted the similarity of race relations in the American South to a caste system.

Castes in Traditional India

The Indian caste system and its relationship to Hinduism are discussed in Dumont (1980), Hiebert (1971), Mandelbaum (1971), and Tyler (1973).

Classes in Industrial Societies: The United States

Material on the distribution of income and assets is from Avery et al. (1987), Joint Economic Committee (1986), Mischel and Bernstein (1994), and U.S. Bureau of the Census (1998).

Maintaining Inequality

The Hawaiian religion is described in Valeri (1985).

Theories of Inequality

Davis and Moore (1945) originated the functionalist theory. Conflict theory goes back to Marx (1967, original 1867). Dahrendorf (1959) was important in formulating the modern version of conflict theory in sociology. Lenski (1966) is an excellent source comparing and evaluating the functionalist and conflict theories. The information on salaries of Chief Executive Officers (CEOs) in Japan and the United States is from *The New York Times* (April 17, 1995).

CHAPTER 13

Defining Religion

An excellent recent summary of *mana* is Shore (1989). The idea that Judeo-Christian myths provide a world view conducive to environmental destruction is taken from Lin White (1967).

Theories of Religion

The Trobriand magic example is from Malinowski (1954). Frazer's intellectual theory is from Frazer (1963). Geertz (1965) argues that religion provides meaning. Malinowski (1954) argues that magic and religion serve to alleviate anxieties during times of stress and uncertainty. Dobu beliefs about the fate of the dead are discussed in Fortune (1963, 179–188). Kwaio pollution is described in Keesing (1982). The theory that ritual behavior creates social solidarity goes back to Durkheim (1915).

The Sphere of Supernatural Intervention

Ethnographic data are from Victor Turner (1967; Ndembu), Rasmussen (1979; Inuit), Omar Moore (1957; Naskapi), Malinowski (1922; Trobriands), and Frigout (1979; Hopi).

Supernatural Explanations of Misfortune

The distinction between imitative and contagious magic is taken from Frazer (1963). Fortune (1932) describes Dobu sorcery. The witchcraft examples are from Kluckhohn (1967; Navajo), Wilson (1951; Nyakyusa), Evans-Pritchard (1976; Zande), Offiong (1983; Ibibio), and Middleton (1965; Lugbara). Kluckhohn (1967) hypothesizes that Navajo witchcraft beliefs reduce overt, socially disruptive hostilities.

Varieties of Religious Organization

Wallace (1966) formulated and named the kinds of cults. The vision quest material is from Lowie (1954, 1956). Harner (1973b) describes Jivaro shamanism. Middleton (1965) describes the Lugbara ancestral cult.

Revitalization Movements

A general description of cargo cults is in Worsley (1968). Lawrence (1964) describes the Garia cults. On Handsome Lake's movement among the Seneca, see Wallace (1969). Stewart (1980) and Anderson (1996) describe peyotism among Native Americans.

CHAPTER 14

Art and the Aesthetic

Many of the ideas for this chapter came from Hunter and Whitten (1976) and Anderson (1989). On Shaker art, we consulted the classic study by Andrews and Andrews (1937). For changes in Chinese art, we consulted the Nelson Gallery (1975). Other sources of general information used in this chapter include Lipman and Winchester (1974), Hobson (1987), and Harvey (1937). Specific information on art in particular cultures is drawn from Colton (1959; Hopi) and Connelly (1979; Hopi), Hoebel (1978; Cheyenne), Kalb (1994; New Mexican Santos), and Hail (1983; Plains Indians).

Forms of Artistic Expression

Body arts. The general discussion of body arts is based primarily on Brain (1979). Information on Polynesian tattooing is from Gell (1993), Hage et al. (1995), and Simmons (1983). A 1998 research paper by undergraduate Maureen McCardel of Ohio Wesleyan University also was helpful on Polynesian tattooing.

Visual arts. Close (1989) provides a good summary of the archaeological debate over style versus function. Material on Northwest Coast art is from our general knowledge, with specific points drawn from Anderson (1989), Boas (1955), Furst and Furst (1982), and Holm (1965, 1972). The comparative information on style in visual arts is from Fischer (1961).

Performance arts. We drew from the studies of Kaeppler (1978) and Lomax (1962, 1968). Good sources on voudon are Metraux (1972) and

Wade Davis' (1985) controversial book. We drew information on !Kung healing from Lee (1993) and Shostak (1983) and on Tumbuka healing from Friedson (1998). A recent source of case studies on various performances and healing is Laderman and Roseman, eds. (1996). An informative and heavily illustrated source for students on Native American dance is Heth (1992). For a discussion of the individual in art see Warner (1986).

Art and Culture

Information on the use of sandpaintings and song/chants in Navajo curing ceremonials is taken from Sandner (1991) and Reichard (1950, 1977). BaMbuti *molimo* is described in Turnbull (1961).

CHAPTER 15

Personality and Culture

Winthrop (1991) provided the definition of personality used in this section. The configurational or thematic approach to culture and personality was elegantly stated in Benedict (1934). DuBois (1944) describes Alorese child-rearing practices and their effects on adult personality. Rohner (1975) conducted the cross-cultural test of the notion that parental rejection during childhood tends to be associated with certain adult personality traits. The social systems model of the relation between personality and the cultural system comes from the work of Kardiner (1945) and is modernized and explicitly formulated by Whiting (1977). Figure 15.1 is drawn from Whiting (1977), but substantially modified to make it compatible with the terminology and concepts developed in Chapters 6 through 15 of *Humanity*.

Age Categories and Age Sets

The information on Hidatsa age sets is from Lowie (1954). Material on the Swazi is from Kuper (1963). Hanson (1988) discusses the idea that age sets function as mechanisms for organizing warfare in decentralized societies.

Life Cycle

The Cheyenne concept of abortion is from Llewellyn and Hoebel (1941). See Jenness (1932) and Hoebel (1954) for a discussion of Eskimo infanticide. The description of the Osage child-naming rite is based on LaFlesche (1928). The material on whether Samoan young women do or do not experience all the stresses and strains typical of American adolescents is based on Mead (1928) and Freeman (1983). The information on New Guinea beliefs about feminine pollution and male initiation rituals is taken from Meggitt (1970–Enga) and Newman and Boyd (1982–Awa). On the Apache girls' ceremony, see Farrer (1996). The data on the Tucuna girl's puberty rite are from Ninuendaju (1948). Wallace and Hoebel (1952) provided the information on the treatment of the elderly among the Comanche. On the Inuit treatment of the elderly, see Hoebel (1954). Data on abandonment and patricide among subarctic peoples are drawn from Vanstone (1974) and Jenness (1932).

CHAPTER 16

Culture Change

The concepts of innovation and invention are from Barnett (1953). For a good discussion of why particular changes are accepted or rejected by a society see Foster (1962).

The World Since 1500

The most important single source is Stavrianos (1982). Secondary information is drawn from E. Wolf (1982), Abu-Lughod (1989), Crosby (1972), and—for the period from the fifteenth through the eighteenth centuries—Braudel (1979a, 1979b). Data on the demographic effects of contact on Native American peoples are from Thronton (1987) and Dobyns (1976). Specific information on historic changes among Native Americans is from Leacock and Lurie (1971), Kehoe (1992), and Wolf (1959). Historical data on Africa and the Africa slave trade are from Davidson (1961, 1969), Oliver and Fage (1962), and Mintz (1986). Data on the effects of New World cultigens on Africa are primarily from Miracle (1966, 1967). Information on the Easter Island slave raids is taken from Goldman (1970) and Heyerdahl (1958). Statistics on the number of Europeans in India during the 1920s is from Mayo (1927). Most of the twentieth-century general economic and population data were drawn from Hepner and McKee (1992), Jackson and Hudman (1990), Stamp (1973), The World Bank (1982, 1992), and the CIA (1993). Data on the changing magnitude of world trade were obtained from Rostow (1978), supplemented with later data from The World Bank (1992). More current data on economic, social, and migration issues has been taken from new reports in the *Washington Post, Christian Science Monitor,* and the *Atlantic Monthly,* as well as other newspapers and periodicals.

CHAPTER 17

There is a vast body of literature in anthropology and sociology on ethnicity and related issues. Our ideas on the nature and significance of ethnicity have been most strongly influenced by the studies of Frederick Barth (1958 and 1969), Joan Vincent (1974), Bud B. Khlief (1979), Nathan Glazer and Daniel Moynihan (1963 and 1975), John Bennett (1975), Robert E. Norris (1990), Joseph Himes (1974), DeVos and Romanusci-Ross (1975), Ronald Cohen (1978), Sol Tax (1967), Bernard Nietschmann (1989), Donald Horowitz (1985), and Richard Jackson and Lloyd Hudman (1990). For discussions of international legal and political issues, see Gudmundur Alfredsson (1989) and Lee Swepton (1989). For additional data concerning particular ethnic groups and historical events, we have drawn on a number of sources: Gerner (1994), Hajda and Beissinger (1990), Charles Foster (1980), John Bodley (1982), Joseph Opala (1987), Eric Wolf (1982), L. S. Stavrianos (1982), Basil Davidson (1968), Robert Carmack (1988), Alice B. Kehoe (1992), John T. McAlister (1973), Dale Eickelmen (1989), Richard Handler (1988), and Richard Price (1979), as well as basic reference sources and discussions with colleagues and students from Saudi Arabia, Oman, Bangladesh, Indonesia, and Malaysia. In addition, one of the authors spent the summer of 1988 in Yugoslavia and the summer of 1989 in Guatemala collecting data on ethnic identity and conflict. For information on current ethnic conflicts we have had to rely upon current news reports from the *Washington Post* and *Christian Science Monitor.* Information on potential regions of ethnic conflict within the former Soviet Union is from *The Moscow News,* June 15–28, 1992. Data for "Other Voices" is from Conrad (1983), Daigle (1982), Brasseaux (1992), and Ross and Deveau (1992), together with materials collected by the author in Nova Scotia and New Brunswick in 1994 and southern Louisiana in 1995.

CHAPTER 18

Applied Anthropology

The ideas about the unique contributions of anthropology to problem solving are our own.

Population Growth

Data on historic world population growth are from Ehrlich, Ehrlich, and Holdren (1977, 182–3). Quantitative information comes from the tables compiled by the World Bank (1999). The economic interpretation of high birth rates in the Punjabi villages was presented by Mamdani (1973). The 1982 study of the same area is reported in Nag and Kak (1984). Data on large Javanese and Nepalese families appear in B. White (1973) and Nag, White, and Peet (1978). Nardi (1981, 1983), Shankman (1976), and Small (1997) discuss the importance of remittances in Samoa and Tonga. Freed and Freed (1985) discuss why Indian couples feel they need more than one son.

World Hunger

The inequality explanation of hunger is stated and defended in laypersons' terms in Lappé and Collins (1977, 1986). The El Salvadoran data are reported and analyzed in Durham (1979). The discussion of the effects of the "green revolution" on Javanese peasants is from Franke (1974). Johnson (1971) discusses risk minimization among peasants. The quantitative data on the energetic efficiency of various food systems are compiled from information given in Pimentel et al. (1973, 1975), and Pimentel and Pimentel (1979).

Agricultural Alternatives

The potential value of traditional farming methods for the modern world is described in volumes by Altieri (1987) and Wilken (1987). The advantages of intercropping and other traditional methods are covered in Innis (1980), Gliessman and Grantham (1990), and Harrison (1987). Traditional resource management is covered by Alcorn (1981) and Posey (1983, 1984, 1985). Nations and Nigh (1980) discuss the potential of Lacandon Maya shifting cultivation.

The Uses of Fieldwork: Two Studies

Murray's involvement in the Haitian agroforestry project is described in Murray (1987). On the Swaziland health project, see Green (1985, 1987, 1994).

CHAPTER 19

Indigenous Peoples Today

For the best general discussion of the evolution of European attitudes to indigenous peoples, see Berkhofer (1978). Germany's policies toward the Herero are discussed in Bodley (1982). S. Davis (1977) discusses the impact on indigenous tribes of Brazil's efforts to develop the Amazon Basin. Specific material on the plight of the Yanomamö is from *Newsweek* magazine (April 9, 1990:34) and from the Commission for the Creation of the Yanomamö Park (1989a, b), published in *Cultural Survival Quarterly*. On San relocation, see Hitchcock (1999). The experiences of the Kayapó are recounted by T. Turner (1989).

Vanishing Knowledge

The Maori claim was reported in the June 15, 1996, edition of *The Columbia Dispatch*. The July 22, 1995, issue of *The Economist* reported the claims of Canada's Nisga'a. The *Business Week* issue referred to is from March 1, 1993. The examples of medicines we have learned about from indigenous peoples are taken from Lewis and Lewis (1977). Farnsworth (1984) argues that many more plants will be discovered to have medical uses. A good discussion of the insights of "traditional medicine" is in Fabrega (1975). The discussion of the erosion of the genetic diversity of major food crops is from our general knowledge and Harlan (1975). The material on amaranth is from Sokolov (1986). The sharpest attack on Afrocentrists has come from Mary Lefkowitz (1996), a renowned classicist, for her interpretations of ancient Greek and Egyptian history. For western interpretations of African and African-American history and culture see Coombes (1994) and Pieterse (1992). For Euro-American images of Native Americans see Berkhofer (1978).

Bibliography

Aberle, David F.
1961 "Matrilineal Descent in Cross-cultural Perspective." In *Matrilineal Kinship,* edited by David M. Schneider and Kathleen Gough, 655–727. Berkeley: University of California Press.

Abu-Lughod, Janet L.
1989 *Before European Hegemony. The World System* A.D. *1250–1350.* New York: Oxford University Press.

Adams, Richard N.
1982 *Paradoxical Harvest.* Cambridge: Cambridge University Press.
1988 "Energy and the Regulation of Nation States." *Cultural Dynamics* 1:46–61.

Albers, Patricia C.
1989 "From Illusion to Illumination: Anthropological Studies of American Indian Women." In Sandra Morgen, ed., 1989, pp. 132–170.

Alcorn, Janice
1981 "Huastec Non-Crop Resource Management." *Human Ecology* 9:395–417.

Alfredsson, Gudmundur
1989 "The United Nations and the Rights of Indigenous Peoples." *Current Anthropology* 30:255–259.

Alkire, William H.
1977 *An Introduction to the Peoples and Cultures of Micronesia.* 2nd ed. Menlo Park, Calif.: Cummings.

Allen, Michael
1984 "Elders, Chiefs, and Big Men: Authority Legitimation and Political Evolution in Melanesia." *American Ethnologist* 11:20–41.

Altieri, Miguel A.
1987 *Agroecology: The Scientific Basis of Alternative Agriculture.* Boulder, Colo.: Westview Press.

American Anthropological Association
1995 *The AAA Guide, 1995–96.* Arlington, Va.: American Anthropological Association.

Anderson, Edward F.
1996 *Peyote: The Divine Cactus.* 2nd ed. Tucson: University of Arizona.

Anderson, Richard L.
1989 *Art in Small-Scale Societies.* 2nd ed. Englewood Cliffs, N.J.: Prentice Hall.

Andrews, Edward Deming, and Faith Andrews
1937 *Shaker Furniture: The Craftsmanship of American Communal Sect.* New Haven: Yale University Press.

Avery, Robert B., Gregory E. Elliehausen, and Arthur B. Kennickell
1987 "Measuring Wealth with Survey Data: An Evaluation of the 1983 Survey of Consumer Finances." Paper presented at the 20th Congress of the International Association for Research on Income and Wealth, Rocca di Papa, Italy.

Aveni, Anthony
1995 *Empires of Time.* New York: Kodansha America.

Bailey, Garrick
1989 "Descent and Social Survival of Native Horticultural Societies of the Eastern United States." Paper presented at the American Anthropological Association meetings, Washington, D.C.
1995 *The Osage and the Invisible World: From the Works of Francis LaFlesche.* Norman: University of Oklahoma Press.

Balikci, Asen
1970 *The Netsilik Eskimo.* Garden City, N.Y.: Natural History Press.

Barnes, Sandra T.
1990 "Women, Property, and Power." In Peggy Reeves Sanday and Ruth Gallagher Goodenough, eds., 1990, pp. 253–280.

Barnett, Homer
1953 *Innovation: The Basis of Cultural Change.* New York: McGraw-Hill.

Barth, Fredrik
1958 "Ecological Relationships of Ethnic Groups in Swat, North Pakistan." *American Anthropologist* 60:1079–89.
1969 *Ethnic Groups and Boundaries.* Boston: Little, Brown and Company.

Benedict, Ruth
1934 *Patterns of Culture.* Boston: Houghton Mifflin Company.

Bennett, John, ed.
1975 "The New Ethnicity: Perspectives from Ethnology." *1973 Proceedings of the American Ethnological Society.* St. Paul, Minn.: West Publishing Co.

Berch, Bettina
1982 *The Endless Days: The Political Economy of Women and Work.* San Diego: Harcourt, Brace, Jovanovich.

Berkhofer, Robert F. Jr.
1978 *The White Man's Indian: Images of the American Indian from Columbus to the Present.* New York: Knopf.

Berlin, Brent, and Paul Kay
1969 *Basic Color Terms—Their Universality and Evolution.* Berkeley: University of California Press.

Berreman, Gerald D.
1959 "Caste in India and the United States." *American Journal of Sociology* 66:120–127.

Bertelsen, Judy S., ed.
1977 *Nonstate Nations in International Politics: Comparative System Analyses.* New York: Praeger.

Black, Nancy Johnson
1991 "What is Anthropology?" In *Introduction to Library Research in Anthropology,* edited by John Weeks, pp. 1–5. Boulder, Colo.: Westview Press.

Boas, Franz
1955 *Primitive Art.* New York: Dover Publications.

Boas, Franz
1966 *Race, Language and Culture.* New York: Free Press (original 1940).

Bodley, John H.
1982 *Victims of Progress.* 2nd ed. Palo Alto, Calif.: Mayfield Publishing Company.

Bohannan, Paul
1955 "Some Principles of Exchange and Investment Among the Tiv." *American Anthropologist* 57:60–70.
1968 *Justice and Judgement Among the Tiv.* London: Oxford University Press.

Boserup, Ester
1965 *The Conditions of Agricultural Growth.* Chicago: Aldine.
1970 *Women's Role in Economic Development.* New York: St. Martin's.

Boyd, Robert, and Peter J. Richerson
1985 *Culture and the Evolutionary Process.* Chicago: University of Chicago Press.

Bradfield, Maitland
1971 "The Changing Pattern of Hopi Agriculture." Royal Anthropological Institute of Great Britain and Ireland Occasional Paper, no. 30. London: Royal Anthropological Institute.

Brain, Robert
1979 *The Decorated Body*. New York: Harper & Row.

Brasseaux, Carl A.
1992 *Acadian to Cajun: Transformation of a People, 1803–1877*. Jackson, Miss.: University Press of Mississippi.

Braudel, Fernand
1979a *The Structures of Everyday Life: Civilization & Capitalism 15th–18th Century*. Vol. 1, New York: Harper & Row.
1979b *The Wheels of Commerce: Civilization & Capitalism 15th–18th Century*. Vol. 2, New York: Harper & Row.

Brown, Donald E.
1991 *Human Universals*. New York: McGraw-Hill, Inc.

Brown, Judith K.
1970a "A Note on the Division of Labor by Sex." *American Anthropologist* 72:1073–1078.
1970b "Economic Organization and the Position of Women among the Iroquois." *Ethnohistory* 17:131–167.
1988 "Cross-Cultural Perspectives on Middle-Aged Women." In *Cultural Constructions of 'Woman,'* edited by Pauline Kolenda, pp. 73–100. Salem, Wisc.: Sheffield.

Burger, Julian
1987 *Report from the Frontier: The State of the World's Indigenous Peoples*. Cambridge, Mass.: Cultural Survival, Inc.
1990 *The GAIA Atlas of First Peoples*. New York: Anchor Books.

Burton, Michael L., and Douglas R. White
1984 "Sexual Division of Labor in Agriculture." *American Anthropologist* 86:568–583.

Callender, Charles, and Lee. M. Kochems
1983 "The North American Berdache." *Current Anthropology*. 24:443–90.

Carmack, Robert, ed.
1988 *Harvest of Violence*. Norman: University of Oklahoma Press.

Casal, Father Gabriel, Regalado Trota Jose, Eric Casino, George Ellis, and Wilhelm Solheim II
1981 *The People and Art of the Philippines*. Los Angeles: Museum of Cultural History, University of California.

Central Intelligence Agency
1993 *The World Factbook 1992*. Washington, D.C.: Government Printing Office.

Chagnon, Napoleon A.
1983 *Yanomamö: The Fierce People*. 3rd ed. New York: Holt, Rinehart and Winston.

Close, Angela E.
1989 "Identifying Style in Stone Artifacts: A Case Study from the Nile Valley." In Donald Henry and George Odell, eds. "Alternative Approaches to Lithic Analysis." *Archaeological Papers of the American Anthropological Association,* no. 1, pp. 3–26.

Cohen, Mark Nathan
1977 *The Food Crisis in Prehistory*. New Haven and London: Yale University Press.
1989 *Health and the Rise of Civilization*. New Haven, Conn.: Yale University Press.

Cohen, Ronald
1978 "Ethnicity: Problem and Focus in Anthropology." In *Annual Review of Anthropology,* vol. 7, 1978, edited by Bernard Siegal. Palo Alto, Calif.: Annual Reviews, Inc.

Cohen, Ronald, and Elman Service
1978 *Origins of the State: The Anthropology of Political Evolution*. Philadelphia: Institute for the Study of Human Issues.

Cohen, Ronald, and John Middleton, eds.
1970 *From Tribe to Nation in Africa*. Scranton, Pa.: Chandler Publishing Company.

Cohen, Theodore F.
1987 "Remaking Men." *Journal of Family Issues* 8:57–77.

Colton, Harold S.
1959 *Hopi Kachina Dolls*. Albuquerque: University of New Mexico Press.

Commission for the Creation of Yanomami Park (CCPY)
1989a "The Threatened Yanomami." *Cultural Survival Quarterly* 13:45–46.
1989b "Brazilian Government Reduces Yanomami Territory by 70 Percent." *Cultural Survival Quarterly* 13:47.

Conklin, Harold C.
1957 "Hanunoó Agriculture." FAO Forestry Development Paper, no. 12. Rome: Food and Agriculture Organization of the United Nations.

Cong, Dachang
1992 "Amish Factionalism and Technological Change: A Case Study of Kerosene Refrigerators and Conservatism." *Ethnology* 31:205–218.

Connelly, John C.
1979 "Hopi Social Organization." In William Sturtevant, ed. *Handbook of North American Indians* 9:539–553.

Conrad, Glenn R., ed.
1983 *The Cajuns: Essays on Their History and Culture*. Lafayette, La.: University of Southwestern Louisiana.

Coombes, Annie E.
1994 *Reinventing Africa: Museum, Material Culture, and Popular Imagination in Late Victorian and Edwardian England*. New Haven, Conn.: Yale University Press.

Crosby, Alfred W.
1972 *The Colombian Exchange*. Westport, Conn.: Greenwood.
1986 *Ecological Imperialism: The Biological Expansion of Europe, 900–1900*. Cambridge: Cambridge University Press.

Dahrendorf, Ralf
1959 *Class and Class Conflict in Industrial Society*. Berkeley: University of California Press.

Daigle, Jean, ed.
1982 *The Acadians of the Maritimes*. Moncton, New Brunswick: Universite de Moncton.

D'Altroy, Terence N.
1987 "Transitions in Power: Centralization of Wanka Political Organization under Inka Rule," *Ethnohistory* 34:78–102.

Davidson, Basil
1961 *The African Slave Trade: Precolonial History 1450–1850*. Boston: Atlantic-Little Brown.
1969 *Africa in History*. New York: Macmillan.

Davis, Kingsley, and Wilbert E. Moore
1945 "Some Principles of Stratification." *American Sociological Review* 10:242–49.

Davis, Shelton H.
1977 *Victims of the Miracle*. Cambridge: Cambridge University Press.

Davis, Wade
1985 *The Serpent and the Rainbow*. New York: Warner Books.

Davis, William G.
1973 *Social Relations in a Philippine Market*. Berkeley: University of California Press.

DeMallie, Raymond J.
1983 "Male and Female in Traditional Lakota Culture." In *The Hidden Half: Studies of Plains Indian Women*, edited by Patricia Albers and Beatrice Medicine, 237–65. Lanham, Md.: University Press of America.

Denevan, William M.
1992 "The Pristine Myth: The Landscape of the Americas in 1492." *Annals of the Association of American Geographers* 82:369–385.

Denig, Edwin Thompson
1961 *Five Indian Tribes of the Upper Missouri*, edited by John Ewers. Norman: University of Oklahoma Press.

Dentan, Robert Knox
1968   *The Semai: A Nonviolent People of Malaya.* New York: Holt, Rinehart and Winston.

DeVos, George, and Lola Romanusci-Ross, eds.
1975   *Ethnic Identity: Cultural Continuities and Change.* Palo Alto, Calif.: Mayfield Publishing Co.

di Leonardo, Micaela, ed.
1991   *Gender at the Crossroads of Knowledge.* Berkeley: University of California Press.

Divale, William T.
1974   "Migration, External Warfare, and Matrilocal Residence." *Behavior Science Research* 9:75–133.

Divale, William T., and Marvin Harris
1976   "Population, Warfare, and the Male Supremacist Complex." *American Anthropologist* 78:521–38.

Dobyns, Henry F.
1976   *Native American Historical Demography: A Critical Bibliography.* Bloomington: Indiana University Press.
1983   *Their Number Become Thinned.* Knoxville: University of Tennessee Press.

Domhoff, G. William
1983   *Who Rules America Now?* Englewood Cliffs, N.J.: Prentice-Hall, Inc.

Donkin, Robin
1979   *Agricultural Terracing in the Aboriginal New World.* Tucson: University of Arizona Press.

Doolittle, William E.
1992   "Agriculture in North America on the Eve of Contact: A Reassessment." *Annals of the Association of American Geographers* 82:386–401.

Douglas, Mary
1966   *Purity and Danger.* Middlesex, England: Penguin.

DuBois, Cora
1944   *The People of Alor.* Minneapolis: University of Minnesota Press.

Dumont, Louis
1980   *Homo Hierarchicus: The Caste System and Its Implications.* Chicago and London: University of Chicago Press.

Durham, William H.
1979   *Scarcity and Survival in Central America.* Stanford, Calif.: Stanford University Press.

Durkheim, Emile
1915   *The Elementary Forms of the Religious Life.* London: George Allen and Unwin Ltd.

Dyson-Hudson, Rada, and Eric Alden Smith
1978   "Human Territoriality: An Ecological Reassessment." *American Anthropologist* 80:21–41.

Dyson-Hudson, Rada, and Neville Dyson-Hudson
1969   "Subsistence Herding in Uganda." *Scientific American* 220:76–89.

Eggan, Fred
1950   *Social Organization of the Western Pueblos.* Chicago: University of Chicago Press.

Ember, Carol
1974   "An Evaluation of Alternative Theories of Matrilocal Versus Patrilocal Residence." *Behavior Science Research* 9:135–149.
1983   "The Relative Decline in Women's Contribution to Agriculture with Intensification." *American Anthropologist* 85:285–304.

Ember, Melvin
1959   "The Nonunilinear Descent Groups of Samoa." *American Anthropologist* 61:573–577.

Ember, Melvin, and Carol R. Ember
1971   "The Conditions Favoring Matrilocal Versus Patrilocal Residence." *American Anthropologist* 73:571–594.
1972   "The Conditions Favoring Multilocal Residence." *Southwestern Journal of Anthropology* 28:382–400.

Ember, Melvin, Carol R. Ember, and Burton Pasternak
1974   "On the Development of Unilineal Descent." *Journal of Anthropological Research* 30:69–94.

Estioko-Griffin, Agnes
1986   "Daughters of the Forest." *Natural History* 95:36–43.

Evans-Pritchard, E. E.
1940   *The Nuer.* Oxford: Clarendon.
1976   *Witchcraft, Oracles, and Magic among the Azande.* Abridged edition. Oxford: Clarendon Press.

Ewers, John
1955   "The Horse in Blackfoot Indian Culture." Bureau of American Ethnology, Bulletin 159, Washington, D.C.: U.S. Government Printing Office.

Fabrega, H. Jr.
1975   "The Need for an Ethnomedical Science." *Science* 189:969–75.

Fagan, Brian M.
1986   *People of the Earth.* Boston: Little, Brown and Company.

Fallers, Lloyd A.
1969   *Law Without Precedent.* Chicago: University of Chicago Press.

Farb, Peter
1974   *Word Play.* New York: Alfred A. Knopf.

Farnsworth, Norman R.
1984   "How Can the Well Be Dry When It Is Filled with Water?" *Economic Botany* 38:4–13.

Farrer, Claire F.
1996   *Thunder Rides a Black Horse.* 2nd ed. Prospect Heights, Ill.: Waveland Press.

Faulkner, Gretchen Fearon, Nancy T. Prince, and Jennifer Sapiel Neptune
1998   "Beautifully Beaded: Northeastern Native American Beadwork." *American Indian Art* 24 (1):32–41.

Ferguson, R. Brian
1984   "A Reexamination of the Causes of Northwest Coast Warfare." In *Warfare, Culture, and Environment*, edited by R. Brian Ferguson, 267–328. Orlando, Fla.: Academic Press.

Firth, Raymond
1936   *We, The Tikopia.* Boston: Beacon Press.
1959   *Economics of the New Zealand Maori.* 2nd ed. Wellington: Government Printer.
1965   *Primitive Polynesian Economy.* New York: Norton.
1968   "A Note on Descent Groups in Polynesia." In *Kinship and Social Organization*, edited by Paul Bohannan and John Middleton, pp. 213–223. Garden City, N.Y.: The Natural History Press.

Fischer, John
1961   "Art Styles as Cultural Cognitive Maps." *American Anthropologist* 63:80–84.

Fogelson, Raymond D.
1989   "The Ethnohistory of Events and Nonevents." *Ethnohistory* 36:133–47.

Fortune, Reo
1932   *Sorcerers of Dobu.* New York: E.P. Dutton.

Foster, Charles R., ed.
1980   *Nations Without a State: Ethnic Minorities of Western Europe.* New York: Praeger.

Foster, George
1962   *Traditional Cultures and the Impact of Technological Change.* New York: Harper & Row.

Franke, Richard W.
1974   "Miracle Seeds and Shattered Dreams in Java." *Natural History* 83:10–18, 84–88.

Frazer, Sir James George
1963   *The Golden Bough.* Abridged ed. Toronto: The Macmillan Company (original 1911–1915).

Freed, Stanley A., and Ruth S. Freed
1985   "One Son Is No Sons." *Natural History* 94:10–15.

Freeman, Derek
1968   "On the Concept of the Kindred." In *Kinship and Social Organization,* edited by Paul Bohannan and John Middleton, pp. 255–272. Garden City, N.Y.: The Natural History Press.
1970   "The Iban of Western Borneo." In *Cultures of the Pacific,* edited by Thomas G. Harding and Ben J. Wallace, 180–200. New York: Free Press.
1983   *Margaret Mead and Samoa.* Cambridge, Mass.: Harvard University Press.

Fried, Morton
1967   *The Evolution of Political Society.* New York: Random House.

Friedl, Ernestine
1975   *Women and Men: An Anthropologist's View.* New York: Holt, Rinehart and Winston.
1978   "Society and Sex Roles." In *Anthropology 98/99,* edited by Elvio Angeloni, 122–126. Guilford, Conn.: Dushkin.

Friedson, Steven
1998   "Tumbuka Healing." In *The Garland Encyclopedia of World Music,* vol. 1, edited by Ruth M. Stone, pp. 271–284. New York: Garland Publishing, Inc.

Frigout, Arlette
1979   "Hopi Ceremonial Organization." In *Southwest,* edited by Alfonso Ortiz, 564–76. *Handbook of North American Indians,* vol. 9. Washington, D.C.: Smithsonian Institution.

Fromkin, Victoria, and Robert Rodman
1988   *An Introduction to Language.* 4th ed. New York: Holt, Rinehart and Winston.

Furst, Peter T., and Jill L. Furst
1982   *North American Indian Art.* New York: Rizzoli International Publications, Inc.

Geertz, Clifford
1963   *Agricultural Involution.* Berkeley: University of California Press.
1965   "Religion As a Cultural System." In *Anthropological Approaches to the Study of Religion,* edited by Michael Banton. Association of Social Anthropologists Monographs, no. 3. London: Tavistock Publications.
1973   *The Interpretation of Cultures.* New York: Basic Books.
1980   *Negara.* Princeton, N.J.: Princeton University Press.

Gell, Alfred
1993   *Wrapping in Images.* Oxford: Clarendon Press.

Gerner, Deborah J.
1994   *One Land, Two Peoples: The Conflict over Palestine.* Boulder, Colo.: Westview Press.

Gilmore, David D.
1980   *The People of the Plain.* New York: Columbia University Press.
1990   *Manhood in the Making.* New Haven, Conn.: Yale University Press.

Gliessman, Stephen, and Robert Grantham
1990   "Agroecology: Reshaping Agricultural Development." In *Lessons of the Rain Forest,* edited by Suzanne Head and Robert Heinzman. San Francisco: Sierra Club Books, pp. 196–207.

Glazer, Nathan, and Daniel P. Moynihan
1963   *Beyond the Melting Pot.* Cambridge: Harvard University Press.

Glazer, Nathan, and Daniel P. Moynihan, eds.
1975   *Ethnicity: Theory and Experience.* Cambridge: Harvard University Press.

Gluckman, Max
1972   *The Ideas in Barotse Jurisprudence.* Manchester: Manchester University Press.
1973   *The Judicial Process Among the Barotse.* Manchester: Manchester University Press.

Goldman, Irving
1970   *Ancient Polynesian Society.* Chicago: University of Chicago Press.

Goldstein, Melvyn C.
1987   "When Brothers Share a Wife." *Natural History* 96(3):38–49.

Goodenough, Ward H.
1961   "Comment on Cultural Evolution." *Daedalus* 90:521–28.

Goody, Jack
1976   *Production and Reproduction.* Cambridge: Cambridge University Press.

Goody, Jack, and S. J. Tambiah
1973   *Bridewealth and Dowry.* Cambridge: Cambridge University Press.

Gough, E. Kathleen
1959   "The Nayars and the Definition of Marriage." *Journal of the Royal Anthropological Institute* 89:23–24.

Graburn, Nelson H. H., ed.
1976   *Ethnic and Tourist Arts: Cultural Expressions from the Fourth World.* Berkeley: University of California Press.

Graham, Susan Brandt
1985   "Running and Menstrual Dysfunction: Recent Medical Discoveries Provide New Insights into the Human Division of Labor by Sex." *American Anthropologist* 87:878–82.

Green, Edward C.
1985   "Traditional Healers, Mothers and Childhood Diarrheal Disease in Swaziland: The Interface of Anthropology and Health Education." *Social Science and Medicine* 20:277–285.
1987   "The Planning of Health Education Strategies in Swaziland." In *Anthropological Praxis,* edited by Robert M. Wulff and Shirley J. Fiske, pp. 15–25. Boulder, Colo.: Westview Press.
1994   "The Integration of Modern and Traditional Health Sectors in Swaziland." In *Applying Cultural Anthropology: An Introductory Reader,* edited by Aaron Podolefsky and Peter J. Brown, pp. 237–242. Mountain View, Calif.: Mayfield.

Grigg, David
1974   *The Agricultural Systems of the World.* Cambridge: Cambridge University Press.

Hage, Per, Frank Harary, and Bojka Milicic
1995   Tatooing, Gender and Social Stratification in Micro-Polynesia. *Journal of the Royal Anthropological Institute (N.S.)* 2:335–350.

Hail, Barbara A.
1983   *Hau, Kola!: The Plains Indian Collection of the Haffenrefer Museum.*

Hajda, Lubomyr, and Mark Beissinger, ed.
1990   *The Nationalities Factor in Soviet Politics and Society.* Boulder, Colo.: Westview Press.

Hall, Edward T.
1959   *The Silent Language.* Greenwich, Conn.: Fawcett Publications.
1966   *The Hidden Dimension.* Garden City, N.Y.: Doubleday.

Hamill, James
1990   *Ethno-Logic: The Anthropology of Human Reasoning.* Urbana: University of Illinois Press.

Handler, Richard
1988   *Nationalism and the Politics of Culture in Quebec.* Madison: University of Wisconsin Press.

Hanson, Jeffery R.
1988   "Age-Set Theory and Plains Indian Age-Grading: A Critical Review and Revision." *American Ethnologist* 15:349–64.

Harlan, Jack R.
1975   "Our Vanishing Genetic Resources." *Science* 188: 618–21.

Harner, Michael J.
1973a   *The Jivaro.* Garden City, N.Y.: Doubleday-Anchor.
1973b   "The Sound of Rushing Water." In *Hallucinogens and Shamanism,* edited by Michael J. Harner, 15–27. London: Oxford University Press.

Harrell, Stevan, and Sara A. Dickey
1985   "Dowry Systems in Complex Societies." *Ethnology* 24:105–120.

Harris, Marvin
    1968 *The Rise of Anthropological Theory*. New York: Thomas Y. Crowell.
    1977 *Cannibals and Kings*. New York: Random House.
    1979 *Cultural Materialism*. New York: Vintage Books.
    1981 *America Now*. New York: Simon & Schuster.
    1985 *Good to Eat*. New York: Simon & Schuster.
    1999 *Theories of Culture in Postmodern Times*. Walnut Creek, Calif.: Altamira Press.

Harrison, Paul
    1987 *The Greening of Africa*. New York: Penguin.

Hart, C. W. M., and Arnold R. Pilling
    1979 *The Tiwi of North Australia*. New York: Holt, Rinehart, and Winston.

Harvey, Paul
    1937 *The Oxford Companion to Classical Literature*. Oxford: Clarendon Press.

Hassrick, Royal B.
    1964 *The Sioux: Life and Customs of a Warrior Society*. Norman: University of Oklahoma Press.

Hepner, George F., and Jesse O. McKee
    1992 *World Regional Geography: A Global Approach*. St. Paul, Minn.: West Publishing Company.

Heth, Charlotte, general editor
    1993 *Native American Dance*. Washington, D.C.: Smithsonian Institution.

Hewlett, Barry S.
    1992 *Intimate Fathers*. Ann Arbor, Mich.: University of Michigan Press.

Heyerdahl, Thor
    1958 *Aku-Aku*. Chicago: Rand McNally & Company.

Hickerson, Harold
    1970 *The Chippewa and Their Neighbors: A Study in Ethnohistory*. New York: Holt, Rinehart and Winston.

Hiebert, P. G.
    1971 *Konduru: Structure and Integration in a Hindu Village*. Minneapolis: University of Minnesota Press.

Himes, Joseph S.
    1974 *Racial and Ethnic Relations*. Dubuque, Ia.: Wm. C. Brown Company.

Hitchcock, Robert K.
    1999 "Resource Rights and Resettlement Among the San of Botswana." *Cultural Survival Quarterly* 22(4):51–55.

Hobson, Christine
    1987 *The World of the Pharaohs*. New York: Thames and Hudson.

Hockett, Charles D.
    1960 "The Origin of Speech." *Scientific American* 203:88–96.

Hoebel, E. Adamson
    1940 *The Political Organization and Law-ways of the Comanche Indians*. American Anthropological Association, Memoir 54.
    1954 *The Law of Primitive Man*. Cambridge: Harvard University Press.
    1978 *The Cheyennes*. 2nd ed. New York: Holt, Rinehart and Winston.

Holm, Bill
    1965 *Northwest Coast Indian Art: An Analysis of Form*. Seattle: University of Washington Press.
    1972 *Crooked Beak of Heaven*. Seattle: University of Washington Press.

Holmes, Lowell D., and Ellen Rhoads Holmes
    1992 *Samoan Village Then and Now*. 2nd ed. Fort Worth: Harcourt Brace Jovanovich College Publishers.

Horowitz, Donald L.
    1985 *Ethnic Groups in Conflict*. Berkeley: University of California Press.

Hostetler, John A., and Gertrude Enders Huntington
    1992 *Amish Children*. 2nd ed. Fort Worth, Tex.: Harcourt Brace Jovanovich College Publishers.

Howard, Alan, and John Kirkpatrick
    1989 "Social Organization." In *Developments in Polynesian Ethnology*, edited by Alan Howard and Robert Borofsky, pp. 47–94. Honolulu: University of Hawaii Press.

Hunter, David E., and Phillip Whitten, eds.
    1976 *Encyclopedia of Anthropology*. New York: Harper & Row.

Innis, Donald Q.
    1980 "The Future of Traditional Agriculture." *Focus* 30:1–8.

Jackson, Richard, and Lloyd E. Hudman
    1990a *Cultural Geography: People, Places and Environment*. St. Paul, Minn.: West Publishing Company.
    1990b *World Regional Geography: Issues for Today*. New York: John Wiley & Sons.

Jenness, Diamond
    1932 *The Indians of Canada*. Ottawa: National Museum of Canada.

Johnson, Allen W.
    1971 "Security and Risk-Taking Among Poor Peasants: A Brazilian Case." In *Studies in Economic Anthropology*, edited by George Dalton, 143–50. American Anthropological Association Special Publication, no. 7. Washington, D.C.: American Anthropological Association.

Johnson, Allen W., and Timothy Earle
    1987 *The Evolution of Human Societies*. Stanford, Conn.: Stanford University Press.

Joint Economic Committee
    1986 *The Concentration of Wealth in the United States: Trends in the Distribution of Wealth Among American Families*.

Julien, Catherine J.
    1988 "How Inca Decimal Administration Worked." *Ethnohistory* 35:257–279.

Jurmain, Robert, Harry Nelson, and Lynn Kilgore
    1995 *Essentials of Physical Anthropology*. 2nd ed.. St. Paul, Minn.: West Publishing Company.

Kaeppler, Adrienne L.
    1978 "Dance in Anthropological Perspective." In Bernard Siegel, ed. *Annual Review of Anthropology*, 7:31–49. Palo Alto, Calif.: Annual Reviews Inc.

Kahn, J., et al., eds.
    1979 *World Economic Development*. Boulder, Colo.: Westview.

Kalb, Laurie Beth
    1994 *Crafting Devotions: Tradition in Contemporary New Mexico Santos*. Albuquerque: University of New Mexico Press.

Kammer, Jerry
    1980 *The Second Long Walk: The Navajo-Hopi Land Dispute*. Albuquerque: University of New Mexico.

Kapur, Akash
    1998 "The Indian State of Kerala Has Everything Against It—Except Success." *The Atlantic Monthly*. Sept. 1, p. 4(1).

Kardiner, Abram
    1945 *The Psychological Frontiers of Society*. New York: Columbia University Press.

Keesing, Roger M.
    1982 *Kwaio Religion*. New York: Columbia University Press.

Kehoe, Alice B.
    1989 *The Ghost Dance*. New York: Holt, Rinehart and Winston.
    1992 *North American Indians: A Comprehensive Account*. 2nd ed. Englewood Cliffs, N.J.: Prentice-Hall, Inc.

Kelly, Robert L.
    1995 *The Foraging Spectrum: Diversity in Hunter-Gatherer Lifeways*. Washington, D.C.: Smithsonian Institution.

Khlief, Bud B.
1979 "Language as Identity: Toward an Ethnography of Welsh Nationalism." *Ethnicity* 6(4):346–57.

Kluckhohn, Clyde
1967 *Navajo Witchcraft*. Boston: Beacon Press.

Kottak, Conrad
1992 *Assault on Paradise: Social Change in a Brazilian Village*. 2nd ed. New York: McGraw-Hill.

Krader, Lawrence
1968 *Formation of the State*. Englewood Cliffs, N.J.: Prentice-Hall.

Kraybill, Donald B.
1989 *The Riddle of Amish Culture*. Baltimore, Md.: Johns Hopkins University Press.
1990 *The Puzzles of Amish Life*. Intercourse, Pa.: Good Books.

Kuper, Hilda
1963 *The Swazi: A South African Kingdom*. New York: Holt, Rinehart and Winston.

Laderman, Carol, and Marina Roseman, eds.
1996 *The Performance of Healing*. New York: Routledge.

LaFlesche, Francis
1905 *Who Was the Medicine Man?* Hampton, Va.: Hampton Institute Press.
1925 "The Osage Tribe: Rite of Vigil." *Thirty-ninth Annual Report of the Bureau of American Ethnology (1917–18)*, pp. 523–833. Washington, D.C.: Government Printing Office.
1928 "The Osage Tribe: Two Versions of the Child-Naming Rite." *43rd Annual Report of the Bureau of American Ethnology, 1925–1926*, 23–164. Washington, D.C.: Government Printing Office.

LaLone, Mary B., and Darrell E. LaLone
1987 "The Inka State in the Southern Highlands: State Administrative and Production Enclaves." *Ethnohistory* 34:47–62.

Lappé, Frances Moore, and Joseph Collins
1977 *Food First*. New York: Ballantine Books.
1986 *World Hunger: Twelve Myths*. New York: Grove Press.

Lawrence, Peter
1964 *Road Belong Cargo*. Manchester: Manchester University Press.

Leach, E. R.
1968 "The Sinhalese of the Dry Zone of Northern Ceylon." In *Economic Anthropology*, edited by Edward E. LeClair, Jr., and Harold K. Schneider, 395–403. New York: Holt, Rinehart and Winston (original 1960).

Leacock, Eleanor
1978 "Women's Status in Egalitarian Society: Implications for Social Evolution." *Current Anthropology* 19:247–75.

Leacock, Eleanor, and Nancy Lurie, eds.
1971 *North American Indians in Historical Perspective*. New York: Random House.

Lee, Richard B.
1968 "What Hunters Do for a Living, or, How to Make Out on Scarce Resources." In *Man the Hunter*, edited by Richard B. Lee and Irven DeVore, 30–48. Chicago: Aldine.
1969 "!Kung Bushman Subsistence: An Input—Output Analysis." In *Environment and Social Behavior*, edited by Andrew P. Vayda, 47–79. Garden City, N.Y.: Natural History Press.
1979 *The !Kung San*. Cambridge: Cambridge University Press.
1993 *The Dobe Ju/'hoansi*, 2nd ed. Fort Worth, Tex.: Harcourt Brace Jovanovich College Publishers.

Lefkowitz, Mary
1995 *Not Out of Africa: How Afrocentrism Became an Excuse to Teach Myth as History*. New York: Basic Books.

Lenski, Gerhard E.
1966 *Power and Privilege*. New York: McGraw-Hill.

LeVine, Terry Yarov
1987 "Inka Labor Service at the Regional Level: The Functional Reality." *Ethnohistory* 34:14–46.

Lewis, Oscar
1941 "Manly-hearted Women Among the South Piegan." *American Anthropologist* 43:173–87.

Lewis, Walter H., and Memory P. F. Elvin-Lewis
1977 *Medical Botany*. New York: John Wiley and Sons.

Lipman, Jean, and Alice Winchester
1974 *The Flowering of American Folk Art*. New York: The Viking Press.

Llewellyn, Karl, and E. Adamson Hoebel
1941 *The Cheyenne Way*. Norman: University of Oklahoma.

Lomax, Alan
1962 "Song Structure and Social Structure." *Ethnology* 1:425–51.
1968 "Folk Song Style and Culture." *American Association for the Advancement of Science Publication*, no. 88. Washington, D.C.

Lowie, Robert H.
1954 *Indians of the Plains*. Garden City, N.Y.: American Museum of Natural History.
1956 *The Crow Indians*. New York: Holt, Rinehart and Winston (original 1935).

Malinowski, Bronislaw
1922 *Argonauts of the Western Pacific*. New York: E. P. Dutton and Company, Inc.
1926 *Crime and Custom in Savage Society*. London: Rutledge and Kegan Paul.
1954 *Magic, Science and Religion*. Garden City, N.Y.: Doubleday and Company, Inc.
1960 *A Scientific Theory of Culture and Other Essays*. New York: Oxford University Press (original 1944).

Mamdani, Mahmood
1973 *The Myth of Population Control: Family, Caste, and Class in an Indian Village*. New York: Monthly Review Press.

Mandelbaum, David G.
1970 *Society in India*. 2 vols. Berkeley: University of California Press.

Mark, Joan
1988 *A Stranger in Her Native Land: Alice Fletcher and the American Indians*. Lincoln: University of Nebraska Press.

Martin, M. Kay, and Barbara Voorhies
1975 *Female of the Species*. New York: Columbia University Press.

Marx, Karl
1967 *Capital*. Volume 1. New York: International Publishers (original 1867).
1970 *A Contribution to the Critique of Political Economy*. New York: International Publishers (original 1859).

Mayo, Katherine
1927 *Mother India*. Harcourt, Brace & Company.

McAlister, John T., ed.
1973 *Southeast Asia: The Politics of National Integration*. New York: Random House.

McDonald, Kim
1995 "Unearthing Sins of the Past." *The Chronicle of Higher Education*, October 6, A12, 20.

McNickle, D'Arcy
1971 "Americans Called Indians." In Eleanor Burke Leacock and Nancy Oestrich Lurie, eds. *North American Indians in Historical Perspective*, pp. 29–63. New York: Random House.

Mead, Margaret
1928 *Coming of Age in Samoa*. New York: Morrow.

Mead, Sidney Moko, ed.
1984 *Te Maori: Maori Art from New Zealand Collections*. New York: Harry N. Abrams, Inc.

Medicine, Beatrice
1983 "'Warrior Women': Sex Role Alternatives for Plains Indian Women." In *The Hidden Half: Studies of Plains Indian Women*, edited by Patricia Albers and Beatrice Medicine, 267–75. Lanham, Md.: University Press of America.

Meggitt, Mervyn
    1970   "Male-Female Relationships in the Highlands of Australian New Guinea." In *Cultures of the Pacific,* edited by Thomas G. Harding and Ben J. Wallace, 125–43. New York: Free Press.

Meigs, Anna S.
    1988   *Food, Sex, and Pollution: A New Guinea Religion.* New Brunswick, N.J.: Rutgers University Press.
    1990   "Multiple Gender Ideologies and Statuses." In Peggy Reeves Sanday and Ruth Gallagher Goodenough, eds., 1990, pp. 99–112.

Metraux, Alfred
    1969   *The History of the Incas.* New York: Pantheon Books.
    1972   *Voodoo in Haiti.* New York: Schocken Books.

Middleton, John
    1965   *The Lugbara of Uganda.* New York: Holt, Rinehart and Winston.

Mintz, Sidney W.
    1986   *Sweetness and Power: The Place of Sugar in Modern History.* New York: Penguin Books.

Miracle, Marvin P.
    1966   *Maize in Tropical Africa.* Madison: University of Wisconsin.
    1967   *Agriculture in the Congo Basin.* Madison: University of Wisconsin.

Mishel, Lawrence, and Jared Bernstein
    1994   *The State of Working America 1994–95.* Economic Policy Institute Series. Armonk: M. E. Sharpe.

Moore, Omar Khayyam
    1957   "Divination—A New Perspective." *American Anthropologist* 59:69–74.

Morgan, Lewis Henry
    1877   *Ancient Society.* New York: World Publishing.

Morgen, Sandra, ed.
    1989   *Gender and Anthropology: Critical Reviews for Research and Teaching.* Washington, D.C.: American Anthropological Association.

Murdock, George Peter
    1949   *Social Structure.* New York: The Free Press.
    1967   *Ethnographic Atlas.* Pittsburgh: University of Pittsburgh Press.

Murdock, George P., and Caterina Provost
    1973   "Factors in the Division of Labor By Sex: A Cross-Cultural Analysis." *Ethnology* 12:203–225.

Murray, Gerald
    1987   "The Domestication of Wood in Haiti: A Case Study in Applied Evolution." In *Anthropological Praxis,* edited by Robert M. Wulff and Shirley J. Fiske, pp. 223–241. Boulder, Colo.: Westview Press.

Nadel, S. F.
    1951   The Foundations of Social Anthropology. London: Cohen & West.

Nag, Moni, and Neeraj Kak
    1984   "Demographic Transition in a Punjab Village." *Population and Development Review* 10:661–678.

Nag, Moni, Benjamin N. F. White, and R. Creighton Peet
    1978   "An Anthropological Approach to the Study of the Economic Value of Children in Java and Nepal." *Current Anthropology* 19:293–306.

Nardi, Bonnie
    1981   "Modes of Explanation in Anthropological Population Theory." *American Anthropologist* 83:28–56.
    1983   "Goals in Reproductive Decision Making." *American Ethnologist* 10:697–714.

Naroll, Raoul
    1962   *Data Quality Control—A New Research Technique.* New York: The Free Press.

Nations, James, and Robert Nigh
    1980   "The Evolutionary Potential of Lacandon Maya Sustained-Yield Tropical Forest Agriculture." *Journal of Anthropological Research* 36:1–30.

Neale, Walter C.
    1976   *Monies in Societies.* San Francisco: Chandler and Sharp.

Nelson Gallery
    1975   *The Chinese Exhibition: The Exhibition of Archaeological Finds of The People's Republic of China.* Kansas City: The Nelson Gallery-Atkins Museum.

Newman, Katherine S.
    1983   *Law and Economic Organization: A Comparative Study of Pre-Industrial Societies.* Cambridge: Cambridge University Press.

Newman, Philip L., and David J. Boyd
    1982   "The Making of Men: Ritual and Meaning in Awa Male Initiation." In *Rituals of Manhood: Male Initiation in Papua New Guinea,* edited by Gilbert Herdt, 239–85. Berkeley and Los Angeles: University of California Press.

Nietschmann, Bernard
    1988   "Third World War: The Global Conflict Over the Rights of Indigenous Nations." *Utne Reader* (Nov./Dec.): 84–91.

Ninuendju, Curt
    1948   "The Tucuna." In *Handbook of South American Indians,* vol. 3, edited by Julian Steward, 713–25. *Handbook of South American Indians: The Tropical Forest Tribes.* Bureau of American Ethnology Bulletin 143. Washington, D.C.: U.S. Government Printing Office.

Obeyesekere, Gananath
    1992   *The Apotheosis of Captain Cook: European Mythmaking in the Pacific.* Princeton, N.J.: Princeton University Press.

Offiong, Daniel
    1983   "Witchcraft Among the Ibibio of Nigeria." *African Studies Review* 26:107–24.

Oliver, Douglas L.
    1989   *Oceania: The Native Cultures of Australia and the Pacific Islands.* Honolulu: University of Hawaii Press.

Oliver, Roland, and J. D. Fage
    1962   *A Short History of Africa.* Baltimore: Penguin.

Oliver, Symmes C.
    1962   "Ecology and Cultural Continuity as Contributing Factors in the Social Organization of the Plains Indians." University of California Publications in American Archaeology and Ethnology 48(1).

Pasternak, Burton
    1976   *Introduction to Kinship and Social Organization.* Englewood Cliffs, N.J.: Prentice-Hall, Inc.

Pasternak, Burton, Carol R. Ember, and Melvin Ember
    1976   "On the Conditions Favoring Extended Family Households." *Journal of Anthropological Research* 32:109–23.

Peoples, James G.
    1982   "Individual or Group Advantage? A Reinterpretation of the Maring Ritual Cycle." *Current Anthropology* 23:291–309.
    1985   *Island in Trust.* Boulder, Colo.: Westview Press.

Piddocke, Stuart
    1965   "The Potlatch System of the Southern Kwakiutl: A New Perspective." *Southwestern Journal of Anthropology* 21:244–64.

Pieterse, Jan Nederveen
    1992   *White on Black: Images of Africa and Blacks in Western Popular Culture.* New Haven, Conn.: Yale University Press.

Pimentel, David, et al.
    1973   "Food Production and the Energy Crisis." *Science* 182:443–49.
    1975   "Energy and Land Constraints in Food Protein Production." *Science* 190:754–61.

Pimentel, David, and Marcia Pimentel
    1979   *Food, Energy and Society.* New York: John Wiley and Sons.

Porter, Philip W.
1965 "Environmental Potentials and Economic Opportunities—A Background for Cultural Adaptation." *American Anthropologist* 67:409–20.

Posey, Darrell
1983 "Indigenous Ecological Knowledge and Development of the Amazon." In *The Dilemma of Amazonian Development*, Emilio Moran, ed. Boulder, Colo.: Westview Press.
1984 "A Preliminary Report on Diversified Management of Tropical Forest by the Kayapó Indians of the Brazilian Amazon." *Advances in Economic Botany* 1:112–126.
1985 "Indigenous Management of Tropical Forest Ecosystems: The Case of the Kayapó Indians of the Brazilian Amazon." *Agroforestry Systems* 3:139–158.

Pospisil, Leopold
1958 *Kapauku Papuans and Their Law*. Yale University Publications in Anthropology, no. 54.
1978 *The Kapauku Papuans of West New Guinea*. 2nd ed. New York: Holt, Rinehart and Winston.

Price, Richard, ed.
1979 *Maroon Societies: Rebel Slave Communities in the Americas*. Baltimore: Johns Hopkins University.

Pulliam, H. Ronald, and Christopher Dunford
1980 *Programmed to Learn*. New York: Columbia University Press.

Quinn, Naomi
1977 "Anthropological Studies on Women's Status." *Annual Review of Anthropology* 6:181–225.

Radcliffe-Brown, A. R.
1922 *The Andaman Islanders*. Cambridge: Cambridge University Press.
1965 *Structure and Function in Primitive Societies*. New York: Free Press.

Rappaport, Roy
1968 *Pigs for the Ancestors*. New Haven: Yale University Press.

Rasmussen, Knud
1979 "A Shaman's Journey to the Sea Spirit." In *Reader in Comparative Religion*, edited by William A. Lessa and Evon Z. Vogt, 308–11. New York: Harper & Row.

Reichard, Gladys A.
1950 *Navaho Religion*. Princeton, N.J.: Princeton University Press.
1977 *Navajo Medicine Man Sandpaintings*. New York: Dover Publications.

Reichel-Dolmatoff, Gerardo
1971 *Amazonian Cosmos*. Chicago: University of Chicago Press.

Rosaldo, Michelle Z., and Louise Lamphere, eds.
1974 *Women, Culture, and Society*. Stanford, Calif.: Stanford University Press.

Ross, Sally, and Alphonse Deveau
1992 *The Acadians of Nova Scotia: Past and Present*. Halifax, N.S.: Nimbus Publishing.

Rostow, W. W.
1978 *The World Economy: History and Prospect*. Austin: University of Texas.

Ruddle, Kenneth
1974 *The Yukpa Autosubsistence System: A Study of Shifting Cultivation and Ancillary Activities in Columbia and Venezuela*. Berkeley: University of California Press.

Sacks, Karen
1982 *Sisters and Wives*. Urbana: University of Illinois Press.

Sahlins, Marshall
1958 *Social Stratification in Polynesia*. Seattle: University of Washington Press.
1965 "On the Sociology of Primitive Exchange." In *The Relevance of Models for Social Anthropology*, edited by Michael Banton, pp. 139–236. London: Tavistock.

1972 *Stone Age Economics*. New York: Aldine Publishing Company.
1981 *Historical Metaphors and Mythical Realities: Structure in the Early History of the Sandwich Island Kingdom*. Ann Arbor: University of Michigan Press.
1995 *How "Natives" Think: About Captain Cook, For Example*. Chicago: University of Chicago Press.

Said, Edward
1978 *Orientalism*. New York: Vintage Books.

Sanday, Peggy R.
1973 "Toward a Theory of the Status of Women." *American Anthropologist* 75:1682–1700.
1981 *Female Power and Male Dominance*. Cambridge: Cambridge University Press.

Sanday, Peggy Reeves, and Ruth Gallagher Goodenough, eds.
1990 *Beyond the Second Sex*. Philadelphia: University of Pennsylvania Press.

Sandner, Donald
1991 *Navajo Symbols of Healing*. Rochester, Vt.: Healing Arts Press.

Sapir, Edward
1964 "The Status of Linguistics as a Science." In *Edward Sapir*, edited by David G. Mandelbaum, 65–77. Berkeley: University of California Press (original 1929).

Schlegel, Alice
1972 *Male Dominance and Female Autonomy*. New Haven, Conn.: HRAF Press.
1991 "Status, Property, and the Value on Virginity." *American Ethnologist* 18:719–734.

Schneider, Harold K.
1981 *The Africans*. Englewood Cliffs, N.J.: Prentice-Hall.

Scudder, Thayer
1982 *No Place to Go: Effects of Compulsory Relocation on Navajos*. Philadelphia: ISHI.

Sen, Amartya
1984 *Resources, Values and Development*. Cambridge, Mass.: Harvard University Press.
1987 *The Standard of Living*. Cambridge: Cambridge University Press.

Shankman, Paul
1976 *Migration and Underdevelopment: The Case of Western Samoa*. Boulder, Colo.: Westview Press.

Shore, Bradd
1989 "Mana and Tapu." In *Developments in Polynesian Ethnology*, Alan Howard and Robert Borofsky, eds., pp. 137–173. Honolulu: University of Hawaii Press.

Shostak, Marjorie
1983 *Nisa: The Life and Words of a !Kung Woman*. New York: Vintage.

Simmons, Dave
1983 "Moko." In *Art and Artists of Oceania*, pp. 226–243. Palmerston North: Dunmore Press.

Small, Cathy
1997 *Voyages*. Ithaca and London: Cornell University Press.

Smith, Bruce
1995 *The Emergence of Agriculture*. New York: Scientific American Library.

Smith, Eric Alden, and Bruce Winterhalder, eds.
1992 *Evolutionary Ecology and Human Behavior*. New York: Aldine de Gruyter.

Snow, Clyde
1995 "Murder Most Foul." *The Sciences* (May/June): 16–20.

Sokolov, Raymond
1986 "The Good Seed." *Natural History* 95:102–105.

Stamp, L. Dudley
1973 *A Commercial Geography*. 9th ed. London: Longman.

Stavrianos, L. S.
1982 *The World Since 1500: A Global History*. 4th ed. Englewood Cliffs, N.J.: Prentice-Hall.

Steward, Julian H.
1938 *Basin-Plateau Sociopolitical Groups*. Bureau of American Ethnology Bulletin 120.
1955 *Theory of Culture Change*. Urbana, Ill.: University of Illinois Press.
1977 *Evolution and Ecology: Essays on Social Transformation,* edited by Jane C. Steward and Robert F. Murphy. Urbana, Ill.: University of Illinois Press.

Stewart, Omer C.
1980 "The Native American Church." In *Anthropology on the Great Plains,* edited by W. Raymond Wood and Margot Liberty, 188–96. Lincoln, Neb.: University of Nebraska Press.

Stone, M. Priscilla, Glenn Davis Stone, and Robert McC. Netting
1995 "The Sexual Division of Labor in Kofyar Agriculture." *American Ethnologist* 22:165–86.

Suttles, Wayne
1960 "Affinal Ties, Subsistence, and Prestige among the Coast Salish." *American Anthropologist* 62:296–305.
1962 "Variations in Habitat and Culture on the Northwest Coast." In *Man in Adaptation: The Cultural Present,* edited by Yehudi A. Cohen, 128–41. Chicago: Aldine.
1968 "Coping with Abundance: Subsistence on the Northwest Coast." In *Man the Hunter,* edited by Richard B. Lee and Irven DeVore, 56–68. Chicago: Aldine.

Swanson, Guy
1960 *The Birth of the Gods*. Ann Arbor: University of Michigan Press.

Swepton, Lee
1989 "Indigenous and Tribal Peoples and International Law: Recent Developments." *Current Anthropology* 30:259–64.

Tax, Sol, ed.
1967 *Acculturation in the Americas*. New York: Cooper Square Publishers.

Thornton, Russell
1987 *American Indian Holocaust and Survival: A Population History since 1492*. Norman: University of Oklahoma Press.

Tischer, Henry L.
1990 *Introduction to Sociology*. 3d ed. Fort Worth, Tex.: Holt, Rinehart and Winston.

Trudgill, Peter
1983 *Sociolinguistics*. Middlesex, England: Penguin.

Turnbull, Colin M.
1962 *The Forest People*. New York: Simon & Schuster.

Turner, Terence
1989 "Kayapo Plan Meeting to Discuss Dams." *Cultural Survival Quarterly* 13:20–22.

Turner, Victor
1967 *The Forest of Symbols*. Ithaca, N.Y.: Cornell University Press.

Tyler, Stephen A., ed.
1969 *Cognitive Anthropology*. New York: Holt, Rinehart and Winston.

Tyler, Stephen A.
1973 *India: An Anthropological Perspective*. Pacific Palisades, Calif.: Goodyear Publishing Company.

Tylor, Edward B.
1865 *Researches into the Early History of Mankind and the Development of Civilization*. London: J. Murray.
1871 *Primitive Culture*. London: J. Murray.

United Nations Development Programme
1995 *Human Development Report 1995*. New York: Oxford University Press.

United States Bureau of the Census
1998 Current Population Reports, pp. 60–200, Money Income in the United States: 1997. Washington, D.C.: U.S. Government Printing Office.

Urban, Greg, and Joel Sherzer, eds.
1992 *Nation-States and Indians in Latin America*. Austin: University of Texas.

Valeri, Valerio
1985 *Kingship and Sacrifice: Ritual and Society in Ancient Hawaii*. Chicago and London: University of Chicago Press.

Van den Berghe, Pierre
1979 *Human Family Systems*. New York: Elsevier.

Vanstone, James W.
1974 *Athapaskan Adaptations: Hunters and Fishermen of the Subarctic Forest*. Chicago: Aldine.

Vincent, Joan
1974 "The Structuring of Ethnicity." *Human Organization* 33:375–79.

Wallace, Anthony F. C.
1966 *Religion: An Anthropological View*. New York: Random House.
1969 *The Death and Rebirth of the Seneca*. New York: Vintage Books.

Wallace, Ernest, and E. Adamson Hoebel
1952 *The Comanches: Lords of the South Plains*. Norman: University of Oklahoma.

Warner, John Anson
1986 "The Individual in Native American Art: A Sociological View." In Edwin L. Wade, ed. *The Arts of the North American Indian: Native Traditions in Evolution,* pp. 171–202. New York: Hudson Hills Press.

Weigle, Marta, and Barbara A. Babcock, eds.
1996 *The Great Southwest of the Fred Harvey Company and the Santa Fe Railway*. Phoenix: The Heard Museum.

Weyler, Rey
1982 *Blood of the Land*. New York: Vintage Books.

White, Benjamin N. F.
1973 "Demand for Labor and Population Growth in Colonial Java." *Human Ecology* 1:217–36.

White, Douglas R., Michael L. Burton, and Malcolm M. Dow
1981 "Sexual Division of Labor in African Agriculture: A Network Autocorrelation Analysis." *American Anthropologist* 83:824–49.

White, Leslie
1949 *The Science of Culture*. New York: Grove Press.
1959 *The Evolution of Culture*. New York: McGraw-Hill.

White, Lynn
1967 "The Historical Roots of Our Ecological Crisis." *Science* 155:1203–1207.

Whiting, Beatrice
1950 *Paiute Sorcery*. Viking Fund Publications in Anthropology 15. New York.

Whiting, John W. M.
1977 "A Model for Psychocultural Research." In *Culture and Infancy,* edited by P. Herbert Leiderman, S. R. Tulkin, and A. Rosenfield, 29–49. New York: Academic Press.

Whitworth, John McKelvie
1975 *God's Blueprints: A Sociological Study of Three Utopian Sects*. Boston: Rutledge and Kegan Paul.

Whyte, Martin King
1978 *The Status of Women in Preindustrial Societies*. Princeton, N.J.: Princeton University Press.

Wilken, Gene C.
1987 *Good Farmers: Traditional Resource Management in Mexico and Central America*. Berkeley: University of California Press.

Wilson, Monica
1951 *Good Company*. Oxford: Oxford University Press.

Winterhalder, Bruce, and Eric Alden Smith, eds.
1981 *Hunter-Gatherer Foraging Strategies*. Chicago: University of Chicago Press.

Winthrop, Robert H.
1991 *Dictionary of Concepts in Cultural Anthropology*. New York: Greenwood Press.

Wolf, Eric
1966 *Peasants*. Englewood Cliffs, N.J.: Prentice-Hall.
1969 *Peasant Wars of the Twentieth Century*. New York: Harper and Row.
1982 *Europe and the People Without History*. Berkeley: University of California Press.

Wolf, Margery
1972 *Women and the Family in Rural Taiwan*. Stanford, Calif.: Stanford University Press.

Woodburn, James
1968 "An Introduction to Hadza Ecology." In *Man the Hunter*, edited by Richard B. Lee and Irven DeVore, 49–55. Chicago: Aldine.
1982 "Egalitarian Societies." *Man* 17:431–51.

World Bank
1999 *World Development Report 1998/9*. New York: Oxford.

Worsley, Peter
1968 *The Trumpet Shall Sound*. New York: Schocken Books.

Photo Credits

Chapter 1
p 1 Marshall Expedition/Documentary Educational Resources
p 3 Karl Ammann/Corbis
p 4 Robert Brenner/Photo Edit
p 8 Jack Fields/Corbis
p 9 Gavriel Jecan/Tony Stone Images
p 10 Brian Vikander/Corbis

Chapter 2
p 15 Jacksonville Museum of Contemporary Art, Florida/Superstock
p 18 A. Ramey/Photo Edit
p 19 Chagnon/Anthro-Photo File
p 21 Michael Newman/Photo Edit
p 27 © Peter Arnold, Inc.
p 30 © Bill O'Conner/Peter Arnold, Inc.

Chapter 3
p 33 Michael Newman/Photo Edit
p 36 Erika Lansner/Tony Stone Images
p 39 Courtesy of Jim Peoples
p 41 © Erika Stone/Peter Arnold, Inc.
p 47 Joseph Nettis/Photo Researchers, Inc.

Chapter 4
p 51 Sarah Steck
p 53 Scala Art Resource 1988
p 54 Bill Bachman/Photo Researchers, Inc.
p 56 Mankato Museum Of Anthropology
p 58 Jenike/Anthro-Photo File
p 61 Mankato Museum Of Anthropology
p 62 Slyvia Howe/Anthro-Photo File
p 64 Randall Hagadorn/Courtesy of Clifford Geertz

Chapter 5
p 68 Documentary Educational Resources
p 70 Crawford/Anthro-Photo File
p 74 National Anthropological Archives/Smithsonian Institution
p 80 Christian Monty/Photo Researchers, Inc.

Chapter 6
p 85 Dr. Charles Hughes/Documentary Educational Resources
p 89 George Holton/Photo Researchers, Inc.
p 90 Washburn/Anthro-Photo File
p 91 Lee/Anthro-Photo File
p 94 Lamont Lindstrom
p 99 Hafner/Anthro-Photo File
p 101 United Nations
p 102 Galen Rowell/Corbis

Chapter 7
p 108 Jeff Greenberg/Photo Edit
p 109 Lee/Anthro-Photo File
p 112 Lamont Lindstrom
p 115 Tom McCarthy/Photo Edit
p 117 Courtesy of Garrick Bailey

Chapter 8
p 120 Nancy Sheehan/Photo Edit
p 122 © Martha Cooper/Peter Arnold, Inc.
p 124 Halpern/Anthro-Photo File
p 126 L. Abu-Lughed/Anthro-Photo File
p 129 Scholer/Anthro-Photo File
p 133 Alan Oddie/Photo Edit

Chapter 9
p 138 Documentary Educational Resources
p 139 ©Jeffrey L. Rotman/Peter Arnold, Inc.
p 143 Tony Stone Images
p 147 Don Smetzer/Tony Stone Images
p 149 Israel Talby 1991/Woodfin Camp & Associates
p 150 George Chan/Photo Researchers, Inc.
p 151 Chris Heller/Anthro-Photo File

Chapter 10
p 160 Blair Seltz/Photo Researchers, Inc.
p 162 Lawrence Migdale/Photo Researchers, Inc.
p 163 © Malcolm S. Kark/Peter Arnold, Inc.
p 167 Stan Wayman/Photo Researchers, Inc.
p 168 Courtesy of Garrick Bailey
p 170 DeVore/Anthro-Photo File
p 171 Robert Brenner/Photo Edit
p 175 © 1992, Stock Montage
p 177 R. Krubner/H. Armstrong Roberts
p 179 Robert Brenner/Photo Edit

Chapter 11
p 184 Courtesy of Garrick Bailey
p 188 Art Wolfe/Tony Stone Images
p 190 Art Resource
p 192 Courtesy of Garrick Bailey
p 194 Bloss/Anthro-Photo File
p 195 Chris Rainier /Corbis
p 198 David Frazier/Photo Library

Chapter 12
p 203 Joseph Sohm, Chromosohm Inc./Corbis
p 204 Art Wolfe/Tony Stone Images
p 206 Bernard Wolfe/Photo Reserachers, Inc.
p 210 Mark Richards/Photo Edit
p 213 Thomas K. Perry
p 215 Adam Woolfit/Corbis

Chapter 13
p 218 Paul Chesley/Tony Stone Images
p 222 Norman Prince
p 224 © Martha Cooper/Peter Arnold, Inc.
p 225 © BIOS(A. Compost)/Peter Arnold, Inc.
p 232 Loren McIntyre/Woodfin Camp & Associates
p 235 Lamont Lindstrom

Chapter 14
p 241 Rafel Salvatore/Documentary Educational Resources
p 242 Kevin R Morris/Corbis

Chapter 15
p 262 Photo Edit
p 265 Shostak/Anthro-Photo File
p 268 Susan Eckert/Tony Stone Images
p 272 Courtesy of David Boyd
p 275 Etter/Anthro-Photo File
p 276 Nobory Kormine/Photo Researchers, Inc.

Chapter 16
p 281 Jacksonville Museum of Contemporary Art, Florida/Superstock
p 282 Courtesy of Garrick Bailey
p 288 Corbis/Bettmann/Corbis
p 289 Iam Murphy/Tony Stone Images
p 290 Corbis/Bettmann/Corbis
p 297 Thomas K. Perry
p 299 Lawernce Manning/Tony Stone Images
p 301 Paul Conklin/Photo Edit
p 302 David Young Wolff/Photo Edit
p 302 United Nations

Chapter 17
p 306 Matthew Neal McVay/Tony Stone Images
p 308 A. Ramey/Photo Edit
p 309 Garrick Bailey
p 311 Hulton-Deutsch Collection/Corbis
p 315 Reuters/Bettmann
p 319 Howard Davies/Corbis
p 323 FPG International
p 326 Smithsonian Institution

Chapter 18
p 331 Steve Lansing/Documentary Educational Resources
p 333 Tronick/Anthro-Photo File
p 336 Bruce Bander/Photo Researchers, Inc.
p 340 Bruce Bander/Photo Researchers, Inc.
p 343 Carl Frank/Photo Researchers, Inc.
p 344 Jim Sugar Photography/Corbis

Chapter 19
p 351 Documentary Educational Resources
p 353 © 1992, Stock Montage
p 354 Victor Englebert/Photo Researchers, Inc.
p 358 Bac Alexander/Photo Researchers, Inc.

Chapter 8 (second column)
p 244 David Young Wolff/Photo Edit
p 246 © John Cancalosi/Peter Arnold, Inc.
p 248 Paul A. Souders/Corbis
p 249 Courtesy of James Peoples
p 250 © Jeff Greenberg/Peter Arnold, Inc.
p 252 Corbis
p 254 Shostal/Anthro-Photo File
p 255 Ted Spiegel/Corbis
p 257 Robert Holmes/Corbis
p 259 Paul Conklin/Photo Edit

Peoples and Cultures Index

Note: Page numbers in *italics* indicate illustrations. Letters *f* and *t* indicate figures and tables, respectively.

A

Acadians, 312–313
Afghanistan, *179*
Africa. *See also specific country*
  in 16th century, *286f*
  body arts in, 245
  bridewealth in, 130–131
  colonization of, 285–287, 290–291
  Dutch in, 310
  ethnic groups and national
      boundaries, 314, *316f*
  fertility rates in, 334
  money objects in, 114
  performance arts in, 253
  slave trade, 283–287, 290
  social complexity of, 178–179
  urbanization of, 298
African-Americans, 28–29, 307, 310
Agta, 167
Aka, 176
Albanians, in Yugoslavia, 325, 328
Alorese, 265–266
Amazonian Indians, *232,* 273, 353–354
Americas. *See also* Latin America; Native
    Americans; *specific country*
  conquest of, 282–285, 289–290
Amish, 220, 360–362
Andalusia, 173
Andean civilizations, 244–245
Angola, 285
Apache, 273, *273,* 284, 356
Argentina, 290
Armenians, 320, 321
Asia. *See also specific country*
  in 16th century, 281, *286f*
  since 1945, 293–295
  bridewealth in, 130
  European expansion in, 287–288, 291
  language regions of, *317f*
  urbanization of, 298
Athabaskan tribes, 275
Australia
  body painting in, 245, *246*
  European expansion and, 288, 292
  Tiwi of, *54*
Awa, *272,* 272–273
Azande, 228, 229, 253
Azeri, 320, 321
Aztec, 234, 282

B

Babylon, 198
BaMbuti, 88, 167, 176, 256
Bangladesh, 317, 319, 334
Bantu-speaking peoples, 310
Barotse, 198

Basques, 325
Bedouins, *126*
Belgium
  colonization by, 291
  ethnic pluralism in, 325
Bengal, 291
Bengalis, 317
Blackfoot Indians
  alternative sex roles among, 164–165
  European contact and, 284
Boers, 310
Bolivia, Tukano people of, 23
Borneo, Iban people of, 149
Bosnia, 300, 318, 322, 328
Botswana, 354–355
Brazil, *336*
  Amazonian Indians in, 273, 353–354
  Kayapó people of, 345, 355
  racial classifications in, 28
Bretons, 245
Bulgaria, 324
Bunyoro, 211
Burma, 291, 317
Burundi, 318

C

Cajuns, 312–313
Canada
  Acadians of, 312–313
  ethnic pluralism in, 325, 326–327
  Naskapi people of, 226
  Nisga'a people of, 355
Cape Coloureds, 310
Carib, 47
Caribbean, 252, 283. *See also specific island*
Caribou Inuits, 193
Catalonians, 325
Ceylon, 288, 291
Cheyenne
  adolescents, 271
  age sets among, 268
  court system of, 196, 197, 269
  and culture change, 79
  elderly, 275
  European contact and, 284
  political organization of, 187–188
China
  body arts in, 245
  elderly in, *276*
  ethnic identity in, 309
  ethnic problems of, 318
  European expansion and, 287, 288, 291
  ideology in, 211
  industrialization of, 295
  marriage in, 122
  nationalities in, 314
  population of, 333
  status of women in, 173, 177–178
Ciguayo Indians, 283
Colombia, 298, *343*
Comanche

European contact and, 284
familial legal system of, 193
peyote religion among, 237
political organization of, 185, 186–187
Congo, *290,* 291
Cossacks, 322
Croatia, 3, 309, 318, 319
Crow
  alternative sex roles among, 165
  kinship terminology, 153–154, *154f*
  vision quest among, 231
Czechoslovakia, 323, 326, 327

D

Dakota, 284
Dobu, 224, 227
Dutch. *See also* Netherlands
  in Africa, 310

E

Easter Island, 292
Ecuador, Jivaro people of, 195, 232
Efe, *58*
Egyptians, ancient, 234, 244, 245, 254
El Salvador, 340–341
Enga, 271
England, *184. See also* Great Britain
  colonization by, 283–284, 286, 288, 291,
    292
  stereotypes about, 310
Eskimo. *See also* Inuit
  kinship terminology, 152, *152f*
Estonia, 322
Ethiopia, nationalities in, 314
Europe. *See also specific country*
  expansion of
    industrial phase, 281, 288–292
    mercantile phase, 281–288
  and nationality problems, 314–315
  immigration to, 298–299
  social complexity of, 178–179
  urbanization of, 298

F

Fiji, 292
Flemish, 325
France
  body art in, 244
  colonization by, 283–284, 286, 291
  cultural heterogeneity in, 185
  Huguenots of, 310
  migratory workers in, 298
  stereotypes about, 265

G

Garia, 236
Germans, ethnic
  refugees from Eastern Europe, 309
  relocation after World War II, 323, *324f*

Great Britain. *See also* England
    income distribution in, 213
    and Ireland, 314
    migratory workers in, 298
Greece, ancient, 244, 254, 256, 270, 358
Gros Ventre, 47
Guam, 288
Guatemala, *117, 168, 222*
    clothing styles in, *309,* 310
    ethnic conflicts in, 7
    passive assimilation in, 325, 326

H

Haiti, 289
    tree-planting program in, 345–347
    voudon religion of, 230
Hanunóo, 22
Hawaiian Islands
    discovery of, 76–77
    European expansion and, 292
    ideology in, 211
    kinship terminology, 152, 153*f*
Herero, 352
Hidatsa, 268
Himalayas, *102,* 128–129, *129*
Hindus, *315,* 315–317
    language of, 39
    religion of, 125, 233
    sacred cattle of, *62*
Hispaniola, 282, 283, 345
Hong Kong, 294
Hopi
    art of, 244, 255–256
    child-rearing among, 263
    language of, 46
    as matrilineal society, 145, 176
    religious beliefs of, 226
Hua, 160–162, 174
Huguenots, 310
Hungary, 314
Hutu, 318

I

Iban, 149
Ibibio, 228
Ibos, 318
Inca civilization, *190,* 190–191
India. *See also* Hindus
    castes in, 205–207
    cultural heterogeneity in, 185
    dowry in, 131
    ethnic boundaries of, 317*f*
    ethnic problems of, 315–317
    European expansion and, 287, 288, 291
    fertility rates in, 334, 337
    ideology in, 211
    Kerala, 342
    Nayar marriage, 123–124
    population of, 333
    status of women in, 179–180
Indonesia, *225*
    Alorese people of, 265–266
    costs and benefits of children in, 337–338
    industrialization of, 295
    Kapauku people of, 115
    languages, 48
    medicine men, *358*
    nationalities in, 314
    threats to indigenous peoples of, 354

Inuit. *See also* Eskimo
    children, 263, 269–270
    elderly, 275
    familial legal system of, 193
    religious beliefs of, 226
Iraq, 319
Ireland, 265, 314, 359
Irian Java, 115, *225*
Iroquois, *175*
    kinship terminology, 152–153, 153*f*
    status of women, 174–175, 176
Islamic peoples
    art of, 256
    Western view of, 300–301
Israel, 314
Italians, 265

J

Jamaica, *177*
Japan
    since 1945, 293, 294
    European expansion and, 291
    income distribution in, 213
    language of, 48
    marriage in, 122
    racial classifications in, 28
    status of women in, 173
Java
    costs and benefits of children in, 337–338
    European expansion and, 288
    Kapauku people of, 115
    languages of, 48
Jews, 309, 314, 325
Jivaro, 195, 232
Jordanians, *150*
Ju/'hoansi. *See* !Kung

K

Kaimanga people, *9*
Kapauku, 115
Karen, 317
Karimojong, 102–103
Kashmir, 315
Kayapó, 345, 355
Kazakhstan, 322
Kenya
    fertility rates in, 334
    Maasai of, 102, *143, 268*
Kerala, India, 342
Kiowa, 237, 284
Kofyar, 171
Kongo, 285, 287
Kosovo, 300, 318, 327
Kosraen, 38–39
!Kung, *90, 91, 109, 170, 204, 265*
    band organization of, 89, 90, 109
    brideservice among, 131
    child-rearing among, 263
    modesty among, 110
    performance arts among, 252–253
    work of, 92
Kurdistan, proposed boundaries of, 318*f*
Kurds, 3, 318, 319
Kwaio, 224–225
Kwakiutl, 264

L

Lacandon Maya, 345
Laotians, *124*

Latin America. *See also specific country*
    crops of, 359
    urbanization of, 298
Lugbara, 228, 233
Lunda, 287
Luzon, Agta people of, 167

M

Maasai, 102, *143, 268*
Madagascar, *151*
Malawi, 253
Malaya, 291
Malaysia
    Iban people of, 149
    industrialization of, 295
    Semai people of, 19
Maori, 246, 247, *248,* 292, 355
Maring, 111
Marquesas, 247
Mayans, 7, *309,* 345
Melanesia
    cargo cults in, 235–236
    Dobu people of, 224, 227
    European expansion and, 288, 292
    money objects in, 114
    peyote religion in, 237–238
Mescalero Apache, 273, *273*
Metis, 310
Mexico
    conquest of, 282, 283
    Lacandon Maya of, 345
Micronesia
    child-rearing in, 263
    European expansion and, 288, 292
    languages in, 38–39, 47
    redistribution systems in, 113–114
    symbols in, 22
Middle East
    banking in, 296
    male relationships in, *139*
    status of women in, 179–180
    Western view of, 300–301
Moldavia, 322
Morocco, 319
Mozambique, 285, 286
Muslims
    in India, 315–317
    in Yugoslavia, 325, 328

N

Naga people, 315
Nagorno-Karabakh, 300, 320, 321
Naskapi, 226
Native Americans, *188. See also specific tribes*
    alternative sex roles among, 164–165
    art of, 248, *249, 250,* 250–251, *252,* 254–256, *255*
    body arts among, 245
    children, 269–270
    church of, 238
    concept of sacred, 221
    European expansion and, 282–285, 289–290, 292
    forced assimilation of, 324
    in Guatemala, 325, 326
    humorous deception by, 72
    linguistic influences of, 42
    matrilineal societies, 80, 145

of Northwest Coast, 204, 250–251
political activism by, 355, 356
relocation of, 323
revitalization movements, 236–237
study of, 74–75
in United States, 326
vision quest among, 231
Navajo, 72, 229, *255*
art of, 254–255, *255*
beliefs of, 23, 228
children, 270
elderly, 275
Nayar, 123–124
Ndembu, 226, 274
Nepal
Buddhist monks in, *30*
child from, *159*
polyandry in, 128, *129*
Netherlands. *See also* Dutch
body art in, 244
colonization by, 283–284, 286, 288, 291
New Caledonia, 292
New Guinea, *195. See also* Papua New Guinea
European expansion and, 292
Hua people of, 160–162, 174
initiation rites in, 271–273
New Zealand, Maori people of, 246, 247, *248,*
292, 355
Nigeria
ethnic problems of, 318
fertility rates in, 334
Ibibio people of, 228
Kofyar people of, 171
Tiv people of, 115–116
Yoruba people of, 176
Nisga'a, 355
Northern Ireland, 314
Northwest Coast peoples, 204, 250–251
art of, *250, 252*
Nuer, *194,* 194–195, 248
Nupe, 40
Nyakyusa, 228, 269

O

Oceania. *See also* Australia; Melanesia;
Micronesia; Polynesia
European expansion and, 288, 292
Omaha, 74–75
body arts of, 244
kinship terminology, 153, 154*f*
Oneida community, 127
Osage
body painting among, 245, 246
humorous deception by, 72
naming rite of, 270
peyote religion and, 237
religious beliefs, 221
rituals of, 251

P

Pacific Islands. *See also specific island*
bridewealth in, 130
Tikopia, 143–145
Pakistan, 315, 316, 334
Palestine, 314
Papago, 359
Papua New Guinea, *163*
art and gender in, 256
body painting in, 245

crops of, 359
Garia people of, 236
Kaimanga people of, *9*
Maring people of, 111
Peru
conquest of, 282
crops of, 359
Inca empire of, *190,* 190–191
Philippines
Agta people of, 167
European expansion and, 287
Hanunóo people of, 22
marketplace, 117
threats to indigenous peoples of, 354
Plains Indians
age sets among, 268
alternative sex roles among, 164–165
art of, 248, 256
European contact and, 284
political organization of, 185, 186–188
vision quest among, 231
Polynesia
child-rearing in, 263
cognatic descent in, 148
European expansion and, 288, 292
languages, 47
mana in, 219
political organization in, 188–189
ranked societies in, 204
redistribution systems, 113–114
tattooing in, 246, 247
Portugal, colonization by, 282–283, 285–286,
287
Pueblos, 72, 94–95

R

Romania, 314
Rome, ancient, 254
Russia, 288. *See also* Soviet Union
Rwanda, *319*

S

Sahrawi, 319
Samoa, *68, 148*
adolescence in, 270
European expansion and, 292
tattooing in, 247
San, 354–355. *See also* !Kung
Scotch-Irish, 314
Semai, 19
Seminole, 310
Seneca, 236–237
Serbs, 3, 309, 327–328
Shakers, 242, 256
furniture of, *242*
Shan, 317
Shoshone, 88
European contact and, 284
Sikhs, *306,* 309, 315
Singapore, 294
Sioux, 164
Slovakia, 327
Slovenia, 318, 319
Solomon Islands, 224–225
Somalia, 319, 338, *340*
Somaliland, 319
Somalis, 314
South Africa, 291, 294–295, 310
South Korea, 294

Southeast Asia
bridewealth in, 130
economic growth in, 294–295
Soviet Union
disintegration of, 320–322
republics and divisions of, 321*f,* 325
Spain
colonization by, 282–283, 286, 287–288
ethnic pluralism in, 325
status of women in, 173
Sub-Saharan Africa
bridewealth in, 130
colonization of, 285–287, 290–291
fertility rates in, 334
social complexity of, 178–179
Sudan
Azande people of, 228, 229
European expansion and, 287
Nuer people of, *194,* 194–195, 248
Surinam, *224*
Swazi, 130–131, 269, 347–348
Sweden, 265
Switzerland, 265, 360

T

Tahiti, 188–189
Taino Indians, 283
Taiwan, *122,* 294
Tajikistan, 322
Tanna, *94, 112*
Tanzania
Maasai of, 102, *143, 268*
Nyakyusa of, 228, 269
Tasmania, 292, 310
Thailand
agriculture in, *98*
industrialization of, 295
language of, 39, 40
Tibet, 128, 318
Tikopia, 143–145, 204
Timor, Alorese people of, 265–266
Tiv, 115–116
Tiwi, *54*
Tonga, 292
Trobriand Islanders, 70–71, 109
religious beliefs of, 222, 226
Tucuna Indians, 273
Tukano, 23
Tumbuka, 253
Turkey, 319
Tutsi, 318

U

Uganda
Karimojong people of, 102–103
Lugbara people of, 228, 233
United States
adolescence in, 270, 271
Cajuns in, 312–313
child rearing in, 267
children in, costs and benefits of, 335–336
classes in, 207–210
corn blight in, 359
court system in, 199
cultural heterogeneity in, 185
economy of, 295–296
ethnic groups in, 307, 311
gender in, 162
immigration to, 298*f,* 299

income distribution in, 209*t*, 213
Indian policy of, 324
Industrial Revolution and, 289
marriage in, 127, 129
Native American population of, 326
occupational prestige in, 208
old age in, 275–276
secular ideologies in, 212
status of women in, 176–177
Urdu-speaking peoples, 317

V

Vanuatu, *94, 112*
Volga Germans, 323

W

Walloons, 325
West Germany, 298
West Indies, 47, 289
Western Sahara, 319

Y

Yąnomamö, *19, 354*
behavior patterns of, 19
brideservice among, 131
marriage alliances, 129
name taboo, 48, 72
personality of, 265
threats to, 353–354

Yana, 47
Yoruba, 176
Yugo Ossetian, 320
Yugoslavia, 309, 318, 319, 322
disintegration of, 326, 327–328
nationalities in, 325, 328
republics and provinces of, 328*f*
Yukaghir, 47

Z

Zaire, BaMbuti pygmies of, 88, 167, 176, 256
Zambia, Ndembu people of, 226, 274
Zulu, 48, 130
Zuni, 264–265

Name Index

Note: Page numbers in *italics* indicate illustrations.

A

Allen, Michael, 80
Anderson, Richard, 242

B

Bailey, Garrick, 75, 221
Barnes, Sandra, 176
Benedict, Ruth, 10, 165, 264–265
Berlin, Brent, 45
Bernstein, Jared, 209
Boahannan, Paul, 115
Boas, Franz, 10, 55–56, 66, 75
Boserup, Ester, 178
Bourassa, Rosa, 75
Boyd, David, 272
Brain, Robert, 245
Brown, Judith, 173
Burton, Michael, 171

C

Callender, Charles, 165
Catherine the Great, 323
Cerroni-Long, E. Liza, 7
Chagnon, Napoleon, 72
Child, Irvin, 266
Clinton, Bill, 26–27
Cohen, T., 268
Collins, Joseph, 340
Columbus, Christopher, 281, 282
Cook, James, 76–77
Cortez, Hernando, 282
Crosby, Alfred W., 93, 292

D

da Gama, Vasco, 287
Darwin, Charles, 52
Davidson, Basil, 287
Davis, William, 117

de las Casas, Bartolome, 283
DeMallie, Raymond J., 165
Denig, Edwin, 165
Dentan, Robert, 19
Diamond, 93
Dorsey, James, 75
Dow, Malcomb, 171
DuBois, Cora, 265–266
Durham, William, 340–341
Durkheim, Emile, 225–226
Dyson-Hudson, Neville, 102
Dyson-Hudson, Rada, 102

E

Ember, Carol, 150, 170
Ember, Melvin, 150
Erickson, Ken, 7
Estioko-Griffin, Agnes, 167
Evans-Pritchard, E. E., 229
Ewers, John, 284

F

Fagan, Brian M., 93
Farnsworth, Norman, 358
Farrer, Claire, 273
Firth, Raymond, 204
Fischer, John, 251
Fletcher, Alice, 74–75
Frazer, James, 223, 227
Freed, Ruth, 338
Freed, Stanley, 338
Freeman, Derek, 270
Fried, Morton, 203
Friedson, Steven, 253
Frum, John, 235

G

Gandhi, Indira, 315
Geertz, Clifford, 63, *64,* 224
Gell, Alfred, 247
Gilmore, David, 173
Glazer, Nathan, 307

Gluckman, Max, 198
Goodall, Jane, *3*
Goodenough, Ward H., 25
Goody, Jack, 178
Green, Edward, 347–348

H

Handsome Lake, 237, 238
Harris, Marvin, 61, *61*
Hassrick, Royal B., 165
Hitchcock, Robert, 355
Hockett, Charles, 34
Hoebel, E. Adamson, 192, 197
Hostetler, John A., 362
Huntington, Gertrude Enders, 362
Huntington, Samuel, 300
Hutton, James, 52
Hyde, Henry, 26

I

Ivan the Terrible, 288

J

Johnson, Samuel, 243

K

Kaeppler, Adrienne, 251
Kak, Neeraj, 337
Kapur, Akash, 342
Kay, Paul, 45
Keller, Helen, 35
Kluckhohn, Clyde, 229
Kochems, Lee M., 165
Kottak, Conrad, 28
Kraybill, Donald B., 361, 362
Kroeber, Alfred, 10

L

LaFlesche, Francis, 74–75, 221, 251
LaFlesche, Susette, 74, 75
Lapp,, Francis Moore, 340

Lee, Richard B., 89, 92, 110
Leopold (King of Belgium), 291
Lewis, Oscar, 165
Llewellyn, Karl, 197
Lomax, Alan, 253–254
Longfellow, Henry Wadsworth, 312
Lyell, Charles, 52

M

Maitland, Frederick, 280
Malinowski, Bronislaw, 56–58, 60, 66,
    70–71, 224
Mamdani, Mahmood, 337
Mark, Joan, 75
Martin, Kay, 170
Martinez, Maria, 258
Marx, Karl, 214
Mead, Margaret, 7, 55, *68,* 247, 270
Medicine, Beatrice, 165
Meggitt, Mervyn, 271
Meigs, Anna, 160, 161
Middleton, John, 233
Milner, 247
Mishel, Lawrence, 209
Morgan, Lewis Henry, 55, 152, 293
Moynihan, Daniel, 307
Murdock, George, 79
Murray, Gerald, 345–346

N

Nag, Moni, 337
Netting, R. McC, 171

Newman, Philip, 272
Noyes, John Humphrey, 127

O

Obeyesekere, Gananath, 77
Oliver, Symmes C., 284

P

Parker, Enoch, 237
Pizarro, Francisco, 282
Plotkin, Mark, 357
Posey, Darrell, 345, 355
Pospisil, Leopold, 115, 192
Putnam, Frederic, 74

R

Radcliffe-Brown, A. R., 57, 66
Ridington, 75

S

Sahlins, Marshall, 76–77, 112
Said, Edward, 300–301
Sanday, Peggy, 176
Sapir, Edward, 45–46
Schlegel, Alice, 177, 178, 179
Sen, Amartya, 342
Snow, Clyde, 3
Stalin, Joseph, 323
Stamp, L. Dudley, 295
Steward, Julian, *56,* 58–59, 60, 66

Stone, G. D., 171
Stone, M. P., 171

T

Tibbles, Henry, 74, 75
Tischer, Henry L. , 208
Tito, Marshal, 327, 328
Turner, Victor, 274
Tylor, Edward B., 16, 54, 219, 293

V

Van den Berghe, Pierre, 127
Voorhies, Barbara, 170

W

Wallace, Anthony, 230
Weatherford, Jack, 42
White, Benjamin, 338
White, Douglas, 171
White, Leslie, 58–59, 60, 66
Whiting, Beatrice, 78–79
Whiting, John, 266
Whittington, Stephen, 7
Whitworth, John McKelvie, 127
Whorf, Benjamin, 45–46
Whyte, Martin, 177, 178
Wilson, John, 237
Winthrop, Robert H., 263
Woodburn, James, 203

Subject Index

Note: Italicized letters *f* and *t* following
page numbers indicate figures and tables,
respectively.

A

Accommodation, 325, 326
Ad hoc systems, 192
Adaptation, 85–86
    and culture, 103
    indigenous peoples and, 358–362
Adolescence, 270–271
Adulthood, 274–275
    initiation into, 271–273
Aesthetic, 242–243
Affinal relatives, 121
Afrocentrism, 356
Age set association, 268–269
Agriculture (cultivation), 86, 92–99
    European expansion and, 287, 288, 291
    horticulture, 94–96, 95*f*
    intensive, 96–99, 97*f*
    and sexual division of labor, 169–172
    preservation of crop varieties, 358–359
    technology transfer and, 341–344

traditional methods, benefits of, 344–345
    "undiscovered" useful species, 359–362
Agroforestry Outreach Project (AOP),
    346–347
Amaranth, 359
American historical particularism, 55–56
Ancestral cults, 233
Androcentric bias, 174
Animism, 219
Anthropological linguistics, 2
Anthropological perspectives, 8–9
Anthropological research
    comparative methods, 77–81
    ethnographic methods, 69–77. *See also*
        Fieldwork
Anthropological thought
    19th-century origins of, 52–55
    early 20th-century, 55–58
    mid 20th-century, 58–59
    contemporary, 59–66
    emphases of, 332
    functionalism, 56–58
    historical particularism, 55–56
    idealism, 59, 61–63

materialism, 59–61
    postmodernism, 63
Anthropology
    applied, 2, 5–6, 332–333
    cognitive, 41–42
    cultural, 2, 4–5, 6–8
    developmental, 5–6
    educational, 6
    establishment as separate discipline, 54–55
    forensic, 3
    history and, 280
    interpretive, 63
    medical, 5
    physical (biological), 2–3, 60
    psychological, 263
    science-humanity dichotomy of, 59, 60
    subfields of, 2–6
    value of, 9–11
AOP. *See* Agroforestry Outreach Project
Applied anthropology, 2, 5–6, 332–333
Archaeology, 2, 3–4, 60
Art(s), 241–259
    body, 244–248
    definition of, 242

forms of, 244–254
gender and, 256
performance, 251–254
pervasiveness of, 243–244
religion and, 251–252, 254–256
social functions of, 256–259
visual, 248–251
Artificial countries, 315
Assimilation, 323–325
effectiveness of, 326
forced, 324
passive, 325
Authority, 186
Avunculocal residence, 132, 146–147

B

Balanced reciprocity, 108–111
Bands, 88–89, 185–187
composite, 186
simple, 185
Behavior
individual, cultural knowledge and, 25–27
patterns of, 17, 18–20
Berdaches, 164
Bias, Eurocentric, 174
Big men, 186
Bilateral kinship, 149
Bilocal residence, 132
Biological (physical) anthropology, 2–3, 60
Biological determinism, 27
Biology, and culture, 27–31
Body arts, 244–248
Bound morphemes, 40–41
Brideservice, 131
Bridewealth, 130–131, 179
British functionalism, 56–58

C

Cargo cults, 235–236
Castes, 205
in traditional India, 205–207
Central Kalahari Game Reserve (CKGR), 354–355
Change. *See* Culture change; Demographic change
Chiefdoms, 188–189
Childhood, 269–270
Child-rearing practices, 263
and personality formation, 263–266
Children, costs and benefits of
in lesser developed countries, 336–338
in North America, 335–336
Christianity. *See* Judeo-Christian tradition
Civilizations, 98
ancient, 98, 99f
CKGR. *See* Central Kalahari Game Reserve
Clans, 142
Classes, 205
in industrial societies, 207–210
Classifications of reality, 22–23
language and, 41–43
Clothing style, as ethnic boundary marker, 310
Code of Hammurabi, 198
Cognatic descent, 147–148
Cognatic descent group, 147
Cognitive anthropology, 41–42
Colonization
of Americas, 282–285, 289–290

of Asia, 287–288, 291
and nationality problems, 314–315
of Oceania, 288, 292
of sub-Saharan Africa, 285–287, 290–291
Communal cults, 230, 233–234
Comparative methods, 77–81
controlled historical comparisons, 79–81
cross-cultural comparisons, 78–79
Comparative perspective, 8–9, 11, 54
Complex societies, 178
Composite bands, 186
Conflict theory of inequality, 212, 214
Consanguineal relatives, 121
Consultants (informants), 72–73
Contagious principle of magic, 227
Contract archaeology, 4
Controlled historical comparisons, 79–81
Court legal systems, 195–199
Cousins, 141
Cranial deformation, 244–245
Cross cousins, 141
Cross-cultural comparisons, 78–79
Cult(s)
communal, 230, 233–234
concept of, 230
ecclesiastical, 230, 234–235
individualistic, 230, 231
shamanistic, 230, 231–233
Cultivation. *See* Agriculture
Cultural alternatives, indigenous peoples and, 362–363
Cultural anthropology, 2, 4–5
present-day status of, 6–8
Cultural identity, 17
Cultural integration, 17
Cultural knowledge, 16–17, 18, 20–24
and individual behavior, 25–27
and speech, 47
Cultural relativism, 9, 10, 56
Cultural resource management, 4
Cultural universals, 30
Culture
adaptation and, 103
behavioral components of, 17
biology and, 27–31
concept of, 10
definitions of, 16, 17–20
evolution of, perspectives on, 53–55, 58–59
and human life, 24–25
language and, 41–45
mental components of, 16–17
and personality, 263–268, 267f
Culture change, 79, 280
European expansion and, 281–288
Industrial Revolution and, 288–292
Culture shock, 73
Curios, 258
Cyclical age sets, 268

D

Dance, 251, 253–254
Demographic changes
European expansion and, 283, 285, 289, 292
post-World War II, 297–299
Descent, 139
cognatic, 147–148
form of, 140
matrilineal, 140, 141, 141f

patrilineal, 140f, 140–141
unilineal, 140
and women's status, 177–178
Descent groups, 142–143
cognatic, 147
examples of, 143–146
segmentation of, 143, 144f
Development, indicators of, 342
Developmental anthropology, 5–6
Dewesternization, 356
Dialects, 37
Diffusion, 280
Division of labor, 86
foraging and, 88
organization of production and, 169–172
pastoralism and, 102–103
sexual, 163–172, 166t
DNA, mitochondrial, 7
Domestic group, 121
Domestication, 91–92
in Old and New worlds, 92–93
Dowry, 131, 178–179
Dry land gardening, 94

E

Ecclesiastical cults, 230, 234–235
Economic classes, 207–208
Economic problems, population growth and, 334–335
Economic progress, cultural alternatives to, 362–363
Economic systems, exchange in, 107–117
Economy, global, 293–297, 294f
Educational anthropology, 6
Egalitarian societies, 203–204
art in, 251
Enculturation, 17, 46
Endogamous rules, 125
Energy subsidy, 343
Environmental problems
deforestation, 345–347
population growth and, 334
Ethnic boundary markers, 308–310
elimination of, forced assimilation and, 324
Ethnic cleansing, 322, 325
Ethnic conflict(s), 311–322
ancient roots of, 7
resolving, 322–329
Ethnic group(s), 307–311
art as expression of, 257–259
attributes of, 307–310
definition of, 307
fluidity of, 310
types of, 310–311
Ethnic homogenization, 322–325
Ethnic pluralism, 325
Ethnocentrism, 9, 10
Ethnogenesis, 310
Ethnographic methods, 69–77
ethnohistory, 69, 73–77
fieldwork. *See* Fieldwork
Ethnography, 5
Ethnology, 4. *See also* Cultural anthropology
Ethnoscience, 41. *See also* Cognitive anthropology
Eurocentric bias, 174
Evolution
cultural, perspectives on, 53–55, 58–59
human, 2, 52–53

Exchange, 107–117
  marital, 130–131
  market, 107, 114–117
  reciprocity, 107–113
  redistribution, 107, 113–114
Exogamous rules, 125
Extended family, 121, 133–134, 134*f*
  unilineally, 142
Extinction
  danger of, 355
  of ethnic groups, 310

F

Faith healers, 232–233
Familial legal systems, 193
Family
  extended, 121, 133–134, 134*f*, 142
  nuclear, 121, 133
Feud, 195
Fieldwork, 5, 69–71
  early 20th-century anthropologists and, 55, 57, 58
  problems in, 71–73
  as rite of passage, 73
  uses of, 345–348
Foraging. *See* Hunting and gathering
Forced assimilation, 324
Forensic anthropology, 3
Form of descent, 140
Free morphemes, 40–41
Functionalism, 56–58
Functionalist theory of inequality, 212–213

G

Gender
  and art, 256
  cultural construction of, 160–163
Generalized reciprocity, 107–108
Genocide, 323
Gerontology, 275
Global economy, 293–297, 294*f*
Global knowledge, 357
Grammar, 37
Group marriage, 125, 127

H

Head shaping, 244–245
Herding (pastoralism), 86, 100–103
  regions of, 101*f*
Hierarchical nesting, 307
Historic archaeology, 3
Historical particularism, 55–56
History
  and anthropology, 280
  political nature of, 356
  world
    since 1500, 281–293, 286*f*
    since 1945, 293–300
Holistic perspective, 8
Homeland, 311
Homogenization
  cultural, 309–310
  ethnic, 322–325
Horticulture, 94–95
  cultural consequences of, 95–96
  regions of, 95*f*
  sexual division of labor in, 169–171
Household forms, 133–134, 134*f*
Human evolution, 2, 52–53

Human uniqueness, 61
Human variation, study of, 2
Humorous deception, 72
Hunger, 338–345
  causes of, 339–341
  inequality explanation of, 339
  scarcity explanation of, 339
  solutions to, 341–345
Hunting and gathering (foraging), 86, 87–91
  and egalitarian society, 203
  regions, 87*f*

I

Idealism, 59, 61–63
Identity
  cultural, 17
  ethnic, 307
  social, 19
Ideologies, 211
  secular, 212
Imitative principle of magic, 227
Immigration, 298–299
Incest taboo, 123
Income distribution
  in industrialized nations, 213
  in U.S., 209*t*, 213
Indigenous peoples
  definition of, 352
  knowledge of, 357–363
  modern-day problems of, 352–356
Individualistic cults, 230, 231
Indunas, 198
Industrial Revolution, 288–292
Industrial societies
  classes in, 207–210
  cultural alternatives to, 362–363
  ideologies in, 212
  income distribution in, 213
  women's status in, 180–181
Inequality, 203
  conflict theory of, 212, 214
  functionalist theory of, 212–213
  maintaining, 210–212
  theories of, 212–216
Inequality explanation of hunger, 339
Influence, 186
Informants (consultants), 72–73
Initiation rites, 271–273
  military service and, 274
Innovation, 280
Intensification, 61
Intensive agriculture, 96–97
  cultural consequences of, 97–99
  regions of, 97*f*
  and sexual division of labor, 169–172
Intercropping, 344–345
International Monetary Fund, 296
Interpretive anthropology, 63
Interviewing, 69–70, 72
Islamic religion
  and usury, 296
  Western view of, 300–301

J

Judeo-Christian tradition
  ecclesiasticism in, 234
  music in, 251
  mythology in, 219–220
  social functions of, 225
  usury in, 296

witches in, 229

K

Kin group, 121
  ranking in, 204
Kin terms, 151
Kindred, 149
Kinship, 137–156
  bilateral, 149
  cultural variations in, 138–139
  diagrams, 131*f*, 131–132
  influences on, 149–150
  terminology, 151–156
  unilateral, 140–148
Knowledge
  cultural, 16–17, 18, 20–24
  and individual behavior, 25–27
  and speech, 47
  global, 357
  of indigenous peoples, 357–363
  local, 357

L

Language
  and culture, 41–45
  as ethnic boundary marker, 309
  grammar, 37
  humanity and, 34
  properties of, 34–36
  sound systems, 37–38
  variations in, 38–40
  study of, 2
  words and meaning, 40–41
  and world views, 45–46
Law, 191–192
  procedural, 192
  and social boundaries, 195
  substantive, 192
LDCs. *See* Lesser developed countries
Legal systems
  court, 195–199
  self-help, 192–195
Lesser developed countries (LDCs), 333
  costs and benefits of children in, 336–338
  hunger in, 338–345
  population growth in, 333–335
Levirate, 130
Life cycle, 269–276
  adolescence, 270–271
  adulthood, 274–275
  childhood, 269–270
  definition of, 269
  initiation rites, 271–273
  old age, 275–276
Likombwa, 198
Limited-purpose money, 115–116
Lineage, 142
Lineal age sets, 269
Linguistics
  anthropological, 2
  sociolinguistics, 47
Local knowledge, 357

M

Magic, 227–228
Mana, 211, 219
Market exchange, 107, 114–117
Marriage, 121–124
  and adult status, 274–275

functions of, 123
group, 125, 127
monogamy, 125
polygamy, 125–129
and residence patterns, 132, 133
rules regarding, 124–125
Marriage alliances, 129–130
Martial exchanges, 130–131
Master status, 147
Materialism, 59–61
Matriarchy, 174
Matrilineal descent, 140, 141*f*
Matrilineal descent group, 142
Matrilineal societies, 79–80
example of, 145–146
Matrilocal residence, 132
Mediator legal systems, 194
Medical anthropology, 5
Medicine man, 231
Medicines, indigenous peoples and, 357–358
Migration
international, 298–299
population growth and, 335
urbanization and, 298
Mitochondrial DNA, 7
Modal personality, 265
Money, 114–116
limited-purpose, 115–116
multipurpose, 115
Monogamy, 125
serial, 129
Morpheme, 40–41
Morphology, 40
Multinational corporations, 296
Multinational countries, 325–329
Multipurpose money, 115
Music, 251–254
Myths, 219–220, 223
origin, 308

N

National Historic Preservation Act (1966), 4
Nationalism, 302
Nationality(ies), 311
countries with multiple, 325–329
stateless, problem of, 311–322
Negative reciprocity, 111–112
Neolocal residence, 132
New World, 281
conquest of, 282–285
domestication in, 92–93
Nomadism, 100
Nonverbal communication, 21–22
Norms, 20
Nuclear family, 121, 133

O

Old age, 275–276
Old World, 281
domestication in, 92–93
Organization of production, 86–87
and division of labor, 169–172
and women's status, 180–181
Orientalism, 300–301
Origin myth, 308

P

Paleoanthropology, 2
Parallel cousins, 141

Parricide, 275
Participant observation, 70
Passive assimilation, 325
Pastoralism (herding), 86, 100–103
regions of, 101*f*
Patrilineal descent, 140, 140*f*
Patrilineal descent group, 142
segmentation of, 143, 144*f*
Patrilineal societies, 79–80
example of, 143–145
Patrilocal residence, 132
Patterns of behavior, 17, 18–20
Peasant marketplaces, 116–117
Peasants, 98–99
Performance arts, 251–254
Personality
culture and, 263–268, 267*f*
definition of, 263
modal, 265
Peyote religion, 237, 238
Phonemes, 38
Phonology, 37
Physical (biological) anthropology, 2–3, 60
Pluralism, ethnic, 325
Political fragmentation, 300, 302
Political organization
forms of, 185–191
sexual asymmetry in, 174
Polyandry, 125, 128–129
Polyculture, 344–345
Polygamy, 125–129
Polygyny, 125, 126–128
sororal, 128
Population
decline, European expansion and, 283, 285, 289, 292
growth, 333–334
anthropological perspectives on, 334–338
consequences of, 334–335
post-World War II, 297
and world hunger, 339–341
terminology, 333
Postmarital residence patterns, 132
and household forms, 133–135
and women's status, 177–178
Postmodernism, 63
Prehistoric archaeology, 3
Priests, 234
Primatology, 2
Primogeniture, 128
Procedural law, 192
Prophets, 235
Protoculture, 24
Psychological anthropology, 263
Puberty rites, 271–273

Q

Quinoa, 359

R

Race, cultural construction of, 28–29
Ranked societies, 204
Rapport, developing, 71–72
Reality, classifications of, 22–23
language and, 41–43
Reasonable-person model, 196
Reciprocal sharing, 89–90
Reciprocity, 107–113
balanced, 108–111
generalized, 107–108

negative, 111–112
and social distance, 112–113
Redistribution, 107, 113–114
Reforestation, 345–347
Refugees, 323
Relatives
affinal, 121
classification of, 151–156
consanguineal, 121
cultural classifications of, 139
Relativistic perspective, 9, 10
historical particularism and, 56
Religion
and art, 251–252, 254–256
components of, 219–221
definition of, 219
as ethnic boundary marker, 309
intellectual/cognitive functions of, 223–224
psychological functions of, 224–225
revitalization movements, 235–238
sexual asymmetry in, 174
social functions of, 225–226
sphere of supernatural intervention, 226
and status quo, preservation of, 212
supernatural explanations of misfortune, 226–230
theories of, 222–226
unilinear evolutionary perspective on, 54
varieties of organization, 230–235
Relocation, 323, 325
Research
comparative methods, 77–81
ethnographic methods, 69–77. *See also*
Fieldwork
Residence patterns, postmarital, 132, 133
and household forms, 133–135
Resources
rights to, among foragers, 90–91
women's control over, 176–177
Respect language, 47
Revelations, 235
Revitalization movements, 235–238
Rite of passage, 269, 274
Rituals, 220, 222, 223, 251–252
Roles, 19–20
of anthropologist, 72

S

Sacred, concept of, 221
SAE. *See* Standard American English
Scarcity explanation of hunger, 339
Scarification, 245, 247–248, 274
Secular ideologies, 212
Self-help legal systems, 192–195
Semantic domains, 44
Serial monogamy, 129
Sex
versus gender, 160
and speech patterns, 47
Sexual division of labor, 163–172
factors influencing, 168–169
patterns in, 165–168, 166*t*
Shamanistic cults, 230, 231–233
Shifting cultivation, 22, 94, 345
Simple bands, 185
Slash and burn cultivation, 22, 94, 345
Slave trade, 283–287, 290
Social control, 191
Social distance, and reciprocity, 112–113
Social solidarity, religion and, 225–226
Social systems model, 266–267, 267*f*

Society(ies), 17
    complex, 178
    egalitarian, 203–204
    ranked, 204
    stratified, 204–205
Sociolinguistics, 47
Sociology, versus cultural anthropology, 6
Sodalities, 187
Sorcery, 227–228
    interpretations of, 228–230
Sororal polygyny, 128
Sororate, 130
Speech, social uses of, 46–49
Spirit helpers, 231
Standard American English (SAE), 37
Standard of living, measures of, 342
States, 189–191
Status
    adult, marriage and, 274–275
    art and, 258–259
    master, 147
Status groups, 207
Status of women, 172–181
    in industrial societies, 180–181
    influences on, 175–180
    universality of, 174–175
Stereotyping, 71
Stratified societies, 204–205
    art in, 251
Subnationalities, 311
Substantive law, 192
Supernatural explanations of misfortune,
    226–230
Supernatural intervention, sphere of, 226

Supernatural powers, 219
Superstition, 223
Surplus, 97–98
Symbols, 21–22

T
Taboos
    applied to language, 48
    incest, 123
Tattooing, 245–248
Technology
    and cultural evolution, 58–59
    and materialism, 59–61
Technology transfer solution, to world hunger,
    341–344
Third World. *See* Lesser developed countries
Tone languages, 39–40
Totemic clans, 142
Totemism, 233–234
Trade partnership, 109
Traditional resource management practices,
    345
Tribes, 187–188
Tribute, 113–114

U
Unilineal descent, 140
Unilineal descent group, 142
Unilineal evolution, 53–54, 55, 58, 293
United States Agency for International
    Development (USAID), 345
    projects funded by, 345–348
Universals, cultural, 30

Urbanization, 298, 300–301
    population growth and, 335
USAID. *See* United States Agency for
    International Development
Usury, 296

V
Values, 20–21
Vision quest, 231
Visual arts, 248–251
Voudon religion, 252

W
Wealth
    accumulation of, 114
    distribution of, in U.S., 208–209, 209*t*
Whorf-Sapir hypothesis, 45–46
Witchcraft, 228
    interpretations of, 228–230
Women, status of, 172–181
    in industrial societies, 180–181
    influences on, 175–180
    universality of, 174–175
Workplace culture, 7
World Bank, 296–297
World history
    since 1500, 281–293, 286*f*
    since 1945, 293–300
World hunger, 338–345
World views, 23–24
    of cultural anthropologists, 332
    language and, 45–46
World War II, 293